PARALLEL PROGRAMMING

TECHNIQUES AND APPLICATIONS USING NETWORKED WORKSTATIONS AND PARALLEL COMPUTERS

2nd Edition

BARRY WILKINSON
University of North Carolina at Charlotte
Western Carolina University

MICHAEL ALLEN
University of North Carolina at Charlotte

Upper Saddle River, NJ 07458

Library of Congress Cataloging-in-Publication Data

CIP DATA AVAILABLE.

Vice President and Editorial Director, ECS: *Marcia Horton*
Executive Editor: *Kate Hargett*
Vice President and Director of Production and Manufacturing, ESM: *David W. Riccardi*
Executive Managing Editor: *Vince O'Brien*
Managing Editor: *Camille Trentacoste*
Production Editor: *John Keegan*
Director of Creative Services: *Paul Belfanti*
Art Director: *Jayne Conte*
Cover Designer: *Kiwi Design*
Managing Editor, AV Management and Production: *Patricia Burns*
Art Editor: *Gregory Dulles*
Manufacturing Manager: *Trudy Pisciotti*
Manufacturing Buyer: *Lisa McDowell*
Marketing Manager: *Pamela Hersperger*

Pearson Prentice Hall
Pearson Education, Inc.
Upper Saddle River, NJ 07458

Printed in the United States of America

10 9 8 7 6 5 4 3 2 1

ISBN: 0-13-140563-2

Pearson Education Ltd., *London*
Pearson Education Australia Pty. Ltd., *Sydney*
Pearson Education Singapore, Pte. Ltd.
Pearson Education North Asia Ltd., *Hong Kong*
Pearson Education Canada, Inc., *Toronto*
Pearson Educación de Mexico, S.A. de C.V.
Pearson Education—Japan, *Tokyo*
Pearson Education Malaysia, Pte. Ltd.
Pearson Education, Inc., *Upper Saddle River, New Jersey*

To my wife, Wendy,
and my daughter, Johanna

Barry Wilkinson

To my wife, Bonnie

Michael Allen

Preface

The purpose of this text is to introduce parallel programming techniques. Parallel programming is programming multiple computers, or computers with multiple internal processors, to solve a problem at a greater computational speed than is possible with a single computer. It also offers the opportunity to tackle larger problems, that is, problems with more computational steps or larger memory requirements, the latter because multiple computers and multiprocessor systems often have more total memory than a single computer. In this text, we concentrate upon the use of multiple computers that communicate with one another by sending messages; hence the term *message-passing* parallel programming. The computers we use can be different types (PC, SUN, SGI, etc.) but must be interconnected, and a software environment must be present for message passing between computers. Suitable computers (either already in a network or capable of being interconnected) are very widely available as the basic computing platform for students, so that it is usually not necessary to acquire a specially designed multiprocessor system. Several software tools are available for message-passing parallel programming, notably several implementations of MPI, which are all freely available. Such software can also be used on specially designed multiprocessor systems should these systems be available for use. So far as practicable, we discuss techniques and applications in a system-independent fashion.

Second Edition. Since the publication of the first edition of this book, the use of interconnected computers as a high-performance computing platform has become widespread. The term "cluster computing" has come to be used to describe this type of computing. Often the computers used in a cluster are "commodity" computers, that is, low-cost personal computers as used in the home and office. Although the focus of this text, using multiple computers and processors for high-performance computing, has not been changed, we have revised our introductory chapter, Chapter 1, to take into account the move towards commodity clusters and away from specially designed, self-contained, multiprocessors. In the first edition, we described both PVM and MPI and provided an appendix for each. However, only one would normally be used in the classroom. In the second edition, we have deleted specific details of PVM from the text because MPI is now a widely adopted standard and provides for much more powerful mechanisms. PVM can still be used if one wishes, and we still provide support for it on our home page.

Message-passing programming has some disadvantages, notably the need for the programmer to specify explicitly where and when the message passing should occur in the program and what to send. Data has to be sent to those computers that require the data through relatively slow messages. Some have compared this type of programming to assembly language programming, that is, programming using the internal language of the computer, a very low-level and tedious way of programming which is not done except under very specific circumstances. An alternative programming model is the shared memory model. In the first edition, shared memory programming was covered for computers with multiple internal processors and a common shared memory. Such shared memory multiprocessors have now become cost-effective and common, especially dual- and quad-processor systems. Thread programming was described using Pthreads. Shared memory programming remains in the second edition and with significant new material added including performance aspects of shared memory programming and a section on OpenMP, a thread-based standard for shared memory programming at a higher level than Pthreads. Any broad-ranging course on practical parallel programming would include shared memory programming, and having some experience with OpenMP is very desirable. A new appendix is added on OpenMP. OpenMP compilers are available at low cost to educational institutions.

With the focus of using clusters, a major new chapter has been added on shared memory programming on clusters. The shared memory model can be employed on a cluster with appropriate distributed shared memory (DSM) software. Distributed shared memory programming attempts to obtain the advantages of the scalability of clusters and the elegance of shared memory. Software is freely available to provide the DSM environment, and we shall also show that students can write their own DSM systems (we have had several done so). We should point out that there are performance issues with DSM. The performance of software DSM cannot be expected to be as good as true shared memory programming on a shared memory multiprocessor. But a large, scalable shared memory multiprocessor is much more expensive than a commodity cluster.

Other changes made for the second edition are related to programming on clusters. New material is added in Chapter 6 on partially synchronous computations, which are particularly important in clusters where synchronization is expensive in time and should be avoided. We have revised and added to Chapter 10 on sorting to include other sorting algorithms for clusters. We have added to the analysis of the algorithms in the first part of the book to include the computation/communication ratio because this is important to message-passing computing. Extra problems have been added. The appendix on parallel computational models has been removed to maintain a reasonable page count.

The first edition of the text was described as course text primarily for an undergraduate-level parallel programming course. However, we found that some institutions also used the text as a graduate-level course textbook. We have also used the material for both senior undergraduate-level and graduate-level courses, and it is suitable for beginning graduate-level courses. For a graduate-level course, more advanced materials, for example, DSM implementation and fast Fourier transforms, would be covered and more demanding programming projects chosen.

Structure of Materials. As with the first edition, the text is divided into two parts. Part I now consists of Chapters 1 to 9, and Part II now consists of Chapters 10 to 13. In Part I, the basic techniques of parallel programming are developed. In Chapter 1, the concept of parallel computers is now described with more emphasis on clusters. Chapter 2 describes message-passing routines in general and particular software (MPI). Evaluating the performance of message-passing programs, both theoretically and in practice, is discussed. Chapter 3 describes the ideal problem for making parallel the embarrassingly parallel computation where the problem can be divided into independent parts. In fact, important applications can be parallelized in this fashion. Chapters 4, 5, 6, and 7 describe various programming strategies (partitioning and divide and conquer, pipelining, synchronous computations, asynchronous computations, and load balancing). These chapters of Part I cover all the essential aspects of parallel programming with the emphasis on message-passing and using simple problems to demonstrate techniques. The techniques themselves, however, can be applied to a wide range of problems. Sample code is usually given first as sequential code and then as parallel pseudocode. Often, the underlying algorithm is already parallel in nature and the sequential version has "unnaturally" serialized it using loops. Of course, some algorithms have to be reformulated for efficient parallel solution, and this reformulation may not be immediately apparent. Chapter 8 describes shared memory programming and includes Pthreads, an IEEE standard system that is widely available, and OpenMP. There is also a significant new section on timing and performance issues. The new chapter on distributed shared memory programming has been placed after the shared memory chapter to complete Part I, and the subsequent chapters have been renumbered.

Many parallel computing problems have specially developed algorithms, and in Part II problem-specific algorithms are studied in both non-numeric and numeric domains. For Part II, some mathematical concepts are needed, such as matrices. Topics covered in Part II include sorting (Chapter 10), numerical algorithms, matrix multiplication, linear equations, partial differential equations (Chapter 11), image processing (Chapter 12), and searching and optimization (Chapter 13). Image processing is particularly suitable for parallelization and is included as an interesting application with significant potential for projects. The fast Fourier transform is discussed in the context of image processing. This important transform is also used in many other areas, including signal processing and voice recognition.

A large selection of "real-life" problems drawn from practical situations is presented at the end of each chapter. These problems require no specialized mathematical knowledge and are a unique aspect of this text. They develop skills in the use of parallel programming techniques rather than simply teaching how to solve specific problems, such as sorting numbers or multiplying matrices.

Prerequisites. The prerequisite for studying Part I is a knowledge of sequential programming, as may be learned from using the C language. The parallel pseudocode in the text uses C-like assignment statements and control flow statements. However, students with only a knowledge of Java will have no difficulty in understanding the pseudocode, because syntax of the statements is similar to that of Java. Part I can be studied immediately after basic sequential programming has been mastered. Many assignments here can be attempted without specialized mathematical knowledge. If MPI is used for the assignments, programs are usually written in C or C++ calling MPI message-passing library routines. The descriptions of the specific library calls needed are given in Appendix A. It is possible to use Java, although students with only a knowledge of Java should not have any difficulty in writing their assignments in C/C++.

In Part II, the sorting chapter assumes that the student has covered sequential sorting in a data structure or sequential programming course. The numerical algorithms chapter requires the mathematical background that would be expected of senior computer science or engineering undergraduates.

Course Structure. The instructor has some flexibility in the presentation of the materials. Not everything need be covered. In fact, it is usually not possible to cover the whole book in a single semester. A selection of topics from Part I would be suitable as an addition to a normal sequential programming class. We have introduced our first-year students to parallel programming in this way. In that context, the text is a supplement to a sequential programming course text. All of Part I and selected parts of Part II together are suitable as a more advanced undergraduate or beginning graduate-level parallel programming/computing course, and we use the text in that manner.

Home Page. A Web site has been developed for this book as an aid to students and instructors. It can be found at www.cs.uncc.edu/par_prog. Included at this site are extensive Web pages to help students learn how to compile and run parallel programs. Sample programs are provided for a simple initial assignment to check the software environment. The Web site has been completely redesigned during the preparation of the second edition to include step-by-step instructions for students using navigation buttons. Details of DSM programming are also provided. The new Instructor's Manual is available to instructors, and gives MPI solutions. The original solutions manual gave PVM solutions and is still available. The solutions manuals are available electronically from the authors. A very extensive set of slides is available from the home page.

Acknowledgments. The first edition of this text was the direct outcome of a National Science Foundation grant awarded to the authors at the University of North Carolina at Charlotte to introduce parallel programming in the first college year.[1] Without the support of the late Dr. M. Mulder, program director at the National Science Foundation, we would not have been able to pursue the ideas presented in the text. A number of graduate students worked on the original project. Mr. Uday Kamath produced the original solutions manual.

We should like to record our thanks to James Robinson, the departmental system administrator who established our local workstation cluster, without which we would not have been able to conduct the work. We should also like to thank the many students at UNC Charlotte who took our classes and helped us refine the material over many years. This

[1]National Science Foundation grant "Introducing parallel programming techniques into the freshman curricula," ref. DUE 9554975.

included "teleclasses" in which the materials for the first edition were classroom tested in a unique setting. The teleclasses were broadcast to several North Carolina universities, including UNC Asheville, UNC Greensboro, UNC Wilmington, and North Carolina State University, in addition to UNC Charlotte. Professor Mladen Vouk of North Carolina State University, apart from presenting an expert guest lecture for us, set up an impressive Web page that included "real audio" of our lectures and "automatically turning" slides. (These lectures can be viewed from a link from our home page.) Professor John Board of Duke University and Professor Jan Prins of UNC Chapel Hill also kindly made guest-expert presentations to classes. A parallel programming course based upon the material in this text was also given at the Universidad Nacional de San Luis in Argentina by kind invitation of Professor Raul Gallard.

The National Science Foundation has continued to support our work on cluster computing, and this helped us develop the second edition. A National Science Foundation grant was awarded to us to develop distributed shared memory tools and educational materials.[2] Chapter 9, on distributed shared memory programming, describes the work. Subsequently, the National Science Foundation awarded us a grant to conduct a three-day workshop at UNC Charlotte in July 2001 on teaching cluster computing,[3] which enabled us to further refine our materials for this book. We wish to record our appreciation to Dr. Andrew Bernat, program director at the National Science Foundation, for his continuing support. He suggested the cluster computing workshop at Charlotte. This workshop was attended by 18 faculty from around the United States. It led to another three-day workshop on teaching cluster computing at Gujarat University, Ahmedabad, India, in December 2001, this time by invitation of the IEEE Task Force on Cluster Computing (TFCC), in association with the IEEE Computer Society, India. The workshop was attended by about 40 faculty. We are also deeply in the debt to several people involved in the workshop, and especially to Mr. Rajkumar Buyya, chairman of the IEEE Computer Society Task Force on Cluster Computing who suggested it. We are also very grateful to Prentice Hall for providing copies of our textbook to free of charge to everyone who attended the workshops.

We have continued to test the materials with student audiences at UNC Charlotte and elsewhere (including the University of Massachusetts, Boston, while on leave of absence). A number of UNC-Charlotte students worked with us on projects during the development of the second edition. The new Web page for this edition was developed by Omar Lahbabi and further refined by Sari Ansari, both undergraduate students. The solutions manual in MPI was done by Thad Drum and Gabriel Medin, also undergraduate students at UNC-Charlotte.

We would like to express our continuing appreciation to Petra Recter, senior acquisitions editor at Prentice Hall, who supported us throughout the development of the second edition. Reviewers provided us with very helpful advice, especially one anonymous reviewer whose strong views made us revisit many aspects of this book, thereby definitely improving the material.

Finally, we wish to thank the many people who contacted us about the first edition, providing us with corrections and suggestions. We maintained an on-line errata list which was useful as the book went through reprints. All the corrections from the first edition have

[2]National Science Foundation grant "Parallel Programming on Workstation Clusters," ref. DUE 995030.

[3]National Science Foundation grant supplement for a cluster computing workshop, ref. DUE 0119508.

been incorporated into the second edition. An on-line errata list will be maintained again for the second edition with a link from the home page. We always appreciate being contacted with comments or corrections. Please send comments and corrections to us at wilkinson@email.wcu.edu (Barry Wilkinson) or cma@uncc.edu (Michael Allen).

BARRY WILKINSON
Western Carolina University

MICHAEL ALLEN
University of North Carolina, Charlotte

About the Authors

Barry Wilkinson is a full professor in the Department of Computer Science at the University of North Carolina at Charlotte, and also holds a faculty position at Western Carolina University. He previously held faculty positions at Brighton Polytechnic, England (1984–87), the State University of New York, College at New Paltz (1983–84), University College, Cardiff, Wales (1976–83), and the University of Aston, England (1973–76). From 1969 to 1970, he worked on process control computer systems at Ferranti Ltd. He is the author of *Computer Peripherals* (with D. Horrocks, Hodder and Stoughton, 1980, 2nd ed. 1987), *Digital System Design* (Prentice Hall, 1987, 2nd ed. 1992), *Computer Architecture Design and Performance* (Prentice Hall 1991, 2nd ed. 1996), and *The Essence of Digital Design* (Prentice Hall, 1997). In addition to these books, he has published many papers in major computer journals. He received a B.S. degree in electrical engineering (with first-class honors) from the University of Salford in 1969, and M.S. and Ph.D. degrees from the University of Manchester (Department of Computer Science), England, in 1971 and 1974, respectively. He has been a senior member of the IEEE since 1983 and received an IEEE Computer Society Certificate of Appreciation in 2001 for his work on the IEEE Task Force on Cluster Computing (TFCC) education program.

Michael Allen is a full professor in the Department of Computer Science at the University of North Carolina at Charlotte. He previously held faculty positions as an associate and full professor in the Electrical Engineering Department at the University of North Carolina at Charlotte (1974–85), and as an instructor and an assistant professor in the Electrical Engineering Department at the State University of New York at Buffalo (1968–74). From 1985 to 1987, he was on leave from the University of North Carolina at Charlotte while serving as the president and chairman of DataSpan, Inc. Additional industry experience includes electronics design and software systems development for Eastman Kodak, Sylvania Electronics, Bell of Pennsylvania, Wachovia Bank, and numerous other firms. He received B.S. and M.S. degrees in Electrical Engineering from Carnegie Mellon University in 1964 and 1965, respectively, and a Ph.D. from the State University of New York at Buffalo in 1968.

Contents

PART I Basic Techniques

Chapter 1

Parallel Computers

In this chapter, we describe the demand for greater computational power from computers and the concept of using computers with multiple internal processors and multiple interconnected computers. The prospects for increased speed of execution by using multiple computers or multiple processors and the limitations are discussed. Then, the various ways that such systems can be constructed are described, in particular by using multiple computers in a cluster, which has become a very cost-effective computer platform for high-performance computing.

1.1 THE DEMAND FOR COMPUTATIONAL SPEED

There is a continual demand for greater computational power from computer systems than is currently possible. Areas requiring great computational speed include numerical simulation of scientific and engineering problems. Such problems often need huge quantities of repetitive calculations on large amounts of data to give valid results. Computations must be completed within a "reasonable" time period. In the manufacturing realm, engineering calculations and simulations must be achieved within seconds or minutes if possible. A simulation that takes two weeks to reach a solution is usually unacceptable in a design environment, because the time has to be short enough for the designer to work effectively. As systems become more complex, it takes increasingly more time to simulate them. There are some problems that have a specific deadline for the computations, for example weather forecasting. Taking two days to forecast the local weather accurately for the next day would make the prediction useless. Some areas, such as modeling large DNA structures and global weather forecasting, are *grand challenge problems*. A grand challenge problem is one that cannot be solved in a reasonable amount of time with today's computers.

Weather forecasting by computer (*numerical weather prediction*) is a widely quoted example that requires very powerful computers. The atmosphere is modeled by dividing it into three-dimensional regions or cells. Rather complex mathematical equations are used to capture the various atmospheric effects. In essence, conditions in each cell (temperature, pressure, humidity, wind speed and direction, etc.) are computed at time intervals using conditions existing in the previous time interval in the cell and nearby cells. The calculations of each cell are repeated many times to model the passage of time. The key feature that makes the simulation significant is the number of cells that are necessary. For forecasting over days, the atmosphere is affected by very distant events, and thus a large region is necessary. Suppose we consider the whole global atmosphere divided into cells of size 1 mile $\times$ 1 mile $\times$ 1 mile to a height of 10 miles (10 cells high). A rough calculation leads to about 5×10^8 cells. Suppose each calculation requires 200 floating-point operations (the type of operation necessary if the numbers have a fractional part or are raised to a power). In one time step, 10^{11} floating point operations are necessary. If we were to forecast the weather over seven days using 1-minute intervals, there would be 10^4 time steps and 10^{15} floating-point operations in total. A computer capable of 1 Gflops (10^9 floating-point operations/sec) with this calculation would take 10^6 seconds or over 10 days to perform the calculation. To perform the calculation in 5 minutes would require a computer operating at 3.4 Tflops (3.4×10^{12} floating-point operations/sec).

Another problem that requires a huge number of calculations is predicting the motion of the astronomical bodies in space. Each body is attracted to each other body by gravitational forces. These are long-range forces that can be calculated by a simple formula (see Chapter 4). The movement of each body can be predicted by calculating the total force experienced by the body. If there are N bodies, there will be $N - 1$ forces to calculate for each body, or approximately N^2 calculations, in total. After the new positions of the bodies are determined, the calculations must be repeated. A snapshot of an undergraduate student's results for this problem, given as a programming assignment with a few bodies, is shown in Figure 1.1. However, there could be a huge number of bodies to consider. A galaxy might have, say, 10^{11} stars. This suggests that 10^{22} calculations have to be repeated. Even using the efficient approximate algorithm described in Chapter 4, which requires $N \log_2 N$ calculations (but more involved calculations), the number of calculations is still enormous ($10^{11} \log_2 10^{11}$). It would require significant time on a single-processor system. Even if each calculation could be done in 1 μs (10^{-6} seconds, an extremely optimistic figure, since it involves several multiplications and divisions), it would take 10^9 years for one iteration using the N^2 algorithm and almost a year for one iteration using the $N \log_2 N$ algorithm. The N-body problem also appears in modeling chemical and biological systems at the molecular level and takes enormous computational power.

Global weather forecasting and simulation of a large number of bodies (astronomical or molecular) are traditional examples of applications that require immense computational power, but it is human nature to continually envision new applications that exceed the capabilities of present-day computer systems and require more computational speed than available. Recent applications, such as virtual reality, require considerable computational speed to achieve results with images and movements that appear real without any jerking. It seems that whatever the computational speed of current processors, there will be applications that require still more computational power.

Figure 1.1 Astrophysical *N*-body simulation by Scott Linssen (undergraduate student, University of North Carolina at Charlotte).

A traditional computer has a single processor for performing the actions specified in a program. One way of increasing the computational speed, a way that has been considered for many years, is by using multiple processors within a single computer (multiprocessor) or alternatively multiple computers, operating together on a single problem. In either case, the overall problem is split into parts, each of which is performed by a separate processor in parallel. Writing programs for this form of computation is known as *parallel programming*. The computing platform, a *parallel computer*, could be a specially designed computer system containing multiple processors or several computers interconnected in some way. The approach should provide a significant increase in performance. The idea is that p processors/computers could provide up to p times the computational speed of a single processor/computer, no matter what the current speed of the processor/computer, with the expectation that the problem would be completed in $1/p$th of the time. Of course, this is an ideal situation that is rarely achieved in practice. Problems often cannot be divided perfectly into independent parts, and interaction is necessary between the parts, both for data transfer and synchronization of computations. However, substantial improvement can be achieved, depending upon the problem and the amount of parallelism in the problem. What makes parallel computing timeless is that the continual improvements in the execution speed of processors simply make parallel computers even faster, and there will always be grand challenge problems that cannot be solved in a reasonable amount of time on current computers.

Apart from obtaining the potential for increased speed on an existing problem, the use of multiple computers/processors often allows a larger problem or a more precise solution of a problem to be solved in a reasonable amount of time. For example, computing many physical phenomena involves dividing the problem into discrete solution points. As we have mentioned, forecasting the weather involves dividing the air into a three-dimensional grid of solution points. Two- and three-dimensional grids of solution points occur in many other applications. A multiple computer or multiprocessor solution will often allow more solution points to be computed in a given time, and hence a more precise solution. A related factor is that multiple computers very often have more total main memory than a single computer, enabling problems that require larger amounts of main memory to be tackled.

Even if a problem can be solved in a reasonable time, situations arise when the same problem has to be evaluated multiple times with different input values. This situation is especially applicable to parallel computers, since without any alteration to the program, multiple instances of the same program can be executed on different processors/computers simultaneously. Simulation exercises often come under this category. The simulation code is simply executed on separate computers simultaneously but with different input values.

Finally, the emergence of the Internet and the World Wide Web has spawned a new area for parallel computers. For example, Web servers must often handle thousands of requests per hour from users. A multiprocessor computer, or more likely nowadays multiple computers connected together as a "cluster," are used to service the requests. Individual requests are serviced by different processors or computers simultaneously. On-line banking and on-line retailers all use clusters of computers to service their clients.

The parallel computer is not a new idea; in fact it is a very old idea. For example, Gill wrote about parallel programming in 1958 (Gill, 1958). Holland wrote about a "computer capable of executing an arbitrary number of sub-programs simultaneously" in 1959 (Holland, 1959). Conway described the design of a parallel computer and its programming in 1963 (Conway, 1963). Notwithstanding the long history, Flynn and Rudd (1996) write that "the continued drive for higher- and higher-performance systems . . . leads us to one simple conclusion: the future is parallel." We concur.

1.2 POTENTIAL FOR INCREASED COMPUTATIONAL SPEED

In the following and in subsequent chapters, the number of processes or processors will be identified as p. We will use the term "*multiprocessor*" to include all parallel computer systems that contain more than one processor.

1.2.1 Speedup Factor

Perhaps the first point of interest when developing solutions on a multiprocessor is the question of how much faster the multiprocessor solves the problem under consideration. In doing this comparison, one would use the best solution on the single processor, that is, the best sequential algorithm on the single-processor system to compare against the parallel algorithm under investigation on the multiprocessor. The *speedup factor*, $S(p)$,[1] is a measure of relative performance, which is defined as:

$$S(p) = \frac{\text{Execution time using single processor system (with the best sequential algorithm)}}{\text{Execution time using a multiprocessor with } p \text{ processors}}$$

We shall use t_s as the execution time of the best sequential algorithm running on a single processor and t_p as the execution time for solving the same problem on a multiprocessor.

[1] The speedup factor is normally a function of both p and the number of data items being processed, n, i.e. $S(p,n)$. We will introduce the number of data items later. At this point, the only variable is p.

Then:

$$S(p) = \frac{t_s}{t_p}$$

$S(p)$ gives the increase in speed in using the multiprocessor. Note that the underlying algorithm for the parallel implementation might not be the same as the algorithm on the single-processor system (and is usually different).

In a theoretical analysis, the speedup factor can also be cast in terms of computational steps:

$$S(p) = \frac{\text{Number of computational steps using one processor}}{\text{Number of parallel computational steps with } p \text{ processors}}$$

For sequential computations, it is common to compare different algorithms using time complexity, which we will review in Chapter 2. Time complexity can be extended to parallel algorithms and applied to the speedup factor, as we shall see. However, considering computational steps alone may not be useful, as parallel implementations may require expense communications between the parallel parts, which is usually much more time-consuming than computational steps. We shall look at this in Chapter 2.

The maximum speedup possible is usually p with p processors (*linear speedup*). The speedup of p would be achieved when the computation can be divided into equal-duration processes, with one process mapped onto one processor and no additional overhead in the parallel solution.

$$S(p) \le \frac{t_s}{t_s/p} = p$$

Superlinear speedup, where $S(p) > p$, may be seen on occasion, but usually this is due to using a suboptimal sequential algorithm, a unique feature of the system architecture that favors the parallel formation, or an indeterminate nature of the algorithm. Generally, if a purely deterministic parallel algorithm were to achieve better than p times the speedup over the current sequential algorithm, the parallel algorithm could be emulated on a single processor one parallel part after another, which would suggest that the original sequential algorithm was not optimal.

One common reason for superlinear speedup is extra memory in the multiprocessor system. For example, suppose the main memory associated with each processor in the multiprocessor system is the same as that associated with the processor in a single-processor system. Then, the total main memory in the multiprocessor system is larger than that in the single-processor system, and can hold more of the problem data at any instant, which leads to less disk memory traffic.

Efficiency. It is sometimes useful to know how long processors are being used on the computation, which can be found from the (system) *efficiency*. The efficiency, E, is defined as

$$E = \frac{\text{Execution time using one processor}}{\text{Execution time using a multiprocessor} \times \text{number of processors}}$$

$$= \frac{t_s}{t_p \times p}$$

which leads to

$$E = \frac{S(p)}{p} \times 100\%$$

when E is given as a percentage. For example, if $E = 50\%$, the processors are being used half the time on the actual computation, on average. The efficiency of 100% occurs when all the processors are being used on the computation at all times and the speedup factor, $S(p)$, is p.

1.2.2 What Is the Maximum Speedup?

Several factors will appear as overhead in the parallel version and limit the speedup, notably

1. Periods when not all the processors can be performing useful work and are simply idle.
2. Extra computations in the parallel version not appearing in the sequential version; for example, to recompute constants locally.
3. Communication time between processes.

It is reasonable to expect that some part of a computation cannot be divided into concurrent processes and must be performed sequentially. Let us assume that during some period, perhaps an initialization period or the period before concurrent processes are set up, only one processor is doing useful work, and for the rest of the computation additional processors are operating on processes.

Assuming there will be some parts that are only executed on one processor, the ideal situation would be for all the available processors to operate simultaneously for the other times. If the fraction of the computation that cannot be divided into concurrent tasks is f, and no overhead is incurred when the computation is divided into concurrent parts, the time to perform the computation with p processors is given by $ft_s + (1 - f)t_s/p$, as illustrated in Figure 1.2. Illustrated is the case with a single serial part at the beginning of the computation, but the serial part could be distributed throughout the computation. Hence, the speedup factor is given by

$$S(p) = \frac{t_s}{ft_s + (1 - f)t_s/p} = \frac{p}{1 + (p - 1)f}$$

This equation is known as *Amdahl's law* (Amdahl, 1967). Figure 1.3 shows $S(p)$ plotted against number of processors and against f. We see that indeed a speed improvement is indicated. However, the fraction of the computation that is executed by concurrent processes needs to be a substantial fraction of the overall computation if a significant increase in speed is to be achieved. Even with an infinite number of processors, the maximum speedup is limited to $1/f$; i.e.,

$$\underset{p \to \infty}{S(p)} = \frac{1}{f}$$

For example, with only 5% of the computation being serial, the maximum speedup is 20, irrespective of the number of processors. Amdahl used this argument to promote single-processor

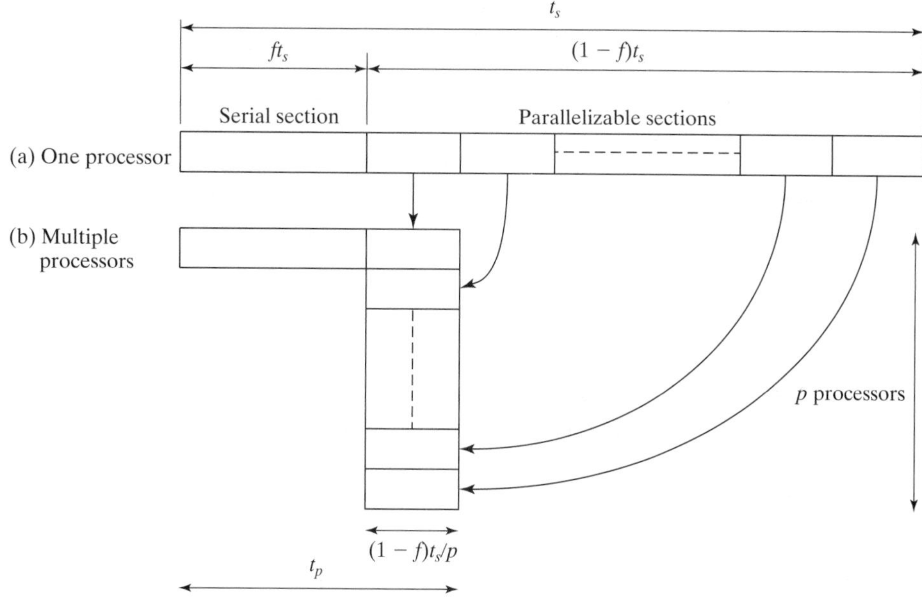

Figure 1.2 Parallelizing sequential problem — Amdahl's law.

systems in the 1960s. Of course, one can counter this by saying that even a speedup of 20 would be impressive.

Orders-of-magnitude improvements are possible in certain circumstances. For example, superlinear speedup can occur in search algorithms. In search problems performed by exhaustively looking for the solution, suppose the solution space is divided among the processors for each one to perform an independent search. In a sequential

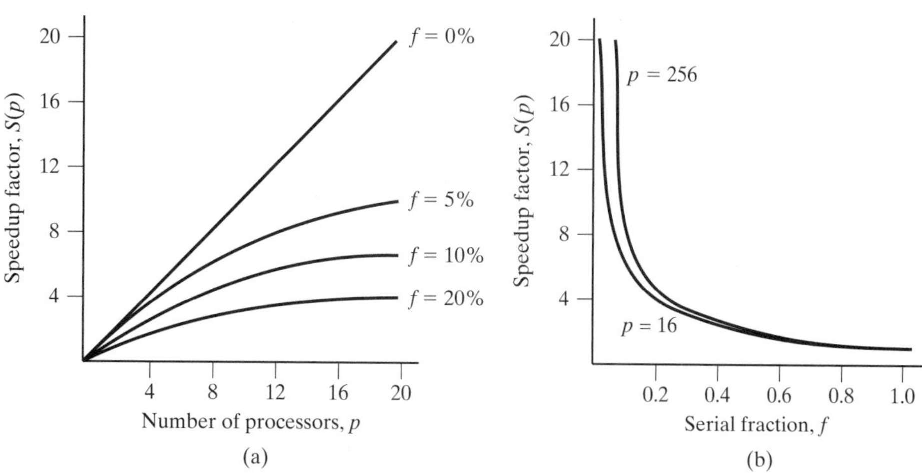

Figure 1.3 (a) Speedup against number of processors. (b) Speedup against serial fraction, f.

implementation, the different search spaces are attacked one after the other. In parallel implementation, they can be done simultaneously, and one processor might find the solution almost immediately. In the sequential version, suppose x sub-spaces are searched and then the solution is found in time Δt in the next sub-space search. The number of previously searched sub-spaces, say x, is indeterminate and will depend upon the problem. In the parallel version, the solution is found immediately in time Δt, as illustrated in Figure 1.4.

The speedup is then given by

$$S(p) = \frac{\left(x \times \frac{t_s}{p}\right) + \Delta t}{\Delta t}$$

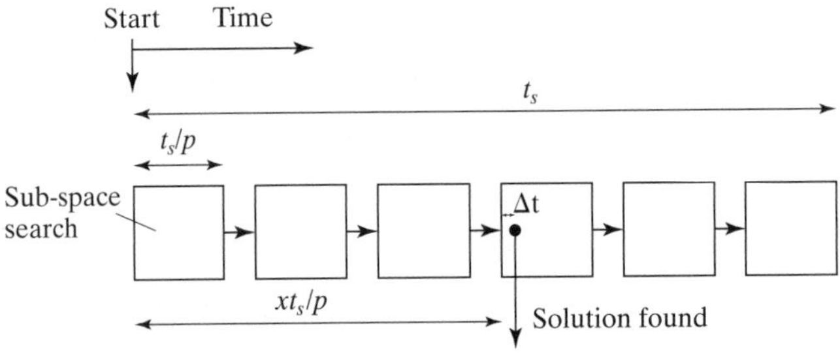

(a) Searching each sub-space sequentially

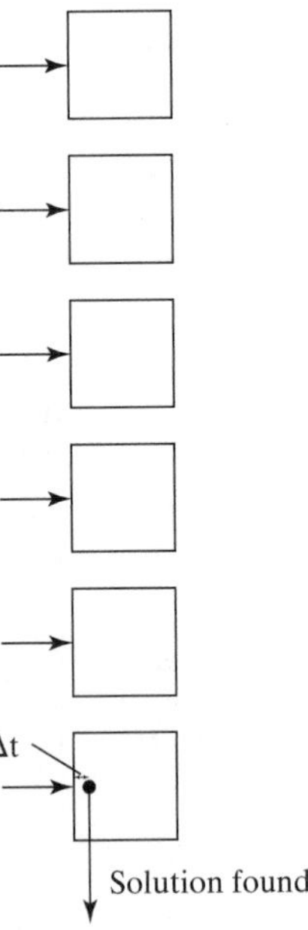

(b) Searching each sub-space in parallel

Figure 1.4 Superlinear speedup.

The worst case for the sequential search is when the solution is found in the last sub-space search, and the parallel version offers the greatest benefit:

$$S(p) = \frac{\left(\frac{p-1}{p}\right) \times t_s + \Delta t}{\Delta t} \rightarrow \infty \quad \text{as } \Delta t \text{ tends to zero}$$

The least advantage for the parallel version would be when the solution is found in the first sub-space search of the sequential search:

$$S(p) = \frac{\Delta t}{\Delta t} = 1$$

The actual speedup will depend upon which sub-space holds the solution but could be extremely large.

Scalability. The performance of a system will depend upon the size of the system, i.e., the number of processors, and generally the larger the system the better, but this comes with a cost. *Scalability* is a rather imprecise term. It is used to indicate a hardware design that allows the system to be increased in size and in doing so to obtain increased performance. This could be described as *architecture* or *hardware scalability.* Scalability is also used to indicate that a parallel algorithm can accommodate increased data items with a low and bounded increase in computational steps. This could be described as *algorithmic scalability.*

Of course, we would want all multiprocessor systems to be *architecturally scalable* (and manufacturers will market their systems as such), but this will depend heavily upon the design of the system. Usually, as we add processors to a system, the interconnection network must be expanded. Greater communication delays and increased contention results, and the system efficiency, *E*, reduces. The underlying goal of most multiprocessor designs is to achieve scalability, and this is reflected in the multitude of interconnection networks that have been devised.

Combined architecture/algorithmic scalability suggests that increased problem size can be accommodated with increased system size for a particular architecture and algorithm. Whereas increasing the size of the system clearly means adding processors, increasing the size of the problem requires clarification. Intuitively, we would think of the number of data elements being processed in the algorithm as a measure of size. However, doubling the problem size would not necessarily double the number of computational steps. It will depend upon the problem. For example, adding two matrices, as discussed in Chapter 11, has this effect, but multiplying matrices does not. The number of computational steps for multiplying matrices quadruples. Hence, scaling different problems would imply different computational requirements. An alternative definition of *problem size* is to equate problem size with the number of basic steps in the best sequential algorithm. Of course, even with this definition, if we increase the number of data points, we will increase the problem size.

In subsequent chapters, in addition to number of processors, *p*, we will also use *n* as the number of input data elements in a problem.[2] These two, *p* and *n*, usually can be altered in an attempt to improve performance. Altering *p* alters the size of the computer system, and altering n alters the size of the problem. Usually, increasing the problem size improves the relative performance because more parallelism can be achieved.

Gustafson presented an argument based upon scalability concepts to show that Amdahl's law was not as significant as first supposed in determining the potential speedup limits (Gustafson, 1988). Gustafson attributed formulating the idea into an equation to E. Barsis. Gustafson makes the observation that in practice a larger multiprocessor usually allows a larger-size problem to be undertaken in a reasonable execution time. Hence in practice, the problem size selected frequently depends of the number of available processors. Rather than assume that the problem size is fixed, it is just as valid to assume that the parallel execution time is fixed. As the system size is increased (p increased), the problem size is increased to maintain constant parallel-execution time. In increasing the problem size, Gustafson also makes the case that the serial section of the code is normally fixed and does not increase with the problem size.

Using the constant parallel-execution time constraint, the resulting speedup factor will be numerically different from Amdahl's speedup factor and is called a *scaled speedup factor* (i.e, the speedup factor when the problem is scaled). For Gustafson's scaled speedup factor, the parallel execution time, t_p, is constant rather than the serial execution time, t_s, in Amdahl's law. For the derivation of Gustafson's law, we shall use the same terms as for deriving Amdahl's law, but it is necessary to separate out the serial and parallelizable sections of the sequential execution time, t_s, into $ft_s + (1 - f)t_s$ as the serial section ft_s is a constant. For algebraic convenience, let the parallel execution time, $t_p = ft_s + (1 - f)t_s/p = 1$. Then, with a little algebraic manipulation, the serial execution time, t_s, becomes $ft_s + (1 - f)t_s = p + (1 - p)ft_s$. The scaled speedup factor then becomes

$$S_s(p) = \frac{ft_s + (1-f)t_s}{ft_s + (1-f)t_s/p} = \frac{p + (1-p)ft_s}{1} = p + (1-p)ft_s$$

which is called *Gustafson's law*. There are two assumptions in this equation: the parallel execution time is constant, and the part that must be executed sequentially, ft_s, is also constant and not a function of p. Gustafson's observation here is that the scaled speedup factor is a line of negative slope $(1 - p)$ rather than the rapid reduction previously illustrated in Figure 1.3(b). For example, suppose we had a serial section of 5% and 20 processors; the speedup is 0.05 + 0.95(20) = 19.05 according to the formula instead of 10.26 according to Amdahl's law. (Note, however, the different assumptions.) Gustafson quotes examples of speedup factors of 1021, 1020, and 1016 that have been achieved in practice with a 1024-processor system on numerical and simulation problems.

Apart from constant problem size scaling (Amdahl's assumption) and time-constrained scaling (Gustafson's assumption), scaling could be memory-constrained scaling. In memory-constrained scaling, the problem is scaled to fit in the available memory. As the number of processors grows, normally the memory grows in proportion. This form can lead to significant increases in the execution time (Singh, Hennessy, and Gupta, 1993).

[2] For matrices, we consider $n \times n$ matrices.

1.2.3 Message-Passing Computations

The analysis so far does not take account of message-passing, which can be a very significant overhead in the computation in message-passing programming. In this form of parallel programming, messages are sent between processes to pass data and for synchronization purposes. Thus,

$$t_p = t_{\text{comm}} + t_{\text{comp}}$$

where t_{comm} is the communication time, and t_{comp} is the computation time. As we divide the problem into parallel parts, the computation time of the parallel parts generally decreases because the parts become smaller, and the communication time between the parts generally increases (as there are more parts communicating). At some point, the communication time will dominate the overall execution time and the parallel execution time will actually increase. It is essential to reduce the communication overhead because of the significant time taken by interprocessor communication. The communication aspect of the parallel solution is usually not present in the sequential solution and considered as an overhead.

The ratio

$$\text{Computation/communication ratio} = \frac{\text{Computation time}}{\text{Communication time}} = \frac{t_{\text{comp}}}{t_{\text{comm}}}$$

can be used as a metric. In subsequent chapters, we will develop equations for the computation time and the communication time in terms of number of processors (p) and number of data elements (n) for algorithms and problems under consideration to get a handle on the potential speedup possible and effect of increasing p and n.

In a practical situation we may not have much control over the value of p, that is, the size of the system we can use (except that we could map more than one process of the problem onto one processor, although this is not usually beneficial). Suppose, for example, that for some value of p, a problem requires c_1n computations and c_2n^2 communications. Clearly, as n increases, the communication time increases faster than the computation time. This can be seen clearly from the computation/communication ratio, (c_1/c_2n), which can be cast in time-complexity notation to remove constants (see Chapter 2). Usually, we want the computation/communication ratio to be as high as possible, that is, some highly increasing function of n so that increasing the problem size lessens the effects of the communication time. Of course, this is a complex matter with many factors. Finally, one can only verify the execution speed by executing the program on a real multiprocessor system, and it is assumed this would then be done. Ways of measuring the actual execution time are described in the next chapter.

1.3 TYPES OF PARALLEL COMPUTERS

Having convinced ourselves that there is potential for speedup with the use of multiple processors or computers, let us explore how a multiprocessor or multicomputer could be constructed. A parallel computer, as we have mentioned, is either a single computer with multiple internal processors or multiple computers interconnected to form a coherent high-performance computing platform. In this section, we shall look at specially designed parallel computers, and later in the chapter we will look at using an off-the-shelf "commodity" computer configured as a cluster. The term *parallel computer* is usually reserved for specially designed components. There are two basic types of parallel computer:

1. Shared memory multiprocessor
2. Distributed-memory multicomputer.

1.3.1 Shared Memory Multiprocessor System

A conventional computer consists of a processor executing a program stored in a (main) memory, as shown in Figure 1.5. Each main memory location in the memory is located by a number called its *address*. Addresses start at 0 and extend to $2^b - 1$ when there are b bits (binary digits) in the address.

A natural way to extend the single-processor model is to have multiple processors connected to multiple memory modules, such that each processor can access any memory module in a so–called *shared memory* configuration, as shown in Figure 1.6. The connection between the processors and memory is through some form of *interconnection network*. A shared memory multiprocessor system employs a *single address space,* which means that each location in the whole main memory system has a unique address that is used by each processor to access the location. Although not shown in these "models," real systems have high-speed cache memory, which we shall discuss later.

Programming a shared memory multiprocessor involves having executable code stored in the shared memory for each processor to execute. The data for each program will also be stored in the shared memory, and thus each program could access all the data if

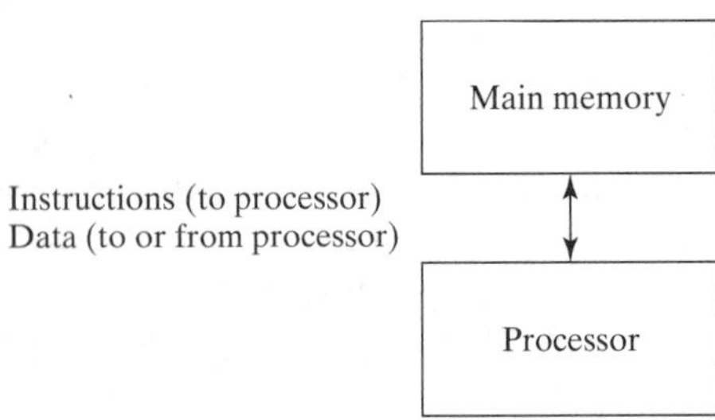

Figure 1.5 Conventional computer having a single processor and memory.

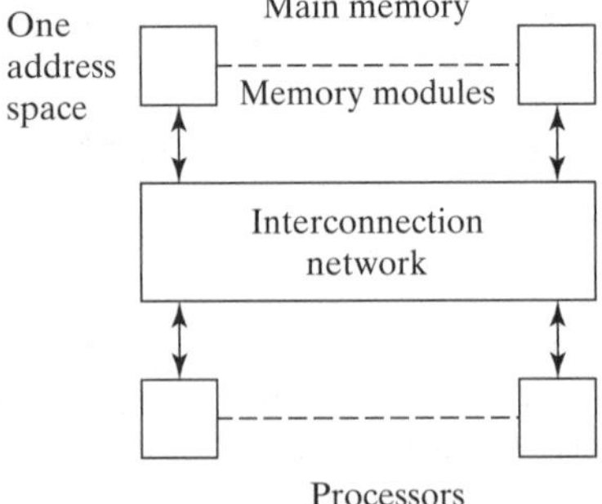

Figure 1.6 Traditional shared memory multiprocessor model.

needed. A programmer can create the executable code and shared data for the processors in different ways, but the final result is to have each processor execute its own program or code sequences from the shared memory. (Typically, all processors execute the same program.)

One way for the programmer to produce the executable code for each processor is to use a high-level parallel programming language that has special parallel programming constructs and statements for declaring shared variables and parallel code sections. The compiler is responsible for producing the final executable code from the programmer's specification in the program. However, a completely new parallel programming language would not be popular with programmers. More likely when using a compiler to generate parallel code from the programmer's "source code," a regular sequential programming language would be used with preprocessor directives to specify the parallelism. An example of this approach is OpenMP (Chandra et al., 2001), an industry-standard set of compiler directives and constructs added to C/C++ and Fortran. Alternatively, so-called *threads* can be used that contain regular high-level language code sequences for individual processors. These code sequences can then access shared locations. Another way that has been explored over the years, and is still finding interest, is to use a regular sequential programming language and modify the syntax to specify parallelism. A recent example of this approach is UPC (Unified Parallel C) (see http://upc.gwu.edu). More details on exactly how to program shared memory systems using threads and other ways are given in Chapter 8.

From a programmer's viewpoint, the shared memory multiprocessor is attractive because of the convenience of sharing data. Small (two-processor and four-processor) shared memory multiprocessor systems based upon a bus interconnection structure-as illustrated in Figure 1.7 are common; for example dual-Pentium® and quad-Pentium systems. Two-processor shared memory systems are particularly cost-effective. However, it is very difficult to implement the hardware to achieve fast access to all the shared memory by all the processors with a large number of processors. Hence, most large shared memory systems have some form of hierarchical or distributed memory structure. Then, processors can physically access nearby memory locations much faster than more distant memory locations. The term *nonuniform memory access* (NUMA) is used in these cases, as opposed to *uniform memory access* (UMA).

Conventional single processors have fast cache memory to hold copies of recently referenced memory locations, thus reducing the need to access the main memory on every memory reference. Often, there are two levels of cache memory between the processor and the main memory. Cache memory is carried over into shared memory multiprocessors by providing each processor with its own local cache memory. Fast local cache memory with each processor can somewhat alleviate the problem of different access times to different main memories in larger systems, but making sure that copies of the same data in different

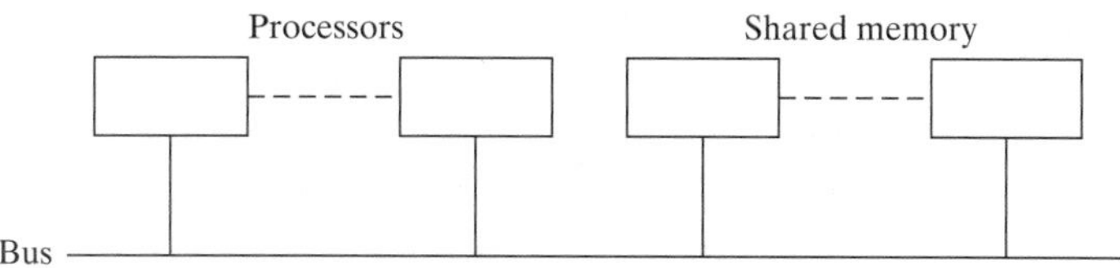

Figure 1.7 Simplistic view of a small shared memory multiprocessor.

caches are identical becomes a complex issue that must be addressed. One processor writing to a cached data item often requires all the other copies of the cached item in the system to be made invalid. Such matters are briefly covered in Chapter 8.

1.3.2 Message-Passing Multicomputer

An alternative form of multiprocessor to a shared memory multiprocessor can be created by connecting complete computers through an interconnection network, as shown in Figure 1.8. Each computer consists of a processor and local memory but this memory is not accessible by other processors. The interconnection network provides for processors to send messages to other processors. The messages carry data from one processor to another as dictated by the program. Such multiprocessor systems are usually called *message-passing multiprocessors*, or simply *multicomputers*, especially if they consist of self-contained computers that could operate separately.

Programming a message-passing multicomputer still involves dividing the problem into parts that are intended to be executed simultaneously to solve the problem. Programming could use a parallel or extended sequential language, but a common approach is to use message-passing library routines that are inserted into a conventional sequential program for message passing. Often, we talk in terms of *processes*. A problem is divided into a number of concurrent processes that may be executed on a different computer. If there were six processes and six computers, we might have one process executed on each computer. If there were more processes than computers, more than one process would be executed on one computer, in a time-shared fashion. Processes communicate by sending messages; this will be the only way to distribute data and results between processes.

The message-passing multicomputer will physically *scale* more easily than a shared memory multiprocessor. That is, it can more easily be made larger. There have been examples of specially designed message-passing processors. Message-passing systems can also employ general-purpose microprocessors.

Networks for Multicomputers. The purpose of the interconnection network shown in Figure 1.8 is to provide a physical path for messages sent from one computer to another computer. Key issues in network design are the *bandwidth*, *latency*, and *cost*. Ease of construction is also important. The *bandwidth* is the number of bits that can be transmitted in unit time, given as bits/sec. The *network latency* is the time to make a message transfer through the network. The *communication latency* is the total time to send the

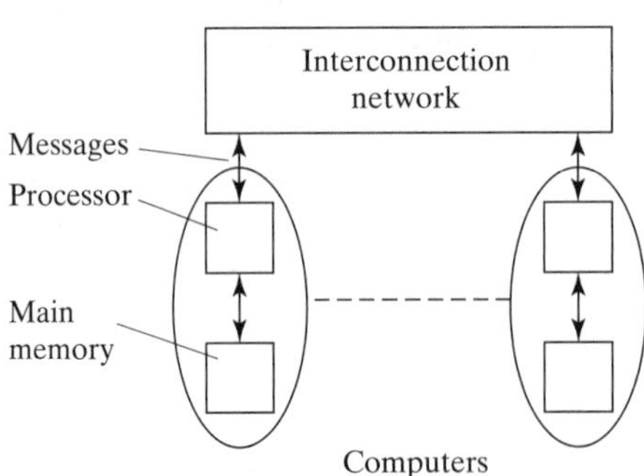

Figure 1.8 Message-passing multiprocessor model (multicomputer).

message, including the software overhead and interface delays. *Message latency,* or *startup time*, is the time to send a zero-length message, which is essentially the software and hardware overhead in sending a message (finding the route, packing, unpacking, etc.) onto which must be added the actual time to send the data along the interconnection path.

The number of physical links in a path between two nodes is an important consideration because it will be a major factor in determining the delay for a message. The *diameter* is the minimum number of links between the two farthest nodes (computers) in the network. Only the shortest routes are considered. How efficiently a parallel problem can be solved using a multicomputer with a specific network is extremely important. The diameter of the network gives the maximum distance that a single message must travel and can be used to find the communication lower bound of some parallel algorithms.

The *bisection width* of a network is the minimum number of links (or sometimes wires) that must be cut to divide the network into two equal parts. The *bisection bandwidth* is the collective bandwidth over these links, that is, the maximum number of bits that can be transmitted from one part of the divided network to the other part in unit time. These factor can also be important in evaluating parallel algorithms. Parallel algorithms usually require numbers to be moved about the network. To move numbers across the network from one side to the other we must use the links between the two halves, and the bisection width gives us the number of links available.

There are several ways one could interconnect computers to form a multicomputer system. For a very small system, one might consider connecting every computer to every other computer with links. With c computers, there are $c(c-1)/2$ links in all. Such exhaustive interconnections have application only for a very small system. For example, a set of four computers could reasonably be exhaustively interconnected. However, as the size increases, the number of interconnections clearly becomes impractical for economic and engineering reasons. Then we need to look at networks with restricted interconnection and switched interconnections.

There are two networks with restricted direct interconnections that have seen wide use — the *mesh* network and the *hypercube* network. Not only are these important as interconnection networks, the concepts also appear in the formation of parallel algorithms.

Mesh. A two-dimensional *mesh* can be created by having each node in a two-dimensional array connect to its four nearest neighbors, as shown in Figure 1.9. The diameter of a $\sqrt{p} \times \sqrt{p}$ mesh is $2(\sqrt{p}-1)$, since to reach one corner from the opposite corner requires a path to made across $(\sqrt{p}-1)$ nodes and down $(\sqrt{p}-1)$ nodes. The free ends of a mesh might circulate back to the opposite sides. Then the network is called a *torus*.

The mesh and torus networks are popular because of their ease of layout and expandability. If necessary, the network can be *folded*; that is, rows are interleaved and columns are interleaved so that the wraparound connections simply turn back through the network rather than stretch from one edge to the opposite edge. Three-dimensional meshes can be formed where each node connects to two nodes in the x-plane, the y-plane, and the z-plane. Meshes are particularly convenient for many scientific and engineering problems in which solution points are arranged in two-dimensional or three-dimensional arrays.

There have been several examples of message-passing multicomputer systems using two-dimensional or three-dimensional mesh networks, including the Intel Touchstone Delta computer (delivered in 1991, designed with a two-dimensional mesh), and the J-machine, a

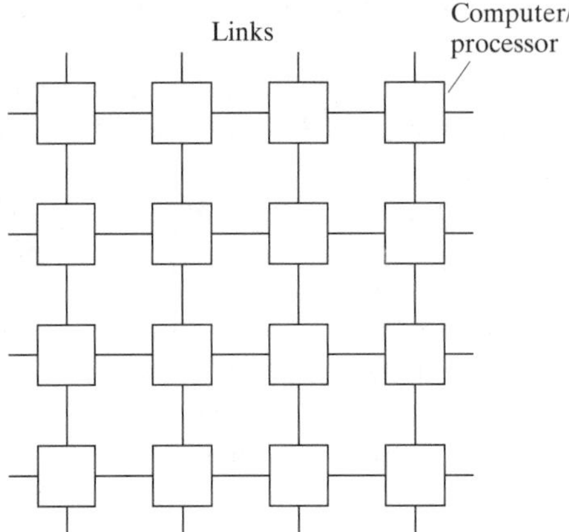

Figure 1.9 Two-dimensional array (mesh).

research prototype constructed at MIT in 1991 with a three-dimensional mesh. A more recent example of a system using a mesh is the ASCI Red supercomputer from the U.S. Department of Energy's Accelerated Strategic Computing Initiative, developed in 1995–97. ASCI Red, sited at Sandia National Laboratories, consists of 9,472 Pentium-II Xeon processors and uses a $38 \times 32 \times 2$ mesh interconnect for message passing. Meshes can also be used in shared memory systems.

Hypercube Network. In a d-dimensional (binary) *hypercube network*, each node connects to one node in each of the dimensions of the network. For example, in a three-dimensional hypercube, the connections in the x-direction, y-direction, and z-direction form a cube, as shown in Figure 1.10. Each node in a hypercube is assigned a d-bit binary address when there are d dimensions. Each bit is associated with one of the dimensions and can be a 0 or a 1, for the two nodes in that dimension. Nodes in a three-dimensional hypercube have a 3-bit address. Node 000 connects to nodes with addresses 001, 010, and 100. Node 111 connects to nodes 110, 101, and 011. Note that each node connects to nodes whose addresses differ by one bit. This characteristic can be extended for higher-dimension hypercubes. For example, in a five-dimensional hypercube, node 11101 connects to nodes 11100, 11111, 11001, 10101, and 01101.

A notable advantage of the hypercube is that the *diameter* of the network is given by $\log_2 p$ for a p-node hypercube, which has a reasonable (low) growth with increasing p. The

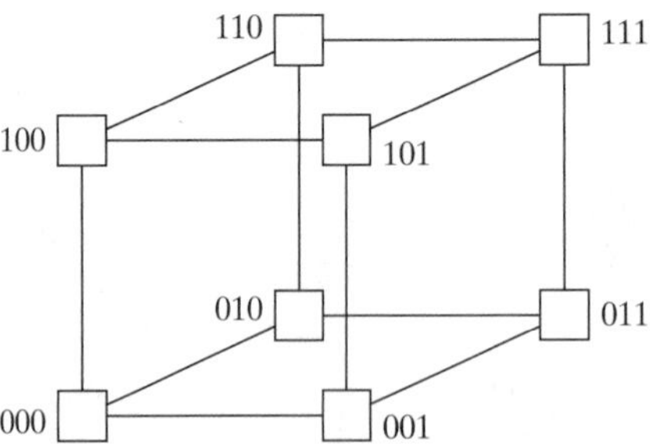

Figure 1.10 Three-dimensional hypercube.

number of links emanating from each node also only grows logarithmically. A very convenient aspect of the hypercube is the existence of a minimal distance deadlock-free routing algorithm. To describe this algorithm, let us route a message from a node X having a nodal address $X = x_{n-1}x_{n-2} \dots x_1x_0$ to a destination node having a nodal address $Y = y_{n-1}y_{n-2} \dots y_1y_0$. Each bit of Y that is different from that of X identifies one hypercube dimension that the route should take and can be found by performing the exclusive-OR function, $Z = X \oplus Y$, operating on pairs of bits. The dimensions to use in the routing are given by those bits of Z that are 1. At each node in the path, the exclusive-OR function between the current nodal address and the destination nodal address is performed. Usually the dimension identified by the most significant 1 in Z is chosen for the route. For example, the route taken from node 13 (001101) to node 42 (101010) in a six-dimensional hypercube would be node 13 (001101) to node 45 (101101) to node 41 (101001) to node 43 (101011) to node 42 (101010). This hypercube routing algorithm is sometimes called the *e-cube routing algorithm*, or *left-to-right routing*.

A d-dimensional hypercube actually consists of two $d - 1$ dimensional hypercubes with dth dimension links between them. Figure 1.11 shows a four-dimensional hypercube drawn as two three-dimensional hypercubes with eight connections between them. Hence, the bisection width is 8. (The bisection width is $p/2$ for a p-node hypercube.) A five-dimensional hypercube consists of two four-dimensional hypercubes with connections between them, and so forth for larger hypercubes. In a practical system, the network must be laid out in two or possibly three dimensions.

Hypercubes are a part of a larger family of k-ary d-cubes; however, it is only the binary hypercube (with $k = 2$) that is really important as a basis for multicomputer construction and for parallel algorithms. The hypercube network became popular for constructing message-passing multicomputers after the pioneering research system called the Cosmic Cube was constructed at Caltech in the early 1980s (Seitz, 1985). However, interest in hypercubes has waned since the late 1980s.

As an alternative to direct links between individual computers, switches can be used in various configurations to route the messages between the computers.

Crossbar switch. The crossbar switch provides exhaustive connections using one switch for each connection. It is employed in shared memory systems more so than

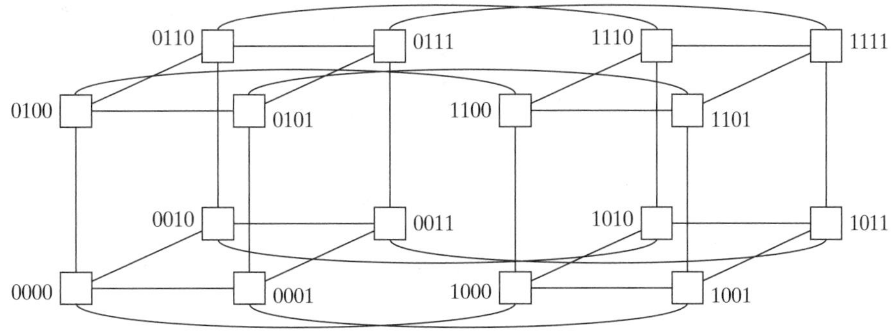

Figure 1.11 Four-dimensional hypercube.

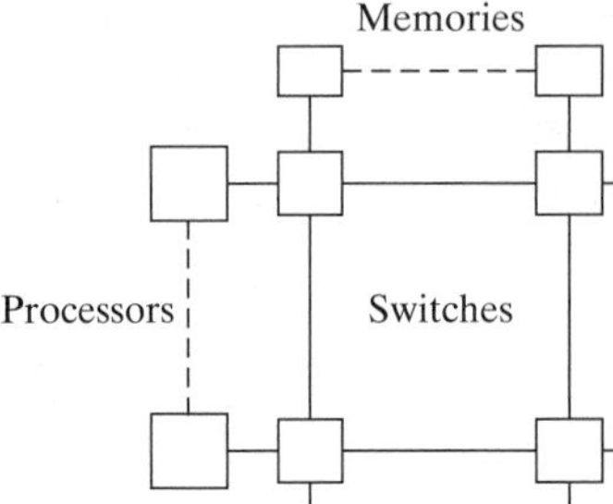

Figure 1.12 Cross-bar switch.

message-passing systems for connecting processor to memories. The layout of the crossbar switch is shown in Figure 1.12. There are several examples of systems using crossbar switches at some level with the system, especially very high performance systems. One of our students built a very early crossbar switch multiple microprocessor system in the 1970s (Wilkinson and Abachi, 1983).

Tree Networks. Another switch configuration is to use a *binary tree*, as shown in Figure 1.13. Each switch in the tree has two links connecting to two switches below it as the network fans out from the root. This particular tree is a *complete binary tree* because every level is fully occupied. The *height* of a tree is the number of links from the root to the lowest leaves. A key aspect of the tree structure is that the height is logarithmic; there are $\log_2 p$ levels of switches with p processors (at the leaves). The tree network need not be complete or based upon the base two. In an m-ary tree, each node connects to m nodes beneath it.

Under uniform request patterns, the communication traffic in a tree interconnection network increases toward the root, which can be a bottleneck. In a *fat tree network* (Leiserson, 1985), the number of the links is progressively increased toward the root. In a *binary fat tree*, we simply add links in parallel, as required between levels of a binary tree, and increase the number of links toward the root. Leiserson developed this idea into the *universal fat tree*, in which the number of links between nodes grows exponentially toward the root, thereby allowing increased traffic toward the root and reducing the communication bottleneck. The most notable example of a computer designed with tree interconnection networks is the Thinking Machine's Connection Machine CM5 computer, which uses a 4-ary fat tree (Hwang, 1993). The fat tree has been used subsequently. For example, the Quadrics QsNet network (see http://www.quadrics.com) uses a fat tree.

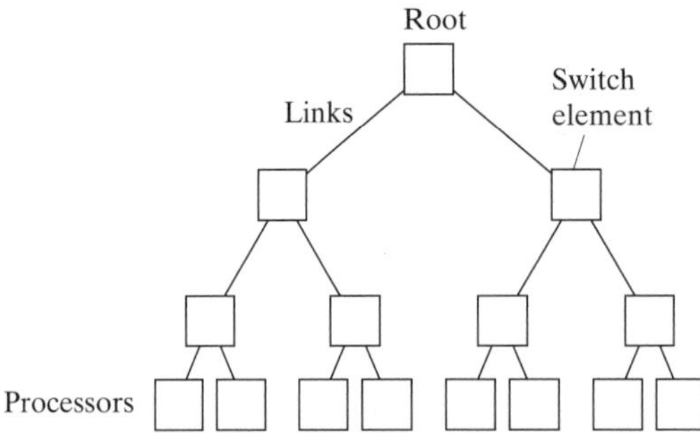

Figure 1.13 Tree structure.

Multistage Interconnection Networks. The multistage interconnection network (MIN) is a classification covering a multitude of configurations with the common characteristic of having a number of levels of switches. Switches in one level are connected to switches in adjacent levels in various symmetrical ways such that a path can made from one side of the network to the other side (and back sometimes). An example of a multistage interconnection network is the Omega network shown in Figure 1.14 (for eight inputs and outputs). This network has a very simple routing algorithm using the destination address. Inputs and outputs are given addresses as shown in the figure. Each switching cell requires one control signal to select either the upper output or the lower output (0 specifying the upper output and 1 specifying the lower). The most significant bit of the destination address is used to control the switch in the first stage; if the most significant bit is 0, the upper output is selected, and if it is 1, the lower output is selected. The next-most significant bit of the destination address is used to select the output of the switch in the next stage, and so on until the final output has been selected. The Omega network is highly blocking, though one path can always be made from any input to any output in a free network.

Multistage interconnection networks have a very long history and were originally developed for telephone exchanges, and are still sometimes used for interconnecting computers or groups of computers for really large systems. For example, the ASCI White supercomputer uses an Omega multistage interconnection network. For more information on multistage interconnection networks see Duato, Yalamanchili, and Ni (1997).

Communication Methods. The ideal situation in passing a message from a source node to a destination node occurs when there is a direct link between the source node and the destination node. In most systems and computations, it is often necessary to route a message through intermediate nodes from the source node to the destination node. There are two basic ways that messages can be transferred from a source to a destination: *circuit switching* and *packet switching*.

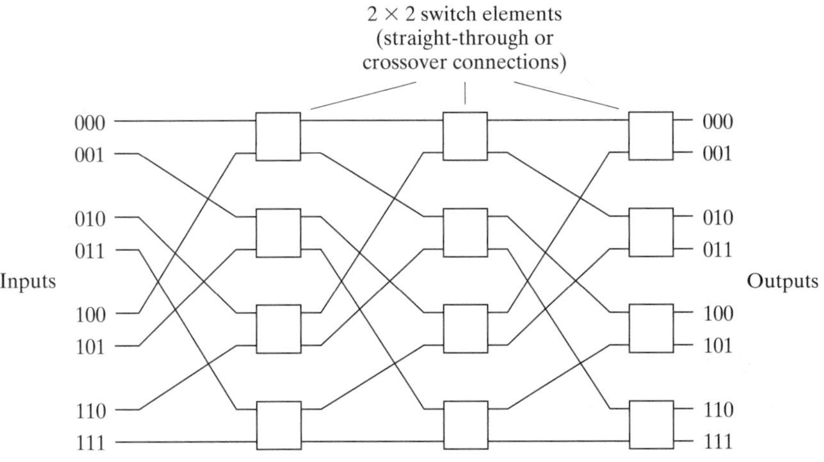

Figure 1.14 Omega network.

Circuit switching involves establishing the path and maintaining all the links in the path for the message to pass, uninterrupted, from the source to the destination. All the links are reserved for the transfer until the message transfer is complete. A simple telephone system (not using advanced digital techniques) is an example of a circuit-switched system. Once a telephone connection is made, the connection is maintained until the completion of the telephone call. Circuit switching has been used on some early multicomputers (e.g., the Intel IPSC-2 hypercube system), but it suffers from forcing all the links in the path to be reserved for the complete transfer. None of the links can be used for other messages until the transfer is completed.

In packet switching, the message is divided into "packets" of information, each of which includes the source and destination addresses for routing the packet through the interconnection network, and the data. There is a maximum size for the packet, say 1000 data bytes. If the message is larger than the maximum size, the message is broken up into separate packets, and each packet is sent through the network separately. Buffers are provided inside nodes to hold packets before they are transferred onward to the next node. A packet remains in a buffer if blocked from moving forward to the next node. The mail system is an example of a packet-switched system. Letters are moved from the mailbox to the post office and handled at intermediate sites before being delivered to the destination. This form of packet switching is called *store-and-forward packet switching* . Store-and-forward packet switching enables links to be used by other packets once the current packet has been forwarded. Unfortunately, store-and-forward packet switching, as described, incurs a significant latency, since packets must first be stored in buffers within each node, whether or not an outgoing link is available. This requirement is eliminated in *cut-through*, a technique originally developed for computer networks (Kermani and Kleinrock, 1979). In cut-through, if the outgoing link is available, the message is immediately passed forward without being stored in the nodal buffer; that is, it is "cut through." Thus, if the complete path were available, the message would pass immediately through to the destination. Note, however, that if the path is blocked, storage is needed for the complete message/packet being received.

Seitz introduced *wormhole* routing (Dally and Seitz, 1987) as an alternative to normal store-and-forward routing to reduce the size of the buffers and decrease the latency. In store-and-forward packet routing, a message is stored in a node and transmitted as a whole when an outgoing link becomes free. In wormhole routing, the message is divided into smaller units called *flits* (flow control digits). A flit is usually one or two bytes (Leighton, 1992). The link between nodes may provide for one wire for each bit in the flit so that the flit can be transmitted in parallel. Only the head of the message is initially transmitted from the source node to the next node when the connecting link is available. Subsequent flits of the message are transmitted when links become available, and the flits can be distributed through the network. When the head flit moves forward, the next one can move forward, and so on. A request/acknowledge signaling system is necessary between nodes to "pull" the flits along. When a flit is ready to move on from its buffer, it makes a request to the next node. When this node has a flit buffer empty, it calls for the flit from the sending node. It is necessary to reserve the complete path for the message as the parts of the message (the flits) are linked. Other packets cannot be interleaved with the flits along the same links.

Wormhole routing requires less storage at each node and produces a latency that is independent of the path length. Ni and McKinley (1993) present an analysis to show the independence of path length on latency in wormhole routing. If the length of a flit is much less than the total message, the latency of wormhole routing will be appropriately constant irrespective of the length of the route. (Circuit switching will produce a similar characteristic.) In contrast, store-and-forward packet switching produces a latency that is approximately proportional to the length of the route, as is illustrated in Figure 1.15.

Interconnection networks, as we have seen, have routing algorithms to find a path between nodes. Some routing algorithms are adaptive in that they choose alternative paths through the network depending upon certain criteria, notably local traffic conditions. In general, routing algorithms, unless properly designed, can be prone to *livelock* and *deadlock*. *Livelock* can occur particularly in adaptive routing algorithms and describes the situation in which a packet keeps going around the network without ever finding its destination. *Deadlock* occurs when packets cannot be forwarded to the next node because they are blocked by other packets waiting to be forwarded, and these packets are blocked in a similar way so that none of the packets can move.

Deadlock can occur in both store-and-forward and wormhole networks. The problem of deadlock appears in communication networks using store-and-forward routing and has been studied extensively in that context. The mathematical conditions and solutions for deadlock-free routing in any network can be found in Dally and Seitz (1987). A general solution to deadlock is to provide *virtual* channels, each with separate buffers, for classes of messages. The *physical* links or channels are the actual hardware links between nodes. Multiple *virtual* channels are associated with a physical channel and time-multiplexed onto the physical channel, as shown in Figure 1.16. Dally and Seitz developed the use of separate virtual channels to avoid deadlock for wormhole networks.

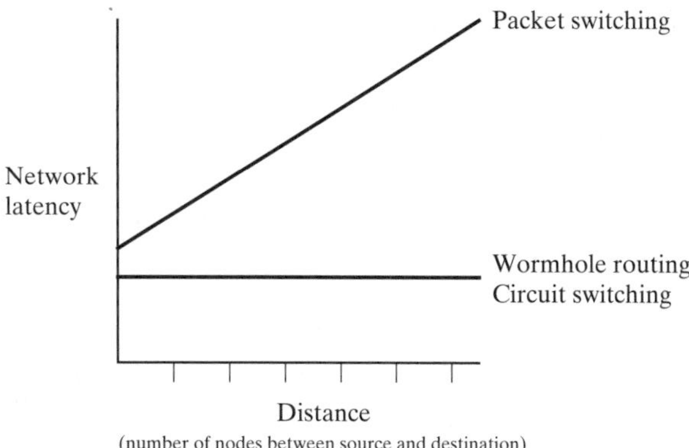

Figure 1.15 Network delay characteristics.

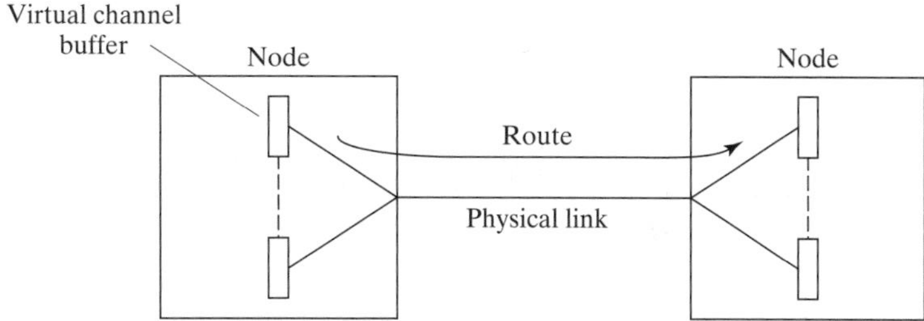

Figure 1.16 Multiple virtual channels mapped onto a single physical channel.

1.3.3 Distributed Shared Memory

The message-passing paradigm is often not as attractive for programmers as the shared memory paradigm. It usually requires the programmers to use explicit message-passing calls in their code, which is very error prone and makes programs difficult to debug. Message-passing programming has been compared to low-level assembly language programming (programming using the internal language of a processor). Data cannot be shared; it must be copied. This may be problematic in applications that require multiple operations across large amounts of data. However, the message-passing paradigm has the advantage that special synchronization mechanisms are not necessary for controlling simultaneous access to data. These synchronization mechanisms can significantly increase the execution time of a parallel program.

Recognizing that the shared memory paradigm is desirable from a programming point of view, several researchers have pursued the concept of a *distributed shared memory system.* As the name suggests, in a distributed shared memory system the memory is physically distributed with each processor, but each processor has access to the whole memory using a single memory address space. For a processor to access a location not in its local memory, message passing occurs to pass data between the processor and the memory location but in some automated way that hides the fact that the memory is distributed. Of course, accesses to remote locations will incur a greater delay, and usually a significantly greater delay, than for local accesses.

Multiprocessor systems can be designed in which the memory is physically distributed but operates as shared memory and appears from the programmer's perspective as shared memory. A number of projects have been undertaken to achieve this goal using specially designed hardware, and there have been commercial systems based upon this idea. Perhaps the most appealing approach is to use networked computers. One way to achieve distributed shared memory on a group of networked computers is to use the existing virtual memory management system of the individual computers which is already provided on almost all systems to manage its local memory hierarchy. The virtual memory management system can be extended to gives the illusion of global shared memory even when it is distributed in different computers.This idea is called *shared virtual memory.* One of the first to develop shared virtual memory was Li (1986). There are other ways to achieve distributed shared memory that do not require the use of the virtual memory management system or special hardware. In any event, physically the system is as given for message-passing multicomputers in Figure 1.8, except that now the local memory becomes part of the shared memory and is accessible from all processors, as illustrated in Figure 1.17.

Implementing and programming a distributed shared memory system is considered in detail in Chapter 9 after the fundamental concepts of shared memory programming in Chapter 8. Shared memory and message passing should be viewed as programming paradigms in that either could be the programming model for any type of multiprocessor, although specific systems may be designed for one or the other.

It should be mentioned that DSM implemented on top of a message-passing system usually will not have the performance of a true shared memory system, nor will using message-passing directly on a message system.

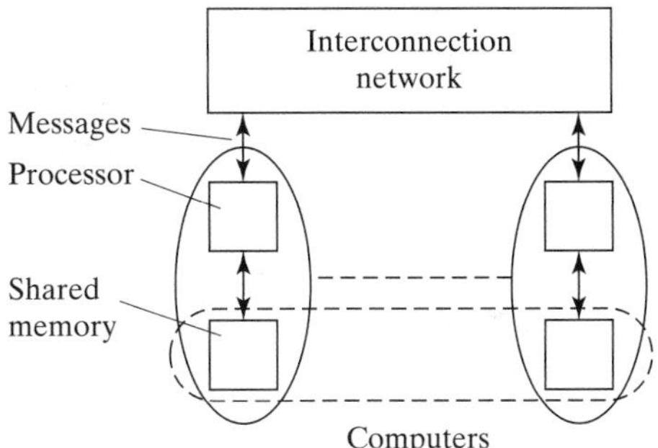

Figure 1.17 Shared memory multiprocessor.

1.3.4 MIMD and SIMD Classifications

In a single-processor computer, a single stream of instructions is generated by the program execution. The instructions operate upon data items. Flynn (1966) created a classification for computers and called this single-processor computer a *single instruction stream-single data stream* (SISD) computer. In a general-purpose multiprocessor system, each processor has a separate program, and one instruction stream is generated from each program for each processor. Each instruction operates upon different data. Flynn classified this type of computer as a *multiple instruction stream-multiple data stream* (MIMD) computer. The shared memory and message-passing multiprocessors so far described are both in the MIMD classification. The term MIMD has stood the test of time and is still widely used for a computer system operating in this mode.

Apart from the two extremes, SISD and MIMD, for certain applications there can be significant performance advantages in designing a computer in which a single instruction stream is from a single program but multiple data streams exist. The instructions from the program are broadcast to more than one processor. Each processor is essentially an arithmetic processor without a (program) control unit. A single control unit is responsible for fetching the instructions from memory and issuing the instructions to the processors. Each processor executes the same instruction in synchronism, but using different data. For flexibility, individual processors can be inhibited from participating in the instruction. The data items form an array, and an instruction acts upon the complete array in one instruction cycle. Flynn classified this type of computer as a *single instruction stream-multiple data stream* (SIMD) computer. The SIMD type of computer was developed because there are a number of important applications that mostly operate upon arrays of data. For example, most computer simulations of physical systems (from molecular systems to weather forecasting) start with large arrays of data points that must be manipulated. Another important application area is low-level image processing, in which the picture elements (pixels) of the image are stored and manipulated, as described in Chapter 12. Having a system that will perform similar operations on data points at the same time will be both efficient in hardware and relatively simple to program. The program simply consists of a single sequence of instructions operating on the array of data points together with normal control instructions executed by the separate control unit. We will not consider SIMD computers in this text as they are specially designed computers, often for specific applications. Computers today can have SIMD instructions for multimedia and graphics applications. For example, the

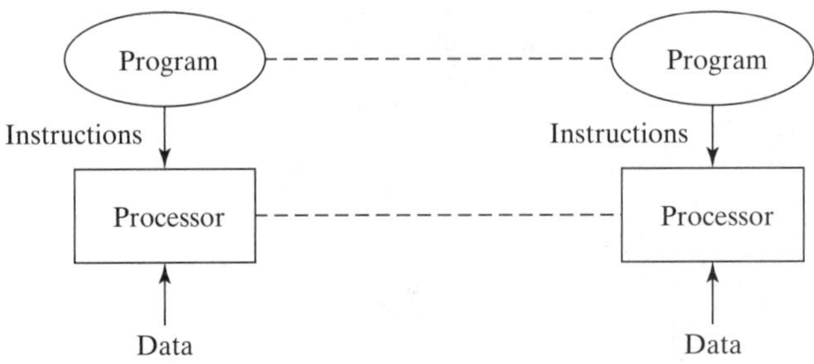

Figure 1.18 MPMD structure.

Pentium family, starting with the Pentium II, now has such SIMD instructions added to speed up multimedia and other applications that require the same operation to be performed on different data, the so-called MMX (MultiMedia eXtension) instructions.

The fourth combination of Flynn's classification, *multiple instruction stream-single data stream* (MISD) computer, does not exist unless one specifically classifies pipelined architectures in this group, or possibly some fault tolerant systems.

Within the MIMD classification, which we are concerned with, each processor has its own program to execute. This could be described as *multiple program multiple data* (MPMD) structure, as illustrated in Figure 1.18. Of course, all of the programs to be executed could be different, but typically only two source programs are written, one for a designated master processor and one for the remaining processors, which are called slave processors. A programming structure we may use, or may have to use, is the *single program multiple data* (SPMD) structure. In this structure, a single source program is written and each processor will execute its personal copy of this program, although independently and not in synchronism. The source program can be constructed so that parts of the program are executed by certain computers and not others depending upon the identity of the computer. For a master-slave structure, the program would have parts for the master and parts for the slaves.

1.4 CLUSTER COMPUTING

1.4.1 Interconnected Computers as a Computing Platform

So far, we have described specially designed parallel computers containing multiple processors or multiple computers as the computing platform for parallel computing. There have been numerous university research projects over the years designing such multiprocessor systems, often with radically different architectural arrangements and different software solutions, each project searching for the best performance. For large systems, the direct links have been replaced with switches and multiple levels of switches (multistage interconnection networks). Computer system manufacturers have come up with numerous designs. The major problem that most manufacturers have faced is the unending progress towards faster and faster processors. Each new generation of processors is faster and able to perform more simultaneous operations internally to boost performance. The most obvious improvement noticed by the computer purchaser is the increase in the clock rate of personal computers. The basic clock rate continues to increase unabated. Imagine purchasing a Pentium (or any other) computer one year and a year later being able to purchase the same system but with twice the clock frequency. And in addition to clock rate, other factors make the system operate even faster. For example, newer designs may employ more internal parallelism within the processor and other ways to achieve faster operation. They often use memory configurations with higher bandwidth. The way around the problem of unending progress of faster processors for "supercomputer" manufacturers has been to use a huge number of available processors. For example, suppose a multiprocessor is designed with state-of-the-art processors in 2004, say 3GHz processors. Using 500 of these processors together should still overtake the performance of any single processor system for some years, but at an enormous cost.

In the late 1980s and early 1990s, another more cost-effective approach was tried by some universities—using workstations and personal computers connected together to form a powerful computing platform. A number of projects explored forming groups of computers from various perspectives. Some early projects explored using workstations as found in laboratories to form a *cluster of workstations* (COWs) or *network of workstations* (NOWs), such as the NOW project at Berkeley (Anderson, Culler, and Patterson, 1995). Some explored using the free time of existing workstations when they were not being used for other purposes, as oftentimes workstations, especially those in offices, are not used continuously or do not require 100% of the processor time even when they are being used.

Initially, using a network of workstations for parallel computing became interesting to many people because networks of workstations already existed for general-purpose computing. Workstations, as the name suggests, were already used for various programming and computer-related activities. It was quickly recognized that a network of workstations, offered a very attractive alternative to expensive supercomputers and parallel computer systems for high-performance computing. Using a network of workstations has a number of significant and well-enumerated advantages over specially designed multiprocessor systems. Key advantages are:

1. Very high performance workstations and PCs are readily available at low cost.
2. The latest processors can easily be incorporated into the system as they become available and the system can be expanded incrementally by adding additional computers, disks, and other resources.
3. Existing application software can be used or modified.

Software was needed to be able to use the workstations collectively, and fortuitously, at around the same time, message-passing tools were developed to make the concept usable. The most important message-passing project to provide parallel programming software tools for these workstations was Parallel Virtual Machine (PVM), started in the late 1980s. PVM was a key enabling technology and led to the success of using networks of workstations for parallel programming. Subsequently, the standard message-passing library, Message-Passing Interface (MPI), was defined.

The concept of using multiple interconnected personal computers (PCs) as a parallel computing platform matured in the 1990s as PCs became very inexpensive and powerful. Workstations, that is, computers particularly targeted towards laboratories, were being replaced in part by regular PCs, and the distinction between workstations and PCs in general-purpose laboratories disappeared. The term "network of workstations" has given way to simply a "cluster" of computers, and using the computers in a cluster collectively on a single problem by the term *cluster computing*.[3]

Ethernet Connections. The communication method for networked computers has commonly been an Ethernet type, which originally consisted of a single wire to which all the computers attach, as shown in Figure 1.19. Shown here is a file server that holds all the files of the users and the system utilities. The use of a single wire was regarded as a cost and layout advantage of the Ethernet design. Nowadays, a single wire has been replaced with various switches and hubs while maintaining the Ethernet protocol. A switch, as the name suggests, provides direct switched connections between the computers to allow multiple simultaneous connections, as illustrated in Figure 1.20, whereas a hub is simply a point where all the computers are connected. The switch automatically routes the packets to their destinations and allows multiple simultaneous connections between separate pairs of computers. Switches are interconnected in various configurations to route messages between the computers in the network.

In the Ethernet type of connection, all transfers between a source and a destination are carried in packets serially (one bit after another on one wire). The packet carries the source address, the destination address, and the data. The basic Ethernet format is shown in

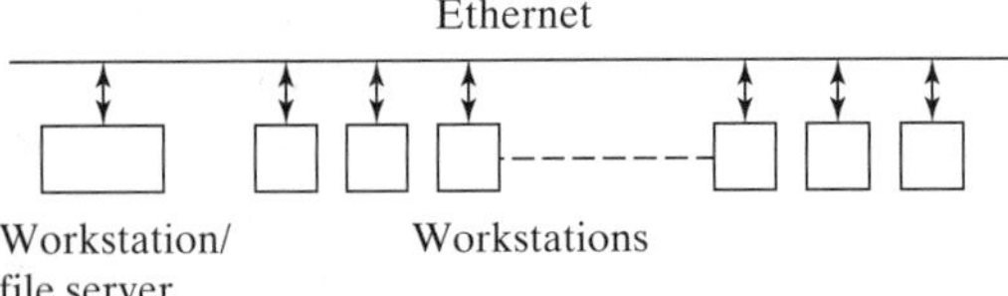

Figure 1.19 Original Ethernet-type single wire network.

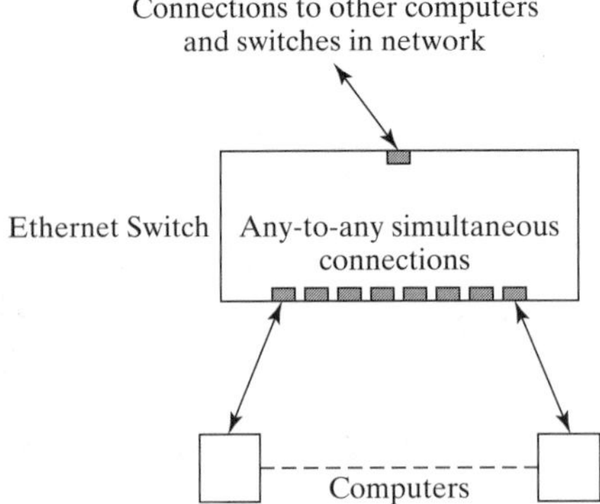

Figure 1.20 Ethernet switch.

[3] Although the term "cluster computing" is now the accepted term, it has been applied to networks of workstations/PCs being used collectively to solve problems since the early 1990s. For example, there were workshops called Cluster Computing at the Supercomputing Computations Research Institute at Florida State University in 1992 and 1993.

Frame check sequence (32 bits)	Data (variable)	Type (16 bits)	Source address (48 bits)	Destination address (48 bits)	Preamble (64 bits)

Direction →

Figure 1.21 Ethernet frame format.

Figure 1.21. The preamble shown in Figure 1.21 is for synchronization. There is a maximum size for the data (1.5 K bytes), and if the data to be sent is larger than that, it is divided in separate packets, each with its source and destination address.[4] Packets could take different paths from the source to the destination and would often do so on a large network or the Internet and have to be reconstituted in the correct order at the destination.

As mentioned, the original Ethernet protocol was designed to use a single wire connecting multiple computers. Since each workstation is operating completely independently and could send messages at any time, the Ethernet line may be needed by one computer while it is already being used to carry packets sent by other another computer. Packets are not sent if it can be detected that information is already being transmitted on the network. It may be that at the time a packet is to be sent, no other information is passing along the Ethernet line at the point where this computer is attached and hence it will launch its packet. However, more than one packet could be launched by different workstations at nearly the same instant. If more than one packet is submitted to the network, the information from them will be corrupted. This is detected at the source by simply comparing the information being sent to that actually on the Ethernet line. If not the same, the individual packets are resubmitted after intervals, all according to the Ethernet protocol (IEEE standard 802.3).

The original speed for Ethernet was 10 Mbits/sec, which has been improved to 100 Mbits/sec and 1000 Mbits/sec (the latter called Gigabit Ethernet). The interconnects can be twisted-pair wire (copper), coax wire, or optical fiber, the latter for higher speed and longer distances. We should mention that the message latency is very significant with Ethernet, especially with the additional overhead caused by some message-passing software.

Network Addressing. TCP/IP (Transmission Control Protocol/Internet Protocol) is a standard that establishes the rules for networked computers to communicate and pass data. On the Internet, each "host" computer is given an address for identification purposes. TCP/IP defines the format of addresses as a 32-bit number divided into four 8-bit numbers (for IPv4, Internet Protocol version 4). With certain constraints, each number is in the range 0–255. The notation for the complete address is to separate each number by a period. For example, a computer might be given the IP address:

```
129.49.82.1
```

In binary, this address would be:

```
10000001.00110001.01010010.00000001
```

[4] It is possible to increase the packet size. Alteron Networks has a propriety technique called jumbo frames to increase the packet size from 1,500 bytes to 9,000 bytes.

The address is divided into fields to select a network, a possible sub-network, and computer ("host") within the sub-network or network. There are several formats identified by the first one, two, three, or four bits of the address. The layout of the IPv4 formats are shown in Figure 1.22. This information is relevant for setting up a cluster.

Class A format is identified with a leading 0 in the address and uses the next seven bits as the network identification. The remaining 24 bits identify the sub-network and "host" (computer). This provides for 16,777,216 (2^{24}) hosts within a network, but only 128 networks are available. The hosts can be arranged in various sub-network configurations. Class A would be used for very large networks.

Class B is for medium-sized networks and identified by the first two bits being 10. The network is identified by the next 14 bits. The remaining 16 bits are used for the sub-network and host. This provides for 65,536 (2^{16}) hosts within a network, and 16,384 (2^{14}) networks are available. Again the hosts can be arranged in various sub-network configurations, but a simple configuration would be to have 256 sub-networks and 256 hosts in each sub-network; that is, the first eight-bits of the sub-network/host part to identify the sub-network and the remaining eight bits to identify the host within the sub-network.

Class C is for small networks and identified by the first three bits being 110. The network is identified by the next 21 bits. The remaining eight bits are used for the host. This provides for 256 (2^8) hosts within a network, and 2,097,152 (2^{21}) networks are available.

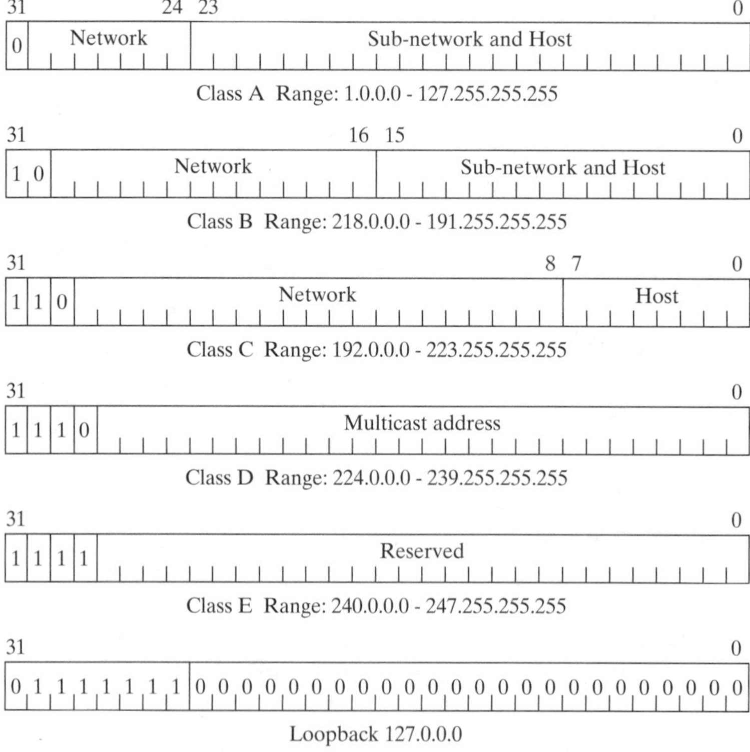

Figure 1.22 IPv4 formats.

The hosts can be arranged in various sub-network configurations, but a simple configuration would not to have a sub-network.

Class D is used to broadcast a message to multiple destinations simultaneously; that is, the transmission is picked up by multiple computers (called multicast). The loopback format is used to send a message back to oneself for testing. Certain addresses are reserved, as indicated in Figure 1.22, and some network addresses within classes A, B, and C are reserved for private networks (10.0.0.0 to 10.255.255.255, 172.16.0.0 to 172.32.255.255, and 192.168.0.0 to 192.168.255.255). Private network addresses can be used on dedicated clusters, as will be discussed later.

IPv4 with its 32-bit addresses provides for about 4 billion hosts (2^{32} = 4,294,967,296, less those not used for specific host addresses). The Internet has grown tremendously, to over 100,000,000 hosts by 2001 by most estimates (Knuckles, 2001), and soon more IP addresses will be needed. Not only are IP addresses used for computers connected to the Internet permanently, as in computer laboratories; IP addresses are also used by Internet Service Providers for dial-up and other connections to customers. IPv6 (Internet Protocol version 6) has been developed to extend the addressability of IPv4 by using 128 bits divided into eight 16-bit sections. This gives 2^{128} possible hosts (a big number!). IPv6 also has a number of other enhancements for message transfers. Network software can be designed to handle both IPv4 and IPv6. For the following, we will assume IPv4 addresses.

The IP addressing information is important to setting up a cluster because IP addressing is usually used to communicate between computers within the cluster and between the cluster and users outside the cluster. Network addresses are assigned to the organization by the Internet Assigned Number Authority. The sub-network and host assignments are chosen by the organization (i.e., its system administrator for the sub-network/host). Masks are set up in the communication software to select the network, sub-network, and host field. The masks are 32-bit numbers with 1's defining the network/sub-network part of the address. For example, the mask for a class B address with bits 8 to 15 (in Figure 1.22) used for the sub-network would be:

```
255.255.255.0
```

or in binary:

```
11111111.11111111.11111111.00000000
```

which is used to separate the host address from the network/sub-network address. Note that the division of sub-network and host field need not be on 8-bit boundaries and is decided by the local system administrator, but the network address (A, B, or C) is allocated to the organization.

Computers connect to an Ethernet cable via a Ethernet network interface card (NIC). The source and destination addresses in the Ethernet format shown in Figure 1.21 are not IP addresses; they are the addresses of network interface cards. These addresses are 48 bits and called MAC (Media Access Controller) addresses. Each network interface card has a predefined and unique 48-bit MAC address that is set up during manufacture of the chip or card. (Allocation of addresses is controlled by the IEEE Registration Authority.) While the IP address of a computer is selected by software, the MAC address of each NIC is unalterable. A translation is necessary between the two to establish a communication path. The higher-level software will use IP addresses, and the lower-level network interface software will use MAC addresses. Actually, both MAC and IP address are contained in the Ethernet packet, the IP addresses are within the data part of the packet in Figure 1.21.

There is a level above IP addressing whereby IP addresses are converted into names for ease of user interaction. For example, `sol.cs.wcu.edu`, is the name of one of Western Carolina University's servers within the Department of Mathematics and Computer Science; its IP address is `152.30.5.10`. The relationship between name and IP address is established using the Domain Naming Service, a distributed name database.[5]

1.4.2 Cluster Configurations

There are several ways a cluster can be formed.

Existing Networked Computers. One of the first ways to form a cluster was to use existing networked workstations in a laboratory, as illustrated in Figure 1.23(a). These workstations were already provided with IP addresses for network communication. Messaging software provided the means of communication. Indeed, the first way tried by the authors for teaching cluster computing in the early 1990s was to use existing networked computers. Using a network of existing computers is very attractive for educational institutions because it can be done without additional resources. However, it can present significant problems in the usage of the computers. Cluster computing involves using multiple computers simultaneously. Clearly, it is possible with modern operating systems to arrange for the computers to run the cluster computing programs in the background while other

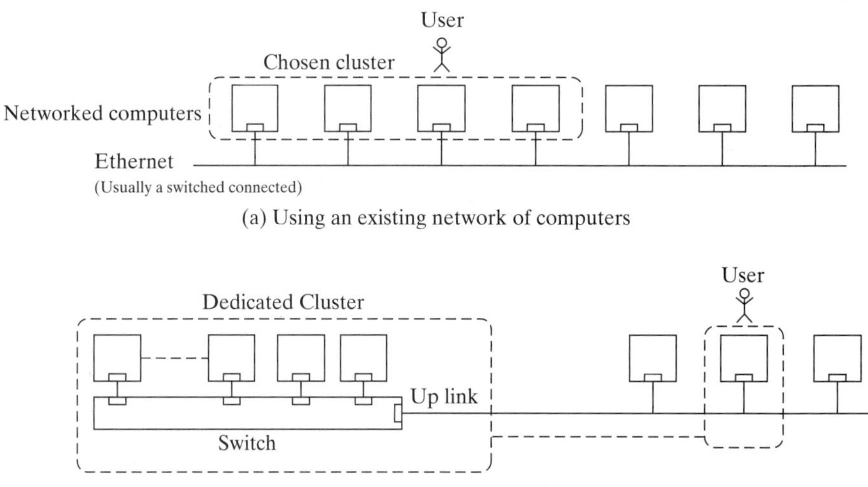

Figure 1.23 Early ways to form a cluster.

[5] In UNIX systems, the relationship between host name and IP address is held in a file called hosts, which can be inspected (e.g., cat /etc/hosts). A look-up table is maintained holding the relationship between the name/IP address and Ethernet MAC address of hosts. This table can be inspected with the address resolution protocol command arp -a.

users are directly working at the computer. Moreover, the structure of the message-passing software then used (PVM) made this easy. In practice, situations arise that make it unworkable. Users at the computer can cause the computer to stop while the cluster computing work is in progress (they can simply turn the computer off!). Conversely, cluster computing activities by students can cause the computers to get into difficulties. It also requires the ability for remote access to the computers, with possible security issues if not done properly. At the time, the common way for remote access (in UNIX) was through "r" commands (`rlogin`, `rsh`) which were used by the message-passing software to start processes remotely. Since these commands are insecure, students would be able to remotely access other computers and cause havoc. (Passwords were transmitted unencrypted.) More recently, of course, remote access has been made secure with the use of `ssh`.

Moving to a Dedicated Computer Cluster. We quickly found it very cost-effective (free!) and less trouble simply to move computers from a laboratory into a dedicated cluster when the computers were upgraded in the laboratory. Every time the laboratory was upgraded, so was the cluster, but with last year's models that were being replaced in the laboratory. The computers forming a cluster need not have displays or keyboards and are linked with the same communication medium as used in the laboratories. Simply moving computers into a dedicated group could be done without any changes to IP addresses. The computers could still belong to the sub-network as before except that each computer would never have local users sitting at its console. All access is done remotely. A user would login to a computer outside the cluster group and enroll the cluster computers together with its own computer to form a cluster, as illustrated in Figure 1.23(b). Note that the computers in the cluster would be the type that were originally selected for the computer laboratory. For example, our cluster formed that way originally consisted of eight SUN IPC computers in the early 1990s, which were upgraded to eight SUN Ultra computers later when these computers were being replaced in the general-purpose laboratories.

Beowulf Clusters. A small but very influential cluster-computing project was started at the NASA Goddard Space Flight Center in 1993, concentrating upon forming a cost-effective computer cluster by the use of readily available low-cost components. Standard off-the-shelf microprocessors were chosen with a readily available operating system (Linux) and connected together with low-cost interconnects (Ethernet). Whereas other projects were also concerned with constructing clusters, they often used some specialized components and software in their design to obtain the best performance. In contrast, the NASA project started with the premise that only widely available low-cost components should be used, chosen on a cost/performance basis. It was entitled the Beowulf project (Sterling, 2002a and 2002b). This name has stuck for describing any cluster of low-cost computers using commodity interconnects and readily available software for the purpose of obtaining a cost-effective computing platform. Originally, Intel processors (486's) were used and the free Linux operating system, and Linux is a still common operating system for Beowulf clusters with Intel processors. Other types of processors can be employed in a Beowulf cluster.

The key attribute for attaching the name Beowulf to a cluster is the use of widely available components to obtain the best cost/performance ratio. The term *commodity computer* is used to highlight the fact that the cost of personal computers is now so low that computers can be bought and replaced at frequent intervals. The mass market for personal computers has made their manufacture much less expensive. And this applies to all the components around the processor, such as memory and network interfaces. We now have commodity Ethernet network interfaces cards (NICs) at minimal cost. Such interconnects can be used to connect the commodity computers to form a cluster of commodity computers.

Beyond Beowulf. Clearly, one would use higher-performance components if that made economic sense, and really high-performance clusters would use the highest-performance components available.

Interconnects. Beowulf clusters commonly use fast Ethernet in low-cost clusters. Gigabit Ethernet is an easy upgrade path; this was the choice made at UNC-Charlotte. However, there are more specialized and higher-performance interconnects, such as Myrinet, a 2.4 Gbits/sec interconnect. There are other interconnects that could be used, including cLan, SCI (Scalable Coherent Interface), QsNet, and Infiniband; see Sterling (2002a) for more details.

Clusters with Multiple Interconnects. The Beowulf project and other projects explored using multiple parallel interconnections to reduce the communication overhead. Clusters can be set up with multiple Ethernet cards or network cards of different types. The original Beowulf project used two regular Ethernet connections per computer and a "channel bonding" technique. Channel bonding associates several physical interfaces with a single virtual channel. Software is available to achieve this effect (e.g., see http://cesdis.gsfc.nasa.gov/beowulf/software). In the context of Beowulf, the resulting structure had to be cost-effective. It did show significant improvement in performance (see Sterling, 2002 for more details). Some recent clusters have used slower Ethernet connections for set-up and faster interconnects such as Myrinet for communication during program execution.

We have worked on the concept of using multiple Ethernet lines configured as shown in Figure 1.24(a), (b), and (c). There are numerous ways that switches can be used. The configurations shown are in the general classification of overlapping connectivity networks (Hoganson, Wilkinson, and Carlisle, 1997; Wilkinson, 1990, 1991, 1992a, 1992b). Overlapping connectivity networks have the characteristic that regions of connectivity are provided and the regions overlap. In the case of overlapping connectivity Ethernets, this is achieved by having Ethernet segments such as shown in the figure, but there are several other ways overlapping connectivity can be achieved; see, for example, Wilkinson and Farmer (1994). It should be mentioned that the structures of Figure 1.24 significantly reduce collisions but the latency and data transmission times remain.

Symmetrical Multiprocessors (SMP) Cluster. Small shared memory multiprocessors based around a bus, as described in Section 1.2.1, have a symmetry between their processors and memory modules and are called symmetric or symmetrical (shared memory) multiprocessors. Small shared memory multiprocessor systems based upon Pentium processors are very cost-effective, especially two-processor systems. Hence, it is also reasonable to form clusters of "symmetrical multiprocessor" (SMP) systems, as illustrated in Figure 1.25. This leads to some interesting possibilities for programming such a cluster. Between SMPs, message passing could be used, and within the SMPs, threads or other

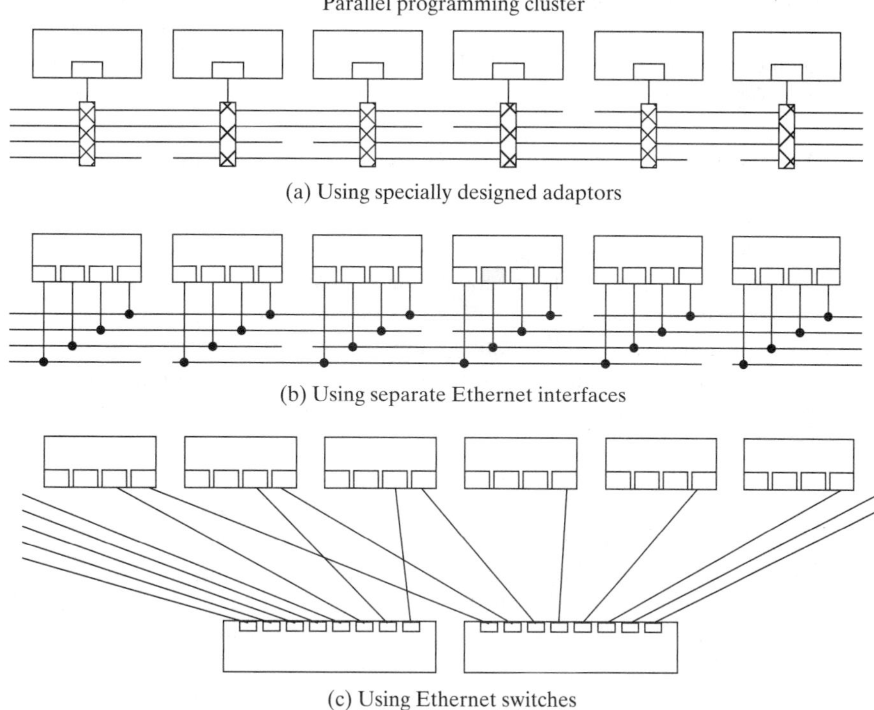

Figure 1.24 Overlapping connectivity Ethernets.

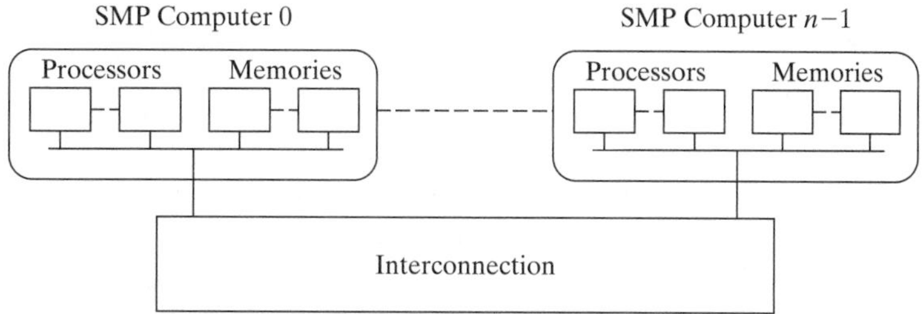

Figure 1.25 Cluster of shared memory computers.

shared memory methods could be used. Often, however, for convenience, message passing is done uniformly. When a message is to pass between processors within a SMP computer, the implementation might use shared memory locations to hold the messages, and communication would be much faster.

Web Clusters. Since the arrival of the Internet and the World Wide Web, computers in different locations and even countries are interconnected. The emergence of the Web has led to the possibility of using computers attached to the Web at various sites for parallel programming. Projects have investigated using the "web" of computers to form a parallel computing platform. The idea was originally called *metacomputing* and is now called *grid computing*. Projects involved in this type of large-scale cluster computing include Globus, Legion, and WebFlow. More details of these three systems can be found in Baker and Fox (1999).

1.4.3 Setting Up a Dedicated "Beowulf Style" Cluster

"Beowulf style" implies commodity components. These are generally PCs that can be bought from well-known suppliers. These suppliers have now embraced cluster computing and offer pre-packaged cluster computing systems, although they may be targeted towards very high performance using multiple dual/quad processor servers. In any event, the setup procedures have been substantially simplified with the introduction of software packages such as Oscar, which automates the procedure of loading the operating system and other procedures. We shall briefly outline Oscar later in this section.

Hardware Configuration. A common hardware configuration is to have one computer operating as a master node with the other computers in the cluster operating as compute nodes within a private network. The master node is traditionally known as the *frontend* and acts as a file server with significant memory and storage capacity. Generally, it is convenient for all the compute nodes to have disk drives, although diskless compute nodes are possible. Connection between the compute nodes and the master node can be by Fast or Gigabit Ethernet (or possibly a more specialized interconnect, such as Myrinet), as illustrated in Figure 1.26. The master node needs a second Ethernet interface to connect to the outside world and would have a globally accessible IP address. The compute nodes would be given private IP addresses; that is, these computers can only communicate within the cluster network and are not directly accessible from outside the cluster.

This model can be enhanced in several ways. Another computer acting as an administrative or management node can be added. This node would be used by the system administrator for monitoring the cluster and testing. The sole purpose of the compute nodes is to perform computations, so they do not need a keyboard or display. However, it may be convenient to be able to access each compute node through its normal console input. Hence, the serial connections of these nodes could be brought back to the master though a serial concentrator switch or, if present, the administrative node. There are various possible connections. Figure 1.27 shows one arrangement whereby a single display and keyboard are present that can be switched between the master node and the administrative node.

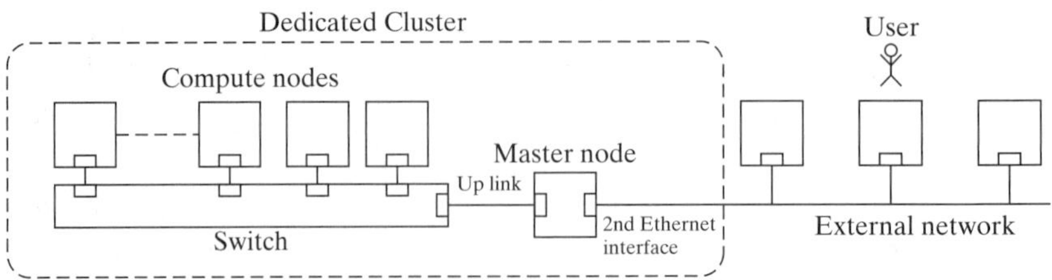

Figure 1.26 Dedicated cluster with a master node.

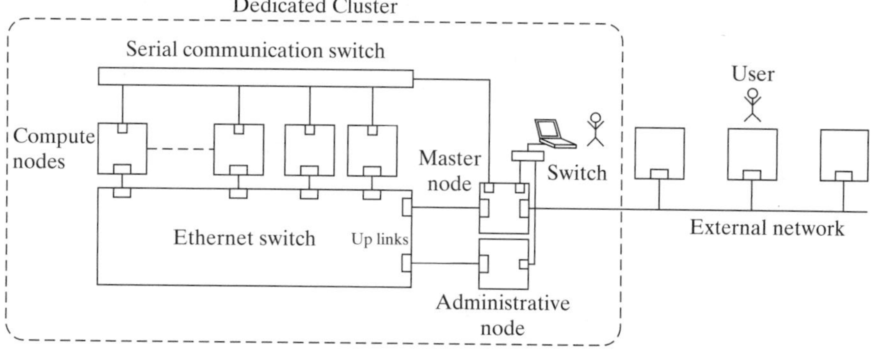

Figure 1.27 Dedicated cluster with a master and administrative nodes and serial connections.

Software Configuration. Normally every computer in the cluster will have a copy of the operating system (traditionally Linux, but Windows clusters can also be formed). The master node will normally also contain all the application files for the cluster and be configured as a file server using a network file system, which allows the compute nodes to see and have direct access to files stored remotely. The most commonly used network file system is NFS. Note that the cluster compute nodes are separated from the outside network and all user access is through the master node via a separate Ethernet interface and IP address. Mounted on the master node will be the message-passing software (MPI and PVM, which will be discussed in Chapter 2), cluster-management tools, and parallel applications. The message-passing software is between the operating system and the user, and is the *middleware*.

Once all the software is established, the user can log onto the master node and enroll compute nodes using the message-passing software, again as will be described in Chapter 2. The challenge here is to set up the cluster in the first place, which involves fairly detailed operating system and networking knowledge (i.e., Linux commands and how to use them). There are books and Web sites dedicated to this task (and even workshops). Fortunately, as mentioned, the task of setting up the software for a cluster has been substantially simplified with the introduction of cluster setup packages, including Oscar (Open Source Cluster Application Resources), which is menu driven and freely available. Before starting with Oscar, the operating system (RedHat Linux) has to be mounted on the master mode. Then, in a number of menu-driven steps, Oscar mounts the required software and configures the cluster. Briefly, NFS and network protocols are set up on the master node. The cluster is defined in a database. The private cluster network is defined with IP addresses selected by the user. The Ethernet interface MAC addresses of the compute nodes are collected. They are obtained by each compute node making a Boot Protocol (BOOTP/DHCP) request to the master node. IP addresses are returned for the compute nodes. Also returned is the name of the "boot" file specifying which kernel (the central part of operating system) to boot. The kernel is then downloaded and booted, and the compute node file system created. The operating system on the compute nodes is installed through the network using the Linux installation utility LUI. Finally, the cluster is configured and middleware installed and configured. Test programs are run. The cluster is then ready. Workload management tools are provided for batch queues, scheduling, and job monitoring. Such tools are very desirable for a cluster. More details of Oscar can be found at http://www.csm.ornl.gov/oscar.

1.5 SUMMARY

This chapter introduced the following concepts:

- Parallel computers and programming
- Speedup and other factors
- Extension of a single processor system into a shared memory multiprocessor
- The message-passing multiprocessor (multicomputer)
- Interconnection networks suitable for message-passing multicomputers
- Networked workstations as a parallel programming platform
- Cluster computing

FURTHER READING

Further information on the internal design of multiprocessor systems can be found in computer architecture texts such as Culler and Singh (1999), Hennessy and Patterson (2003), and Wilkinson (1996). A great deal has been published on interconnection networks. Further information on interconnection networks can be found in a significant textbook by Duato, Yalamanchili, and Ni (1997) devoted solely to interconnection networks. An early reference to the Ethernet is Metcalfe and Boggs (1976).

Anderson, Culler, and Patterson (1995) make a case for using a network of workstations collectively as a multiple computer system. Web-based material on workstation cluster projects includes http://cesdis.gsfc.nasa.gov/beowulf. An example of using shared memory on networked workstations can be found in Amza et al. (1996).

Recognizing the performance limitation of using commodity interfaces in workstation clusters has led several researchers to design higher-performance network interface cards (NICs). Examples of work in this area includes Blumrich et al. (1995), Boden et al. (1995), Gillett and Kaufmann (1997), and Minnich, Burns, and Hady (1995). Martin et al. (1997) have also made a detailed study of the effects of communication latency, overhead, and bandwidth in clustered architecture. One point they make is that it may be better to improve the communication performance of the communication system rather than invest in doubling the machine performance.

The two-volume set edited by Buyya (1999a and 1999b) provides a wealth of information on clusters. Williams (2001) wrote an excellent text on computer system architecture with an emphasis on networking. Details about building a cluster can be found in Sterling (2002a and 2002b).

BIBLIOGRAPHY

AMDAHL, G. (1967), "Validity of the Single-Processor Approach to Achieving Large-Scale Computing Capabilities," *Proc. 1967 AFIPS Conf.*, Vol. 30, p. 483.

AMZA, C., A. L. COX, S. DWARKADAS, P. KELEHER, H. LU, R. RAJAMONY, W. YU, AND W. ZWAENEPOEL (1996), "TreadMarks: Shared Memory Computing on Networks of Workstations," *Computer*, Vol. 29, No. 2, pp. 18–28.

ANDERSON, T. E., D. E. CULLER, AND D. PATTERSON (1995), "A Case for NOW (Networks of Workstations," *IEEE Micro*, Vol. 15, No. 1, pp. 54–64.

BLUMRICH, M. A., C. DUBNICKI, E. W. FELTON, K. LI, AND M. R. MESRINA (1995), "Virtual-Memory-Mapped Network Interface," *IEEE Micro*, Vol. 15, No. 1, pp. 21–28.

BAKER, M., AND G. FOX (1999), "Chapter 7 Metacomputing: Harnessing Informal Supercomputers," *High Performance Cluster Computing,* Vol. 1 *Architecture and Systems*, (Editor BUYYA, R.), Prentice Hall PTR, Upper Saddle River, NJ.

BODEN, N. J., D. COHEN, R. E. FELDERMAN, A. E. KULAWIK, C. L. SEITZ, J. N. SEIZOVIC, AND W.-K. SU (1995), "Myrinet: A Gigabit-per-Second Local Area Network," *IEEE Micro*, Vol. 15, No. 1, pp. 29–36.

BUYYA, R., Editor (1999a), *High Performance Cluster Computing,* Vol. 1 *Architecture and Systems*, Prentice Hall PTR, Upper Saddle River, NJ.

BUYYA, R. Editor (1999b), *High Performance Cluster Computing,* Vol. 2 *Programming and Applications*, Prentice Hall PTR, Upper Saddle River, NJ.

CHANDRA, R., L. DAGUM, D. KOHR. D. MAYDAN, J. MCDONALD, AND R. MENON (2001), *Parallel Programming in OpenMP,* Morgan Kaufmann Publishers, San Francisco, CA.

CONWAY, M. E. (1963), "A Multiprocessor System Design," *Proc. AFIPS Fall Joint Computer Conf.*, Vol. 4, pp. 139–146.

CULLER, D. E., AND J. P. SINGH (1999), *Parallel Computer Architecture A Hardware/Software Approach*, Morgan Kaufmann Publishers, San Francisco, CA.

DALLY, W., AND C. L. SEITZ (1987), "Deadlock-free Message Routing in Multiprocessor Interconnection Networks," *IEEE Trans. Comput.*, Vol. C-36, No. 5, pp. 547–553.

DUATO, J., S. YALAMANCHILI, AND L. NI (1997), *Interconnection Networks: An Engineering Approach*, IEEE CS Press, Los Alamitos, CA.

FLYNN, M. J. (1966), "Very High Speed Computing Systems," *Proc. IEEE*, Vol. 12, pp. 1901–1909.

FLYNN, M. J., AND K. W. RUDD (1996), "Parallel Architectures," *ACM Computing Surveys*, Vol. 28, No. 1, pp. 67–70.

GILL, S. (1958), "Parallel Programming," *Computer Journal*, Vol. 1, April, pp. 2–10.

GILLETT, R., AND R. KAUFMANN (1997), "Using the Memory Channel Network," *IEEE Micro*, Vol. 17, No. 1, pp 19–25.

GUSTAFSON, J. L. (1988), "Reevaluating Amdahl's Law," *Comm. ACM*, Vol. 31, No. 1, pp. 532–533.

HENNESSY, J. L., AND PATTERSON, D. A. (2003), *Computer Architecture: A Quantitative Approach* 3rd edition, Morgan Kaufmann Publishers, San Francisco, CA.

HOGANSON, K., B. WILKINSON, AND W. H. CARLISLE (1997), "Applications of Rhombic Multiprocessors," *Int.Conf. on Parallel and Distributed Processing Techniques and Applications 1997*, Las Vegas, NV, June 30–July 2.

HOLLAND, J. (1959), "A Universal Computer Capable of Executing an Arbitrary Number of Subprograms Simultaneously," *Proc. East Joint Computer Conference*, Vol. 16, pp. 108–113.

KERMANI, P., AND L. KLEINROCK (1979), "Virtual Cut-Through: A New Communication Switching Technique," *Computer Networks*, Vol. 3, pp. 267–286.

KNUCKLES, C. D. (2001), *Introduction to Interactive Programming on the Internet using HTML and JavaScript*, John Wiley, New York.

LEIGHTON, F. T. (1992), *Introduction to Parallel Algorithms and Architectures: Arrays, Trees, Hypercubes*, Morgan Kaufmann, San Mateo, CA.

LEISERSON, C. L. (1985), "Fat-Trees: Universal Networks for Hardware-Efficient Supercomputing," *IEEE Trans. Comput.*, Vol. C-34, No. 10, pp. 892–901.

LI, K. (1986), "Shared Virtual Memory on Loosely Coupled Multiprocessor," Ph.D. thesis, Dept. of Computer Science, Yale University.

MARTIN, R. P., A. M. VAHDAT, D. E. CULLER, AND T. E. ANDERSON (1997), "Effects of Communication Latency, Overhead, and Bandwidth in a Cluster Architecture," *Proc 24th Ann. Int. Symp. Comput. Arch.*, ACM, pp. 85–97.

METCALFE, R., AND D. BOGGS (1976), "Ethernet: Distributed Packet Switching for Local Computer Networks," *Comm. ACM*, Vol. 19, No. 7, pp. 395–404.

MINNICH, R., D. BURNS, AND F. HADY (1995), "The Memory-Integrated Network Interface," *IEEE Micro*, Vol. 15, No. 1, pp. 11–20.

NI, L. M., AND P. K. MCKINLEY (1993), "A Survey of Wormhole Routing Techniques in Direct Networks," *Computer*, Vol. 26, No. 2, pp. 62–76.

PACHECO, P. (1997), *Parallel Programming with MPI*, Morgan Kaufmann, San Francisco, CA.

SEITZ, C. L. (1985), "The Cosmic Cube," *Comm. ACM*, Vol. 28, No. 1, pp. 22–33.

SINGH, J. P., J. L. HENNESSY, AND A. GUPTA (1993), "Scaling Parallel Programs for Multiprocessors: Methodology and Examples," *Computer*, Vol. 26, No. 7, pp. 43–50.

STERLING, T., editor (2002a), *Beowulf Cluster Computing with Windows*, MIT Press, Cambridge, MA.

STERLING, T., editor (2002b), *Beowulf Cluster Computing with Linux*, MIT Press, Cambridge, MA.

WILLIAMS, R. (2001), *Computer Systems Architecture A Networking Approach*, Addison-Wesley, Harlow, England.

WILKINSON, B. (1990), "Cascaded Rhombic Crossbar Interconnection Networks," *Journal of Parallel and Distributed Computing,* Vol. 10, No. 1, pp. 96–101.

WILKINSON, B. (1991), "Comparative Performance of Overlapping Connectivity Multiprocessor Interconnection Networks," *Computer Journal*, Vol. 34, No. 3, pp. 207–214.

WILKINSON, B. (1991), "Multiple Bus Network with Overlapping Connectivity," *IEE Proceedings Pt. E: Computers and Digital Techniques*, Vol. 138, No. 4, pp. 281–284.

WILKINSON, B. (1992a), "Overlapping Connectivity Interconnection Networks for Shared Memory Multiprocessor Systems," *Journal of Parallel and Distributed Computing*, Vol. 15, No. 1, pp. 49–61.

WILKINSON, B. (1992b), "On Crossbar Switch and Multiple Bus Interconnection Networks with Overlapping Connectivity," *IEEE Transactions on Computers*, Vol. 41, No. 6, pp. 738–746.

WILKINSON, B. (1996), *Computer Architecture Design and Performance*, 2nd ed., Prentice Hall, London.

WILKINSON, B., AND H. R. ABACHI (1983), "Cross-bar Switch Multiple Microprocessor System," *Microprocessors and Microsystems*, Vol. 7, No. 2, pp. 75–79.

WILKINSON, B., AND J. M. FARMER (1994), "Reflective Interconnection Networks," *Computers and Elect. Eng.*, Vol. 20, No. 4, pp. 289–308.

PROBLEMS

1-1. A multiprocessor consists of 100 processors, each capable of a peak execution rate of 2 Gflops. What is the performance of the system as measured in Gflops when 10% of the code is sequential and 90% is parallelizable?

1-2. Is it possible to have a system efficiency (E) of greater than 100%? Discuss.

1-3. Combine the equation for Amdahl's law with the superlinear speedup analysis in Section 1.2.1 to obtain an equation for speedup given that some of a search has to be done sequentially.

1-4. Identify the host names, IP addresses, and MAC addresses on your system. Determine the IPv4 or IPv6 format used for the network.

1-5. Identify the class of each of the following IPv4 addresses:

(i) 152.66.2.3

(ii) 1.2.3.4

(iii) 192.192.192.192

(iv) 247.250.0.255

given only that class A starts with a 0, class B starts with the pattern 10, class C starts with the pattern 110, and class D starts with the pattern 1110 (i.e., without reference to Figure 1.22).

1-6. Suppose the assigned (IPv4) network address is 153.78.0.0 and it is required to have 6 sub-networks each having 250 hosts. Identify the class of the network address and division of the addresses for the sub-network and hosts. Two addresses must be set aside for the server node.

1-7. A cluster of 32 computers is being set up. The server node has two Ethernet connections, one to the Internet and one to the cluster. The Internet IP address is 216.123.0.0. Devise an IP address assignment for the cluster using C class format.

1-8. A company is proposing an IPv8 format using 512 bits. Do you think this is justified? Explain.

1-9. It is possible to construct a system physically that is a hybrid of a message-passing multicomputer and a shared memory multiprocessor. Write a report on how this might be achieved and its relative advantages over a pure message-passing system and a pure shared memory system.

1-10. (Research project) Write a report on the prospects for a truly incrementally scalable cluster computer system which can accept faster and faster processors without discarding older ones. The concept is to start with a system with a few state-of-the art processors and add a few newer processors each year. Each subsequent year, the processors available naturally get better. At some point the oldest are discarded, but one keeps adding processors. Hence, the system never gets obsolete, and the older processors left still provide useful service. The key issue is how to design the system architecture to accept faster processors and faster interconnects. Another issue is when to discard older processors. Perform an analysis on the best time to discard processors and interconnects.

Chapter 2

Message-Passing Computing

In this chapter, we outline the basic concepts of message-passing computing. The structure of message-passing programs is introduced and how to specify message-passing between processes. We discuss these first in general, and then outline one specific system, MPI (message-passing interface).[1] Finally, we discuss how to evaluate message-passing parallel programs, both theoretically and in practice.

2.1 BASICS OF MESSAGE-PASSING PROGRAMMING

2.1.1 Programming Options

Programming a message-passing multicomputer can be achieved by

1. Designing a special parallel programming language
2. Extending the syntax/reserved words of an existing sequential high-level language to handle message-passing
3. Using an existing sequential high-level language and providing a library of external procedures for message-passing

There are examples of all three approaches. Perhaps the only common example of a special message-passing parallel programming language is the language called *occam*, which was designed to be used with the unique message-passing processor called the *transputer*

[1] Web-based materials for this book include support for two systems, MPI and PVM.

(Inmos, 1984). There are several examples of language extensions for parallel programming, although most, such as High Performance Fortran (HPF), are more geared toward shared memory systems (see Chapter 8). One example of a language extension with explicit message-passing facilities is Fortran M (Foster, 1995).

It is also possible to use a special parallelizing compiler to convert a program written in a sequential programming language, such as Fortran, into executable parallel code. This option was proposed many years ago but is not usually practical for message-passing because traditional sequential programming languages alone do not have the concept of message-passing. Parallelizing compilers are considered briefly in Chapter 8 in the context of shared memory programming.

Here we will concentrate upon the option of programming by using a normal high-level language such as C, augmented with message-passing library calls that perform direct process-to-process message-passing. In this method, it is necessary to say explicitly what processes are to be executed, when to pass messages between concurrent processes, and what to pass in the messages. In this form of programming a message-passing system, we need:

1. A method of creating separate processes for execution on different computers
2. A method of sending and receiving messages

2.1.2 Process Creation

Before continuing, let us reiterate the concept of a *process*. In Chapter 1, the term *process* was introduced for constructing parallel programs. In some instances, especially when testing a program, more than one process may be mapped onto a single processor. Usually, this will not produce the fastest execution speed, as the processor must then time-share between the processes given to it, but it allows a program to be verified before executing the program on a multiple-processor system. There is one situation in which it may be desirable to construct a program to have more than one process on one processor: in order to hide network latencies (this will be discussed in Section 2.3.1). Nevertheless, we will assume that one process is mapped onto each processor and use the term *process* rather than *processor* unless it is necessary to highlight the operation of the processor. First, it is necessary to create processes and begin their execution.

Two methods of creating processes are:

- Static process creation
- Dynamic process creation

In *static process creation*, all the processes are specified before execution and the system will execute a fixed number of processes. The programmer usually explicitly identifies the processes or programs prior to execution by command-line actions. In *dynamic process creation*, processes can be created and their execution initiated during the execution of other processes. Process creation constructs or library/system calls are used to create processes. Processes can also be destroyed. Process creation and destruction may be done conditionally, and the number of processes may vary during execution. Clearly, dynamic process creation is a more powerful technique than static process creation, but it does incur very significant overhead when the processes are created. The term *process creation* is somewhat misleading because in all cases the code for the processes has to be written and compiled prior to the execution of any process.

In most applications, the processes are neither all the same nor all different; usually there is one controlling process, a "master process," and the remainder are "slaves," or "workers," which are identical in form, only differentiated by their process identification (ID). The process ID can be used to modify the actions of the process or compute different destinations for messages. The processes are defined by programs written by the programmer.

The most general programming model is the *multiple-program, multiple-data* (MPMD) model, in which a completely separate and different program is written for each processor, as shown in Figure 2.1. However, as we have mentioned, normally it is sufficient to have just two different programs, a master program and a slave program. One processor executes the master program, and multiple processors execute identical slave programs. Usually, even though the slave programs are identical, process IDs may be used to customize the execution—for example, to specify the destination of generated messages.

For static process creation especially, the so-called *single-program, multiple-data* (SPMD) model is convenient. In the SPMD model, the different programs are merged into one program. Within the program are control statements that will select different parts for each process. After the source program is constructed with the required control statements to separate the actions of each processor, the program is compiled into executable code for each processor, as illustrated in Figure 2.2. Each processor will load a copy of this code into its local memory for execution, and all processors can start executing their code together. If the processors are of different types, the source code has to be compiled into executable code for each processor type, and the correct type must be loaded for execution by each processor. We will describe the SPMD programming in more detail later (Section 2.2.2), as it is the main approach for one of the most common message-passing systems, MPI.

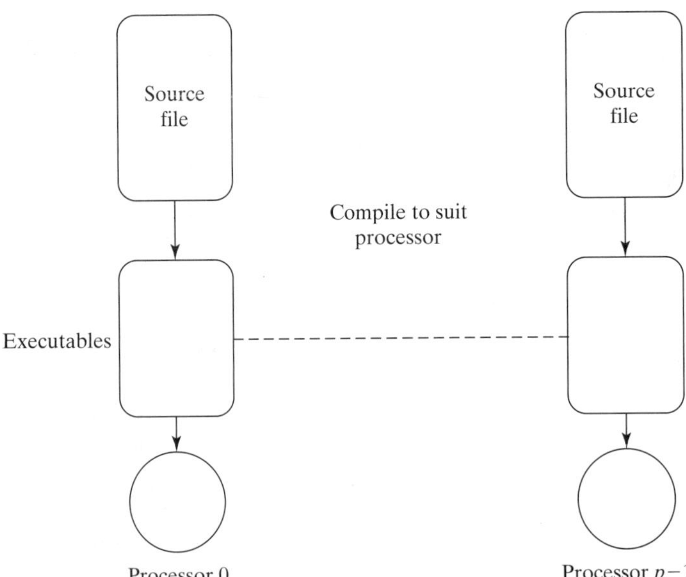

Figure 2.1 Multiple-program, multiple-data (MPMD) model.

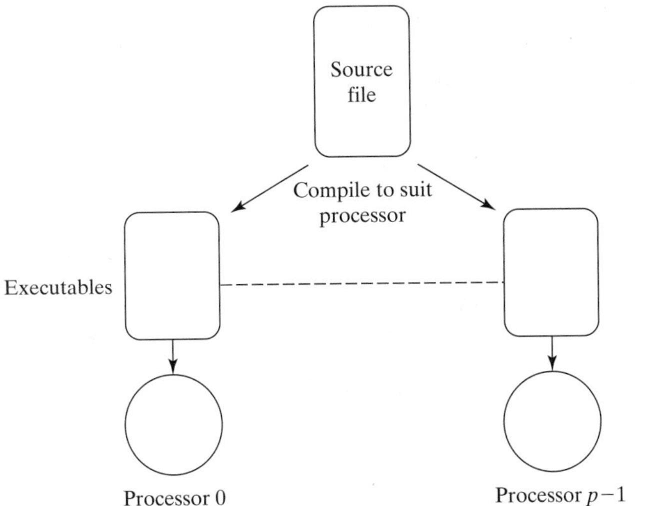

Figure 2.2 Single-program, multiple-data (SPMD) model.

For dynamic process creation, two distinct programs may be written, a master program and a slave program separately compiled and ready for execution. An example of a library call for dynamic process creation might be of the form

```
spawn(name_of_process);
```

which immediately starts another process[2], and both the calling process and the called process proceed together, as shown in Figure 2.3. The process being "spawned" is simply a previously compiled and executable program.

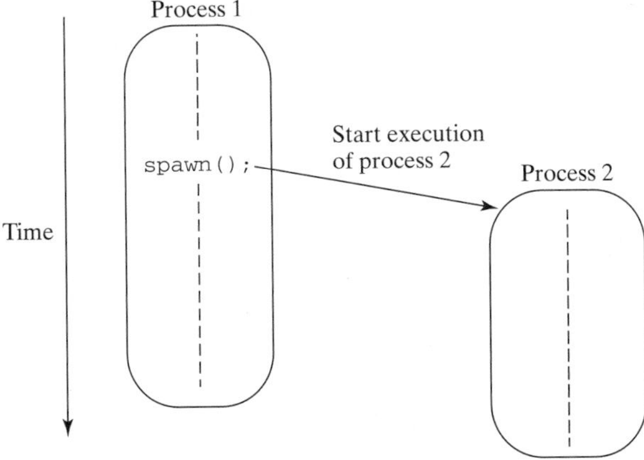

Figure 2.3 Spawning a process.

[2] Courier typeface is used to highlight code, either pseudocode or using a specific language or system.

2.1.3 Message-Passing Routines

Basic Send and Receive Routines. Send and receive message-passing library calls often have the form

```
send(parameter_list)
recv(parameter_list)
```

where `send()` is placed in the source process originating the message, and `recv()` is placed in the destination process to collect the messages being sent. The actual parameters will depend upon the software and in some cases can be complex. The simplest set of parameters would be the destination ID and message in `send()` and the source ID and the name of the location for the receiving message in `recv()`. For the C language, we might have the call

```
send(&x, destination_id);
```

in the source process, and the call

```
recv(&y, source_id);
```

in the destination process, to send the data `x` in the source process to `y` in the destination process, as shown in Figure 2.4. The order of parameters depends upon the system. We will show the process identification after the data and use an `&` with a single data element, as the specification usually calls for a pointer here. In this example, `x` must have been preloaded with the data to be sent, and `x` and `y` must be of the same type and size. Often, we want to send more complex messages than simply one data element, and then a more powerful message formation is needed. The precise details and variations of the parameters of real message-passing calls will be described in Section 2.2, but first we will develop the basic mechanisms. Various mechanisms are provided for send/receive routines for efficient code and flexibility.

Synchronous Message-Passing. The term *synchronous* is used for routines that return when the message transfer has been completed. A synchronous send routine will wait until the complete message that it has sent has been accepted by the receiving process before returning. A synchronous receive routine will wait until the message it is expecting arrives and the message is stored before returning. A pair of processes, one with a synchronous send operation and one with a matching synchronous receive operation, will be synchronized, with neither the source process nor the destination process able to

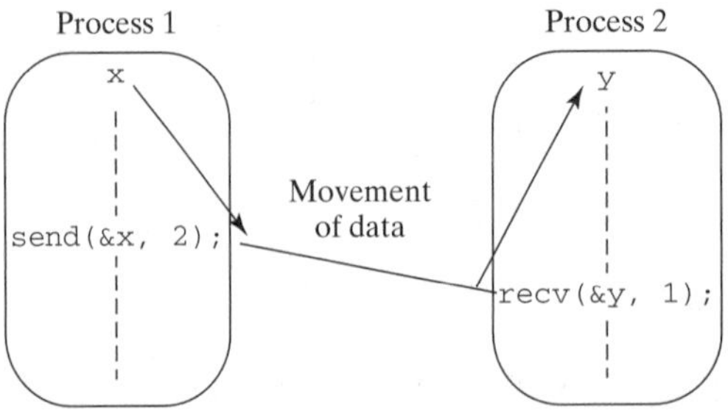

Figure 2.4 Passing a message between processes using `send()` and `recv()` library calls.

proceed until the message has been passed from the source process to the destination process. Hence, synchronous routines intrinsically perform two actions: They transfer data, and they synchronize processes. The term *rendezvous* is used to describe the meeting and synchronization of two processes through synchronous send/receive operations.

Synchronous send and receive operations do not need message buffer storage. They suggest some form of signaling, such as a three-way protocol in which the source first sends a "request to send" message to the destination. When the destination is ready to accept the message, it returns an acknowledgment. Upon receiving this acknowledgment, the source sends the actual message. Synchronous message-passing is shown in Figure 2.5 using the three-way protocol. In Figure 2.5(a), process 1 reaches its `send()` before process 2 has reached the corresponding `recv()`. Process 1 must be suspended in some manner until process 2 reaches its `recv()`. At that time, process 2 must awaken process 1 with some form of "signal," and then both can participate in the message transfer. Note that in Figure 2.5(a), the message is kept in the source process until it can be sent. In Figure 2.5(b), process 2 reaches its `recv()` before process 1 has reached its `send()`. Now, process 2 must be suspended until both can participate in the message transfer. The exact mechanism for suspending and awakening processes is system dependent.

Blocking and Nonblocking Message-Passing. The term *blocking* was formerly also used to describe routines that do not allow the process to continue until the transfer is completed. The routines are "blocked" from continuing. In that sense, the terms *synchronous* and *blocking* were synonymous. The term *nonblocking* was used to describe routines

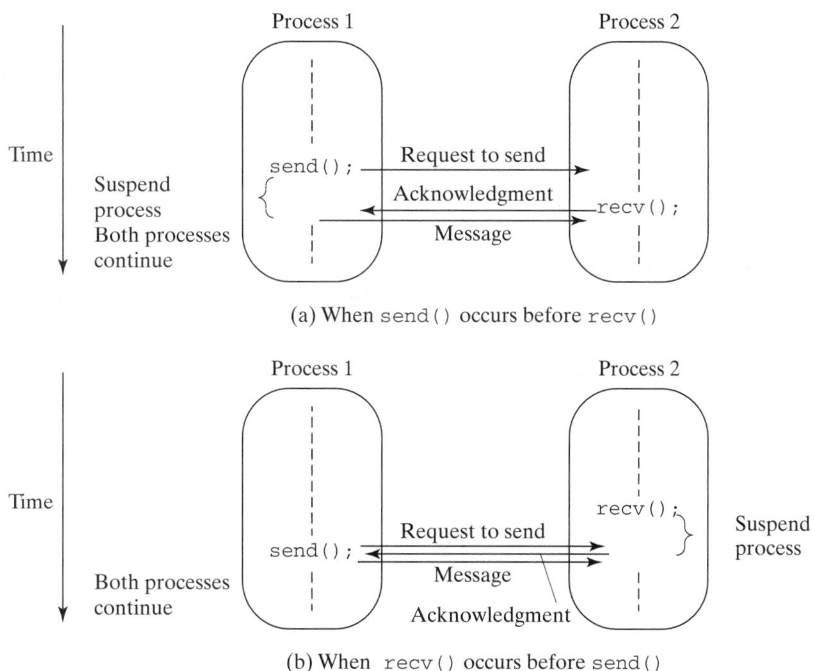

Figure 2.5 Synchronous `send()` and `recv()` library calls using a three-way protocol.

that return whether or not the message had been received. However, the terms *blocking* and *nonblocking* have been redefined in systems such as MPI. We will look into the precise MPI specification later, but for now, let us mention how a send message-passing routine can return before the message transfer has been completed. Generally, a *message buffer* is needed between the source and destination to hold messages, as shown in Figure 2.6. Here, the message buffer is used to hold messages being sent prior to being accepted by `recv()`. For a receive routine, the message has to have been received if we want the message. If `recv()` is reached before `send()`, the message buffer will be empty and `recv()` waits for the message. But for a send routine, once the local actions have been completed and the message is safely on its way, the process can continue with subsequent work. In this way, using such send routines can decrease the overall execution time. In practice, buffers can only be of finite length, and a point could be reached when a send routine is held up because all the available buffer space has been exhausted. It may be necessary to know at some point if the message has actually been received, which will require additional message-passing.

We shall conform to MPI's definitions of terms: Routines that return after their local actions complete, even though the message transfer may not have been completed, are *blocking* or, more accurately, *locally blocking*. Those that return immediately are *nonblocking*. In MPI, nonblocking routines assume that the data storage used for the transfer is not modified by the subsequent statements prior to the data storage being used for the transfer, and it is left to the programmer to ensure this. The term *synchronous* will be used to describe the situation in which the send and receive routines do not return until both occur and the message has been transmitted from the source to the destination. For the most part, *(locally) blocking* and *synchronous* are sufficient for the code in this text.

Message Selection. So far, we have described messages being sent to a specified destination process from a specified source process, where the destination ID is given as a parameter in the send routine and the source ID is given as a parameter in the receive routine. The `recv()` in the destination process will only accept messages from a source process specified as a parameter in `recv()` and will ignore other messages. A special symbol or number may be provided as a *wild card* in place of the source ID to allow the destination to accept messages from any source. For example, the number −1 might be used as a source ID wild card.

To provide greater flexibility, messages can be selected by a *message tag* attached to the message. The *message tag* `msgtag` is typically a user-chosen positive integer (including

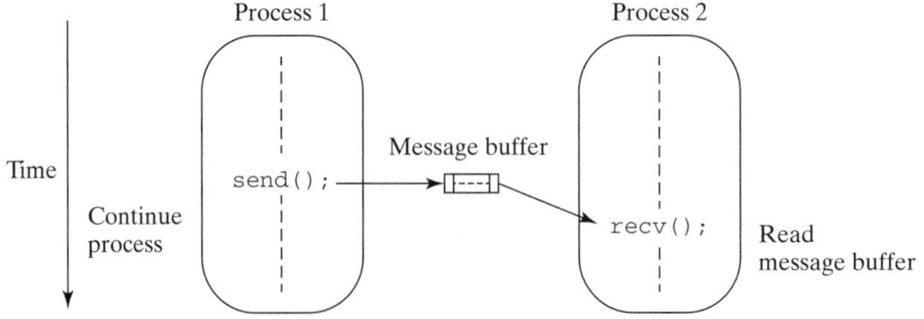

Figure 2.6 Using a message buffer.

zero) that can be used to differentiate between different types of messages being sent. Then specific receive routines can be made to accept only messages with a specific message tag and ignore other messages. A message tag will be an additional parameter in `send()` and `recv()`, usually immediately following the source/destination identification. For example, to send a message, `x`, with message tag 5 from a source process, 1, to a destination process, 2, and assign to `y`, we might have

```
send(&x, 2, 5);
```

in the source process and

```
recv(&y, 1, 5);
```

in the destination process. The message tag is carried within the message. If special type matching is not required, a *wild card* can be used in place of a message tag, so that the `recv()` will match with any `send()`.

The use of message tags is very common. However, it require the programmer to keep track of the message tag numbers used in the program and in any included programs written by others or in library routines that are called. A more powerful message-selection mechanism is needed to differentiate between messages sent within included programs or library routines and those in the user processes. This mechanism will be described later.

Broadcast, Gather, and Scatter. There are usually many other message-passing and related routines that provide desirable features. A process is frequently required to send the same message to more than one destination process. The term *broadcast* is used to describe sending the same message to all the processes concerned with the problem. The term *multicast* is used to describe sending the same message to a defined group of processes. However, this differentiation will not be used here, so it will simply be called broadcast in either case.

Broadcast is illustrated in Figure 2.7. The processes that are to participate in the broadcast must be identified, typically by first forming a named group of processes to be used as a parameter in the broadcast routines. In Figure 2.7, process 0 is identified as the

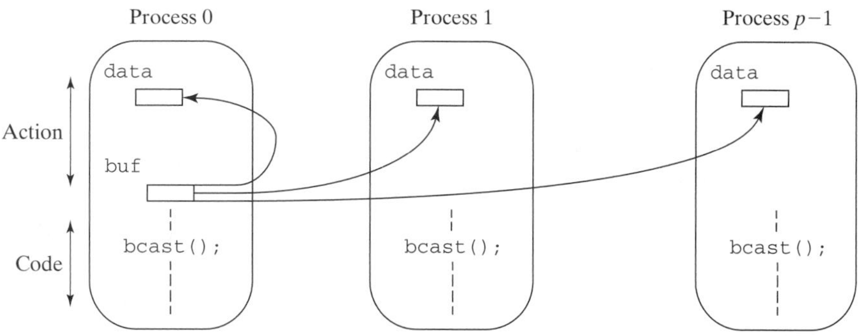

Figure 2.7 Broadcast operation.

root process within the broadcast parameters. The root process could be any process in the group. In this example, the root process holds the data to be broadcast in `buf`. Figure 2.7 shows each process executing the same `bcast()` routine, which is very convenient for the SPMD model, in which all the processes have the same program. Figure 2.7 also shows the root receiving the data, which is the arrangement used in MPI but it depends upon the message-passing system. For the MPMD model, an alternative arrangement is for the source to execute a broadcast routine and destination processes to execute regular message-passing receive routines. In this event, the root process would not receive the data, which is not necessary anyway since the root process already has the data.

As described, the broadcast action does not occur until all the processes have executed their broadcast routine. The broadcast operation will have the effect of synchronizing the processes. The actual implementation of the broadcast will depend upon the software and the underlying architecture. We will look at the implementation later in this chapter and in subsequent chapters. It is important to have an efficient implementation, given the widespread use of broadcast in programs.

The term *scatter* is used to describe sending each element of an array of data in the root to a separate process. The contents of the ith location of the array are sent to the ith process. Whereas broadcast sends the same data to a group of processes, scatter distributes different data elements to processes. Both are common requirements at the start of a program to send data to slave processes. Scatter is illustrated in Figure 2.8. As with broadcast, a group of processes needs to be identified as well as the root process. In this example, the root process also receives a data element. Figure 2.8 shows each process executing the same `scatter()` routine, which again is convenient for the SPMD model.

The term *gather* is used to describe having one process collect individual values from a set of processes. Gather is normally used after some computation has been done by these processes. Gather is essentially the opposite of scatter. The data from the ith process is received by the root process and placed in the ith location of the array set aside to receive the data. Gather is illustrated in Figure 2.9. Process 0 in this example is the root process for the gather. In this example, data in the root is also gathered into the array.

Sometimes the gather operation can be combined with a specified arithmetic or logical operation. For example, the values could be gathered and then added together by the

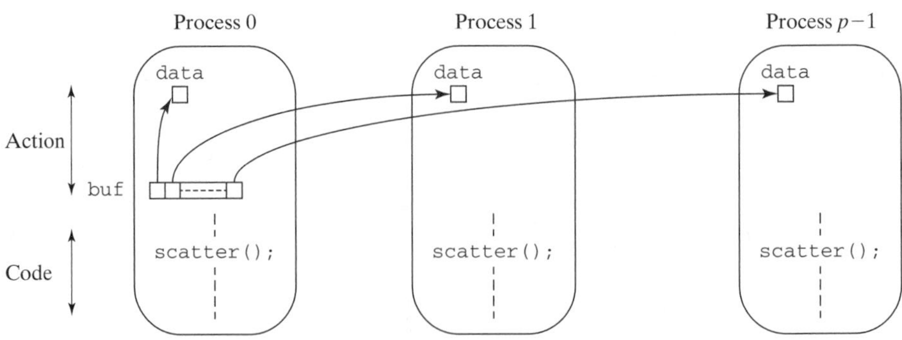

Figure 2.8 Scatter operation.

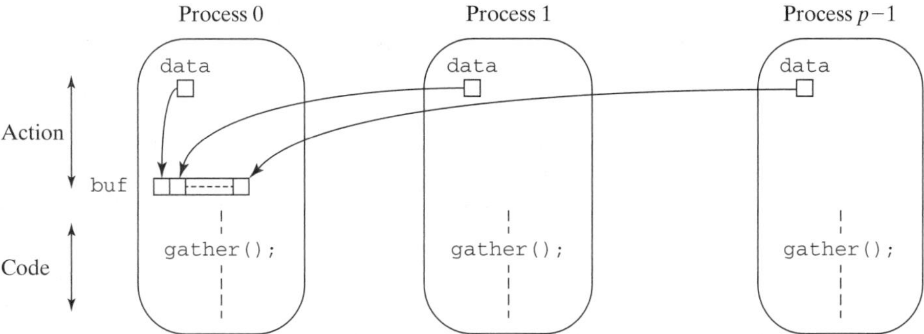

Figure 2.9 Gather operation.

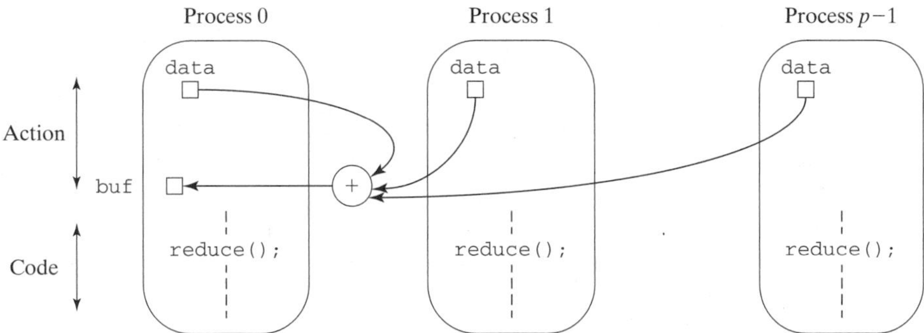

Figure 2.10 Reduce operation (addition).

root, as illustrated in Figure 2.10. Another arithmetic/logical operation could be performed by the root. All such operations are sometimes called *reduce* operations. Most message-passing systems provide for these operations and other related operations. The actual way that the reduce operation is implemented depends upon the implementation. A centralized operation in the root is not the only solution. Partial operations could be distributed among the processes. Whatever the implementation, the idea is to have common collective operations implemented as efficiently as possible.

2.2 USING A CLUSTER OF COMPUTERS

2.2.1 Software Tools

Now let us relate the basic message-passing ideas to a cluster of computers (cluster computing). There have been several software packages for cluster computing, originally described as for networks of workstations. Perhaps the first widely adopted software for using a network of workstations as a multicomputer platform was PVM (parallel virtual machine) developed by Oak Ridge National Laboratories in the late 1980s and used widely in the 1990s. PVM provides a software environment for message-passing between homogeneous or heterogeneous computers and has a collection of library routines that the user can employ with C or Fortran programs. PVM became widely used, partly because it was made readily available at no charge (from http://www.netlib.org/pvm3). Windows implementations are now available. PVM used dynamic process creation from the start. Apart from PVM, there have also been proprietary message-passing libraries from IBM and others for specific systems. However, it was PVM which made using a network of workstations for parallel programming really practical for most people in the early 1990s.

2.2.2 MPI

To foster more widespread use and portability, a group of academics and industrial partners came together to develop what they hoped would be a "standard" for message-passing systems. They called it MPI (Message-Passing Interface). MPI provides library routines for message-passing and associated operations. A fundamental aspect of MPI is that it defines a standard but not the implementation, just as programming languages are defined but not how the compilers for the languages are implemented. MPI has a large number of routines (over 120 and growing), although we will discuss only a subset of them. An important factor in developing MPI is the desire to make message-passing portable and easy to use. Some changes were also made to correct technical deficiencies in earlier message-passing systems such as PVM. The first version of MPI, version 1.0, was finalized in May 1994 after two years of meetings and discussions. Version 1 purposely omitted some advances that were added to subsequent versions. There have been enhancements to version 1.0 in version1.2. Version 2.0 (MPI-2) was introduced in 1997 and included dynamic process creation, one-sided operations, and parallel I/O.

The large number of functions, even in version 1, is due to the desire to incorporate features that applications programmers can use to write efficient code. However, programs can be written using a very small subset of the available functions. It has been suggested by Gropp, Lusk, and Skjellum (1999a) that successful programs could be written with only six of the 120+ functions. We will mention a few more than just these six "fundamental" functions. Function calls are available for both C and Fortran. We will only consider the C versions. All MPI routines start with the prefix `MPI_` and the next letter is capitalized. Generally, routines return information indicating the success or failure of the call. Such detail is omitted here and can be found in Snir et al. (1998).

Several free implementations of the MPI standard exist, including MPICH from Argonne National Laboratories and Mississippi State University, and LAM from the Ohio Supercomputing Center (now supported by the University of Notre Dame). There are also numerous vender implementations, from Hewlett-Packard, IBM, SGI, SUN, and others. Implementation for Windows clusters exist. A list of MPI implementations and their sources can be found at http://www.osc.edu/mpi/ and http://www.erc.msstate.edu/misc/mpi/implementations.html. A key factor in choosing an implementation is continuing support, because a few early implementations are now not supported at all. A good indicator of support is whether the implementation includes features of the most recent version of the MPI standard (currently MPI-2). The features of available implementations can be found at http://www.erc.msstate.edu/misc/mpi/implementations.html (24 implementations listed here at the time of writing). Most, if not all, implementations do not include every feature of MPI-2. For example, at the time of writing, MPICH did not support MPI one-sided communication at all. The extended collective operations of MPI-2 are only supported in two implementations (commercial implementations from Hitachi and NEC Corporation). Not having full support can be problematic for writing state-of-the art programs, especially one-sided communication, which is a useful feature.

Process Creation and Execution. As with parallel programming in general, parallel computations are decomposed into concurrent processes. Creating and starting MPI processes is purposely not defined in the MPI standard and will depend upon the implementation. Only static process creation was supported in MPI version 1. This means that all the processes must be defined prior to execution and started together. MPI version 2 introduced dynamic process creation as an advanced feature and has a spawn routine, `MPI_Comm_spawn()`. Even so, one may choose not to use it because of the overhead of dynamic process creation.

Using the SPMD model of computation, one program is written and executed by multiple processors. The way that different programs are started is left to the implementation. Typically, an executable MPI program will be started on the command line. For example, the same executable might be started on four separate processors simultaneously by

```
mpirun prog1 -np 4
```

or

```
prog1 -np 4
```

These commands say nothing about where the copies of `prog1` will be executed. Again, mapping processes onto processors is not defined in the MPI standard. Specific mapping may be available on the command line or by the use of a file holding the names of the executables and the specific processors to run each executable. MPI has support for defining topologies (meshes, etc.), and hence it has the potential for automatic mapping.

Before any MPI function call, the code must be initialized with `MPI_Init()`, and after all MPI function calls, the code must be terminated with `MPI_Finalize()`. Command-line arguments are passed to `MPI_Init()` to allow MPI setup actions to take place. For example,

```
main (int argc, char *argv[])
{
  MPI_Init(&argc, &argv);                          /* initialize MPI */
      .
      .
      .
  MPI_Finalize();                                  /* terminate MPI */
}
```

(As in sequential C programs, `&argc`, argument count, provides the number of arguments, and `&argv`, argument vector, is a pointer to an array of character strings.)

Initially, all processes are enrolled in a "universe" called `MPI_COMM_WORLD`, and each process is given a unique rank, a number from 0 to $p - 1$, where there are p processes. In MPI terminology, `MPI_COMM_WORLD` is a *communicator* that defines the *scope* of a communication operation, and processes have ranks associated with the communicator. Other communicators can be established for groups of processes. For a simple program, the default communicator, MPI_COMM_WORLD, is sufficient. However, the concept allows programs, and especially libraries, to be constructed with separate scopes for messages.

Using the SPMD Computational Model. The SPMD model is ideal where each process will actually execute the same code. Normally, though, one or more processors in all applications need to execute different code. To facilitate this within a single program, statements need to be inserted to select which portions of the code will be executed by each processor. Hence, the SPMD model does not preclude a master-slave approach, but both the master code and the slave code must be in the same program. The following MPI code segment illustrates how this could be achieved:

```
main (int argc, char *argv[])
{
   MPI_Init(&argc, &argv);

   MPI_Comm_rank(MPI_COMM_WORLD, &myrank);        /* find process rank */
   if (myrank == 0)
      master();
   else
      slave();

   MPI_Finalize();
}
```

where master() and slave() are procedures to be executed by the master process and slave process, respectively. The approach could be used for more than two code sequences. The SPMD model would be inefficient in memory requirements if each processor were to execute completely different code, but fortunately this is unlikely to be required. One advantage of the SPMD model is that command-line arguments can be passed to each process.

Given the SPMD model, any global declarations of variables will be duplicated in each process. Variables that are not to be duplicated could be declared locally; that is, declared within code executed only by that process. For example,

```
MPI_Comm_rank(MPI_COMM_WORLD, &myrank);/* find process rank */
if (myrank == 0) {                /* process 0 actions/local variables */
   int x, y;
      .
      .
      .
} else if (myrank == 1) {         /* process 1 actions/local variables */
   int x, y;
      .
      .
      .
}
```

Here, x and y in process 0 are different local variables from x and y in process 1. However such declarations are not favored in C because the scope of a variable in C is from its declaration to the end of the program or function rather than from the declaration to the end of the current block, which one would want to achieve by declaring the variables within a block. In most instances, one would declare all the variables at the top of the program, and these are then duplicated for each process and essentially are local variables to each process.

Message-Passing Routines. Message-passing communications can be a source of erroneous operation. An intent of MPI is to provide a *safe* communication environment. An example of unsafe communication is shown in Figure 2.11. In this figure, process 0 wishes to send a message to process 1, but there is also message-passing between library routines, as shown. Even though each `send`/`recv` pair has matching source and destination, incorrect message-passing occurs. The use of wild cards makes incorrect operation or deadlock even more likely. Suppose that in one process a nonblocking receive has wild cards in both the tag and source fields. A pair of other processes call library routines that require message-passing. The first send in this library routine may match with the nonblocking receive that is using wild cards, causing erroneous actions.

Communicators are used in MPI for all point-to-point and collective MPI message-passing communications. A communicator is a *communication domain* that defines a set of

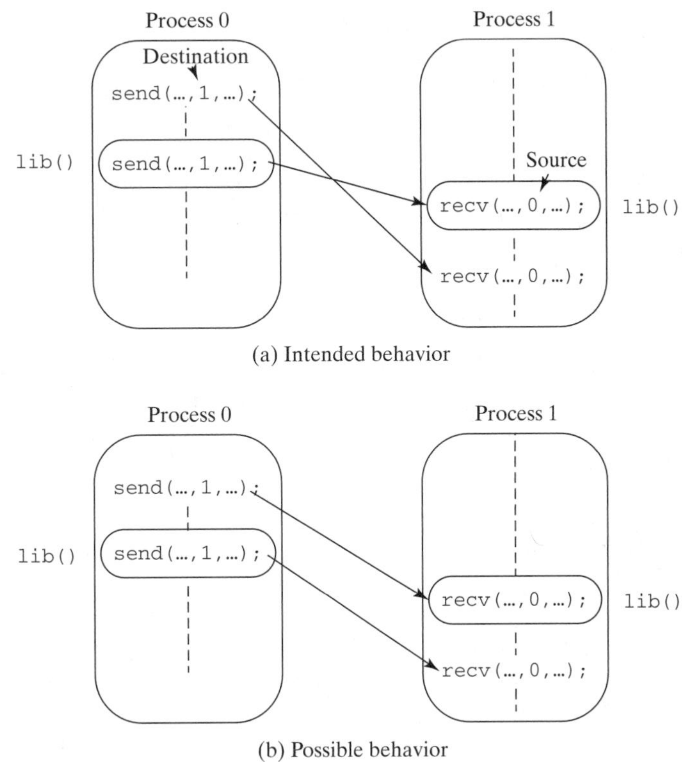

Figure 2.11 Unsafe message-passing with libraries.

processes that are allowed to communicate with one another. In this way, the communication domain of the library can be separated from that of a user program. Each process has a rank within the communicator, an integer from 0 to $p - 1$, where there are p processes. Two types of communicators are available, an *intracommunicator* for communicating within a group, and an *intercommunicator* for communication between groups. A *group* is used to define a collection of processes for these purposes. A process has a unique *rank* in a group (an integer from 0 to $m - 1$, where there are m processes in the group), and a process could be a member of more than one group. For simple programs, only intracommunicators are used, and the additional concept of a group is unnecessary.

A default intracommunicator, `MPI_COMM_WORLD`, exists as the first communicator for all the processes in the application. In simple applications, it is not necessary to introduce new communicators. `MPI_COMM_WORLD` can be used for all point-to-point and collective operations. New communicators are created based upon existing communicators. A set of MPI routines exists for forming communicators from existing communicators (and groups from existing groups); see Appendix A.

Point-to-Point Communication. Message-passing is done by the familiar send and receive calls. Message tags are present, and wild cards can be used in place of the tag (`MPI_ANY_TAG`) and in place of the source ID in receive routines (`MPI_ANY_SOURCE`).

The datatype of the message is defined in the send/receive parameters. The datatype can be taken from a list of standard MPI datatypes (`MPI_INT`, `MPI_FLOAT`, `MPI_CHAR`, etc.) or can be user created. User-defined datatypes are derived from existing datatypes. In this way, a data structure can be created to form a message of any complexity. For example, a structure could be created consisting of two integers and one float if that is to be sent in one message. Apart from eliminating the need for packing/unpacking routines, as found in the earlier PVM message-passing system, declared datatypes have the advantage that the datatype can be reused. Also, explicit send and receive buffers are not required. This is very useful in reducing the storage requirements of large messages; messages are not copied from the source location to an explicit send buffer. Copying to an explicit send buffer would incur twice the storage space as well as time penalties. (MPI does provide routines for explicit buffers if required.)

Completion. There are several versions of send and receive. The concepts of being *locally complete* and *globally complete* are used in describing the variations. A routine is locally complete if it has completed all of its part in the operation. A routine is globally complete if all those involved in the operation have completed their parts of the operation and the operation has taken place in its entirety.

Blocking Routines. In MPI, blocking send or receive routines return when they are locally complete. The local completion condition for a blocking send routine is that the location used to hold the message can be used again or altered without affecting the message being sent. A blocking send will send the message and return. This does not mean that the message has been received, just that the process is free to move on without adversely affecting the message. Essentially the source process is blocked for the minimum time that is required to access the data. A blocking receive routine will also return when it is locally complete, which in this case means that the message has been received into the destination location and the destination location can be read.

The general format of parameters of the blocking send is

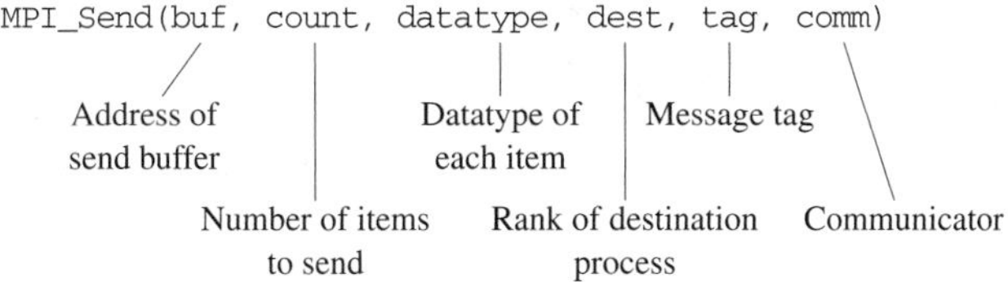

The general format of parameters of the blocking receive is

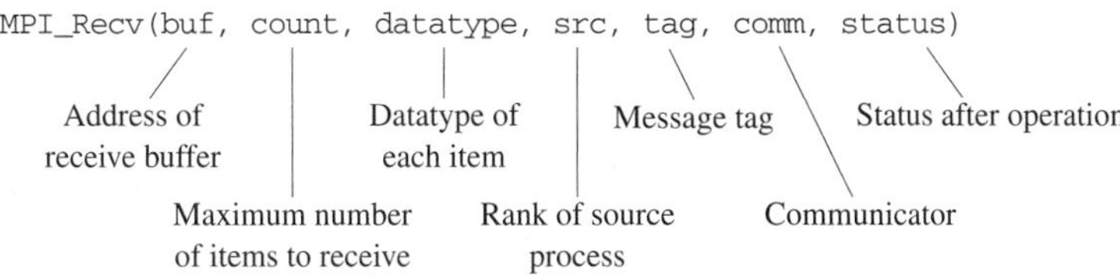

Note that a maximum message size is specified in `MPI_Recv()`. If a message is received that is larger than the maximum size, an overflow error occurs. If the message is less than the maximum size, the message is stored at the front of the buffer and the remaining locations are untouched. Usually, though, we would expect to send messages of a known size.

Example

To send an integer x from process 0 to process 1,

```
int x;
MPI_Comm_rank(MPI_COMM_WORLD, &myrank);            /* find process rank */
if (myrank == 0) {
  MPI_Send(&x, 1, MPI_INT, 1, msgtag, MPI_COMM_WORLD);
} else if (myrank == 1) {
  MPI_Recv(&x, 1, MPI_INT, 0, msgtag, MPI_COMM_WORLD, status);
}
```

Nonblocking Routines. A nonblocking routine returns immediately; that is, allows the next statement to execute, whether or not the routine is locally complete. The nonblocking send, `MPI_Isend()`, where `I` refers to the word *immediate*, will return even before the source location is safe to be altered. The nonblocking receive, `MPI_Irecv()`, will return even if there is no message to accept. The formats are

```
MPI_Isend(buf, count, datatype, dest, tag, comm, request)
MPI_Irecv(buf, count, datatype, source, tag, comm, request)
```

Completion can be detected by separate routines, `MPI_Wait()` and `MPI_Test()`. `MPI_Wait()` waits until the operation has actually completed and will return then. `MPI_Test()` returns immediately with a flag set indicating whether the operation has completed at that time.

These routines need to be associated with a particular operation, which is achieved by using the same `request` parameter. The nonblocking receive routine provides the ability for a process to continue with other activities while waiting for the message to arrive.

Example

To send an integer `x` from process 0 to process 1 and allow process 0 to continue,

```
int x;
MPI_Comm_rank(MPI_COMM_WORLD, &myrank);          /* find process rank */
if (myrank == 0) {
  MPI_Isend(&x, 1, MPI_INT, 1, msgtag, MPI_COMM_WORLD, req1);
  compute();
  MPI_Wait(req1, status);
} else if (myrank == 1) {
  MPI_Recv(&x, 0, MPI_INT, 1, msgtag, MPI_COMM_WORLD, status);
}
```

Send Communication Modes. MPI send routines can have one of four communication modes that define the send/receive protocol. The modes are *standard*, *buffered*, *synchronous*, and *ready*.

In the *standard* mode send, it is not assumed that the corresponding receive routine has started. The amount of buffering, if any, is implementation dependent and not defined by MPI. If buffering is provided, the send could complete before the receive is reached. (If nonblocking, completion occurs when the matching `MPI_Wait()` or `MPI_Test()` returns.)

In the *buffered* mode, send may start and return before a matching receive. It is necessary to provide specific buffer space in the application for this mode. Buffer space is supplied to the system via the MPI routine `MPI_Buffer_attach()` and removed with `MPI_Buffer_detach()`.

In the *synchronous* mode, send and receive can start before each other but can only complete together.

In the *ready* mode, a send can only start if the matching receive has already been reached, otherwise an error will occur. The ready mode must be used with care to avoid erroneous operation.

Each of the four modes can be applied to both blocking and nonblocking send routines. The three nonstandard modes are identified by a letter in the mnemonics (buffered – `b`; synchronous – `s`, and ready – `r`). For example, `MPI_Issend()` is a nonblocking synchronous send routine. This is an unusual combination but has significant uses. The send will return immediately and hence will not directly synchronize the process with the one that has the corresponding receive. The message transfer will presumably complete at some point, which can be determined, as with all immediate mode routines, through the use of `MPI_Wait()` or `MPI_Test()`. This would allow for example to time how long it would take to synchronize processes or to determine whether there is a problem, such as lack of buffer storage. There are some disallowed combinations. Only the standard mode is available for the blocking and nonblocking receive routines, and it is not assumed that the corresponding send has started. Any type of send routine can be used with any type of receive routine.

Collective Communication. Collective communication, such as broadcast, involves a set of processes, as opposed to point-to-point communication involving one source process and one destination process. The processes are those defined by an intracommunicator. Message tags are not present.

Broadcast, Gather, and Scatter Routines. MPI provides a broadcast routine and a range of gather and scatter routines. The communicator defines the collection of processes that will participate in the collection operation. The principal collective operations operating upon data are

```
MPI_Bcast()            - Broadcasts from root to all other processes
MPI_Gather()           - Gathers values for group of processes
MPI_Scatter()          - Scatters buffer in parts to group of processes
MPI_Alltoall()         - Sends data from all processes to all processes
MPI_Reduce()           - Combines values on all processes to single value
MPI_Reduce_scatter()   - Combines values and scatter results
MPI_Scan()             - Computes prefix reductions of data on processes
```

The processes involved are those in the same communicator. There are several variations of the routines. Details of the parameters can be found in Appendix A.

Example

To gather items from the group of processes into process 0, using dynamically allocated memory in the root process, we might use

```
int data[10];                        /*data to be gathered from processes*/
      .
      .
      .
MPI_Comm_rank(MPI_COMM_WORLD, &myrank);                 /* find rank */
if (myrank == 0) {
   MPI_Comm_size(MPI_COMM_WORLD, &grp_size);            /*find group size*/
   buf = (int *)malloc(grp_size*10*sizeof(int));        /*allocate memory*/
}
MPI_Gather(data,10,MPI_INT,buf,grp_size*10,MPI_INT,0, MPI_COMM_WORLD);
```

Note that `MPI_Gather()` gathers from all processes, including the root.

Barrier. As in all message-passing systems, MPI provides a means of synchronizing processes by stopping each one until they all have reached a specific "barrier" call. We will look at barriers in detail in Chapter 6 when considering synchronized computations.

Sample MPI Program. Figure 2.12 shows a simple MPI program. The purpose of this program to add a group of numbers together. These numbers are randomly generated and held in a file. The program can be found at http://www.cs.uncc.edu/par_prog and can be used to become familiar with the software environment.

```
#include "mpi.h"
#include <stdio.h>
#include <math.h>
#define MAXSIZE 1000

void main(int argc, char **argv)
{
  int myid, numprocs;
  int data[MAXSIZE], i, x, low, high, myresult, result;
  char fn[255];
  char *fp;

  MPI_Init(&argc,&argv);
  MPI_Comm_size(MPI_COMM_WORLD,&numprocs);
  MPI_Comm_rank(MPI_COMM_WORLD,&myid);

  if (myid == 0) {             /* Open input file and initialize data */
     strcpy(fn,getenv("HOME"));
     strcat(fn,"/MPI/rand_data.txt");
     if ((fp = fopen(fn,"r")) == NULL) {
        printf("Can't open the input file: %s\n\n", fn);
        exit(1);
     }
     for(i = 0; i < MAXSIZE; i++) fscanf(fp,"%d", &data[i]);
  }

/* broadcast data */
   MPI_Bcast(data, MAXSIZE, MPI_INT, 0, MPI_COMM_WORLD);

/* Add my portion Of data */
   x = MAXSIZE/numprocs;           /* must be an integer */
   low = myid * x;
   high = low + x;
   myresult = 0;
   for(i = low; i < high; i++)
      myresult += data[i];
   printf("I got %d from %d\n", myresult, myid);

/* Compute global sum */
   MPI_Reduce(&myresult, &result, 1, MPI_INT, MPI_SUM, 0, MPI_COMM_WORLD);
   if (myid == 0) printf("The sum is %d.\n", result);

   MPI_Finalize();
}
```

Figure 2.12 Sample MPI program.

2.2.3 Pseudocode Constructs

In the preceding sections, we saw specific MPI routines for implementing basic message-passing. Additional code is required for the sometimes numerous parameters, and often many other detailed aspects are involved. For example, error detection code may need to be incorporated. In C, almost all MPI routines return an integer error code in the event of an error;[3] in C++ exception is thrown and error handlers provided. In any

[3] The notable MPI routine that does not have an error code is `MPI_Wtime()` which returns the elapsed time as a double. Presumably this routine cannot cause an error.

event, the code can be identified from a list of error classes and the appropriate action taken. Such additions, although necessary for structurally sound programs, substantially detract from readability. Rather than use real code, we will use a pseudocode for describing algorithms. Our pseudocode will omit the clutter of parameters that are secondary to understanding the code.

The process identification is placed last in the list (as in MPI). To send a message consisting of an integer `x` and a float `y`, from the process called `master` to the process called `slave`, assigning to `a` and `b`, we simply write in the master process

```
send(&x, &y, Pslave);
```

and in the slave process

```
recv(&a, &b, Pmaster);
```

where `x` and `a` are declared as integers and `y` and `b` are declared as floats. The integer `x` will be copied to `a`, and the float `y` copied to `b`. (Note that we have allowed ourselves the flexibility of specifying more than one data item of different types; in actual code, separate routines may be necessary, or data types created.) We have retained the `&` symbol to indicate that the data parameters are pointers (as they must be for `recv()` at least, and for sending arrays). Where appropriate, the *i*th process will be given the notation P_i, and a tag may be present that would follow the source or destination name. Thus

```
send(&x, P2, data_tag);
```

sends `x` to process 2, with the message tag `data_tag`. The corresponding receive will have the same tag (or a wide card tag). Sometimes more complex data structures need to be defined, and additional specification is also needed in collective communication routines.

The most common form of basic message-passing routine needed in our pseudocode is the locally blocking `send()` and `recv()`, which will be written as given:

```
send(&data1, Pdestination);          /* Locally blocking send */
recv(&data1, Psource);               /* Locally blocking receive */
```

In many instances, the locally blocking versions are sufficient. Other forms will be differentiated with prefixes:

```
ssend(&data1, Pdestination);         /* Synchronous send */
```

Virtually all of the code segments given, apart from the message-passing routines, are in the regular C language, although not necessarily in the most optimized or concise manner. For example, for clarity we have refrained from using compressed assignments (e.g., `x += y;`), except for loop counters. Some artistic license has been taken. Exponentiation is written in the normal mathematical way. Generally, initialization of variables is not shown. However, translation of pseudocode to actual message-passing code in MPI or any other message-passing "language" is straightforward.

2.3 EVALUATING PARALLEL PROGRAMS

In subsequent chapters, we will describe various methods of achieving parallelism, and we will need to evaluate these methods. As a prelude to this, let us give a brief overview of the key aspects.

2.3.1 Equations for Parallel Execution Time

Our first concern is how fast the parallel implementation is likely to be. We might begin by estimating the execution time on a single computer, t_s, by counting the computational steps of the best sequential algorithm. For a parallel algorithm, in addition to determining the number of computational steps, we need to estimate the communication overhead. In a message-passing system, the time to send messages must be considered in the overall execution time of a problem. The parallel execution time, t_p, is composed of two parts: a computation part, say t_{comp}, and a communication part, say t_{comm}. Thus we have

$$t_p = t_{\text{comp}} + t_{\text{comm}}$$

Computational Time. The computation time can be estimated in much the same way as for a sequential algorithm, by counting the number of computational steps. When more than one process is being executed simultaneously, we only need to count the computational steps of the most complex process. Often, all the processes are performing the same operation, so we simply count the number of computation steps of one process. In other situations, we would find the greatest number of computation steps of the concurrent processes. Generally, the number of computational steps will be a function of n and p. Thus

$$t_{\text{comp}} = f(n, p)$$

The time units of t_p are those of a computational step. For convenience, we will often break down the computation time into parts separated by message-passing, and then determine the computation time of each part. Then

$$t_{\text{comp}} = t_{\text{comp1}} + t_{\text{comp2}} + t_{\text{comp3}} + \ldots$$

where $t_{\text{comp1}}, t_{\text{comp2}}, t_{\text{comp3}} \ldots$ are the computation times of each part.

Analysis of the computation time usually assumes that all the processors are the same and operating at the same speed. This may be true for a specially designed multicomputer/multiprocessor but may not be true for a cluster. One of the powerful features of clusters is that the computers need not be the same. Taking into account a heterogeneous system would be difficult in a mathematical analysis, so our analysis will assume identical computers. Different types of computers will be taken into account by choosing implementation methods that balance the computational load across the available computers (*load balancing*), as described in Chapter 7.

Communication Time. The communication time will depend upon the number of messages, the size of each message, the underlying interconnection structure, and the mode of transfer. The communication time of each message will depend upon many factors, including network structure and network contention. For a first approximation, we will use

$$t_{\text{comm1}} = t_{\text{startup}} + wt_{\text{data}}$$

for the communication time of a message 1, where $t_{startup}$ is the *startup time*, sometimes called the *message latency*. The startup time is essentially the time needed to send a message with no data. (It could be measured by simply doing that.) It includes the time to pack the message at the source and unpack the message at the destination. The term *latency* is also used to describe a complete communication delay, as in Chapter 1, so we will use the term *startup* time here. The startup time is assumed to be constant. The term t_{data} is the transmission time to send one data word, also assumed to be constant, and there are w data words. The transmission rate is usually measured in bits/second and would be b/t_{data} bits/second when there are b bits in the data word. The equation is illustrated in Figure 2.13. Of course, we do not get such a perfect linear relationship in a real system. Many factors can affect the communication time, including contention on the communication medium. The equation ignores the fact that the source and destination may not be directly linked in a real system so that the message must pass through intermediate nodes. It also assumes that the overhead incurred by including information other than data in the packet is constant and can be part of $t_{startup}$.

The final communication time, t_{comm} will be the summation of the communication times of all the sequential messages from a process. Thus

$$t_{comm} = t_{comm1} + t_{comm2} + t_{comm3} + \dots$$

where t_{comm1}, t_{comm2}, t_{comm3} … are the communication times of the messages. (Typically, the communication patterns of all the processes are the same and assumed to take place together, so that only one process need be considered.)

Since the startup and data transmission times, $t_{startup}$ and t_{data}, are both measured in units of one computational step, we can add t_{comp} and t_{comm} together to obtain the parallel execution time, t_p.

Benchmark Factors. Once we have the sequential execution time t_s, the computational time t_{comp}, and the communication time t_{comm}, we can establish the speedup factor and computation/communication ratio described in Chapter 1 for any given algorithm/implementation, namely:

$$\text{Speedup factor} = \frac{t_s}{t_p} = \frac{t_s}{t_{comp} + t_{comm}}$$

$$\text{Computation/communication ratio} = \frac{t_{comp}}{t_{comm}}$$

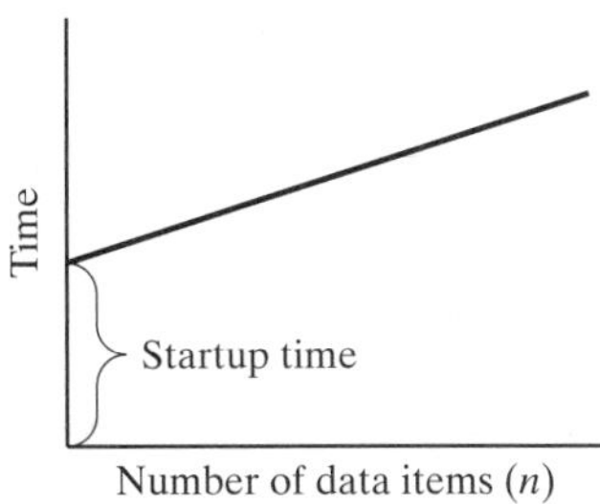

Figure 2.13 Idealized communication time.

Both factors will be functions of the number of processors, p, and the number of data elements, n, and will give an indication of the scalability of the parallel solution with increasing number of processors and increasing problem size. The computation/communication ratio in particular will highlight the effect of communication with increasing problem size and system size.

Important Notes on Interpretation of Equations. There are many assumptions in the analysis given in subsequent chapters, and the analysis is only intended to give a starting point to how an algorithm might perform in practice. The parallel execution time, t_p, will be normalized to be measured in units of an arithmetic operation, which of course will depend upon the computer system. For ease of analysis, it will be assumed that the system is a homogeneous system. Every processor is identical and operating at the same speed. Also, all arithmetic operations are considered to require the same time; for example division requires the same time as addition. Although this is very unlikely in practice, it is a common assumption for analysis. Any additional operations necessary in the formation of the program, such as counting iterations, are not considered.

We will not differentiate between sending an integer and sending a real number, or other formats. All are assumed to require the same time. (This is also not true in practice — in most practical implementations, an 8-bit character will require less time to send than a 64-bit float.) However in many problems, the data type of the data been sent is often the same throughout. The actual startup and transmission times are also dependent upon the computer system and can vary widely between systems. Often the startup time is at least one or two orders of magnitude greater than the transmission time, which is also much greater than the arithmetic operation time. In practice, it is the startup time that will dominate the communication time in many cases. We cannot ignore this term unless n is quite large. (It would, however, be ignored when the equations are converted to order notation; see Section 2.3.2.)

Example

Suppose a computer can operate at a maximum of 1 GFLOPs (10^9 floating point operations per second) and the startup time is 1 μs. The computer could execute 1000 floating point operations in the time taken in the message startup.

Latency Hiding. In the preceding example, one would need 1000 floating point operations between each message just to spend as much time in computing as in message startup. This effect is often cited by shared memory supporters as the Achilles' heel of message-passing multicomputers. One way to ameliorate the situation is to overlap the communication with subsequent computations; that is, by keeping the processor busy with useful work while waiting for the communication to be completed, which is known as *latency hiding*. The nonblocking send routines are provided particularly to enable latency hiding, but even the (locally) blocking send routines allow for subsequent computations to take place while waiting for the destination to receive the message and perhaps return a message. Problem 2-8 explores latency hiding empirically using this approach.

Latency hiding can also be achieved by mapping multiple processes on a processor and using a time-sharing facility that switches from one process to another when the first process is stalled because of incomplete message-passing or for some other reason.

Sometimes the processes are called *virtual processors*. An m-process algorithm implemented on an p-processor machine is said to have a *parallel slackness* of m/p for that machine, where $p < m$. Using parallel slackness to hide latency relies upon an efficient method of switching from one process to another. *Threads* offer an efficient mechanism. See Chapter 8 for further details.

2.3.2 Time Complexity

As with sequential computations, a parallel algorithm can be evaluated through the use of time complexity (notably the O notation — "order of magnitude," "big-oh") (Knuth, 1976). This notation should be familiar from sequential programming and is used to capture characteristics of an algorithm as some variable, usually the data size, tends to infinity. This is especially useful in comparing the execution time of algorithms (*time complexity*) but can also be applied to other computational aspects, such as memory requirements (*space complexity*) as well as speed-up and efficiency in parallel algorithms. Let us first review time complexity as applied to sequential algorithms.

When using the notations for execution time, we start with an estimate of the number of computational steps, considering all the arithmetic and logical operations to be equal and ignoring other aspects of the computation, such as computational tests. An expression of the number of computational steps is derived, often in terms of the number of data items being handled by the algorithm. For example, suppose an algorithm, A1, requires $4x^2 + 2x + 12$ computational steps for x data items. As we increase the number of data items, the total number of operations will depend more and more upon the term $4x^2$. This term will "dominate" the other terms, and eventually the other terms will be insignificant. The growth of the function in this example is *polynomial*. Another algorithm, A2, for the same problem might require $5 \log x + 200$ computational steps.[4] For small x, this has more steps than the first function, A1, but as we increase x, a point will be reached whereby the second function, A2, requires fewer computational steps and will be preferred. In the function $5 \log x + 200$, the first term, $5 \log x$, will eventually dominate the second term, 200, and the second term can be ignored because we only need to compare the dominating terms. The growth of function $\log x$ is *logarithmic*. For a sufficiently large x, logarithmic growth will be less than polynomial growth. We can capture growth patterns in the O notation (big-oh). Algorithm A1 has a big-oh of $O(x^2)$. Algorithm A2 has a big-oh of $O(\log x)$.

Formal Definitions.

O notation. Formally, the O notation can be defined as follows:

> $f(x) = O(g(x))$ if and only if there exist positive constants, c and x_0, such that $0 \le f(x) \le cg(x)$ for all $x \ge x_0$

where $f(x)$ and $g(x)$ are functions of x. For example, if $f(x) = 4x^2 + 2x + 12$, the constant $c = 6$ would work with the formal definition to establish that $f(x) = O(x^2)$, since $0 < 4x^2 + 2x + 12 \le 6x^2$ for $x \ge 3$.

[4] Throughout the text, logarithms are assumed to have the base 2 unless otherwise stated, although the base here does not matter.

Unfortunately, the formal definition also leads to alternative functions for $g(x)$ that will also satisfy the definition. For example, $g(x) = x^3$ also satisfies the definition $4x^2 + 2x + 12 \le 2x^3$ for $x \ge 3$. Normally, we would use the function that grows the least for $g(x)$. In fact, in many cases we have a "tight bound" in that the function $f(x)$ equals $g(x)$ to within a constant factor. This can be captured in the Θ notation.

Θ notation. Formally, the Θ notation can be defined as follows:

$f(x) = \Theta(g(x))$ if and only if there exist positive constants c_1, c_2, and x_0 such that $0 \le c_1 g(x) \le f(x) \le c_2 g(x)$ for all $x \ge x_0$.

If $f(x) = \Theta(g(x))$, it is clear that $f(x) = O(g(x))$ is also true. One way of satisfying the conditions for the function $f(x) = 4x^2 + 2x + 12$ is illustrated in Figure 2.14. We can actually satisfy the conditions in many ways with $g(x) = x^2$, but can see that $c_1 = 2$, $c_2 = 6$, and $x_0 = 3$ will work; that is, $2x^2 \le f(x) \le 6x^2$. Thus, we can say that $f(x) = 4x^2 + 2x + 12 = \Theta(x^2)$, which is more precise than using $O(x^2)$. We should really use the big-oh notation if and only if the upper bound on growth can be satisfied. However, it is common practice to use big-oh in any event.

Ω notation. The lower bound on growth can be described by the Ω notation, which is formally defined as

$f(x) = \Omega(g(x))$ if and only if there exist positive constants c and x_0 such that $0 \le cg(x) \le f(x)$ for all $x \ge x_0$.

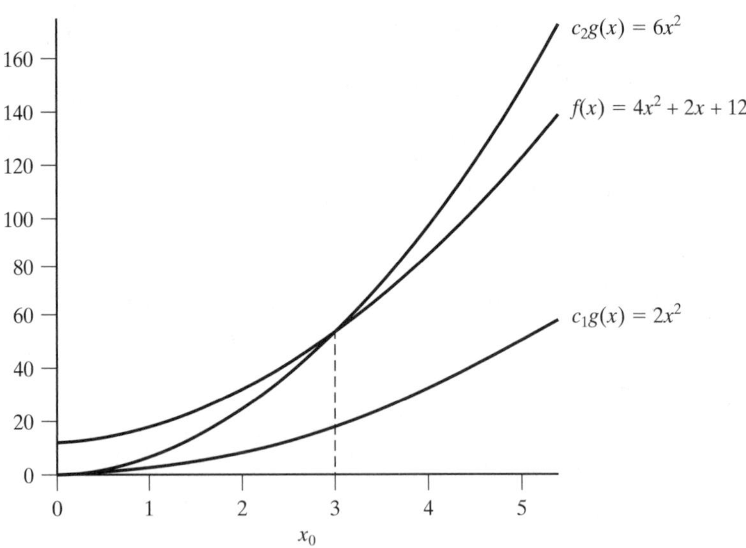

Figure 2.14 Growth of function $f(x) = 4x^2 + 2x + 12$.

It follows from this definition that $f(x) = 4x^2 + 2x + 12 = \Omega(x^2)$ (see Figure 2.14). We can read O() as "grows at most as fast as" and Ω() as "grows at least as fast as." The function $f(x) = \Theta(g(x))$ is true if and only if $f(x) = \Omega(g(x))$ and $f(x) = O(g(x))$.

The Ω notation can be used to indicate the best-case situation. For example, the execution time of a sorting algorithm often depends upon the original order of the numbers to be sorted. It may be that it requires at least $n \log n$ steps, but could require n^2 steps for n numbers depending upon the order of the numbers. This would be indicated by a time complexity of $\Omega(n \log n)$ and $O(n^2)$.

In this text, we often deal with functions of two variables, p and n. In such cases, the time complexity is also a function of the two variables.

Time Complexity of a Parallel Algorithm. If we use time complexity analysis, which hides lower terms, t_{comm} will have a time complexity of $O(n)$. The time complexity of t_p will be the sum of the complexity of the computation and the communication.

Example

Suppose we were to add n numbers on two computers, where each computer adds $n/2$ numbers together, and the numbers are initially all held by the first computer. The second computer submits its result to the first computer for adding the two partial sums together. This problem has several phases:

1. Computer 1 sends $n/2$ numbers to computer 2.
2. Both computers add $n/2$ numbers simultaneously.
3. Computer 2 sends its partial result back to computer 1.
4. Computer 1 adds the partial sums to produce the final result.

As in most parallel algorithms, there is computation and communication, which we will generally consider separately:

Computation (for steps 2 and 4):

$$t_{comp} = n/2 + 1$$

Communication (for steps 1 and 3):

$$t_{comm} = (t_{startup} + n/2t_{data}) + (t_{startup} + t_{data}) = 2t_{startup} + (n/2 + 1)t_{data}$$

The computational complexity is $O(n)$. The communication complexity is $O(n)$. The overall time complexity is $O(n)$.

Computation/Communication Ratio. Normally, communication is very costly. If both the computation and communication have the same time complexity, increasing n is unlikely to improve the performance. Ideally, the time complexity of the computation should be *greater* than that of the communication, for in that case increasing n will improve the performance. For example, suppose the communication time complexity is $O(n)$ and the computation time complexity is $O(n^2)$. By increasing n, eventually an n can be found that will cause the computation time to dominate the overall execution time. There are notable examples where this can be true. For example, the N-body problem mentioned in Chapter 1, and discussed in Chapter 4, has a communication time complexity of $O(N)$ and a computation time complexity of $O(N^2)$ (using a direct parallel algorithm). This is one of the few problems where the size can be really large.

Cost and Cost-Optimal Algorithms. The *processor-time* product or *cost* (or *work*) of a computation can be defined as

$$\text{Cost} = (\text{execution time}) \times (\text{total number of processors used})$$

The cost of a sequential computation is simply its execution time, t_s. The cost of a parallel computation is $t_p \times p$. A *cost-optimal* parallel algorithm is one in which the cost to solve a problem is proportional to the execution time on a single processor system (using the fastest known sequential algorithm). Thus,

$$\text{Cost} = t_p \times p = k \times t_s$$

where k is a constant. Using time complexity analysis, we can say that a parallel algorithm is cost-optimal algorithm if

Parallel time complexity × number of processors = sequential time complexity

Example

Suppose the best-known sequential algorithm for a problem with n numbers has time complexity of $O(n \log n)$. A parallel algorithm for the same problem that uses p processors and has a time complexity of $O\left(\frac{n}{p}\log n\right)$ is cost-optimal, whereas a parallel algorithm that uses p^2 processors and has time complexity of $O\left(\frac{n^2}{p}\right)$ is not cost-optimal.

2.3.3 Comments on Asymptotic Analysis

Whereas time complexity is widely used for sequential program analysis and for theoretical analysis of parallel programs, the time complexity notation is *much* less useful for evaluating the potential performance of parallel programs. The big-oh and other complexity notations use asymptotic methods (allowing the variable under consideration to tend to infinity), which may not be completely relevant. The conclusions reached from the analyses are based upon the variable under consideration, usually either the data size or the number of processors growing toward infinity. However, often the number of processors is constrained and we are therefore unable to expand the number of processors toward infinity. Similarly, we are interested in finite and manageable data sizes. In addition, the analysis ignores lower terms that could be very significant. For example, the communication time equation

$$t_{\text{comm}} = t_{\text{startup}} + wt_{\text{data}}$$

has a time complexity of $O(w)$, but for reasonable values of w, the startup time would completely dominate the overall communication time. Finally, the analysis also ignores other factors that appear in real computers, such as communication contention.

Shared Memory Programs. Much of our discussion is centered on message-passing programs. For shared memory programs, the communication aspect, of course, does not exist and the time complexity is simply that of the computation, as in a sequential program. In that respect, time complexity might be more relevant. However, an additional aspect of a shared memory program is that the shared data must be accessed in a controlled fashion, causing additional delays. This aspect is considered in Chapter 8.

2.3.4 Communication Time of Broadcast/Gather

Notwithstanding our comments about theoretical analysis, let us look at broadcast/gather operations and their complexity. Almost all problems require data to be broadcast to processes and data to be gathered from processes. Most software environments provide for broadcast and gather. The actual algorithm used will depend upon the underlying architecture of the multicomputer. In the past, the programmer might have been given some knowledge of the interconnection architecture (mesh, etc.) and been able to take advantage of it, but nowadays this is usually hidden from the programmer.

In this text, we concentrate upon using clusters. Again the actual interconnection structure will be hidden from the user, although it is much more likely to provide full simultaneous connections between pairs of computers using switches. In the distant past, Ethernet used a single wire connecting all computers. Broadcast on a single Ethernet connection could be done using a single message that was read by all the destinations on the network simultaneously, (Ethernet protocols provide for this form of communication.) Hence, broadcast could be very efficient and just require a single message:

$$t_{\text{comm}} = t_{\text{startup}} + wt_{\text{data}}$$

with an O(1) time complexity for one data item; for w data items it was O(w).

Of course, most clustered computers will use a variety of network structures, and the convenient broadcast medium available in a single Ethernet will not generally be applicable. Typically messages are sent from the originating computer to multiple destinations, which themselves send the message on to multiple destinations. Once a message arrives at a destination it is converted into a 1-to-N fan-out broadcast call, where the same message is sent to each of the destinations in turn, as shown in Figure 2.15. The same construction will be necessary for gather, except that the messages pass in the opposite direction. In either case, the limiting factor will be whether the messages sent or received are sequential, leading to:

$$t_{\text{comm}} = N(t_{\text{startup}} + wt_{\text{data}})$$

an O(N) communication time complexity for one source connecting to N destinations. We are assuming that the messages at each level occur at the same time (which of course would not happen in practice).

The 1-to-N fan-out broadcast applied to a tree structure is shown in Figure 2.16. The complexity here will depend upon the number of nodes at each level and the number

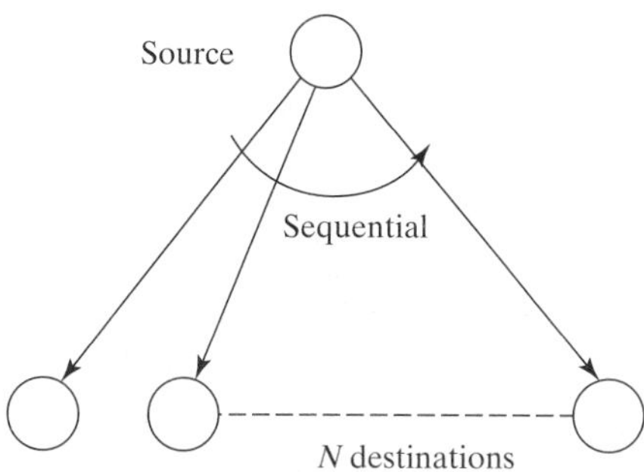

Figure 2.15 1-to-N fan-out broadcast.

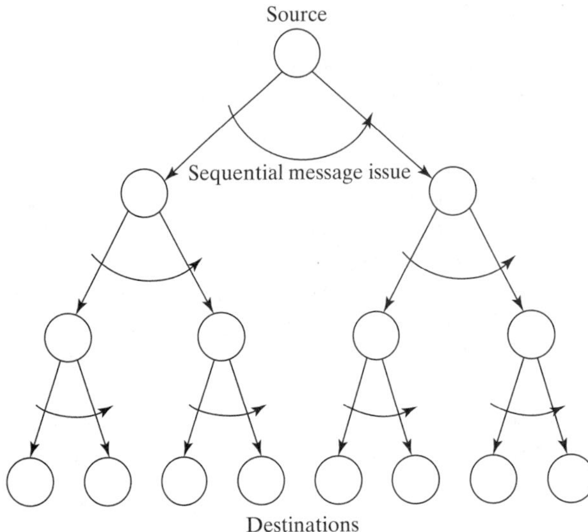

Figure 2.16 1-to-N fan-out broadcast on a tree structure.

of levels. For a binary tree N = 2 and log p levels if there are p final destinations. This leads to

$$t_{\text{comm}} = 2(\log p)(t_{\text{startup}} + wt_{\text{data}})$$

assuming again that the messages at each level occur at the same time. (It is left as an exercise to determine the communication time if this assumption is not made.)

One disadvantage of a binary tree implementation of broadcast is that if a node fails in the tree, all the nodes below it will not receive the message. In addition, a binary tree would be difficult to implement in a library call. The programmer can, of course, achieve it with explicit coding in the processes.

2.4 DEBUGGING AND EVALUATING PARALLEL PROGRAMS EMPIRICALLY

In writing a parallel program, we first want to get it to execute correctly. Then we will become interested in how fast the program executes. Finally, we would like to see whether it can be made to execute faster.

2.4.1 Low-Level Debugging

Getting a parallel program to work properly can be a significant intellectual challenge. It is useful to write a sequential version first, based upon the ultimate parallel algorithm. Having said that, the parallel code still has to be made to work. Errors in sequential programs are found by *debugging*. A common way is to instrument the code; that is, to insert code that outputs intermediate calculated values as the program executes. Print statements are used to output the intermediate values. Similar techniques could be used in parallel programs, but this approach has some very significant consequences. First and foremost, instrumenting a sequential program makes it execute slower, but it still functions deterministically and produces the same answer. Instrumenting a parallel program by inserting code in the different processes will certainly slow down the computations. It also may cause the instructions to be executed in a different interleaved order, as generally each process will be affected differently. It is possible for a nonworking program to start working after the instrumentation code is inserted — which would certainly indicate that the problem lies within interprocess timing.

We should also mention that since processes might be executing on a remote computer, output from print statements may need to be redirected to a file in order to be seen at the local computer. Message-passing software often has facilities to redirect output.

The lowest level of debugging (in desperation) is to use a debugger. Primitive sequential-program debugging tools, such as `dbx`, exist (but are rarely used) to examine registers and perhaps set "breakpoints" to stop the execution. Applying these techniques to parallel programs would be of little value because of such factors as not knowing the precise interleaved order of events in different processes. One scenario would be to run the debugger on individual processors and watch the output in separate display windows. A parallel computation could have many simultaneous processes, which would make this approach unwieldy. In the case of dynamic process creation, system facilities may be needed to start spawned processes through a debugger.

Parallel computations have characteristics that are not captured by a regular sequential debugger, such as timing of events. Events may be recognized when certain conditions occur. In addition to what might appear in a sequential program, such as access to a memory location, an event in this context may be a message being sent or received. Parallel debuggers are available (McDowell and Helmbold, 1989).

2.4.2 Visualization Tools

Parallel computations lend themselves to visual indication of their actions, and message-passing software often provides visualization tools as part of the overall parallel programming environment. Programs can be watched as they are executed in a *space-time diagram* (or *process-time diagram*). A hypothetical example is shown in Figure 2.17. Each waiting period indicates a process being idle, often waiting for a message to be received. Such visual presentations may help spot erroneous actions. The events that created the space-time diagram can be captured and saved so that the presentation can be replayed without having to reexecute the program. Also of interest is a *utilization-time diagram*, which shows the amount of time spent by each process on communication, waiting, and message-passing library routines. Apart from its help in debugging, the utilization-time diagram also indicates the efficiency of the computation. Finally, animation may be useful where processes are shown in a two-dimensional display and changes of state are shown in a movie form.

Implementations of visualization tools are available for MPI. An example is the Upshot program visualization system (Herrarte and Luske, 1991). All forms of visualization imply software "probes" into the execution, which may alter the characteristics of the computation. It certainly makes the computation proceed much slower. (Hardware performance monitors are possible that do not usually affect the performance. For example, there are some that simply monitor the system bus, but these are not widely deployed.)

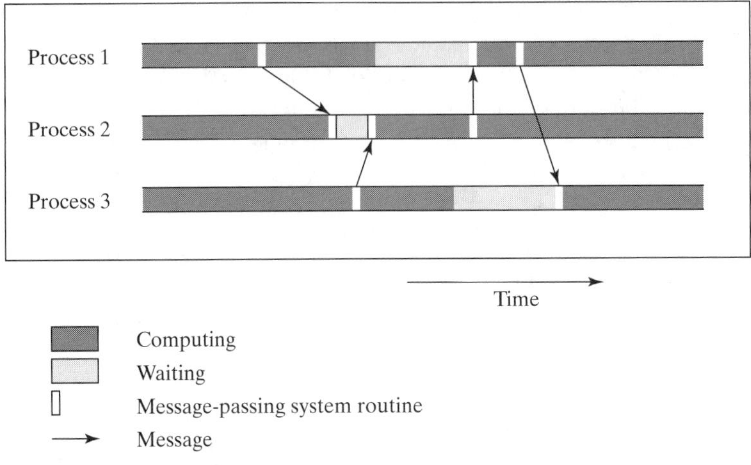

Figure 2.17 Space-time diagram of a parallel program.

2.4.3 Debugging Strategies

Geist et al. (1994a) suggest a three-step approach to debugging message-passing programs:

1. If possible, run the program as a single process and debug as a normal sequential program.
2. Execute the program using two to four multitasked processes on a single computer. Now examine actions, such as checking that messages are indeed being sent to the correct places. Very often mistakes are made with message tags and messages are sent to the wrong places.
3. Execute the program using the same two to four processes but now across several computers. This step helps find problems that are caused by network delays related to synchronization and timing.

Placing error-checking code in the program is always important as good programming practice, but is particularly important in parallel programs to ensure that faulty conditions can be handled and not cause deadlock. Many message-passing routines return an error code if an error is detected. Though not necessary for these routines to execute, error codes should be recognized if they occur. They are also useful in debugging. MPI also can be made to return error codes, but the default situation is for the program to abort when an error is encountered.

2.4.4 Evaluating Programs

Measuring Execution Time. Time-complexity analysis might give an insight into the potential of a parallel algorithm and is useful in comparing different algorithms. However, given our comments in Section 2.3.4 about time-complexity analysis, only when the algorithm is coded and executed on a multiprocessor system will it be truly known how well the algorithm actually performs. As with low-level debugging (Section 2.4), programs can be instrumented with additional code. To measure the execution time of a program or the *elapsed time* between two points in the code in seconds, we could use regular system calls, such as `clock()`, `time()`, or `gettimeofday()`. Thus, to measure the execution time between point `L1` and point `L2` in the code, we might have a construction such as

```
        .
        .
        .
L1:  time(&t1);                          /* start timer */
        .
        .
        .
L2:  time(&t2);                          /* stop timer */
        .
        .
        .
     elapsed_time = difftime(t2, t1);    /* elapsed_time = t2 - t1 */
     printf("Elapsed time = %5.2f seconds", elapsed_time);
```

Elapsed time will include the time waiting for messages, and it is assumed that the processor is not executing any other program at the same time.

Often the message-passing software itself includes facilities for timing; for example, by providing library calls that return the time or by displaying time on space-time diagrams (as described in Section 2.4). MPI provides the routine `MPI_Wtime()` for returning time in seconds. In general, each processor will be using its own clock, and the time returned will not necessarily be synchronized with the clocks of other processors unless clock synchronization is available. Clock synchronization is defined in MPI as an environment attribute but may not be implemented in a system because it usually incurs a very significant system overhead.

Communication Time by the Ping-Pong Method. Point-to-point communication time of a specific system can be found using the *ping-pong method* as follows. One process, say P_0, is made to send a message to another process, say P_1. Immediately upon receiving the message, P_1 sends the g back to P_0. The time involved in this message communication is recorded at P_0. This time is divided by two to obtain an estimate of the time of one-way communication:

Process P_0

```
        .
        .
        .
L1:  time(&t1);
     send(&x, P1);
     recv(&x, P1);
L2:  time(&t2);
     elapsed_time = 0.5 * difftime(t2, t1);
     printf("Elapsed time = %5.2f seconds", elapsed_time);
        .
        .
        .
```

Process P_1

```
    .
    .
    .
recv(&x, P0);
send(&x, P0);
    .
    .
    .
```

Problem 2-5 explores measuring communication times.

Profiling. A *profile* of a program is a histogram or graph showing the time spent on different parts of the program. A profile can show the number of times certain source statements are executed, as illustrated in Figure 2.18. The *profiler* actually producing the results must capture the information from the executing program and in doing so will affect the execution time. To count the appearance of each instruction would probably be too invasive. Instead, the executing code is usually probed or sampled at intervals to give statistical results. Probing in any form will affect the execution characteristics. This is especially important in parallel programs that have interrelationships between concurrent processes.

Profiling can be used to identify "hot spot" places in a program visited many times during the program execution. These places should be optimized first, a technique that is applicable to both sequential and parallel programs.

2.4.5 Comments on Optimizing Parallel Code

Once the performance has been measured, structural changes may need to be made to the program to improve its performance. Apart from optimizations that apply to regular single-processor programs, such as moving constant calculations to the outside of loops, several parallel optimizations are possible. These usually relate to the architecture of the multiprocessor system. The number of processes can be changed to alter the process granularity. The amount of data in the messages can be increased to lessen the effects of startup times. It may often be better to recompute values locally than to send computed values in additional messages from one process to other processes needing these values. Communication and

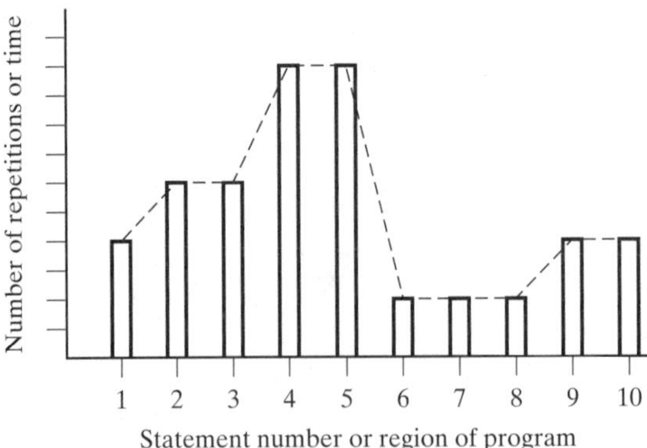

Figure 2.18 Program profile.

computation can be overlapped (latency hiding, Section 2.3.1). One can perform a *critical path analysis* on the program; that is, determine the various concurrent parts of the program and find the longest path that dominates the overall execution time.

A much less obvious factor than those just mentioned is the effect of the memory hierarchy. Processors usually have high-speed cache memory. A processor first accesses its cache memory, and only afterward accesses the main memory if the information is not already in the cache. The information is brought into the cache from the main memory by a previous reference to it, but only a limited amount of data can be held in the cache. The best performance will result if as much of the data as possible resides in the cache when needed. This can sometimes be achieved by a specific strategy for parallelization and sometimes by simply reordering the memory requests in the program. In Chapter 11, some numerical algorithms are presented. Simply performing the sequence of arithmetic operations in a different order can result in more of the data being in the cache when subsequent references to the data occur.

2.5 SUMMARY

This chapter introduced the following concepts:

- Basic message-passing techniques
- Send, receive, and collective operations
- Software tools for harnessing a network of workstations
- Modeling communication
- Communication latency and latency hiding
- Time complexity of parallel algorithms
- Debugging and evaluating parallel programs

FURTHER READING

We have concentrated upon message-passing routines in general and on one system in particular, MPI. Another system that is widely used is PVM (Parallel Virtual Machine). One of the earliest articles on PVM is Sunderam (1990). More details on PVM can be found in Geist et al. (1994a and 1994b). Further details on MPI can be found in Gropp, Lusk, and Skjellum (1999) and Snir et al. (1998). MPI-2 can be found specifically in Gropp et al (1998), and Gropp, Lusk, and Thakur (1999). The home page for the MPI forum, http://www.mpi-forum.org, provides many official documents and information about MPI. Other sources include Dongarra et al. (1996), which gives references to several earlier message-passing systems in addition to PVM. Programming in PVM and MPI is described in several chapters of Sterling (2002a and b). Papers on scattering and gathering messages include Bhatt et al. (1993).

Fundamental design and analysis of sequential algorithms can be found in the classic text by Knuth (1973). Other texts include Aho, Hopcroft, and Ullman (1974). There have been many others since. A modern, comprehensive, and very well written text on this subject is Cormen, Leiserson, and Rivest (1990), which contains over 1000 pages. Design and analysis of parallel algorithms can be found in several texts, including Akl (1989) and JáJá (1992). A rather unique book that integrates sequential and parallel algorithms is Berman and Paul (1997).

Details of parallel debugging can be found in McDowell and Helmbold (1989) and Simmons et al. (1996). Other papers include Kraemer and Stasko (1993) and Sistare et al. (1994). A special issue of the *IEEE Computer* on parallel and distributed processing tools (November. 1995) contained several useful articles on performance-evaluation tools for parallel systems.

BIBLIOGRAPHY

AHO, A. V., J. E. HOPCROFT, AND J. D. ULLMAN (1974), *The Design and Analysis of Computer Algorithms*, Addison-Wesley Publishing Company, Reading, MA.

AKL, S. G. (1989), *The Design and Analysis of Parallel Algorithms*, Prentice Hall, Englewood Cliffs, NJ.

BERMAN, K. A., AND J. L. PAUL (1997), *Fundamentals of Sequential and Parallel Algorithms*, PWS Publishing Company, Boston, MA.

BHATT, S. N., ET AL. (1993), "Scattering and Gathering Messages in Networks of Processors, *IEEE Trans. Comput.*, Vol. 42, No. 8, pp. 938–949.

CORMEN, T. H., C. E. LEISERSON, AND R. L. RIVEST (1990), *Introduction to Algorithms*, MIT Press, Cambridge, MA.

DONGARRA, J., S. W. OTTO, M. SNIR, AND D. WALKER (1996), "A Message-Passing Standard for MMP and Workstations," *Comm. ACM*, Vol. 39, No. 7, pp. 84–90.

FAHRINGER, T. (1995), "Estimating and Optimizing Performance for Parallel Programs," *Computer*, Vol. 28, No. 11, pp. 47–56.

FOSTER, I. (1995), *Designing and Building Parallel Programs*, Addison-Wesley, Reading, MA.

GEIST, A., A. BEGUELIN, J. DONGARRA, W. JIANG, R. MANCHEK, AND V. SUNDERAM (1994a), *PVM3 User's Guide and Reference Manual*, Oak Ridge National Laboratory, TN.

GEIST, A., A. BEGUELIN, J. DONGARRA, W. JIANG, R. MANCHEK, AND V. SUNDERAM (1994b), *PVM: Parallel Virtual Machine*, MIT Press, Cambridge, MA.

GRAMA, A., A. GUPTA, G. KARYPIS, AND V. KUMAR (2003), *Introduction to Parallel Computing,* 2nd edition, Benjamin/Cummings, Redwood City, CA.

GROPP, W., S. HUSS-LEDERMAN, A. LUMSDAINE, E. LUSK, B. NITZBERG, W. SAPHIR, AND M. SNIR (1998), *MPI, The Complete Reference,* Volume 2, *The MPI-2 Extensions,* MIT Press, Cambridge, MA.

GROPP, W., E. LUSK, AND A. SKJELLUM (1999a), *Using MPI Portable Parallel Programming with the Message-Passing Interface,* 2nd edition, MIT Press, Cambridge, MA.

GROPP, W., E. LUSK, AND RAJEEV THAKUR (1999b), *Using MPI-2 Advanced Features of the Message-Passing Interface*, MIT Press, Cambridge, MA.

HERRARTE, V., AND LUSKE, E. (1991), "Studying Parallel Program Behavior with Upshot," Technical Report ANL-91/15, Mathematics and Computer Science Division, Argonne National Laboratory.

INMOS LTD. (1984), *Occam Programming Manual*, Prentice Hall, Englewood Cliffs, NJ.

JÁJÁ, J. (1992), *An Introduction to Parallel Algorithms*, Addison Wesley, Reading, MA.

KARONIS, N. T. (1992), "Timing Parallel Programs That Use Message-Passing," *J. Parallel & Distributed Computing*, Vol. 14, pp. 29–36.

KNUTH, D. E. (1973), *The Art of Computer Programming*, Addison-Wesley, Reading, MA.

KNUTH, D. E. (1976), "Big Omicron, Big Omega and Big Theta," *SIGACT News* (April–June), pp. 18–24.

KRAEMER, E., AND J. T. STASKO (1993), "The Visualization of Parallel Systems: An Overview," *J. Parallel & Distribut. Computing*, Vol. 18, No. 2 (June), pp. 105–117.

KRONSJO, L. (1985), *Computational Complexity of Sequential and Parallel Algorithms*, Wiley, NY.

MCDOWELL, C. E., AND D. P. HELMBOLD (1989), "Debugging Concurrent Programs," *Computing Surveys*, Vol. 21, No. 4, pp. 593–622.

SIMMONS, M., A. HAYES, J. BROWN, AND D. REED (EDS.) (1996), *Debugging and Performance Tools for Parallel Computing Systems*, IEEE CS Press, Los Alamitos, CA.

SISTARE, S., D. ALLEN, R. BOWKER, K. JOURDENAIS, J. SIMONS, AND R. TITLE (1994), "A Scalable Debugger for Massively Parallel Message-Passing Programs," *IEEE Parallel & Distributed Technology*, (Summer), pp. 50–56.

SNIR, M., S. W. OTTO, S. HUSS-LEDERMAN, D. W. WALKER, AND J. DONGARRA (1998), *MPI - The Complete Reference Volume 1, The MPI Core, 2nd edition*, MIT Press, Cambridge, MA.

STERLING, T., editor (2002a), *Beowulf Cluster Computing with Windows*, MIT Press, Cambridge, MA.

STERLING, T., editor (2002b), *Beowulf Cluster Computing with Linux*, MIT Press, Cambridge, MA.

SUNDERAM, V. (1990), "PVM: A Framework for Parallel Distributed Computing," *Concurrency: Practice & Experience*, Vol. 2, No. 4, pp. 315–339.

PROBLEMS

2-1. Develop an equation for message communication time, t_{comm}, that incorporates a delay through multiple links as would occur in a static interconnection network. Develop the equation for a mesh assuming that all message destinations are randomly chosen.

2-2. Pointers are used in the send and receive used in book and in MPI, but they can be avoided by passing the arguments by value. For example, pointers can be eliminated in the receive routine by having the routing return the message data, which then can be assigned to a variable, i.e., `x = recv(sourceID)`. Write new routines to "wrap" around regular MPI send and receive routines to avoid pointers and demonstrate their use.

2-3. To send a message from a specific source process to a specific destination process, it is necessary for the source process to know the destination TID (task identification) or rank and for the destination to know the source TID or rank. Explain how each process can obtain the TID or rank of the other process in MPI. Give a program example.

2-4. (A suitable first assignment) Compile and run the MPI program to add numbers, as given in Figures 2.14 and 2.16 (or as found in http://www.cs.uncc.edu/par_prog as the "sample program" in the compiling instructions) and execute on your system. Modify the program so that the maximum number is found and output as well as the sum.

2-5. Measure the time to send a message in a parallel programming system by using code segments of the form

Master

```
          .
          .
          .
L1:   time(&t1);
      send(&x, Pslave);
L2:   time(&t2);
      tmaster = difftime(t2, t1);
      recv(&tslave, Pslave);
      printf("Master Time = %d", tmaster);
      printf("Slave Time = %d", tslave);
          .
          .
          .
```

Slave

```
          .
          .
          .
L1:   time(&t1);
      recv(&x, Pmaster);
L2:   time(&t2);
      tslave = difftime(t2, t1);
      send(&tslave, Pmaster);
          .
          .
          .
```

Repeat with the ping-pong method described in Section 2.4.4. Experiment with sending groups of multiple messages and messages of different sizes to obtain a good estimate for the time of message transfers. Plot the time for sending a message against the size of the message, and fit a line to the results. Estimate the startup time, $t_{startup}$ (latency), and the time to send one data item, t_{data}.

2-6. Repeat Problem 2-5 for broadcast and other collective routines as available on your system.

2-7. Compare the use of broadcast and gather routines using individual send and receive routines empirically.

2-8. Experiment with latency hiding on your system to determine how much computation is possible between sending messages. Investigate using both nonblocking and locally blocking send routines.

2-9. Develop an equation for communication time and time complexity for the binary tree broadcast described in Section 2.3.4 assuming the messages at each level do not occur at the same time (as would happen in practice). Extend for an m-ary tree broadcast (each node having m destinations).

2-10. If you have both PVM and MPI available (or any two systems), make a comparative study of the communication times on the systems by passing messages between processes that have been instrumented to measure the communication times.

Chapter 3

Embarrassingly Parallel Computations

In this chapter, we will consider the "ideal" computation from a parallel computing standpoint — a computation that can be divided into a number of completely independent parts, each of which can be executed by a separate processor. This is known as an *embarrassingly parallel* computation. We will look at sample embarrassingly parallel computations before moving on in other chapters to computations that do not decompose as well. The material in this chapter can form the basis of one's first parallel program.

3.1 IDEAL PARALLEL COMPUTATION

Parallel programming involves dividing a problem into parts in which separate processors perform the computation of the parts. An ideal parallel computation is one that can be immediately divided into completely independent parts that can be executed simultaneously. This is picturesquely called *embarrassingly parallel* (a term coined by Geoffrey Fox; Wilson, 1995) or perhaps more aptly called *naturally parallel*. Parallelizing these problems should be obvious and requires no special techniques or algorithms to obtain a working solution. Ideally, there would be no communication between the separate processes; that is, a completely disconnected computational graph, as shown in Figure 3.1. Each process requires different (or the same) data and produces results from its input data without any need for results from other processes. This situation will give the maximum possible speedup if all the available processors can be assigned processes for the total duration of the computation. The only constructs required here are simply to distribute the data and to start the processes. Interesting, there are many significant real applications that

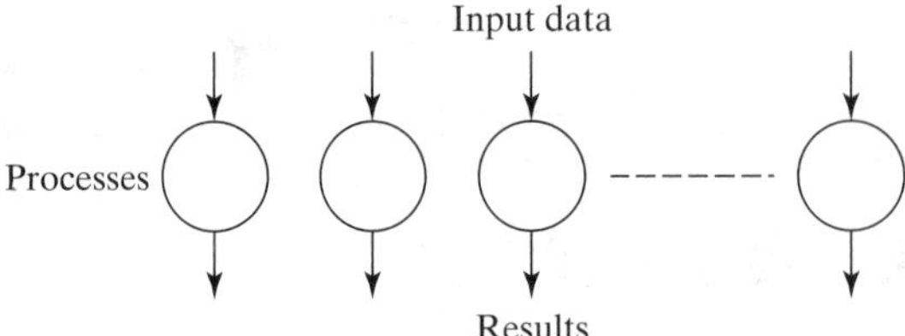

Figure 3.1 Disconnected computational graph (embarrassingly parallel problem).

are embarrassingly parallel, or at least nearly so. Often the independent parts are identical computations and the SPMD (single-program multiple-data) model is appropriate, as suggested in Figure 3.1. The data is not shared, and hence distributed memory multiprocessors or message-passing multicomputers are appropriate. If the same data is required, the data must be copied to each process. The key characteristic is that there is no interaction between the processes.

In a practical embarrassingly parallel computation, data has to be distributed to the processes and results collected and combined in some way. This suggests that initially, and finally, a single process must be operating alone. A common approach is the master-slave organization. If dynamic process creation is used, first, a master process will be started that will spawn (start) identical slave processes. The resulting structure is shown in Figure 3.2. (The master process could take on a computation after spawning, although often this is not done when the master is needed for the results as soon as they arrive.) As noted in Section 2.2.3, the master-slave approach can be used with static process creation. There, we simply put both the master and the slave in the same program and use `IF` statements to select either the master code or the slave code based upon the process identification, ID (the master ID or a slave ID). The actual details of master and slave startup are omitted from the example pseudocode sequences given later.

In this chapter, we consider applications where there is minimal interaction between slave processes. Even if the slave processes are all identical, it may be that statically assigning processes to processors will not provide the optimum solution. This holds especially when the processors are different, as is often the case with networked workstations, and then load-balancing techniques offer improved execution speed. We will introduce load balancing in this chapter, but only for cases in which there is no interaction between slave processes. When there is interaction between processes, load balancing requires a significantly different treatment, and this is addressed in Chapter 7.

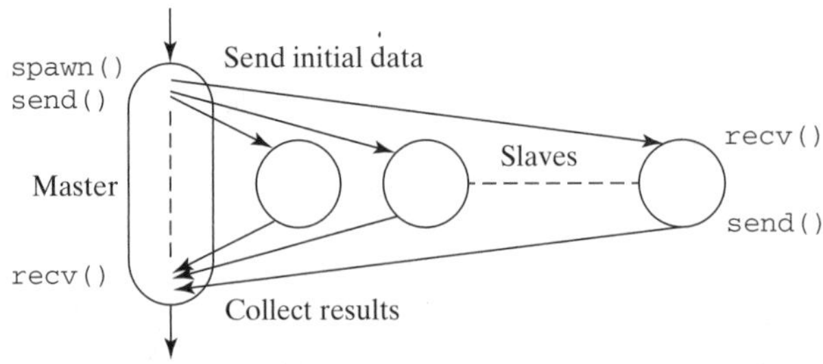

Figure 3.2 Practical embarrassingly parallel computational graph with dynamic process creation and the master-slave approach.

3.2 EMBARRASSINGLY PARALLEL EXAMPLES

3.2.1 Geometrical Transformations of Images

Images are often stored within a computer so that they can be altered in some way. Displayed images originate in two ways. Images are obtained from external sources such as video cameras and may need to be altered in some way (*image processing*). Displayed images may also be artificially created, an approach that is usually associated with the term *computer graphics*. In any event, a number of graphical operations can be performed upon the stored image. For example, we might want to move the image to a different place in the display space, decrease or increase its size, or rotate it in two or three dimensions. Such graphical transformations must be done at high speed to be acceptable to the viewer. Frequently, other image-processing operations, such as smoothing and edge detection, are also done on images, especially externally originated images that are "noisy." and are often embarrassingly parallel. Chapter 11 considers these image-processing operations. Here, we shall consider simple graphical transformations.

The most basic way to store a two-dimensional image is a *pixmap*, in which each pixel (picture element) is stored as a binary number in a two-dimensional array. For purely black-and-white images, a single binary bit is sufficient for each pixel, a 1 if the pixel is white and a 0 if the pixel is black; this is a *bitmap*. *Grayscale* images require more bits, typically using 8 bits to represent 256 different monochrome intensities. Color requires more specification. Usually, the three primary colors, red, green, and blue (RGB), as used in a monitor, are stored as separate 8-bit numbers. Three bytes could be used for each pixel, one byte for red, one for green, and one for blue, 24 bits in all. A standard image file format using this representation is the "tiff" format.

The storage requirements for color images can be reduced by using a look-up table to hold the RGB representation of the specific colors that happen to be used in the image. For example, suppose only 256 different colors are present. A table of 256 24-bit entries could hold the representation of the colors used. Then each pixel in the image would only need to be 8 bits to select the specific color from the look-up table. This method can be used for external image files, in which case the look-up table is held in the file together with the image. The method can also be used for internally generated images to reduce the size of the video memory, though this is becoming less attractive as video memory becomes less expensive. For this section, let us assume a simple grayscale image. (Color images can be reduced to grayscale images, and this is often done for image processing; see Chapter 11.) The terms *bitmap* and *bit-mapped* are used very loosely for images stored in binary as an array of pixels.

Geometrical transformations require mathematical operations to be performed on the coordinates of each pixel to move the position of the pixel without affecting its value. Since the transformation on each pixel is totally independent from the transformations on other pixels, we have a truly embarrassingly parallel computation. The result of a transformation is simply an updated bitmap. A sample of some common geometrical transformations is given here (Wilkinson and Horrocks, 1987):

(a) Shifting

The coordinates of a two-dimensional object shifted by Δx in the x-dimension and Δy

in the y-dimension are given by

$$x' = x + \Delta x$$
$$y' = y + \Delta y$$

where x and y are the original and x' and y' are the new coordinates.

(b) Scaling

The coordinates of an object scaled by a factor S_x in the x-direction and S_y in the y-direction are given by

$$x' = xS_x$$
$$y' = yS_y$$

The object is enlarged in size when S_x and S_y are greater than 1 and reduced in size when S_x and S_y are between 0 and 1. Note that the magnification or reduction does not need to be the same in both x- and y-directions.

(c) Rotation

The coordinates of an object rotated through an angle θ about the origin of the coordinate system are given by

$$x' = x\cos\theta + y\sin\theta$$
$$y' = -x\sin\theta + y\cos\theta$$

(d) Clipping

This transformation applies defined rectangular boundaries to a figure and deletes from the displayed picture those points outside the defined area. This may be useful after rotation, shifting, and scaling have been applied to eliminate coordinates outside the field of view of the display. If the lowest values of x, y in the area to be displayed are x_l, y_l, and the highest values of x, y are x_h, y_h, then

$$x_l \le x' \le x_h$$
$$y_l \le y' \le y_h$$

need to be true for the point (x', y') to be displayed; otherwise the point (x', y') is not displayed.

The input data is the bitmap that is typically held in a file and copied into an array. The contents of this array can easily be manipulated without any special programming techniques. The main parallel programming concern is the division of the bitmap into groups of pixels for each processor because there are usually many more pixels than processes/processors. There are two general methods of grouping: by square/rectangular regions and by columns/rows. We can simply assign one process(or) to one area of the display. For example, with a 640×480 image and 48 processes, we could divide the display area into 48 80×80 rectangular areas and assign one process for each 80×80 rectangular area. Alternatively, we might divide the area into 48 rows of 640×10 pixels for each process. The concept of dividing an area into either rectangular/square areas of rows (or columns), as shown in Figure 3.3, appears in many applications involving processing two-dimensional information. We explore the trade-offs between dividing a region into square blocks or rows (or columns) in Chapter 6. For the case where there is no communication between adjacent areas, as here, it does not matter which partitioning we use, except perhaps for ease of programming.

Suppose we use a master process and 48 slave processes and partition in groups of 10 rows. Each slave process processes one 640×10 area, returning the new coordinates to the master for displaying. If the transformation is shifting, as described in (a) previously, a master-slave approach could start with the master sending the first row number of the 10 rows to be processed by each process. Upon receiving its row number, each process steps through each pixel coordinate in its group of rows, transforming the coordinates and sending the old and new coordinates back to the master. For simplicity, this could be done with individual messages rather than a single message. The master then updates the bitmap.

Let the original bitmap be held in the array `map[][]`. A temporary bitmap is declared, `temp_map[][]`. Usually, the coordinate system of the display has its origin at the top left corner, as shown in Figure 3.3. It is simple matter to transform an image with its origin at

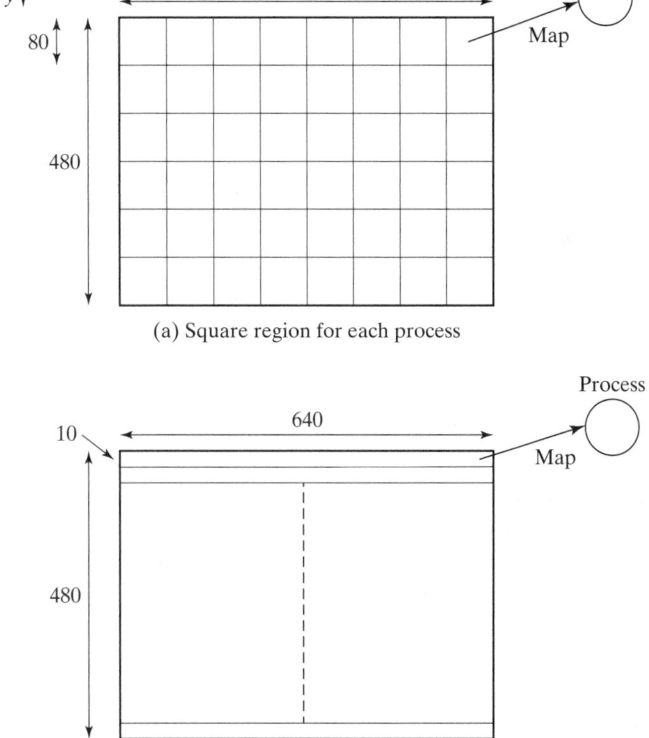

Figure 3.3 Partitioning into regions for individual processes.

the lower-left corner to the display coordinate system. Such details are omitted. Note that in the C programming language, elements are stored row by row, with the first index being the row and the second index being the column. The pseudocode to perform an image shift might look like this:

Master

```
for (i = 0, row = 0; i < 48; i++, row = row + 10)    /* for each process*/
   send(row, Pi);                                     /* send row no.*/

for (i = 0; i < 480; i++)                             /* initialize temp */
   for (j = 0; j < 640; j++)
      temp_map[i][j] = 0;

for (i = 0; i < (640 * 480); i++) {                   /* for each pixel */
   recv(oldrow,oldcol,newrow,newcol, PANY);           /* accept new coords */
   if !((newrow < 0)||(newrow >= 480)||(newcol < 0)||(newcol >= 640))
      temp_map[newrow][newcol]=map[oldrow][oldcol];
}
for (i = 0; i < 480; i++)                             /* update bitmap */
   for (j = 0; j < 640; j++)
      map[i][j] = temp_map[i][j];
```

Slave

```
recv(row, Pmaster);                                   /* receive row no. */
for (oldrow = row; oldrow < (row + 10); oldrow++)
   for (oldcol = 0; oldcol < 640; oldcol++) {         /* transform coords */
      newrow = oldrow + delta_x;                      /* shift in x direction */
      newcol = oldcol + delta_y;                      /* shift in y direction */
      send(oldrow,oldcol,newrow,newcol, Pmaster);     /* coords to master */
   }
```

In the master's receive section, we show a wildcard, P_{any}, indicating that data may be accepted from any slave and in any order. It also may be possible for images to be shifted past the edges of the display area. Wherever the new image does not appear in the display area, the bitmap is set to 0 (black).

In this example, the master sends the starting row numbers to the slaves. However, since the starting numbers are related to the process ID, each slave can determine its starting row itself. The results are returned one at a time rather than as one group, which would have reduced the message overhead time. No code is shown for terminating the slaves, and all results must be generated or the master will wait forever. Slaves here can terminate themselves after they have completed their fixed number of tasks; in other cases, they might be terminated by the master sending them a message to do so. The code is not completely satisfactory because the size of the display area, number of rows for each process, and number of processes are permanently coded for ease of discussion. For complete generality, these factors should be made easily alterable.

Analysis. Suppose each pixel requires two computational steps and there are $n \times n$ pixels. If the transformations are done sequentially, there would be $n \times n$ steps so that

$$t_s = 2n^2$$

and a sequential time complexity of $O(n^2)$.

The parallel time complexity is composed of two parts, communication and computation, as are all message-passing parallel computations. Throughout the text, we will deal with communication and computation separately and sum the components of each to form the overall parallel time complexity.

Communication. To recall our basis for communication analysis, as given in Section 2.3.2, we assume that processors are directly connected and start with the formula

$$t_{\text{comm}} = t_{\text{startup}} + mt_{\text{data}}$$

where t_{startup} is the (constant) time to form the message and initiate the transfer, t_{data} is the (constant) time to send one data item, and there are m data items. The parallel time complexity of the communication time, as given by t_{comm}, is $O(m)$. However, in practice, we usually cannot ignore the communication startup time, t_{startup}, because the startup time is significant unless m was really large.

Let the number of processes be p. Before the computation, the starting row number must be sent to each process. In our pseudocode, we send the row numbers sequentially; that is, p `send()`s, each with one data item. The individual processes have to send back the transformed coordinates of their group of pixels, shown here with individual `send()`s. There are $4n^2$ data items returned to the master, which it will have to accept sequentially. Hence, the communication time is

$$t_{\text{comm}} = p(t_{\text{startup}} + t_{\text{data}}) + n^2(t_{\text{startup}} + 4t_{\text{data}}) = O(p + n^2)$$

Computation. The parallel implementation (using groups of rows or columns or square/rectangular regions) divides the image into groups of n^2/p pixels. Each pixel requires two additions (see slave pseudocode on page 84). Hence, the parallel computation time is given by

$$t_{\text{comp}} = 2\left(\frac{n^2}{p}\right) = O(n^2/p)$$

Overall execution time. The overall execution time is given by

$$t_p = t_{\text{comp}} + t_{\text{comm}}$$

For a fixed number of processors, this is $O(n^2)$.

Speedup factor. The speedup factor is

$$\text{Speedup factor} = \frac{t_s}{t_p} = \frac{2n^2}{2\left(\frac{n^2}{p}\right) + p(t_{\text{startup}} + t_{\text{data}}) + n^2(t_{\text{startup}} + 4t_{\text{data}})}$$

Computation/communication ratio. As introduced in Chapter 1, the ratio of the computation and communication times:

$$\text{Computation/communication ratio} = \frac{\text{Computation time}}{\text{Communication time}} = \frac{t_{\text{comp}}}{t_{\text{comm}}}$$

enables one to see the effects of the communication overhead, especially for increasing problem size. In the problem under consideration, the ratio is

$$\text{Computation/communication ratio} = \frac{2(n^2/p)}{p(t_{\text{startup}} + 2t_{\text{data}}) + 4n^2(t_{\text{startup}} + t_{\text{data}})}$$

$$= \mathrm{O}\left(\frac{n^2/p}{p + n^2}\right)$$

which is constant as the problem size grows with a fixed number of processors. This is not good for a computation/communication ratio! The ideal time complexity of sequential algorithms is one of smallest order (least growth). Conversely, the ideal computation/communication ratio is one of largest order, as then increasing the problem size reduces the effect of the communication, which is usually very significant. (One could use the communication/computation ratio and then the most desirable ratio will be of smallest order as sequential time complexity.)

In fact, the constant hidden in the communication part far exceeds the constants in the computation in most practical situations. Here, we have $4n^2 + p$ startup times in t_{comm}. This code will perform badly. It is very important to reduce the number of messages. We could broadcast the set of row numbers to all processes to reduce the effects of the startup time. Also, we could send the results back in groups. Even then, the communication dominates the overall execution time since the computation is minimal. This application is probably best suited for a shared memory multiprocessor in which the bitmap would be stored in the shared memory, which would be immediately available to all processors.

3.2.2 Mandelbrot Set

Displaying the Mandelbrot set is another example of processing a bit-mapped image. However, now the image must be computed, and this involves significant computation. A Mandelbrot set is a set of points in a complex plane that are quasi-stable (will increase and decrease, but not exceed some limit) when computed by iterating a function, usually the function

$$z_{k+1} = z_k^2 + c$$

where z_{k+1} is the $(k + 1)$th iteration of the complex number $z = a + bi$ (where $i = \sqrt{-1}$), z_k is the kth iteration of z, and c is a complex number giving the position of the point in the complex plane. The initial value for z is zero. The iterations are continued until the magnitude of z is greater than 2 (which indicates that z will eventually become infinite) or the number of iterations reaches some arbitrary limit. The magnitude of z is the length of the vector given by

$$z_{\text{length}} = \sqrt{a^2 + b^2}$$

Computing the complex function, $z_{k+1} = z_k^2 + c$, is simplified by recognizing that

$$z^2 = a^2 + 2abi + bi^2 = a^2 - b^2 + 2abi$$

or a real part that is $a^2 - b^2$ and an imaginary part that is $2ab$. Hence, if z_{real} is the real part of z, and z_{imag} is the imaginary part of z, the next iteration values can be produced by computing:

$$z_{real} = z_{real}^2 - z_{imag}^2 + c_{real}$$

$$z_{imag} = 2z_{real}z_{imag} + c_{imag}$$

where c_{real} is the real part of c, and c_{imag} is the imaginary part of c.

Sequential Code. For coding, a structure can be used holding both the real and imaginary parts of z:

```
structure complex {
   float real;
   float imag;
};
```

A routine for computing the value of one point and returning the number of iterations could be of the form

```
int cal_pixel(complex c)
{
int count, max_iter;
complex z;
float temp, lengthsq;
max_iter = 256;
z.real = 0;
z.imag = 0;
count = 0;                                 /* number of iterations */
do {
   temp = z.real * z.real - z.imag * z.imag + c.real;
   z.imag = 2 * z.real * z.imag + c.imag;
   z.real = temp;
   lengthsq = z.real * z.real + z.imag * z.imag;
   count++;
} while ((lengthsq < 4.0) && (count < max_iter));
return count;
}
```

The square of the length, `lengthsq`, is compared against 4, rather than the length against 2, to avoid a square root operation. Given the termination conditions, all the Mandelbrot points must be within a circle with its center at the origin and of radius 2.

The code for computing and displaying the points requires some scaling of the coordinate system to match the coordinate system of the display area. The actual viewing area will usually be a rectangular window of any size and sited anywhere of interest in the complex plane. The resolution is expanded at will to obtain fascinating images. Suppose the display height is disp_height, the display width is disp_width, and the point in this display area is (x, y). If this window is to display the complex plane with minimum values of (real_min, imag_min) and maximum values of (real_max, imag_max), each (x, y) point needs to be scaled by the factors

```
c.real = real_min + x * (real_max - real_min)/disp_width;
c.imag = imag_min + y * (imag_max - imag_min)/disp_height;
```

to obtain the actual complex plane coordinates. For computational efficiency, let

```
scale_real = (real_max - real_min)/disp_width;
scale_imag = (imag_max - imag_min)/disp_height;
```

Including scaling, the code could be of the form

```
for (x = 0; x < disp_width; x++)          /* screen coordinates x and y */
  for (y = 0; y < disp_height; y++) {
    c.real = real_min + ((float) x * scale_real);
    c.imag = imag_min + ((float) y * scale_imag);
    color = cal_pixel(c);
    display(x, y, color);
  }
```

where display() is a routine suitably written to display the pixel (x, y) at the computed color (taking into account the position of origin in the display window, if necessary). Typical results are shown in Figure 3.4. A sequential version of the program to generate

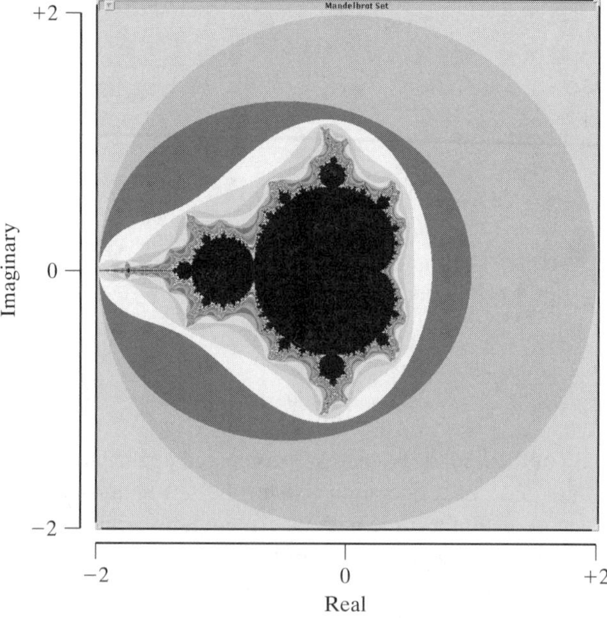

Figure 3.4 Mandelbrot set.

the Mandelbrot set using Xlib calls for the graphics is available at http://www.cs.uncc.edu/par_prog and could be the basis of a simple parallel program (Problem 3-7).

The Mandelbrot set is a widely used test in parallel computer systems (and, for that matter, sequential computers) because it is computationally intensive. It can take several minutes to compute the complete image, depending upon the speed of the computer and the required resolution of the image. Also, it has interesting graphical results. A selected area can be magnified by repeating the computation over that area and scaling the results for the display routine.

Parallelizing the Mandelbrot Set Computation. The Mandelbrot set is particularly convenient to parallelize for a message-passing system because each pixel can be computed without any information about the surrounding pixels. The computation of each pixel itself is less amenable to parallelization. In the previous example of transforming an image, we assigned a fixed area of the display to each process. This is known as *static assignment*. Here, we will consider both static assignment and *dynamic assignment* when the areas computed by a process vary.

Static Task Assignment. Grouping by square/rectangular regions or by columns/rows, as shown in Figure 3.3, is suitable. Each process needs to execute the procedure, `cal_pixel()`, after being given the coordinates of the pixels to compute. Suppose the display area is 640×480 and we were to compute 10 rows in a process (i.e., a grouping of 10×640 pixels and 48 processes). The pseudocode might look like the following:

```
Master

for (i = 0, row = 0; i < 48; i++, row = row + 10)/* for each process*/
   send(&row, Pi);                                /* send row no.*/
for (i = 0; i < (480 * 640); i++) {      /* from processes, any order */
   recv(&c, &color, PANY);               /* receive coordinates/colors */
   display(c, color);                    /* display pixel on screen */
}

Slave (process i)

recv(&row, Pmaster);                     /* receive row no. */
for (x = 0; x < disp_width; x++)         /* screen coordinates x and y */
   for (y = row; y < (row + 10); y++) {
      c.real = min_real + ((float) x * scale_real);
      c.imag = min_imag + ((float) y * scale_imag);
      color = cal_pixel(c);
      send(&c, &color, Pmaster);         /* send coords, color to master */
   }
```

We expect all 640×480 pixels to be sent, but this may occur in any order dependent upon the number of iterations to compute the pixel value and the speed of the computer. The implementation has the same serious disadvantage as that for transformations in Section 3.2.1; it sends results back one at a time rather than in groups. Sending the data in groups reduces the number of communication startup times (one for each message). It is a simple matter to save results in an array and then send the whole array to the master in one message. Note that the master uses a wild card to accept messages from slaves in any order (the notation P_{ANY} indicates a source wild card).

Dynamic Task Assignment—Work Pool/Processor Farms. The Mandelbrot set requires significant iterative computation for each pixel. The number of iterations will generally be different for each pixel. In addition, the computers may be of different types or operate at different speeds. Thus, some processors may complete their assignments before others. Ideally, we want all processors to complete together, achieving a system efficiency of 100 percent, which can be addressed using *load balancing*. This is a complex and extremely important concept in all parallel computations and not just the one we are considering here. Ideally, each processor needs to be given sufficient work to keep it busy for the duration of the overall computation. Regions of different sizes could be assigned to different processors, but this would not be very satisfactory for two reasons: We may not know a priori each processor's computational speed, and we would have to know the exact time it takes for each processor to compute each pixel. The latter depends upon the number of iterations, which differs from one pixel to the next. Some problems may be more uniform in their computational time, but, in any event, a more system-efficient approach will involve some form of dynamic load balancing.

Dynamic load balancing can be achieved using a *work-pool* approach, in which individual processors are supplied with work when they become idle. Sometimes the term *processor farm* is used to describe this approach, especially when all the processors are of the same type. The work pool holds a collection, or pool, of tasks to be performed. In some work-pool problems, processes can generate new tasks; we shall look at the implications of this in Chapter 7.

In our problem, the set of pixels (or, more accurately, their coordinates) forms the tasks. The number of tasks is fixed in that the number of pixels to compute is known prior to the start of the computation. Individual processors request a pair of pixel coordinates from the work pool. When a processor has computed the color for the pixel, it returns the color and requests a further pair of pixel coordinates from the work pool. When all the pixel coordinates have been taken, we then need to wait for all the processors to complete their tasks and report in for more pixel coordinates.

Sending pairs of coordinates of individual pixels will result in excessive communication. Normally, rather than a single coordinate comprising a task, a group of coordinates representing several pixels will form the task to be taken from the work pool in order to reduce the communication overhead. At the start, the slaves are told the size of the group of pixels (assumed to be a fixed size). Then only the first pair of coordinates of the group need be sent to the slaves as a task. This approach reduces the communication to an acceptable level. The overall arrangement is depicted in Figure 3.5.

When the Mandelbrot-set calculation is coded for a work-pool solution, we will find that the pixels will not be generated together. Some will appear before others. (Actually, this will also happen in our example code for the static assignment because some pixels will require more time than others and the order in which messages are received is not constrained.)

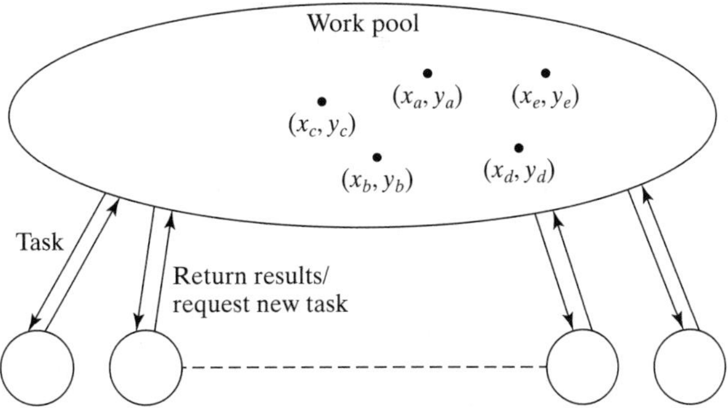

Figure 3.5 Work-pool approach.

Suppose the number of processes is given by `num_proc`, and processes compute one row at a time. In this case, the work pool holds row numbers rather than individual pixel coordinates. Coding for a work pool could be of the form

Master

```
count = 0;                                   /* counter for termination*/
row = 0;                                     /* row being sent */
for (k = 0; k < num_proc; k++) {          /* assuming num_proc<disp_height */
   send(&row, P_k, data_tag);                /* send initial row to process */
   count++;                                  /* count rows sent */
   row++;                                    /* next row */
}

do {
   recv (&slave, &r, color, P_ANY, result_tag);
   count--;                               /* reduce count as rows received */
   if (row < disp_height) {
      send (&row, P_slave, data_tag);                  /* send next row */
      row++;                                           /* next row */
      count++;
   } else
      send (&row, P_slave, terminator_tag);            /* terminate */
   display (r, color);                                 /* display row */
} while (count > 0);
```

Slave

```
recv(y, P_master, ANYTAG, source_tag);      /* receive 1st row to compute */
while (source_tag == data_tag) {
   c.imag = imag_min + ((float) y * scale_imag);
   for (x = 0; x < disp_width; x++) {              /* compute row colors */
      c.real = real_min + ((float) x * scale_real);
      color[x] = cal_pixel(c);
   }
```

```
        send(&x, &y, color, P_master, result_tag);      /* row colors to master */
        recv(&y, P_master, source_tag);                 /* receive next row */
    };
```

In this code, each slave is first given one row to compute and, from then on, gets another row when it returns a result, until there are no more rows to compute. The master sends a terminator message when all the rows have been taken. To differentiate between different messages, tags are used with the message `data_tag` for rows being sent to the slaves, `terminator_tag` for the terminator message, and `result_tag` for the computed results from the slaves. It is then necessary to have a mechanism to recognize different tags being received. Here we simply show a `source_tag` parameter. Note that the master receives and sends messages before displaying results, which can allow the slaves to restart as soon as possible. Locally blocking sends are used. Note also that in order to terminate, the number of rows outstanding in the slaves is counted (`count`), as illustrated in Figure 3.6. It is also possible simply to count the number of rows returned. There are, of course, other ways to code this problem. Termination is considered further in Chapter 7.

Analysis. Exact analysis of the Mandelbrot computation is complicated by not knowing how many iterations are needed for each pixel. Suppose there are n pixels. The number of iterations for each pixel is some function of `c` but cannot exceed `max_iter`. Therefore, the sequential time is

$$t_s \leq \texttt{max\_iter} \times n$$

or a sequential time complexity of $O(n)$.

For the parallel version, let us just consider the static assignment. The total number of processors is given by p, and there are $p - 1$ slave processors. The parallel program has essentially three phases: communication, computation, and communication.

Phase 1: Communication. First, the row number is sent to each slave, one data item to each of $p - 1$ slaves:

$$t_{\text{comm1}} = (p - 1)(t_{\text{startup}} + t_{\text{data}})$$

Separate messages are sent to each slave, causing duplicated startup times. It would be possible to use a scatter routine, which should reduce this effect (Problem 3-6).

Phase 2: Computation. Then the slaves perform their Mandelbrot computation in parallel:

$$t_{\text{comp}} \leq \frac{\texttt{max\_iter} \times n}{p - 1}$$

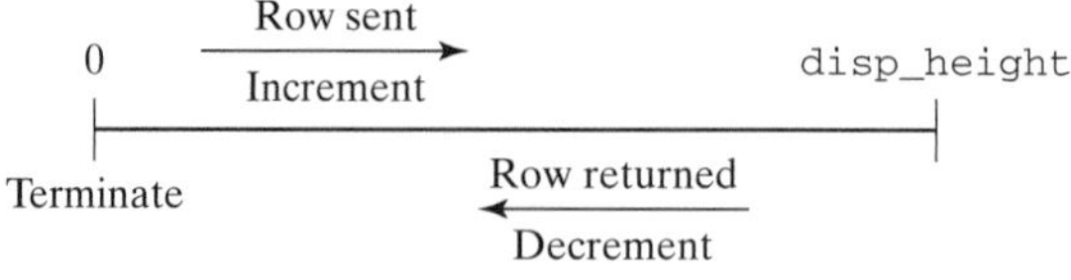

Figure 3.6 Counter termination.

assuming the pixels are evenly divided across all the processors. At least some of the pixels will require the maximum number of iterations, and these will dominate the overall time.

Phase 3: Communication. In the final phase, the results are passed back to the master, one row of pixel colors at a time. Suppose each slave handles u rows and there are v pixels on a row. Then:

$$t_{\text{comm2}} = u(t_{\text{startup}} + vt_{\text{data}})$$

The startup time overhead could be reduced by collecting results into fewer messages. For static assignment, both the value for v (pixels on a row) and value for u (number of rows) would be fixed (unless the resolution of the image was changed). Let us assume that $t_{\text{comm2}} = k$, a constant.

Overall Execution Time. Overall, the parallel time is given by

$$t_p \leq \frac{\texttt{max\_iter} \times n}{p-1} + (p-1)(t_{\text{startup}} + t_{\text{data}}) + k$$

Speedup Factor. The speedup factor is

$$\text{Speedup factor} = \frac{t_s}{t_p} = \frac{\texttt{max\_iter} \times n}{\dfrac{\texttt{max\_iter} \times n}{p-1} + (p-1)(t_{\text{startup}} + t_{\text{data}}) + k}$$

The potential speedup approaches p if `max_iter` is large.

Computation/communication Ratio. The computation/communication ratio

$$\text{Computation/communication ratio} = \frac{(\texttt{max\_iter} \times n)}{(p-1)((p-1)(t_{\text{startup}} + t_{\text{data}}) + k)}$$

$$= \text{O}(n) \text{ with a fixed number of processors}$$

The preceding analysis is only intended to give an indication of whether parallelism is worthwhile. It appears worthwhile.

3.2.3 Monte Carlo Methods

The basis of Monte Carlo methods is the use of random selections in calculations that lead to the solution to numerical and physical problems. Each calculation will be independent of the others and therefore amenable to embarrassingly parallel methods. The name *Monte Carlo* comes from the similarity of statistical simulation methods to the randomness of games of chance; Monte Carlo, the capital of Monaco, is a center for gambling. (The name is attributed to Metropolis on the Manhattan Project during World War II.)

An example that has reappeared in the literature many times (Fox et al., 1988; Gropp, Lusk, and Skjellum, 1999; Kalos and Whitlock, 1986) is to calculate π as follows. A circle is formed within a square, as shown in Figure 3.7. The circle has unit radius, so that the square has sides 2×2. The ratio of the area of the circle to the square is given by

$$\frac{\text{Area of circle}}{\text{Area of square}} = \frac{\pi(1)^2}{2 \times 2} = \frac{\pi}{4}$$

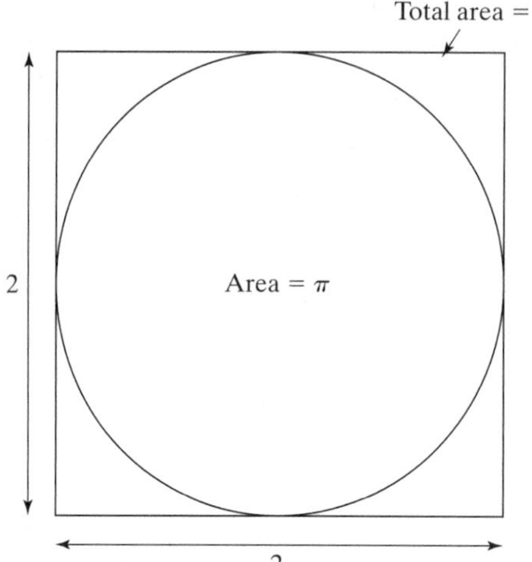

Figure 3.7 Computing π by a Monte Carlo method.

(The same result is obtained for a circle of any dimensions so long as the circle fits exactly inside the square.) Points within the square are chosen randomly and a score is kept of how many points happen to lie within the circle. The fraction of points within the circle will be π/4, given a sufficient number of randomly selected samples.

The area of any shape within a known bound area could be computed by the preceding method, or any area under a curve; that is, an integral. One quadrant of the construction in Figure 3.7 as a function is illustrated in Figure 3.8, which can be described by the integral

$$\int_0^1 \sqrt{1-x^2}\,dx = \frac{\pi}{4}$$

(positive square roots). A random pair of numbers, (x_r, y_r), would be generated, each between 0 and 1, and then counted as in the circle if $y_r \le \sqrt{1-x_r^2}$; that is, $y_r^2 + x_r^2 \le 1$.

The method could be used to compute any definite integral. Unfortunately, it is very inefficient and also requires the maximum and minimum values of the function within the region of interest. An alternative probabilistic method for finding an integral is to use the random values of x to compute $f(x)$ and sum the values of $f(x)$:

$$\text{Area} = \int_{x_1}^{x_2} f(x)\,dx = \lim_{N \to \infty} \frac{1}{N} \sum_{r=1}^{N} f(x_r)(x_2 - x_1)$$

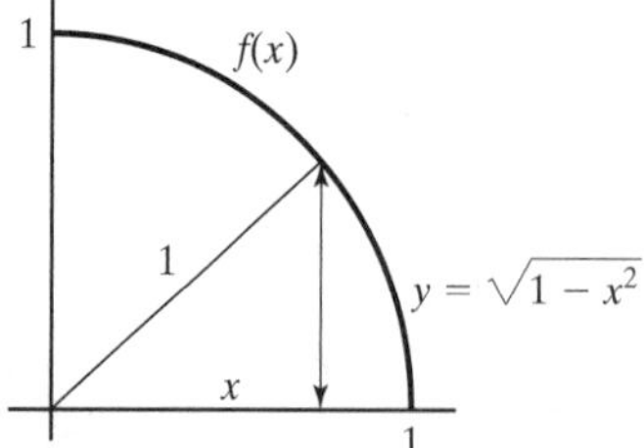

Figure 3.8 Function being integrated in computing π by a Monte Carlo method.

where x_r are randomly generated values of x between x_1 and x_2. This method could also be considered a Monte Carlo method, though some would limit Monte Carlo methods to those that select random values not in the solution as well as those in the solution. The substantial mathematical underpinning to Monte Carlo methods can be found in texts such as Kalos and Whitlock (1986). Monte Carlo methods would not be used in practice for one-dimensional integrals, for which quadrature methods (Section 4.2.2) are better. However, they would be very useful for integrals with a large number of variables and become practical in these circumstances.

Let us briefly look at how a Monte Carlo method could be implemented using $f(x) = x^2 - 3x$ as a concrete example; that is, computing the integral

$$I = \int_{x_1}^{x_2} (x^2 - 3x)\, dx$$

Sequential Code. The sequential code might be of the form

```
sum = 0;
for (i = 0; i < N; i++) {                  /* N random samples */
   xr = rand_v(x1, x2);                    /* generate next random value */
   sum = sum + xr * xr - 3 * xr;           /* compute f(xr) */
}
area = (sum / N) * (x2 - x1);
```

The routine `rand_v(x1, x2)` returns a pseudorandom number between `x1` and `x2`. A fixed number of samples have been taken; in reality, the integral should be computed to some prescribed precision, which requires a statistical analysis to determine the number of samples required. Texts on Monte Carlo methods, such as Kalos and Whitlock (1986), explore statistical factors in great detail.

Parallel Code. The problem is embarrassingly parallel, since the iterations are independent of each other. The main concern is how to produce the random numbers in such a way that each computation uses a different random number and there is no correlation between the numbers. Standard library pseudorandom-number generators such as `rand()`, could be used (but see later). One approach, as used in Gropp, Lusk, and Skjellum (1999), is to have a separate process responsible for issuing the next random number. This structure is illustrated in Figure 3.9. First, the master process starts the slaves, which request a random number from the random-number process for each of their computations. The slaves form their partial sums, which are returned to the master for final accumulation. If each slave is asked to perform the same number of iterations and the system is homogeneous (identical processors), the slaves should complete more or less together.

The random-number process can only service one slave at a time, and this approach has the significant communication cost of sending individual random numbers to the slaves. Groups of random numbers could be sent to reduce the effects of the startup times. The random-number generator could also be incorporated into the master process, since this process is not otherwise active throughout the computation. All this leads to parallel pseudocode of the following form:

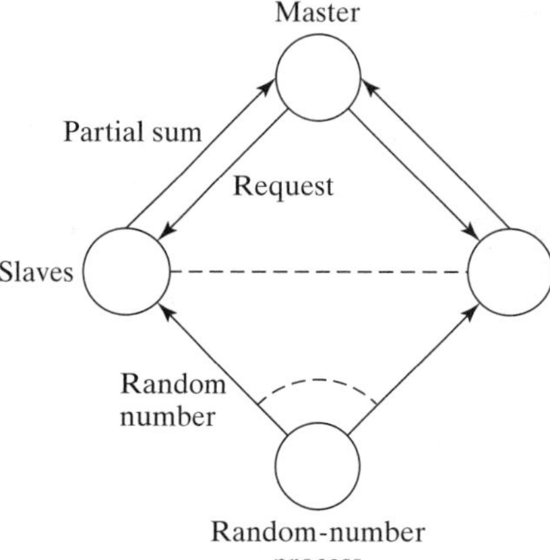

Figure 3.9 Parallel Monte Carlo integration.

Master

```
for(i = 0; i < N/n; i++) {
   for (j = 0; j < n; j++)        /*n=number of random numbers for slave */
      xr[j] = rand();               /* load numbers to be sent */
   recv(PANY, req_tag, Psource);    /* wait for a slave to make request */
   send(xr, &n, Psource, compute_tag);
}
for(i = 0; i < num_slaves; i++) {   /* terminate computation */
   recv(Pi, req_tag);
   send(Pi, stop_tag);
}
sum = 0;
reduce_add(&sum, Pgroup);
```

Slave

```
sum = 0;
send(Pmaster, req_tag);
recv(xr, &n, Pmaster, source_tag);
while (source_tag == compute_tag) {
   for (i = 0; i < n; i++)
      sum = sum + xr[i] * xr[i] - 3 * xr[i];
   send(Pmaster, req_tag);
   recv(xr, &n, Pmaster, source_tag);
};
reduce_add(&sum, Pgroup);
```

In this code, the master waits for any slave to respond using a source wild card (P_{ANY}). The rank of the actual slave responding can be obtained from a status call or parameter. We simply show the source within the message envelope. The type of handshaking is reliable but does have more communication than simply sending data without a request; as we have seen, reducing the communication overhead is perhaps the most important aspect for obtaining high execution speed. It is left as an exercise to eliminate the handshaking. The routine `reduce_add()` is our notation to show a reduce routine that collectively performs addition. The notation to specify a group of processes is P_{group}.

Parallel Random-Number Generation. For successful Monte Carlo simulations, the random numbers must be independent of each other. The most popular way of creating a pseudorandom-number sequence, $x_1, x_2, x_3, \ldots, x_{i-1}, x_i, x_{i+1}, \ldots, x_{n-1}, x_n$, is by evaluating x_{i+1} from a carefully chosen function of x_i. The key is to find a function that will create a very large sequence with the correct statistical properties. The function used is often of the form

$$x_{i+1} = (ax_i + c) \bmod m$$

where a, c, and m are constants chosen to create a sequence that has similar properties to truly random sequences. A generator using this form of equation is known as a *linear congruential generator.* There are many possible values of a, c, and m, and much has been published on the statistical properties of these generators. (See Knuth, 1981, the standard reference, and Anderson, 1990.) A "good" generator is with $a = 16807$, $m = 2^{31} - 1$ (a prime number), and $c = 0$ (Park and Miller, 1988). This generator creates a repeating sequence of $2^{31} - 2$ different numbers (i.e., the maximum for these generators, $m - 1$). A disadvantage of such generators for Monte Carlo simulation is that they are relatively slow.

Even though the pseudorandom-number computation appears to be sequential in nature, each number is calculated from the preceding number and a parallel formulation is possible to increase the speed of generating the sequence. It turns out that

$$x_{i+1} = (ax_i + c) \bmod m$$

$$x_{i+k} = (Ax_i + C) \bmod m$$

where $A = a^k \bmod m$, $C = c(a^{k-1} + a^{k-2} + \ldots + a^1 + a^0) \bmod m$, and k is a selected "jump" constant. Some care is needed to compute and use A and C because of the large numbers involved, but they need be computed only once. (C would not be needed for the good generator described earlier.) Given m processors, the first m numbers of the sequence are generated sequentially. Then each of these numbers can be used to create the next m numbers in parallel, as shown in Figure 3.10, and so on, for the next m numbers.

The computation can be simplified if m is a power of 2, because then the mod operation simply returns the lower m digits. Unfortunately, generators of this type often use a prime number for m to obtain good pseudorandom-number characteristics. Fox, Williams, and Messina (1994) describe a different type of random-number generator using the formula $x_i = (x_{i-63}+x_{i-127}) \bmod 2^{31}$, which naturally generates numbers from distant preceding numbers.

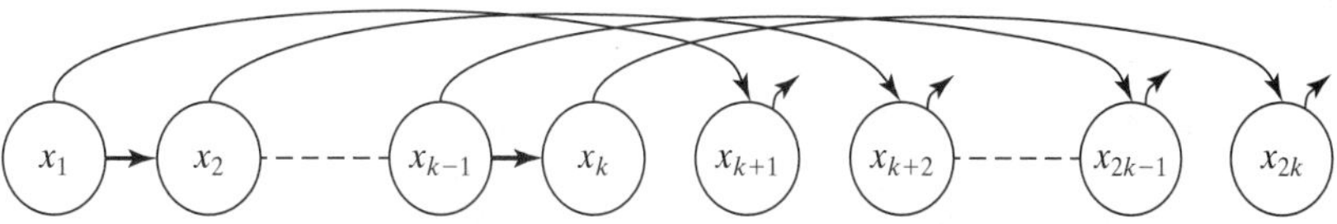

Figure 3.10 Parallel computation of a sequence.

There are several types of pseudorandom-number generators, each using different mathematical formulas. In general, the formula uses previously generated numbers in computing the next number in the sequence, and thus all are deterministic and repeatable. Being repeatable can be advantageous for testing programs, but the formula must produce statistically good random-number sequences. The area of testing random-number generators has a very long history and is beyond the scope of this text. However, one needs to take great care in the choice and use of random-number generators. Some early random-number generators turned out to be quite bad when tested against statistical figures of merit. Even if a random-number generator appears to create a series of random numbers from statistical tests, we cannot assume that different subsequences or samplings of numbers from the sequences are not correlated. This makes using random-number generators in parallel programs fraught with difficulties, because simple naive methods of using them in parallel programs might not produce random sequences and the programmer might not realize this.

In parallel programs in general, one might try to rely on a centralized linear congruential pseudorandom-number generator to send out numbers to slaves processes when they request numbers, as we have described. Apart from incurring a communication overhead and a bottleneck in the centralized communication point, there is a big question mark over whether the subsequence that each slave obtains is truly a random sequence and the sequences themselves are not correlated in some fashion. (One could do statistical tests to confirm this.) Also, all random-number generators repeat their sequences at some point, and using a single random number-generator will make it more likely that the sequence repeats. Alternatively, one might consider a separate pseudorandom-number generator within each slave. However, if the same formula is used even starting at a different number, parts of the same sequence might appear in multiple processors, and even if this does not happen, one cannot immediately assume there is no correlation between sequences. One can see that it is challenging problem to come up with good pseudorandom-sequences for parallel programs.

Because of the importance of pseudorandom-number generators in parallel Monte Carlo computations, effort has gone into finding solid parallel versions of pseudorandom-number generators. SPRNG (Scalable Pseudorandom Number Generator) is a library specifically for parallel Monte Carlo computations and generates random-number streams for parallel processes. This library has several different generators and features for minimization of interprocess correlation and an interface for MPI.

For embarrassingly parallel Monte Carlo simulations where there is absolutely no interaction between concurrent processes, it may be satisfactory to use subsequences which may be correlated if the full sequence is random and the computation is exactly the same as if it were done sequentially. It is left as an exercise to explore this further (Problem 3-14).

3.3 SUMMARY

This chapter introduced the following concepts:

- An (ideal) embarrassingly parallel computation
- Embarrassingly parallel problems and analyses

- Partitioning a two-dimensional data set
- Work-pool approach to achieve load balancing
- Counter termination algorithm
- Monte Carlo methods
- Parallel random-number generation

FURTHER READING

Fox, Williams, and Messina (1994) provide substantial research details on embarrassingly parallel applications (independent parallelism). Extensive details of graphics can be found in Foley et al. (1990). Image processing can be found in Haralick and Shapiro (1992), and we also pursue that topic in Chapter 11. Dewdney (1985) wrote a series of articles on writing programs for computing the Mandelbrot set. Details of Monte Carlo simulations can be found in Halton (1970), Kalos and Whitlock (1986), McCracken (1955), and Smith (1993). Parallel implementations are discussed in Fox et al. (1988) and Gropp, Lusk, and Skjellum (1999). Discussion of parallel random-number generators can be found in Bowan and Robinson (1987), Foster (1995), Fox, Williams, and Messina (1994), Hortensius, McLeod, and Card (1989), and Wilson (1995). Random-number generators must be very carefully used even in sequential programs. A study of different random number generators in this application can be found in Wilkinson (1989). Masuda and Zimmermann (1996) describe a library of random-number generators specifically for parallel computing. Examples are given using MPI. Details of SPRNG can be found at http://sprng.cs.fsu.edu/main.html.

BIBLIOGRAPHY

ANDERSON, S. (1990), "Random Number Generators," *SIAM Review*, Vol. 32, No. 2, pp. 221–251.

BOWAN, K. O., AND M. T. ROBINSON (1987), "Studies of Random Generators for Parallel Processing," *Proc. 2nd Int. Conf. on Hypercube Multiprocessors*, Philadelphia, pp. 445–453.

BRÄUNL, T. (1993), *Parallel Programming:An Introduction*, Prentice Hall, London.

DEWDNEY, A. K. (1985), "Computer Recreations," *Scientific American*, Vol. 253, No. 2 (August), pp. 16–24.

FOLEY, J. D., A. VAN DAM, S. K. FEINER, AND J. F. HUGHES (1990), *Computer Graphics Principles and Practice,* 2nd ed., Addison-Wesley, Reading, MA.

FOSTER, I. (1995), *Designing and Building Parallel Programs*, Addison-Wesley, Reading, MA.

FOX, G., M. JOHNSON, G. LYZENGA, S. OTTO, J. SALMON, AND D. WALKER (1988), *Solving Problems on Concurrent Processors, Vol. 1*, Prentice Hall, Englewood Cliffs, NJ.

FOX, G. C., R. D. WILLIAMS, AND P. C. MESSINA (1994), *Parallel Computing Works*, Morgan Kaufmann, San Francisco, CA.

GROPP, W., E. LUSK, AND A. SKJELLUM (1999), *Using MPI Portable Parallel Programming with the Message-Passing Interfaces,* 2nd edition, MIT Press, Cambridge, MA.

HALTON, J. H. (1970), "A Retrospective and Perspective Survey of the Monte Carlo Method," *SIAM Review*, Vol. 12, No. 1, pp. 1–63.

HARALICK, R. M., AND L. G. SHAPIRO (1992), *Computer and Robot Vision* Volume 1, Addison-Wesley, Reading, MA.

HORTENSIUS, P. D., R. D. MCLEOD, AND H. C. CARD (1989), "Parallel Random Number Generation for VLSI Systems Using Cellular Automata," *IEEE Trans. Comput.*, Vol. 38, No. 10, pp. 1466–1473.

KALOS, M. H., AND P. A. WHITLOCK (1986), *Monte Carlo Methods,* Volume 1, *Basics*, Wiley, NY.

KNUTH, D. (1981), *The Art of Computer Programming,* Volume 2, *Seminumerical Algorithms*, Addison-Wesley, Reading, MA.

MASUDA, N., AND F. ZIMMERMANN (1996), *PRNGlib: A Parallel Random Number Generator Library*, Technical report TR-96-08, Swiss Center for Scientific Computing (available at http://www.cscs.ch/Official/).

MCCRACKEN, D. D. (1955), "The Monte Carlo Method," *Scientific American*, May, pp. 90–96.

PARK, S. K., AND K. W. MILLER (1988), "Random Number Generators: Good Ones Are Hard to Find," *Comm. ACM*, Vol. 31, No. 10, pp. 1192–1201.

SMITH, J. R. (1993), *The Design and Analysis of Parallel Algorithms*, Oxford University Press, Oxford, England.

WILKINSON, B. (1989), "Simulation of Rhombic Cross-Bar Switch Networks for Multiprocessor Systems," *Proc. 20th Annual Pittsburgh Conf. on Modeling and Simulation*, Pittsburgh, May 4–5, pp. 1213–1218.

WILKINSON B., AND D. HORROCKS (1987), *Computer Peripherals,* 2nd edition, Hodder and Stoughton, London.

WILSON, G. V. (1995), *Practical Parallel Programming*, MIT Press, Cambridge, MA.

PROBLEMS

Scientific/Numerical

3-1. Write a parallel program that reads an image file in a suitable uncompressed format (e.g., the PPM format) and generates a file of the image shifted N pixels right, where N is an input parameter.

3-2. Implement the image transformations described in this chapter.

3-3. Rewrite the pseudocode described in Section 3.2.1 to operate on 80×80 square regions rather than groups of rows.

3-4. The windowing transformation involves selecting a rectangular region of interest in an undisplayed picture and transplanting the view obtained onto the display in a specific position. Consider that a rectangular area is selected measuring ΔX by ΔY, with the lower left-hand corner having the coordinates (X, Y) in the undisplayed picture coordinate system. The points within this rectangle, (x, y), are transformed into a rectangle measuring $\Delta X'$ by $\Delta Y'$ by the transformation

$$x' = (\Delta X'/\Delta X)(x - X) + X'$$

$$y' = (\Delta Y'/\Delta Y)(y - Y) + Y'$$

Scaling is involved if $\Delta X'$ is not equal to ΔX and ΔY is not equal to ΔY. Performing the windowing transformation before other transformations, where possible, may reduce the amount of computation on the subsequent transformations. Write a program to perform the windowing transformation.

3-5. A three-dimensional drawing, represented with coordinates of the form (x, y, z), can be projected onto a two-dimensional surface by a perspective transformation. While doing this, hidden lines need to be removed. Beforehand, three-dimensional shifting, scaling, and rotation transformations can be performed. Rotating a three-dimensional object θ degrees about the x-axis requires the transformation

$$x' = x$$

$$y' = y \cos \theta + z \sin \theta$$

$$z' = z \cos \theta - y \sin \theta$$

Similar transformations give rotation about the y- and z-axes. Write a parallel program to perform three-dimensional transformations.

3-6. Rewrite parallel pseudocode for the Mandelbrot computation in Section 3.2.2 using a scatter routine in place of the individual sends for passing the starting rows to each slave. Use a single message in each slave to return its collected results. Analyze your code.

3-7. Download the sequential Mandelbrot program from http/www.cs.uncc.edu/par_prog/ and follow the instructions to compile and run it. (This program uses Xlib calls for the graphics. It is necessary to link the appropriate libraries.) Modify the program to operate a parallel program using static load balancing (i.e., simply divide the image into fixed areas). Instrument the code to obtain the parallel execution time when executing on your system.

3-8. Same as Problem 3-7, only use dynamic load balancing instead.

3-9. Continue Problems 3-7 and 3-8 by experimenting with different starting values for z in the Mandelbrot computation.

3-10. Write a sequential program and a parallel program that compute the fractal ("fractional dimension") image based upon the function

$$z_{i+1} = z_i^3 + c$$

and based upon the function (Bräunl, 1993)

$$z_{i+1} = z_i^3 + (c - 1)z_i - c$$

where $z_0 = 0$ and c provide the coordinates of a point of the image as a complex number.

3-11. Compare the two Monte Carlo ways of computing an integral described in Section 3.2.3 empirically. Use the integral

$$\int_0^1 \sqrt{1 - x^2}\, dx$$

which computes $\pi/4$.

3-12. Rewrite the code for Monte Carlo integration given in Section 3.2.3, eliminating the master process having to request for data explicitly. Analyze your solution.

3-13. Read the paper by Hortensius, McLeod, and Card (1989) and develop code for a parallel random-number generator based upon the method it describes.

3-14. Investigate the effects of using potentially correlated subsequences taken from a random-number generator in embarrassingly parallel Monte Carol simulations. Make a literature search on this subject and write a report.

3-15. The collapse of a set of integers is defined as the sum of the integers in the set. Similarly, the collapse of a single integer is defined as the integer that is the sum of its digits. For example, the collapse of the integer 134957 is 29. This can clearly be carried out recursively, until a single digit results: the collapse of 29 is 11, and its collapse is the single digit 2. The ultimate collapse of a set of integers is just their collapse followed by the result being collapsed recursively until only a single digit {0, 1, ... , 9} remains. Your task is to write a program that will find the ultimate collapse of a one-dimensional array of N integers. Alternative approaches are as follows:

1. Use K computers in parallel, each adding up approximately N/K of the integers and passing its local sum to the master, which then totals the partial sums and forms the ultimate collapse of that integer.
2. Use K computers in parallel, each doing a collapse of its local set of N/K integers and passing the partial result to a master, which then forms the ultimate collapse of the partial collapses.
3. Use K computers in parallel, each doing an ultimate collapse on each one of its local set of N/K integers individually, then adding the local collapsed integers and collapsing the result recursively to obtain a single digit. Each of the K then sends its digit on to the master for final summing and ultimate collapse.
4. Use one computer to process all N integers according to any of the first three approaches.
5. Extra credit: Prove that the first three approaches are equivalent in that they produce the same digit for the ultimate collapse of the set of N integers.

Real Life

3-16. As Kim knew from her English courses, palindromes are phrases that read the same way right-to-left as they do left-to-right, when disregarding capitalization. The problem title, she recalled, was attributed to Napoleon, who was exiled and died on the island of Elba. Being the mathematically minded type, Kim likened that to her hobby of looking for palindromes on her vehicle odometer: 245542 (her old car), or 002200 (her new car).

Now, in her first job after completing her undergraduate program in computer science, Kim is once again working with palindromes. As part of her work, she is exploring alternative security-encoding algorithms based on the premise that the encoding strings are not palindromes. Her first task is to examine a large set of strings to identify those that are palindromes, so they may be deleted from the list of potential encoding strings.

The strings consist of letters, (a ... z, A ... Z), and numbers, (0 ... 9). Kim has a one-dimensional array of pointers, `mylist[]`, in which each element points to the start of a string. As with all character strings, the sequence of chars terminates with the null character, '`\0`'. Kim's program is to examine each string and print out all string numbers (the subscripts of `mylist[]` identifying the strings) that correspond to palindromes.

3-17. Andy, Tom, Bill, and Fred have spent most of their freshman year playing a simple card game. They deal out a deck of 52 regular playing cards, 13 to each person. The rules are similar to bridge or spades: teams of two players, seated so that each player has a member of the other team to his left and right. All 52 cards are dealt one at a time in a clockwise manner. The dealer leads first; players take turns playing in a clockwise manner, and must follow suit if possible; the highest card played of the suit led wins the four-card trick unless a trump is played, in which case the highest trump wins. Dealer passes to the left after each hand of 13 tricks has been played. The object is to win the most tricks for your team. Trump is determined by the player who bids the most tricks; that is, who calls out the highest number of tricks he thinks his team can win. Bidding starts with the dealer and moves clockwise until four consecutive players have announced "no further bid." Each successive bid must be at least one higher than its predecessor. If no one makes a bid, the dealer is stuck with a minimum bid of seven.

Lately, however, one of the group has taken a renewed interest in studying. The result is that fewer than four players are available to play some evenings. Tom decided to write a small game-playing program to fill in for the missing player. Fred wants to make it a parallel computing implementation to allow for the possibility that more than one may be missing. Your job is to assist Fred.

3-18. A small company is having difficulty keeping up with the demand for its services: retrieval of data from a huge database. The company used to just hand a clerk the list of items to be retrieved, and he or she would manually look through the files to find them. The company has progressed far beyond that; now it hands a program a list of items, and the program looks through the database and finds them. Lately the list of items has grown so large, and the retrieval process has become so time-consuming, that customers have begun to complain. The company has offered you the job of reimplementing its retrieval process by using multiple machines in parallel and dividing up the list of items to be retrieved among the machines.

Part 1: Identify all the pitfalls or roadblocks facing you in moving the retrieval process to a parallel processing implementation that are not present in the existing serial/single processor one.

Part 2: Identify one or more solutions to each item identified in Part 1.

Part 3: Simulate a composite solution, retrieving (from a large database) all the items on a list, using multiple processors working in parallel.

3-19. Over the past 35 years a series of unmanned radar-mapping missions have produced a very detailed topographic map of the moon's surface. This information has been digitized and is available in a gridlike format known as a Mercator projection. The topographical data for the next unmanned landing area is contained in a 100×100 array of grid points denoting the height above (or below) the average moon surface level for that 10 km $\times$ 10 km region. This particular landing region was chosen for its gradually changing topography; you may assume that linearly interpolating between any two adjacent grid-points will accurately describe the landscape between the grid points.

Upon the rocket landing somewhere within the designated 10 km $\times$ 10 km region, it will discharge a number of autonomous robots. They will conduct a detailed exploration of the region and report their results back to the rocket via a line-of-sight lightwave communications link (flashes of light emitted by the robots and detected by the rocket). Once its exploration is complete, it is essential that a robot be able to find quickly the nearest location from which line-of-sight communication can occur, since it will have only a short battery life.

The rocket designers have assured us that their receiving antenna will be 20 m above the site of the landing; the transmitting antenna on the robot will be 1 m above its site, wherever that may be in the region. Thus, given only the 100×100 array and the grid-point locations of the rocket and a robot, your job is to determine the grid point nearest the robot that will permit line-of-sight communication with the rocket. You may assume that the topographical data array contains only heights in integer values between +100 m and −100 m, and that both the rocket and the robots will be located on grid points when accessing your program.

3-20. You are given a array of 100×10000 floating point values representing data collected in a series of bake-offs making up the final exam at the Nella School for the Culinary Arts. As with all grading systems, this data must be massaged (normalized) prior to actually assigning grades. For each of the 100 students (whose data is in a row of 10,000 values), the following operations must be performed:

INS (initial normalized score)

The average of the squares of all data values in a given row that are greater than zero but less than 100.

FNS (final normalized score)

The value computed for this student's INS, compared to all other students' INS scores. The students whose INS scores are in the top 10 percent overall get an FNS of 4.0; those in the next 20 percent get an FNS of 3.0; those in the next 30 percent get an FNS of 2.0; those in the next 20 percent get an FNS of 1.0; the rest get an FNS of 0.0 and have to enter the bake-off again next year as a result.

Your program is to print out the FNS scores two ways:

1. A list of FNS scores, by student (row number, FNS) for all students
2. A list of students, by FNS (FNS, list of all rows [students] with this FNS) for all FNS values

3-21. Recently, there has been somewhat of a public health scare related to the presence of a bacterium, cryptosporidium, in the water supply system of several municipalities. It has come to our attention that a band of literary terrorists is spreading the bacterium by cleverly and secretly embedding it in novels. You have been hired by a major publishing company to search a new novel for the presence of the word *cryptosporidium*. It is known that the terrorists have resorted to insertion of punctuation, capitalization, and spacing to disguise the presence of *cryptosporidium*; finding instances of the word requires more than doing a simple word search of the text. For example, in a highly publicized case, one page ended with the sentence

"Leaving his faithful companion, Ospor, to guard the hallway, Tom crept slowly down the stairs and entered the darkened crypt"

while the next page began with

"Ospor, I dium, HELP!" cried Tom, as the giant bats he had disturbed flew around his head. Disaster was narrowly averted when a clerk luckily caught what he thought was a typo and changed "I dium" to "I'm dying" just as the book went to press. Since this publisher handles many books, it is essential that each one be scanned as quickly as possible. To accomplish this you have proposed to use many computers in parallel to divide the task into smaller chunks; each computer would search only a portion of a text. If successful, you stand to make a sizeable commission from the sale of networked computers to the publisher.

Alternative approaches are as follows:

1. Divide the text into sections of equal size and assign each section to a single processor. Each processor checks its section and passes information (about whether it found *cryptosporidium* in its section, portions of the bacterium as the first or last characters of its section, or no evidence of the bacterium at all) back to a master, which examines what was passed back to it and reports on the book as a whole.

2. Divide the text into many more small sections than there are processors and use a work-pool approach, in which faster processors effectively do more of the total work, but in essentially the same manner as described in the preceding approach.

3-22. Nanotechnology is the latest hot field. One of its objectives is to utilize massive numbers of tiny devices operating in parallel to solve problems ranging from environmental decontamination (e.g., cleaning up oil spills), to battlefield cleanup, (removing unexploded ordnance or mines), to exploration and analysis of the Martian surface.

As an expert in parallelism, choose one of these application areas of nanotechnology and discuss the requirements for interdevice communications if it is to ensure that fewer than X percent of whatever it is looking for will be missed.

Chapter 4

Partitioning and Divide-and-Conquer Strategies

In this chapter, we explore two of the most fundamental techniques in parallel programming, *partitioning* and *divide and conquer*. The techniques are related. In partitioning, the problem is divided into separate parts and each part is computed separately. Divide and conquer usually applies partitioning in a recursive manner by continually dividing the problem into smaller and smaller parts before solving the smaller parts and combining the results. First, we will review the technique of partitioning. Then we discuss recursive divide-and-conquer methods. Next we outline some typical problems that can be solved with these approaches. As usual, there is a selection of scientific/numerical and real-life problems at the end of the chapter.

4.1 PARTITIONING

4.1.1 Partitioning Strategies

Partitioning divides the problem into parts. It is the basis of all parallel programming, in one form or another. The embarrassingly parallel problems in the last chapter used partitioning without any interaction between the parts. Most partitioning formulations, however, require the results of the parts to be combined to obtain the desired result. Partitioning can be applied to the program data (i.e., to dividing the data and operating upon the divided data concurrently). This is called *data partitioning* or *domain decomposition*. Partitioning can also be applied to the functions of a program (i.e., dividing it into independent functions and executing them concurrently). This is *functional decomposition*. The idea of performing a task by dividing it into a number of smaller tasks that when completed will complete the overall task is, of course, well known and can be applied in many situations, whether the smaller tasks operate upon parts of the data or are separate concurrent functions. It is much less common to find concurrent functions in a problem, but data partitioning is a main strategy for parallel programming.

To take a really simple data-partitioning example, suppose a sequence of numbers, x_0 … x_{n-1}, are to be added. This is a problem recurring in the text to demonstrate a concept; unless there were a huge sequence of numbers, a parallel solution would not be worthwhile. However, the approach can be used for more realistic applications involving complex calculations on large databases.

We might consider dividing the sequence into p parts of n/p numbers each, (x_0 … $x_{(n/p)-1}$), ($x_{n/p}$ … $x_{(2n/p)-1}$), …, ($x_{(p-1)n/p}$ … x_{n-1}), at which point p processors (or processes) can each add one sequence independently to create partial sums. The p partial sums need to be added together to form the final sum. Figure 4.1 shows the arrangement in which a single processor adds the p partial sums. (The final addition could be parallelized using a tree construction, but that will not be done here.) Note that each processor requires access to the numbers it has to accumulate. In a message-passing system, the numbers would need to be passed to the processors individually. (In a shared memory system, each processor could access the numbers it wanted from the shared memory, and in this respect, a shared memory system would clearly be more convenient for this and similar problems.)

The parallel code for this example is straightforward. For a simple master-slave approach, the numbers are sent from the master processor to the slave processors. They add their numbers, operating independently and concurrently, and send the partial sums to the master processor. The master processor adds the partial sums to form the result. Often, we talk of processes rather than processors for code sequences, where one process is best mapped onto one processor.

It is a moot point whether broadcasting the whole list of numbers to every slave or only sending the specific numbers to each slave is best, since in both cases all numbers must be sent from the master. The specifics of the broadcast mechanism would need to be known in order to decide on the relative merits of the mechanism. A broadcast will have a single startup time rather than separate startup times when using multiple send routines and may be preferable.

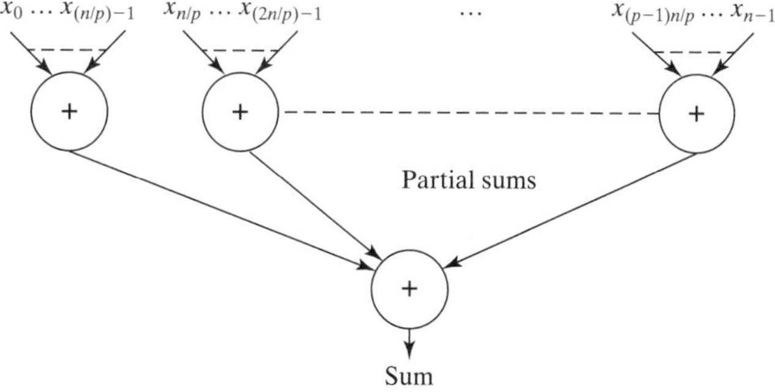

Figure 4.1 Partitioning a sequence of numbers into parts and adding them.

First, we will send the specific numbers to each slave using individual `send()`s. Given n numbers divided into p groups, where n/p is an integer and one group is assigned to one slave process, there would be p slaves. The code using separate `send()`s and `recv()`s might look like the following:

Master

```
s = n/p;                                /* number of numbers for slaves*/
for (i = 0, x = 0; i < p; i++, x = x + s)
   send(&numbers[x], s, Pi);            /* send s numbers to slave */

sum = 0;
for (i = 0; i < p; i++) {               /* wait for results from slaves */
   recv(&part_sum, PANY);
   sum = sum + part_sum;                /* accumulate partial sums */
}
```

Slave

```
recv(numbers, s, Pmaster);              /* receive s numbers from master */
part_sum = 0;
for (i = 0; i < s; i++)                 /* add numbers */
   part_sum = part_sum + numbers[i];
send(&part_sum, Pmaster);               /* send sum to master */
```

If a broadcast or multicast routine is used to send the complete list to every slave, code is needed in each slave to select the part of the sequence to be used by the slave, adding additional computation steps within the slaves, as in

Master

```
s = n/p;                                /* number of numbers for slaves */
bcast(numbers, s, Pslave_group);        /* send all numbers to slaves */
sum = 0;
for (i = 0; i < p; i++) {               /* wait for results from slaves */
   recv(&part_sum, PANY);
   sum = sum + part_sum;                /* accumulate partial sums */
}
```

Slave

```
bcast(numbers, s, Pmaster);             /* receive all numbers from master*/
start = slave_number * s;               /* slave number obtained earlier */
end = start + s;
part_sum = 0;
for (i = start; i < end; i++)           /* add numbers */
   part_sum = part_sum + numbers[i];
send(&part_sum, Pmaster);               /* send sum to master */
```

Slaves are identified by a process ID, which can usually be obtained by calling a library routine. Most often, a group of processes will first be formed and the slave number is an instance or rank within the group. The instance or rank is an integer from 0 to $m - 1$, where there are m processes in the group. MPI requires communicators to be established, and processes have rank within a communicator, as described in Chapter 2. Groups can be associated within communicators, and processes have a rank within groups.

If scatter and reduce routines are available, as in MPI, the code could be

Master

```
s = n/p;                                       /* number of numbers */
scatter(numbers,&s,Pgroup,root=master);        /* send numbers to slaves */
reduce_add(&sum,&s,Pgroup,root=master);        /* results from slaves */
```

Slave

```
scatter(numbers,&s,Pgroup,root=master);        /* receive s numbers */
.                                              /* add numbers */
.
.
reduce_add(&part_sum,&s,Pgroup,root=master);   /* send sum to master */
```

Remember, a simple pseudocode is used throughout. Scatter and reduce (and gather when used) have many additional parameters in practice that include both source and destination IDs. Normally, the operation of a reduce routine will be specified as a parameter and not as part of the routine name as here. Using a parameter does allow different operations to be selected easily. Code will also be needed to establish the group of processes participating in the broadcast, scatter, and reduce.

Although we are adding numbers, many other operations could be performed instead. For example, the maximum number of the group could be found and passed back to the master in order for the master to find the maximum number of all those passed back to it. Similarly, the number of occurrences of a number (or character, or string of characters) can be found in groups and passed back to the master.

Analysis. The sequential computation requires $n - 1$ additions with a time complexity of $O(n)$. In the parallel implementation, there are p slaves. For the analysis of the parallel implementation, we shall assume that the operations of the master process are included in one of the slaves in a SPMD model as this is probably done in a real implementation. (Remember that in MPI, data in the root is used in collective operations.) Thus, the number of processors is p. Our analyses throughout separate communication and computation. It is easier to visualize if we also separate the actions into distinct phases. As with many problems, there is a communication phase followed by a computation phase, and these phases are repeated.

Phase 1 — Communication. First, we need to consider the communication aspect of the p slave processes reading their n/p numbers. Using individual send and receive routines requires a communication time of

$$t_{\text{comm1}} = p(t_{\text{startup}} + (n/p)t_{\text{data}})$$

where t_{startup} is the constant time portion of the transmission, and t_{data} is the time to transmit one data word. Using scatter might reduce the number of startup times. Thus,

$$t_{\text{comm1}} = t_{\text{startup}} + nt_{\text{data}}$$

depending upon the implementation of scatter. In any event, the time complexity is still O(n).

Phase 2 — Computation. Next, we need to estimate the number of computational steps. The slave processes each add n/p numbers together, requiring $n/p - 1$ additions. Since all p slave processes are operating together, we can consider all the partial sums obtained in the $n/p - 1$ steps. Hence, the parallel computation time of this phase is

$$t_{\text{comp1}} = n/p - 1$$

Phase 3 — Communication. Returning partial results using individual send and receive routines has a communication time of

$$t_{\text{comm2}} = p(t_{\text{startup}} + t_{\text{data}})$$

Using gather and reduce has:

$$t_{\text{comm2}} = t_{\text{startup}} + pt_{\text{data}}$$

Phase 4 — Computation. For the final accumulation, the master has to add the p partial sums, which requires $p - 1$ steps:

$$t_{\text{comp2}} = p - 1$$

Overall Execution Time. The overall execution time for the problem (with send and receive) is

$$\begin{aligned} t_{\text{p}} &= (t_{\text{comm1}} + t_{\text{comm2}}) + (t_{\text{comp1}} + t_{\text{comp2}}) \\ &= p(t_{\text{startup}} + (n/p)t_{\text{data}} + p(t_{\text{startup}} + t_{\text{data}}) + (n/p - 1 + p - 1) \\ &= 2pt_{\text{startup}} + (n + p)t_{\text{data}} + p + n/p - 2 \end{aligned}$$

or

$$t_p = \text{O}(n)$$

for a fixed number of processors. We see that the parallel time complexity is the same as the sequential time complexity of O(n). Of course, if we consider only the computation aspect, the parallel formulation is better than the sequential formulation.

Speedup Factor. The speedup factor is

$$\text{Speedup factor} = \frac{t_s}{t_p} = \frac{n-1}{2pt_{\text{startup}} + (n+p)t_{\text{data}} + p + n/p - 2}$$

which suggests little speedup for a fixed number of processors.

Computation/communication ratio. The computation/communication ratio is given by

$$\text{Computation/communication ratio} = \frac{t_{\text{comp}}}{t_{\text{comm}}} = \frac{p + n/p - 2}{2pt_{\text{startup}} + (n+p)t_{\text{data}}}$$

which again, for a fixed number of processors, does not suggest significant opportunity for improvement.

Ignoring the communication aspect, the speedup factor is given by

$$\text{Speedup factor} = \frac{t_s}{t_p} = \frac{n-1}{n/p + p - 2}$$

The speedup tends to p for large n. However, for smaller n, the speedup will be quite low and worsen for an increasing number of slaves, because the $p - 1$ slaves are idle during the fourth phase, forming the final result if one is used for that.

Ideally, we want all the processes to be active all of the time, which cannot be achieved with this formulation of the problem. However, another formulation is helpful and is applicable to a very wide range of problems — namely, the divide-and-conquer approach.

4.1.2 Divide and Conquer

The divide-and-conquer approach is characterized by dividing a problem into subproblems that are of the same form as the larger problem. Further divisions into still smaller subproblems are usually done by recursion, a method well known to sequential programmers. The recursive method will continually divide a problem until the tasks cannot be broken down into smaller parts. Then the very simple tasks are performed and results combined, with the combining continued with larger and larger tasks. JáJá (1992) differentiates between when the main work is in dividing the problem and when it is in combining the results. He categorizes the method as divide and conquer when the main work is combining the results, and as partitioning when the main work is dividing the problem. We will not make this distinction but will use the term *divide and conquer* anytime the partitioning is continued on smaller and smaller problems.

A sequential recursive definition for adding a list of numbers is[1]

```
int add(int *s)                                  /* add list of numbers, s */
{
   if (number(s) <= 2) return (n1 + n2);         /* see explanation */
   else {
      Divide (s, s1, s2);          /* divide s into two parts, s1 and s2 */
      part_sum1 = add(s1);         /*recursive calls to add sub lists */
      part_sum2 = add(s2);
      return (part_sum1 + part_sum2);
   }
}
```

As in all recursive definitions, a method must be present to terminate the recursion when the division can go no further. In the code, `number(s)` returns the number of numbers in the list pointed to by `s`. If there are two numbers in the list, they are called `n1` and `n2`. If there is one number in the list, it is called `n1`, and `n2` is zero. If there are no numbers, both `n1` and `n2`

[1] As in all of our pseudocode, implementation details are omitted. For example, the length of a list may need to be passed as an argument.

are zero. Separate `if` statements could be used for each of the cases: 0, 1, or 2 numbers in the list. Each would cause termination of the recursive call.

This method can be used for other global operations on a list, such as finding the maximum number. It can also be used for sorting a list by dividing it into smaller and smaller lists to sort. Mergesort and quicksort sorting algorithms are usually described by such recursive definitions; see Cormen, Leiserson, and Rivest (1990). One would never actually use recursion to add a list of numbers when a simple iterative solution exists, but the following is applicable to any problem that is formulated by a recursive divide-and-conquer method.

When each division creates two parts, a recursive divide-and-conquer formulation forms a binary tree. The tree is traversed downward as calls are made and upward when the calls return (a preorder traversal given the recursive definition). A binary tree construction showing the "divide" part of divide and conquer is shown in Figure 4.2, with the final tasks at the bottom and the root at the top. The root process divides the problem into two parts. These two parts are each divided into two parts, and so on until the leaves are reached. There the basic operations of the problem are performed. This construction can be used in the preceding problem to divide the list of numbers first into two parts, then into four parts, and so on, until each process has one equal part of the whole. After adding pairs at the bottom of the tree, the accumulation occurs in a reverse tree construction.

Figure 4.2 shows a complete binary tree; that is, a perfectly balanced tree with all bottom nodes at the same level. This occurs if the task can be divided into a number of parts that is a power of 2. If not a power of 2, one or more bottom nodes will be at one level higher than the others. For convenience, we will assume that the task can be divided into a number of parts that is a power of 2, unless otherwise stated.

Parallel Implementation. In a sequential implementation, only one node of the tree can be visited at a time. A parallel solution offers the prospect of traversing several parts of the tree simultaneously. Once a division is made into two parts, both parts can be processed simultaneously. Though a recursive parallel solution could be formulated, it is easier to visualize it without recursion. The key is realizing that the construction is a tree.

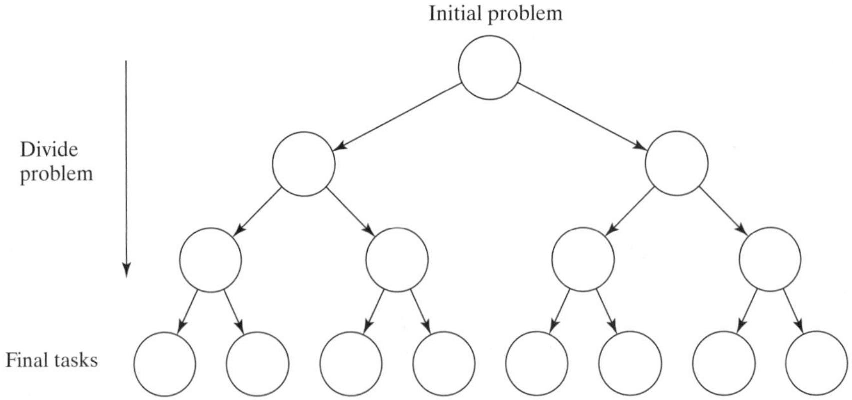

Figure 4.2 Tree construction.

One could simply assign one processor to each node in the tree. That would ultimately require $2^{m+1} - 1$ processors to divide the tasks into 2^m parts. Each processor would only be active at one level in the tree, leading to a very inefficient solution. (Problem 4-5 explores this method.)

A more efficient solution is to reuse processors at each level of the tree, as illustrated in Figure 4.3, which uses eight processors. The division stops when the total number of processors is committed. Until then, at each stage each processor keeps half of the list and passes on the other half. First, P_0 communicates with P_4, passing half of the list to P_4. Then P_0 and P_4 pass half of the list they hold to P_2 and P_6, respectively. Finally, P_0, P_2, P_4, and P_6 pass half of the list they hold to P_1, P_3, P_5, and P_7, respectively. Each list at the final stage will have $n/8$ numbers, or n/p in the general case of p processors. There are $\log p$ levels in the tree.

The "combining" act of summation of the partial sums can be done as shown in Figure 4.4. Once the partial sums have been formed, each odd-numbered processor passes its partial sum to the adjacent even-numbered processor; that is, P_1 passes its sum to P_0, P_3 to P_2, P_5 to P_4, and so on. The even-numbered processors then add the partial sum with its own partial sum and pass the result onward, as shown. This continues until P_0 has the final result.

We can see that these constructions are the same as the binary hypercube broadcast and gather algorithms described in Chapter 2, Section 2.3.3. The constructions would map onto a hypercube perfectly but are also applicable to other systems. As with the hypercube broadcast/gather algorithms, processors that are to communicate with other processors can be found from their binary addresses. Processors communicate with processors whose addresses differ in one bit, starting with the most significant bit for the division phase and with the least significant bit for the combining phase (see Chapter 2, Section 2.3.3).

Suppose we statically create eight processors (or processes) to add a list of numbers. The parallel code for process P_0 might take the form

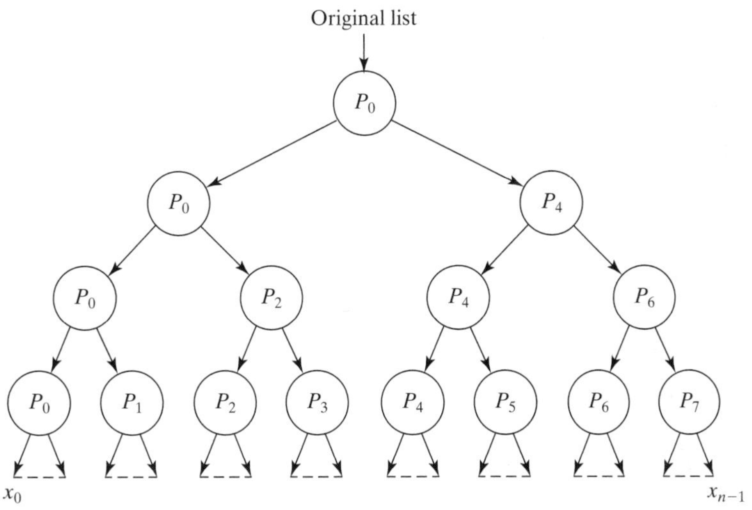

Figure 4.3 Dividing a list into parts.

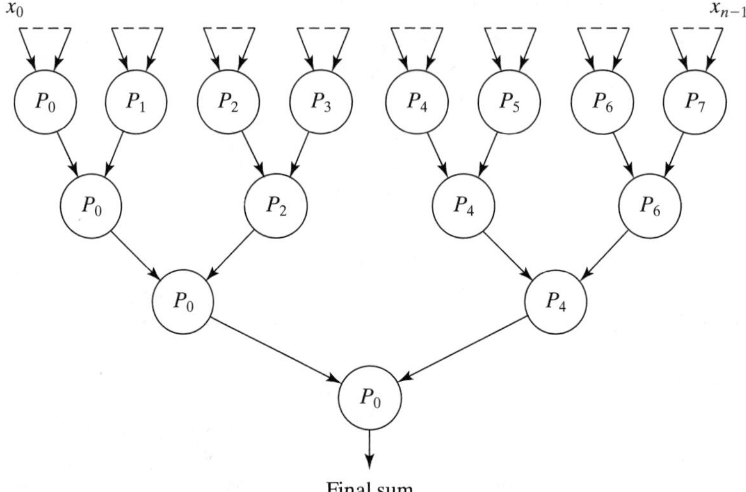

Figure 4.4 Partial summation.

Process P_0

```
                                  /* division phase */
divide(s1, s1, s2);               /* divide s1 into two, s1 and s2 */
send(s2, P4);                     /* send one part to another process */
divide(s1, s1, s2);
send(s2, P2);
divide(s1, s1, s2);
send(s2, P1};
part_sum = *s1;                   /* combining phase */
recv(&part_sum1, P1);
part_sum = part_sum + part_sum1;
recv(&part_sum1, P2);
part_sum = part_sum + part_sum1;
recv(&part_sum1, P4);
part_sum = part_sum + part_sum1;
```

The code for process P_4 might take the form

Process P_4

```
recv(s1, P0);                       /* division phase */
divide(s1, s1, s2);
send(s2, P6);
divide(s1, s1, s2);
send(s2, P5);
part_sum = *s1;                     /* combining phase */
recv(&part_sum1, P5);
part_sum = part_sum + part_sum1;
recv(&part_sum1, P6);
part_sum = part_sum + part_sum1;
send(&part_sum, P0);
```

Similar sequences are required for the other processes. Clearly, another associative operator, such as multiplication, logical OR, logical AND, minimum, maximum, or string concatenation, can replace the addition operation in the preceding example. The basic idea can also be applied to evaluating arithmetic expressions where operands are connected with an arithmetic operator. The tree construction can also be used for such operations as searching. In this case, the information passed upward is a Boolean flag indicating whether or not the specific item or condition has been found. The operation performed at each node is an OR operation, as shown in Figure 4.5.

Analysis. We shall assume that n is a power of 2. The communication setup time, t_{startup}, is not included in the following for simplicity. It is left as an exercise to include the startup time.

The division phase essentially consists only of communication if we assume that dividing the list into two parts requires minimal computation. The combining phase requires both computation and communication to add the partial sums received and pass on the result.

Communication. There is a logarithmic number of steps in the division phase; that is, $\log p$ steps with p processes. The communication time for this phase is given by

$$t_{\text{comm1}} = \frac{n}{2}t_{\text{data}} + \frac{n}{4}t_{\text{data}} + \frac{n}{8}t_{\text{data}} + \ldots + \frac{n}{p}t_{\text{data}} = \frac{n(p-1)}{p}t_{\text{data}}$$

where t_{data} is the transmission time for one data word. The time t_{comm1} is marginally better than a simple broadcast. The combining phase is similar, except that only one data item is sent in each message (the partial sum); that is,

$$t_{\text{comm2}} = (\log p)t_{\text{data}}$$

for a total communication time of

$$t_{\text{comm}} = t_{\text{comm1}} + t_{\text{comm2}} = \frac{n(p-1)}{p}t_{\text{data}} + (\log p)t_{\text{data}}$$

or a time complexity of $O(n)$ for a fixed number of processors.

Computation. At the end of the divide phase, the n/p numbers are added together. Then one addition occurs at each stage during the combining phase, leading to

$$t_{\text{comp}} = \frac{n}{p} + \log p$$

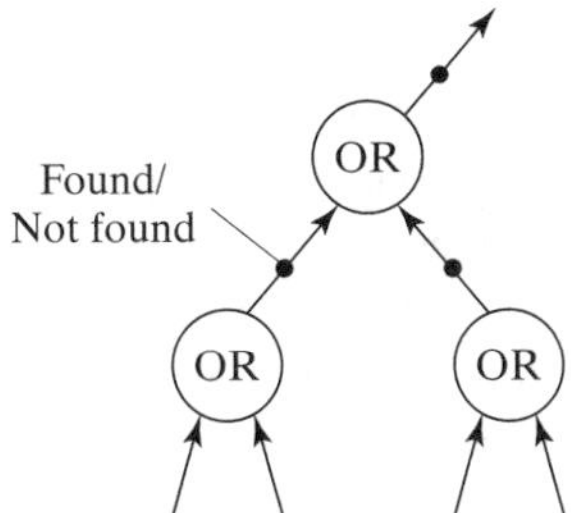

Figure 4.5 Part of a search tree.

again a time complexity of O(n) for a fixed number of processors. For large n and variable p, we get O(n/p).

Overall Execution Time. The total parallel execution time becomes

$$t_p = \left(\frac{n(p-1)}{p} + \log p\right)t_{\text{data}} + \frac{n}{p} + \log p$$

Speedup Factor. The speedup factor is

$$\text{Speedup factor} = \frac{t_s}{t_p} = \frac{n-1}{((n/p)(p-1) + \log p)t_{\text{data}} + n/p + \log p}$$

The very best speedup we could expect with this method is, of course, p when all p processors are computing their partial sums. The actual speedup will be less than this due to the division and combining phases.

Computation/communication Ratio. The computation/communication ratio is given by

$$\text{Computation/communication ratio} = \frac{t_{\text{comp}}}{t_{\text{comm}}} = \frac{n/p + \log p}{((n/p)(p-1) + \log p)t_{\text{data}}}$$

4.1.3 *M*-ary Divide and Conquer

Divide and conquer can also be applied where a task is divided into more than two parts at each stage. For example, if the task is broken into four parts, the sequential recursive definition would be

```
int add(int *s)                          /* add list of numbers, s */
{
  if (number(s) =< 4) return(n1 + n2 + n3 + n4);
  else {
    Divide (s,s1,s2,s3,s4);              /* divide s into s1,s2,s3,s4*/
    part_sum1 = add(s1);                 /*recursive calls to add sublists */
    part_sum2 = add(s2);
    part_sum3 = add(s3);
    part_sum4 = add(s4);
    return (part_sum1 + part_sum2 + part_sum3 + part_sum4);
  }
}
```

A tree in which each node has four children, as shown in Figure 4.6, is called a *quadtree*. A quadtree has particular applications in decomposing two-dimensional regions into four subregions. For example, a digitized image could be divided into four quadrants, and then each of the four quadrants divided into four subquadrants, and so on, as shown in Figure 4.7. An *octtree* is a tree in which each node has eight children and has application for dividing a three-dimensional space recursively. An m-ary tree would be formed if the division is into m parts (i.e., a tree with m links from each node), which suggests that greater

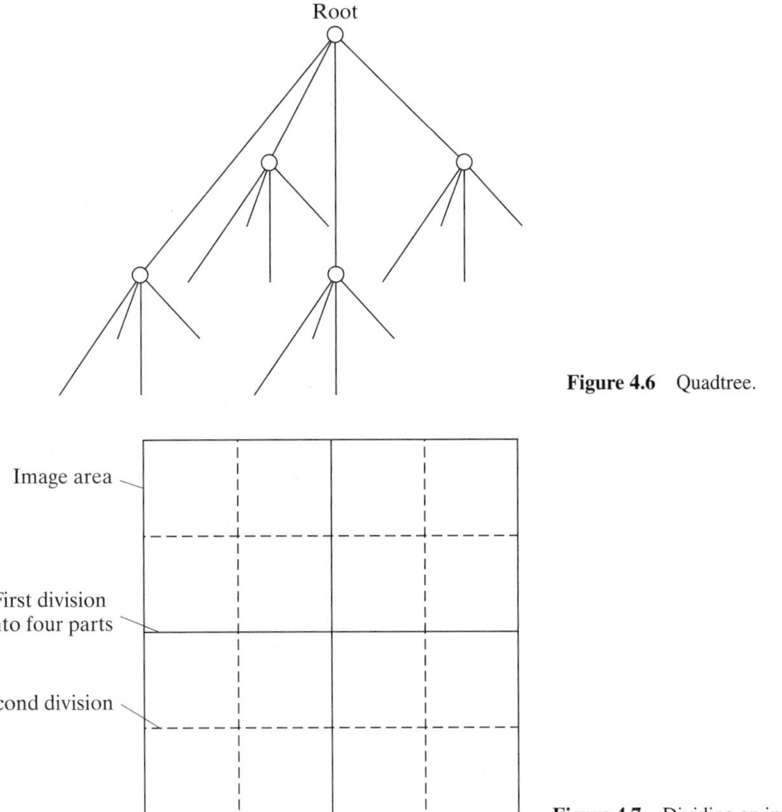

Figure 4.6 Quadtree.

Figure 4.7 Dividing an image.

parallelism is available as m is increased because there are more parts that could be considered simultaneously. It is left as an exercise to develop the equations for computation time and communication time (Problem 4-7).

4.2 PARTITIONING AND DIVIDE-AND-CONQUER EXAMPLES

4.2.1 Sorting Using Bucket Sort

Suppose the problem is not simply to add together numbers in a list, but to sort them into numerical order. There are many practical situations that require numbers to be sorted, and in consequence, sequential programming classes spend a great deal of time developing the various ways that numbers can be sorted. Most of the sequential sorting algorithms are based upon the compare and exchange of pairs of numbers, and we will look at parallelizing such classical sequential sorting algorithms in Chapter 10. Let us look here at the sorting algorithm called *bucket sort*. Bucket sort is not based upon compare and exchange, but is naturally a partitioning method. However, bucket sort only works well if the original numbers are uniformly distributed across a known interval, say 0 to $a - 1$. This interval is divided into m equal regions, 0 to $a/m - 1$, a/m to $2a/m - 1$, $2a/m$ to $3a/m - 1$, … and one "bucket" is assigned to hold numbers that fall within each region. There will be m buckets. The numbers are simply placed into the appropriate buckets. The algorithm could be used with one bucket for each number (i.e., $m = n$). Alternatively, the algorithm could be developed into a divide-and-conquer method by continually dividing the buckets into smaller buckets. If the process is continued in this fashion until each bucket can only contain one number, the method is similar to quicksort, except that in quicksort the regions are divided into regions defined by "pivots" (see Chapter 10). Here we will use a limited number of buckets. The numbers in each bucket will be sorted using a sequential sorting algorithm, as shown in Figure 4.8.

Sequential Algorithm. To place a number into a specific bucket it is necessary to identify the region in which the number lies. One way to do this would be to compare the number with the start of regions; i.e., a/m, $2a/m$, $3a/m$, … . This could require as many as $m - 1$ steps for each number on a sequential computer. A more effective way is to divide the number by m/a and use the result to identify the buckets from 0 to $m - 1$, one computational step for each number (although division can be rather expensive in time). If m/a is a power of 2, one can simply look at the upper bits of the number in binary. For example, if $m/a = 2^3$ (eight), and the number is 1100101 in binary, it falls into region 110 (six), by considering the most significant three bits. In any event, let us assume that placing a number into a bucket requires one step, and that placing all the numbers requires n steps. If the numbers are uniformly distributed, there should be n/m numbers in each bucket.

Next, each bucket must be sorted. Sequential sorting algorithms, such as quicksort or mergesort, have a time complexity of $O(n \log n)$ to sort n numbers (average time complexity for quicksort). The lower bound on any compare and exchange sorting algorithm is about $n \log n$ comparisons (Aho, Hopcroft, and Ullman, 1974). Let us assume that the sequential sorting algorithm actually requires $n \log n$ comparisons, one comparison being regarded as one computational step. Thus, it will take $(n/m)\log(n/m)$ steps to sort the n/m numbers in each bucket using these sequential sorting algorithms. The sorted numbers must be concatenated into the final sorted list. Let us assume that this concatenation requires no additional steps. Combining all the actions, the sequential time becomes

$$t_s = n + m((n/m)\log(n/m)) = n + n\log(n/m) = O(n\log(n/m))$$

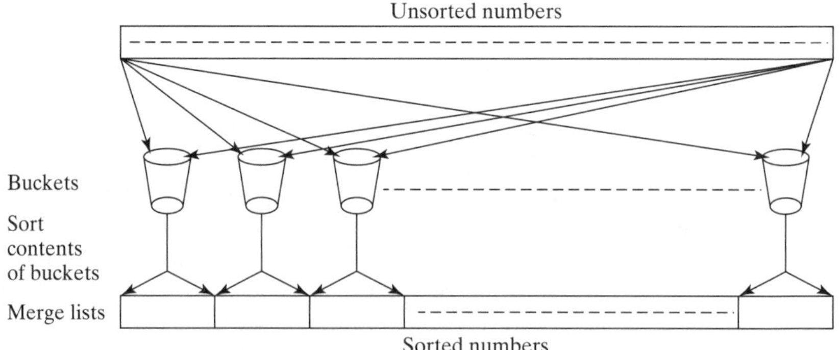

Figure 4.8 Bucket sort.

If $n = km$, where k is a constant, we get a time complexity of $O(n)$. Note that this is much better than the lower bound for sequential compare and exchange sorting algorithms. However, it only applies when the numbers are uniformly distributed.

Parallel Algorithm. Clearly, bucket sort can be parallelized by assigning one processor for each bucket, which reduces the second term in the preceding equation to $(n/p)\log(n/p)$ for p processors (where $p = m$). This implementation is illustrated in Figure 4.9. In this version, each processor examines each of the numbers, so that a great deal of wasted effort takes place. The implementation could be improved by having the processors actually remove numbers from the list into their buckets so that they are not reconsidered by other processors.

We can further parallelize the algorithm by partitioning the sequence into m regions, one region for each processor. Each processor maintains p "small" buckets and separates the numbers in its region into its own small buckets. These small buckets are then "emptied" into the p final buckets for sorting, which requires each processor to send one small bucket to each of the other processors (bucket i to processor i). The overall algorithm is shown in Figure 4.10. Note that this method is a simple partitioning method in which there is minimal work to create the partitions.

The following phases are needed:

1. Partition numbers.
2. Sort into small buckets.
3. Send to large buckets.
4. Sort large buckets.

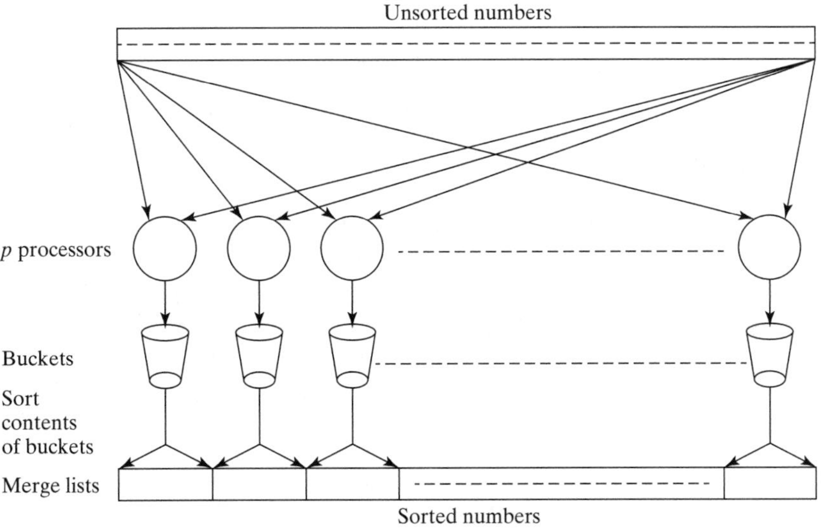

Figure 4.9 One parallel version of bucket sort.

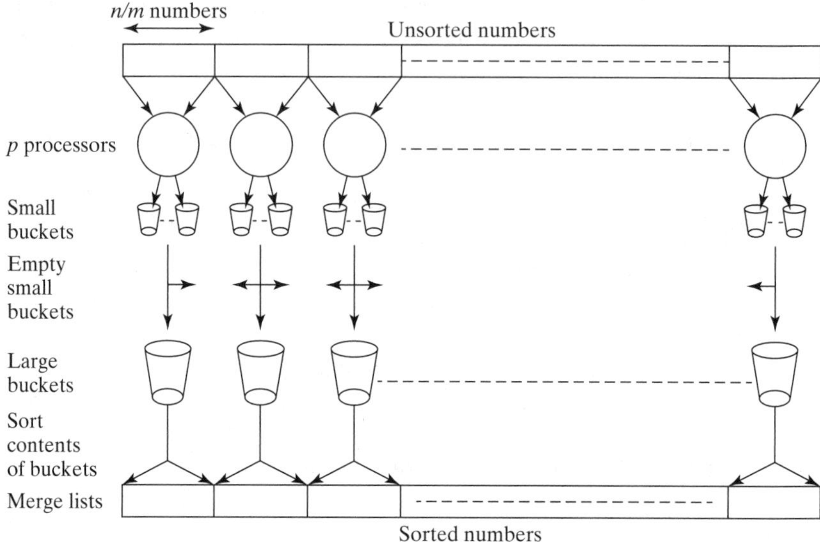

Figure 4.10 Parallel version of bucket sort.

Phase 1 — Computation and Communication. The first step is to send groups of numbers to each processor. Marking a group of numbers into partitions can be done in constant time. This time will be ignored in the overall compassion time. Rather than make the partitions and then send a partition to each processor, a more efficient solution is to simply broadcast all the numbers to each processor and let each processor make its partition. (One must ensure that each partition so created is disjoint but the partitions together include all the numbers.) Using a broadcast or scatter routine, the communication time is:

$$t_{\text{comm1}} = t_{\text{startup}} + nt_{\text{data}}$$

including the communication startup time.

Phase 2 — Computation. To separate each partition of n/p numbers into p small buckets requires the time

$$t_{\text{comp2}} = n/p$$

Phase 3 — Communication. Next, the small buckets are distributed. (There is no computation in Phase 3.) Each small bucket will have about n/p^2 numbers (assuming uniform distribution). Each process must send the contents of $p - 1$ small buckets to other processes (one bucket being held for its own large bucket). Since each process of the p processes must make this communication, we have

$$t_{\text{comm3}} = p(p - 1)(t_{\text{startup}} + (n/p^2)t_{\text{data}})$$

if these communications cannot be overlapped in time and individual `send()`s are used. This is the upper bound on this phase of communication. The lower bound would occur if all the communications could overlap, leading to

$$t_{\text{comm3}} = (p - 1)(t_{\text{startup}} + (n/p^2)t_{\text{data}})$$

In essence, each processor must communicate with every other processor, and an "all-to-all" mechanism would be appropriate. An all-to-all routine sends data from each process to every other process, as illustrated in Figure 4.11. This type of routine is available in MPI (`MPI_Alltoall()`), which we assume would be implemented more efficiently than using individual `send()`s and `recv()`s. The all-to-all routine will actually transfer the rows of an array to columns, as illustrated in Figure 4.12 (and hence transpose a matrix; see Section 10.2.3).

Phase 4 — Computation. In the final phase, the large buckets are sorted simultaneously. Each large bucket contains about n/p numbers. Thus

$$t_{comp4} = (n/p)\log(n/p)$$

Overall Execution Time. The overall run time, including communication, is

$$t_p = t_{comm1} + t_{comp2} + t_{comm3} + t_{comp4}$$

$$\begin{aligned} t_p &= t_{startup} + nt_{data} + n/p + (p-1)(t_{startup} + (n/p^2)t_{data}) + (n/p)\log(n/p) \\ &= (n/p)(1 + \log(n/p)) + pt_{startup} + (n + (p-1)(n/p^2))t_{data} \end{aligned}$$

Speedup Factor. The speedup factor, when compared to sequential bucket sort, is

$$\text{Speedup factor} = \frac{t_s}{t_p} = \frac{n + n\log(n/m)}{(n/p)(1 + \log(n/p)) + pt_{startup} + (n + (p-1)(n/p^2))t_{data}}$$

Speedup factor is actually defined where t_s is the time for the best sequential algorithm for the problem. The lower bound for a sequential sorting algorithm using compare and exchange operations and no requirement upon the distribution or special features of the sequence is $n \log n$ steps. However, bucket sort is better than this and is used for t_s, but it has the assumption of uniformly distributed numbers.

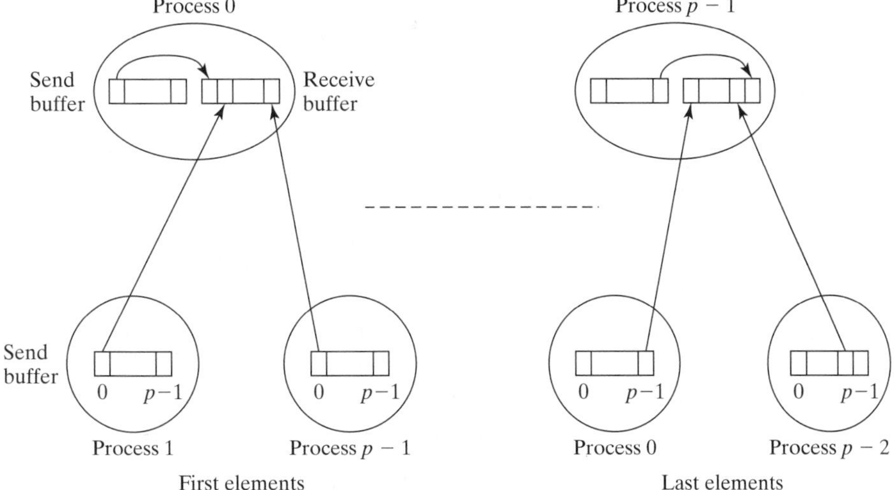

Figure 4.11 All-to-all broadcast.

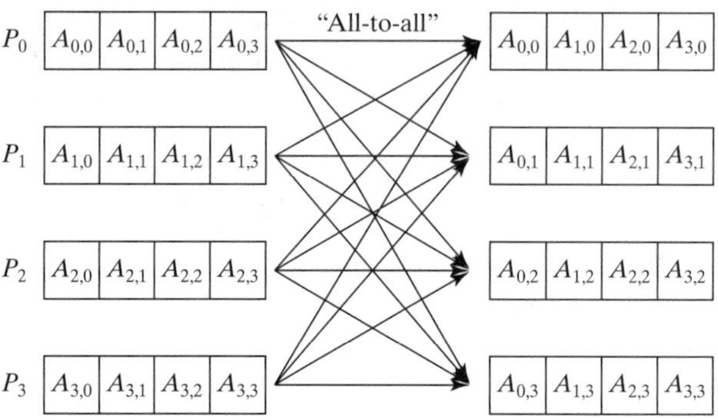

Figure 4.12 Effect of all-to-all on an array.

Computation/communication Ratio. The computation/communication ratio is given by

$$\text{Computation/communication ratio} = \frac{t_{\text{comp}}}{t_{\text{comm}}} = \frac{(n/p)(1 + \log(n/p))}{pt_{\text{startup}} + (n + (p-1))(n/p^2)t_{\text{data}}}$$

It is assumed that the numbers are uniformly distributed to obtain these formulas. If the numbers are not uniformly distributed, some buckets would have more numbers than others, and sorting them would dominate the overall computation time. The worst-case scenario would occur when all the numbers fell into one bucket!

4.2.2 Numerical Integration

Previously, we divided a problem and solved each subproblem. The problem was assumed to be divided into equal parts, and partitioning was employed. Sometimes such simple partitioning will not give the optimum solution, especially if the amount of work in each part is difficult to estimate. Bucket sort, for example, is only effective when each region has approximately the same number of numbers. (Bucket sort can be modified to equalize the work.)

A general divide-and-conquer technique divides the region continually into parts and lets an optimization function decide when certain regions are sufficiently divided. Let us take a different example, numerical integration:

$$I = \int_a^b f(x)\,dx$$

To integrate this function (i.e., to compute the "area under the curve"), we can divide the area into separate parts, each of which can be calculated by a separate process. Each region could be calculated using an approximation given by rectangles, as shown in Figure 4.13, where $f(p)$ and $f(q)$ are the heights of the two edges of a rectangular region, and δ is the width (the *interval*). The complete integral can be approximated by the summation of the rectangular regions from a to b. A better approximation can be obtained by aligning the rectangles so that the upper midpoint of each rectangle intersects with the function, as

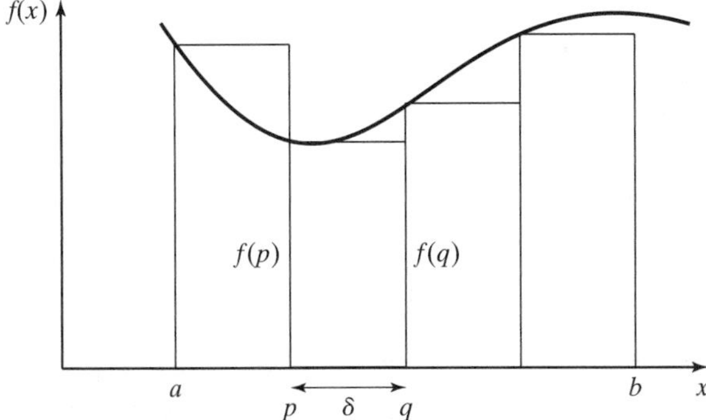

Figure 4.13 Numerical integration using rectangles.

shown in Figure 4.14. This construction has the advantage that the errors on each side of the midpoint end tend to cancel. Another more obvious construction is to use the actual intersections of the vertical lines with the function to create trapezoidal regions, as shown in Figure 4.15. Each region is now calculated as $1/2(f(p) + f(q))\delta$. Such approximate numerical methods for computing a definite integral using a linear combination of values are called *quadrature* methods.

Static Assignment. Let us consider the *trapezoidal* method. Prior to the start of the computation, one process is statically assigned to be responsible for computing each region. By making the interval smaller, we come closer to attaining the exact solution.

Since each calculation is of the same form, the SPMD (single-program multiple-data) model is appropriate. Suppose we were to sum the area from $x = a$ to $x = b$ using p processes numbered 0 to $p - 1$. The size of the region for each process is $(b - a)/p$. To calculate the area in the described manner, a section of SPMD pseudocode could be

Process P_i

```
if (i == master) {                /* read number of intervals required */
   printf("Enter number of intervals ");
   scanf(%d",&n);
}
```

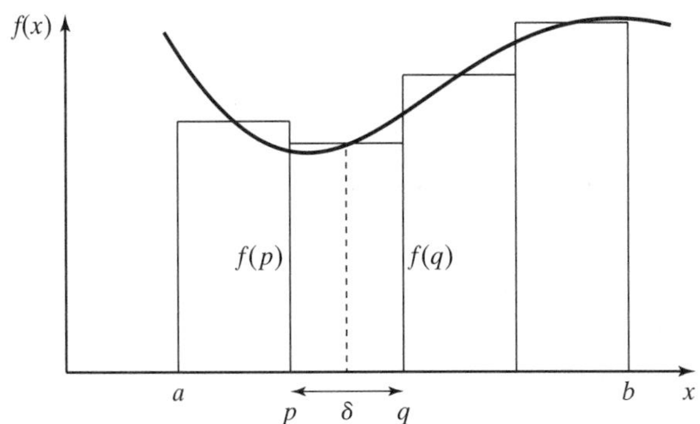

Figure 4.14 More accurate numerical integration using rectangles.

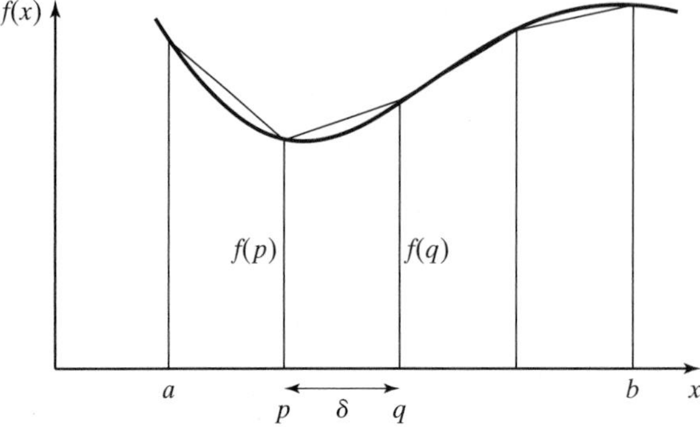

Figure 4.15 Numerical integration using the trapezoidal method.

```
bcast(&n, Pgroup);            /* broadcast interval to all processes */
region = (b - a)/p;              /* length of region for each process */
start = a + region * i;          /* starting x coordinate for process */
end = start + region;            /* ending x coordinate for process */
d = (b - a)/n;                                  /* size of interval */
area = 0.0;
for (x = start; x < end; x = x + d)
   area = area + 0.5 * (f(x) + f(x+d)) * d;
reduce_add(&integral, &area, Pgroup);           /* form sum of areas */
```

A reduce operation is used to add the areas computed by the individual processes. For computational efficiency, computing each area is better if written as

```
area = 0.0;
for (x = start; x < end; x = x + d)
   area = area + f(x) + f(x+d);
area = 0.5 * area * d;
```

We assume that the variable `area` does not exceed the allowable maximum value (a possible disadvantage of this variation). For further efficiency, we can simplify the calculation somewhat by algebraic manipulation, as follows:

$$\text{Area} = \frac{\delta(f(a) + f(a+\delta))}{2} + \frac{\delta(f(a+\delta) + f(a+2\delta))}{2} \ldots + \frac{\delta(f(a+(n-1)\delta) + f(b))}{2}$$

$$= \delta\left(\frac{f(a)}{2} + f(a+\delta) + f(a+2\delta) \ldots + f(a+(n-1)\delta) + \frac{f(b)}{2}\right)$$

given n intervals each of width δ. One implementation would be to use this formula for the region handled by each process:

```
area = 0.5 * (f(start) + f(end));
for (x = start + d; x < end; x = x + d)
   area = area + f(x);
area = area * d;
```

Adaptive Quadrature. The methods used so far are fine if we know beforehand the size of the interval δ that will give a sufficiently close solution. We also assumed that a fixed interval is used across the whole region. If a suitable interval is not known, some form of iteration is necessary to converge on the solution. For example, we could start with one interval and reduce it until a sufficiently close approximation is obtained. This implies that the area is recomputed with different intervals, so we cannot simply divide the total region into a fixed number of subregions, as in the summation example.

One approach is for each process to double the number of intervals successively until two successive approximations are sufficiently close. The tree construction could be used for dividing regions. The depth of the tree will be limited by the number of available processes/processors. In our example, it may be possible to allow the tree to grow in an unbalanced fashion as regions are computed to a sufficient accuracy. The phrase *sufficiently close* will depend upon the accuracy of the arithmetic and the application.

Another way to terminate is use three areas, A, B, and C, as shown in Figure 4.16. The computation is terminated when the area computed for the largest of the A and B regions is sufficiently close to the sum of the areas computed for the other two regions. For example, if region B is the largest, terminate when the area of B is sufficiently close to the area of A plus the area of C. Alternatively, we could simply terminate when C is sufficiently small. Such methods are known as *adaptive quadrature* because the solution adapts to the shape of the curve. (Simplified formulas can be derived for adaptive quadrature methods; see Freeman and Phillips, 1992.)

Computations of areas under slowly varying parts of the curve stop earlier than computations of areas under more rapidly varying parts. The spacing, δ, will vary across the interval. The consequence of this is that a fixed process assignment will not lead to the most efficient use of processors. The load-balancing techniques described in Chapter 3, Section 3.2.2, and in more detail in Chapter 7 are more appropriate. We should point out that some care might be needed in choosing when to terminate. For example, the function shown in Figure 4.17 might cause us to terminate early, as two large regions are the same (i.e., $C = 0$).

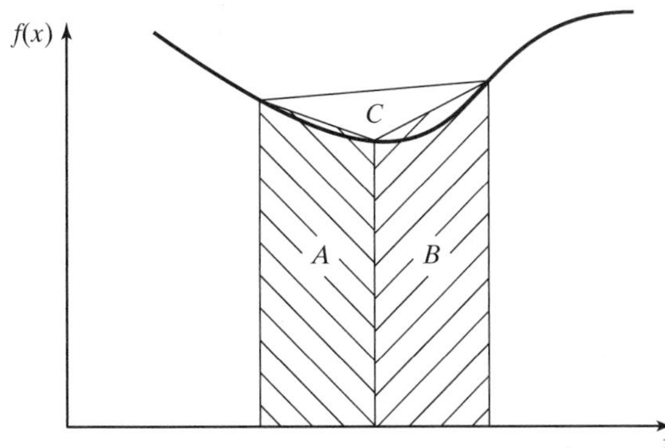

Figure 4.16 Adaptive quadrature construction.

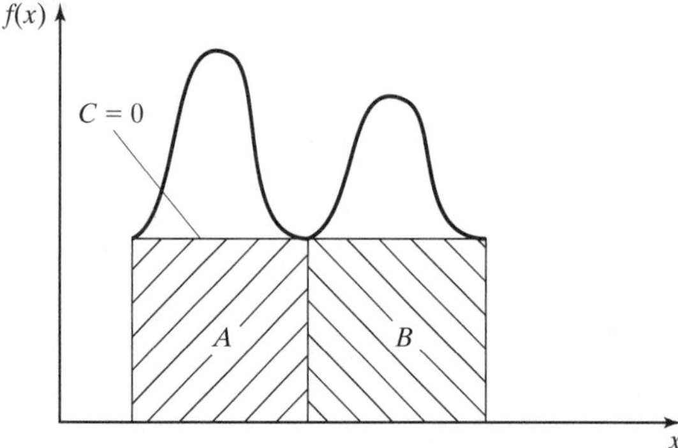

Figure 4.17 Adaptive quadrature with false termination.

4.2.3 *N*-Body Problem

Another problem that can take advantage of divide and conquer is the *N*-body problem. The *N*-body problem is concerned with determining the effects of forces between bodies such as astronomical bodies attracted to each other through gravitational forces. The *N*-body problem also appears in other areas, including molecular dynamics and fluid dynamics. Let us examine the problem in terms of astronomical systems, although the techniques apply to other applications. We provide the basic equations to enable the application to be coded as a programming exercise that could use the same graphic routines as the Mandelbrot problem of Chapter 3 for interesting graphical output.

Gravitational *N*-Body Problem. The objective is to find the positions and movements of bodies in space (e.g., planets) that are subject to gravitational forces from other bodies using Newtonian laws of physics. The gravitational force between two bodies of masses m_a and m_b is given by

$$F = \frac{Gm_am_b}{r^2}$$

where G is the gravitational constant and r is the distance between the bodies. We see that gravitational forces are described by an inverse square law. That is, the force between a pair of bodies is proportional to $1/r^2$, where r is the distance between the bodies. Each body will feel the influence of each of the other bodies according to the inverse square law, and the forces will sum together (taking into account the direction of each force). Subject to forces, a body will accelerate according to Newton's second law:

$$F = ma$$

where m is the mass of the body, F is the force it experiences, and a is the resultant acceleration. All the bodies will move to new positions due to these forces and have new velocities. For a precise numeric description, differential equations would be used (i.e., $F = mdv/dt$ and $v = dx/dt$, where v is the velocity). However, an exact "closed" solution to the *N*-body problem is not known for systems with more than three bodies.

For a computer simulation, we use values at particular times, t_0, t_1, t_2, and so on, the time intervals being as short as possible to achieve the most accurate solution. Let the time interval be Δt. Then, for a particular body of mass m, the force is given by

$$F = \frac{m(v^{t+1} - v^t)}{\Delta t}$$

and a new velocity

$$v^{t+1} = v^t + \frac{F\Delta t}{m}$$

where v^{t+1} is the velocity of the body at time $t + 1$, and v^t is the velocity of the body at time t. If a body is moving at a velocity v over the time interval Δt, its position changes by

$$x^{t+1} - x^t = v\Delta t$$

where x^t is its position at time t. Once bodies move to new positions, the forces change and the computation has to be repeated.

The velocity is not actually constant over the time interval, Δt, so only an approximate answer is obtained. It can help to use a "leap-frog" computation in which velocity and position are computed alternately:

$$F^t = \frac{m(v^{t+1/2} - v^{t-1/2})}{\Delta t}$$

and

$$x^{t+1} - x^t = v^{t+1/2}\Delta t$$

where the positions are computed for times t, $t + 1$, $t + 2$, and so on, and the velocities are computed for times $t + 1/2$, $t + 3/2$, $t + 5/2$, and so on.

Three-Dimensional Space. Since the bodies are in a three-dimensional space, all values are vectors and have to be resolved into three directions, x, y, and z. In a three-dimensional space having a coordinate system (x, y, z), the distance between the bodies at (x_a, y_a, z_a) and (x_b, y_b, z_b) is given by

$$r = \sqrt{(x_b - x_a)^2 + (y_b - y_a)^2 + (z_b - z_a)^2}$$

The forces are resolved in the three directions, using, for example,

$$F_x = \frac{Gm_a m_b}{r^2}\left(\frac{x_b - x_a}{r}\right)$$

$$F_y = \frac{Gm_a m_b}{r^2}\left(\frac{y_b - y_a}{r}\right)$$

$$F_z = \frac{Gm_a m_b}{r^2}\left(\frac{z_b - z_a}{r}\right)$$

where the particles are of mass m_a and m_b and have the coordinates (x_a, y_a, z_a) and (x_b, y_b, z_b). Finally, the new position and velocity are computed. The velocity can also be resolved in three directions. For a simple computer solution, we usually assume a three-dimensional space with fixed boundaries. Actually, the universe is continually expanding and does not have fixed boundaries!

Other Applications. Although we describe the problem in terms of astronomical bodies, the concept can be applied to other situations. For example, charged particles are also influenced by each other, in this case according to Coulomb's electrostatic law (also an inverse square law of distance); particles of opposite charge are attracted and those of like charge are repelled. A subtle difference between the problem and astronomical bodies is that charged particles may move away from each other, whereas astronomical bodies are only attracted and thus will tend to cluster.

Sequential Code. The overall gravitational N-body computation can be described by the algorithm

```
for (t = 0; t < tmax; t++) {                    /* for each time period */
   for (i = 0; i < N; i++) {                    /* for each body */
      F = Force_routine(i);                     /* compute force on ith body */
      v[i]new = v[i] + F * dt / m;              /* compute new velocity and */
      x[i]new = x[i] + v[i]new * dt;            /* new position (leap-frog) */
   }
   for (i = 0; i < N; i++) {                    /* for each body */
      x[i] = x[i]new;                           /* update velocity and position*/
      v[i] = v[i]new;
   }
}
```

Parallel Code. Parallelizing the sequential algorithm code can use simple partitioning whereby groups of bodies are the responsibility of each processor, and each force is "carried" in distinct messages between processors. However, a large number of messages could result. The algorithm is an $O(N^2)$ algorithm (for one iteration) as each of the N bodies is influenced by each of the other $N - 1$ bodies. It is not feasible to use this direct algorithm for most interesting N-body problems where N is very large.

The time complexity can be reduced using the observation that a cluster of distant bodies can be approximated as a single distant body of the total mass of the cluster sited at the center of mass of the cluster, as illustrated in Figure 4.18. This clustering idea can be applied recursively.

Barnes-Hut Algorithm. A clever divide-and-conquer formation to the problem using this clustering idea starts with the whole space in which one cube contains the bodies (or particles). First, this cube is divided into eight subcubes. If a subcube contains no particles, it is deleted from further consideration. If a subcube contains more than one body, it is recursively divided until every subcube contains one body. This process creates an *octtree*; that is, a tree with up to eight edges from each node. The leaves represent cells each containing one body. (We assumed the original space is a cube so that cubes result at each level of recursion, but other assumptions are possible.)

For a two-dimensional problem, each recursive subdivision will create four subareas and a *quadtree* (a tree with up to four edges from each edge; see Section 4.1.3). In general,

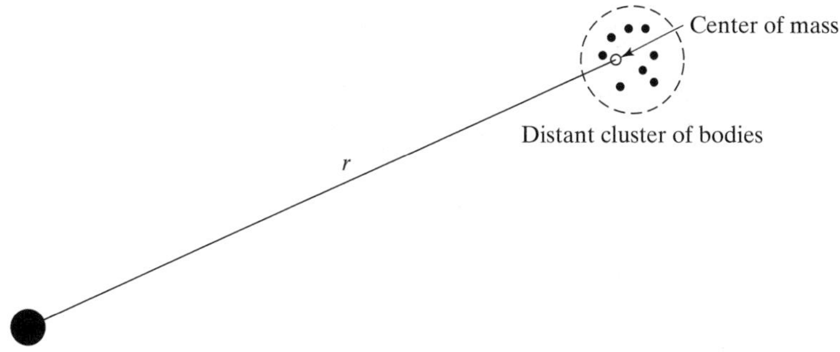

Figure 4.18 Clustering distant bodies.

the tree will be very unbalanced. Figure 4.19 illustrates the decomposition for a two-dimensional space (which is easier to draw) and the resultant quadtree. The three-dimensional case follows the same construction except that it has up to eight edges from each node.

In the *Barnes-Hut algorithm* (Barnes and Hut, 1986), after the tree has been constructed, the total mass and center of mass of the subcube is stored at each node. The force on each body can then be obtained by traversing the tree, starting at the root, stopping at a node when the clustering approximation can be used for the particular body, and otherwise continuing to traverse the tree downward. In astronomical N-body simulations, a simple criterion for when the approximation can be made is as follows. Suppose the cluster is enclosed in a cubic volume given by the dimensions $d \times d \times d$, and the distance to the center of mass is r. Use the clustering approximation when

$$r \geq \frac{d}{\theta}$$

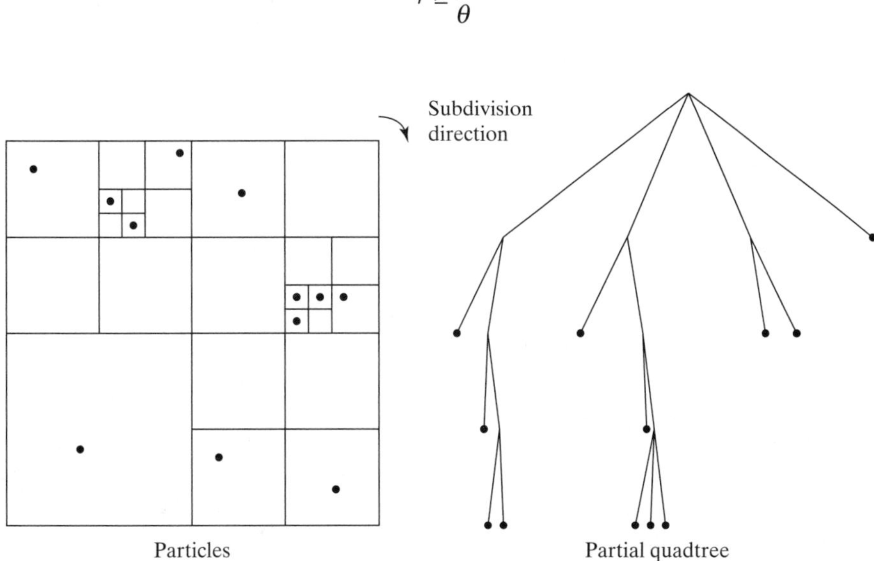

Figure 4.19 Recursive division of two-dimensional space.

where θ is a constant typically 1.0 or less (θ is called the opening angle). This approach can substantially reduce the computational effort.

Once all the bodies have been given new positions and velocities, the process is repeated for each time period. This means that the whole octtree must be reconstructed for each time period (because the bodies have moved). Constructing the tree requires a time of O($n$log$n$), and so does computing all the forces, so that the overall time complexity of the method is O($n$log$n$) (Barnes and Hut, 1986).

The algorithm can be described by the following:

```
for (t = 0; t < tmax; t++) {            /* for each time period */
   Build_Octtree();                     /* construct Octtree (or Quadtree) */
   Tot_Mass_Center();                   /* compute total mass & center /*
   Comp_Force();                        /* traverse tree/computing forces */
   Update();                            /* update position/velocity */
}
```

The `Build_Octtree()` routine can be constructed from the positions of the bodies, considering each body in turn. The `Tot_Mass_Center()` routine must traverse the tree, computing the total mass and center of mass at each node. This could be done recursively. The total mass, M, is given by the simple sum of the total masses of the children:

$$M = \sum_{i=0}^{7} m_i$$

where m_i is the total mass of the ith child. The center of mass, C, is given by

$$C = \frac{1}{M}\sum_{i=0}^{7} (m_i \times c_i)$$

where the positions of the centers of mass have three components, in the x, y, and z directions. The `Comp_Force()` routine must visit nodes ascertaining whether the clustering approximation can be applied to compute the force of all the bodies in that cell. If the clustering approximation cannot be applied, the children of the node must be visited.

The octtree will, in general, be very unbalanced, and its shape changes during the simulation. Hence, a simple static partitioning strategy will not be very effective in load balancing. A better way of dividing the bodies into groups is called *orthogonal recursive bisection* (Salmon, 1990). Let us describe this method in terms of a two-dimensional square area. First, a vertical line is found that divides the area into two areas, each with an equal number of bodies. For each area, a horizontal line is found that divides it into two areas, each with an equal number of bodies. This is repeated until there are as many areas as processors, and then one processor is assigned to each area. An example of the division is illustrated in Figure 4.20.

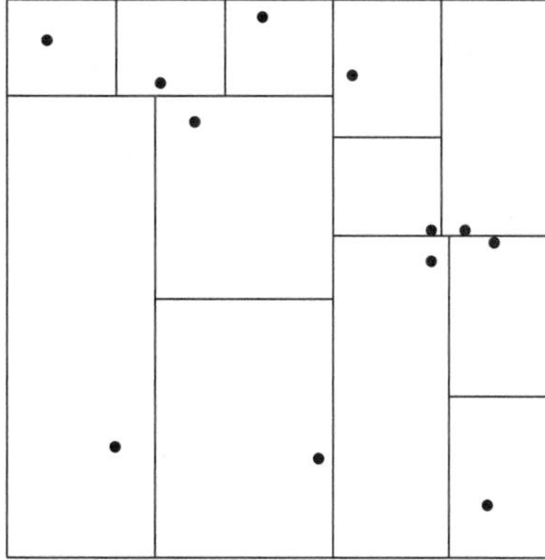

Figure 4.20 Orthogonal recursive bisection method.

4.3 SUMMARY

This chapter introduced the following concepts:

- Partitioning and divide-and-conquer as the basis for parallel computing techniques
- Tree constructions
- Examples of partitioning and divide-and-conquer problems — namely, bucket sort, numerical integration, and the *N*-body problem

FURTHER READING

The divide-and-conquer technique is described in many data structure and algorithms texts (e.g., Cormen Leiserson and Rivest, 1990). As we have seen, this technique results in a tree structure. It is possible to construct a multiprocessor with a tree network that would then be amenable to divide-and-conquer problems. One or two tree network machines have been constructed with the thought that most applications can be formulated as divide and conquer. However, as we have seen in Chapter 1, trees can be embedded into meshes and hypercubes so that it is not necessary to have tree network. Mapping divide-and-conquer algorithms onto different architectures is the subject of research papers like the one by Lo and Rajopadhye (1990).

Once a problem is partitioned, a scheduling algorithm is appropriate in some contexts for allocating processors to partitions or processes. One text dedicated to partitioning and scheduling is Sarkar (1989). Mapping (static scheduling) is not considered in this text. However, dynamic load balancing, in which tasks are assigned to processors during the execution of the program, is considered in Chapter 7.

Bucket sort is described in texts on sorting algorithms (see Chapter 9) and can be found specifically in Lindstrom (1985) and Wagner and Han (1986). Numerical evaluation of integrals in the context of parallel programs can be found in Freeman and Phillips (1992),

Gropp, Lusk, and Skjellum (1999), and Smith (1993) and is often used as a simple application of parallel programs. The original source for the Barnes-Hut algorithm is Barnes and Hut (1986). Other papers include Bhatt et al. (1992) and Warren and Salmon (1992). Liu and Wu (1997) consider programming the algorithm in C++. Apart from the Barnes-Hutt divide-and-conquer algorithm, another approach is the fast multipole method (Greengard and Rokhlin, 1987). Hybrid methods exist.

BIBLIOGRAPHY

AHO, A. V., J. E. HOPCROFT, AND J. D. ULLMAN (1974), *The Design and Analysis of Computer Algorithms*, Addison-Wesley, Reading, MA.

BARNES, J. E., AND P. HUT (1986), "A Hierarchical O(Nlog$N$) Force Calculation Algorithm," *Nature*, Vol. 324, No. 4 (December), pp. 446–449.

BHATT, S., M. CHEN, C. Y. LIN, AND P. LIU (1992), "Abstractions for Parallel N-Body Simulations," *Proc. Scalable High Performance Computing Conference*, pp. 26–29.

BLELLOCH, G. E. (1996), "Programming Parallel Algorithms," *Comm. ACM*, Vol. 39, No. 3, pp. 85–97.

BOKHARI, S. H. (1981), "On the Mapping Problem," *IEEE Trans. Comput.*, Vol. C-30, No. 3, pp. 207–214.

CORMEN, T. H., C. E. LEISERSON, AND R. L. RIVEST (1990), *Introduction to Algorithms*, MIT Press, Cambridge, MA.

FREEMAN, T. L., AND C. PHILLIPS (1992), *Parallel Numerical Algorithms*, Prentice Hall, London.

GREENGARD, L., AND V. ROKHLIN (1987), "A Fast Algorithm for Particle Simulations," *J. Comp. Phys.*, Vol. 73, pp. 325–348.

GROPP, W., E. LUSK, AND A. SKJELLUM (1999), *Using MPI Portable Parallel Programming with the Message-Passing Interface*, MIT Press, Cambridge, MA.

JÁJÁ, J. (1992), *An Introduction to Parallel Algorithms*, Addison Wesley, Reading, MA.

LINDSTROM, E. E. (1985), "The Design and Analysis of BucketSort for Bubble Memory Secondary Storage," *IEEE Trans. Comput.*, Vol. C-34, No. 3, pp. 218–233.

LIU, P., AND J.-J. WU (1997), "A Framework for Parallel Tree-Based Scientific Simulations," *Proc. 1997 Int. Conf. Par. Proc.*, pp. 137–144.

LO, V. M., AND S. RAJOPADHYE (1990), "Mapping Divide-and-Conquer Algorithms to Parallel Architectures," *Proc. 1990 Int. Conf. Par. Proc.*, Part III, pp. 128–135.

MILLER, R., AND Q. F. STOUT (1996), *Parallel Algorithms for Regular Architectures: Meshes and Pyramids*, MIT Press, Cambridge, MA.

PREPARATA, F. P., AND M. I. SHAMOS (1985), *Computational Geometry: An Introduction*, Springer-Verlag, NY.

SALMON, J. K. (1990), *Parallel Hierarchical N-Body Methods*, Ph.D. thesis, California Institute of Technology.

SARKAR, V. (1989), *Partitioning and Scheduling Parallel Programs for Multiprocessing*, MIT Press, Cambridge, MA.

SMITH, J. R. (1993), *The Design and Analysis of Parallel Algorithms*, Oxford University Press, Oxford, England.

WAGNER, R. A., AND Y. HAN (1986), "Parallel Algorithms for Bucket Sorting and Data Dependent Prefix Problem," *Proc. 1986 Int. Conf. Par. Proc.*, pp. 924–929.

WARREN, M., AND J. SALMON (1992), "Astrophysical *N*-Body Simulations Using Hierarchical Tree Data Structures," *Proc. Supercomputing 92*, IEEE CS Press, Los Alamitos, pp. 570–576.

PROBLEMS

Scientific/Numerical

4-1. Write a program that will prove that the maximum speedup of adding a series of numbers using a simple partition described in Section 4.1.1 is $p/2$, where there are p processes.

4-2. Using the equations developed in Section 4.1.1 for partitioning a list of numbers into m partitions that are added separately, show that the optimum value for m to give the minimum parallel execution time is when $m = \sqrt{p/(1 + t_{\text{startup}})}$, where there are p processors. (Clue: Differentiate the parallel execution time equation.)

4-3. Section 4.1.1 gives three implementations of adding numbers, using separate `send()`s and `recv()`s, using a broadcast routine with separate `recv()`s to return partial results, and using scatter and reduce routines. Write parallel programs for all three implementations, instrumenting the programs to extract timing information (Chapter 2, Section 2.3.4), and compare the results.

4-4. Suppose the structure of a computation consists of a binary tree with n leaves (final tasks) and $\log n$ levels. Each node in the tree consists of one computational step. What is the lower bound of the execution time if the number of processors is less than n?

4-5. Analyze the divide-and-conquer method of assigning one processor to each node in a tree for adding numbers (Section 4.1.2) in terms of communication, computation, overall parallel execution time, speedup, and efficiency.

4-6. Complete the parallel pseudocode given in Section 4.1.2 for the (binary) divide-and-conquer method for all eight processes.

4-7. Develop the equations for computation and communication times for m-ary divide and conquer, following the approach used in Section 4.1.2.

4-8. Develop a divide-and-conquer algorithm that finds the smallest value in a set of n values in $O(\log n)$ steps using $n/2$ processors. What is the time complexity if there are fewer than $n/2$ processors?

4-9. Write a parallel program with a time complexity of $O(\log n)$ to compute the polynomial

$$f = a_0x^0 + a_1x^1 + a_2x^2 + \dots + a_{n-1}x^{n-1}$$

to any degree, n, where the a's, x, and n are input.

4-10. Write a parallel program that uses a divide-and-conquer approach to find the first zero in a list of integers stored in an array. Use 16 processes and 256 numbers.

4-11. Write parallel programs to compute the summation of n integers in each of the following ways and assess their performance. Assume that n is a power of 2.

(a) Partition the n integers into $n/2$ pairs. Use $n/2$ processes to add together each pair of integers resulting in $n/2$ integers. Repeat the method on the $n/2$ integers to obtain $n/4$ integers and continue until the final result is obtained. (This is a binary tree algorithm.)

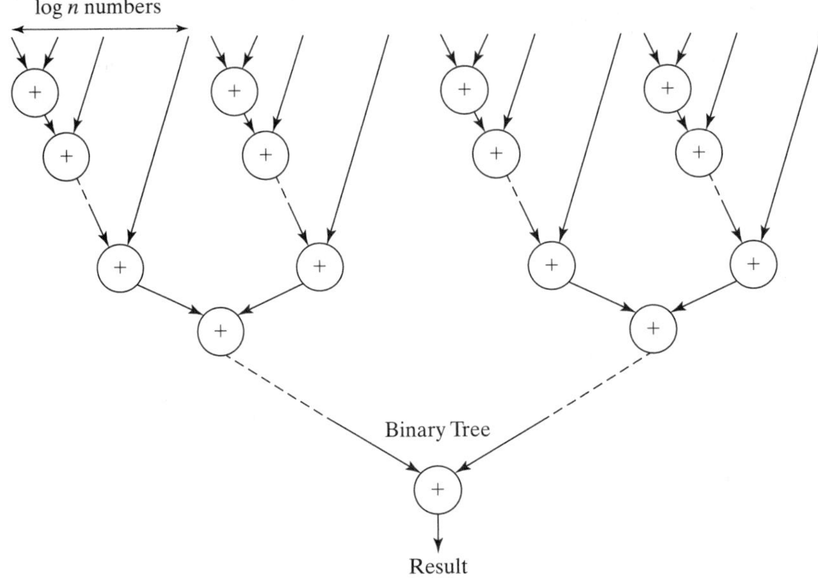

Figure 4.21 Process diagram for Problem 4-12(b).

(b) Divide the n integers into $n/\log n$ groups of $\log n$ numbers each. Use $n/\log n$ processes, each adding the numbers in one group sequentially. Then add the $n/\log n$ results using method (a). This algorithm is shown in Figure 4.21.

4-12. Write parallel programs to compute $n!$ in each of the following ways and assess their performance. The number, n, may be odd or even but is a positive constant.

(a) Compute $n!$ using two concurrent processes, each computing approximately half of the complete sequence. A master process then combines the two partial results.

(b) Compute $n!$ using a producer process and a consumer process connected together. The producer produces the numbers 1, 2, 3, … n in sequence. The consumer accepts the sequence of numbers from the producer and accumulates the result; i.e., $1 \times 2 \times 3 \ldots$.

4-13. Write a divide-and-conquer parallel program that determines whether the number of 1's in a binary file is even or odd (i.e., create a parity checker). Modify the program so that a bit is attached to the contents of the file, and set to a 0 or a 1 to make the number of 1's even (a parity generator).

4-14. Bucket sort and its parallel implementations suffer for poor performance if the numbers are not uniformly distributed, because more numbers will fall into the same bucket for subsequent sorting. Modify the algorithm so that the regions that each bucket collects are altered. This could be done as the algorithm is executed or before in a preprocessing step. Implement your algorithm.

4-15. One way to compute π is to compute the area under the curve $f(x) = 4/(1 + x^2)$ between 0 and 1, which is numerically equal to π. Write a parallel program to calculate π this way using 10 processes. Another way to compute π is to compute the area of a circle of radius $r = 1$ (i.e., $\pi r^2 = \pi$). Determine the appropriate equation for a circle, and write a parallel program to compute π this way. Comment on the two ways of computing π.

4-16. Derive a formula to evaluate numerically an integral using the adaptive quadrature method described in Section 4.2.2. Use the approach given for the trapezoidal method.

4-17. Using any method, write a parallel program that will compute the integral

$$I = \int_{0.01}^{1} \left(x + \sin\left(\frac{1}{x}\right)\right) dx$$

4-18. Write a static assignment parallel program to compute π using the formula

$$\int_{0}^{1} \sqrt{1 - x^2}\, dx = \frac{\pi}{4}$$

using each of the following ways:

1. Rectangular decomposition, as illustrated in Figure 4.13
2. Rectangular decomposition, as illustrated in Figure 4.14
3. Trapezoidal decomposition, as illustrated in Figure 4.15

Evaluate each method in terms of speed and accuracy.

4-19. Find the zero crossing of a function by a bisection method. In this method, two points on the function are computed, say $f(a)$ and $f(b)$, where $f(a)$ is positive and $f(b)$ is negative. The function must cross somewhere between a and b, as illustrated in Figure 4.22. By

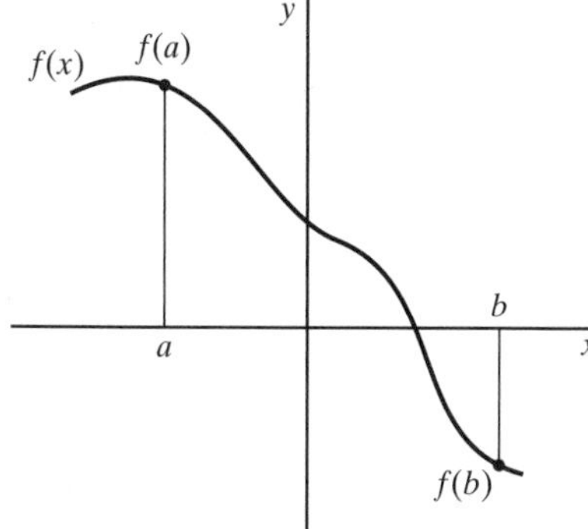

Figure 4.22 Bisection method for finding the zero crossing location of a function.

successively dividing the interval, the exact location of the zero crossing can be found. Write a divide-and-conquer program that will find the zero crossing locations of the function $f(x) = x^2 - 3x + 2$. (This function has two zero crossing locations, $x = 1$ and $x = 2$.)

4-20. Write a parallel program to integrate a function using Simpson's rule, which is given as follows:

$$I = \int_{a}^{b} f(x)\, dx =$$

$$\frac{\delta}{3}[f(a) + 4f(a + \delta) + 2f(a + 2\delta) + 4f(a + 3\delta) + 2f(a + 4\delta) + \ldots 4f(a + (n - 1)\delta) + f(b)]$$

where δ is fixed [$\delta = (b - a)/n$ and n must be even]. Choose a suitable function (or arrange it so that the function can be input).

4-21. Write a sequential program and a parallel program to simulate an astronomical N-body system, but in two dimensions. The bodies are initially at rest. Their initial positions and masses are to be selected randomly (using a random-number generator). Display the movement of the bodies using the graphical routines used for the Mandelbrot program found in http://www.cs.uncc.edu/par_prog, or otherwise, showing each body in a color and size to indicate its mass.

4-22. Develop the N-body equations for a system of charged particles (e.g., free electrons and positrons) that are governed by Coulumb's law. Write a sequential and a parallel program to model this system, assuming that the particles lie in a two-dimensional space. Produce graphical output showing the movement of the particles. Provide your own initial distribution and movement of particles and solution space.

4-23. (Research problem) Given a set of n points in a plane, develop an algorithm and parallel program to find the points that are on the perimeter of the smallest region containing all of the points, and join the points, as illustrated in Figure 4.23. This problem is known as the planar convex hull problem and can be solved by a recursive divide-and-conquer approach very similar to quicksort, by recursively splitting regions into two parts using "pivot" points. There are several sources for information on the planar convex hull problem, including Blelloch (1996), Preparata and Shamos (1985), and Miller and Stout (1996).

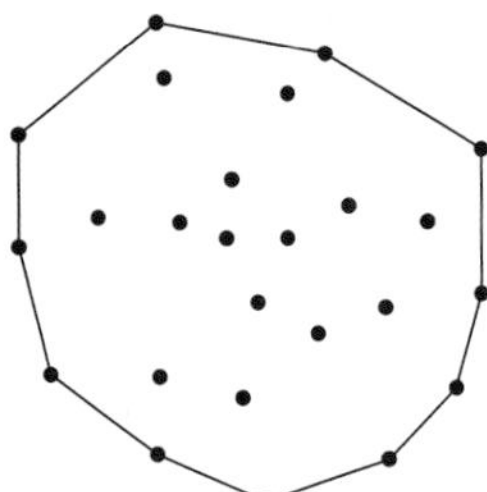

Figure 4.23 Convex hull (Problem 4-23).

Real Life

4-24. Write a sequential and a parallel program to model the planets around the sun (or another astronomical system). Produce graphical output showing the movement of the planets. Provide your own initial distribution and movement of planets. (Use real data if available.)

4-25. A major bank in your state processes an average of 30 million checks a day for its 2 million customer accounts. One time-consuming problem is that of sorting the checks into individual customer-account bundles so they can be returned with the monthly statements. (Yes, the bank handles check sorting for several client banks in addition to its own.) The bank has been using a very fast mainframe-based check sorter and the quicksort method. However, you have told the bank that you know of a way to use N smaller computers in parallel; each will sort $1/N$th of the 30 million checks, and then the partial sorts will be merged into a single sorted result. Before investing in the new technology, the bank hires you as a consultant to simulate the process using message-passing parallel programming. Under the following assumptions, simulate this new approach for the bank.

Assumptions:

1. Each check has three identification numbers: a nine-digit bank-identification number, a nine-digit account-identification number, and a three-digit check number (leading zeros are not printed or shown).

2. All checks with the same bank-identification number are to be sorted by customer account for transmittal to the client bank.

Estimate the speedup if N is 10 and if N is 1000. Estimate the percentage of time spent in communications versus time spent in processing.

4-26. Sue, 21 years old, comes from a very financially astute family. She has been watching her parents save and invest for several years now, reads the *Wall Street Journal* daily in the university library (for free!), and has concluded that she will not be able to rely on social security when she retires in 49 years. For graduation from college, her parents got her a CD-ROM containing historical daily closing prices covering every exchange-listed security, from January 1, 1900 to the end of last month.

For simplicity you may think of the data on the CD-ROM as organized into date/symbol/closing price records for each of the 358,000 securities that have been listed since 1900. (Only a fraction are listed at any given date; firms go out of business and new ones start daily.) Similarly, you may assume that the format of a record is given by

date	Last three digits of the year, followed by the "Julian date" (where January 15 is Julian 15, February 1 is Julian 32, etc.)
symbol	Up to 10 characters, such as PCAI, KAUFX, or IBM.AZ, representing a NASDAQ stock (PCA International), a mutual fund (Kaufman Aggressive Growth), and an option to buy IBM stock at a certain price for a certain length of time, respectively.
closing price	Three integers, X (representing a whole number of dollars per unit), Y (representing the numerator of a fractional dollar per unit), and Z (representing the denominator of a fractional dollar per unit).

For example, "996033/PCAI/10/3/4" indicates that on February 2, 1996, PCA International stock closed at $10.75 per share. Sue wants to know how many of the stocks that were listed as of last month's end have had 50 or more consecutive trading days in which they closed either unchanged from the previous day or at a higher price, anytime in the CD-ROM's recorded history.

4-27. The more Samantha recalled her grandfather's stories about the time he won the 1963 World Championship Dominos Match, the more she wanted to improve her skills at the game. She had a basic problem, though; she had no playing partners left, having already improved to the point where she consistently won every game against the few friends who still remained!

Samantha knew that computerized versions of go, chess, bridge, poker, and checkers had been developed, and saw no reason someone skilled in the science of computers could not do the same for dominos. One of her computer science professors at the second campus of the University of Canada, U-Can-2, had told her she could do anything she wanted (within theoretical limits, of course), and she really wanted to win that next world championship!

Pulling out her slow, nearly ancient 2-cubed Itanium (2 GHz, 2GB RAM, 2 TB hard disk), she quickly developed a straightforward single-processor simulator that she could practice against. The basic outline of her approach was to have the program compare every one of its pieces to the pieces already played in order to determine the computer's best move. This appeared to involve so many computations, including rotations and trial placements of pieces that Samantha found herself waiting for the program to produce the computer's next move, and becoming as bored with its game performance as with that of her old friends. Thus, she is seeking your assistance in developing a parallel-processor version.

1. Outline her single-processor algorithm.
2. Outline your parallel-processor algorithm.

3. Estimate the speedup that could be obtained if you were to network 50 old computers like hers. Then make a recommendation to her about either going ahead with the task or spending $800 to buy the latest processor, reputed to be at least 50 times faster than her old Itanium for these types of simulations: the new 14GHz dual processor Octium with its standard 1024-bit front-side data bus and 2-way simultaneous access to its 16TB of 0.5ns main memory.

4-28. Area, Inc., provides a numerical integration service for several small engineering firms in the region. When any of these firms has a continuous function defined over a domain and is unable to integrate it, Area, Inc., gets the call. You have just been hired to help Area, Inc., improve its slow delivery of computed integration results. Area, Inc. has lost money each year of its existence and is so "nonprofit" that payment of next week's payroll is in question. Given your desire to continue eating (and for that Area, Inc., has to pay you), you have considerable incentive to help Area, Inc.

Given also that you have a considerable background in parallel computing, you recognize the problem immediately: Area, Inc., has been using a single processor to implement a standard numerical integration algorithm.

Step 1: Divide the independent axis into N even intervals.

Step 2: Approximate the area under the function in any interval (its integral over the interval), by the product of the interval width times the function value when it is evaluated at the left edge of the interval.

Step 3: Add up all N approximations to get the total area.

Step 4: Divide the interval width in half.

Step 5: Repeat steps 1 – 4 until the total from the ith repetition differs from the $(i - 1)th$ repetition by less than 0.001 percent of the magnitude of the ith total.

Since your manager is skeptical about newfangled parallel computing approaches, she wants you to simulate two different machine configurations: two processors in the first, and eight processors in the second. She has told you that a successful demonstration is key to being able to buy more processors and to your getting paid next week.

4-29. The Search for Extra-Terrestrial Intelligence (SETI) project employs millions of computers to analyze radio-telescope signals from the Arecibo Observatory in Puerto Rico. Each is given a time- and frequency-limited portion of the signals recorded by the world's largest radio telescope and asked to perform a computationally intense analysis to determine the likelihood of that portion containing intelligent communications from another life form. This is clearly an example of a divide-and-conquer approach.

Discuss how this approach could be applied to the more local problem of analysis of radio-frequency communications in the world's anti-terrorism struggle.

4-30. Rafic loves to solve crossword puzzles. Lately, he has begun to create them when he cannot find a suitably challenging one on which to work. This process has two parts: laying out the pattern of open squares into which individual letters will go, and blackened squares that form breaks between words or phrases. He has a word and phrase dictionary containing over 100,000 words and phrases ranging from ancient Greek and Roman references to such modern things as the Itanium-III and pico-technology. Rafic needs your help.

Develop a sequential algorithm that will produce a crossword puzzle of size $N \times N$, and then convert the algorithm to its parallel counterpart.

4-31. On occasion, beginning computer science students are tempted to copy work done by others and submit it as their own, a practice, known as plagiarism, that typically results in severe academic penalties when detected. Sometimes the more creative students will make small changes to the work before submitting it: changing variable names, changing indentation, and sometimes even changing looping structures (substituting a "while" for a "for"). For a typical first-year course with 400 students, this requires approximately 80,000 program comparisons per programming assignment. As a result, total checking is rarely done.

(Easy) Develop a parallel approach using N computers that can exhaustively check for exact duplicates among the 400 submissions on a typical programming assignment.

(Harder) Pre-process each program to tokenize the variable names, thereby converting each program to a standard set of variable names. Then apply the approach from the "easy" part.

(Hardest) Pre-process each program to put all loops into the same structure: a "for". Then implement both of the earlier parts.

4-32. Sarah, a friend of Tom's has puzzle-creation as her hobby. On her home CAD system tied to the computer-controlled milling machine in her workshop she designed three elementary shapes and fabricated thousands of each. The first is a right triangle whose shortest sides are 1 unit in length. The second is a square whose edges are 1 unit in length. The third is a combination of a rectangle 4 units by 13 units attached to a right triangle whose shortest sides are 4 units. Given an arbitrary combination of pieces (F of type first, S of type second, and T of type third), Sarah needs you to develop and implement an algorithm that will determine the area of the largest right triangle that can be formed by placing some or all of these $F + S + T$ pieces together ... initially as a sequential algorithm and then as a parallel algorithm with N computers working on the solution. Sample combinations of these pieces are shown in Figure 4.24 to get you started.

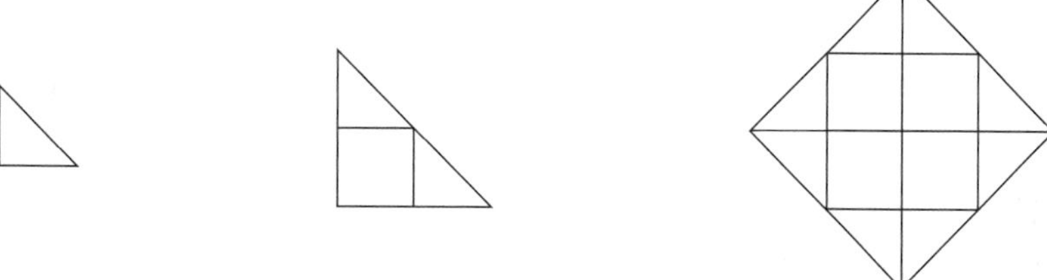

(a) Single triangle. (b) Pair of triangles plus one square. (c) Four instances of (b), each area is 0.5 sq units area is 2 sq units rotated 90 degrees to form a square whose sides are each $2\sqrt{2}$ in length, area is 8 sq units.

Figure 4.24 Triangles (Problem 4-32).

Chapter 5

Pipelined Computations

In this chapter, we present a parallel processing technique called *pipelining*, which is applicable to a wide range of problems that are partially sequential in nature; that is, a sequence of steps must be undertaken. Hence, pipelining can be used to parallelize sequential code. Certain requirements are necessary for improved performance, as will be outlined.

5.1 PIPELINE TECHNIQUE

In the pipeline technique, the problem is divided into a series of tasks that have to be completed one after the other. In fact, this is the basis of sequential programming. In pipelining, each task is executed by a separate process or processor, as shown in Figure 5.1. We sometimes refer to each pipeline process as a pipeline *stage*. Each stage contributes to the overall problem and passes on information that is needed for subsequent stages. This parallelism can be viewed as a form of *functional decomposition*. The problem is divided into separate functions that must be performed, but in this case, the functions are performed in succession. As we shall see, the input data is often broken up and processed separately.

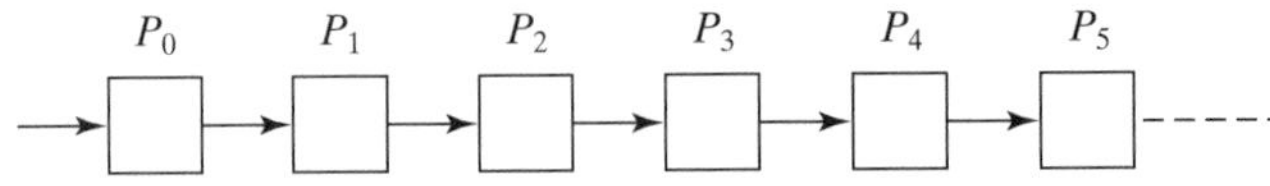

Figure 5.1 Pipelined processes.

As an example of a sequential program that can be formulated as a pipeline, consider a simple loop:

```
for (i = 0; i < n; i++)
   sum = sum + a[i];
```

which adds all the elements of array `a` to an accumulating sum. The loop could be "unrolled" to yield

```
sum = sum + a[0];
sum = sum + a[1];
sum = sum + a[2];
sum = sum + a[3];
sum = sum + a[4];
      .
      .
      .
```

One pipeline solution would have a separate stage for each statement, as shown in Figure 5.2. Each stage accepts the accumulating sum on its input, s_{in}, and one element of `a[]` on its input, a, and produces the new accumulating sum on its output, s_{out}. Therefore, stage i performs

```
sout = sin + a[i];
```

Instead of simple statements, a series of functions can be performed in a pipeline fashion. A frequency filter is a more realistic example in which the problem is divided into a series of functions (functional decomposition). The objective here is to remove specific frequencies (say the frequencies f_0, f_1, f_2, f_3, etc.) from a (digitized) signal, $f(t)$. The signal could enter the pipeline from the left, as shown in Figure 5.3. Each stage is responsible for removing one of the frequencies.

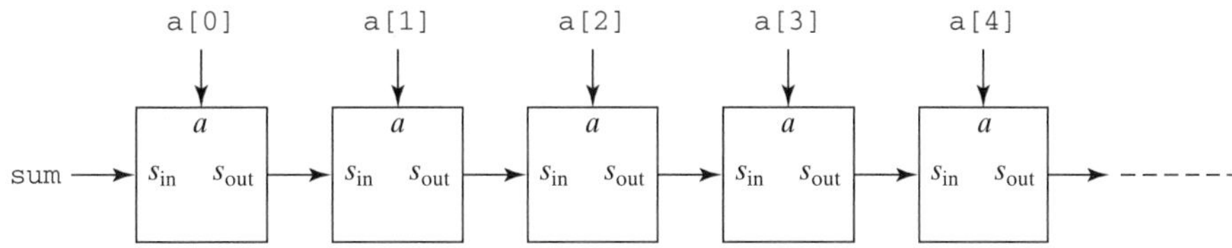

Figure 5.2 Pipeline for an unrolled loop.

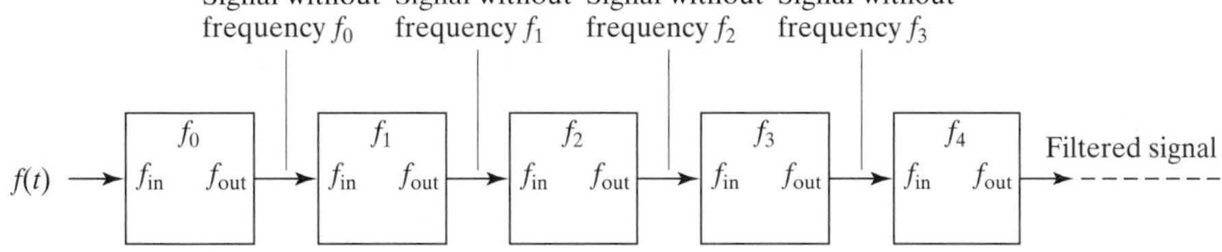

Figure 5.3 Pipeline for a frequency filter.

A similar application is to recognize certain frequencies in a signal. In home and professional sound systems, for example, there often is a display showing the specific frequencies in the audio output. Each stage of a pipeline could recognize one frequency and display its amplitude as part of a frequency-amplitude histogram. Problem 5-13 explores this application.

Given that the problem can be divided into a series of sequential tasks, the pipelined approach can provide increased speed under the following three types of computations:

1. If more than one instance of the complete problem is to be executed
2. If a series of data items must be processed, each requiring multiple operations
3. If information to start the next process can be passed forward before the process has completed all its internal operations.

We will identify these three solutions as Type 1, Type 2, and Type 3.

The Type 1 arrangement is utilized widely in the internal hardware design of computers. It also appears in simulation exercises where many simulation runs must be completed with different parameters to obtain the comparative results. A Type 1 pipeline is illustrated in the *space-time diagram* shown in Figure 5.4. In this diagram, each process is assumed to have been given the same time to complete its task. Each time period is one *pipeline cycle*. Each instance of the problem requires six sequential processes, P_0, P_1, P_2, P_3, P_4, and P_5. Note the staircase effect at the beginning. After the staircase effect, one instance of the problem is completed in each pipeline cycle. The same information shown in Figure 5.4 is shown in an alternative space-time diagram in Figure 5.5, where the instances are listed along the vertical axis. This form of diagram is sometimes useful if it is necessary to show information passing from one task instance to another (as would occur in processor pipelines).

With p processes constituting the pipeline and m instances of the problem to execute, the number of pipeline cycles to execute all m instances is given by $m + p - 1$ cycles. The average number of cycles is $(m + p - 1)/m$ cycles, which tends to one cycle per problem instance for large m. In any event, one instance of the problem will be completed in each pipeline cycle after the first $p - 1$ cycles (the *pipeline latency*). The formula $m + p - 1$ for a p-stage pipeline computing m instances of a problem will be used in our analyses later.

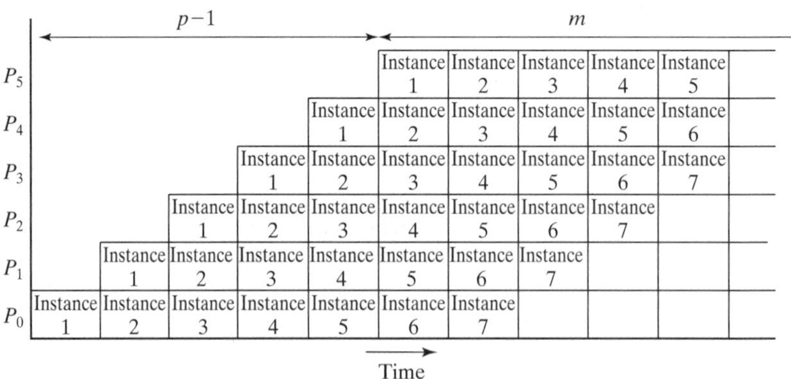

Figure 5.4 Space-time diagram of a pipeline.

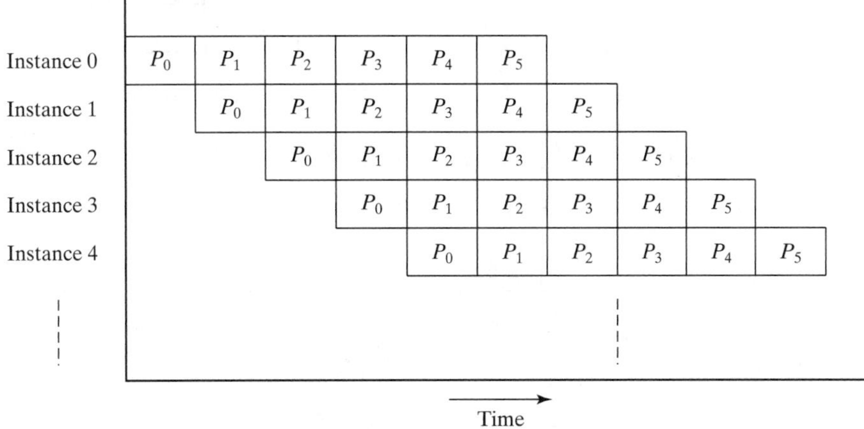

Figure 5.5 Alternative space-time diagram.

The Type 2 arrangement, in which a series of data items must be processed in a sequence, appears in arithmetic calculations, such as multiplying elements of an array where individual elements enter the pipeline as a sequential series of numbers. The arrangement is shown in Figure 5.6, where in this case ten processes form the pipeline and ten

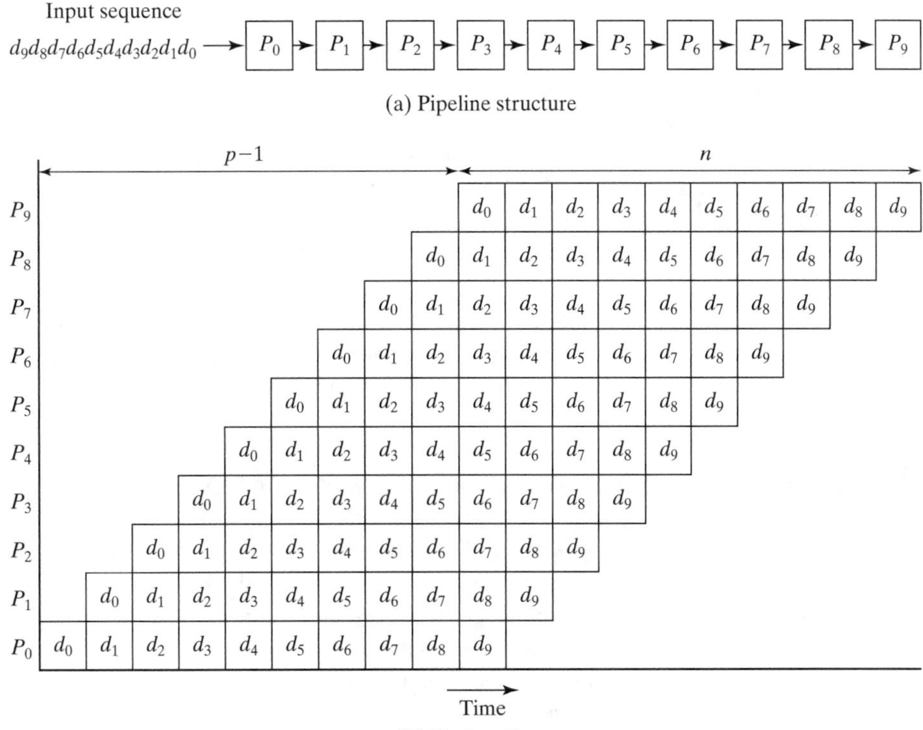

Figure 5.6 Pipeline processing ten data elements.

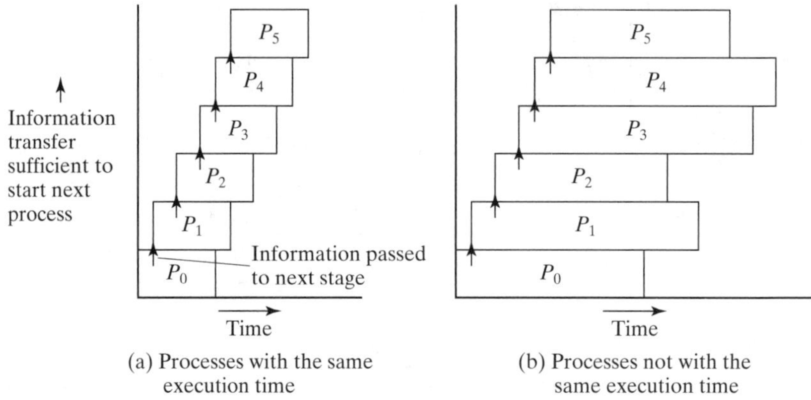

Figure 5.7 Pipeline processing where information passes to next stage before end of process.

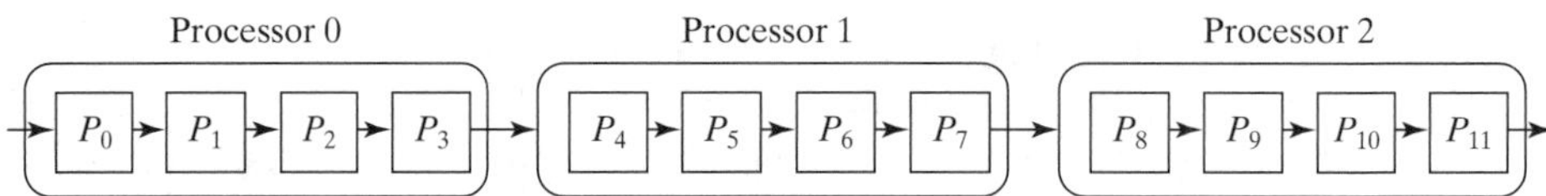

Figure 5.8 Partitioning processes onto processors.

elements, d_0, d_1, d_2, d_3, d_4, d_5, d_6, d_7, d_8, and d_9, are being processed. With p processes and n data items, the overall execution time is again given by $(p - 1) + n$ pipeline cycles, assuming these are all equal.

It is often the third arrangement, Type 3, that is utilized in parallel programs where there is only one instance of the problem to execute, but each process can pass on information to the next process before it has completed. Figure 5.7 shows space-time diagrams when information can pass from one process to another before the end of the execution of a process.

If the number of stages is larger than the number of processors in any pipeline, a group of stages can be assigned to each processor, as shown in Figure 5.8. Of course, now the pipeline stages within one processor are executed sequentially.

5.2 COMPUTING PLATFORM FOR PIPELINED APPLICATIONS

A key requirement for pipelining is the ability to send messages between adjacent processes in the pipeline. This suggests direct communication links between the processors onto which adjacent processes are mapped. An ideal interconnection structure is a line or ring structure, such as a line of processors connected to a host system, as shown in Figure 5.9. Lines and rings can be embedded into meshes and hypercubes, thereby making them suitable platforms. The seemingly inflexible line configuration is, in fact, very convenient for many applications, yet at very low cost. To use pipelining with networked computers and computer clusters efficiently requires an interconnection structure that can provide

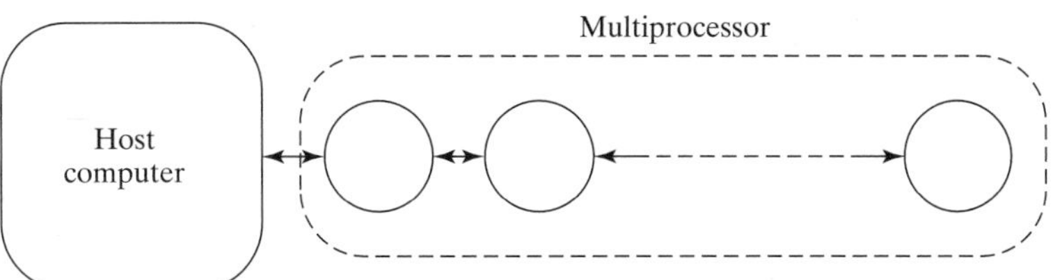

Figure 5.9 Multiprocessor system with a line configuration.

simultaneous transfers between adjacent processes or processors. Most computer clusters employ a switched interconnection structure that allows such transfers. A single shared Ethernet connection would not provide such simultaneous transfers. A little flexibility can be achieved on this matter by using (locally) blocking `send()`s (the `send()`s that are normally used). Then a process can continue with the next operation without waiting for the destination to be ready.

5.3 PIPELINE PROGRAM EXAMPLES

In this section we will examine sample problems that can be pipelined and classify the solutions as Type 1, Type 2, or Type 3.

5.3.1 Adding Numbers

For our first example, consider the problem of adding a list of numbers. (The problem could use any associative operation on a sequence of numbers.) A pipeline solution could have each process in the pipeline add one number to an accumulating sum, as shown in Figure 5.10, when one number is held in each process ($p = n$). The partial sum is passed from one process to the next, each process adding its number to the accumulating sum.

The basic code for process P_i is simply

```
recv(&accumulation, Pi-1);
accumulation = accumulation + number;
send(&accumulation, Pi+1);
```

except for the first process, P_0, which is

```
send(&number, P1);
```

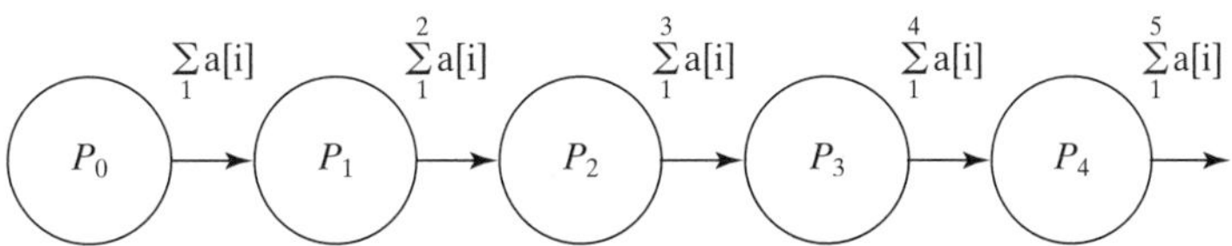

Figure 5.10 Pipelined addition.

and the last process, P_{p-1}, which is

```
recv(&number, Pp-2);
accumulation = accumulation + number;
```

Thus, an SPMD program could have the form

```
if (process > 0) {
   recv(&accumulation, Pi-1);
   accumulation = accumulation + number;
}
if (process < p-1) send(&accumulation, Pi+1);
```

The final result is in the last process. Instead of addition, other arithmetic operations could be done. For example, a single number, x, could be raised to a power by multiplying the input number by x and passing on the result. Hence, a five-stage pipeline could be used to obtain x^6. Problem 5-1 explores the advantages of this approach compared to using a divide-and-conquer tree structure for the same computation.

In our general description of pipelines, we show the data being entered into the first process rather than already in the appropriate processes. If the input data is entered into the first process, it would be natural to return the result through the last process, as shown in Figure 5.11. This would be particularly appropriate if the processors were connected in a ring architecture.

For a master-slave organization, the organization shown in Figure 5.12 would also be appropriate. The numbers of one problem are entered into each process when they are needed by the processes. The first process gets its number before the others. The second process gets its number one cycle later, and so on. As we will see in Chapter 11, this form of message-passing appears in several numeric problems. In Chapter 11, we will also see pipelines where the information is entered from both ends simultaneously and two-dimensional pipeline structures.

Coming back to our problem of adding numbers, it does not make sense to have one process for each number because then to add, say, 1000 numbers, 1000 slave processes would be needed. Generally, a group of numbers would be added together in each process and the result passed onward. Such *data partitioning* is used in most numeric applications to reduce the communication overhead and is assumed in all our examples.

Analysis. Our first pipeline example is Type 1; it is efficient only if we have more than one instance of the problem to solve (i.e., more than one set of numbers to add together).

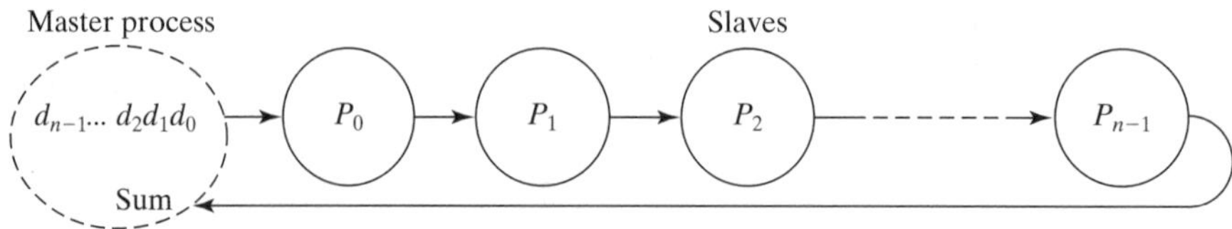

Figure 5.11 Pipelined addition numbers with a master process and ring configuration.

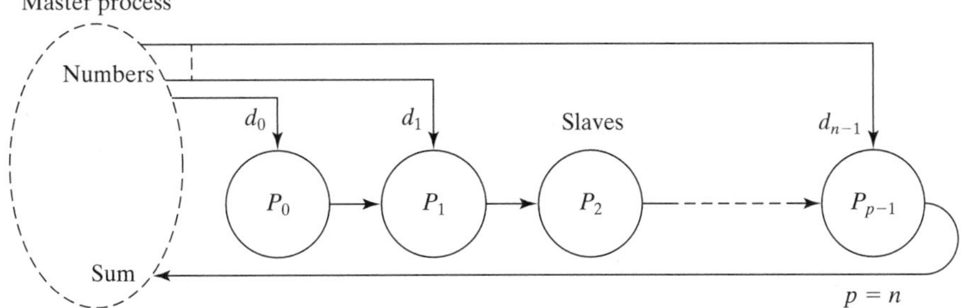

Figure 5.12 Pipelined addition of numbers with direct access to slave processes.

For analyses of pipelines, it may not be appropriate to consider all the processes as having simultaneous communication and computation phases, as in previous chapters, because each instance of a problem starts at a different time and ends at a different time. Instead, we will assume that each process performs similar actions in each pipeline cycle. Then we will work out the computation and communication required in a pipeline cycle. The total execution time, t_{total}, is then obtained by using our pipeline formula for the number of cycles multiplied by the time of one cycle; that is,

$$t_{\text{total}} = (\text{time for one pipeline cycle})(\text{number of cycles})$$

$$t_{\text{total}} = (t_{\text{comp}} + t_{\text{comm}})(m + p - 1)$$

where there are m instances of the problem and p pipeline stages (processes). The computation and communication times are given by t_{comp} and t_{comm}, respectively. The average time for a computation is given by

$$t_a = \frac{t_{\text{total}}}{m}$$

Let us assume that the structure shown in Figure 5.11 is used, and there are n numbers.

Single Instance of Problem. Let us first consider a single number being added in each stage; that is, n is equal to p. The period of one pipeline cycle will be dictated by the time of one addition and two communications, one communication from the left and one communication to the right,

$$t_{\text{comp}} = 1$$

$$t_{\text{comm}} = 2(t_{\text{startup}} + t_{\text{data}})$$

and each pipeline cycle, t_{cycle}, requires at least $t_{\text{comp}} + t_{\text{comm}}$.

$$t_{\text{cycle}} = 2(t_{\text{startup}} + t_{\text{data}}) + 1$$

The term t_{data} is the usual time to transfer one data word, and t_{startup} is the communication startup time. The last process only has one communication, but this may not help because all the processes are allocated the same time period.

If we were to have only one set of numbers ($m = 1$), the total execution time, t_{total}, would be given by

$$t_{total} = (2(t_{startup} + t_{data}) + 1)n$$

(i.e., n pipeline cycles, because each process must wait for the preceding process to complete its computation and pass on its results). The time complexity is $O(n)$.

Multiple Instances of Problem. If, however, we have m groups of n numbers to add, each group resulting in a separate answer, the time of one pipeline cycle remains the same, but now we have $m + n - 1$ cycles, leading to

$$t_{total} = (2(t_{startup} + t_{data}) + 1)(m + n - 1)$$

For large m, the average execution time, t_a, is approximately

$$t_a = \frac{t_{total}}{m} \approx 2(t_{startup} + t_{data}) + 1$$

that is, one pipeline cycle.

Data Partitioning with Multiple Instances of Problem. Now let us consider data partitioning with each stage processing a group of d numbers. The number of processes is given by $p = n/d$. Each communication will still transfer one result, but the computation will also now require d numbers to be accumulated ($d - 1$ steps) plus the incoming number, so that the following applies:

$$t_{comp} = d$$

$$t_{comm} = 2(t_{startup} + t_{data})$$

$$t_{total} = (2(t_{startup} + t_{data}) + d)(m + n/d - 1)$$

Obviously, as we increase d, the data partition, the impact of the communication on the overall time diminishes. But increasing the data partition decreases the parallelism and often increases the execution time. It is left as an exercise to explore the trade-offs of these effects (Problem 5-5).

5.3.2 Sorting Numbers

The objective of sorting numbers is to reorder a set of numbers in increasing (or decreasing) numeric order (strictly, nondecreasing/nonincreasing order if there are duplicate numbers). A pipeline solution for sorting is to have the first process, P_0, accept the series of numbers one at a time, store the largest number so far received, and pass onward all numbers smaller than the stored number. If a number received is larger than the currently stored number, it replaces the currently stored number and the original stored number is passed onward. Each subsequent process performs the same algorithm, storing the largest number so far received. When no more numbers are to be processed, P_0 will have the largest number, P_1 the next-largest number, P_2 the next-largest number, and so on. This algorithm is a parallel version of *insertion sort*. The sequential version is akin to placing playing cards in order by moving cards over to insert a card in position (see Cormen, Leiserson, and Rivest, 1990). (The sequential insertion sort algorithm is only efficient for sorting a small quantity of numbers.)

Figure 5.13 shows the actions in sorting five numbers. The basic algorithm for process P_i is

```
recv(&number, Pi-1);
if (number > x) {
   send(&x, Pi+1);
   x = number;
} else send(&number, Pi+1);
```

With n numbers, how many the ith process is to accept is known; it is given by $n - i$. How many to pass onward is also known; it is given by $n - i - 1$, since one of the numbers received is not passed onward. Hence, a simple loop could be used:

```
right_procNum = n - i - 1;          /* number of processes to the right */
recv(&x, Pi-1);
for (j = 0; j < right_procNum; j++) {
   recv(&number, Pi-1);
   if (&number > x) {
      send(&x, Pi+1);
      x = number;
   } else send(&number, Pi+1);
}
```

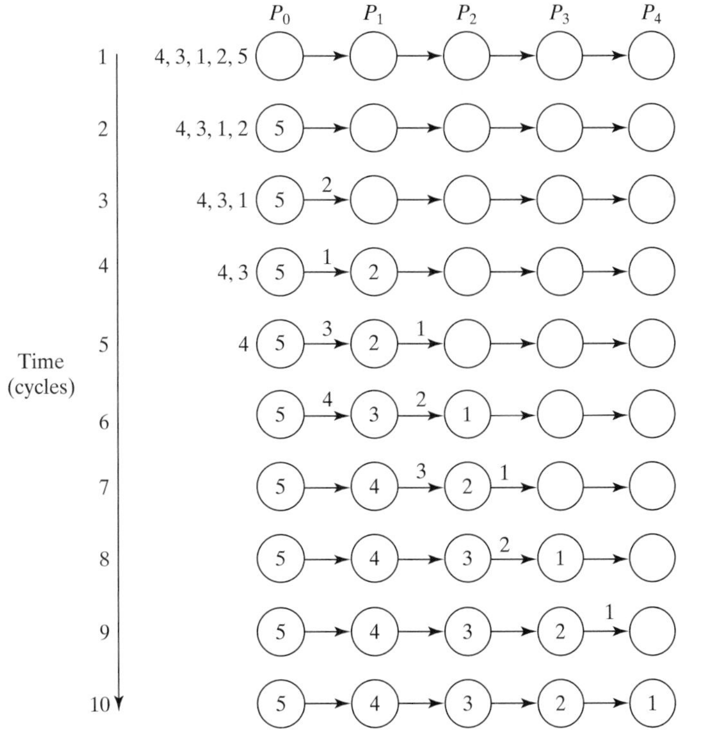

Figure 5.13 Steps in insertion sort with five numbers.

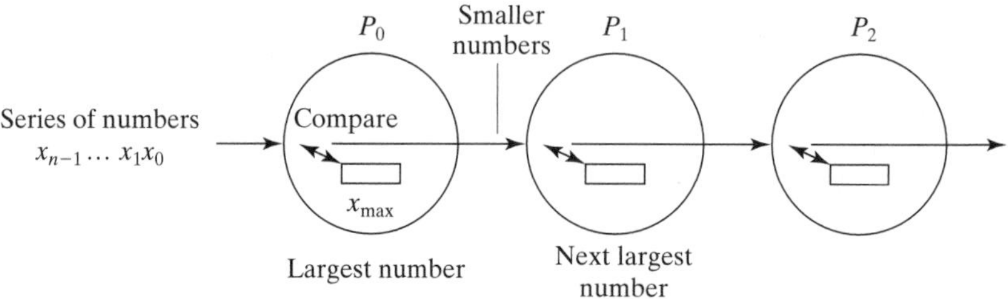

Figure 5.14 Pipeline for sorting using insertion sort.

The pipeline is illustrated in Figure 5.14. A message-passing program using an SPMD or a master-slave approach is straightforward, especially since each pipeline process executes essentially the same code. We see from the code that there is virtually no opportunity for a process to continue with useful work in one pipeline cycle after passing on a number (Type 3). However, a series of operations is performed on a series of data items (Type 2), and this leads to a significant speedup even on one instance of the problem.

Results of the sorting algorithm can be extracted from the pipeline using either the ring configuration of Figure 5.11 or the bidirectional line configuration of Figure 5.15. The latter is advantageous because a process can return its result as soon as the last number is passed through it. The process does not have to wait for all the numbers to be sorted. Leighton (1992) describes this and three other ways that the results could be collected, but concludes that the way described here is best.

Incorporating results being returned, process i could have the form

```
right_procNum = n - i - 1;          /* number of processes to the right */
recv(&x, Pi-1);
for (j = 0; j < right_procNum; j++) {
   recv(&number, Pi-1);
   if (number > x) {
      send(&x, Pi+1);
      x = number;
   } else send(&number, Pi+1);
}
send(&x, Pi-1);                                  /* send number held */
for (j = 0; j < right_procNum; j++) {            /* pass on other numbers */
   recv(&number, Pi+1);
   send(&number, Pi-1);
}
```

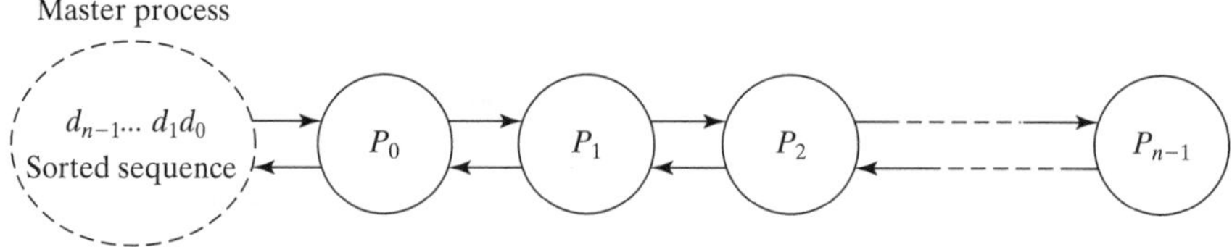

Figure 5.15 Insertion sort with results returned to the master process using a bidirectional line configuration.

Now more numbers pass through a process as processes get nearer the master process. Great care is needed in programming to ensure that the correct number of `send()`s and `recv()`s are present in each process. Process $n - 1$ has no `recv()`s and one `send()` (to process $n - 2$). Process $n - 2$ has one `recv()` (from process $n - 1$) and two `send()`s (to process $n - 3$), and so on. It would be very easy to mismatch `send()`s and `recv()`s, in which case a deadlock situation would occur.

Analysis. Assuming that the compare-and-exchange operation is regarded as one computational step, a sequential implementation of the algorithm requires

$$t_s = (n-1) + (n-2) + \ldots + 2 + 1 = \frac{n(n-1)}{2}$$

as it takes $n - 1$ steps to find the largest number, $n - 2$ steps to find the next-largest number using the remaining numbers, and so on. The approximate number of steps is $n^2/2$, obviously a very poor sequential sorting algorithm and unsuitable except for very small n.

The parallel implementation has $n + n - 1 = 2n - 1$ pipeline cycles during the sorting if there are n pipeline processes and n numbers to sort. Each cycle has one compare and exchange operation. Communication consists of one `recv()` and one `send()`, except for the last process, which only has a `recv()`; this minor difference can be ignored. Therefore, each pipeline cycle requires at least

$$t_{\text{comp}} = 1$$

$$t_{\text{comm}} = 2(t_{\text{startup}} + t_{\text{data}})$$

The total execution time, t_{total}, is given by

$$t_{\text{total}} = (t_{\text{comp}} + t_{\text{comm}})(2n - 1) = (1 + 2(t_{\text{startup}} + t_{\text{data}}))(2n - 1)$$

If the results are returned by communication to the left through to the master, a timing diagram is obtained, as shown in Figure 5.16, leading to $3n - 1$ pipeline cycles (Leighton, 1992). Of course, a real parallel program does not operate completely in synchronism, as suggested in these diagrams, because of the delays in the communication media and other variations.

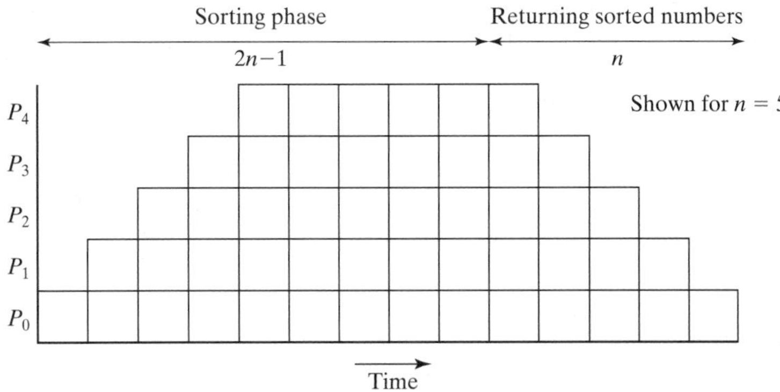

Figure 5.16 Insertion sort with results returned.

5.3.3 Prime Number Generation

A classical method of extracting prime numbers is the sieve of Eratosthenes, described by Eratosthenes of Cyrene more than two thousand years ago (Bokhari, 1987). In this method, a series of all integers is generated from 2. The first number, 2, is prime and kept. All multiples of this number are deleted because they cannot be prime. The process is repeated with each remaining number. The algorithm removes nonprimes, leaving only primes.

For example, suppose we want the prime numbers from 2 to 20. We start with all the numbers:

$$2, 3, 4, 5, 6, 7, 8, 9, 10, 11, 12, 13, 14, 15, 16, 17, 18, 19, 20$$

After considering 2, we get

$$2, 3, \not{4}, 5, \not{6}, 7, \not{8}, 9, \not{1}0, 11, 1\not{2}, 13, 1\not{4}, 15, 1\not{6}, 17, 1\not{8}, 19, 2\not{0}$$

where the numbers with / are marked as not prime and not to be considered further. After considering 3, we get

$$2, 3, \not{4}, 5, \not{6}, 7, \not{8}, \not{9}, 1\not{0}, 11, 1\not{2}, 13, 1\not{4}, 1\not{5}, 1\not{6}, 17, 1\not{8}, 19, \not{2}0$$

Subsequent numbers are considered in a similar fashion. However, to find the primes up to n, it is only necessary to start at numbers up to $\sqrt{n}$. All multiples of numbers greater than $\sqrt{n}$ will have been removed because they are also a multiple of some number equal to or less than $\sqrt{n}$. For example, if $n = 256$, ($\sqrt{n} = 16$), it is not necessary to consider multiples of the number 17 because 17×2 will have been removed as 2×17, 17×3 will have been removed as 3×17, and so on for other numbers beyond 16. Therefore in our example we have all the primes up to 20 by using 2 and 3.

We should mention in passing that the basic method as described is not suitable for finding very large primes (which are of most interest) sequentially because the sequential time complexity is significant and is dominated by the early passes through the list. A simple way to improve the performance is to consider odd numbers only (a way which is left as an exercise).

Sequential Code. A sequential program for this problem usually employs an array with elements initialized to 1 (TRUE) and set to 0 (FALSE) when the index of the element is not a prime number. Letting the square root of `n` be `sqrt_n`, we might have

```
for (i = 2; i <= n; i++)
   prime[i] = 1;                          /* Initialize array */
for (i = 2; i <= sqrt_n; i++)             /* for each number */
   if (prime[i] == 1)                     /* identified as prime */
      for (j = i + i; j <= n; j = j + i)  /* strike out all multiples */
         prime[j] = 0;                    /* includes already done */
```

The elements in the array still set to 1 identify the primes (given by the array indices). Then, the primes are found by examining the array for 1s.

The number of iterations striking out multiples of primes will depend upon the prime. There are $\lfloor n/2 - 1 \rfloor$ multiples of 2, $\lfloor n/3 - 1 \rfloor$ multiples of 3, and so on. Hence, the total sequential time is given by

$$t_s = \left\lfloor \frac{n}{2} - 1 \right\rfloor + \left\lfloor \frac{n}{3} - 1 \right\rfloor + \left\lfloor \frac{n}{5} - 1 \right\rfloor + \ldots + \left\lfloor \frac{n}{\sqrt{n}} - 1 \right\rfloor$$

assuming the computation in each iteration equates to one computational step. The sequential time complexity is $O(n^2)$.

This implementation is very inefficient in that the inner loop will strike out numbers that may have already been deleted by a previous number. In fact, each sweep need only start at i^2 rather than $2i$, where i is the prime number. For example, considering multiples of 5, the sweep can start at 25 (i.e., 5×5) as 5×2, 5×3, and 5×4 will have been considered with previous prime numbers. The analysis of this version of the sieve of Eratosthenes can be found in Quinn (1994).

Parallel Code. Note that the early terms in the preceding expression will dominate the overall time. (There are more multiples of 2 than 3, more multiples of 3 than 4, and so on.) A parallel implementation based upon partitioning, where each process strikes out multiples of one number, will not be very effective. In fact, Quinn (1994) shows that the maximum speedup using this method is limited to about 2.83 irrespective of the number of processors (using certain assumptions). Bohkari (1987) also finds that this method can only use a limited number of processors in a practical situation. There are other ways this problem can be tackled. For example, each process could be assigned a range of numbers and strike out multiples in that range (see Problem 5-11).

A pipelined implementation can be quite effective. First, a series of consecutive numbers is generated that feeds into the first pipeline stage. This stage extracts all multiples of 2 and passes the remaining numbers onto the second stage. The second stage extracts all multiples of 3 and passes the remaining numbers onto the next stage, and so on. The implementation is illustrated in Figure 5.17. There have to be as many stages in the pipeline as prime numbers (unless a "block" partition is used, in which each process handles a group of numbers in the list). The pipeline implementation does not have the disadvantage of reconsidering numbers already identified as prime, as does the simple sequential version.

The code for a process, P_i, could be based upon

```
recv(&x, Pi-1);
/* repeat following for each number */
recv(&number, Pi-1);
if ((number % x) != 0) send(&number, Pi+1);
```

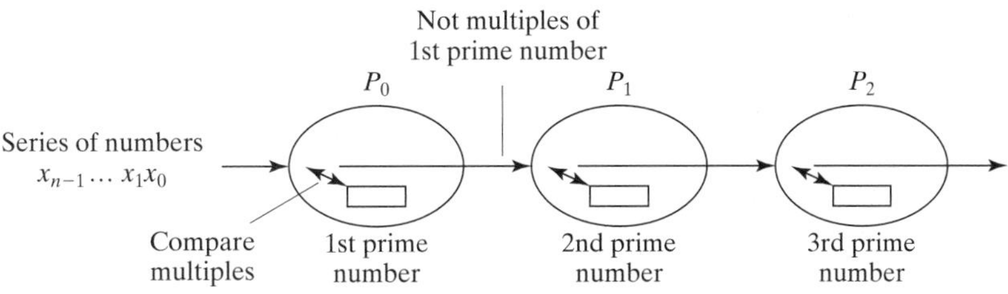

Figure 5.17 Pipeline for sieve of Eratosthenes.

A simple `for` loop is not sufficient for repeating the actions because each process will not receive the same amount of numbers and the amount is not known beforehand. A general technique for dealing with this situation in pipelines is to use a "terminator" message, which is sent at the end of the sequence. Then each process could be

```
recv(&x, Pi-1);
for (i = 0; i < n; i++) {
   recv(&number, Pi-1);
   if (number == terminator) break;
   if (number % x) != 0) send(&number, Pi+1);
}
```

Note. The use of the mod operator, %, to detect whether a number is a multiple of another number is expensive (in execution time). We intentionally avoided its use in the sequential code. Avoiding its use in the parallel code is left as an exercise (Problem 5-7).

Analysis. As with the sorting example, the pipeline implementation is a Type 2. Analysis of the algorithm is similar to the sorting algorithm except that each process in the pipeline will complete fewer steps than the preceding process because it will not receive all the numbers that the preceding process receives.

5.3.4 Solving a System of Linear Equations — Special Case

The final example is Type 3, in which the process can continue with useful work after passing on information. The objective here is to solve a system of linear equations of the so-called *upper-triangular* form:

$$
\begin{aligned}
a_{n-1,0}x_0 + a_{n-1,1}x_1 + a_{n-1,2}x_2 \quad \cdots \quad + a_{n-1,n-1}x_{n-1} &= b_{n-1} \\
&\vdots \\
a_{2,0}x_0 + a_{2,1}x_1 + a_{2,2}x_2 &= b_2 \\
a_{1,0}x_0 + a_{1,1}x_1 &= b_1 \\
a_{0,0}x_0 &= b_0
\end{aligned}
$$

where the *a's* and *b's* are constants and the *x*'s are unknowns to be found. The method used to solve for the unknowns $x_0, x_1, x_2, \ldots, x_{n-1}$ is a simple repeated "back" substitution. First, the unknown x_0 is found from the last equation:

$$x_0 = \frac{b_0}{a_{0,0}}$$

The value obtained for x_0 is substituted into the next equation to obtain x_1:

$$x_1 = \frac{b_1 - a_{1,0}x_0}{a_{1,1}}$$

The values obtained for x_1 and x_0 are substituted into the next equation to obtain x_2:

$$x_2 = \frac{b_2 - a_{2,0}x_0 - a_{2,1}x_1}{a_{2,2}}$$

and so on until all the unknowns are found.

Clearly, this algorithm can be implemented as a pipeline. The first pipeline stage computes x_0 and passes x_0 onto the second stage, which computes x_1 from x_0 and passes both x_0 and x_1 onto the next stage, which computes x_2 from x_0 and x_1, and so on, as shown in Figure 5.18. Each stage is implemented with one process. There are n processes for n equations (i.e., $p = n$). The ith process ($0 < i < p$) receives the values $x_0, x_1, x_2, \ldots, x_{i-1}$ and computes x_i from the equation

$$x_i = \frac{b_i - \sum_{j=0}^{i-1} a_{i,j}x_j}{a_{i,i}}$$

Sequential Code. Given the constants $a_{i,j}$ and b_k stored in arrays `a[][]` and `b[]`, respectively, and the values for unknowns to be stored in an array, `x[]`, the sequential code could be

```
x[0] = b[0]/a[0][0];                    /* x[0] computed separately */
for (i = 1; i < n; i++) {               /* for remaining unknowns */
   sum = 0;
   for (j = 0; j < i; j++)
      sum = sum + a[i][j]*x[j];
   x[i] = (b[i] - sum)/a[i][i];
}
```

Parallel Code. The pseudocode of process P_i ($1 < i < p$) of one pipelined version could be

```
for (j = 0; j < i; j++) {
   recv(&x[j], Pi-1);
   send(&x[j], Pi+1);
}
sum = 0;
for (j = 0; j < i; j++)
   sum = sum + a[i][j]*x[j];
x[i] = (b[i] - sum)/a[i][i];
send(&x[i], Pi+1);
```

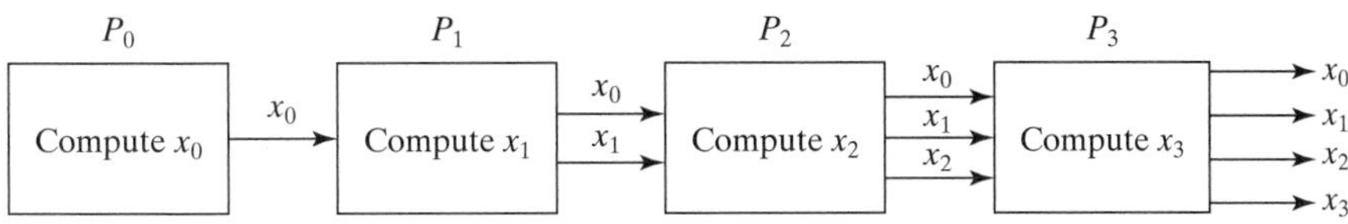

Figure 5.18 Solving an upper triangular set of linear equation using a pipeline.

P_0 simply computes x_0 and passes x_0 on. Now we have additional computations to do after receiving and resending values. This leads to a timing characteristic, as shown in Figure 5.19.[1]

The code for P_i can be written as

```
sum = 0;
for (j = 0; j < i; j++) {
   recv(&x[j], Pi-1);
   send(&x[j], Pi+1);
   sum = sum + a[i][j]*x[j];
}
x[i] = (b[i] - sum)/a[i][i];
send(&x[i], Pi+1);
```

Analysis. For this pipeline, we cannot assume that the computational effort is the same at each pipeline stage (see Figure 5.19). The first process, P_0, performs one divide and one `send()`. The ith process $(0 < i < p - 1)$ performs i `recv()`s, i `send()`s, i multiply/add, one divide/subtract, and a final `send()`, a total of $2i + 1$ communication times and $2i + 2$ computational steps, assuming that multiply, add, divide, and subtract are each one step. The last process, P_{p-1}, performs $p - 1$ `recv()`s, $p - 1$ multiply/add, and one divide/subtract, a total of $p - 1$ communication times and $2p - 1$ computational steps. Figure 5.20 shows the operations in which the communication time and combined multiply/add or divide/subtract are the same. In that case, we get a perfect synchronization of the `send()`s and `recv()`s, and the parallel execution time will be given by the final process plus the $p - 1$ `send()`s plus one divide (to compute x_0).

In essence, the parallel implementation has an $O(n)$ time complexity as $p = n$. The sequential version has a time complexity of $O(n^2)$. The actual speedup is not n, however. It would depend heavily on the actual system parameters. We would expect a computational step, even division, to be much faster than the time of a communication step. To reduce the overhead of communication, we have applied nonblocking send routines to allow the source process to continue as soon as possible with the next computation. The processors will, in general, be constrained by the blocking receives.

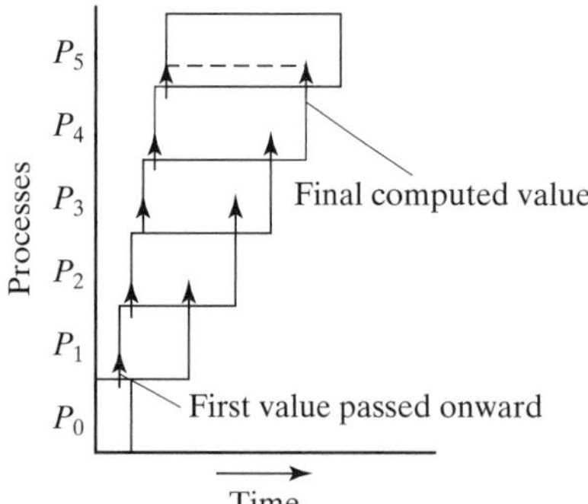

Figure 5.19 Pipeline processing using back substitution.

[1] There is another pipeline solution of implementing back substitution; see Chapter 10.

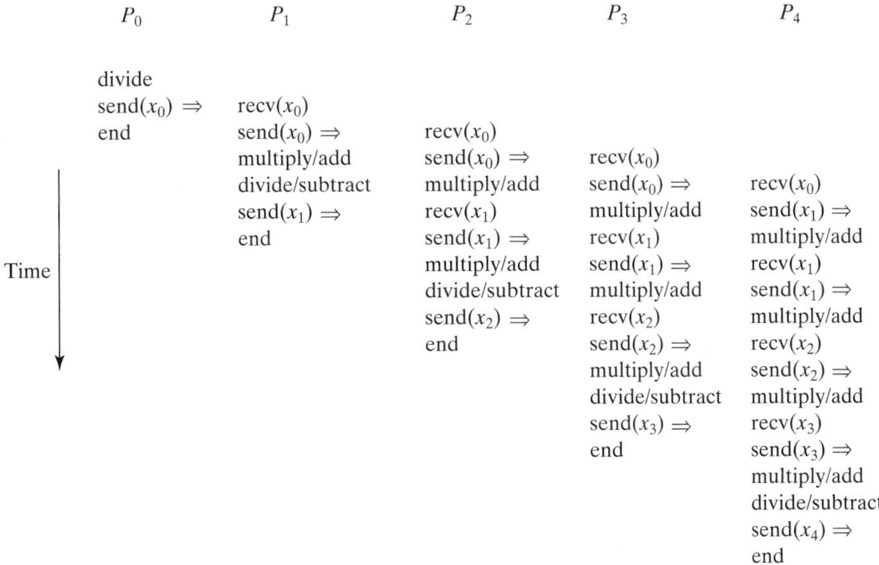

Figure 5.20 Operations in back substitution pipeline.

Final Comments on Solution to Linear Equations. We have studied how to parallelize the solution of a set of linear equations having upper triangular form (which obviously also applies to a set of linear equations having lower triangular form). Such equations do occur in practice; for example, Quinn (1994) describes an upper triangular set of equations for solving for the currents in an electrical circuit consisting of resistors and voltage sources. More important, however, back substitution is an essential component of solving a general set of linear equations when using Gaussian elimination. We describe the solution of linear equations using Gaussian elimination in Chapter 10. Gaussian elimination converts a set of linear equations into triangular form, after which back substitution is used to solve the equations.

5.4 SUMMARY

This chapter introduced the following:

- The pipeline concept and its application areas
- Analysis of pipelines
- Examples illustrating the potential of pipelining, including
  - Insertion sort
  - Prime number generation
  - Solving an upper triangular system of linear equations

FURTHER READING

Pipeline processing most often is seen in specialized very large scale integration (VLSI) components designed to implement arithmetic algorithms. Apart from the simple one-dimensional pipelines with data entered at one side only, more complex pipelines or linear arrays can be devised in which the data is entered from the left and right simultaneously and information moves in both directions. Also, two-dimensional arrays can be devised, especially for implementation in VLSI. We will consider such arrays in Chapter 10 for operating on vectors and matrices. The arrays in that chapter come under the classification of systolic arrays. Pipelines can also be designed to operate upon bits of numbers to achieve various arithmetic operations. Leighton (1992) explores this use of pipelines.

The sieve of Eratosthenes is the fundamental way of finding prime numbers and has been used many times as a programming example in sequential programming texts. Bokhari (known for his early work on the multiprocessor mapping problem) describes the results of using the sieve of Eratosthenes as a benchmark program for a shared memory multiprocessor (Bokhari, 1987). Lansdowne, Cousins, and Wilkinson (1987) continue on this topic and demonstrate a way to program the sieve that improves its performance.

BIBLIOGRAPHY

BOKHARI, S. H. (1987), "Multiprocessing the Sieve of Eratosthenes," *Computer*, Vol. 20, No. 4, pp. 50–58.

CORMEN, T. H., C. E. LEISERSON, AND R. L. RIVEST (1990), *Introduction to Algorithms*, MIT Press, Cambridge, MA.

HENNESSY, J. L., AND D. A. PATTERSON (2003), *Computer Architecture: A Quantitative Approach,* 3rd edition, Morgan Kaufmann, San Mateo, CA.

LANSDOWNE, S. T., R. E. COUSINS, AND D. C. WILKINSON (1987), "Reprogramming the Sieve of Eratosthenes," *Computer*, Vol. 24, No. 8, pp. 90–91.

LEIGHTON, F. T. (1992), *Introduction to Parallel Algorithms and Architectures: Arrays, Trees, Hypercubes*, Morgan Kaufmann, San Mateo, CA.

QUINN, M. J. (1994), *Parallel Computing Theory and Practice*, McGraw-Hill, NY.

WILKINSON, B. (1996), *Computer Architecture Design and Performance*, 2nd edition, Prentice Hall, London.

PROBLEMS

Scientific/Numerical

5-1. Write a parallel program to compute x^{16} using a pipeline approach. Repeat by applying a divide-and-conquer approach. Compare the two methods analytically and experimentally.

5-2. Develop a pipeline solution to compute $\sin\theta$ according to

$$\sin\theta = \theta - \frac{\theta^3}{3!} + \frac{\theta^5}{5!} - \frac{\theta^7}{7!} + \frac{\theta^9}{9!} - \ldots$$

A series of values are input, $\theta_0, \theta_1, \theta_2, \theta_3, \ldots$.

5-3. Modify the program in Problem 5-2 to compute $\cos\theta$ and $\tan\theta$.

5-4. Write a parallel program using pipelining to compute the polynomial

$$f = a_0x^0 + a_1x^1 + a_2x^2 + \ldots + a_{n-1}x^{n-1}$$

to any degree, n, where the a's, x, and n are input. Compare the pipelined approach with the divide-and-conquer approach (Problem 4-8 in Chapter 4).

5-5. Explore the trade-offs of increasing the data partition in the pipeline addition described in Section 5.3.1. Write parallel programs to find the optimum data partition for your system.

5-6. Compare insertion sort (Section 5.3.2) implemented sequentially and implemented as a pipeline, in terms of speedup and time complexity.

5-7. Rework the parallel code for finding prime numbers in Section 5.3.3 to avoid the use of the mod operator to make the algorithm more efficient.

5-8. Radix sort is similar to the bucket sort described in Chapter 4, Section 4.2.1, but specifically uses the bits of the number to identify the bucket into which each number is placed. First the most significant bit is used to place each number into one of two buckets. Then the next-most significant bit is used to place each number in each bucket into one of two buckets, and so on until the least significant bit is reached. Reformulate the algorithm to become a pipeline where all the numbers are passed reordered from stage to stage until finally sorted. Write a parallel program for this method and analyze the method.

5-9. A pipeline consists of four stages, as shown in Figure 5.21. Each stage performs the operation

$$y_{out} = y_{in} + a \times x$$

Determine the overall computation performed.

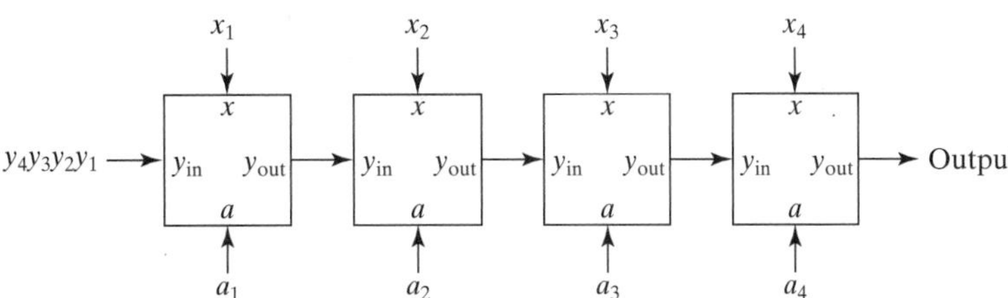

Figure 5.21 Pipeline for Problem 5-9.

5-10. The outer product of two vectors (one-dimensional arrays), A and B, produces a matrix (a two-dimensional array), C, as given by

$$\begin{matrix} & A & B^T & & C \end{matrix}$$

$$AB^T = \begin{bmatrix} a_0 \\ \cdot \\ \cdot \\ a_{n-1} \end{bmatrix} \begin{bmatrix} b_0 & \ldots & b_{n-1} \end{bmatrix} = \begin{bmatrix} a_0b_0 & \ldots & a_0b_{n-1} \\ \cdot & \ldots & \cdot \\ \cdot & \ldots & \cdot \\ a_{n-1}b_0 & \ldots & a_{n-1}b_{n-1} \end{bmatrix}$$

Formulate pipeline implementation for this calculation given that the elements of A (a_0, a_1, …, a_{n-1}) enter together from the left of the pipeline and one element of B is stored in one pipeline stage (P_0 stores b_0, P_1 stores b_1, etc.). Write a parallel program for this problem.

5-11. Compare implementing the sieve of Eratosthenes by each of the following ways:

(i) By the pipeline approach as described in Section 5.3.3

(ii) By having each process strike multiples of a single number

(iii) By dividing the range of numbers into m regions and assigning one region to each process to strike out multiples of prime numbers. Use a master process to broadcast each prime number as found to processes

Perform an analysis of each method.

5-12. (For those with knowledge of computer architecture.) Write a parallel program to model a five-stage RISC processor (reduced instruction set computer), as described in Hennessy and Patterson (2003). The program is to accept a list of machine instructions and shows the flow of instructions through the pipeline, including any pipeline stalls due to dependencies/resource conflicts. Use a single valid bit associated with each register to control access to registers, as described in Wilkinson (1996).

Real Life

5-13. As mentioned in Section 5.1, pipelining could be used to implement an audio frequency-amplitude histogram display in a sound system, as shown in Figure 5.22(a). This application could also be implemented by an embarrassingly parallel, functional decomposition, where each process accepts the audio input directly, as shown in Figure 5.22(b). For each method, write a parallel program to produce a frequency-amplitude histogram display using an audio file as input. Analyze both methods. (Some research may be necessary to develop how to recognize frequencies in a digitized signal.)

5-14. Due to an unprecedented rise in both automobiles and state-mandated auto inspection requirements, the citizens of the state of New Caroltucky have been complaining that it takes too long to complete the inspection process. Typically, the 35-point inspection checks for brakes (six

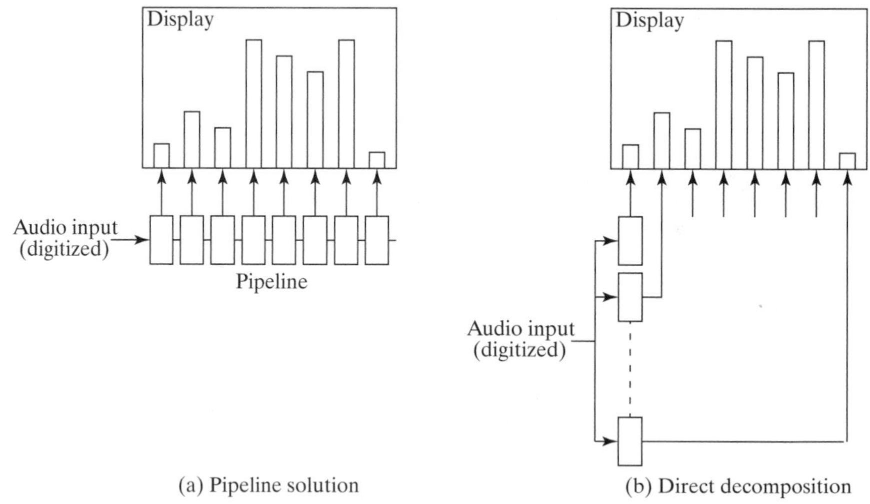

(a) Pipeline solution

(b) Direct decomposition

Figure 5.22 Audio histogram display.

checks there alone: each wheel is pulled and brake lining/pad thickness measured, the master cylinder integrity and performance are checked, and general brakeline leaks and cracks are looked for), along with 29 other time-consuming checks. Once a vehicle begins the inspection process, it typically takes a full hour; some claim they have had to wait in a queue just to get to the inspection bay. Legislators have been told of 72-hour queue delays in extreme cases.

The legislature of New Caroltucky is trying to decide whether the state-run inspection stations need a revamping of their operations. Since the legislature has heard that you are taking a course that includes both sequential and parallel programming concepts, it has decided to hire you to do a simulation of both the present inspection system and a proposed system. You are expected to determine the reduction in total time (queue waiting times plus inspection times) if the state revises the inspection process to implement pipelining instead of the present purely sequential approach.

The present inspection process begins with a driver entering a queue at the inspection station. When an inspector is free, the vehicle at the head of the queue is driven into the inspection bay by the inspector. The inspector then carries out each of the 35 inspections, one at a time. Assuming the vehicle passes, the inspector drives the vehicle out and puts an inspection sticker on it an hour after it was driven into the bay.

The two proposed inspection processes begin the same way, with vehicles entering a single queue. In the proposed new modified-sequential system, there will be three inspectors working in three separate bays doing inspections on three vehicles simultaneously. Each draws a vehicle from the head of the queue when ready to begin a new inspection, but sticks with that vehicle until the inspection is complete. Due to space constraints (there are only three bays), it is not possible to add more inspectors to handle more vehicles simultaneously.

In the proposed new pipelined system, the state will add some automation to the process so that a vehicle is moved automatically through the inspection bays: entering bay no. 1, moving out of it into bay no. 2 as a new vehicle is moved into bay no. 1, and moving out of it and into bay no. 3 as the second vehicle moves into bay no. 2 and a third vehicle moves into bay no. 1. Under this approach there is plenty of room to add additional inspectors in each bay to speed up the inspection steps handled in that bay. For example, if it would help, inspectors could be added for each wheel (each pulls one wheel, measures the pads/shoes, checks for wheel cylinder leaks, replaces that wheel, etc.) plus a fifth who looks for leaks in the lines. Naturally, the state is concerned about cost and efficiency; only the minimum number of inspectors required to achieve the greatest throughput are to be hired. Extra inspectors just standing around will not be tolerated unless eliminating one would cause an increase in the total inspection time once a vehicle enters the first bay.

A table of the tasks assigned to each bay, together with the times each task requires follows. In addition, the loaded labor rate for each inspector (taking into account basic salary, fringe benefits, office and paperwork costs) is given.

Your task is to simulate both new inspection systems to determine several results:

(i) What is the minimum number of inspectors needed under the proposed new pipelined system to achieve the maximum inspection throughput?

(ii) What are the labor costs per inspection performed under each proposed system?

(iii) By how much is the expected inspection delay reduced under each proposed system?

(iv) Without conducting any further simulations (analyzing only what you have obtained from this first part), give an argument for the state investing in additional facilities to expand the number of bays under both systems in order to reduce further the average inspection time. (Naturally, the tasks assigned to each bay under the pipelined approach would have to be changed, but it is assumed that the state inspectors are retrainable.)

Task table

1.	Pull left front wheel	1 minute
2.	Pull left rear wheel	1 minute
3.	Measure the pads/shoes (per wheel)	1 minute
	⋮	
i.	Replace left front wheel	1 minute
j.	Check wheel alignment	5 minutes
k.	Check exhaust system for leaks	1 minute
l.	Check engine emissions at idle	4 minutes
m.	Check engine emissions under load	3 minutes
	⋮	
z.	Remove old sticker and replace with new one	2 minutes
	Total:	60 minutes

Loaded labor rate table

1.	Line inspectors (the "worker bees")	$40,000/yr
2.	Managers (the "drone bees")	$60,000/yr
3.	Senior managers (the "chairman bees")	$80,000/yr

Note 1: One manager is needed for every five (or fraction thereof) line inspectors, as well as a senior manager for every four (or fraction thereof) managers beyond the first two. For example, if there are 13 line inspectors, there would be three managers required plus one senior manager.

Note 2: This is an open-ended problem and requires the student to make some assumptions about arrival rates, randomness of arrival times, and so on, and is probably more suited to a final project in a course than simply being one of several assigned during a term.

5-15. Recall films or news reporting video in which a human chain is passing items from a stockpile area to where they are needed. (Examples include passing filled sandbags hand-to-hand up to the riverbank to build a dike to prevent the river from overflowing its banks, and a bucket-brigade in which buckets of water are being passed hand-to-hand from the water supply to the fire scene.) Given the following data, simulate an N-person chain and compare it to N persons working independently, each moving an item from the stockpile area to where it is needed. The objective is to determine the speedup, that is, the increase in the rate of delivery of the needed items, attainable through the pipelining solution versus that obtainable through the independently operating individuals' solution. Given that there are 1 million items to be moved, determine the speedup for cases in which the number of available people is 150, 300, and 3000.

Data: It is 300 meters from the stockpile to where the items are needed; a human working individually can carry one item at a time and travel at a speed of 1 meter per second carrying that item and 1.5 meters per second when traveling without an item (the return trip). Working cooperatively, the humans stand 1 meter apart and hand the item from hand-to-hand; it takes 1.25 seconds to grab an item from the person behind you, turn, and hand it to the person in front of you. Obviously, if there are only a few humans, the chain, or pipelining, approach is not practical. Similarly, if there are multiples of 300 people, multiple chains can operate in parallel.

Chapter 6

Synchronous Computations

In this chapter, we consider problems solved by a group of separate computations that must at times wait for each other before proceeding, thereby becoming synchronized. A very important class of such applications is called *fully synchronous* applications. In a fully synchronous application, all the processes are synchronized at regular points. Generally, the same computation or operation is applied to a set of data points. All the operations start at the same time in a lock-step manner analogous to SIMD computations. Seventy percent of the first set of applications studied by Fox and colleagues in the ground-breaking Caltech project were classified as synchronous applications (Fox, Williams, and Messina, 1994). First, synchronizing processes are considered and then fully synchronous applications. Finally, we describe how to reduce the amount of synchronization needed in order to increase the computational speed, which we call *partially synchronous* methods. Partially synchronous methods are very important to obtain high computational speed.

6.1 SYNCHRONIZATION

6.1.1 Barrier

Imagine a number of processes computing values. Eventually, each process must wait until all the processes have reached a particular reference point in their computations. This commonly arises when processes need to exchange data and then continue from a known state together. A mechanism is needed that prevents any process from continuing past a specified point until all the processes are ready. The basic mechanism for regulating this situation is called a *barrier*. A barrier is inserted at the point in each process where it must wait. The processes can continue from this point when they have all reached it (or, in some implementations, when a stated number of processes have reached it.) The concept is illustrated in Figure 6.1. In this example, process P_2 is the last to reach the barrier. Therefore, all the other processes must wait and are placed in an inactive state until process P_2 reaches its barrier. Then the inactive processes are awakened (restarted) and all the processes proceed from that point.

Barriers apply to both shared memory and message-passing systems. We will discuss barriers in shared memory systems in Chapters 8 and 9. In message-passing systems, barriers are often provided with library routines. For example, MPI has the barrier routine, `MPI_Barrier()`, with a named communicator as the only parameter. `MPI_Barrier()` is called by each process in the group, blocking until every member of the group has reached the barrier call and only returning then. Although not in MPI, barriers can be defined where the number of processes that must reach the barrier to release the processes is specified and can be less than the total number of processes in the group, but using this feature would be rare. Barriers are naturally synchronous, and message tags are not used.

Figure 6.2 illustrates the library call approach for a barrier. Since a single barrier call is reused for every situation in which a barrier is required, it is essential for barriers to match with the correct barrier in other processes. This characteristic has to be ensured by the implementation. The way that the barrier call is implemented will depend upon the implementer, who in turn will be influenced by the underlying architecture. Certain underlying architectures will suggest specific efficient implementations. As usual, MPI does not specify internal implementation. However, we need to know something about the implementation to assess the complexity of the barrier. Let us review some of the common implementations of a barrier.

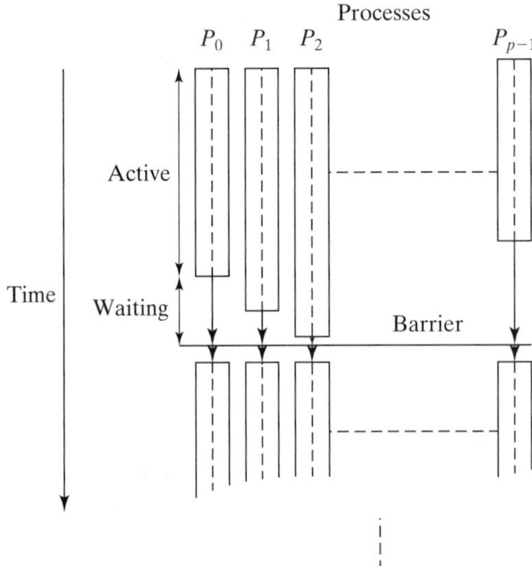

Figure 6.1 Processes reaching the barrier at different times.

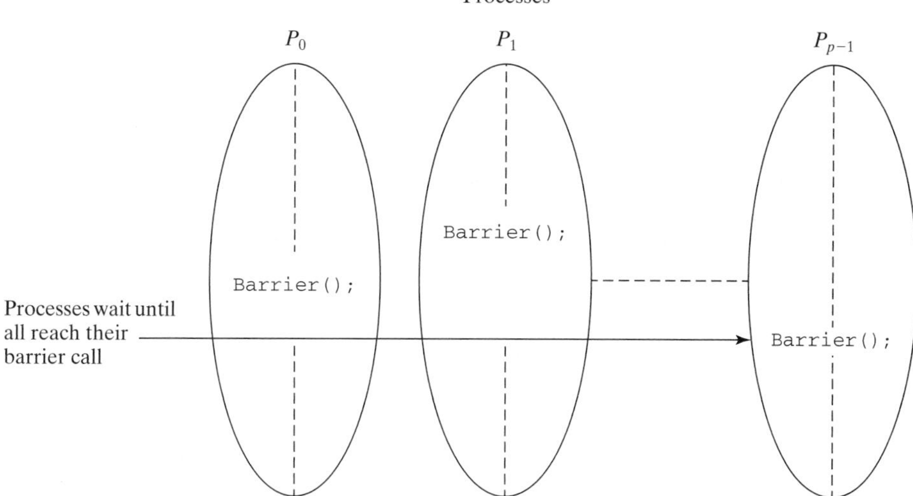

Figure 6.2 Library call barriers.

6.1.2 Counter Implementation

Figure 6.1 suggests one implementation of a barrier, a centralized counter implementation (sometimes called a *linear barrier*), as shown in Figure 6.3. A single counter is used to count the number of processes reaching the barrier. Before any process reaches its barrier, the counter is first initialized to zero. Then each process calling a barrier will increment the counter and check whether the correct number has been reached, say p. If the counter has

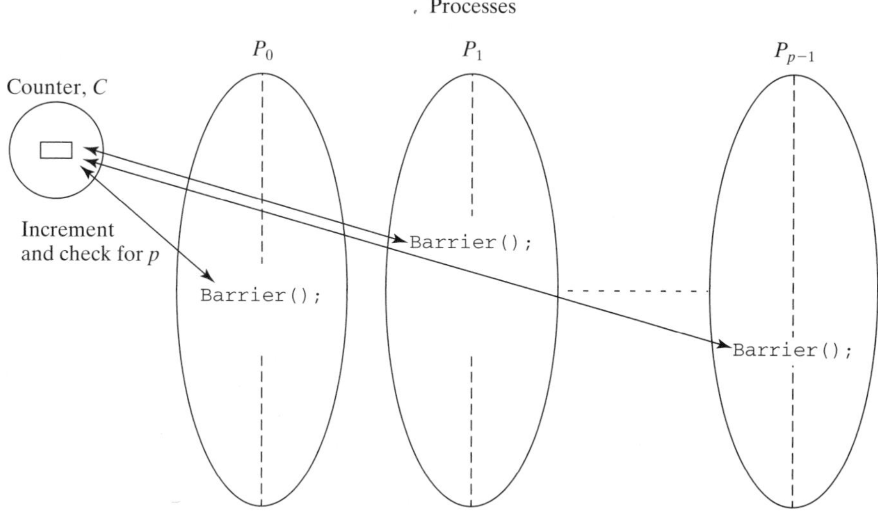

Figure 6.3 Barrier using a centralized counter.

not reached p, the process is stalled or placed in an inactive or "idle" state. If the counter has reached p, the process and all other processes waiting for the counter are released. A mechanism must be in place to release idle processes.

Counter-based barriers often have two phases, an arrival phase (or trapping) and a departure (or release) phase. A process enters the arrival phase and does not leave it until all processes have arrived in this phase. Then processes move to the departure phase and are released. Good implementations of a barrier must take into account that a barrier might be used more than once in a process. A process may enter the barrier for a second time before previous processes have left it for the first time. The two-phase design handles this scenario.

Suppose the master process maintains the barrier counter. The master process counts the messages received from "slave" processes when they reach their barrier during the arrival phase and releases slave processes in the departure phase. The code using (locally) blocking `send()`s and `recv()`s and counting using `for` loops could be of the form

```
for (i = 0; i < p; i++)       /* count slaves as they reach their barrier */
   recv(P_any);
for (i = 0; i < p; i++)       /* release slaves */
   send(P_i);
```

The variable `i` is the barrier counter. The barrier code for the slave processes is simply

```
send(P_master);
recv(P_master);
```

The complete arrangement is illustrated in Figure 6.4. Messages can be received from slave processes in any order and are accepted as received, but messages are sent to slave processes in numeric order in this code. Our implementation allows the barrier to be called repeatedly in a process because we have a clearly defined arrival phase that all processes must reach before continuing on to a clearly defined departure phase. However, note that locally blocking `send()`s do not stop the process. The slave processes will move directly to

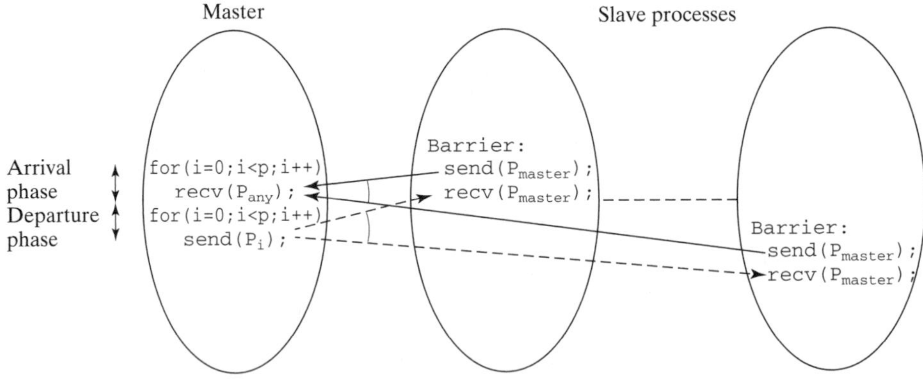

Figure 6.4 Barrier implementation in a message-passing system.

their `recv()`s after the message has been constructed for sending but before it has been received. The `recv()`s are blocking in that the processes will not move out of their departure phase until they receive their messages. The arrival phase could also be implemented with a gather routine, and the departure phase with a broadcast routine. The `send()`s and `recv()`s in Figure 6.4 do not have specific data in the message. A simple NULL message could be sent.

6.1.3 Tree Implementation

Barriers implemented with a counter have a time complexity of $O(p)$ with p processes (both the computational complexity of the master process and the communication complexity, i.e., number of messages). A more efficient barrier can be implemented using the decentralized tree construction introduced in Chapter 2 (Section 2.3.4). Suppose there are eight processes, P_0, P_1, P_2, P_3, P_4, P_5, P_6, and P_7. Essentially, the algorithm performs as follows:

First stage: P_1 sends message to P_0 (when P_1 reaches its barrier)
P_3 sends message to P_2 (when P_3 reaches its barrier)
P_5 sends message to P_4 (when P_5 reaches its barrier)
P_7 sends message to P_6 (when P_7 reaches its barrier)

Second stage: P_2 sends message to P_0 (P_2 and P_3 have reached their barrier)
P_6 sends message to P_4 (P_6 and P_7 have reached their barrier)

Third stage: P_4 sends message to P_0 (P_4, P_5, P_6, and P_7 have reached their barrier)
P_0 terminates arrival phase (when P_0 reaches barrier and has received message from P_4)

The processes now must be released from the barrier, which can be done with a reverse tree construction. The complete barrier construction is shown in Figure 6.5. In this case, the algorithm only involves sending and receiving messages without explicit computations. An eight-process algorithm with the arrival phase and departure phase both implemented with trees requires $2\log 8$ steps, or, in general, $2\log p$ steps, a communication time complexity of $O(\log p)$.

6.1.4 Butterfly Barrier

The tree construction can be developed into a so-called butterfly, in which pairs of processes synchronize at each stage in the following manner (assuming eight processes as an example):

First stage $P_0 \leftrightarrow P_1, P_2 \leftrightarrow P_3, P_4 \leftrightarrow P_5, P_6 \leftrightarrow P_7$
Second stage $P_0 \leftrightarrow P_2, P_1 \leftrightarrow P_3, P_4 \leftrightarrow P_6, P_5 \leftrightarrow P_7$
Third stage $P_0 \leftrightarrow P_4, P_1 \leftrightarrow P_5, P_2 \leftrightarrow P_6, P_3 \leftrightarrow P_7$

as shown in Figure 6.6 with two "links" between synchronizing processes, which implies two pairs of `send()/recv()`. This would be used if data were exchanged between the

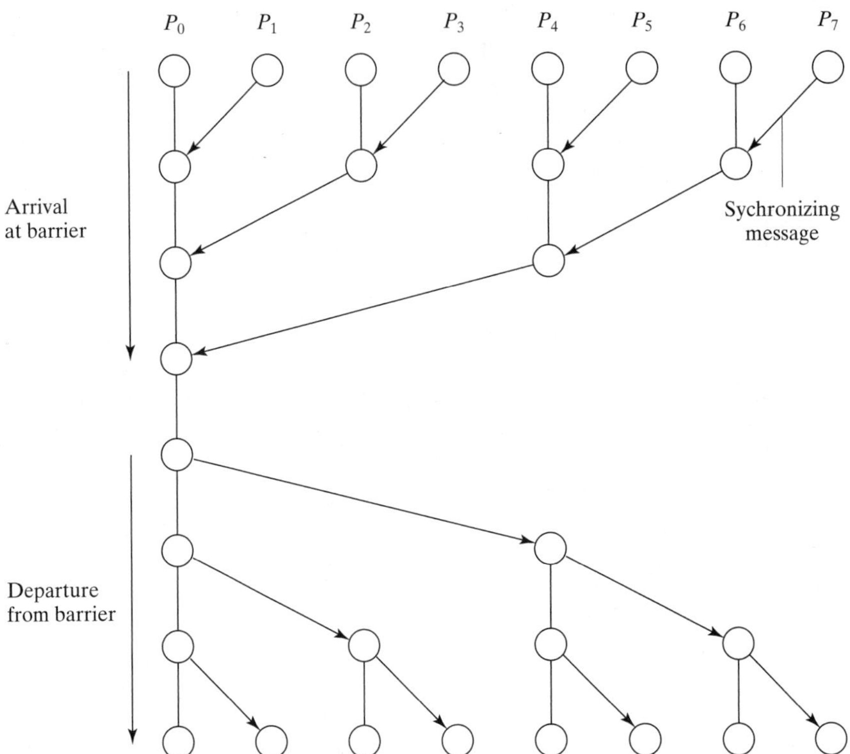

Figure 6.5 Tree barrier.

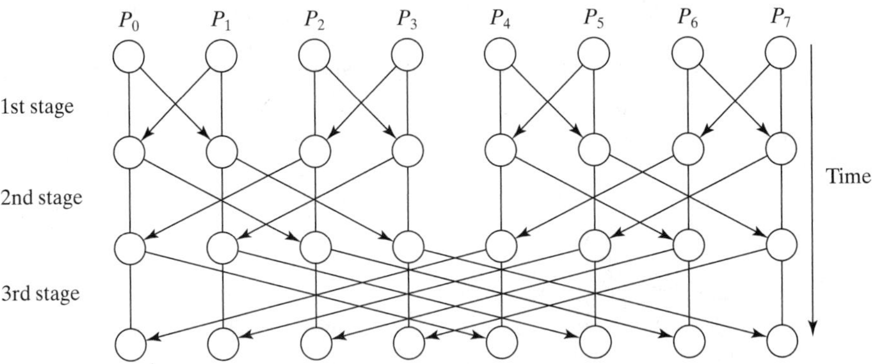

Figure 6.6 Butterfly construction.

processes (as in other applications of the butterfly). For a barrier, each synchronization requires only a single pair of `send()`/`recv()`. After all the synchronizing stages, each process will have been synchronized with each other process, and all processes can continue.

At stage s, process i synchronizes with process $i + 2^{s-1}$ if p is a power of 2. If p is not a power of 2, the communication is between process i and process $(i + 2^{s-1}) \bmod p$. With p processes, the butterfly has $\log p$ steps (p being a power of 2), half the number of steps of the tree implementation, but the same communication time complexity of $O(\log p)$.

6.1.5 Local Synchronization

Some problems can be formulated so that processes need only be synchronized with a few other processes, and not the complete set of processes working on the problem. This often comes about in algorithms where processes are organized as a mesh or a pipeline, and a process needs only to be synchronized to its neighbors. The message-passing technique used in Section 6.1.2 can be reduced to sending messages between individual processes that need to be synchronized. For example, suppose a process P_i needs to be synchronized and to exchange data with process P_{i-1} and process P_{i+1} before continuing. The code for this could be

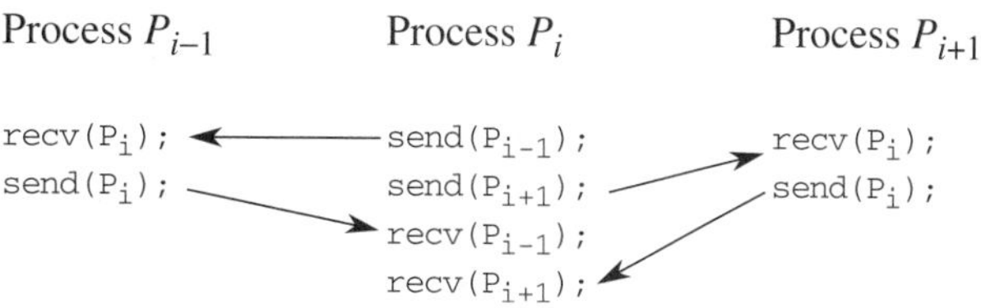

Process P_{i-1}
Process P_i
Process P_{i+1}
recv(P_i);
send(P_i);
send(P_{i-1});
send(P_{i+1});
recv(P_{i-1});
recv(P_{i+1});
recv(P_i);
send(P_i);

Note that this is not a perfect three-process barrier because process P_{i-1} will only synchronize with P_i and continue as soon as P_i allows. Similarly, process P_{i+1} only synchronizes with P_i. However, in many applications this synchronization will be sufficient.

6.1.6 Deadlock

The tree, butterfly, and local synchronization algorithms described here employ synchronous routines to obtain the synchronization between the processes. When a pair of processes send and receive from each other, deadlock may occur. Deadlock will occur using synchronous routines (or blocking routines without sufficient buffering) if both processes perform the send first. This is because neither will return; they will wait for matching receives that are never reached. Clearly, a solution to this problem is to arrange for one process to receive first and then send and the other process to send first and then receive. In situations where even-numbered processes only communicate with odd-numbered processes, and vice versa, as in a linear pipeline, deadlock can be avoided by arranging for the even-numbered processes to perform their sends first and the odd-numbered processes to perform their receives first.

Since bidirectional data transfers are very common, a combined blocking `sendrecv()` routine can be provided in which the internal implementation details avoid deadlock. A `sendrecv()` routine sends a message to a destination process and receives a message from a source process. For flexibility, the source and destination may be different or may be the same process. MPI provides this type of routine `MPI_Sendrecv()`. It also provides `MPI_Sendrecv_replace()`, which uses a single buffer for the sending and receiving message, replacing the send message with receive message. These routines should be implemented so that deadlock cannot occur. Applying `sendrecv()` to the preceding example would simply be

Process P_{i-1}		Process P_i		Process P_{i+1}
`sendrecv(P_i);`	↔	`sendrecv(P_i-1);`		
		`sendrecv(P_i+1);`	↔	`sendrecv(P_i);`

As a matter of detail and to give credence to those who object to the sometimes overwhelming MPI parameter list, the `MPI_Sendrecv()` routine has 12 parameters:

```
MPI_Sendrecv(sendbuf, sendcount, sendtype, dest, sendtag, recvbuf,
             recvcount, recvtype, source, recvtag, comm, status)
```

These parameters are essentially a concatenation of the parameter lists of `MPI_Send()` and `MPI_Recv()`.

6.2 SYNCHRONIZED COMPUTATIONS

6.2.1 Data Parallel Computations

A form of computation that implicitly has synchronization requirements is the *data parallel* computation. In a data parallel computation, the same operation is performed on different data elements simultaneously; that is, in parallel. Data parallel programming is very convenient for two reasons. The first is its ease of programming (essentially only one program). The second is that it can scale easily to larger problems. Many numeric and some non-numeric problems can be cast in a data parallel form. SIMD (single instruction stream multiple data stream) computers, briefly mentioned in Chapter 1, Section 1.3.4, operate as data parallel computers by having the same instruction executed by different processors but on different data, all in synchronism. In an SIMD computer, the synchronism is built into the hardware; the processors operate in lock-step fashion.

A simple example of a computation that can be formed into a data parallel computation is to add the same constant to each element of an array:

```
for (i = 0; i < n; i++)
  a[i] = a[i] + k;
```

The statement `a[i] = a[i] + k` could be executed simultaneously by multiple processors, each using a different index `i` ($0 < i < n$), as illustrated in Figure 6.7. On an SIMD computer the same instruction, equivalent to `a[] = a[] + k`, would be sent to each processor simultaneously.

A special "parallel" construct exists in parallel programming languages to specify data parallel operations — namely, the `forall` statement. The `forall` statement

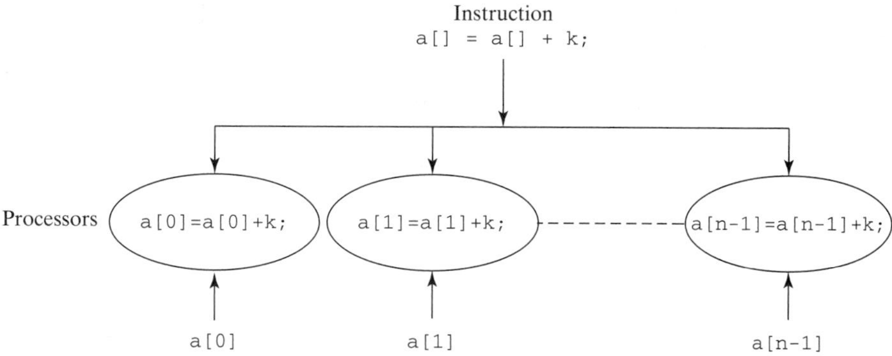

Figure 6.7 Data parallel computation.

```
forall (i = 0; i < n; i++) {
   body
}
```

states that n instances of the statements of the body can be executed simultaneously. One value of the loop variable `i` is valid in each instance of the body; the first instance has `i` = 0, the next `i` = 1, and so on. The loop variable can be used within the body to "personalize" each copy (e.g., to access different elements of an array). To illustrate this, we can add `k` to each element of an array, `a`, by writing

```
forall (i = 0; i < n; i++)
   a[i] = a[i] + k;
```

In all cases, each instance of the body must be independent of the other instances. (We explore how this can be established mathematically in Chapter 8.) The term `forall` is unfortunate, since there is no iteration here; the notation simply states that there are n copies of the body, each assigned a different value of `i`.

Although we do not consider programs for SIMD computers, the data parallel technique can be applied to multiprocessors and multicomputers. On such parallel computers, instances of the body can be executed on different processors, but the whole construct will not be completed until all instances of the body have been executed. Hence, a form of barrier is implicit within the `forall` construct. On a message-passing computer using library routines, the `forall` construct is not generally available and an explicit barrier is needed. For example, to add `k` to the elements of an array in the SPMD (single-program multiple-data) style of programming, we might write

```
i = myrank;
a[i] = a[i] + k;          /* body */
barrier(mygroup);
```

where `myrank` is a process rank between 0 and $n - 1$. It is assumed that each process has access to the required element of the array. Normally, having such a small body would not be efficient because of the barrier overhead.

We can construct much more complex SIMD computations than adding a constant to the elements of an array. Hillis and Steele (1986) describe several data parallel algorithms, including those for summing numbers, sorting, and operating on linked lists. Some SIMD computers and data parallel algorithms operate on bit patterns rather than complete numbers. Many of the image-processing algorithms described in Chapter 12 are data parallel algorithms operating upon bit patterns.

Prefix Sum Problem. An example of a data parallel algorithm is the *prefix sum* problem. In the *prefix sum* problem, given a list of numbers, $x_0, \ldots, x_{n-1}$, all the partial summations (i.e., x_0; $x_0 + x_1$; $x_0 + x_1 + x_2$; $x_0 + x_1 + x_2 + x_3$; …) are computed. The prefix calculation can also be defined with associative operations other than addition; for example, multiplication, maximum, minimum, string concatenation, and logical (Boolean) operations (AND, OR, exclusive OR, etc.). It is widely studied in connection with various computational models. It does have practical applications in areas such as processor allocation, data compaction, sorting, and polynomial evaluation (Wagner and Han, 1986).

The sequential code for the prefix sum problem could be

```
sum[0] = x[0];
for (i = 1; i < n; i++)
  sum[i] = sum[i-1] + x[i];
```

This is an O(n) algorithm.

Figure 6.8 shows a data parallel method of adding all the partial sums of 16 numbers described by Hillis and Steele (1986). This method has a multiple treelike construction and computes the partial sums in the locations $x[i]$ ($0 \le i < 16$). The original numbers are lost. (A separate array could be used to save the numbers.) A different number of computations occurs in each step. First, 15 (16 – 1) additions occur in which $x[i-1]$ is added to $x[i]$ for $1 \le i < 16$. Then 14 (16 – 2) additions occur in which $x[i-2]$ is added to $x[i]$ for $2 \le i < 16$. Then 12 (16 – 4) additions occur in which $x[i-4]$ is added to $x[i]$ for $4 \le i < 16$.

In general, the method requires $\log n$ steps, where there are n numbers (and n is a power of 2). In step j ($0 \le j < \log n$), $n - 2^j$ additions occur in which $x[i - 2^j]$ is added to $x[i]$ for $2^j \le i < n$. Hence, sequential code might be written as

```
for (j = 0; j < log(n); j++)          /* at each step */
  for (i = 2^j; i < n; i++)           /* add to accumulating sum */
    x[i] = x[i] + x[i - 2^j];
```

Because SIMD computers must send the same instruction to all processors, a mechanism is provided to inhibit certain processors from executing the instruction. To indicate this, parallel code might be written as

```
for (j = 0; j < log(n); j++)          /* at each step */
  forall (i = 0; i < n; i++)          /* add to accumulating sum */
    if (i >= 2^j) x[i] = x[i] + x[i - 2^j];
```

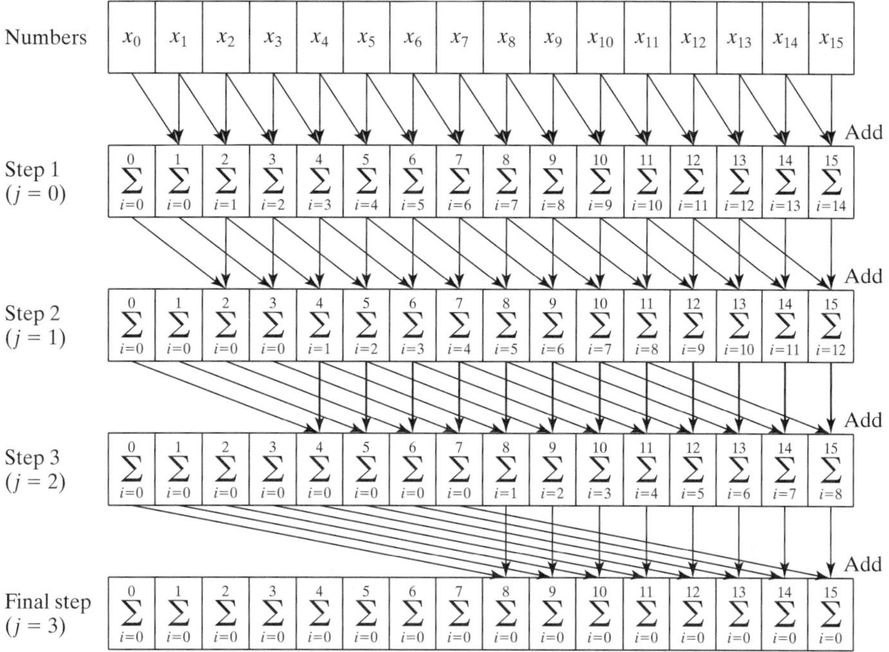

Figure 6.8 Data parallel prefix sum operation.

which uses a maximum of $n - 1$ processors and requires $\log n$ steps. The time complexity of this parallel algorithm is $O(\log n)$ in terms of both computations and communications. The efficiency is less than 1 because fewer processors are used at each step.

There is a prefix sum algorithm using a balanced tree that is also an $O(\log n)$ algorithm but requires $O(n)$ operations in total, instead of $O(n \log n)$ operations in total. See JáJá (1992) for a description of the balanced tree prefix sum algorithm.

6.2.2 Synchronous Iteration

Iteration whereby an operation is performed repeatedly is a key technique in sequential programming. Constructs are provided in all programming languages for iteration (e.g., `for`, `while`, or `do-while`). Iteration is a powerful tool for solving numerical problems, especially those which are not amenable to closed numeric solutions. Generally a result obtained on one iteration is used in the next iteration to get closer to the actual solution. The process is repeated until a sufficiently close solution is obtained. The basic idea of the iterative method is sequential in nature and appears not suited to parallel implementation. However, parallel implementation can be successfully employed to iterative methods when there are multiple independent instances of the iteration. Sometimes this is part of the problem specification. Sometimes we must rearrange the problem to obtain multiple independent instances.

The term *synchronous iteration* or *synchronous parallelism* is used to describe solving a problem by iteration where each iteration is composed of several processes that start together at the beginning of each iteration and the next iteration cannot begin until all the processes have finished the preceding iteration. The `forall` construct could be used to specify the parallel bodies of the synchronous iteration:

```
for (j = 0; j < n; j++)              /* for each synchronous iteration */
   forall (i = 0; i < p; i++) {      /* p processes each executing */
      body(i);                       /* body using specific value of i */
   }
```

In our case for an SPMD program, we will need a specific barrier:

```
for (j = 0; j < n; j++) {            /* for each synchronous iteration */
   i = myrank;                       /* find value of i to be used */
   body(i);                          /* body using specific value of i */
   barrier(mygroup);
}
```

Let us look at some specific synchronous iteration examples.

6.3 SYNCHRONOUS ITERATION PROGRAM EXAMPLES

6.3.1 Solving a System of Linear Equations by Iteration

We saw in Chapter 5, Section 5.3.4, how to solve a system of linear equations if it was of a special triangular form. Suppose the equations were not specifically of that form, but of a general form with n equations and n unknowns

$$\begin{array}{llll}
a_{n-1,0}x_0 + a_{n-1,1}x_1 + a_{n-1,2}x_2 & \cdots & + a_{n-1,n-1}x_{n-1} & = b_{n-1} \\
 & \vdots & & \\
a_{2,0}x_0 + a_{2,1}x_1 + a_{2,2}x_2 & \cdots & + a_{2,n-1}x_{n-1} & = b_2 \\
a_{1,0}x_0 + a_{1,1}x_1 + a_{1,2}x_2 & \cdots & + a_{1,n-1}x_{n-1} & = b_1 \\
a_{0,0}x_0 + a_{0,1}x_1 + a_{0,2}x_2 & \cdots & + a_{0,n-1}x_{n-1} & = b_0
\end{array}$$

where the unknowns are x_0, x_1, x_2, … x_{n-1}. One way to solve these equations for the unknowns is by iteration. By rearranging the ith equation $(0 \le i < n)$:

$$a_{i,0}x_0 + a_{i,1}x_1 + a_{i,2}x_2 \quad \cdots \quad + a_{i,n-1}x_{n-1} \quad = b_i$$

to

$$x_i = (1/a_{i,i})[b_i - (a_{i,0}x_0 + a_{i,1}x_1 + a_{i,2}x_2 \cdots a_{i,i-1}x_{i-1} + a_{i,i+1}x_{i+1} \cdots + a_{i,n-1}x_{n-1})]$$

or

$$x_i = \frac{1}{a_{i,i}}\left[b_i - \sum_{j \ne i} a_{i,j}x_j\right]$$

$(0 < i < n, 0 < j < n)$. This equation gives x_i in terms of the other unknowns and can be used as an iteration formula for each of the unknowns to obtain better approximations.

The iterative method described here is called a *Jacobi iteration*. In this method, all the values of x are updated together. (Alternative methods, such as Gauss-Seidel, are described in Chapter 11.) It can be proven that the Jacobi method will converge if the diagonal values of a have an absolute value greater than the sum of the absolute values of the other a's on the row (the array of a's is *diagonally dominant*). Therefore, convergence is guaranteed if

$$\sum_{j \neq i} |a_{i,j}| < |a_{i,i}|$$

This condition is a sufficient but not a necessary condition. The method may converge even if the array is not diagonally dominant. However, the iteration formula will not work if any of the diagonal elements are zero because it would require dividing by zero.

An iterative method begins with an initial guess for all the unknowns. A possible initialization would be to set $x_i = b_i$. Then calculate new values for the unknowns using the iteration equation. These values are substituted into the iteration formulas; then the action is repeated. The iterations are continued until sufficiently accurate values for all the unknowns are obtained (assuming that the iteration formula converges). There are also "direct" methods for solving linear equations, which we discuss in Chapter 11. Iterative methods are applicable when such direct methods require excessive computations. They also have the advantage of small memory requirements, but the disadvantage is that they may not always converge.

Termination. Termination can be especially problematic in parallel formulations. We look at this topic in detail in Chapter 7 in the context of load balancing. A simple, commonly used approach is to compare the values computed in each iteration to the values obtained from the preceding iteration, and then to terminate the computation in the tth iteration when all values are within a given tolerance; that is, when

$$\left| x_i^t - x_i^{t-1} \right| < \text{error tolerance}$$

for all i, where x_i^t is the value of x_i after the tth iteration, and x_i^{t-1} is the value of x_i after the $(t - 1)$th iteration. However, this does not guarantee the solution to that accuracy. Suppose the error tolerance is 1 percent and a value is computed to 1 percent of its last computed value. This is not 1 percent of the exact value of the solution. If the calculation is converging, we would expect the next computation of x_i to be less than 1 percent different from the present value, but it could be 0.9999 percent different from the present value. The next value could be 0.9998 percent different. We can see that errors might compound and the computed value could be very significantly different from the final exact value. This is illustrated in Figure 6.9 for a hypothetical problem. In addition, errors of one computed value will affect the accuracy of other computed values that use it in their calculations.

Pacheco (1997) suggests a more complex vector termination condition:

$$\sqrt{\sum_{i=0}^{n-1} (x_i^t - x_i^{t-1})^2} < \text{error tolerance}$$

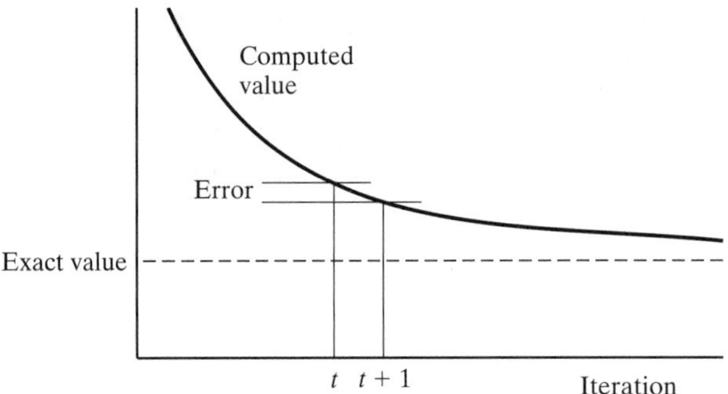

Figure 6.9 Convergence rate.

Bertsekas and Tsitsiklis (1989) suggest the termination condition

$$\left|\sum_{j=0}^{n-1} a_{i,j}x_j^t - b_i\right| < \text{error tolerance}$$

for all i. This method only uses the currently computed values and not values from the preceding iteration. For all equations, it essentially computes the left side of the equation and compares the result with the constant right side. This is not computationally intensive, since the summation without $a_{i,i}x_i$ has already been computed during the iteration. A full treatment of convergence and the effectiveness of different termination formulas can be found in texts on numerical methods.

Whatever method, since the iteration may not terminate, iterations should be stopped when a maximum number of iterations has been reached. There is a trade-off between using a complex termination calculation with potentially fewer iterations and using a less complex termination calculation with more iterations. It may be a good strategy to allow a number of iterations between checking for termination. Since the parallel formulation requires each iteration to use all the values of the preceding iteration, the calculations have to be synchronized globally. Jacobi iterations can be slow to converge. Problem 6-12 explores the convergence characteristics of Jacobi iterations empirically. Faster methods are considered in Chapter 10.

Sequential Code. Given the arrays `a[][]` and `b[]` holding the constants in the equations, `x[]` holding the unknowns, and a fixed number of iterations, the code might look like the following:

```
for (i = 0; i < n; i++)
   x[i] = b[i];                                   /*initialize unknowns*/
for (iteration = 0; iteration < limit; iteration++) {
   for (i = 0; i < n; i++) {                      /* for each unknown */
      sum = 0;
      for (j = 0; j < n; j++)            /* compute summation of a[][]x[] */
         if (i != j) sum = sum + a[i][j] * x[j];
      new_x[i] = (b[i] - sum) / a[i][i];          /* compute unknown */
   }
   for (i = 0; i < n; i++)
      x[i] = new_x[i];                            /* update values */
}
```

It is important to have efficient sequential code. There are other ways the sequential algorithm could be coded that may be preferred for efficiency. We have used an `if` statement so as not to use `a[i][i] * x[j]` in the summation of `a[i][j] * x[j]`. Another solution to avoid the overhead of repeated `if` statements would be to include `a[i][j] * x[j]` in the loop and subtract it afterwards (or before):

```
for (i = 0; i < n; i++)
  x[i] = b[i];                                  /*initialize unknowns*/
for (iteration = 0; iteration < limit; iteration++) {
  for (i = 0; i < n; i++) {                     /* for each unknown */
    sum = -a[i][i] * x[i];
    for (j = 0; j < n; j++)                     /* compute summation */
      sum = sum + a[i][j] * x[j];
    new_x[i] = (b[i] - sum) / a[i][i];          /* compute unknown */
  }
  for (i = 0; i < n; i++) x[i] = new_x[i];      /* update values */
}
```

Yet another solution is to have two loops for computing the summation, the first from 0 to $i-1$ and the second from $i+1$ to $n-1$. We prefer our second version as a reasonably readable solution.

Parallel Code. Suppose that one process is allocated for each unknown ($p = n$) and each process will iterate the same number of times. On each iteration, the newly computed values of the unknowns need to be broadcast to all the other processes. In sequential code, the iteration `for` loop is a natural barrier between iterations. In parallel code, we need to insert a specific barrier. Process P_i could be of the form

```
x[i] = b[i];                                /*initialize unknown*/
for (iteration = 0; iteration < limit; iteration++) {
  sum = -a[i][i] * x[i];
  for (j = 0; j < n; j++)                   /* compute summation */
    sum = sum + a[i][j] * x[j];
  new_x[i] = (b[i] - sum) / a[i][i];        /* compute unknown */
  broadcast_receive(&new_x[i]);             /* broadcast value */
  global_barrier();                         /* wait for all processes */
}
```

The broadcast routine, `broadcast_receive()`, sends the newly computed value of `x[i]` from process i to every other process and collects data broadcast from the other processes. A single broadcast will not work here since there must be matching "broadcast receives" in each process for each newly computed value. Hence, `broadcast_receive()` would have to consist of n broadcasts, each with specific parameters.

An alternative simple solution is to return to basic `send()`s and `recv()`s, for `broadcast_receive()`; that is, process i might have

```
for (j = 0; j < n; j++) if (i != j) send(&x[i], Pj);
for (j = 0; j < n; j++) if (i != j) recv(&x[j], Pj);
```

In MPI, it is allowable to send a message to yourself so that the `if` construct could be removed. A separate barrier may not be necessary since the process would not continue until it has received all the newly computed values.

Earlier, we saw how a butterfly barrier would naturally broadcast and gather values in one composite construction. The butterfly could be coded for our problem. However, since its efficiency depends upon the underlying architecture, a predefined routine would be helpful. MPI has such a routine, called `MPI_Allgather`. Allgather is illustrated in Figure 6.10. The same number of items are gathered from each process. The number is defined in the parameter list. A variation of `MPI_Allgather` called `MPI_Allgatherv` allows a different number of items to be gathered from each process.

Typically, we want to iterate until the approximations are sufficiently close, rather than for a fixed number of times (which may not provide a sufficiently accurate solution). Each process could check its own computed value with, say,

```
x[i] = b[i];                                    /*initialize unknown*/
iteration = 0;
do {
   iteration++;
   sum = -a[i][i] * x[i];
   for (j = 0; j < n; j++)                      /* compute summation */
      sum = sum + a[i][j] * x[j];
   new_x[i] = (b[i] - sum) / a[i][i];           /* compute unknown */
   broadcast_receive(&new_x[i]);                /* broadcast value and wait */
} while (tolerance() && (iteration < limit));
```

where `tolerance()` returns `FALSE` if ready to terminate; otherwise it returns `TRUE`.

The simplest mechanism is to allow the processes to continue until they have all converged. Then `tolerance()` is a routine returning `FALSE` to each process in the same iteration, so that they all stop together. If we were to stop each process as it reaches its solution to the stated tolerance, the processes would have different numbers of iterations. In that case, some care would be needed here to avoid deadlock because broadcast routines broadcast to all the processes in a group and expect all the processes to have matching routines.

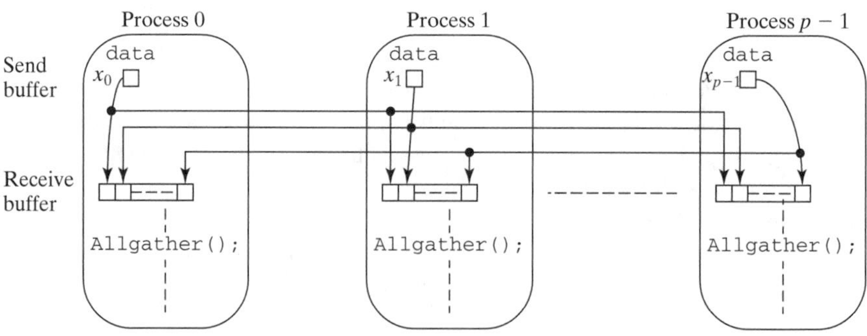

Figure 6.10 Allgather operation.

Partitioning. As with all parallel formulations, the number of processors is usually much smaller than the number of data items to be processed (computing unknowns in this case). We would normally partition the problem so that the processors take on more than one data item. In the problem at hand, each process can be responsible for computing a group of unknowns. Typically, we would allocate unknowns to processors in simple increasing order; that is, with p processors and n unknowns. Processor P_0 would be given the task of computing the unknowns x_0 to $x_{(n/p)-1}$, processor P_1 unknowns $x_{n/p}$ to $x_{(2n/p)-1}$, and so on, assuming that n/p is an integer — this is the so-called *block* allocation used in Chapter 4 for adding numbers. There is usually no advantage here in a *cyclic* allocation where processors are allocated one unknown in order; that is, processor P_0 is allocated $x_0, x_p, x_{2p}, \ldots, x_{((n/p)-1)p}$, processor P_1 is allocated $x_1, x_{p+1}, x_{2p+1}, \ldots, x_{((n/p)-1)p+1}$, and so on. Indeed, cyclic allocation may be disadvantageous because the indices of unknowns have to be computed in a more complex way, and it may require more effort to group the unknowns into one message.

Analysis. The sequential execution time of this problem will be given by the time of one iteration multiplied by the number of iterations. Suppose there are τ iterations. There are two loops, one nested inside the other. The outer loop has n iterations, and the inner loop has n^2 iterations in total. Each inner loop consists of one multiplication and one addition; that is, two computational steps. The outer loop has a multiplication and a subtraction prior to the inner loop, and a subtraction and division after the inner loop for a total of four computational steps. Thus, the sequential time is given by

$$t_s = n(2n + 4)\tau$$

which has a time complexity of $O(n^2)$ if there is a constant number of iterations.

The parallel execution time is the time of one processor when we assume that all processors execute the same number of iterations. Suppose there are n equations and p processors. A processor operates upon n/p unknowns. One iteration has a computational phase and a broadcast communication phase.

Computation. In the computational phase, there is an inner loop with n iterations and an outer loop with n/p iterations, both with the same computational effort as the nested sequential loops. Hence, the computation time is given by

$$t_{\text{comp}} = (n/p)(2n + 4)\tau$$

which has a time complexity of $O(n^2/p)$ if there is a constant number of iterations. As p is increased, the computation time decreases.

Communication. Communication occurs at the end of each iteration and consists of multiple broadcasts. In essence, all the n values computed by each processor must be relayed to every other processor. Given p separate broadcasts, each of the size n/p data items, and requiring t_{data} units of time to send each data item, the time could be of the form

$$t_{\text{comm}} = p(t_{\text{startup}} + (n/p)t_{\text{data}})\tau = (pt_{\text{startup}} + nt_{\text{data}})\tau$$

The communication time is a linearly increasing function of p, given a fixed value for n.

Overall Execution Time. The total parallel execution time is given by

$$t_p = ((n/p)(2n + 4) + pt_{\text{startup}} + nt_{\text{data}})\tau$$

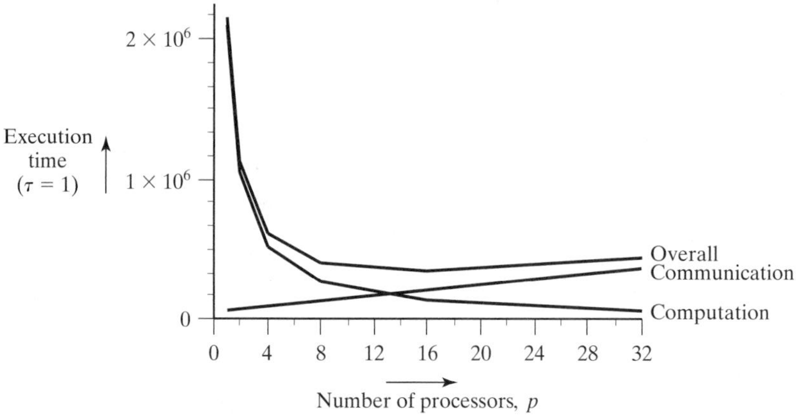

Figure 6.11 Effects of computation and communication in Jacobi iteration.

For non-negligible $t_{startup}$ times, the overall parallel execution time consists of one function that is a decreasing function of p (t_{comp}) and one function that is an increasing function of p (t_{comm}). The resulting total execution time has a minimum value. This characteristic is common to most partitioning situations. The minimum can be found by differentiation. To give a concrete example, suppose $t_{startup}$ = 10,000 and t_{data} = 50 (representative of real systems; see Chapter 2). Figure 6.11 shows the overall execution time, the computation, and communication components, given that n/p must be an integer. The minimum execution time occurs when $p = 16$.

Speedup Factor. The speedup factor is given by

$$\text{Speedup factor} = \frac{t_s}{t_p} = \frac{n(2n+4)}{(n/p)(2n+4) + pt_{startup} + nt_{data}}$$

which is p if the communication is ignored. However, we have already established that there is an optimum number of processors for this problem, dependent upon the values for $t_{startup}$ and t_{data}.

Computation/communication Ratio. The computation/communication ratio is given by

$$\text{Computation/communication ratio} = \frac{t_{comp}}{t_{comm}} = \frac{(n/p)(2n+4)}{pt_{startup} + nt_{data}}$$

which suggests improvement with larger n (scalable).

6.3.2 Heat-Distribution Problem

The preceding problem required global synchronization. Now let us consider a local synchronization problem. Consider a square metal sheet that has known temperatures along each of its edges. The temperature of the interior surface of the sheet will depend upon the temperatures around it. We can find the temperature distribution by dividing the area into a fine mesh of points, $h_{i,j}$. The temperature at an inside point can be taken to be the average of the temperatures of the four neighboring points, as illustrated in Figure 6.12. For this calculation, it is convenient to describe the edges by points adjacent to the interior points. The interior points of $h_{i,j}$ are where $0 < i < n$, $0 < j < n$ [$(n - 1) \times (n - 1)$ interior points]. The edge points are when $i = 0$, $i = n$, $j = 0$, or $j = n$, and have fixed values corresponding to the fixed temperatures of the edges. Hence, the full range of $h_{i,j}$ is $0 \leq i \leq n$, $0 \leq j \leq n$, and there are $(n + 1) \times (n + 1)$ points. We can compute the temperature of each interior point by iterating the equation

$$h_{i,j} = \frac{h_{i-1,j} + h_{i+1,j} + h_{i,j-1} + h_{i,j+1}}{4}$$

$(0 < i < n, 0 < j < n)$ for a fixed number of iterations or until the difference between iterations of a point is less than some very small prescribed amount.

This iteration equation occurs in several other similar problems; for example, with pressure and voltage. More complex versions appear for solving important problems in science and engineering. In fact, we are solving a system of linear equations. Each point is an unknown dependent upon a few other unknowns, rather than all the other unknowns in the general case. To clarify this relationship, consider the array of points as numbered in so-called *natural order* at the top left corner and in rows of m points, as shown in Figure 6.13. The points are numbered from 1 for convenience and include those representing the edges. (Note that $m = n$ here. However, m is used to differentiate the numbering system.) Each point will then use the equation

$$x_i = \frac{x_{i-1} + x_{i+1} + x_{i-m} + x_{i+m}}{4}$$

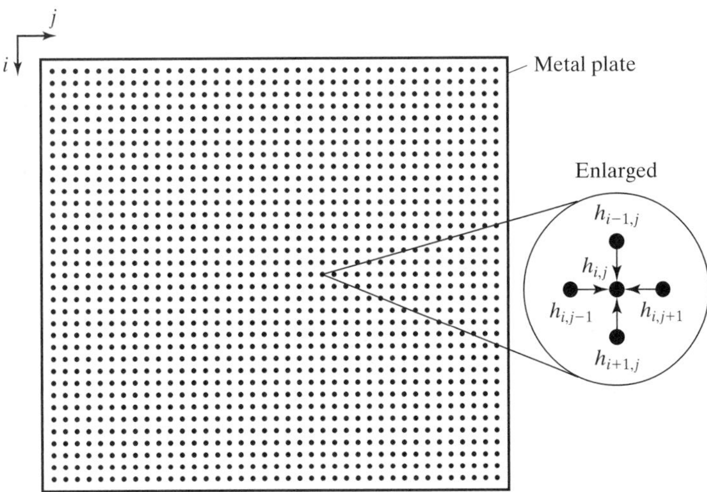

Figure 6.12 Heat distribution problem.

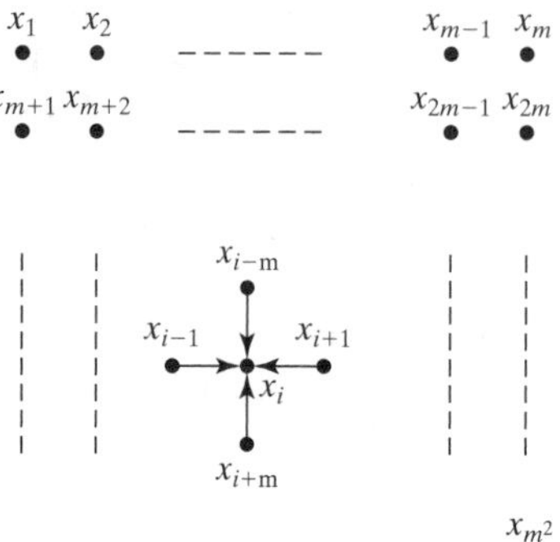

Figure 6.13 Natural ordering of heat-distribution problem.

This equation could be written as a linear equation containing the unknowns x_{i-m}, x_{i-1}, x_{i+1}, and x_{i+m}:

$$x_{i-m} + x_{i-1} - 4x_i + x_{i+1} + x_{i-m} = 0$$

$0 < i \leq m^2$, that is, m^2 equations. The method is known as the *finite difference* method. It can be extended into three dimensions by taking the average of six neighboring points, two in each dimension. We are also solving Laplace's equation. Chapter 11 explores further the relationship with linear equations. (In Chapter 11, n is used for the number of equations.)

Sequential Code. Returning to the original numbering system for the points, suppose that the temperature of each point is held in an array `h[i][j]`, and the boundary points `h[0][x]`, `h[x][0]`, `h[n][x]`, and `h[x][n]` ($0 \leq x \leq n$) have been initialized to the edge temperatures. The calculation as sequential code could be

```
for (iteration = 0; iteration < limit; iteration++) {
  for (i = 1; i < n; i++)
    for (j = 1; j < n; j++)
      g[i][j] = 0.25 * (h[i-1][j] + h[i+1][j] + h[i][j-1] + h[i][j+1]);
  for (i = 1; i < n; i++)             /* update points */
    for (j = 1; j < n; j++)
      h[i][j] = g[i][j];
}
```

using a fixed number of iterations. We multiply by 0.25 to compute the new value of the point rather than divide by 4 because multiplication is usually more efficient than division. Such normal methods to improve efficiency in sequential code carry over to parallel code and should be done where possible in all instances. (Of course, a good optimizing compiler would make such changes.)

There are several ways the code could be written if we want to stop at some precision, but in all cases, all points must have reached their precision. With properly initialized arrays, the sequential code could be

```
do {
  for (i = 1; i < n; i++)
    for (j = 1; j < n; j++)
      g[i][j] = 0.25*(h[i-1][j] + h[i+1][j] + h[i][j-1] + h[i][j+1]);
```

```
    for (i = 1; i < n; i++)          /* update points */
      for (j = 1; j < n; j++)
        h[i][j] = g[i][j];

    continue = FALSE;               /* indicates whether to continue */
    for (i = 1; i < n; i++)         /* check each point for convergence */
      for (j = 1; j < n; j++)
        if (!converged(i,j) {      /* point found not converged */
          continue = TRUE;
          break;
        }

  } while (continue == TRUE);
```

Convergence is checked after all the points have been computed, which allows several possible convergence algorithms. The routine `converged(i,j)` returns `TRUE` if the element `g[i][j]` has converged to the required precision; otherwise it returns `FALSE`. The Boolean flag `continue` will be set to `TRUE` if at least one point in an iteration has not converged. Normally, we would want to ensure that the loop terminates even if convergence does not occur. This can also be done by incorporating a loop counter.

Improvements. In the above code, a second array, `g[][]`, is used to hold the newly computed values of the points from the old values. The array `h[][]` is updated with the new values held in `g[][]` after all the values have been computed in `g[][]`. Using the values of one iteration to compute the values for the next iteration in this fashion is known as a Jacobi iteration. A significant improvement is to eliminate the second array:

```
for (iteration = 0; iteration < limit; iteration++) {
  for (i = 1; i < n; i++)
    for (j = 1; j < n; j++)
      h[i][j] = 0.25 * (h[i-1][j] + h[i+1][j] + h[i][j-1] + h[i][j+1]);
```

Given the sequential order of the computation, two of the values used to compute `h[i][j]` have already been computed in that iteration (`h[i-1][j]` and `h[i][j-1]`) and are used, and two values have not yet been computed in that iteration and were computed from the preceding iteration (`h[i+1][j]` and `h[i][j+1]`). Thus, we are using the most recent values available. This is know as a Gauss-Seidel iteration and usually produces a faster convergence. However, it relies upon the sequential order of computation.

In the Gauss-Seidel method, the unknowns (points) to be computed, say x_i $(0 < i < n-1)$, are ordered so that those before the current unknown, $x_j, j < i$, have already been computed for that iteration and are used, and those after the current point, x_k, $k > i$, have not yet been computed in the current iteration, and therefore the values computed in the preceding iteration are used. The basic Gauss-Seidel method is an excellent match for a sequential program in which unknowns are computed in some sequential order, but as described it is not a good basis for parallel program in which unknowns are computed simultaneously. However, there are specific orderings that allow for simultaneous computations. We shall explore different orderings and faster iteration methods that are amenable to parallelization at the end of this chapter and in more detail in Chapter 11. For now, we shall concentrate upon the Jacobi iteration because it allows us to investigate local synchronization, but one should be aware that it is usually neither the best sequential algorithm nor the best basis for a parallel algorithm.

Parallel Code. The sequential code is "unnatural" in that we have used `for` loops to visit each point, whereas the points can be visited simultaneously without any change to the algorithm:

```
for (iteration = 0; iteration < limit; iteration++) {
  forall (i = 1; i < n; i++)
    forall (j = 1; j < n; j++)
      h[i][j] = 0.25 * (h[i-1][j] + h[i+1][j] + h[i][j-1] + h[i][j+1]);
}
```

In this construction, it is understood that all the values on the right side of the computation are computed from the preceding iteration without any need of an explicit array `g[][]`. We would usually partition the problem so that more than one point is processed by each process. However, in the first instance, suppose that we have one process for each point.

Each process requires the four neighboring points, and the most convenient organization is to arrange the processes conceptually into a mesh. Let us refer to processes by subscripts on the mesh by using row major order, where the first subscript is the row, and the second, the column. For the version with a fixed number of iterations, process $P_{i,j}$ (except for the boundary points) could be of the form

```
for (iteration = 0; iteration < limit; iteration++) {
   g = 0.25 * (w + x + y + z);
   send(&g, Pi-1,j);            /* non-blocking sends */       |
   send(&g, Pi+1,j);                                            |
   send(&g, Pi,j-1);                                            |
   send(&g, Pi,j+1);                                            |  Local
   recv(&w, Pi-1,j);            /* synchronous receives */      |  barrier
   recv(&x, Pi+1,j);                                            |
   recv(&y, Pi,j-1);                                            |
   recv(&z, Pi,j+1);                                            v
}
```

after suitable initialization of `w`, `x`, `y`, and `z`. Each process has its own iteration loop. The number of iterations must be sent to each process. It is important to use `send()`s that do not block while waiting for the `recv()`s; otherwise the processes would deadlock, each waiting for a `recv()` before moving on. The `recv()`s must be synchronous and wait for the `send()`s. Each process will be synchronized with its four neighbors by the `recv()`s. We are using a local synchronization technique here. It is unnecessary to have a separate iteration to update the array. The transfer between four processes is shown in Figure 6.14.

Implementing the version where processes stop when they reach their required precision requires a master process to be notified when all the (slave) processes have

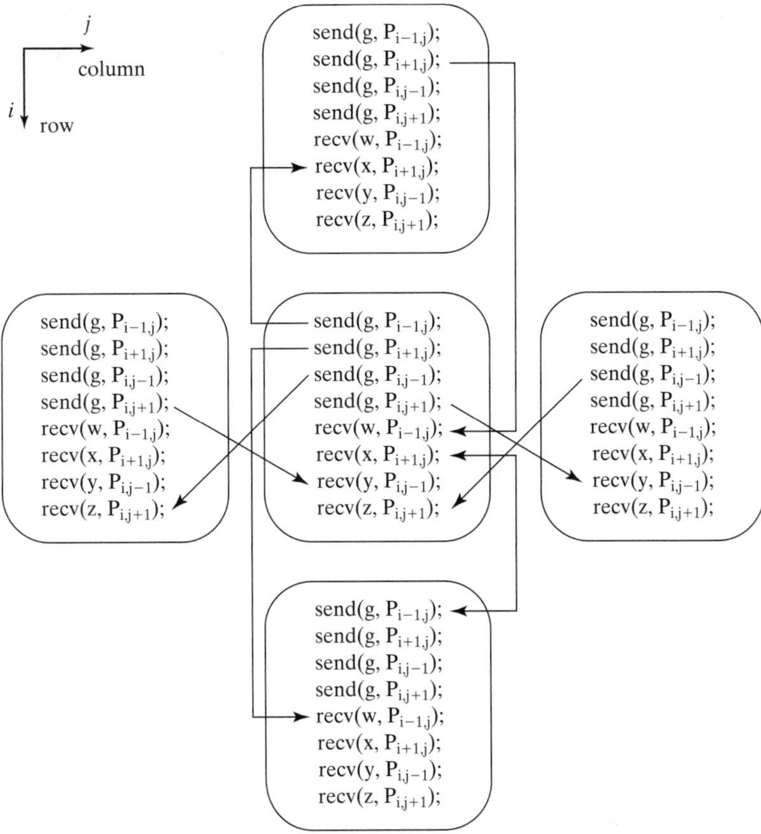

Figure 6.14 Message-passing for heat-distribution problem.

stopped. A process could send data to the master when the precision has been reached locally; for example,

```
iteration = 0;
do {
   iteration++;
   g = 0.25 * (w + x + y + z);
   send(&g, P_{i-1,j});                   /* locally blocking sends */
   send(&g, P_{i+1,j});
   send(&g, P_{i,j-1});
   send(&g, P_{i,j+1});
   recv(&w, P_{i-1,j});                   /* locally blocking receives */
   recv(&x, P_{i+1,j});
   recv(&y, P_{i,j-1});
   recv(&z, P_{i,j+1});
} while((!converged(i, j)) && (iteration < limit));
send(&g, &i, &j, &iteration, P_{master});
```

To handle the processes operating at the edges, we could use the process ID to determine the location of the process in the array, leading to code such as

```
if (last_row) w = bottom_value;
if (first_row) x = top_value;
if (first_column) y = left_value;
if (last_column) z = right_value;
iteration = 0;
do {
   iteration++;
   g = 0.25 * (w + x + y + z);
   if !(first_row) send(&g, Pi-1,j);
   if !(last_row) send(&g, Pi+1,j);
   if !(first_column) send(&g, Pi,j-1);
   if !(last_column) send(&g, Pi,j+1);
   if !(last_row) recv(&w, Pi-1,j);
   if !(first_row) recv(&x, Pi+1,j);
   if !(first_column) recv(&y, Pi,j-1);
   if !(last_column) recv(&z, Pi,j+1);
} while((!converged) && (iteration < limit));
send(&g, &i, &j, iteration, Pmaster);
```

It is a simple matter for us to convert the process indices to actual numbers. Given processes numbered starting at the top left corner of the mesh and numbered across rows (natural ordering), process P_i communicates with P_{i-1} (left), P_{i+1} (right), P_{i-k} (up), and P_{i-k} (down) $(0 \le i < k^2)$.

Partitioning. Obviously, we would normally allocate more than one point to each processor, because there would be many more points than processors. The mesh of points could be partitioned into square blocks or strips (columns), as shown in Figure 6.15 (p partitions). The partitions are the same options as for the image bitmap in Chapter 3, but now there is communication between partitions. Therefore, we would like to minimize the communication. With n^2 points, p processors, and equal partitions, each partition holds n^2/p points. The communication consequences of the two arrangements are shown in Figure 6.16.

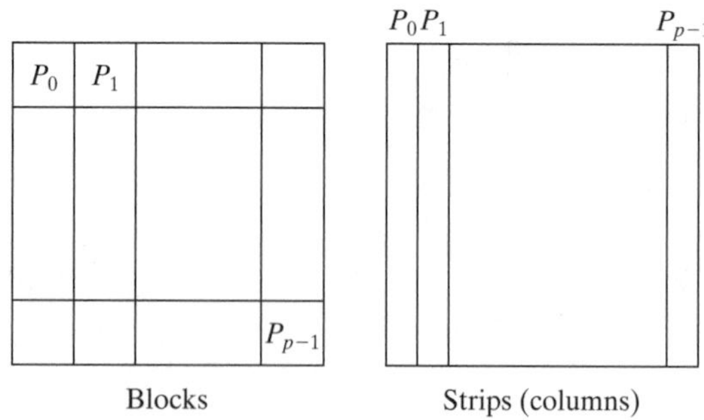

Figure 6.15 Partitioning heat-distribution problem.

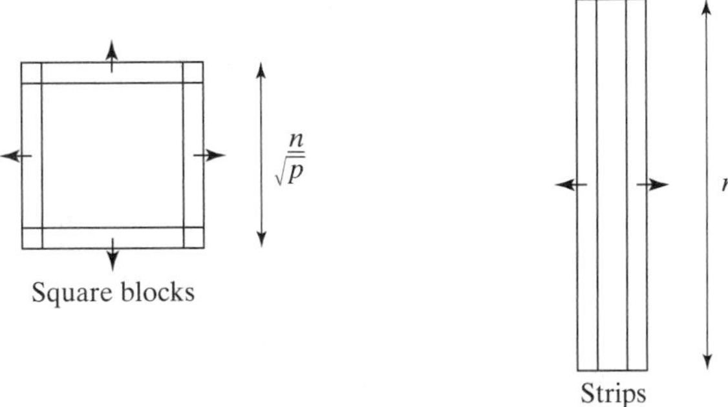

Figure 6.16 Communication consequences of partitioning.

In the block partition, there are four edges where data points are exchanged. Each process generates four messages and receives four messages in each iteration (assuming that the data points along one edge are packed into one message). Thus, the communication time is given by

$$t_{\text{commsq}} = 8\left(t_{\text{startup}} + \frac{n}{\sqrt{p}}t_{\text{data}}\right)$$

This equation is only valid for $p \geq 9$ when at least one block has four communicating edges.

In the strip partition, there are two edges where data points are exchanged. Each process generates two messages and receives two messages in each iteration (assuming again that all the data points along one edge are packed into one message). Thus, the communication time is given by

$$t_{\text{commcol}} = 4(t_{\text{startup}} + nt_{\text{data}})$$

Note that the communication time is independent of the number of processors *p;* that is, the number of partitions.

These communication times will be heavily influenced by the startup time. For example, suppose $t_{\text{startup}} = 10{,}000$, $t_{\text{data}} = 50$ (as used for Figure 6.11), and $n^2 = 1024$. Under these circumstances, the strip partition has a communication time of 46,400 (time units) irrespective of the value of p. The block partition has a communication time of 80,000 + $12800/\sqrt{p}$. For any number of processors, this will be greater than the strip partition. But suppose the startup time is 100. The strip partition now has a communication time of 6800, whereas the block partition has a communication time of 800 + $12800/\sqrt{p}$. Now the strip partition always has a greater communication time for $p > 4$.

In general, the strip partition is best for a large startup time, and a block partition is best for a small startup time. With the previous equations, the block partition has a larger communication time than the strip partition if

$$8\left(t_{\text{startup}} + \frac{n}{\sqrt{p}}t_{\text{data}}\right) > 4(t_{\text{startup}} + nt_{\text{data}})$$

or

$$t_{\text{startup}} > n\left(1 - \frac{2}{\sqrt{p}}\right)t_{\text{data}}$$

($p \geq 9$). The right side tends to nt_{data}, or 1600 with our numbers, as p increases modestly. For example, the crossover point between block partition being best and strip partition being best is reached with $p = 64$ when $t_{\text{startup}} = 1200$. Figure 6.17 shows the characteristics for $p = 9$, 16, 64, 256, and 1024.

The startup time will be large in most systems, especially in workstation clusters. Hence, the strip partition seems the appropriate choice. It is also the easiest partition for us to program, since messages simply pass left and right rather than left, right, up, and down.

Implementation Details. It will be necessary for us to send a complete column of points to an adjacent process in one message. For convenience, we might divide the two-dimensional array of points into rows rather than columns when the array is stored in row major order (as in C). Then a row can be sent in a message simply by specifying the starting address of the row and the number of data elements stored in it (a contiguous group of elements). If we do not want to utilize the actual storage structure, then a separate one-dimensional array could be used to hold the points being transmitted to an adjacent process. We could have started our discussion by dividing into rows rather than columns, but this implementation detail is not an algorithmic matter.

In addition to the division of points into rows, Figure 6.18 shows each process having an additional row of points at each edge, called *ghost points*, that hold the values from the adjacent edge. Each array of points is increased to accommodate the ghost rows. Ghost points are provided for programming convenience.

The code for process P_i (not including the processes at the borders) could take the form

```
for (k = 1; k <= n/p; k++)        /* compute points in partition */
  for (j = 1; j <= n; j++)
   g[k][j] = 0.25 * (h[k-1][j] + h[k+1][j] + h[k][j-1] + h[k][j+1]);
```

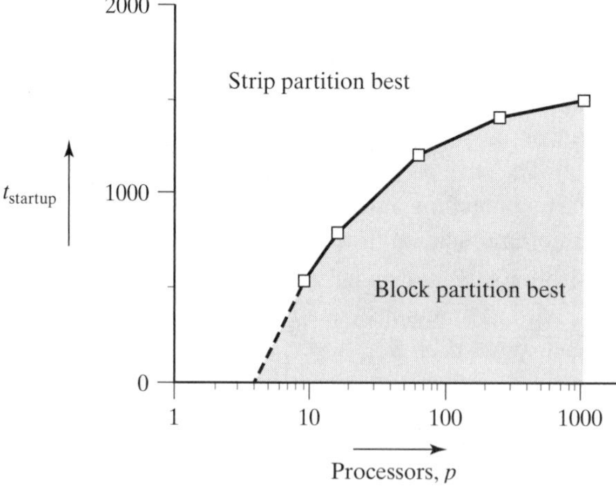

Figure 6.17 Startup times for block and strip partitions.

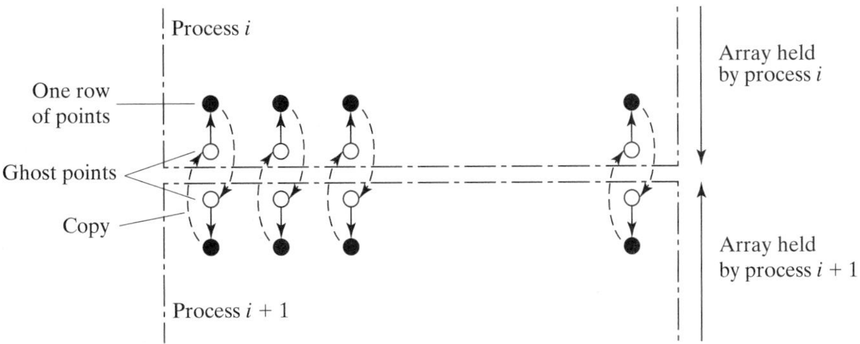

Figure 6.18 Configurating array into contiguous rows for each process, with ghost points.

```
for (k = 1; k <= n/p; k++)          /* update points */
  for (j = 1; j <= n; j++)
   h[k][j] = g[k][j];
send(&g[1][1], n, Pi-1);            /* send row to adjacent process */
send(&g[n/p][1], n, Pi+1);
recv(&h[0][1], n, Pi-1);            /* receive row from adjacent process */
recv(&h[n/p + 1][1], n, Pi+1);
```

Safety and Deadlock. The arrangement when all the processes send their messages first and then receive all of their messages, as in all the code so far, is described as unsafe in the MPI literature. This is because it relies upon buffering in the `send()`s. The amount of buffering is not specified in MPI. If a send routine has insufficient storage available when it is called, the implementation should be such as to delay the routine from returning until storage becomes available or until the message can be sent without buffering. Hence, the locally blocking `send()` could behave as a synchronous `send()`, only returning when the matching `recv()` is executed. Since a matching `recv()` would never be executed if all the `send()`s are synchronous, deadlock would occur. In our case, it is likely that sufficient storage is available if n/p is relatively small — and you might question why an implementation would have a locally blocking send available if it cannot be used with safety!

A way of making the code safe is to alternate the order of the `send()`s and `recv()`s in adjacent processes. This is so that only one process performs the `send()`s first. Then even synchronous `send()`s would not cause deadlock. In fact, a good way you can test for safety is to replace message-passing routines in a program with synchronous versions.

Safe code, by alternating the `send()`s and `recv()`s, could be of the form

```
if ((i % 2) == 0) {                          /* even-numbered processes */
   send(&g[1][1], n, Pi-1);
   recv(&h[0][1], n, Pi-1);
   send(&g[n/p][1], n, Pi+1);
   recv(&h[n/p + 1][1], n, Pi+1);
} else {                                     /* odd-numbered processes */
   recv(&h[n/p + 1][1], n, Pi+1);
   send(&g[n/p][1], n, Pi+1);
```

```
    recv(&h[0][1], n, Pi-1);
    send(&g[1][1], n, Pi-1);
}
```

Alternating the `send()`s and `recv()`s can easily be done here but could be more difficult in other circumstances.

MPI offers several alternative methods for safe communication:

- Combined send and receive routines: `MPI_Sendrecv()` (which is guaranteed not to deadlock)
- Buffered send()s: `MPI_Bsend()` — here the user provides explicit storage space
- Nonblocking routines: `MPI_Isend()` and `MPI_Irecv()` — here the routine returns immediately, and a separate routine is used to establish whether the message has been received (`MPI_Wait()`, `MPI_Waitall()`, `MPI_Waitany()`, `MPI_Test()`, `MPI_Testall()`, or `MPI_Testany()`)

A pseudocode segment using the third method is

```
isend(&g[1][1], n, Pi-1);
isend(&g[n/p][1], n, Pi+1);
irecv(&h[0][1], n, Pi-1);
irecv(&h[n/p + 1][1], n, Pi+1);
waitall(4);
```

Essentially, the wait routine becomes a barrier, waiting for all the message-passing routines to complete.

6.3.3 Cellular Automata

A concept that is particularly suitable for synchronous iteration is called *cellular automaton.* In cellular automation, the problem space is first divided into cells. Each cell can be in one of a finite number of states. Cells are affected by their neighbors according to certain rules, and all cells are affected simultaneously in a "generation." The rules are reapplied in subsequent generations so that cells evolve, or change state, from generation to generation.

The most famous cellular automaton is the "Game of Life," devised by John Horton Conway, a Cambridge mathematician, and published by Gardner (Gardner, 1967). Gardner points out that the concept of cellular automata can be traced back to Von Neuman's work in the early 1950s. The Game of Life is a board game; the board consists of a (theoretically infinite) two-dimensional array of cells. Each cell can hold one "organism" and has eight neighboring cells, including those diagonally adjacent. Initially, some of the cells are occupied in a pattern. The following rules apply:

1. Every organism with two or three neighboring organisms survives for the next generation.
2. Every organism with four or more neighbors dies from overpopulation.

3. Every organism with one neighbor or none dies from isolation.
4. Each empty cell adjacent to exactly three occupied neighbors will give birth to an organism.

These rules were derived by Conway "after a long period of experimentation."

Another simple fun example of cellular automata is "Sharks and Fishes" in the sea, each with different behavioral rules. A two-dimensional version of this problem is studied in detail in Fox et al. (1988). An ocean could be modeled as a three-dimensional array of cells. Each cell can hold one fish or one shark (but not both). Fish might move around according to these rules:

1. If there is one empty adjacent cell, the fish moves to this cell.
2. If there is more than one empty adjacent cell, the fish moves to one cell chosen at random.
3. If there are no empty adjacent cells, the fish stays where it is.
4. If the fish moves and has reached its breeding age, it gives birth to a baby fish, which is left in the vacated cell.
5. Fish die after x generations.

The sharks might be governed by the following rules:

1. If one adjacent cell is occupied by a fish, the shark moves to this cell and eats the fish.
2. If more than one adjacent cell is occupied by a fish, the shark chooses one fish at random, moves to the cell occupied by the fish, and eats the fish.
3. If there are no fish in adjacent cells, the shark chooses an unoccupied adjacent cell to move to in the same way that fish move.
4. If the shark moves and has reached its breeding age, it gives birth to a baby shark, which is left in the vacated cell.
5. If a shark has not eaten for y generations, it dies.

Problem 6-21 describes a similar problem with foxes and rabbits. The behavior of the rabbits is to move around happily, whereas the behavior of the foxes is to eat any rabbits they come across.

There are serious applications for cellular automata, because they avoid the need for differential equations. For example, given the rules of fluid/gas dynamics, the movement of fluids and gases around objects or diffusion of gases can be modeled by this method. Biological growth can also be modeled. Examples given in the problems include airflow across an airplane wing (Problem 6-24) and erosion/movement of sand at a beach or riverbank (Problem 6-23). No doubt there are many other possible applications for cellular automata (Problem 6-22).

6.4 PARTIALLY SYNCHRONOUS METHODS

It is clear that synchronization causes a significant degradation of performance. In this final section, we will explore ways to reduce the amount of synchronization in the synchronous iteration problems explored earlier. Let us take the heat-distribution problem as an example.

The parallel code was written as

```
for (iteration = 0; iteration < limit; iteration++) {
  forall (i = 1; i < n; i++)
    forall (j = 1; j < n; j++)
      h[i][j] = 0.25 * (h[i-1][j] + h[i+1][j] + h[i][j-1] + h[i][j+1]);
}
```

with the assumption that the values on the right side of the computation are computed from the preceding iteration. The code computes the next iteration values based on the immediately preceding iteration values. This is the traditional Jacobi iteration method, which requires a global synchronization point (barrier) for processes to wait until all processes have performed their calculations. It is not the calculation that causes the performance reduction but the time it takes to perform the barrier synchronization. We have already mentioned the possibility of using some of the present iteration values in the calculation, as in the Gauss-Seidel iteration method, but a barrier is still present because all the processes operate on the same iteration together. Suppose the barrier was removed altogether, allowing processes to continue with subsequent iterations before other processes have completed their present iteration. Then the processes moving forward would use values computed from not only the preceding iteration but from earlier iterations and not only the last iteration. The method is called an *asynchronous iterative method.* The mathematical conditions for convergence may be more strict in asynchronous iteration; that is, the calculation may not converge unless certain mathematical conditions exist. Each process may not be allowed to use any previous iteration values if the method is to converge. A form of asynchronous iterative method called *chaotic relaxation* was introduced by Chazan and Miranker (1969) in which the convergence conditions are stated as:

> "there must be a fixed positive integer s such that, in carrying out the evaluation of the ith iterate, a process cannot make use of any value of the components of the jth iterate if $j < i - s$" (Baudet, 1978).

This suggests a simple alteration to the parallel code to allow processes to continue until they try to use a value which is more than s iteration cycles previously. Each stored value will need a "time stamp," the iteration number associated with the stored value.

The final part of the code, checking for convergence of every iteration, can also be reduced. It may be better to allow iterations to continue for several iterations before checking for convergence. Combining the chaotic relaxation and delayed convergence testing, each process is allowed to perform s iterations before being synchronized but will also update its locally stored values as it goes. At every s iterations, the maximum divergence is recorded. Convergence is checked then. The actual iteration corresponding to the elements of the array being used at any time may be from an earlier iteration but only up to s iterations previously. In a message-passing solution, all the data values that are obtained from other processes will be from s iterations previously when the processes last communicated. Data values being used that are computed within the process will be from the present iteration or the previous iteration, depending upon the sequence in which the data values are computed sequentially.

Note that the method described cannot be applied to all synchronous problems. For example, cellular automation does not lend itself to this approach.

6.5 SUMMARY

This chapter introduced the following:

- The concept of a barrier and its implementations (global barriers and local barriers)
- Data parallel computations
- The concept of synchronous iteration
- Examples of using global and local barriers
- The concept of safe communication
- Cellular automata
- Partially synchronous methods

FURTHER READING

The concept of a barrier is discussed in most parallel programming texts. Apart from the software implementations of barriers described here, some multiprocessor systems (e.g., the CRAY T3D) have hardware support for barriers. Pacheco (1997) develops MPI code for Jacobi iterations. MPI code for Jacobi iterations can also be found in Snir et al. (1996), with significant discussion about safe programs and alternative coding when you use special features of MPI, such as the `MPI_Sendrecv()` routine, posting routines, and null processes. Significant MPI details for Jacobi iterations can also be found in the other MPI "reference," Gropp, Lusk, and Skjellum (1999), which also includes the use of MPI features such as topologies. A discussion of the trade-off between computation and communication can be found in Snir et al. (1996) and Wilson (1995). In addition to the fully synchronous technique discussed in this chapter, synchronization can be applied in a less structured or loosely synchronous manner, whereby processes are synchronized occasionally. Several loosely synchronous applications are discussed in detail in Fox, Williams, and Messina (1994).

Since its introduction by Chazan and Miranker (1969), chaotic relaxation has been studied by several authors, including Baudet (1978) and Evans and Yousif (1992), although it was ignored in textbooks on parallel programming and algorithms in the past. It offers the potential for very significant improvement in execution speed over fully synchronous methods, when it can be applied.

BIBLIOGRAPHY

BAUDET, G. M. (1978), Asynchronous Iterative Methods for Multiprocessors, *J. ACM*, Vol. 25, pp 226–244.

BERTSEKAS, D. P., AND J. N. TSITSIKLIS (1989), *Parallel and Distributed Computation Numerical Methods*. Prentice Hall, Englewood Cliffs, NJ.

CHAZAN, D, AND W. MIRANKER (1969), Chaotic Relaxation, *Linear Algebra and Its Applications*, Vol 2, pp. 199–222.

EVANS, D. J, AND N. Y. YOUSIF (1992), "Asynchronous Parallel Algorithms for Linear Equations," in *Parallel Processing in Computational Mechanics* (editor H. Adeli), Marcel Dekker, NY, pp. 69–130.

FOX, G. C., M. A. JOHNSON, G. A. LYZENGA, S. W. OTTO, J. K. SALMON, AND D. W. WALKER (1988), *Solving Problems on Concurrent Processors*, Volume 1, Prentice Hall, Englewood Cliffs, NJ.

FOX, G. C., R. D. WILLIAMS, AND P. C. MESSINA (1994), *Parallel Computing Works*, Morgan Kaufmann, San Francisco, CA.

GARDNER, M. (1967), "Mathematical Games," *Scientific American*, October, pp. 120–123.

GROPP, W., E. LUSK, AND A. SKJELLUM (1999), *Using MPI Portable Parallel Programming with the Message-Passing Interface*, MIT Press, Cambridge, MA.

HILLIS, W. D., AND G. L. STEELE, JR. (1986), "Data Parallel Algorithms," *Comm. ACM*, Vol. 29, No. 12, pp. 1170–1183.

JÁJÁ, J. (1992), *An Introduction to Parallel Algorithms*, Addison Wesley, Reading, MA.

PACHECO, P. (1997), *Parallel Programming with MPI*, Morgan Kaufmann, San Francisco, CA.

SNIR, M., S. W. OTTO, S. HUSS-LEDERMAN, D. W. WALKER, AND J. DONGARRA (1996), *MPI: The Complete Reference*, MIT Press, Cambridge, MA.

WAGNER, R. A., AND Y. HAN (1986), "Parallel Algorithms for Bucket Sorting and the Data Dependent Prefix Problem," *Proc. 1986 Int. Conf. Par. Proc.*, IEEE CS Press, pp. 924–929.

WILSON, G. V. (1995), *Practical Parallel Programming*, MIT Press, Cambridge, MA.

PROBLEMS

Scientific/Numerical

6-1. Implement the counter barrier described in Figure 6.4, and test it. Is it necessary to use blocking or synchronous routines for both send and receive? Explain.

6-2. Write a barrier, `barrier(procNum)`, which will block until `procNum` processes reach the barrier and then release the processes. Allow for the barrier to be called with different numbers of processes and with different values for `procNum`.

6-3. Investigate the time that a barrier takes to operate by using code such as

```
t1 = time();
Barrier(group);
t2 = time();
printf("Elapsed time = %", difftime(t2, t1));
```

(In MPI the barrier routine is `MPI_Barrier(Communicator)`. The time routine is `MPI_Wtime()`.) Investigate different numbers of processes.

6-4. Write code to implement an eight-process barrier using the tree construction described in Section 6.1.3 and compare with any available barrier calls (e.g., in MPI `MPI_Barrier()`).

6-5. Implement the butterfly barrier described in Section 6.1.4, and compare with any available barrier calls.

6-6. Determine experimentally at what point in your system the limit to buffering is reached when using nonblocking sends. Establish the effects of requesting more buffering than is available. (It may be that the amount of buffering available is related to the amount of memory being used for other purposes.)

6-7. Can noncommutative operators such as division be used in the prefix calculation of Figure 6.8?

6-8. Determine the efficiency of the prefix calculation of Figure 6.8.

6-9. Given a fixed rectangular area with sides x and y and a communication that is proportional to the perimeter, $2(x + y)$, show that the minimum communication is given by $x = y$ (i.e., a square).

6-10. Write a parallel program to solve the one-dimensional problem based upon the finite difference equation

$$x_i = \frac{x_{i-1} + x_{i+1}}{2}$$

for $0 \le i \le 1000$, given that $x_0 = 10$ and $x_{1000} = 250$.

6-11. In the text, we have assumed a square array for the heat-distribution problem of Section 6.3.2. What are the mathematical conditions for choosing blocks or strips as the partition if the array has a length of n points and a width of m points?

6-12. Investigate the accuracy of convergence of the heat-distribution problem using the different termination methods described in Section 6.3.1. Determine whether it is sufficient to use the difference between the present and next values of the points or whether it is necessary to use a more complex termination calculation. The basic question being investigated here is, "If each point is computed until each is within 1 percent (say) of its previous computed value, what is the accuracy of the solution?"

6-13. Write a parallel program to simulate the Game of Life as described in Section 6.3.3 and experiment with different initial populations.

6-14. Compare experimentally a fully synchronous implementation and a partially synchronous implementation of the heat-distribution problem described in Section 6.3.1. Try different values of s in the convergence condition specified in Section 6.4. Write a report on your findings that includes the specific speed improvements you obtained.

Real Life

6-15. Figure 6.19 shows a room that has four walls and a fireplace. The temperature of the wall is 20°C, and the temperature of the fireplace is 100°C. Write a parallel program using Jacobi iteration to compute the temperature inside the room and plot (preferably in color) the temperature contours at 10°C intervals using Xlib calls or similar graphics calls as available on your system. Instrument the code so that the elapsed time is displayed. (This programming assignment is convenient after a Mandelbrot assignment because it can use the same graphics calls.)

6-16. Repeat Problem 6-15 but with a round room of diameter 20 ft and a point heat source in the center at 100°C; the walls are at 20°C.

6-17. Simulate a road junction controlled by traffic lights, as shown in Figure 6.20. Vehicles come from all four directions along the roads and wish either to pass straight through the junction to the other side, or turn left, or turn right. On average, 70 percent of the vehicles wish to pass straight through, 10 percent wish to turn right, and 20 percent wish to turn left. Each vehicle moves at the same speed up to the junction. Develop a set of driving rules to solve this problem by a cellular automata approach, and implement them in a parallel program using your own test data (vehicle numbers and positions).

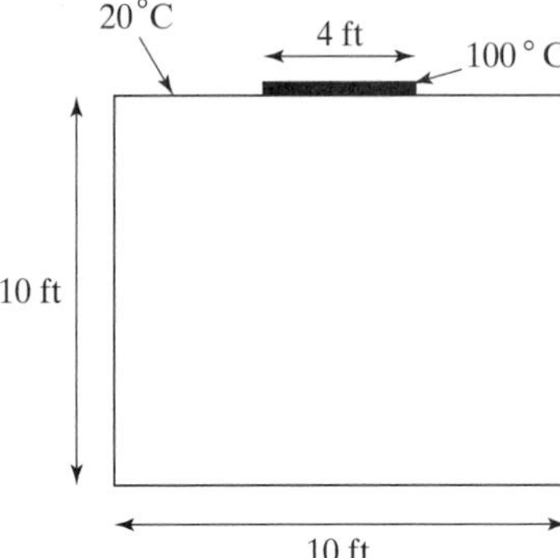

Figure 6.19 Room for Problem 6-15.

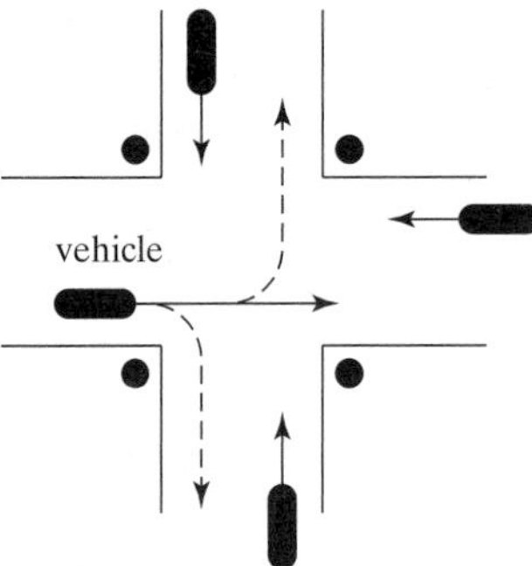

Figure 6.20 Road junction for Problem 6-17.

6-18. Write a parallel program to simulate the actions of the sharks and fish as described in Section 6.3.3. The parameters that are input are size of ocean, number of fish and sharks, their initial placement in the ocean, breeding ages, and shark starvation time. Adjacent cells do not include diagonally adjacent cells. Therefore, there are six adjacent cells, except for the edges. For every generation, the fishes' and sharks' ages are incremented by 1. Modify the simulation to take into account currents in the water.

6-19. Dr. Michaels was known across campus for being somewhat absent-minded. Thus, it was no surprise when he went on a camping trip into the Uwharrie National Forest, but left his map and compass behind. Luckily for him, he had packed his new portable computer that included one of the new cellular modems. Luckier still, he left you sitting back in the computer science building working on a research project!

You had a premonition about this trip, so you downloaded a detailed map of the forest that showed the location of every tree, cliff, and road/path through the forest from the latest NASA satellite pictures. The data is in the form of an array of "cells," with rectangular areas of 0.3 meters on an edge. Each cell contains a 'T', 'C', 'O', or 'R,' which designates what is in that area of the forest:

'T' The area contains an impassable tree.

'C' The area contains an abrupt drop-off (a cliff).

'O' The area is open and passable by the professor.

'R' The area is a roadway or marked path and is passable by the professor.

Thus, you were not particularly surprised when Dr. Michaels's e-mail message came through asking for your help. It seems he is suffering from a medical condition that necessitates his exiting the forest as rapidly as possible. He has asked you to write a program to do two things:

1. Identify where in the forest he happens to be.
2. Direct him out of the forest anywhere along the road that borders the southern edge.

Your program can query the professor about what is immediately ahead, behind, left, and right of his present cell. In response to each query, he will send back four letters. For example, the results of Query() might be 'T', 'O', 'O', 'C' and indicate that he is facing a tree blocking his movement forward, that he can move backward or to his left, and that he finds an impassable cliff to his right. By implication, the cell he is standing in contains 'O' or 'R.'

Your program can tell the professor to move one cell in any of the four directions by sending him an 'F' (move forward), a 'B' (move backward), 'L' (move left), or 'R' (move right). The syntax is Move('L') for a move left, and so on. Keep in mind that if you tell him to move into a cell containing a tree, your grade will suffer when he finally returns. However, if you direct him to move into a cell containing a cliff, it will not only be on your conscience but also appear as an 'F' on your grade report (which will be filed by Dr. Michaels's next of kin).

Your program is to be able to identify the professor's location in as few query/movement combinations as possible, and then direct him by way of the shortest route possible from that location to the road that runs along the forest's southern boundary.
Prototypes of the Query() and Move() functions are as follows:

```
char * Query(void)
/* Query returns a pointer to a string of four characters */

int Move(char direction);
/* if the move is successful, Move returns the value 0. If it is unsuccessful
because you directed him into a tree, Move returns a -1. If Move is
unsuccessful because you directed the professor off a cliff, Move returns a
-100 indicating you just failed your research project work and need to call
the coroner. */
```

Hint: The professor may be facing any of four directions, north, east, south, or west, and does not have a compass. Thus, you will have to match the pattern he returns in response to a Query() to your map data in four possible orientations to narrow down the set of possible locations he is in. Then you will have to Move() him and again Query() him. When you have finally determined where he is located, you have to find the shortest route out of the forest to the southern boundary road.

6-20. Eric was fascinated by the latest episode of "Who Done It?", a mystery thriller he had watched on tape-delay last night. It seems the key to solving the mystery was the ability of Sam Shovel, the detective, to match patterns in various handwriting samples. Eric decided to write a simple program to mimic Sam's pattern-matching behavior. The first thing Eric did was to create a set of 26 "perfect" printed letters on 15×21 grids. These templates would then be compared to actual printing samples, one after the other, to deduce the actual printed characters. His first attempt at writing this program was a total flop! He soon had discovered that none of the actual printed characters was an exact match for his "perfect" characters; he had not recognized any part of the suspect's message.

He then decided to try three radically different approaches. In the first, he used a pipelined solution: scaled the character to a nominal size, centered it in a grid, determined its axes of symmetry, and rotated it to a standard orientation; then compared it to the set of "perfect" characters. In the second, he smoothed the printed character to eliminate noise from the suspect's jittery printing by blurring it slightly using a mathematics-based filter operation, by applying still more mathematics to look at the character in a transform domain, and finally by comparing that to the transforms of the "perfect" characters. In the third approach, Eric decided to simplify things still further; he just counted the number of matches between cells on the 15×21 grid and the grid containing the printed character. He moved the printed character around over the "perfect" one until he got the best match, recorded the number of matches, and then repeated with the next "perfect" character until all 26 had been compared; the best match must be the winner, he thought.

Give a brief analysis of each of his approaches with respect to the one with the best prospects for parallel processing.

6-21. Once upon a time there was an island populated only by rabbits, foxes, and vegetation. The island (conveniently enough!) was the exact shape of a chessboard. Some local geographers have even drawn gridlines that serve to divide the island into 64 squares to facilitate their demographic studies on the populations of each inhabitant.

Within each square the populations of rabbits and foxes are governed by several factors:

- the populations of rabbits and foxes in each square at the start of this "day"
- the reproduction rates of rabbits and foxes (the same over the entire island) during this day
- the vegetation growth rate
- the death rates of "old" rabbits and foxes during this day
- the eating habits of foxes (foxes live entirely on rabbits; when the vegetation is dense, rabbits are more difficult to find)
- the eating habits of rabbits (they live on the vegetation; too many rabbits in a square could lead to their starving and/or a lower reproduction rate and/or being easier for foxes to find and eat)
- the migration (from day to day) of rabbits from one square to other squares that are immediately adjacent
- the migration of foxes from one square to any other square within two "leaps"

Since this is an island, there are certain boundary conditions: The 28 squares on the water's edge have no migration possible into or out of the water for either rabbits or foxes. Similarly, there are certain initial conditions representing the starting populations of rabbits and foxes in the various squares at the time your program begins its execution.

Your job is to simulate 10 years of life on the island, using time steps of a day in length, and to determine the populations of rabbits and foxes at the end of the period in each square on the island. For each pair of rabbits in a square at the start of a birthing day, which occurs every nine weeks, a litter of babies is born. The size of the litter ranges between two and nine and varies based on both the food supply (vegetation level) and the number of rabbits in that square at the start of the day (population density), as given in Table 6.1. For each pair of foxes in a square at the start of a birthing day, which occurs every six months, a litter of kits is born. The size of the litter ranges between zero and five and varies based on both the food supply (rabbit population) and the number of foxes in that square at the start of the day (population density), as given in Table 6.2.

A fox can survive on as little as two rabbits per week, but will eat as many as four if they can be found. If the vegetation level is below 0.6, rabbits are more easily found. In that case, on any given day, there is a four in seven chance that a fox will eat a rabbit if there are sufficient rabbits available; if there are fewer rabbits than that, or if the vegetation level is at or above 0.6, the foxes will have to make do with a two in seven chance of having a meal — provided there are sufficient rabbits available at that consumption level. (If there are fewer rabbits than the

TABLE 6.1 RABBIT BIRTHS FOR PROBLEM 6-21

Vegetation at start of day	Number of rabbits at start of day				
	< 2	2 to 200	201 to 700	701 to 5000	> 5000
< 0.2	0	3	3	2	2
≥ 0.2 but < 0.5	0	4	4	3	3
≥ 0.5 but < 0.8	0	6	5	4	4
≥ 0.8	0	9	8	7	5

TABLE 6.2 RABBIT AND FOX POPULATIONS FOR PROBLEM 6-21

Rabbit population at start of day (per fox)	Number of foxes at start of day				
	< 2	2 to 10	11 to 50	51 to 100	> 100
< 3.0	0	2	2	1	0
≥3.0 but < 10	0	3	3	2	1
≥10 but < 40	0	4	3	3	2
≥40	0	5	4	3	3

number needed to keep the fox population alive, foxes that didn't get fed have a 10 percent chance that they will die off; that is, in addition to their natural death rate.) The lifespan of a fox is estimated to be four years. Use a random-number generator each day to determine whether one or more foxes die a natural death.

A rabbit consumes vegetation; each rabbit consumes 0.1 percent of the vegetation in a square per day, under non-food-constrained situations. The normal lifespan of a rabbit is estimated to be 18 months. If the vegetation level is less than 0.35, the death rate due to starvation rises dramatically, as given in Table 6.3.

TABLE 6.3 RABBIT LIFESPAN

Vegetation Level	Rabbit Lifespan
0.1 to 0.15	3 months
0.15 to 0.25	6 months
0.25 to 0.3	12 months
over 0.35	18 months

Use a random-number generator each day to determine the number of rabbits that die from a combination of starvation and natural causes. The vegetation level rises quite rapidly when not being eaten by rabbits; growing conditions are ideal on the semitropical island. The vegetation level follows the growth/consumption formula:

Vegetation at end of day =

(110% of vegetation at start of day) – (0.001 × number of rabbits at start of day)

within the limits that the vegetation level will not drop below 0.1 or grow to be more than 1.0. At the end of each day, 20 percent of the rabbit population randomly emigrates to adjoining squares. Use a random-number generator to determine the number that actually emigrate to each of the possible adjoining squares. Similarly, since foxes range more widely, at the end of each day, every fox randomly emigrates zero, one, or two squares distant from its location at the start of that day. Note: All possible migrations are to be considered uniformly likely among the choices available.

Case 1: Uniformly, there are two foxes and 100 rabbits per square initially; the vegetation level is 1.0 everywhere.

Case 2: There are 20 foxes in one corner square and none elsewhere; there are 10 rabbits in every square except in the corner square diagonally opposite the foxes, and it contains 800 rabbits; the vegetation level is 0.3 everywhere.

Case 3: There are no foxes on the island, but there are two rabbits in each square; the initial vegetation level is 0.5 everywhere.

6-22. Develop a cellular automaton solution to a real problem and implement it.

6-23. (A research assignment) Develop the rules necessary to model the movement (erosion) of sand dunes at a beach when affected by the waves. (A similar problem is modeling the erosion of the banks of a river due to the water.)

6-24. (A research assignment) Develop the rules necessary to model the airflow across a wing as shown in Figure 6.21 (two dimensions). Select your own dimensions for the solution space and object. Select the number of grid points and write code to solve the problem.

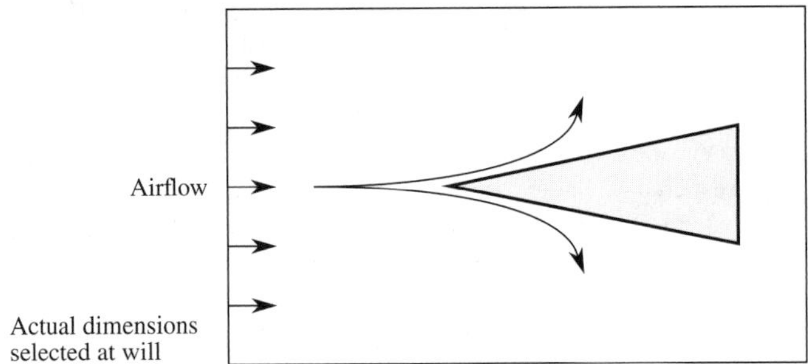

Figure 6.21 Figure for Problem 6-24.

Chapter 7

Load Balancing and Termination Detection

In this chapter, we introduce the concept of *load balancing*, which is used to distribute computations fairly across processors in order to obtain the highest-possible execution speed. A related issue is detecting when a computation has been completed, so-called *termination detection*. Termination detection becomes a significant issue when the computation is distributed, and it is considered here with load balancing. After developing the various load-balancing termination and detection techniques, an application example is described in detail.

7.1 LOAD BALANCING

So far, we have divided a problem into a fixed number of processes that are to be executed in parallel. Each process performs a known amount of work. In addition, it was assumed that the processes were simply distributed among the available processors without any discussion of the effects of the types of processors and their speeds. However, it may be that some processors will complete their tasks before others and become idle because the work is unevenly divided, or perhaps some processors will operate faster than others (or both situations). Ideally, we want all the processors to be operating continuously on tasks that would lead to the minimum execution time. Achieving this goal by spreading the tasks evenly across the processors is called *load balancing*. Load balancing was mentioned in Chapter 3 for the Mandelbrot calculation, in which there was no interprocess communication. Now we will develop load balancing further to include the case in which there is communication between processors. Load balancing is particularly useful when the amount of work is not known prior to execution. It also helps mitigate the effects of differences in processor speeds even when the amount of work is known in advance.

Figure 7.1 illustrates how load balancing will produce the minimum execution time (the true goal). In Figure 7.1(a), one processor, P_1, is operating for a longer period, and one processor, P_4, completes its work early. The total execution time is longer. Ideally, part of P_1's work should be given to P_4 to equalize the workload. In Figure 7.1(b), all the processors are executing for the duration of the execution, t seconds, and perfect load balancing exists. Another way of viewing this problem is that the total computation using a single processor may require k clock cycles. With p processors and no additional overhead for a parallel implementation, the execution time should be reduced to k/p clock cycles.

Load balancing can be attempted *statically* before the execution of any process or *dynamically* during the execution of the processes. Static load balancing is usually referred to as the *mapping problem* (Bokhari, 1981) or *scheduling problem*. Substantial literature exists on the problem, mostly using optimization techniques, starting from estimated execution times of parts of the program and their interdependencies. The following are some potential static load-balancing techniques:

- *Round robin algorithm* — passes out tasks in sequential order of processes, coming back to the first when all the processes have been given a task
- *Randomized algorithms* — selects processes at random to take tasks
- *Recursive bisection* — recursively divides the problem into subproblems of equal computational effort while minimizing message-passing
- *Simulated annealing* — an optimization technique
- *Genetic algorithm* — another optimization technique, described in Chapter 12

Figure 7.1 could also be viewed as a form of *bin packing* (i.e., placing objects into boxes to reduce the number of boxes), and scheduling can be approached with bin-packing

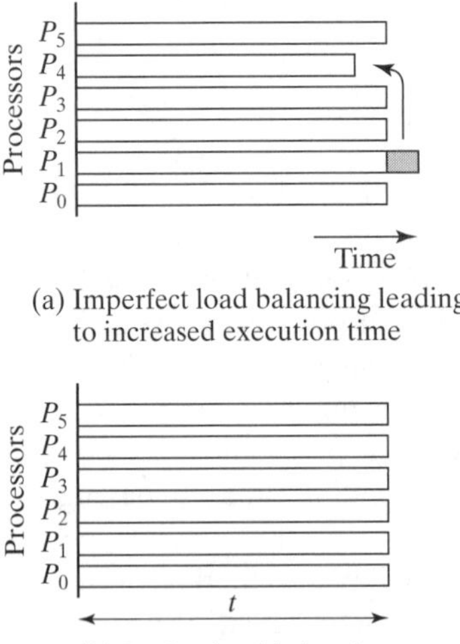

Figure 7.1 Load balancing.

algorithms (Coffman, Garey, and Johnson, 1978). In our case, there would be a fixed number of equal-sized boxes (processes) and the object is to minimize the size of the boxes.

For processors/computers interconnected by a static-link interconnection network, communicating processes should be executed on processors with direct communication paths to reduce the communication delays. This is an essential part of the "mapping" problem for such systems. The solution may require different mappings for different networks. In general, there is probably no polynomial-time algorithm for solving the problem, and therefore it is regarded as a computationally intractable problem. Hence, heuristics are often used to select processors for processes.

There are several fundamental flaws with static load balancing even if a mathematical solution exists. First and foremost, it is very difficult to estimate accurately the execution times of various parts of a program without actually executing the parts. Therefore, scheduling these parts without using actual execution times is innately inaccurate. In addition, some systems may also have communication delays that vary under different circumstances, and it could be difficult to incorporate variable communication delays in static load balancing. Some problems have an indeterminate number of steps to reach their solution. For example, search algorithms commonly traverse a graph looking for the solution, and it is unknown how many paths must be searched beforehand, whether done in parallel or sequentially. Since static load balancing would not work well under these circumstances, we need to turn to dynamic load balancing.

In dynamic load balancing, all these factors are taken into account by making the division of load dependent upon the execution of the parts as they are being executed. This incurs an additional overhead during execution but is much more effective than static load balancing. In this chapter, we will concentrate upon dynamic load balancing and describe different ways that it can be achieved. We will also discuss in detail how a computation finally comes to an end, which can be a significant problem in dynamic loading balancing. This aspect is called *termination detection.*

The computation will be divided into *work* or *tasks* to be performed, and processes perform these tasks. As usual, the processes are mapped onto processors. Since our objective is to keep the processors busy, we are interested in the activity of the processors. However, we often map a single process onto each processor, so we will use the terms *process* and *processor* somewhat interchangeably.

7.2 DYNAMIC LOAD BALANCING

In dynamic load balancing, tasks are allocated to processors during the execution of the program. Dynamic load balancing can be classified as one of the following:

- Centralized
- Decentralized

In centralized dynamic load balancing, tasks are handed out from a centralized location. A clear master-slave structure exists in which a master process controls each of a set of slave processes directly. In decentralized dynamic load balancing, tasks are passed between arbitrary processes. A collection of worker processes operate upon the problem and interact among themselves, finally reporting to a single process. A worker process may receive tasks from other worker processes and may send tasks to other worker processes to complete or pass on at their discretion.

7.2.1 Centralized Dynamic Load Balancing

In centralized dynamic load balancing, the master process holds the collection of tasks to be performed. Tasks are sent to the slave processes. When a slave process completes one task, it requests another task from the master process. This mechanism is the essential part of the so-called *work-pool* approach first introduced in Chapter 3 to generate the Mandelbrot image. In that case, the work pool held the tasks as specified by the coordinates of the pixels. The term *replicated worker* is sometimes used to describe the methodology, because all the slaves are the same. (This idea can be developed into having specialized slaves capable of performing certain tasks.) Another term used for the same methodology is *processor farm.*

The work-pool technique can be readily applied to simple divide-and-conquer problems. It can also be applied to problems in which the tasks are quite different and of different sizes. Generally, it is best to hand out the larger or most complex tasks first. If a larger task were handed out later in the computation, the slaves that completed the smaller tasks would then sit idly by waiting for the larger task to be completed.

The work-pool technique can also be readily applied when the number of tasks may change during execution. In some applications, especially search algorithms, the execution of one task may generate new tasks, though finally the number of tasks must reduce to zero, signaling that the computation is completing. A queue can be used to hold the currently waiting tasks, as shown in Figure 7.2. If all the tasks are of equal size and importance, a simple first-in-first-out queue may be acceptable. If some tasks are more important than others (e.g., are expected to lead to a solution more quickly), they would be passed to the slave processes first. Other information, such as the current best solution, may be kept by the master process.

Termination. Stopping the computation when the solution has been reached is called *termination.* A great advantage of centralized dynamic load balancing is that it is a simple matter for the master process to recognize when to terminate. For a computation in

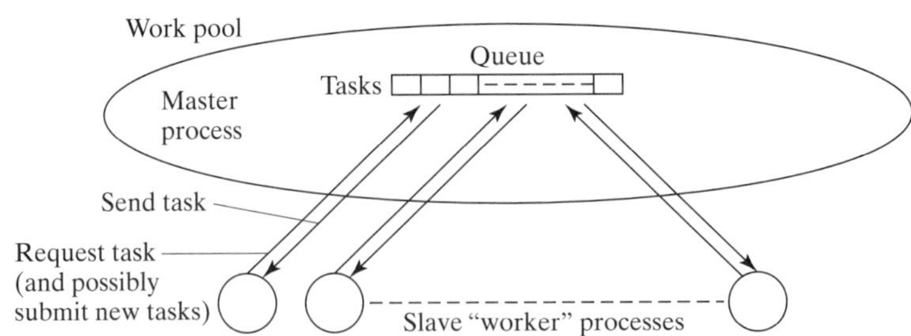

Figure 7.2 Centralized work pool.

which tasks are taken from a task queue, the computation terminates when both of the following are satisfied:

- The task queue is empty
- Every slave process is idle and has made a request for another task without any new tasks being generated

Note that it is necessary to establish that no new tasks have been generated. (Problems that do not generate new tasks during the execution, such as the Mandelbrot calculation, would terminate when the task queue is empty and all slaves have finished.)

In some applications, a slave may detect the program termination condition by some local termination condition, such as finding the item in a search algorithm. In that case, the slave process would send a termination message to the master. Then the master would close down all the other slave processes. In some applications, each slave process must reach a specific local termination condition, such as convergence on its local solutions, as in the synchronous iteration problems of Chapter 6.

7.2.2 Decentralized Dynamic Load Balancing

Although widely used, a significant disadvantage of the centralized work pool is that the master process can only issue one task at a time, and after the initial tasks have been sent, it can only respond to requests for new tasks one at a time. Thus the potential exists for a bottleneck when there are many slave processes making simultaneous requests. The centralized work pool will be satisfactory if there are few slaves and the tasks are computationally intensive. For finer-grained tasks and many slaves, it may be more appropriate to distribute the work pool into more than one site.

One approach is to distribute the work pool as shown in Figure 7.3. Here, the master has divided its initial work pool into parts and sent one part to each of a set of "mini-masters" processes (M_0 to M_{p-1}). Each mini-master controls one group of slaves. For an optimization problem, the mini-masters might find a local optimum that they would pass back the master. The master would select the best solution. It is clear that this approach

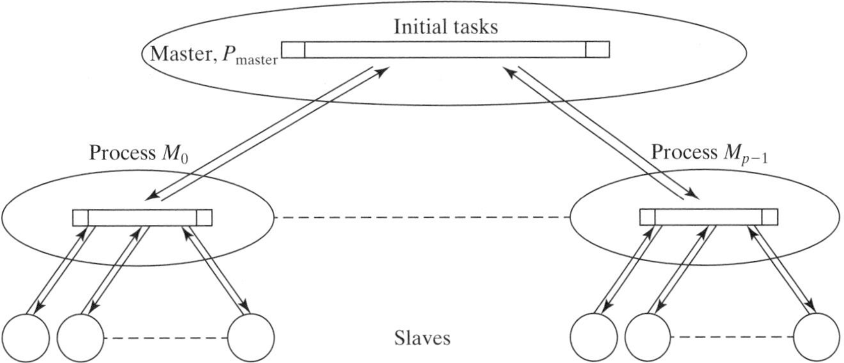

Figure 7.3 A distributed work pool.

could be developed by having several levels of decomposition; a tree could be formed with the slave processes at the leaves and internal nodes dividing up the work. This is the basic method of decomposing a task into equal subtasks. At each level in the tree, the process passes on half of the tasks to one subtree and the other half to the other subtree, assuming a binary tree. Another distributed approach would be to have the slaves actually hold a portion of the work pool and solve for this portion.

Fully Distributed Work Pool. Once the workload is distributed with processes having and generating their own tasks, the possibility exists for processes to execute tasks from each other, as illustrated in Figure 7.4. The tasks could be transferred by

1. The *receiver-initiated* method
2. The *sender-initiated* method

In the *receiver-initiated* method, a process requests tasks from other processes it selects. Typically, a process would request tasks from other processes when it has few or no tasks to perform. The method has been shown to work well at high system load. In the *sender-initiated* method, a process sends tasks to other processes it selects. Typically, in this method, a process with a heavy load passes out some of its tasks to others that are willing to accept them. This method has been shown to work well for light overall system loads. Another option is to have a mixture of both methods. Unfortunately, it can be expensive to determine process loads. In very heavy system loads, load balancing can also be difficult to achieve because of the lack of available processes.

Let us discuss load balancing in the context of the receiver-initiated method, though it can also apply to the sender-initiated method. Several strategies are feasible. Processes could be organized as a ring with a process requesting tasks from its nearest neighbors. A ring organization would suit a multiprocessor system using a ring interconnection network. Similarly, in a hypercube, processes could request tasks from those processes directly interconnected, one in each dimension. Of course, as with any strategy, one would need to be careful not to keep passing on the same task that is received.

Process Selection. Without the constraints (and advantages) of a specific interconnection network, all processes are equal candidates, and any process could select any other process. For distributed operation, each process would have its own selection algorithm, as shown in Figure 7.5. When implemented locally, this algorithm could be

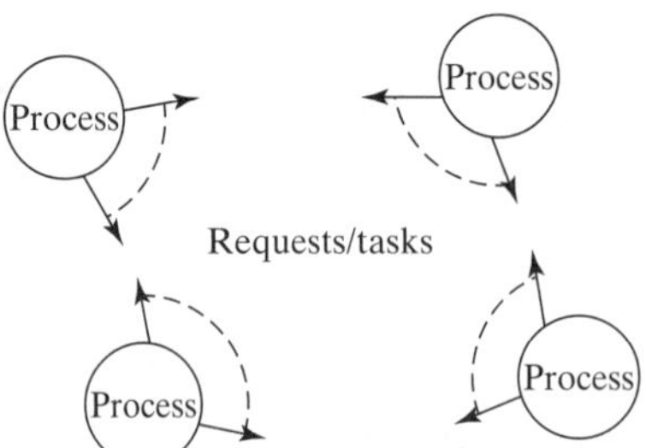

Figure 7.4 Decentralized work pool.

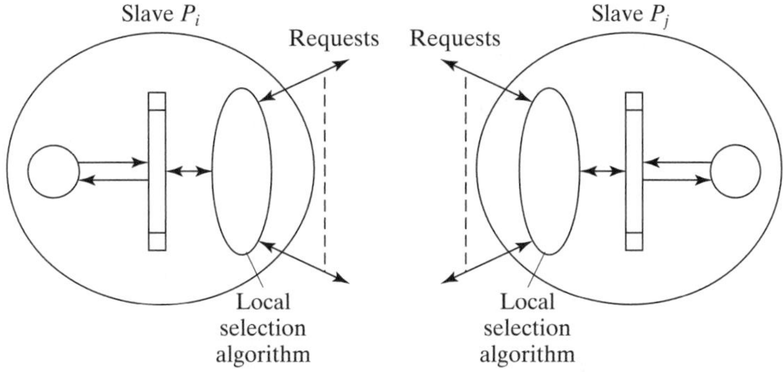

Figure 7.5 Decentralized selection algorithm requesting tasks between slaves.

applied to all the processes working on the problem or to different subsets, if the problem or network makes it desirable. Algorithms for selecting a process include the *round robin algorithm*. In the round robin algorithm, process P_i requests tasks from process P_x, where x is given by a counter that is incremented after each request, using modulo p arithmetic (p processes). If $p = 8$, x takes on the values 0, 1, 2, 3, 4, 5, 6, 7, 0, 1, 2, 3, 4, 5, 6, 7, … . The process does not select itself ($x = i$) and would cause the counter to be incremented once more when $x = i$. In the *random polling algorithm*, process P_i requests tasks from process P_x, where x is a number that is selected randomly between 0 and $p - 1$ (excluding i).

When a process receives a request for tasks, it will send a portion of the tasks it has yet to undertake to the requesting process. For example, suppose the problem is one of traversing a search tree using a depth first search. Nodes will be visited in a downward fashion from the root. A list of unvisited nodes leading from the edges of a node a process visits will be maintained. The process will select from this list a suitable set of unvisited nodes to return to the requesting process. Various strategies can be used to determine how many nodes and which nodes to return.

7.2.3 Load Balancing Using a Line Structure

Wilson (1995) describes a load-balancing technique that is particularly applicable to processors connected in a line structure (or pipeline), but the technique could be extended to other interconnection structures. He describes the technique in connection with transputers, which are often connected as a line. We consider the technique here to show the possibilities of a specific interconnection network. The basic idea is to create a queue of tasks with individual processors accessing locations in the queue, as shown in Figure 7.6. The master process (P_0 in Figure 7.6) feeds the queue with tasks at one end, and the tasks are shifted down the queue. When a worker process, P_i ($1 \le i < p$), detects a task at its input from the queue and the process is idle, it takes the task from the queue. Then the tasks to the left shuffle down the queue so that the space held by the task is filled. A new task is inserted into the left-side end of the queue. Eventually, all the processes will have a task and the queue is filled with new tasks. This mechanism will clearly keep worker processes busy. High-priority or larger tasks could be placed in the queue first.

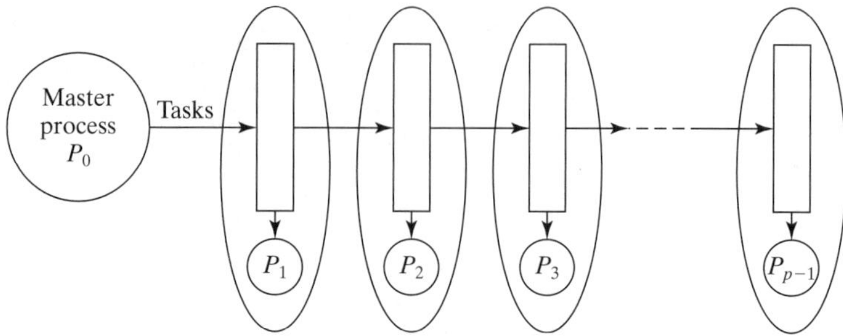

Figure 7.6 Load balancing using a pipeline structure.

The shifting actions could be orchestrated by using messages between adjacent processes. Perhaps the most elegant method is to have two processes running on each processor:

- For left and right communication
- For the current task

as shown in Figure 7.7. Three processes could also be constructed

- For left communication
- For right communication
- For the current task

These constructions are typical of transputer programs where concurrent processes are supported within the hardware of the transputer and are expected. There is no difficulty in applying the idea to some implementations of MPI that allow multiple processes on a single processor. However, some implementations of MPI do not allow multiple processes on a single processor, and in any event it might incur a very significant and possibly unacceptable overhead. (A more attractive alternative is to use threads, as described in Chapter 8.)

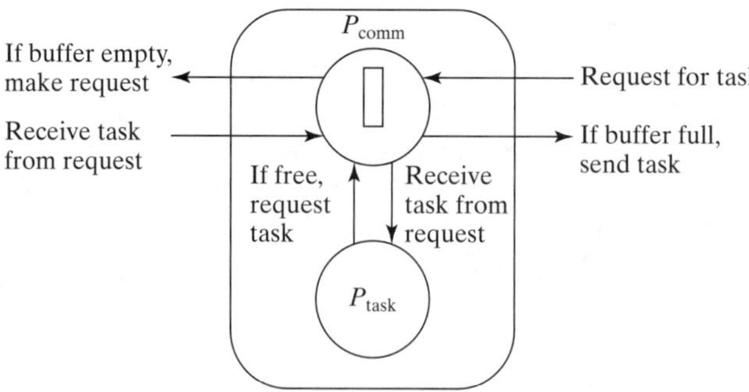

Figure 7.7 Using a communication process in line load balancing.

We could hand-code the time sharing between communication and task computation as follows:

Master process (P_0)

```
for (i = 0; i < num_tasks; i++) {
   recv(P1, request_tag);                     /* request for task */
   send(&task, P1, task_tag);                 /* send tasks into queue */
}
recv(P1, request_tag);                        /* request for task */
send(&empty, P1, task_tag);                   /* end of tasks */
```

Process P_i $(1 < i < p)$

```
if (buffer == empty) {
   send(Pi-1, request_tag);                   /* request new task */
   recv(&buffer, Pi-1, task_tag);             /* task from left proc */
}
if ((buffer == full) && (!busy)) {            /* get next task */
   task = buffer;                             /* get task*/
   buffer = empty;                            /* set buffer empty */
   busy = TRUE;                               /* set process busy */
}
nrecv(Pi+1, request_tag, request);            /* check message from right */
if (request && (buffer == full)) {
   send(&buffer, Pi+1);                       /* shift task forward */
   buffer = empty;
}
if (busy) {                                   /* continue on current task */
   Do some work on task.
   If task finished, set busy to false.
}
```

A combined `sendrecv()` might be applied if available rather than a `send()`/`recv()` pair.

Nonblocking Receive Routines. In the previous code, a nonblocking `nrecv()` is necessary to check for a request being received from the right. In our pseudocode, we have simply added the parameter `request`, which is set to `TRUE` if a message has been received. In actual programming systems, specific mechanisms are present. In MPI, the nonblocking receive, `MPI_Irecv()`, returns (in a parameter) a request "handle," which is used in subsequent completion routines to wait for the message or to establish whether the message has actually been received at that point (`MPI_Wait()` and `MPI_Test()`, respectively). In effect, the nonblocking receive, `MPI_Irecv()`, posts a request for message and returns immediately.

Other Structures. Though not mentioned in Wilson (1995), it is clearly possible to extend the approach to a tree, as shown in Figure 7.8. Tasks are passed from a node into one of the two nodes below it when a node buffer becomes empty.

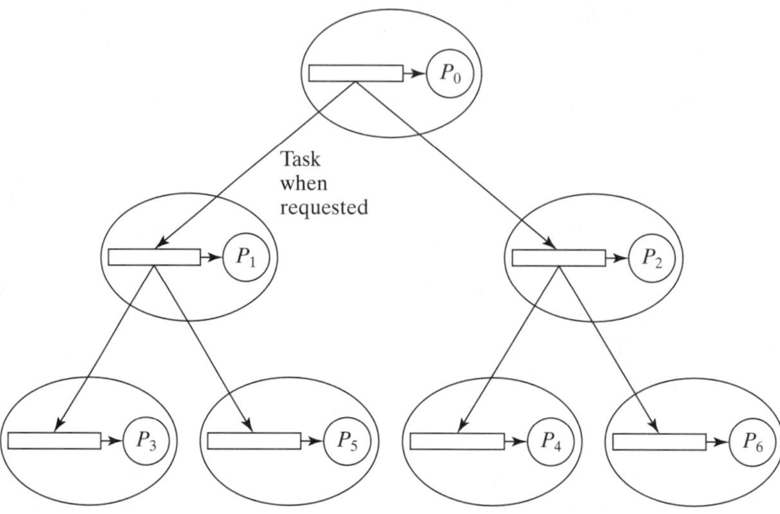

Figure 7.8 Load balancing using a tree.

7.3 DISTRIBUTED TERMINATION DETECTION ALGORITHMS

So far, we have considered distributing the tasks. Now let us look at how to terminate these distributed tasks. Various distributed termination algorithms have been proposed, but first let us examine the termination conditions.

7.3.1 Termination Conditions

When a computation is distributed, recognizing that the computation has come to an end may be difficult unless the problem is such that one process reaches a solution. In general, distributed termination at time t requires the following conditions to be satisfied (Bertsekas and Tsitsiklis, 1989):

- Application-specific local termination conditions exist throughout the collection of processes, at time t.
- There are no messages in transit between processes at time t.

The subtle difference between these termination conditions and those given for a centralized load-balancing system is the need to take into account messages in transit. The second condition is necessary for the distributed termination system because a message in transit might restart a terminated process. One could imagine a process reaching its local termination condition and terminating while a message is being sent to it from another process. The first condition is usually relatively easy to recognize. Each process can send a message to the master when its local termination conditions are satisfied. However, the second condition is more difficult to recognize. The time that it takes for messages to travel between processes will not be known in advance. One could conceivably wait a long enough period to allow any message in transit to arrive. This approach would not be favored and would not permit portable code on different architectures.

7.3.2 Using Acknowledgment Messages

Bertsekas and Tsitsiklis (1989) describe a distributed termination method using request and acknowledgment messages. The method is very general, mathematically sound, and copes with messages being in transit when a process is about to terminate locally. Bertsekas and Tsitsiklis give formal mathematical arguments in detail.

The method is illustrated in Figure 7.9. Each process is in one of two states:

1. Inactive
2. Active

Initially, without any task to perform, the process is in the inactive state. Upon receiving a task from a process, it changes to the active state. The process that sent the task to make it enter the active state becomes its "parent." If the process passes on a task to an inactive process, it similarly becomes the parent of this process, thus creating a tree of processes, each with a unique parent. An active process could potentially receive more tasks from other active processes while it is in the active state, but these other processes are not parents of the process. Hence, the computation itself need not be a tree structure. On every occasion when a process sends a task to another process, it expects an acknowledgment message from that process. On every occasion when it receives a task from a process, it immediately sends an acknowledgment message, except if the process it receives the task from is its parent process. It only sends an acknowledgment message to its parent when it is ready to become inactive. It becomes inactive when

- Its local termination condition exists (all tasks are completed).
- It has transmitted all its acknowledgments for tasks it has received.
- It has received all its acknowledgments for tasks it has sent out.

The last condition means that a process must become inactive before its parent process. When the first process becomes idle, the computation can terminate.

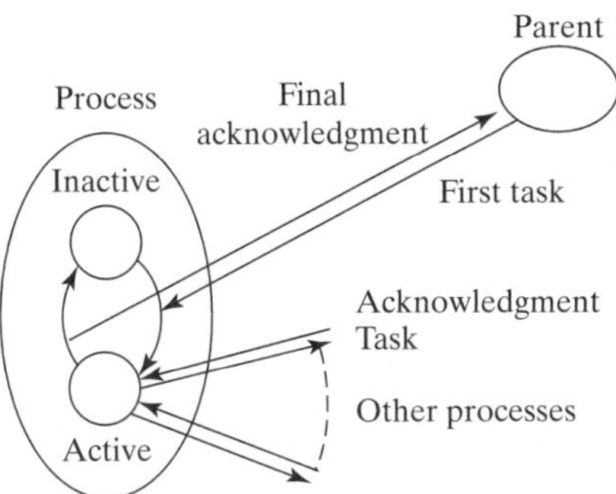

Figure 7.9 Termination using message acknowledgments.

This algorithm is perhaps the best to use because of its generality and its proven soundness. However, a particular application may lend itself to another solution, and certain interconnection structures may suggest alternative termination mechanisms.

7.3.3 Ring Termination Algorithms

For termination purposes, the processes are organized in a ring structure, as shown in Figure 7.10. The single-pass ring termination algorithm is as follows:

1. When P_0 has terminated, it generates a token that is passed to P_1.
2. When P_i ($1 \leq i < p$) receives the token and has already terminated, it passes the token onward to P_{i+1}. Otherwise, it waits for its local termination condition and then passes the token onward. P_{p-1} passes the token to P_0.
3. When P_0 receives a token, it knows that all the processes in the ring have terminated. A message can then be sent to all the processes informing them of the global termination, if necessary.

Each process, except the first process, implements a function, as illustrated in Figure 7.11. The algorithm assumes that a process cannot be reactivated after reaching its local termination condition. This does not apply to work-pool problems in which a process can pass a new task to an idle process.

The dual-pass ring termination algorithm (Dijkstra, Feijen, and Gasteren, 1983) can handle processes being reactivated but requires two passes around the ring. The reason for reactivation is for process P_i to pass a task to P_j where $j < i$ and after a token has passed P_j, as shown in Figure 7.12. If this occurs, the token must recirculate through the ring a second time. To differentiate these circumstances, tokens are colored white or black. Processes are also colored white or black. Receiving a black token means that global termination may not

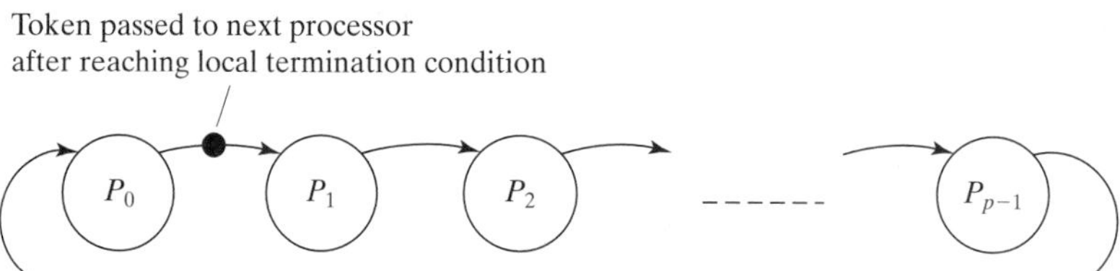

Figure 7.10 Ring termination detection algorithm.

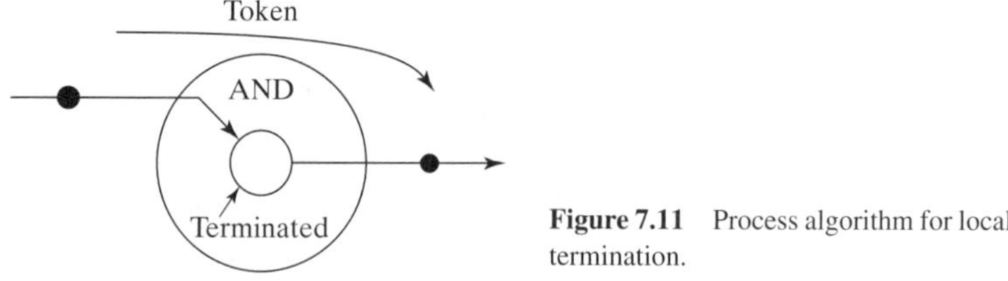

Figure 7.11 Process algorithm for local termination.

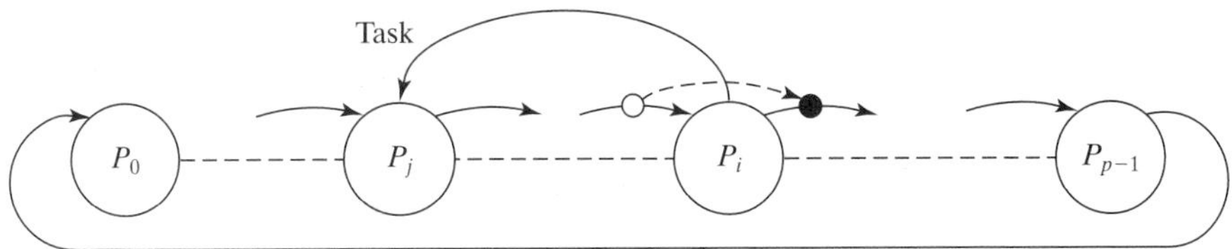

Figure 7.12 Passing task to previous processes.

have occurred and the token must be recirculated around the ring again. The algorithm is as follows, again starting at P_0:

1. P_0 becomes white when it has terminated and generates a white token to P_1.
2. The token is passed through the ring from one process to the next when each process has terminated, but the color of the token may be changed. If P_i passes a task to P_j where $j < i$ (i.e., before this process in the ring), it becomes a *black process*; otherwise it is a *white process*. A black process will color a token black and pass it on. A white process will pass on the token in its original color (either black or white). After P_i has passed on a token, it becomes a white process. P_{p-1} passes the token to P_0.
3. When P_0 receives a black token, it passes on a white token; if it receives a white token, all processes have terminated.

Note that in both ring algorithms, P_0 becomes the central point for global termination. Also, it is assumed that an acknowledge signal is generated to each request.

Tree Algorithm. The local actions described in Figure 7.11 can be applied to various interconnection structures, notably a tree structure, to indicate that processes up to that point have terminated. Two branches of a tree using this mechanism are shown in Figure 7.13. Now a token is passed forward when the tokens are received from each branch of the tree and the local termination condition exists. When the root receives its

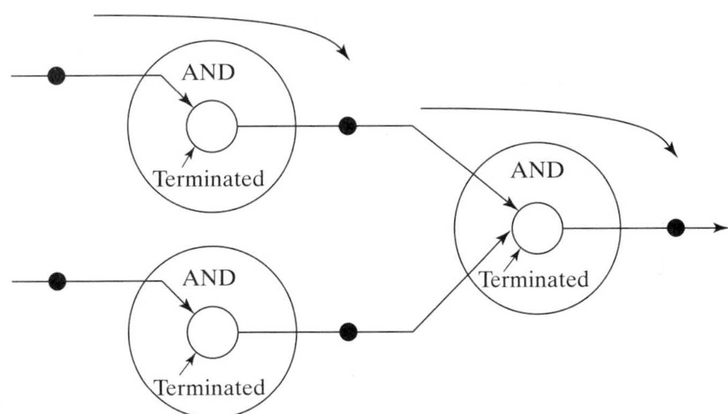

Figure 7.13 Tree termination.

full complement of tokens and has terminated, global termination has occurred. Again all other processes must then be informed, perhaps by a tree broadcast algorithm.

7.3.4 Fixed Energy Distributed Termination Algorithm

Another termination algorithm uses the notation of a fixed quantity within the system, colorfully termed "energy." This energy is similar to a token but has a numeric value. The system starts with all the energy being held by one process, the master process. The master process passes out portions of the energy with the tasks to processes making requests for tasks. Similarly, if these processes receive requests for tasks, the energy is divided further and passed to them. When a process becomes idle, it passes the energy it holds back before requesting a new task. This energy could be passed directly back to the master process or to the process giving it the original task. In the latter case, the algorithm will create a treelike structure, and a process will not hand back its energy until all the energy it has handed out is returned and combined to the total energy held. When all the energy is returned to the root and the root becomes idle, all the processes must be idle and the computation can terminate.

A significant disadvantage of the fixed energy method is that dividing the energy will be of finite precision and adding the partial energies may not equate to the original energy if floating-point arithmetic is used. In addition, one can only divide the energy so far before it becomes essentially zero. Integer arithmetic with verification can generally overcome the first problem if the original integer energy is large enough to cope with the number of divisions.

7.4 PROGRAM EXAMPLE

In this section, we will discuss how the various load-balancing strategies can be applied to a representative problem. There are several application areas, including the obvious search and optimization areas. Other areas include image processing, ray tracing, and volume rendering. In fact, any problem that can be divided and conquered is a candidate for a work-pool approach. For the most part, problems that can take greatest advantage of dynamic load balancing are those in which the number of tasks is variable and unknown. Of course, dynamic load balancing is also very advantageous to a heterogeneous network of computers.

7.4.1 Shortest-Path Problem

We will investigate the problem of finding the shortest distance between two points on a graph. This is a very well known problem appearing in some form in most sequential programming classes. It can be stated as follows:

> Given a set of interconnected nodes where the links between the nodes are marked with "weights," find the path from one specific node to another specific node that has the smallest accumulated weights.

The interconnected nodes can be described by a *graph*. In graph terminology, the nodes are called *vertices*, and the links are called *edges*. If the edges have implied directions, that is, if an edge can only be traversed in one direction, the graph is a *directed graph*. The problem is one of searching for the best path through the graph. The graph itself could be used to find the solution to many different problems; for example,

1. The shortest distance between two towns or other points on a map, where the weights represent distance
2. The quickest route to travel, where the weights represent time (the quickest route may not be the shortest route if different modes of travel are available; for example, flying to certain towns)
3. The least expensive way to travel by air, where the weights represent the cost of the flights between cities (the vertices)
4. The best way to climb a mountain given a terrain map with contours
5. The best route through a computer network for minimum message delay (the vertices represent computers, and the weights represent the delay between two computers)
6. The most efficient manufacturing system, where the weights represent hours of work

"The best way to climb a mountain" will be used as an example, as illustrated in Figure 7.14. The corresponding graph is shown in Figure 7.15, where the weights indicate the amount of effort that would be expended in traversing the route between two connected camp sites. Note in this example that the graph is a directed graph and the weights are associated with traversing the path in a particular direction. Theoretically, we should make paths between all the camps in both directions, an exhaustively connected graph, though it would still be a directed graph since the weights would be different in each direction. The effort in one direction may be different from the effort in the opposite direction (downhill instead of uphill!). In some problems, the weights would be the same in both directions. For example, in finding the shortest route to drive, the distance is the same in both directions. The weights would be the same, an *undirected graph.*

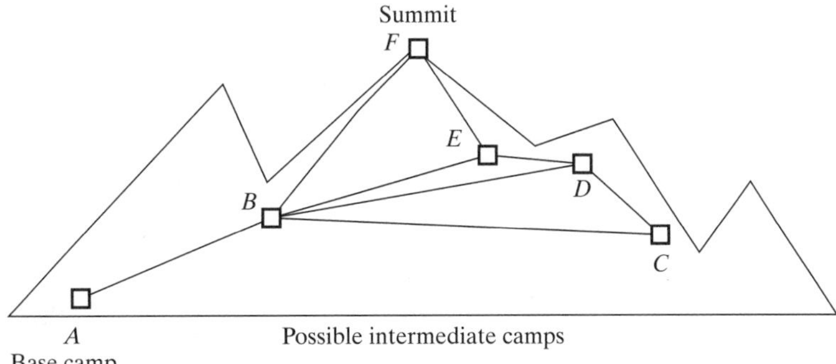

Figure 7.14 Climbing a mountain.

7.4.2 Graph Representation

We first need to establish the way that the graph is to be represented in the program. As will be familiar from sequential programming, there are two basic ways that a graph can be represented in a program:

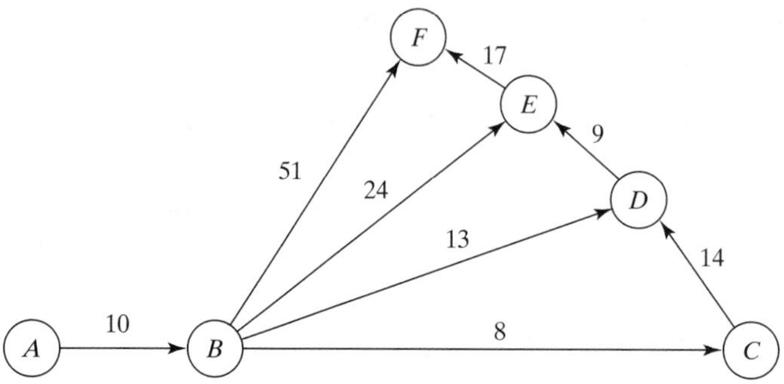

Figure 7.15 Graph of mountain climb.

1. Adjacency matrix — a two-dimensional array, `a`, in which `a[i][j]` holds the weight associated with the edge between vertex i and vertex j if one exists
2. Adjacency list — for each vertex, a list of vertices directly connected to the vertex by an edge and the corresponding weights associated with the edges

Both methods are shown in Figure 7.16 for our mountain-climbing problem. The adjacency list is implemented as a linked list. The order of the edges in the adjacency list is arbitrary.

Source \ Destination	*A*	*B*	*C*	*D*	*E*	*F*
A	∞	10	∞	∞	∞	∞
B	∞	∞	8	13	24	51
C	∞	∞	∞	14	∞	∞
D	∞	∞	∞	∞	9	∞
E	∞	∞	∞	∞	∞	17
F	∞	∞	∞	∞	∞	∞

(a) Adjacency matrix

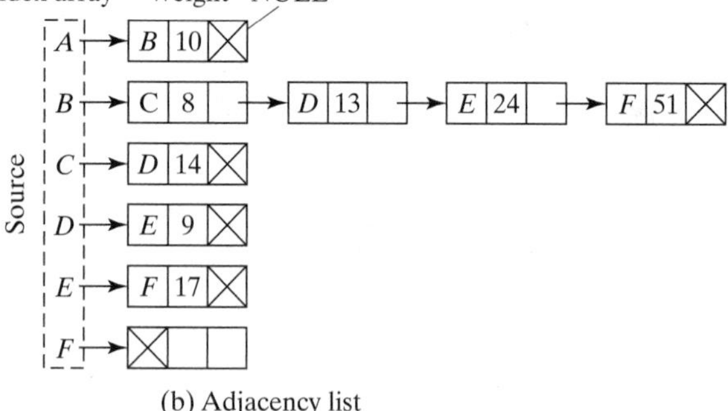

(b) Adjacency list

Figure 7.16 Representing a graph.

The method chosen will depend upon characteristics of the graph and the structure of the program. For sequential programs, the adjacency matrix is normally used for dense graphs—graphs where there are many edges from each vertex. The adjacency list is used for sparse graphs—graphs where there are few edges from each vertex. The difference is based upon space (storage) requirements. An adjacency matrix has an $O(v^2)$ space requirement, and an adjacency list has an $O(ve)$ space requirement, where there are e edges from each vertex and v vertices in all. In general, e will be different for each vertex, and therefore the upper bound on the space requirement of an adjacency list is given by $O(ve_{max})$. Accessing the adjacency list is regarded as slower than accessing the adjacency matrix, as it requires the linked list to be traversed sequentially, which potentially requires v steps. For parallel programs, an adjacency list could be accessed in parallel to speed up the process. In addition to space and time characteristics, for parallel programs we need to consider the partitioning of tasks and its effect on accessing the information. For now, let us assume an adjacency matrix representation (even though our graph is sparse).

7.4.3 Searching a Graph

In our example, the search to the summit is quite simple because there are only a few ways to the summit. But in more complex problems, the search is not so manageable, and an algorithmic approach is necessary. Single-source shortest-path graph algorithms find the minimum accumulation of weights from a source vertex to a destination vertex. Two well-known single-source shortest-path algorithms are candidates for identifying the best way to the summit:

- Moore's single-source shortest-path algorithm (Moore, 1957)
- Dijkstra's single-source shortest-path algorithm (Dijkstra, 1959)

The two algorithms are similar. Moore's is chosen because it is more amenable to parallel implementation, although it may do more work (Adamson and Tick, 1992). The weights must all be positive values for the algorithm to work. (Other algorithms exist that will work with both positive and negative weights.)

Moore's Algorithm. Starting with the source vertex, the basic algorithm implemented when vertex i is being considered is as follows: Find the distance to vertex j through vertex i and compare with the current minimum distance to vertex j. Change the minimum distance if the distance through vertex i is shorter. In mathematical notation, if d_i is the current minimum distance from the source vertex to vertex i, and $w_{i,j}$ is the weight of the edge from vertex i to vertex j, we have

$$d_j = \min(d_j, d_i + w_{i,j})$$

The algorithm is illustrated in Figure 7.17. Interestingly, the problem could be solved by simply applying the preceding formula repeatedly (an iterative solution). See Bertsekas and Tsitsiklis (1989) for further details.

The formula here is implemented using a directed search. A first-in-first-out vertex queue is created and holds a list of vertices to examine. Vertices are considered only when they are in the vertex queue. Initially, only the source vertex is in the queue. Another

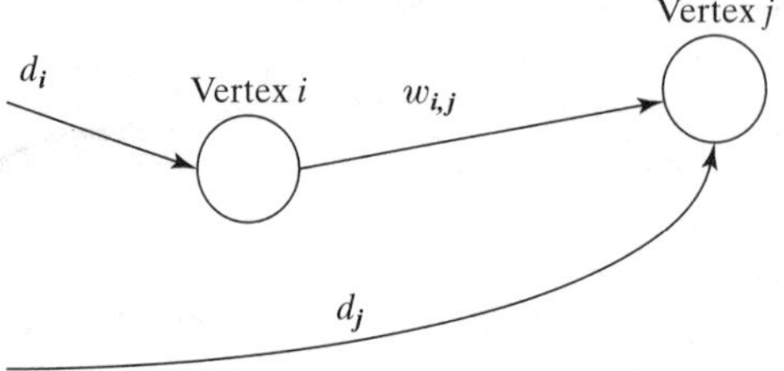

Figure 7.17 Moore's shortest-path algorithm.

structure is needed to hold the current shortest distance from the source vertex to each of the other vertices. Suppose there are n vertices, and vertex 0 is the source vertex. The current shortest distance from the source vertex to vertex i will be stored in the array `dist[i]` ($1 \le i < n$). At first, none of these distances will be known and the array elements are initialized to infinity. Suppose `w[i][j]` holds the weight of the edge from vertex i and vertex j (infinity if no edge). The code could be of the form

```
newdist_j = dist[i] + w[i][j];
if (newdist_j < dist[j]) dist[j] = newdist_j;
```

When a shorter distance is found to vertex j, vertex j is added to the queue (if not already in the queue), which will cause vertex j to be examined again. This is an important aspect of this algorithm, which is not present in Dijkstra's algorithm.

Stages in Searching a Graph. To see how this algorithm proceeds from the source vertex, let us follow the steps using our mountain-climbing graph as the example.

The initial values of the two key data structures are

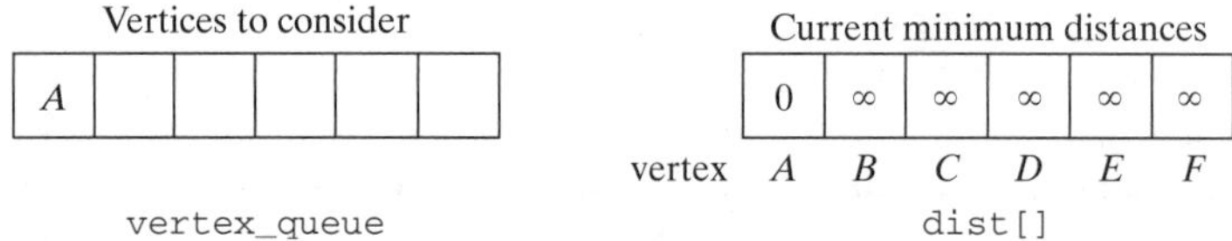

The element `dist[A]` will always be zero when A is the source, but the structure provides for complete generality should a vertex other than A be selected as the source vertex.

First, each of the edges emanating from vertex A is examined. In our graph, that will be vertex B. The weight to vertex B is 10, which will provide the first (and actually the only distance) to vertex B. Both data structures, `vertex_queue` and `dist[]`, are updated as follows:

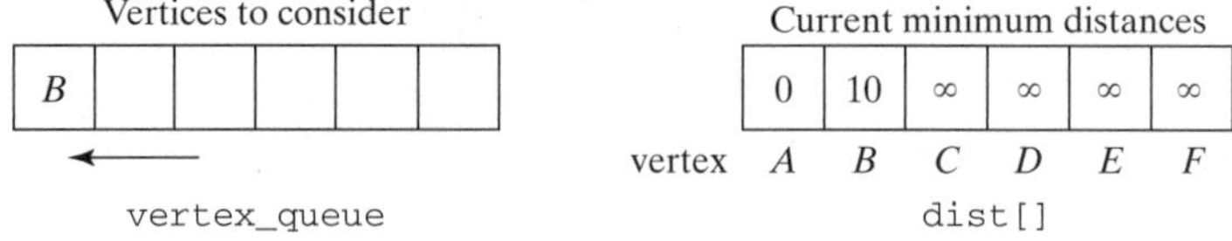

Once a new vertex, B, is placed in the vertex queue, the task of searching around vertex B begins. Now we have four edges to examine: to C, to D, to E, and to F. In this

algorithm, it is not necessary to examine these edges in any specific order. Dijkstra's algorithm requires the nearest vertex to be examined first, which imposes sequential processing. However, Moore's algorithm may require vertices to be reexamined. To demonstrate, let us examine the edges in the order *F*, *E*, *D*, and *C*.

The distances through vertex *B* to the vertices are `dist[F]` = 10 + 51 = 61, `dist[E]` = 10 + 24 = 34, `dist[D]` = 10 + 13 = 23, and `dist[C]` = 10 + 8 = 18. Since all were new distances, all the vertices are added to the queue (except *F*), as follows:

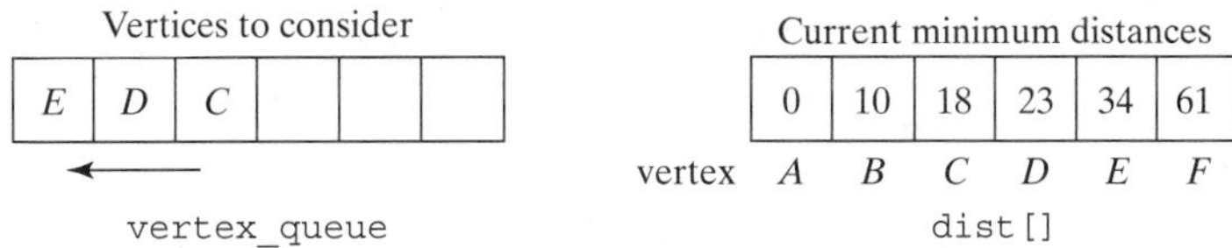

Vertex *F* need not be added because it is the destination with no outgoing edges and requires no processing. (If *F* were added, it would be discovered that there were no outgoing edges.)

Starting with vertex *E*, which has one edge to vertex *F* with a weight of 17, the distance to vertex *F* through vertex *E* is `dist[E]` + 17 = 34 + 17 = 51, which is less than the current distance to vertex *F* and replaces this distance, leading to

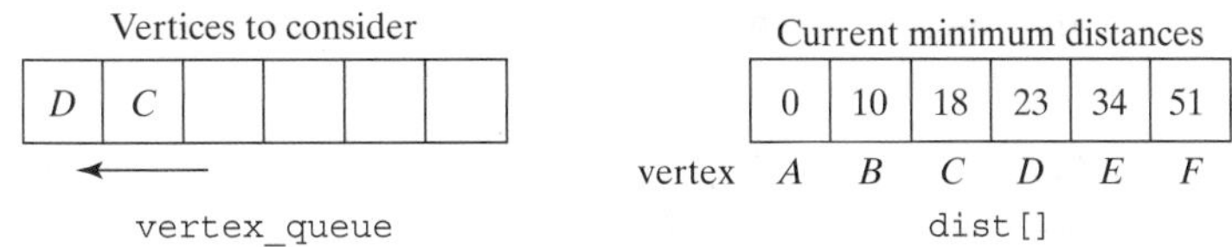

Next is vertex *D*. There is one edge to vertex *E* with the weight of 9, giving the distance to vertex *E* through vertex *D* of `dist[D]` + 9 = 23 + 9 = 32, which is less than the current distance to vertex *E* and replaces this distance. Vertex *E* is added to the queue, as follows:

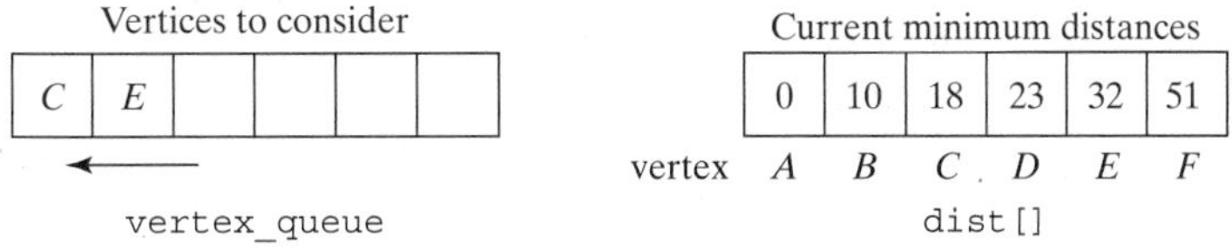

Next is vertex *C*. We have one edge to vertex *D* with a weight of 14. Hence, the (current) distance through vertex *C* to vertex *D* is `dist[C]` + 14 = 18 + 14 = 32. This is greater than the current distance to vertex *D* of 23, so this distance is left stored.

Next is vertex *E* (again). There is one edge to vertex *F* with the weight of 17, giving the distance to vertex *F* through vertex *E* of `dist[E]` + 17 = 32 + 17 = 49, which is less than the current distance to vertex *F* and replaces this distance, as follows:

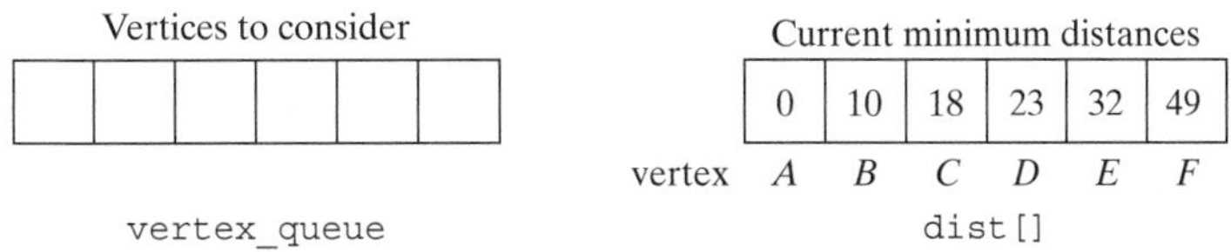

There are no more vertices to consider. We have the minimum distance from vertex A to each of the other vertices, including the destination vertex, F. Usually, the actual path is also required in addition to the distance. Then the path needs to be stored as the distances are recorded. The path in our case is $A \rightarrow B \rightarrow D \rightarrow E \rightarrow F$.

Sequential Code. The specific details of maintaining the vertex queue are omitted. Let `next_vertex()` return the next vertex from the vertex queue, or `num_vertex` if none. We will assume that an adjacency matrix is used, named `w[][]`, which is accessed sequentially to find the next edge. The sequential code could then be of the form

```
while ((i = next_vertex()) != num_vertex)                /* while a vertex */
   for (j = 0; j < n; j++)                               /* get next edge */
      if (w[i][j] != infinity) {                         /* if an edge */
         newdist_j = dist[i] + w[i][j];
         if (newdist_j < dist[j]) {
            dist[j] = newdist_j;
            append_queue(j);                /* vertex to queue if not there */
         }
      }                                     /* no more vertices to consider */
```

Parallel Implementations. We will look at both the centralized work pool and decentralized work pool solutions.

Centralized Work Pool. The first parallel implementation to consider uses a centralized work pool holding the vertex queue, `vertex_queue[]`, as tasks. Each slave takes vertices from the vertex queue and returns new vertices in the manner illustrated previously in Figure 7.2. For the slaves to identify edges and compute distances, they need access to both the structure holding the graph weights (adjacency matrix or adjacency list) and the array holding the current minimum distances, `dist[]`. If this information is held by the master process, messages will need to be sent to the master to access the information. This could lead to a very significant communication overhead. Since the structure holding the graph weights is fixed, this structure could be copied into each slave. We will assume a copied adjacency matrix. For now, let us assume that the distance array, `dist[]`, is held centrally and simply copied with the vertex in its entirety. Instead, individual requests for distances could also be made. The code could be of the form

Master

```
while (vertex_queue() != empty) {
   recv(P_ANY, source = P_i);                   /* request task from slave */
   v = get_vertex_queue();
   send(&v, P_i);                               /* send next vertex and */
   send(&dist, &n, P_i);                        /* current dist array */
   recv(&j, &dist[j], P_ANY, source = P_i);     /* new distance received */
   append_queue(j, dist[j]);                    /* append vertex to queue */
                                                /* and update distance array */
};
recv(P_ANY, source = P_i);                      /* request task from slave */
send(P_i, termination_tag);                     /* termination message*/
```

Slave (process *i*)

```
send(Pmaster);                              /* send request for task */
recv(&v, Pmaster, tag);                     /* get vertex number */
if (tag != termination_tag) {
   recv(&dist, &n, Pmaster);                /* and dist array */
   for (j = 0; j < n; j++)                  /* get next edge */
      if (w[v][j] != infinity) {            /* if an edge */
         newdist_j = dist[v] + w[v][j];
         if (newdist_j < dist[j]) {
            dist[j] = newdist_j;
            send(&j, &dist[j], Pmaster);    /* add vertex to queue */
         }                                  /* send updated distance */
      }
}
```

Clearly, the vertex number and distance array could be sent in one message. Note too that individual slaves may have distances that are not exactly the same because they are being updated continually by different slaves.

The master waits for requests from any slave but must respond to the specific slave that makes a request. In our pseudocode notation, `source = Pi` is used to indicate the source of the message. In an actual programming system, the source could be identified by making each slave send its identification (possibly as a unique tag). In the case of MPI, the actual source of the message can be found by reading the status word returned by the `MPI_Recv()` routine.

Decentralized Work Pool. One of the distributed work-pool approaches can be applied to our problem. The task queue, in our case `vertex_queue[]`, could also be distributed. A convenient approach is to assign slave process *i* to search around vertex *i* only and for it to have the vertex queue entry for vertex *i* if this exists in the queue. In other words, one element of the queue is reserved specifically to hold vertex *i*, and this entry is in process *i*. The array `dist[]` will also be distributed among the processes so that process *i* maintains the current minimum distance to vertex *i*. Process *i* also stores an adjacency matrix/list for vertex *i*, for the purpose of identifying the edges from vertex *i*.

With our arrangements, the algorithm can proceed as follows: The search will be activated by a coordinating process loading the source vertex into the appropriate process. In our case, vertex *A* is the first vertex to search. The process assigned to vertex *A* is activated. This process will immediately begin searching around its vertex to find distances to connected vertices. The distances will then be sent to the appropriate processes. The distance to vertex *j* will be sent to process *j* to be compared with its currently stored value and replaced if the currently stored value is larger. In our case, the process responsible for vertex *B* will be contacted with the distance to vertex *B*. In this fashion, all minimum distances will be updated during the search. If the contents of `d[i]` changes, process *i* will be reactivated to search again. Figure 7.18 shows the message-passing. Message-passing will distribute across many of the slave processes, rather than be focused on the master process.

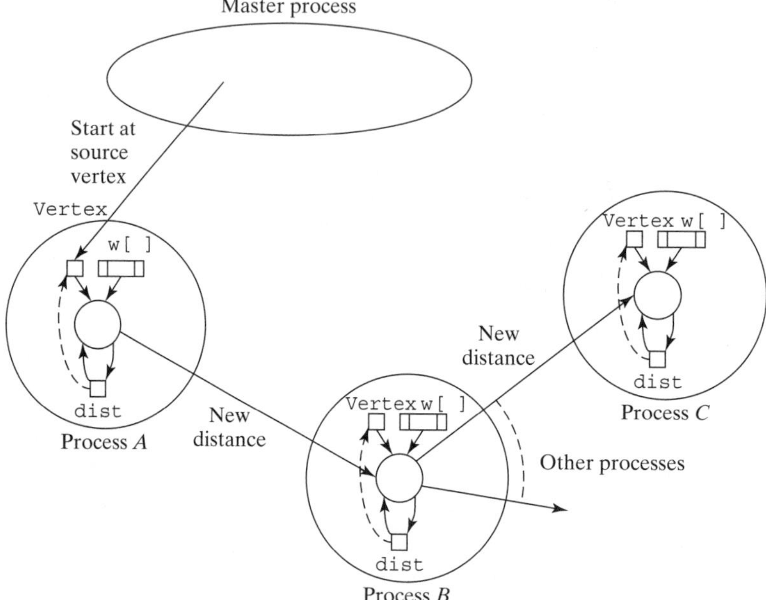

Figure 7.18 Distributed graph search.

A code segment for the slave processes might take the form

Slave (process *i*)

```
recv(newdist, P_ANY);
if (newdist < dist) {
   dist = newdist;
   vertex_queue = TRUE;                 /* add to queue */
} else vertex_queue == FALSE;
if (vertex_queue == TRUE)               /* start searching around vertex */
   for (j = 0; j < n; j++)              /* get next edge */
      if (w[j] != infinity) {
         d = dist + w[j];
         send(&d, P_j);                 /* send distance to proc j */
      }
```

This could certainly be simplified to:

Slave (process *i*)

```
recv(newdist, P_ANY);
if (newdist < dist) {
   dist = newdist;                      /* start searching around vertex */
   for (j = 1; j < n; j++)              /* get next edge */
      if (w[j] != infinity) {
         d = dist + w[j];
         send(&d, P_j);                 /* send distance to proc j */
      }
}
```

A mechanism is necessary to repeat the actions and terminate when all the processes are idle. The mechanism must cope with messages in transit. The simplest solution is to use synchronous message-passing, in which a process cannot proceed until the destination has received the message. It is left as an exercise to investigate this method and the more powerful method of identifying the unique parent that receives an acknowledgment last, as described in Section 7.3.

Note that a process is only active after its vertex is placed on the queue, and it is possible for many processes to be inactive, leading to an inefficient solution. The method is also impractical for a large graph if one vertex is allocated to each processor. In that case, a group of vertices could be allocated to each processor.

7.5 SUMMARY

This chapter introduced the following:

- Centralized and distributed work pools and load-balancing techniques
- Several distributed termination algorithms
- Shortest-path graph-searching application

FURTHER READING

There have been a large number of research papers on static and dynamic scheduling of tasks over the years. Static load balancing is found in Graham (1972). Another early task-allocation paper is Chu et al. (1980), with references to previous work. Heuristic methods are described in Efe (1982), Lo (1988), and Shirazi and Wang (1990). Static and dynamic methods are compared in Iqbal, Salz, and Bokhari (1986). Other details and methods of static load balancing can be found in Lewis and El-Rewini (1992) and El-Rewini (1996). Textbooks solely on scheduling include Bharadwaj et al. (1996), which provides a detailed mathematical treatment.

Load balancing in distributed systems is also described in many papers; for example, Tantawi and Towsley (1985), Shivaratri, Krueger, and Singhal (1992), and El-Rewini, Ali, and Lewis (1995). A collection of papers is published in Shirazi, Hurson, and Kavi (1995). Jacob (1996) considers load balancing specifically in a network of workstations. The powerful dynamic load-balancing technique using the concept of a single parent that receives an acknowledgment last is described fully, with its mathematical underpinning, in Bertsekas and Tsitsiklis (1989). The method is also used in parallel programs in Lester (1993). The concept of viewing load balancing as a physical system optimizing for minimum energy is described in Fox et al. (1988). Termination detection is treated in Barbosa (1996).

Mateti and Deo (1982), Paige (1985), and Adamson and Tick (1992) consider parallel algorithms for the shortest-path problem. Lester (1993) considers parallel programming aspects of the shortest-path problem.

BIBLIOGRAPHY

ADAMSON, P., AND E. TICK (1992), "Parallel Algorithms for the Single-Source Shortest-Path Problem," *Proc. 1992 Int. Conf. Par. Proc.*, Vol. 3, pp. 346–350.

BARBOSA, V. C. (1996), *An Introduction to Distributed Algorithms*, MIT Press, Cambridge, MA.

BERMAN, K. A., AND J. L. PAUL (1997), *Fundamentals of Sequential and Parallel Algorithms*, PWS, Boston, MA.

BERTSEKAS, D. P., AND J. N. TSITSIKLIS (1989), *Parallel and Distributed Computation Numerical Methods*, Prentice Hall, Englewood Cliffs, NJ.

BHARADWAJ, V., D. GHOSE, V. MANI, AND T. G. ROBERTAZZI (1996), *Scheduling Divisible Loads in Parallel and Distributed Systems*, IEEE CS Press, Los Alamitos, CA.

BOKHARI, S. H. (1981), "On the Mapping Problem," *IEEE Trans. Comput.*, Vol. C-30, No. 3, pp. 207–214.

CHU, W. W., L. J. HOLLOWAY, M.-T. LAN, AND K. EFE (1980), "Task Allocation in Distributed Data Processing," *Computer*, Vol. 13, No. 11, pp. 57–69.

COFFMAN, E. G., JR., M. R. GAREY, AND D. S. JOHNSON (1978), "Application of Bin-Packing to Multiprocessor Scheduling," *SIAM J. on Computing*, Vol. 7, No. 1, pp. 1–17.

DIJKSTRA, E. W. (1959), "A Note on Two Problems in Connexion with Graphs," *Numerische Mathematik*, Vol. 1, pp. 269–271.

DIJKSTRA, E. W., W. H. FEIJEN, AND A. J. M. V. GASTEREN (1983), "Derivation of a Termination Detection Algorithm for a Distributed Computation," *Information Processing Letters*, Vol. 16, No. 5, pp. 217–219.

EFE, K. (1982), "Heuristic Models of Task Assignment Scheduling in Distributed Systems," *Computer*, Vol. 15, No. 6, pp. 50–56.

EL-REWINI, H. (1996), "Partitioning and Scheduling," Chap. 9 in *Parallel and Distributed Computing Handbook*, Zomaya, A. Y., ed., McGraw-Hill, NY.

EL-REWINI, H., H. H. ALI, AND T. LEWIS (1995), "Task Scheduling in Multiprocessor Systems," *Computer*, Vol. 28, No. 12, pp. 27–37.

FOX, G., M. JOHNSON, G. LYZENGA, S. OTTO, J. SALMON, AND D. WALKER (1988), *Solving Problems on Concurrent Processors*, Volume 1, Prentice Hall, Englewood Cliffs, NJ.

GRAHAM, R. L. (1972), "Bounds on Multiprocessing Anomalies and Packing Algorithms," *Proc. AFIPS 1972 Spring Joint Computer Conference*, pp. 205–217.

IQBAL, M. A., J. H. SALZ, AND S. H. BOKHARI (1986), "A Comparative Analysis of Static and Dynamic Load Balancing Strategies," *Proc. 1986 Int. Conf. Par. Proc.*, pp. 1040–1047.

JACOB, J. C. (1996), "Task Spreading and Shrinking on a Network of Workstations with Various Edge Classes," *Proc. 1996 Int. Conf. Par. Proc.*, Part III, pp. 174–181.

LESTER, B. (1993), *The Art of Parallel Programming*, Prentice Hall, Englewood Cliffs, NJ.

LEWIS, T. G., AND H. EL-REWINI (1992), *Introduction to Parallel Computing*, Prentice Hall, Englewood Cliffs, NJ.

LO, V. M. (1988), "Heuristic Algorithms for Task Assignment in Distributed Systems," *IEEE Trans. Comput.*, Vol. 37, No. 11, pp. 1384–1397.

LO, V. M., AND S. RAJOPADHYE (1990), "Mapping Divide-and-Conquer Algorithms to Parallel Architectures," *Proc. 1990 Int. Conf. Par. Proc.*, Part III, pp. 128–135.

MATETI, P., AND N. DEO (1982), "Parallel Algorithms for the Single Source Shortest Path Problem," *Computing*, Vol. 29, pp. 31–49.

MATTSON, T. G. (1996), "Scientific Computation," Chap. 34 in *Parallel and Distributed Computing Handbook*, Zomaya, A. Y., ed., McGraw-Hill, NY.

MOORE. E. F. (1957), "The Shortest Path Through a Maze," *Proc. Int. Symp. on Theory of Switching Circuits*, pp. 285–292.

PAIGE, R. C. (1985), "Parallel Algorithms for Shortest Path Problems," *Proc. 1985 Int. Conf. Par. Proc.*, pp. 14–20.

SHIRAZI, B., AND M. WANG (1990), "Analysis and Evaluation of Heuristic Methods for Static Task Scheduling," *J. Par. Dist. Comput.*, Vol. 10, pp. 222–232.

SHIRAZI, B. A., A. R. HURSON, AND K. M. KAVI (1995), *Scheduling and Load Balancing in Parallel and Distributed Systems*, IEEE CS Press, Los Alamitos, CA.

SHIVARATRI, N. G., P. KRUEGER, AND M. SINGHAL (1992), "Load Distribution for Locally Distributed Systems," *Computer*, Vol. 25, No. 12, pp. 33–44.

TANTAWI, A. N., AND D. TOWSLEY (1985), "Optimal Load Balancing in Distributed Computer Systems," *J. ACM*, Vol. 32, No. 2, pp. 445–465.

WILSON, G. V. (1995), *Practical Parallel Programming*, MIT Press, Cambridge, MA.

ZOMAYA, A. Y., ed. (1996), *Parallel and Distributed Computing Handbook*, McGraw-Hill, NY.

PROBLEMS

Scientific/Numerical

7-1. One approach for assigning processes to processors is to make the assignment random using a random-number generator. Investigate this technique by applying it to a parallel program that adds together a sequence of numbers.

7-2. Write a parallel program that will implement the load-balancing technique using the pipeline structure described in Section 7.2.3 for any arbitrary set of independent arithmetic tasks.

7-3. The traveling salesperson problem is a classical computer science problem (though it might also be regarded as a real-life problem). Starting at one city, the objective is to visit each of n cities exactly once and return to the first city on a route that minimizes the distance traveled. The n cities can be regarded as variously connected. The connections can be described by a weighted graph. Write a parallel program to solve the traveling salesperson problem with real data obtained from a map to include 25 major cities.

7-4. Implement Moore's algorithm using the load-balancing line structure described in Section 7.2.3.

7-5. As noted in the text, the decentralized work-pool approach described in Section 7.4 for searching a graph is inefficient in that processes are only active after their vertex is placed on the queue. Develop a more efficient work-pool approach that keeps processes more active.

7-6. Write a load-balancing program using Moore's algorithm and a load-balancing program using Dijkstra's algorithm for searching a graph. Compare the performance of each algorithm and make conclusions.

Real Life

7-7. Single-source shortest-path algorithms can be used to find the shortest route for messages through any interconnection network one would like to devise. Write a parallel program that will find all the shortest routes through an arbitrary interconnection network and the specific one of your computer cluster if not fully switched.

7-8. Quality-of-service (QOS) describes how well a communication network, most notably the Internet, can provide data transfers within constraints. There may be several parameters (initial response time, maximum data transmission delay, etc.) that could be specified by the user and could be modeled by separate weights on each arc. Write a parallel program that can search a graph in which each arc has two weights and attempts to find a path which minimizes both accumulated weights. It may not be possible to obtain the absolute minimum of both accumulated weights, and one may need to provide an acceptable maximum value for each of the accumulated weights.

7-9. You have been commissioned to develop a challenging maze to be constructed at a stately home. The maze is to be laid out on a grid such as shown in Figure 7.19. Develop a parallel program that will find the positions of the hedges that result in the *longest time* in the maze if one uses the maze algorithm "Keep to the path where there is a hedge or wall on the left," as illustrated in Figure 7.19, which is guaranteed to find the exit eventually (Berman and Paul, 1997).

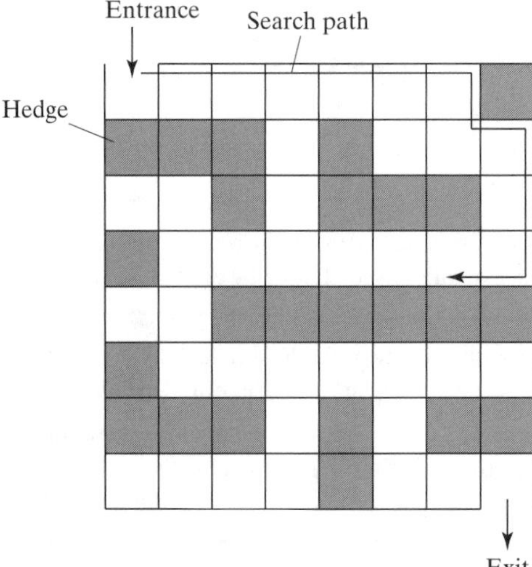

Figure 7.19 Sample maze for Problem 7-9.

7-10. A building has a number of interconnected rooms with a pot of gold in one, as illustrated in Figure 7.20. Draw a graph describing the plan of rooms where each vertex is a room. Doors connecting rooms are shown as edges between the rooms, as illustrated in Figure 7.21. Write a program that will find the path from the outside door to the chamber holding the gold. Notice that edges are bidirectional, and cycles may exist in the graph.

7-11. Historically, banks have used one or the other of two competing algorithms to handle the flow of customers at the teller stations within a bank: multiple-queue and single-queue. In the multiple-queue approach, each teller has a separate queue, similar to the lines at supermarkets.

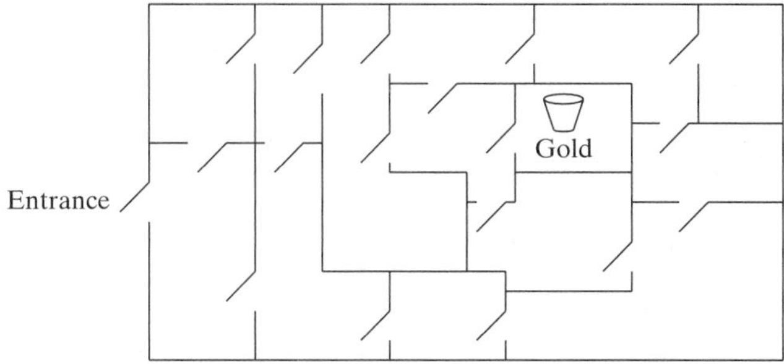

Figure 7.20 Plan of rooms for Problem 7-10.

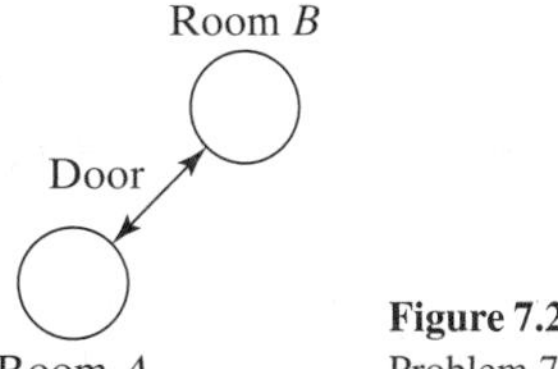

Figure 7.21 Graph representation for Problem 7-10.

In the purest form of this model, customers enter the bank, choose a queue to enter, and remain in it until served by the teller. One variation that is popular is to permit "queue hopping"; each person in each queue is constantly evaluating whether his or her chances of being served sooner would be enhanced by jumping to another queue. In the single-queue approach, there is only one queue.

The customer at the head of the queue is selected by the first teller completing a transaction. Your task is to simulate the pure multiple-queue and the single-queue approaches using a parallel program and prepare a one-page summary (management report) outlining the perceived advantages and disadvantages of each method given the following set of assumptions. In addition to such items as the average customer waiting times and maximum waiting times, gather whatever other statistics you feel are relevant in documenting your report's conclusions.

Assumptions:

1. There are five tellers.
2. All the queues are unlimited in size; customers will snake around the parking lot if necessary. However, the queues are empty at the start of business each day, and although no new customers are allowed into a queue after closing time, those already in the queue are permitted to complete their transactions.
3. Customers arrive randomly at the bank. Due to the bank's location near a major university, customers tend to be concentrated around the end of class times: 10 new customers arrive per minute (on average) between 10 minutes before and 10 minutes after the hour. Two new customers arrive per minute (on average) at all other times. The actual arrivals are random and are distributed evenly in the range of one to 19 arrivals per minute near the top of the hour and zero to four arrivals per minute at other times.
4. Each transaction takes a random amount of time to complete. On average, transactions take five minutes but are evenly distributed in the range from one to nine minutes. Each customer is considered a single transaction.

5. Run the simulations between the 9:00 A.M. and 6:00 P.M. (bank opening and closing times) for 100 days to generate the data from which you will draw conclusions for your summary report.

7-12. You are the president of a very large corporation employing nearly a million people. Your firm's personnel department has cleverly organized all the employees in a tree-style organization chart in which every employee reports to a supervisor but no supervisor has more than eight or fewer than two employees reporting to him or her. While it may be irrelevant, assume that the average number of employees reporting to a supervisor is five. Thus the average depth of the tree structure is roughly nine. (A little under 1,000,000 lowest-level employees report to about 200,000 first-level supervisors, who report to about 40,000 second-level supervisors, who report to about 8,000 third-level supervisors, etc.)

You have just heard from the U.S. Attorney General that one of your employees was indicted for something that may or may not affect your firm. You did not get the employee's name. Your task is to search the organization for the employee by following the official organization-chart personnel hierarchy. You are to do a breadth-first search, starting with the employees you directly supervise, until you identify the individual indicted. Note: You may assume that any nonindicted employee will answer "Not me!", while the employee who was indicted will answer "Yep, the feds got me!"

7-13. A table defines a collection of streets in a section of a major city. Many of the streets are one-way. In addition, there are several tunnels and bridges that allow the driver to skip over or under cross streets. The streets are all numbered. Even numbers are oriented east-west, while odd ones are oriented north-south. Each row of the table has the form

- street number being described
- cross street
- cross street
- mode (one-way or bidirectional)

As an example, one row might look like 13, 4, 6, 1, indicating that it is describing street number 13 in the block where it spans between streets 4 and 6, and is one-way in the direction from street 4 to street 6. (If the line had been 13, 6, 4, 1, then the street would have been one-way between streets 6 and 4.) Another row might look like 13, 6, 22, 2, indicating that street 13 is a two-way street and either a tunnel or a bridge in the section where it links streets 6 and 22 (with no entrances or exits from/to other cross streets between 6 and 22). Complete one (or more) of the following:

1. Find the number of paths that a taxi could use to get from one intersection to another in the city without passing through any intersection more than once.
2. Find the shortest path (fewest blocks traveled) that a taxi could use to get from one intersection to another without passing through any intersection more than once. Note: The only intersections that are associated with bridges or tunnels are those at the two ends.
3. Find the longest path (most blocks traveled) that a taxi could use to get from one intersection to another without passing through any intersection more than once. Note: The only intersections that are associated with bridges or tunnels are those at the two ends.

7-14. A brilliant, yet color-blind, researcher in the biology department has been growing cultured specimens of a dreaded bacterium in Petri dishes. While the culture solution is an opaque white, the bacteria are a pastel pink under visible light. This has hindered her greatly in the daily task of estimating the bacteria growth because she cannot discern yellow/orange/red hues.

She has rigged a digitizing camera that feeds data directly into a computer, and has hired you to write a scanning program that will calculate the percentage of the surface of the Petri dish covered by the bacteria. In addition, your program is to display the surface of the Petri dish in hues of blue/green.

After some initial experimentation, you have determined that an area of the Petri dish, center coordinates (x, y), has an average hue in the range from white to pink that depends upon both the (x, y) coordinates and the length of time, t, that the experiment has been running. For reasons that are not entirely clear, the exact relationship seems to be

$$\frac{t}{100} + \frac{(x+y)}{x_{max} + y_{max}} = Z$$

where the hue throughout a region is white if $Z < 0.95$ and pink otherwise. Your program is to compute and display the bacterium distribution across the Petri dish at a particular experiment time, t. Implement it so that you may zoom in on any particular point. Note: This should be computationally similar to a time-varying fractal, although the picture will not be nearly as jagged.

7-15. Lately, the TV, newspapers, and movies had been filled with stories about aliens, or so it seemed to Tom. Thus, when he was approached by an odd-looking stranger who was posing a multidimensional recursion problem to the people who lived in his apartment complex, Tom simply took it in stride. While it was vaguely discomforting to know that his family might never see him again if he failed to solve the problem, he was confident enough in his math skills to put aside all worries.

The only concern Tom had about the problem was that the aliens seemed much more at ease in dealing with dimensions greater than 3 than he was. But Tom was confident in his abilities and immediately dug into it.

Given an N-dimensional sphere of radius r, centered at the origin of an N-dimensional coordinate system, compute the number of integer coordinate points inside the sphere. The following are examples provided by the aliens for checking work:

(i) A three-dimensional sphere of radius 1.5 has 19 integer coordinate points within the sphere:

five points in the circle formed when the first coordinate is −1:

(−1, 0, 0), (−1, 0, 1), (−1, 0, −1), (−1, −1, 0), (−1, 1, 0),

five more in the circle when the first coordinate is 1:

(1, 0, 0), (1, 0, 1), (1, 0, −1), (1, −1, 0), (1, 1, 0),

and nine points in the circle when the first coordinate is 0:

(0, 0, 0), (0, 1, 0), (0, 1, 1), (0, 1, −1), (0, −1, 0), (0, −1, 1), (0, −1, −1), (0, 0, −1), and (0, 0, 1).

(ii) A two-dimensional sphere of radius 2.05 has 13 integer coordinate points within the sphere:

(0, 0), (−1, 0), (−2, 0), (1, 0), (2, 0), (−1, −1), (−1, 1), (1, −1), (1, 1), (0, −2), (0 −1), (0, 1), (0, 2).

(iii) A one-dimensional sphere of radius 25.5 has 51 integer coordinate points:

(±25, ±24, ±23, … ±1, 0).

Chapter 8

Programming with Shared Memory

In this chapter, we outline the methods of programming systems that have shared memory, including the use of processes, threads, parallel programming languages, and sequential languages with compiler directives and library routines. We will start with the standard UNIX process. The UNIX process approach introduces the "fork-join" model, which is used in OpenMP, discussed later. We then describe the IEEE thread standard Pthreads in some detail, which is widely available on a variety of multiprocessor and single-processor platforms. For the parallel programming language approach, we limit the discussion to general features and techniques rather than describe a specific parallel programming language. For an example of the use of compiler directives (coupled with library routines), we describe OpenMP, a widely accepted industry standard for parallel programming on a shared memory multiprocessor. Further, we describe performance issues in parallel programming whatever programming tools are used, covering shared data and synchronization issues, including sequential consistency. Finally, we provide some parallel code examples. Shared memory programming on a cluster, which uses many of the same concepts, is considered in Chapter 9.

8.1 SHARED MEMORY MULTIPROCESSORS

In Chapter 1, Section 1.3, two fundamental types of multiprocessor systems were identified — namely, the shared memory multiprocessor and the message-passing multicomputer. So far, we have concentrated on the message-passing multicomputer or a cluster of computers. Now we will look at programming shared memory systems. Shared memory systems are usually specially designed and manufactured but can be very cost-effective, especially small shared memory multiprocessor systems such as dual- and quad-Pentium systems.

In a shared memory system, any memory location is accessible to any of the processors. A *single address space* exists, meaning that each memory location is given a unique address within a single range of addresses. For a small number of processors, a common architecture is the single-bus architecture, in which all processors and memory modules attach to the same set of wires (the bus), as shown in Figure 8.1. This architecture is only suitable for perhaps up to eight processors because the bus can only be used by one processor at a time. Bus contention increases with increasing numbers of processors and soon saturates the bus. The use of cache memory reduces the need to access the main memory as much, and each processor usually has multiple levels of cache memory, as in a single processor system, but still a single bus is limited in its bandwidth.

For more than a few processors, to obtain sufficient bandwidth, multiple interconnects can be used, including a full crossbar switch, as shown in Figure 8.2. A crossbar switch provides full connectivity between the processors and individual memory modules but is expensive. Other interconnection structures are also possible, including multistage interconnection networks (see Chapter 1) and combinations of crossbar switches and buses. Ideally, the system has uniform memory access (UMA), that is, the same high speed access time to any memory location from any processor. It is possible to construct UMA systems with perhaps 100 or more processors (e.g., the SUN Fire 15K server with up to 106 processors). Alternatively for reduced cost and increased scalability, interconnection networks are used in which some memory is physically closer to certain processors than others, and the time to access a main memory location varies with the separation distance, that is, a non-uniform access (NUMA) system. In any event, high-speed cache memory is

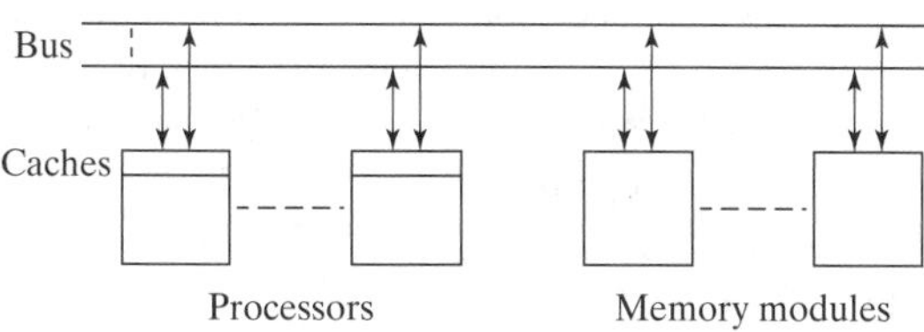

Figure 8.1 Shared memory multiprocessor using a single bus.

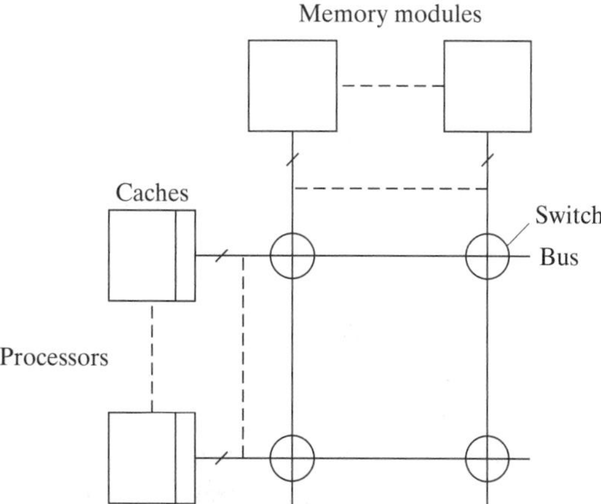

Figure 8.2 Shared memory multiprocessor using a crossbar switch.

always present in all systems to hold the contents of recently referenced main memory locations. In this chapter, we will describe the general features of programming a shared memory multiprocessor system. Aspects of caches that are important to know when programming shared memory systems are discussed in Section 8.6.1.

There are several alternatives for programming shared memory multiprocessor systems:

- Using a completely new programming language for parallel programming
- Modifying the syntax of an existing sequential programming language to create a parallel programing language
- Using an existing sequential programming language supplemented with compiler directives for specifying parallelism
- Using library routines with an existing sequential programming language
- Using heavyweight processes
- Using threads

One could also use a regular sequential programming language and ask a *parallelizing compiler* to convert the sequential program into parallel executable code. In that case, the compiler establishes which statements can be executed simultaneously. It might rearrange the statements to achieve concurrency, but the original intent of the programmer must be left intact. This method was investigated extensively in the 1970s. Using a completely new parallel programming language is of very limited appeal, for it requires one to learn a new language from scratch. Only one example of this has been used to any extent, the Ada language promoted by the U.S. Department of Defense.

Taking an existing sequential language and modifying it is more attractive, because then one only needs to learn the modifications. The most appealing way of doing this is to use compiler directives and library routines rather than modifying the syntax. An accepted standard for doing this is OpenMP. A special compiler is still needed.

Interestingly, Stroustrup, the inventor of C++, in the preface to Wilson and Lu (1996), says that he did not include any concurrency features in the original C++ specification though he could have done so. His conclusion was that "no single model of concurrency would serve more than a small fraction of the user community well." He also has a "weakness for the library approaches because these offer a higher degree of portability than approaches based upon language extensions."

In this chapter, we will start with traditional processes and then introduce the *thread* using the thread Pthreads standard. Pthreads is readily available on a multitude of platforms (single workstations and multiprocessor systems). Java also provides thread-based capabilities and offers some high-level features that are described here. It is perfectly feasible to use Java for thread-based parallel programming if an implementation is provided for the target multiprocessor system.

8.2 CONSTRUCTS FOR SPECIFYING PARALLELISM

8.2.1 Creating Concurrent Processes

Perhaps the first example of a structure to specify concurrent processes is the FORK-JOIN group of statements, described by Conway (1963). (Conway refers to earlier work, and it appears that the idea was known before 1960.) FORK-JOIN constructs have been applied as extensions to FORTRAN and to the UNIX operating system. In the original FORK-JOIN construct, a FORK statement generates one new path for a concurrent process and the concurrent processes use JOIN statements at their ends. When both JOIN statements have been reached, processing continues in a sequential fashion. For more concurrent processes, additional FORK statements are necessary. The FORK-JOIN constructs are shown nested in Figure 8.3. Each spawned process requires a JOIN statement at its end, which brings together the concurrent processes to a single terminating point. Only when all the concurrent processes have completed can the subsequent statements of the main process be executed. Typically a counter is used to keep a record of processes not completed. FORK/JOIN is essentially the same as the spawn/exit operations in message-passing and can be a library/system routine or a language construct.

UNIX Heavyweight Processes. Operating systems such as UNIX are based upon the notion of a process. On a single-processor system, the processor has to be time-shared between processes, switching from one process to another. This might occur at regular intervals, or when an active process becomes delayed. Time-sharing also offers the opportunity to deschedule processes that are blocked from proceeding for some reason, such as waiting for an I/O operation to complete. On a multiprocessor, there is an opportunity to execute processes truly concurrently. UNIX provides system calls to create processes, and it is possible to use these facilities to write parallel programs. We would not get an increased execution speed on a single processor. (Actually, the speed would reduce because of the overhead of creating the processes and handling context changes as we swap between processes.)

The UNIX system call `fork()` creates a new process. The new process (child process) is an *exact copy* of the calling process except that it has a unique process ID. It has its own copy of the parent's variables. On success, `fork()` returns 0 to the child process and returns the process ID of the child process to the parent process. (On failure, `fork()`

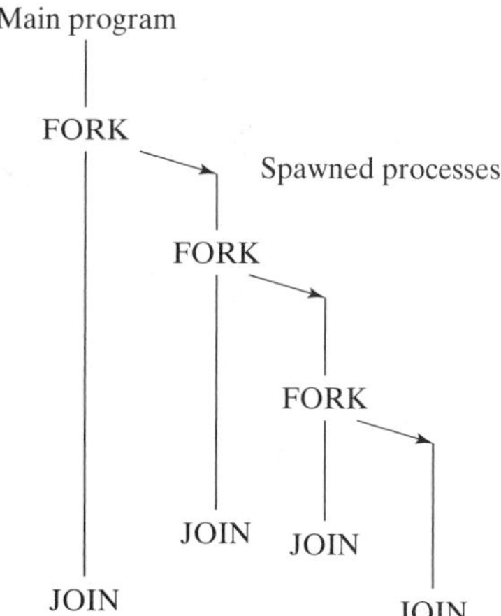

Figure 8.3 **FORK-JOIN** construct.

returns –1 to the parent process and no child process is created.) Processes are "joined" using the system calls `wait()` (or `waitpid()`) and `exit()`, defined as

```
wait(statusp);  /*delays caller until signal received or one of its */
                /*child processes terminates or stops */
exit(status);   /*terminates a process. */
```

Hence, a single child process can be created by

```
      :
pid = fork();                                         /* fork */
   Code to be executed by both child and parent
if (pid == 0) exit(0); else wait(0);                  /* join */
      :
```

(Checking for fork errors is not shown.) The parent will wait for the slave to finish if it reaches the join point first; if the slave reaches the join point first, it will terminate. The program construction is basically a SPMD (single-program multiple-data) model. As in other examples of this model, control statements are used to separate the code for different processes. If the child is to execute different code, we could use

```
pid = fork();
if (pid == 0) {
   code to be executed by slave
} else {
   Code to be executed by parent
}
if (pid == 0) exit(0); else wait(0);
      :
```

All the variables in the original program are duplicated in each process, becoming local variables for the process. They are initially assigned the same values as the original variables. The forked process starts execution at the point of the fork.

8.2.2 Threads

The process created with UNIX fork is a "heavyweight" process; it is a completely separate program with its own variables, stack, and personal memory allocation. Memory can be shared among processes through the use of system calls (see the program example in Section 8.7), but heavyweight processes are expensive in time and memory space. A complete copy of the process, with its own memory allocation, variables, stack, and so on, is created even though execution only starts from the forked position. Often a complete copy of a process is not required. A much more efficient mechanism is one in which independent concurrent sequences are defined within a process, so-called threads.[1] The threads all share the same memory space and global variables of the process and are much less

[1] Some authors differentiate lightweight processes and threads, describing a lightweight process as a kernel thread or a type of thread within the operating system.

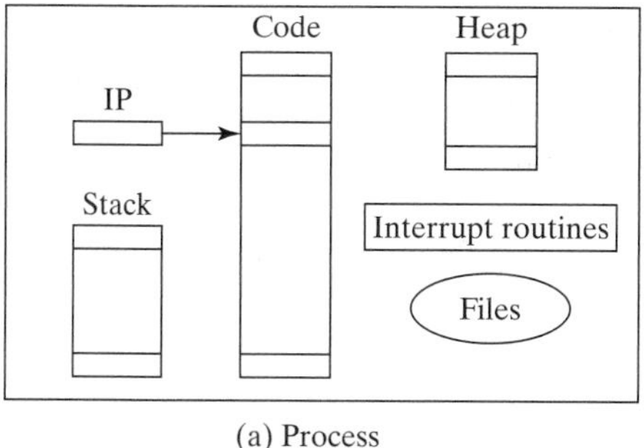

(a) Process

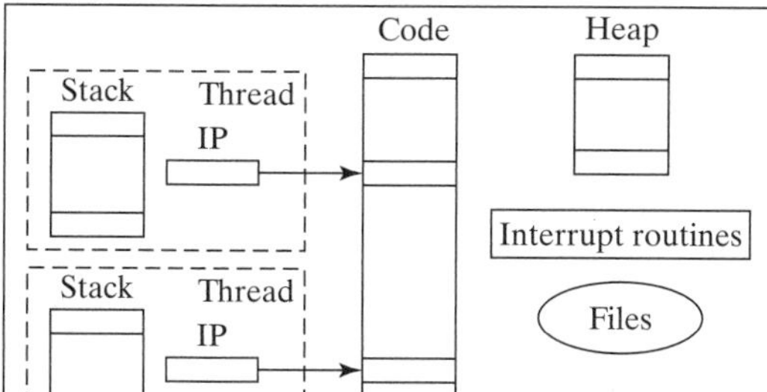

(b) Threads

Figure 8.4 Differences between a process and threads.

expensive in time and memory space than the processes themselves. The differences between processes and threads are illustrated in Figure 8.4. The basic parts of a process are shown in Figure 8.4(a). An instruction pointer (IP) holds the address of the next instruction to be executed. A stack is present for procedure calls, and also a heap, system routines, and files. As shown in Figure 8.4(b), each thread in the process has its own instruction pointer pointing to the next instruction of the thread to be executed. Each thread needs its own stack and also stores information regarding registers but shares the code and other parts.

Creation of a thread can take three orders of magnitude less time than process creation. In addition, a thread will immediately have access to shared global variables. Equally important, threads can be synchronized much more efficiently than processes. Synchronization of processes requires time-consuming system actions, whereas synchronization of threads can be done by accessing a variable. We will look at synchronization later.

Manufacturers have used threads in their operating systems for some time because they offer a powerful and elegant solution to handling concurrent activities within the operating system. Whenever an activity of a thread is delayed or blocked, such as waiting for I/O, another thread can take over. Examples of multithreaded operating systems include SUN Solaris, IBM AIX, SGI IRIX, and Windows XP. Within such operating systems are facilities for users to employ threads in their programs, but each system is different. Fortunately, a standard now exists, *Pthreads* (from the IEEE Portable Operating System Interface, POSIX, section 1003.1), which is widely available. We will concentrate upon Pthreads. Appendix C provides an abbreviated list of Pthread routines.

Multithreading also helps alleviate the long latency of message-passing; the system can switch rapidly from one thread to another while waiting for messages and provides a powerful mechanism for latency hiding. Solaris threads have message-passing routines, but this is not provided with Pthreads (SunSoft, 1994).

Executing a Pthread Thread. In Pthreads, the main program is a thread itself. A separate thread can be created and terminated with the routines

```
pthread_t thread1;            /* handle of special Pthread datatype */
      ⋮
pthread_create(&thread1, NULL, (void *) proc1, (void *) &arg);
      ⋮
pthread_join(thread1, void *status);
      ⋮
```

as illustrated in Figure 8.5.The new thread starts executing the routine `proc1` and is passed one argument, in this case `&arg`. (The `NULL` parameter in `pthread_create()` causes default thread "attributes" to be used.) A thread ID or "handle" is assigned and obtained from `&thread1` that can be used in subsequent references to the thread. It is used in `pthread_join()` to cause the calling thread to wait for the new thread to terminate if it has not already done so when the call is made. The thread is destroyed when it terminates, releasing resources. A completion status can be returned (`*status`) in `pthread_join()`. The status could be used if the thread is to return a value (which would need to be cast into a void). If none is required, `NULL` would be specified. A thread will also terminate naturally at the end of its routine (`return()`) and then return its status. It can be terminated and destroyed with `pthread_exit(void *status)`. It can be destroyed ("canceled") by another process, in which case the status returned is `PTHREAD_CANCELED`. If status were used to return a value, note that in certain situations there might be confusion with `PTHREAD_CANCELED`.

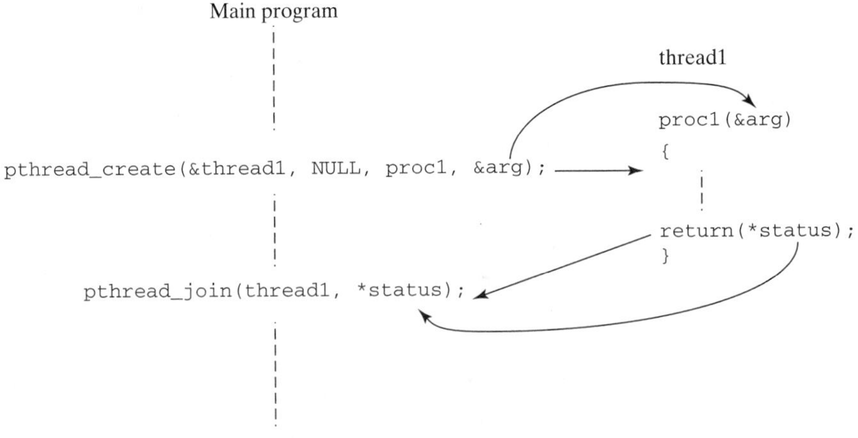

Figure 8.5 `pthread_create()` and `pthread_join()`.

The routine pthread_join() waits for one specific thread to terminate. To create a barrier waiting for all threads, pthread_join() could be repeated:

```
        :
for (i = 0; i < p; i++)
   pthread_create(&thread[i], NULL, (void *) slave, (void *) &arg);
        :
for (i = 0; i < p; i++)
   pthread_join(thread[i], NULL);
        :
```

An array of thread IDs is created, and p slave threads are started and terminated together. A thread can obtain its thread ID by calling the routine pthread_self(). A specific thread can be identified by comparing thread IDs using the routine pthread_equal(thread1, thread2), where thread1 and thread2 are thread IDs.

Detached Threads. If a thread is not bothered when a thread it creates terminates, a join will not be needed. Threads that are not joined are called *detached threads*. When detached threads terminate, they are destroyed and their resource released. Detached threads are illustrated in Figure 8.6. They can be specified in a thread attribute when created. A detached thread is more efficient and thus should be used unless the threads must be joined.

Thread Pools. All of the configurations that have been described for processes are applicable to threads. A master thread can control a collection of slave threads. A work pool of threads can be formed. Threads can communicate through shared locations or, as we shall see, using *signals*.

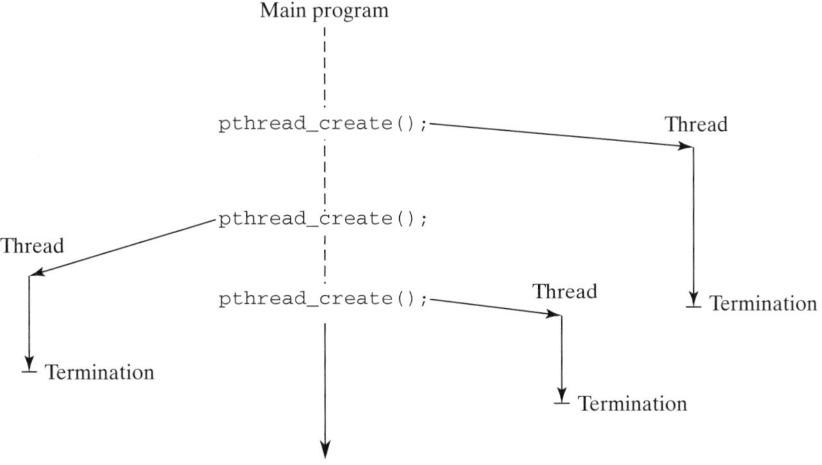

Figure 8.6 Detached threads.

Statement Execution Order. Once processes or threads are created, their execution order will depend upon the system. On a single-processor system, the processor will be time-shared between the processes/threads, in an order determined by the system if not specified, although typically a thread executes to completion if not blocked. On a multiprocessor system, the opportunity exists for different processes/threads to execute on different processors. In any event, one should be aware that the instructions of individual processes/threads may be interleaved in time. For example, if there were two processes with the machine instructions

Process 1	Process 2
Instruction 1.1	Instruction 2.1
Instruction 1.2	Instruction 2.2
Instruction 1.3	Instruction 2.3

there are several possible orderings, including

Instruction 1.1
Instruction 1.2
Instruction 2.1
Instruction 1.3
Instruction 2.2
Instruction 2.3

assuming that an instruction cannot be divided into smaller interruptible steps. If two processes were to print messages, for example, the messages could appear in different orders depending upon the scheduling of the processes calling the print routine. Worse, the individual characters of each message could be interleaved if the machine instructions of instances of the print routine could be interleaved.

In addition to interleaved execution of machine instructions in processes/threads, a compiler (or the processor) might reorder the instructions of your program for optimization purposes while preserving the logical correctness of the program. For example, the statements

```
a = b + 5;
x = y + 4;
```

could be compiled to execute in reverse order:

```
x = y + 4;
a = b + 5;
```

and still be logically correct. It may be advantageous to delay statement `a = b + 5` because some previous instruction currently being executed in the processor needs more time to produce the value for `b`. It is very common for modern superscalar processors to execute machine instructions out of order for increased speed of execution.

Thread-Safe Routines. System calls or library routines/functions are called *thread-safe* if they can be called from multiple threads simultaneously and always produce correct results; for example, print messages without interleaving the characters. Fortunately, standard I/O is designed to be thread-safe. However, routines that access shared data and static data may require special care to be made thread-safe. For example, system routines that return time may not be thread-safe. A list of POSIX thread-safe routines can be found in Pthreads reference books such as Kleiman, Shah, and Smaalders (1996). In fact, almost all POSIX routines are defined as thread-safe except those which are technically difficult to make thread-safe. Generally though, the thread-safety of functions is dependent on the operating system. The thread-safety aspect of any routine can be avoided by forcing only one thread to execute the routine at a time. This can be achieved by simply enclosing the routine in a critical section (see Section 8.3.2) but is very inefficient.

8.3 SHARING DATA

The key aspect of shared memory programming is that shared memory provides the possibility of creating variables and data structures that can be accessed directly by every processor. There is no need to pass the data in messages, as in message-passing environments.

8.3.1 Creating Shared Data

If UNIX heavyweight processes are to share data, additional shared memory system calls are necessary. Typically, each process has its own virtual address space within the virtual memory management system. The shared memory system calls allow processes to attach a segment of physical memory to their virtual memory space. The shared memory segment is created using the `shmget()` system call ("get shared memory segment identifier"), which returns a shared memory identifier. Once created, the shared segment is attached to the data segment of the calling process using the `shmat()` system call, which returns the starting address of the data segment. A code sequence using these calls will be found in Section 8.7.1.

It is not necessary to create shared data items explicitly when using threads. Variables declared at the top of the main program (main thread) are global and are available to all threads. Variables declared within routines are naturally local.

8.3.2 Accessing Shared Data

Accessing shared data needs careful control if the data is ever altered by a process. (We use the term *process*, but everything also applies to threads.) Reading the variable by different processes does not cause conflicts, but writing new values may do so. Consider two processes each of which is to add 1 to a shared data item, `x`. To add 1 to `x`, we might write `x++;` or `x = x + 1;`. In either case, it will be necessary for the contents of the `x` location to be read, `x + 1` computed, and the result written back to the location. With two processes doing this at approximately the same time, we have

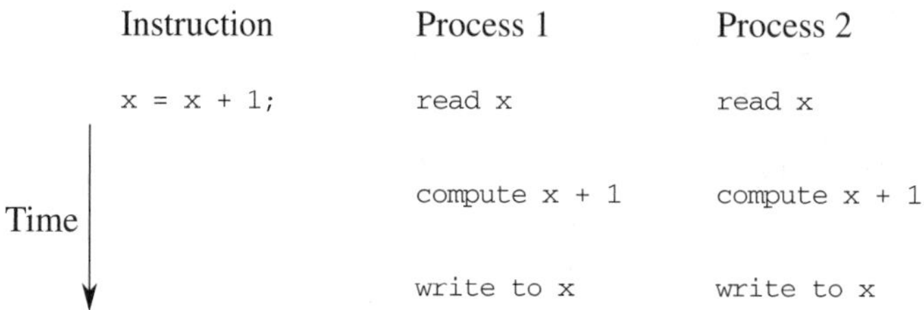

as illustrated in Figure 8.7. Suppose that the value of `x` was originally 10. The desired outcome after both process 1 and process 2 have completed this section is for `x` to be 12. But both processes read the original value of `x` as 10, and both will write back the value 11. Situations when more than one process might perform arithmetic operations on shared data appear in shared databases. An example given by Nichols, Buttlar, and Farrell (1996) is with two automatic teller machines (ATMs) (one being accessed by the husband and one by the wife simultaneously). A similar situation might arise with automatic debits occurring from different sources.

The problem of accessing shared data can be generalized by considering shared resources. In addition to shared data, the resource might also be a physical device, such as an input/output device. A mechanism for ensuring that only one process accesses a particular resource at a time is to establish sections of code involving the resource as so-called *critical sections* and arrange that only one such critical section is executed at a time. The first process to reach a critical section for a particular resource enters and executes the critical section. The process prevents all other processes from entering their critical sections for the same resource. Once the process has finished its critical section, another process is allowed to enter a critical section for the same resource. This mechanism is known as *mutual exclusion*.

Locks. The simplest mechanism for ensuring mutual exclusion of critical sections is by the use of a *lock*. A lock is a 1-bit variable that is a 1 to indicate that a process has entered the critical section and a 0 to indicate that no process is in the critical section. The lock operates much like a door lock. A process coming to the "door" of a critical section and finding it open may enter the critical section, locking the door behind it to prevent other

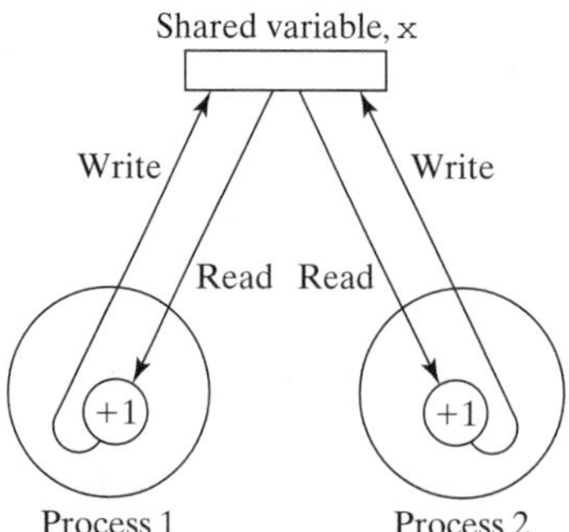

Figure 8.7 Conflict in accessing shared variable.

processes from entering. Once the process has finished the critical section, it unlocks the door and leaves.

Suppose that a process reaches a lock that is set, indicating that the process is excluded from the critical section. It now has to wait until it is allowed to enter the critical section. The process might examine the lock bit continually in a tight loop, for example, equivalent to

```
while (lock == 1) do_nothing;        /* no operation in while loop */
lock = 1;                            /* enter critical section */

   critical section

lock = 0;                            /* leave critical section */
```

Such locks are called *spin locks*, and the mechanism is called *busy waiting*. Figure 8.8 shows the serialization of critical sections by a lock. Busy waiting is an inefficient use of processors, as no useful work is being done while waiting for the lock to open. In some cases, it may be possible to deschedule the process from the processor and schedule another process, though this in itself incurs an overhead in saving and reading process information. If more than one process is waiting for a lock to open, and the lock opens, a mechanism is necessary to choose the best or highest-priority process to enter the critical section first, rather than let this be resolved by indeterminate busy waiting.

It is important to make sure that two or more processes do not simultaneously enter the critical section. Similarly, if one process finds the lock open but has not yet closed it, so that another process finds it open, it is necessary to ensure that both do not enter their critical sections at one time. Hence, the actions of examining whether a lock is open and closing it must be done as one uninterruptable operation, during which no other process can operate upon the lock. This exclusion mechanism is generally implemented in hardware by having special indivisible machine instructions (e.g., test-and-set instructions), although locks can be implemented without indivisible machine instructions (see Ben-Ari, 1990). In the following, when we say "lock" or "unlock," it is implied that these actions are done

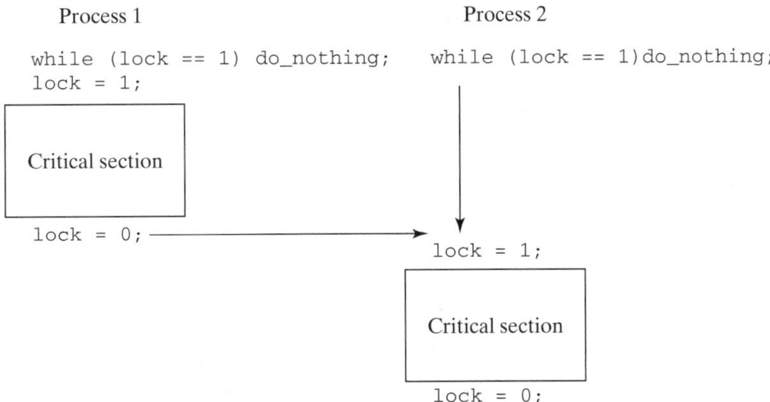

Figure 8.8 Control of critical sections through busy waiting.

atomically (as uninterruptable operations); that is, without any other process having access to the lock or being able to influence the outcome of the operation.

Pthread Lock Routines. Locks are implemented in Pthreads with what are called *mutually exclusive lock* variables, or "mutex" variables. To use a mutex, first it must be declared as of type `pthread_mutex_t` and initialized, usually in the "main" thread:

```
pthread_mutex_t mutex1;
pthread_mutex_init(&mutex1, NULL);
```

NULL specifies a default attribute for the mutex. A mutex can also be created dynamically using malloc and can be destroyed with `pthread_mutex_destroy()`. A critical section can then be protected using `pthread_mutex_lock()` and `pthread_mutex_unlock()`:

```
        .
        .
        .
pthread_mutex_lock(&mutex1);

  critical section

pthread_mutex_unlock(&mutex1);
        .
        .
        .
```

If a thread reaches a mutex lock and finds it locked, it will wait for the lock to open. If more than one thread is waiting for the lock to open when it opens, the system will select one thread to be allowed to proceed. Only the thread that locks a mutex can unlock it. (If another thread tries, an error condition will occur.)

Deadlock. An important consideration is being able to avoid deadlock, which prevents processes from proceeding. Deadlock can occur with two processes when one requires a resource held by the other, which in turn requires a resource held by the first process, as shown in Figure 8.9(a). In this figure, each process has acquired one of the resources. Both processes are delayed, and unless one process releases a resource wanted by the other, neither process will ever proceed. Deadlock can also occur in a circular fashion, as shown in Figure 8.9(b), with several processes having a resource wanted by another. Process P_1 requires resource R_2, which is held by P_2, process P_2 requires resource R_3, which is held by process P_3, and so on, with process P_n requiring resource R_1 held by P_1, thus forming a deadlock situation. These forms of deadlock are known as *deadly embrace*. Given a set of processes having various resource requests, a circular path between any group indicates a potential deadlock situation. Deadlock can be eliminated between two processes accessing more than one resource if both processes make requests for the same set of resources in the same order.

Pthreads offers one routine that can test whether a lock is actually closed without blocking the thread — namely, `pthread_mutex_trylock()`. This routine will lock an unlocked mutex and return 0 or will return with `EBUSY` if the mutex is already locked. The routine may find a use in overcoming deadlock.

Semaphores. Dijkstra (1968) devised the concept of a *semaphore*, which is a positive integer (including zero) operated upon by two operations named **P** and **V**. The **P**

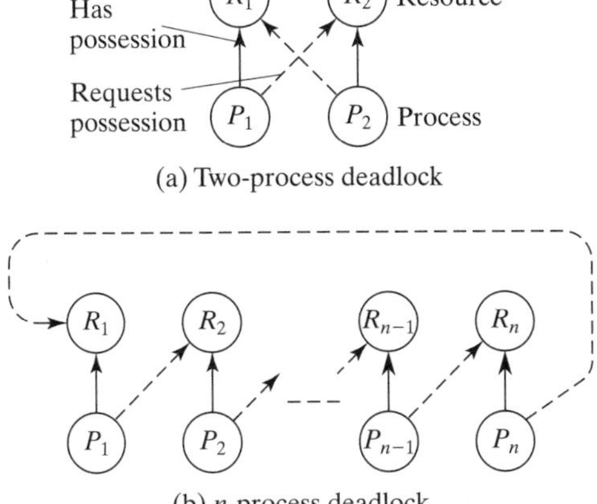

Figure 8.9 Deadlock (deadly embrace).

operation on a semaphore, s, written as **`P`**`(s)`, waits until s is greater than 0 and then decrements s by 1 and allows the process to continue. The **`V`** operation increments s by 1 to release one of the waiting processes (if any). The **`P`** and **`V`** operations are performed indivisibly. (The letter **`P`** is from the Dutch word *passeren*, meaning "to pass," and the letter **`V`** is from the Dutch word *vrijgeven*, meaning "to release.")

A mechanism for activating waiting processes is also implicit in the **`P`** and **`V`** operations. Though the exact algorithm is not specified, the algorithm is expected to be fair. Processes delayed by **`P`**`(s)` are kept in abeyance until released by a **`V`**`(s)` on the same semaphore. Processes might be delayed using a spin lock (busy waiting) or more likely by descheduling processes from processors and allocating in their place a process that is ready.

Mutual exclusion of critical sections of more than one process accessing the same resource can be achieved with one semaphore having the value 0 or 1 (a *binary semaphore*), which acts as a lock variable, but the **`P`** and **`V`** operations include a process-scheduling mechanism. The semaphore is initialized to 1, indicating that no process is in its critical section associated with the semaphore. Each mutually exclusive critical section is preceded by a **`P`**`(s)` and terminated with a **`V`**`(s)` on the same semaphore, as shown below:

Process 1	Process 2	Process 3
Noncritical section	Noncritical section	Noncritical section
⋮	⋮	⋮
`P``(s)`	**`P`**`(s)`	**`P`**`(s)`
Critical section	Critical section	Critical section
`V``(s)`	**`V`**`(s)`	**`V`**`(s)`
⋮	⋮	⋮
Noncritical section	Noncritical section	Noncritical section

Any process may reach its **`P`**`(s)` operation first (or more than one process may reach it simultaneously). The first process to reach its **`P`**`(s)` operation, or to be accepted, will set the semaphore to 0, inhibiting the other processes from proceeding past their **P**(s) operations, but any process reaching its **P**(s) operation will be recorded so that one can be selected when the critical section is released. The accepted process executes its critical section. When the process reaches its **V**(s) operation, it sets the semaphore *s* to 1, and one of the processes waiting is allowed to proceed into its critical section.

A general semaphore (or counting semaphore) can take on positive values other than 0 and 1. Such semaphores provide, for example, a means of recording the number of "resource units" available or used and can be used to solve producer/consumer problems.

Semaphore routines exist for UNIX processes. They do not exist in Pthreads as such, though they can be written, but they do exist in the real-time extension to Pthreads. Example code for UNIX semaphores is given in Section 8.7.1. Briefly, semaphores are created using `semget(key,nsems,semflg)`, which returns the semaphore identifier associated with key. The call `semctl()` is used to set a semaphore to a value. **P** and **V** operations are achieved using `semop()` semaphore operations, which perform atomic operations on an array of semaphores.

Monitor. It is widely recognized that semaphores, though capable of implementing most critical-section applications, are open to human errors in use. For every **P** operation on a given semaphore, there must be a corresponding **V** operation on the same semaphore, which could be done by a different process. Omission of a **P** or **V** operation, or misnaming the semaphore, would create havoc. A higher-level technique is to use a *monitor* (Hoare, 1974), which is a suite of procedures that provides the only method to access a shared resource. Essentially the data and the operations that can operate upon the data are encapsulated into one structure. Reading and writing can only be done by using a monitor procedure, and only one process can use a monitor procedure at any instant. If a process requests a monitor procedure while another process is using one, the requesting process is suspended and placed on a queue. When the active process has finished using the monitor, another process is allowed to use a monitor procedure.

A monitor procedure could be implemented using a semaphore to protect its entry; that is,

```
monitor_proc1()
{
   P(monitor_semaphore);

      monitor body

   V(monitor_semaphore);
   return;
}
```

The concept of a monitor exists in Java. The keyword `synchronized` in Java makes a block of code in a method thread-safe, preventing more than one thread inside the method. A simple program using the Java monitor method is given in Section 8.7.3. The reader is referred to books on Java for more details as given under Further Reading.

Condition Variables. Often, a critical section is to be executed if a specific global condition exists; for example, if a certain value of a variable has been reached. With locks, the global variable would need to be examined at frequent intervals ("polled") within a critical section. This is a very time-consuming and unproductive exercise. The problem can be overcome by introducing so-called *condition variables*, which appear in the context of a monitor. Three operations are defined for a condition variable:

`Wait(cond_var)` — wait for a condition to occur

`Signal(cond_var)` — signal that the condition has occurred

`Status(cond_var)` — return the number of processes waiting for the condition to occur

The wait operation will also release a lock or semaphore and can be used to allow another process to alter the condition. When the process calling `wait()` is finally allowed to proceed, the lock or semaphore is again set. We shall see why unlocking and locking are necessary. It is left to the program to recognize that the condition has occurred before calling `signal()`.

As an example of the use of condition variables, consider one or more processes (or threads) designed to take action when a counter, `x`, is zero. Another process or thread is responsible for decrementing the counter. The routines could be of the form

```
action()                          counter()
{                                 {
      ⋮                                 ⋮
   lock();                           lock();
   while (x != 0)                    x--;
      wait(s);  <-------------------  if (x == 0) signal(s);
   unlock();                         unlock();
   take_action();
      ⋮                                 ⋮
}                                 }
```

The same lock is used to access the shared counter variable, `x`, in both the counter routine and the action routine. It is assumed that the action routine reaches its critical section first, since signals are not remembered and could be missed if the counter routine reaches its critical section first. In the action routine, `wait()` will unlock the lock and wait to be released by the signal, `s`. When `signal()` generates the signal `s`, `wait()` is released. The `while` statement in the action routine will cause the condition to be tested again even after it has supposedly occurred. This double-checking is generally necessary for good error checking and is particularly important if multiple threads/processes can be woken up simultaneously or other signals could have woken up the thread/process.

Pthread Condition Variables. Pthreads provide condition variables that are associated with a specific mutex. To use a condition variable, first a variable must be declared to be of type `pthread_cond_t` and initialized, again usually in the "main" thread:

```
pthread_cond_t cond1;
pthread_cond_init(&cond1, NULL);
```

NULL specifies a default attribute for the mutex. Condition variables can be destroyed with `pthread_cond_destroy()`.

Two routines are provided to make a thread wait on a condition variable signal:

```
pthread_cond_wait(cond1, mutex1);
pthread_cond_timedwait(cond1, mutex1, abstime);
```

The routine `pthread_cond_wait()` suspends the calling thread until another thread signals on the condition variable and unlocks the specified mutex. (These two actions are "atomic.") When the signal is received, the mutex is locked and the call returns. The routine `pthread_cond_timedwait()` is similar except that the call also returns if the system time reaches or exceeds the time `abstime`.

Two routines are provided to send a signal from the calling thread to another thread to release it:

```
pthread_cond_signal(cond1);
pthread_cond_broadcast(cond1);
```

The routine `pthread_cond_signal()` releases one thread that was blocked waiting for the condition variable, `cond1`. The routine `pthread_cond_broadcast()` signals all the threads that were blocked waiting for the condition variable, `cond1`. However, only one waiting thread can acquire the mutex; the others are placed in a waiting state for the mutex.

Given the declarations and initializations

```
pthread_cond_t cond1;
pthread_mutex_t mutex1;
      .
      .
      .
pthread_cond_init(&cond1, NULL);
pthread_mutex_init(&mutex1, NULL);
```

the Pthreads arrangement for signal and wait is as follows:

```
action()                                   counter()
{                                          {
      .                                          .
      .                                          .
      .                                          .
pthread_mutex_lock(&mutex1);               pthread_mutex_lock(&mutex1);
while (c !=0)                              c--;
  pthread_cond_wait(cond1,mutex1);       <-if (c == 0) pthread_cond_signal(cond1);
pthread_mutex_unlock(&mutex1);             pthread_mutex_unlock(&mutex1);
take_action();
      .                                          .
      .                                          .
      .                                          .
}                                          }
```

Signals are *not* remembered, which means that threads must already be waiting for a signal to receive it.

Barriers. As with message-passing systems, process/thread synchronization is often needed in shared memory programs. Pthreads do not have a native barrier (except in the POSIX 1003.1j extension), so barriers have to be hand-coded using a condition variable and mutex, the full details of which are beyond the scope of this book. Code examples can be found in Butenhof (1997), Kleiman, Shah, and Smaalders (1996), and Prasad (1997). The implementation often uses a centralized counter approach, as described in Chapter 6, Section 6.1.2. A global counter variable is incremented each time a thread reaches the barrier, and all the threads are released when the counter has reached a defined number of threads. The threads are released by the last thread reaching the barrier using broadcast signal (`pthread_cond_broadcast()`) received by the other waiting threads (using `pthread_cond_wait()` in a loop). The counter is set to zero for the next time the barrier is used.

As with barriers in message-passing systems, one must taken into account that barriers may be called more than once and the implementation must handle the situation of a thread entering the barrier for a second time while other threads are still in the barrier for the first time. We saw one way of preventing that in Chapter 6, a design having a two phases, an arrival phase and a departure phase.

Butenhof (1997) provides a different implementation, which uses a variable called `count` associated with the barrier to count the threads arriving at the barrier, and a second variable called `cycle`, which is 0 or 1. The variable `cycle` saved in each thread is a local variable when the thread arrives at the barrier. When one cycle of the barrier is complete, the variable `cycle` is inverted (i.e., changed from 0 to 1 or from 1 to 0) by the final thread arriving at the barrier. Only when the value of `cycle` stored in the thread is different from the actual value of `cycle` is the thread released (`pthread_cond_wait()` is in a `while` loop which only terminates when the local value of `cycle` is different to `cycle`). Several other aspects of coding a shared memory barrier are not described here; for example, how to avoid erroneous conditions such as threads accessing barriers before they exist and are initialized. Full details can be found in Butenhof (1997).

8.4 PARALLEL PROGRAMMING LANGUAGES AND CONSTRUCTS

8.4.1 Languages

Using a specially designed parallel programming language seems appealing, especially for a shared memory system. Shared memory variables can be declared and accessed in the same way as any variable in the program. Parallel programming languages provide a high level of abstraction and can hide some of the architectural details of the actual computing platform. They have a very long history. A large number of parallel programming languages have been proposed over the years, but none of them has been universally accepted. Table 8.1 lists a few early languages. Bal, Steiner, and Tanenbaum (1989) list a great number of references to systems/languages until 1989. Some languages are for general control parallelism (where instructions in different processes are separately controlled). Some languages are specifically for data parallelism (where a single instruction specifies the same operation across a set of data items). Karp and Babb (1988) describe 12 parallel Fortran languages. Foster (1995) describes three parallel programming languages in detail: Compositional C++, Fortran M, and High Performance Fortran (HPF). In the large book edited by Wilson and Lu (1996), 15 different languages for writing parallel programs are

TABLE 8.1 SOME EARLY PARALLEL PROGRAMMING LANGUAGES

Language	Originator/date	Comments
Concurrent Pascal	Brinch Hansen, 1975[a]	Extension to Pascal
Ada	U.S. Dept. of Defense, 1979[b]	Completely new language
Modula-P	Bräunl, 1986[c]	Extension to Modula 2
C*	Thinking Machines, 1987[d]	Extension to C for SIMD systems
Concurrent C	Gehani and Roome, 1989[e]	Extension to C
Fortran D	Fox et al., 1990[f]	Extension to Fortran for data parallel programming

a. Brinch Hansen, P. (1975), "The Programming Language Concurrent Pascal," *IEEE Trans. Software Eng.*, Vol. 1, No. 2 (June), pp. 199–207.

b. U.S. Department of Defense (1981), "The Programming Language Ada Reference Manual," *Lecture Notes in Computer Science*, No. 106, Springer-Verlag, Berlin.

c. Bräunl, T., R. Norz (1992), *Modula-P User Manual*, Computer Science Report, No. 5/92 (August), Univ. Stuttgart, Germany.

d. Thinking Machines Corp. (1990), *C* Programming Guide, Version 6*, Thinking Machines System Documentation.

e. Gehani, N., and W. D. Roome (1989), *The Concurrent C Programming Language*, Silicon Press, New Jersey.

f. Fox, G., S. Hiranandani, K. Kennedy, C. Koelbel, U. Kremer, C. Tseng, and M. Wu (1990), *Fortran D Language Specification*, Technical Report TR90-141, Dept. of Computer Science, Rice University.

described in detail, all using C++ as the base language. (Only one language is targeted toward shared memory multiprocessor systems.) Of all the languages proposed in the 1980s and 1990s, only HPF is still seen to any extent.

There is continuing interesting in providing language extensions for parallel programming. A recent example is Unified Parallel C (UPC), which is a parallel extension to C developed by a consortium of academia, industry, and government (see http://www.gwu.edu/~upc). Such team efforts are more likely to find acceptance. UPC is a relatively small extension to the base language and is particularly targeted toward distributed shared memory systems as found in clusters (see Chapter 9). Rather than select one language extension such as UPC, let us briefly review the constructs that usually appear in such extensions or parallel programming languages for shared memory systems, and mention the languages/extensions that use them.

8.4.2 Language Constructs

Shared Data. In a parallel programming language supporting shared memory, variables might be declared as shared with, say,

```
shared int x;
```

or, if a pointer

```
shared int* p;
```

In the above, `p` is a pointer to a shared integer. Such declarations do not necessarily mean that the variable can be accessed simultaneously by more than one process; they simply mean that any process may access the variable. An appropriate mechanism must be in place to ensure that only one process at a time does actually access the variable. UPC has the `shared` declarations above and also ones for declaring arrays where the elements of the array are distributed in different threads. The concept of `shared` can be extended to shared objects in an object-oriented language.

`par` Construct. Parallel languages offer the possibility of specifying concurrent statements, as in the `par` construct:

```
par {
   S1;
   S2;
    .
    .
    .
   Sn;
}
```

The keyword `par` indicates that statements in the body are to be executed concurrently. This is *instruction-level parallelism.* In instruction-level parallelism, concurrent processes can be as short as a single statement. Single statements may incur an unacceptable overhead in many systems, although the construct allows this possibility.

Multiple concurrent processes or threads could be specified by listing the routines that are to be executed concurrently:

```
par {
   proc1();
   proc2();
      .
      .
      .
   procn();
}
```

Here, `proc1()`, `proc2()`, ..., `procn()` are executed simultaneously if possible.

The `par { ... }` construction can be found in various parallel languages; for example, CC++ (Foster, 1995). For Pascal-like parallel languages, we might find the constructs `PARBEGIN ... PAREND` or `COBEGIN ... COEND`, both of which delimit a group of statements to be executed concurrently. An earlier example can be found in ALGOL-68. The order of execution of statements (or compound statements) separated by commas instead of semicolons was not defined; that is, the statements would be executed in any order in a single-processor system and could be executed simultaneously in a multiprocessor system.

`forall` Construct. Sometimes multiple similar processes need to be started together. This can be obtained with the `forall` construct (or `parfor` construct):

```
forall (i = 0; i < p; i++) {
   S1;
   S2;
    .
    .
    .
   Sm;
}
```

which generates p processes each consisting of the statements forming the body of the `for` loop, `S1`, `S2`, ..., `Sm`. Each process uses a different value of i. For example,

```
forall (i = 0; i < 5; i++)
  a[i] = 0;
```

clears `a[0]`, `a[1]`, `a[2]`, `a[3]`, and `a[4]` to zero concurrently. An example of the `forall` construct for parallel languages based upon the C language can be found in Terrano, Dunn, and Peters (1989). The similar `parfor` construct can be found in CC++ (Foster, 1995). High Performance Fortran (HPF) includes a `forall` construct. UPC has a `forall` construct with the unusual feature of specifying how the body is distributed among the threads.

8.4.3 Dependency Analysis

One of the key issues in parallel programming is to identify which processes can be executed together. When using a parallel programming language, one hopes that the compiler can spot problems that would prevent concurrent execution. Processes cannot be executed together if there is some dependency between them that requires the processes to be executed in a sequential order. The process of finding the dependencies in a program is called *dependency analysis*. For example, we can see immediately in the code

```
forall (i = 0; i < 5; i++)
  a[i] = 0;
```

that every instance of the body is independent of the other instances and all instances can be executed simultaneously. However, it may not be obvious. For example,

```
forall (i = 2; i < 6; i++) {
  x = i - 2*i + i*i;
  a[i] = a[x];
}
```

In this case, it is not at all obvious whether different instances of the body can be executed simultaneously. Preferably, we need an algorithmic way of recognizing the dependencies that can be used by a *parallelizing compiler* (a compiler that converts sequential code into parallel code).

Bernstein's Conditions. Bernstein (1966) established a set of conditions that are sufficient to determine whether two processes can be executed simultaneously. These conditions, which we will reduce to a simple form, relate to memory locations used by the processes to hold variables that are altered and read during the execution of the processes. Let us define two sets of memory locations, I (input) and O (output), such that

I_i is the set of memory locations read by process P_i.
O_j is the set of memory locations altered by process P_j.

For two processes, P_1 and P_2, to be executed simultaneously, the inputs to process P_1 must not be part of the outputs of P_2, and the inputs of P_2 must not be part of the outputs of P_1; that is,

$$I_1 \cap O_2 = \phi$$
$$I_2 \cap O_1 = \phi$$

where ϕ is an empty set. The set of outputs of each process must also be different:

$$O_1 \cap O_2 = \phi$$

We will refer to these three conditions as Bernstein's conditions.

If the three conditions are all satisfied, the two processes can be executed concurrently. The conditions can be applied to processes of any complexity. A process can be a single statement allowing us to determine whether the two statements can be executed simultaneously. Then I_i corresponds to the variables on the right-hand side of the statements, and O_j corresponds to the variables on the left-hand side of the statements.

Example: Suppose the two statements are (in C)

```
a = x + y;
b = x + z;
```

We have

$$I_1 = (\mathrm{x, y})$$
$$I_2 = (\mathrm{x, z})$$
$$O_1 = (\mathrm{a})$$
$$O_2 = (\mathrm{b})$$

and the conditions

$$I_1 \cap O_2 = \phi$$
$$I_2 \cap O_1 = \phi$$
$$O_1 \cap O_2 = \phi$$

are satisfied. Hence, the statements `a = x + y` and `b = x + z` can be executed simultaneously. Suppose the statements are

```
a = x + y;
b = a + b;
```

Then $I_2 \cap O_1 \neq \phi$ and the two statements cannot be executed simultaneously.

The technique can be extended to determine whether several statements can be executed in parallel. Bernstein's conditions can be automated in a compiler and could conceivably be used by the programmer. The conditions are completely general and do not use any special characteristics of the computation in finding the parallelism. They can be used to identify instruction-level parallelism or coarser parallelism, where a set of routines is being considered for concurrent operation. In that case, the inputs are the parameters to the routines, and the outputs are the variables/values returned.

Some common programming constructs have a natural parallelism that a compiler or the programmer can utilize, in particular program loops. For example, the C loop

```
for (i = 1; i <= 20; i++)
  a[i] = b[i];
```

could be expanded to

```
a[1] = b[1];
a[2] = b[2];
     ⋮
a[19] = b[19];
a[20] = b[20];
```

Given 20 processors, these statements could all be executed simultaneously (Bernstein's conditions being satisfied).

Dependencies in loops can sometimes be handled by decomposing the loop into multiple loops that are independent of each other. For example, the C loop

```
for (i = 3; i <= 20; i++)
  a[i] = a[i-2] + 4;
```

computes

```
a[3]  = a[1] + 4;
a[4]  = a[2] + 4;
      ⋮
a[19] = a[17] + 4;
a[20] = a[18] + 4;
```

Hence `a[5]` can only be computed after `a[3]`, `a[6]` after `a[4]`, and so on. The computation can be split into two independent sequences:

```
a[3]  = a[1] + 4;                a[4]  = a[2] + 4;
a[5]  = a[3] + 4;                a[6]  = a[4] + 4;
      ⋮                                ⋮
a[17] = a[15] + 4;               a[18] = a[16] + 4;
a[19] = a[17] + 4;               a[20] = a[18] + 4;
```

or written as two `for` loops:

```
for (i = 3; i <= 20; i+=2) {
  a[i] = a[i-2] + 4;
}
```

and

```
for (i = 4; j <= 20; i+=2) {
  a[i] = a[i-2] + 4;
}
```

Bernstein's conditions can be used to identify the two loops. There are many other techniques that a parallelizing compiler can use to recognize or create parallelism. More details on techniques for parallelizing compilers can be found in Wolfe (1996).

8.5 OPENMP

In the preceding two sections, we discussed language constructs that might be found in parallel programming languages for specifying parallelism. Typically, these constructs are extensions to existing sequential languages. Although such parallel programming constructs appear to be an attractive approach, and several such extensions have been developed over the years, they have met with limited success. An alternative approach is to start with a normal sequential programming language but create the parallel specifications by the judicious use of embedded compiler directives. These compiler directives can specify such things as the `par` and `forall` operations described in Section 8.3.3. This approach is taken by OpenMP, an accepted standard developed in the late 1990s by a group of industry specialists. OpenMP consists of a small set of compiler directives, augmented with a small set of library routines and environment variables using the base languages Fortran and C/C++. Several OpenMP compilers are available, some at no cost to academics.

For C/C++, the OpenMP directives are contained in `#pragma` statements. The OpenMP `#pragma` statements have the format:

```
#pragma omp directive_name ...
```

where `omp` is an OpenMP keyword, and there may be additional parameters (clauses) after the directive name for different options. Some directives require code to specified in a structured block (a statement or statements) that follows the directive, and then the directive and structured block form a "construct." The `#pragma` statements would be ignored by a regular C/C++ compiler. If the `#pragma` statements are carefully used, it is possible to write a parallel program with them such that a regular C/C++ compiler would create an executable sequential program and an OpenMP compiler would create a parallel version of the same program. Another advantage of the directive approach is that the OpenMP compiler can do dependency analysis and rearrangements, as described in Section 8.3.4 (and also much more advanced analysis and rearrangements). Programmers can get the results of this analysis and help the compiler by making their own rearrangements. Directives alone are sometimes awkward for specifying parallelism, so OpenMP also has a few library routines, most notably for creating locks and setting the level of concurrency.

In this section, we will briefly describe the main features provided in OpenMP. Appendix C gives a summary of all the features, and additional details can be found in OpenMP Architecture Review Board (2002) and Chandra et al. (2001).

OpenMP uses the fork-join model described in Section 8.2.1, but thread-based. Initially, a single thread is executed by a master thread. Parallel regions are sections of code that can be executed by multiple threads (a team of threads). The `parallel` directive (see below) is the directive for creating a team of threads and specifies a block of code that will be executed by the multiple threads in parallel. The exact number of threads in the team is determined in one of several ways. Other directives are used within a `parallel` construct to specify parallel for loops and different blocks of code for threads. Data can be declared as private through the `private()` clause in directives, the `thread_private` directive, or in other ways. When created with the `thread_private` directive, the private variable persists from one parallel region to the next; that is, values of these variables are maintained. Other data is shared.

Parallel Directive. The fundamental directive is the `parallel` directive

```
#pragma omp parallel
   structured_block
```

which creates multiple threads, each one executing the specified `structured_block`. The `structured_block` is either a single statement or a compound statement created with { ...} but must have a single entry point and a single exit point. There is an implicit barrier at the end of the construct. The directive corresponds to the previous `forall` construct

```
forall(i = 0; i < OMP_NUM_THREADS; i++)
   structured_block
```

if `OMP_NUM_THREADS` is defined, except that the local variable `i` does not exit.

Example

```
#pragma omp parallel private(x, num_threads)
{
   x = omp_get_thread_num();
   num_threads = omp_get_num_threads();
   a[x] = 10*num_threads;
}
```

Two library routines are used here, `omp_get_num_threads()`, which returns the number of threads that are currently being used in the parallel directive, and `omp_get_thread_num()`, which returns the thread number (an integer from 0 to `omp_get_num_threads()` – 1 where thread 0 is the master thread). The array `a[]` is a global array, and `x` and `num_threads` are declared as private to the threads.

The number of threads in a team is established by either:

1. a `num_threads` clause after the `parallel` directive
2. the `omp_set_num_threads()` library routine being previously called
3. the environment variable `OMP_NUM_THREADS` is defined

in the order given; the number is system-dependent if none of the above applies. The number of threads available may also be altered automatically to achieve the best use of the system resources through a "dynamic adjustment" mechanism. Usually, the best performance is not obtained when the number of threads is greater than the number of available processors, because then they would have to time-share on the processors. Often, the best use of resources is when the number of threads is the same as the number of available processors, given sufficient parallelism in the code. (Note that the system may be operating on other tasks so that the number of available processors may be less than the total number of processors in the system.) Dynamic adjustment can be enabled before program execution, if not done by default, by setting the environment variable `OMP_DYNAMIC`. It can also be enabled and disabled during program execution outside parallel regions with the library function `omp_set_num_dynamic(int num_threads)`. If enabled, each parallel region will use the number of threads that best utilizes the system resources. Using this option means that the program must be written to work with different numbers of threads in the parallel regions.

Work-Sharing. There are three constructs in this classification, `sections`, `for`, and `single`. In all cases, there is an implicit barrier at the end of the construct unless a `nowait` clause is included. Note that these constructs do not start a new team of threads. That should have already been done by an enclosing `parallel` construct.

Sections. The construct

```
#pragma omp sections
{
   #pragma omp section
      structured_block
   #pragma omp section
      structured_block
            .
            .
            .
}
```

causes the structured blocks to be shared among threads in the team. Note that two directives are used, `#pragma omp sections` and `#pragma omp section`. `#pragma omp sections` precedes the set of structured blocks, and `#pragma omp section` prefixes each structured block. The first section directive is optional.

This construct corresponds to the `par` construct described earlier:

```
par {
   structured_block
   structured_block
        .
        .
        .
   structured_block
}
```

which specifies that all structured blocks can and should be executed concurrently. Whether they are will depend upon the number of available processors.

For Loop. The directive

```
#pragma omp for
   for_loop
```

causes the `for` loop to be divided into parts, and the parts are shared among threads in the team. The `for` loop must be of canonical form; that is, a simple form with an initial expression, a single Boolean condition, and a simple increment expression (as fully described in the OpenMP specification documentation). The way the `for` loop is divided can be specified by an additional "schedule" clause. For example, the clause `schedule(static, chunk_size)` causes the for loop be divided into sizes specified by `chunk_size` and allocated to threads in a round robin fashion.

Single. The directive

```
#pragma omp single
   structured block
```

causes the structured block to be executed by one thread only.

Combined Parallel Work-sharing Constructs. If a `parallel` directive is followed by a single `for` directive, it can be combined into

```
#pragma omp parallel for
   for_loop
```

with similar effects, that is, it has the effect of each thread executing the same `for` loop.

If a `parallel` directive is followed by a single `sections` directive, it can be combined into

```
#pragma omp parallel sections {
   #pragma omp section
      structured_block
   #pragma omp section
      structured_block
            .
            .
            .
}
```

with similar effect. (In both cases, the `nowait` clause is not allowed.)

Master Directive. The `master` directive

```
#pragma omp master
   structured_block
```

causes the master thread to execute the structured block. This directive is different from those in the work-sharing group in that there is no implied barrier at the end of the construct (or the beginning). Other threads encountering this directive will ignore it and the associated structured block, and will move on.

Synchronization Constructs. There are five constructs in this classification, `critical`, `barrier`, `atomic`, `flush`, and `ordered`.

Critical. The critical directive will only allow one thread to execute the associated structured block. When one or more threads reach the critical directive

```
#pragma omp critical name
   structured_block
```

they will wait until no other thread is executing the same critical section (one with the same name), and then one thread will proceed to execute the structured block. name is optional. All critical sections with no name map to one undefined name.

Barrier. When a thread reaches the barrier

```
#pragma omp barrier
```

it waits until all the other threads have reached the barrier, and then they all proceed together. There are restrictions on the placement of barrier directives in a program. In particular, all the threads must be able to reach the barrier.

Atomic. The atomic directive

```
#pragma omp atomic
   expression_statement
```

implements a critical section efficiently when the critical section simply updates a variable (adds 1, subtracts 1, or does some other simple arithmetic operation as defined by expression_statement). Often processors have efficient atomic instructions for doing this. Of course, a good compiler should be able to spot this in a critical section anyway. The arithmetic operation is given in expression_statement, which must be in a simple form as defined by OpenMP (see Appendix C).

Flush. Shared objects are initially stored in shared memory and may be brought into local storage (processor registers or cache memory) when accessed by processors. The flush directive is a synchronization point which causes the thread to have a "consistent" view of certain or all shared variables in memory. All current read and write operations on the variables are allowed to complete, and values are written back to memory, but any memory operations in the code after the flush are not started, thereby creating a "memory fence." Flush has the format

```
#pragma omp flush (variable_list)
```

Flush occurs automatically at the entry and exit of parallel and critical directives (and combined parallel for and parallel sections directives), and at the exit of for, sections, and single (if a nowait clause is not present). Note that it does not occur at all in master or at the entry of for, section, or single. Also, it only applies to the thread executing the flush, not to all the threads in the team which do not automatically get a consistent view of memory. For that, each thread would have to execute a flush directive.

Ordered. The ordered directive is used in conjunction with for and parallel for directives to cause an iteration to be executed in the order that it would have occurred if written as a sequential loop. See Appendix C for further details.

8.6 PERFORMANCE ISSUES

8.6.1 Shared Data Access

Even though processors have the ability to access any location within the shared memory, it is still very important to try to organize the data for the best performance, given that all modern computer systems have cache memory, high-speed memory closely attached to each processor. Cache memory is used because the speed at which a processor can make references to memory locations greatly exceeds the time that the main memory requires to respond. A higher-speed, but smaller, cache memory can be matched more closely to the speed of the processor. Systems can even have more than one level of cache memory; a small on-chip first-level (L1) cache with the processor, and a larger off-chip second-level (L2) cache after the first-level cache. It is even possible to have a shared third-level (L3) cache, especially in a symmetric shared memory multiprocessors (SMP). In the following, we shall only consider a single cache with each processor.

Programs consist of executable instructions (code) and associated data. In current practice, executable instructions are not altered when the program is executed. In contrast, the data may be altered, which may cause significant complexities to the system design and significantly affect the overall performance. When a processor first references a main memory location, a copy of the contents is transferred to the cache memory of the processor. Suppose the information being brought into the cache is data. When the processor subsequently references the data, it accesses the cache for it in the first instance. If another processor then references the same main memory location, a copy of the data is also transferred to the cache associated with that processor, thus creating more than one copy of the data. This is not a problem until a processor alters its cached copy; that is, writes a new data value. Then a *cache coherence protocol* must ensure that subsequently processors obtain the newly altered data when they reference it.

Cache coherence protocols use either an update policy or, more commonly, an invalidate policy. In the update policy, copies of the data in all caches are updated at the time one copy is altered. In the invalidate policy, when one copy of data is altered, the same data in any other cache is invalidated by resetting a valid bit in the cache. An invalid copy is updated when a processor tries to access it. There are several different cache coherence protocols (see Tomasevic and Milutinovic, 1993, for further details). The programmer can assume that an effective cache coherence protocol is present in the system and that it will have an impact upon the performance of the system.

Knowing that caches are present may suggest an alteration to the parallel algorithm for greater performance. The key characteristic is that caches are organized in blocks of contiguous locations (also called lines). When a processor first references one or more bytes in the block, the whole block is transferred into the cache from the main memory. Hence, if another part of the block is referenced, it will already be in the cache, and there will be no need to transfer it from the main memory. A parallel algorithm could take this into account if the size of the block and the way data is stored by the compiler are known. Such tweaking, of course, makes the performance highly dependent upon the actual computer system being used to execute the program.

Blocks are used in caches because a basic characteristic of sequential programs is that memory references tend to be near previous memory references (which is known as temporal locality). However, it may be that different parts of a block may be required by different processors but not the same bytes in the block. If one processor writes to one part of the block, copies of the complete block in other caches must be updated or invalidated, but the actual data is not shared. This is known as *false sharing* and can have a deleterious effect on performance. False sharing is illustrated in Figure 8.10. In this figure, a block consists of eight words, 0 to 7. Two processors access the same block, but different bytes in the block (processor 1 accesses word 3, and processor 2 accesses word 5). Suppose processor 1 alters word 3. The cache coherence protocol will update or invalidate the block in the cache of processor 2 even though processor 2 may never reference word 3. Suppose now that processor 2 alters word 5. Now the cache coherence protocol will update or invalidate the block in the cache of processor 1 even though processor 1 may never reference word 5, resulting in an unfortunate ping-ponging of cache blocks.

A solution for this problem is for the compiler to alter the layout of the data stored in the main memory, separating data only altered by one processor into different blocks. This may be difficult to satisfy in all situations. For example, the code

```
forall (i = 0; i < 5; i++)
  a[i] = 0;
```

is likely to create false sharing because the elements of `a`, `a[0]`, `a[1]`, `a[2]`, `a[3]`, and `a[4]`, are likely to be stored in consecutive locations in memory. The only way to avoid false sharing would be to place each element in a different block, which would create significant wastage of storage for a large array. But even code such as

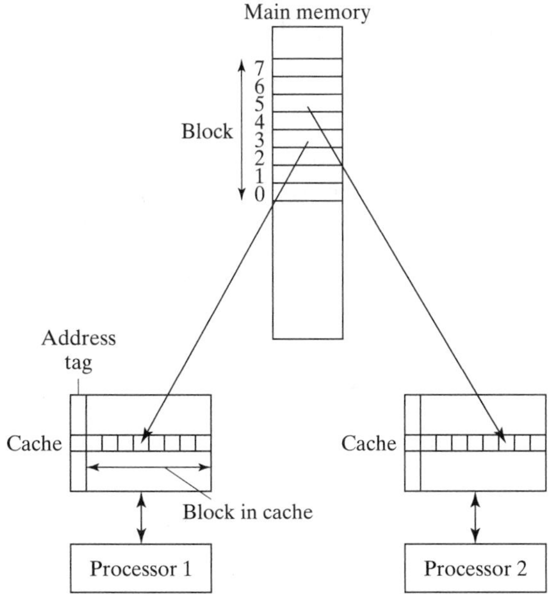

Figure 8.10 False sharing in caches.

```
par {
   x = 0;
   y = 0;
}
```

where `x` and `y` are shared variables, could create false sharing because the variables `x` and `y` are likely to be stored together in a data segment.

In general, the programmer needs to arrange their parallel algorithms so that the caching characteristics are exploited fully and false sharing is reduced (that nonshared data items are not grouped in the same block).

8.6.2 Shared Memory Synchronization

A major cause for reduced performance of shared memory programs is the use of synchronization primitives. Synchronization in shared memory programs is used for one of three main purposes:

- Mutual exclusion synchronization
- Process/thread synchronization
- Event synchronization

Mutual exclusion synchronization is used to control access to critical sections and can be implemented with lock/unlock routines. High-performance programs should have as few critical sections as possible, because their use can serialize the code, as illustrated in Figure 8.11. Let us assume as usual that each processor is executing one process, and all the processors happen to come to their critical sections together. The critical sections will be executed one after the other. In this situation, the execution time becomes almost that of a single processor. As pointed out by Pfister (1998), increasing the number of processors may be counterproductive. For example, suppose there are p processors, and each has a critical section taking t_{crit} time units, and a computation outside the critical section taking t_{comp} time units, and these two parts are repeated. When $t_{\text{comp}} < pt_{\text{crit}}$, fewer than p processors will be active at some time (see Figure 8.11).

As we have seen, barriers are used in both message-passing programs and shared memory programs. Barriers sometimes cause processors to wait needlessly. For example, some synchronous algorithms can modified to be asynchronous or partially so, as described at the end of Chapter 6, resulting in fewer barriers and very significant reductions in execution time.

Event synchronization is used to signal that some condition or value has occurred in one process/thread to another process/thread. Event synchronization can be achieved by code such as

```
Process 1                         Process 2

    :
data = new;
flag = TRUE;                          :
    :                             while (flag != TRUE) { };
                                  data_copy = data;
                                      :
```

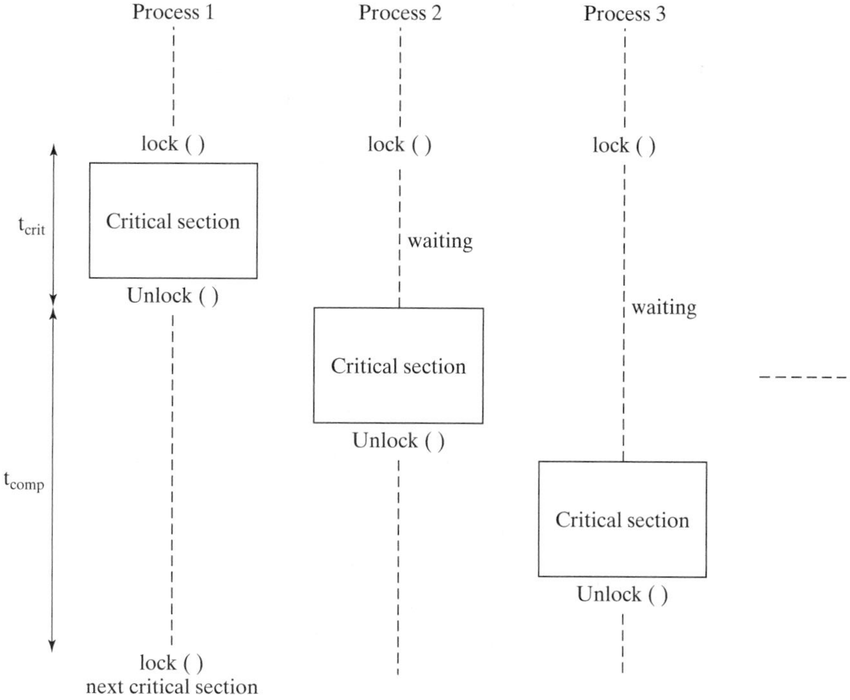

Figure 8.11 Critical sections serializing code.

Here, process 2 is told that data has been updated by process 1. `Flag` is a shared variable, but it is not necessary to restrict access to it to within a critical section. As noted by Culler and Singh (1999), rather than use a separate flag variable, the data variable itself could be used:

```
Process 1                           Process 2

    .
    .
    .
data = new;
    .
    .                                   .
    .                                   .
                                        .
                                    while (data != new) { };
                                    data_copy = data;
                                        .
                                        .
                                        .
```

although the code does become less readable, and one has to be *extremely* careful to study the possibilities and implications. One assumption here is that `data` cannot equal `new` before being set to that value by process 1, or if that can happen, it does not matter. Another assumption here is that statements in each process are executed in the order given in the program. Finally, the existence of cache memory is a very significant factor. It may be that the values held in the caches are not up-to-date values unless the cache is explicitly brought up-to-date. In the next section, we will explore the aspect of program order and memory operations further.

8.6.3 Sequential Consistency

In any (MIMD) multiprocessor system, each processor will be executing its own program held in local memory, and thus more than one program will be executed simultaneously. The term *sequential consistency* describes when the final result of these programs is the same irrespective of the time-relationship of the individual programs. That is, at any point in time, the actual progress of the executions of the individual instructions of each program may be different and could be interleaved in any order. The only constraint is that the instructions of each program are executed in program order. Formally, sequential consistency was defined by Lamport (1979) as:

> A multiprocessor is sequentially consistent if the result of any execution is the same as if the operations of all the processors were executed in some sequential order, and the operations of each individual processor occur in this sequence in the order specified by its program.

In other words, the overall effect of a parallel program is not changed by any arbitrary interleaving of instruction execution in time.

The key aspect for the final result of the programs to correct is the order in which the processors make requests for memory locations. For a system to be sequentially consistent, it must still produce the results that the program is designed to produce even though the individual requests from different processors can be interleaved in any order. One might picture this situation as shown in Figure 8.12. Clearly, if a processor is to read a shared

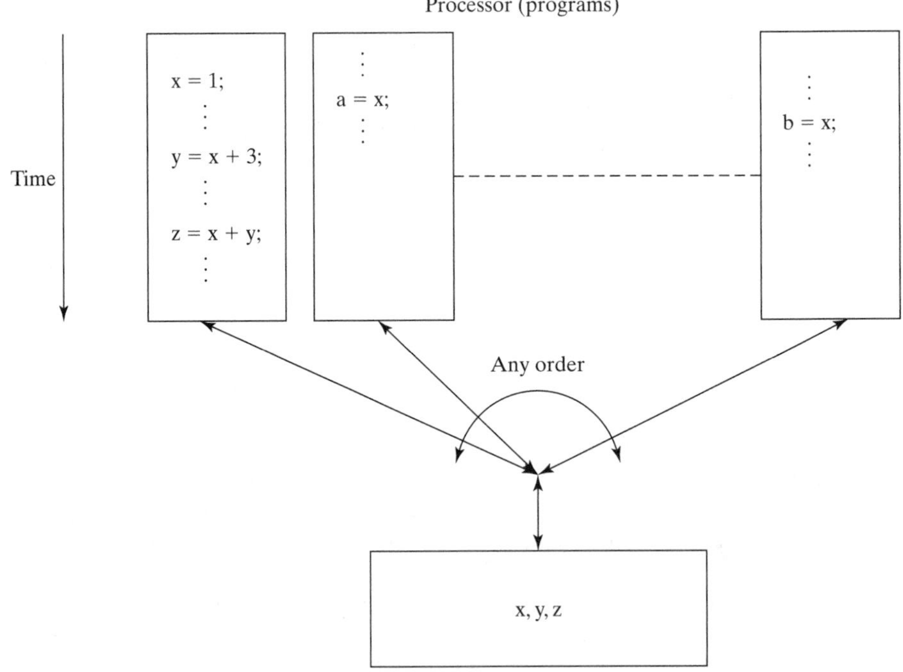
Processor (programs)
Time
x = 1;
y = x + 3;
z = x + y;
a = x;
b = x;
Any order
x, y, z

Figure 8.12 Sequentially consistent system.

variable, such as x in Figure 8.12, it usually requires the most up-to-date value of the variable. Sequential consistency will provide this value within the timing variations that could occur when each program is being executed.

Writing a parallel program for a system which is known to be sequentially consistent enables us to reason about the result of the program. In the code sequence given in Section 8.3.1

```
Process 1                          Process 2

    :
data = new;
flag = TRUE;                           :
    :                              while (flag != TRUE) { };
                                   data_copy = data;
                                       :
```

we would expect `data_copy` to be `set to new` because we expect the statement `data = new` to be executed before `flag = TRUE`, and the statement `while (flag != TRUE) { }` to be executed before `data_copy = data` (Hill, 1998). This code sequence can be used in sequentially consistent systems to ensure that a process (process 2 above) reads specific new data from another process (process 1 above). Process 2 will simple wait for the new data to be produced.

Program Order. Lamport's definition of sequential consistency says that "operations of each individual processor occur . . . in the order specified in its program," or *program order.* In Figure 8.12, this order is that of the stored machine instructions to be executed. However, the order of stored machine instructions may not be the same as the order of the corresponding high-level statements in the source program if the compiler is allowed to reorder statements for improved performance. In that case, the preceding example could fail.

Even if the compiler is instructed not to reorder the code, the order of execution of machine instructions in modern high-performance processors is also not necessarily the same as the order of the machine instructions in memory, because modern processors usually reorder machine instructions internally during execution for increased performance. However, the fact that a processor might not execute machine instructions in program order does not alter a multiprocessor's sequential consistency if the processor produces the final results in program order; that is, retires values to registers and memory locations in program order, which processors usually do to maintain sequential consistency.

As an example of processor reordering, suppose the new data in the preceding example is computed as follows:

```
Process 1                          Process 2

    :
new = a * b;
data = new;
flag = TRUE;                           :
    :                              while (flag != TRUE) { };
                                   data_copy = data;
                                       :
```

The multiply operation in `new = a * b` would correspond to a multiply machine instruction in the executable program. The next instruction corresponding to `data = new` must not be issued until the multiply has completed and produced its result. The next statement, `flag = TRUE`, is completely independent, and a clever processor not adhering to sequential consistency could start this operation before the multiply has completed (in fact it would), leading to the sequence:

```
Process 1                        Process 2

   :
new = a * b;
flag = TRUE;
data = new;
   :                                :
                                 while (flag != TRUE) { };
                                 data_copy = data;
                                    :
```

Now the while statement might occur before `new` is assigned to `data`, and the code would fail.

All multiprocessors will have the option of operating under the sequential consistency model, that is, forcing instructions to store their results in program order. A memory fence can be used explicitly; for example, using the `flush` directive in OpenMP. However, it can significantly limit compiler optimizations and processor performance. (This conclusion has been questioned by Hill (1998).)

Relaxing Read/Write Orders. Processors may be provided with facilities allowing them to relax their consistency in terms of the order of reads and writes with respect to those of another processor. For example, the term *processor consistency* describes the situation in which individual processors write in program order but the interleaved writes of different processors can appear in different orders. This relaxation would allow some opportunities for improved performance (through buffering and reordering instructions).

To support general relaxed read and write orders, special machine instructions, variously called *memory fences* or *memory barriers*, are provided to synchronize the memory operations when necessary in the program. For example, the Alpha processor has a memory barrier instruction that waits for all previously issued memory-access instructions to complete before issuing any new memory operations. It also has a write memory barrier instruction, which is similar to the memory barrier instruction but only considers memory write operations. The SUN Sparc V9 processor has a memory barrier instruction with four bits for variations. The write-to-read bit prevents any reads that follow it from being issued before all the writes that precede it have completed. The other bits are write-to-write, read-to-read, and read-to-write. The IBM PowerPC processor has a sync instruction, which is similar to the Alpha memory barrier instruction.

8.7 PROGRAM EXAMPLES

In this section, we will demonstrate the use of UNIX system calls, Pthreads, and Java by writing simple programs to sum the elements of an array, `a[1000]`:

```
int sum, a[1000];
  sum = 0;
  for (i = 0; i < 1000; i++)
    sum = sum + a[i];
```

using more than one process/thread. Of course, normally we would not want to use UNIX heavyweight processes for this purpose, but doing so shows the techniques for critical sections. For the UNIX process example, tasks will be statically assigned. For Pthreads and Java, a dynamic load-balancing approach will be used. For both UNIX processes and Pthreads, a critical section is necessary to protect access to shared variables. Java uses the monitor method.

8.7.1 UNIX Processes

For this example, the calculation will be divided into two parts, one doing the even *i* and one doing the odd *i*.

Process 1

```
sum1 = 0;
for (i = 0; i < 1000; i = i + 2)
  sum1 = sum1 + a[i];
```

Process 2

```
sum2 = 0;
for (i = 1; i < 1000; i = i + 2)
  sum2 = sum2 + a[i];
```

Each process will add its result (`sum1` or `sum2`) to an accumulating result, `sum` (after `sum` is initialized):

```
sum = sum + sum1;                    sum = sum + sum2;
```

producing the final answer. The result location, `sum`, will need to be shared and access protected by a lock. For this program, a shared data structure is created, as shown in Figure 8.13. Only one process accesses a given element of `a[]`, and in any event the access is a read access, so that access to `a[]` need not be protected. However, each process can alter `sum`, and this must be done within a critical section. A binary semaphore is used.

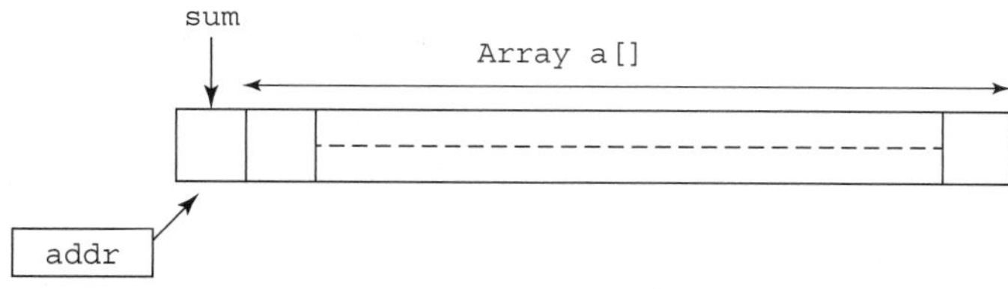

Figure 8.13 Shared memory locations for Section 8.7.1 program example.

```
#include <sys/types.h>
#include <sys/ipc.h>
#include <sys/shm.h>
#include <sys/sem.h>
#include <stdio.h>
#include <errno.h>
#define array_size 1000          /* no of elements in shared memory */
extern char *shmat();
void P(int *s);
void V(int *s);
int main() {
int shmid, s, pid;               /* shared memory, semaphore, proc id */
char *shm;                       /*shared mem. addr returned by shmat()*/
int *a, *addr, *sum;             /* shared data variables*/
int partial_sum;                 /* partial sum of each process */
int i;
                                 /* initialize semaphore set */
int init_sem_value = 1;
s = semget(IPC_PRIVATE, 1, (0600 | IPC_CREAT))
if (s == -1) {                   /* if unsuccessful*/
  perror("semget");
  exit(1);
}
if (semctl(s, 0, SETVAL, init_sem_value) < 0) {
  perror("semctl");
  exit(1);
}
                                 /* create segment*/
shmid = shmget(IPC_PRIVATE,(array_size*sizeof(int)+1),
  (IPC_CREAT|0600));
if (shmid == -1) {
  perror("shmget");
  exit(1);
}
                                 /* map segment to process data space */
shm = shmat(shmid, NULL, 0);
                                 /* returns address as a character*/
if (shm == (char*)-1) {
  perror("shmat");
  exit(1);
}

addr = (int*)shm;                /* starting address */
sum = addr;                      /* accumulating sum */
addr++;
a = addr;                        /* array of numbers, a[] */

*sum = 0;
for (i = 0; i < array_size; i++)    /* load array with numbers */
  *(a + i) = i+1;
```

```
pid = fork();                        /* create child process */
if (pid == 0)    {                   /* child does this */
   partial_sum = 0;
   for (i = 0; i < array_size; i = i + 2)
      partial_sum += *(a + i);
else {                               /* parent does this */
   partial_sum = 0;
   for (i = 1; i < array_size; i = i + 2)
      partial_sum += *(a + i);
}
P(&s);                               /* for each process, add partial sum */
   *sum += partial_sum;
V(&s);

printf("\nprocess pid = %d, partial sum = %d\n", pid, partial_sum);
if (pid == 0) exit(0); else wait(0);           /* terminate child proc */
printf("\nThe sum of 1 to %i is %d\n", array_size, *sum);


                                               /* remove semaphore */
if (semctl(s, 0, IPC_RMID, 1) == -1) {
   perror("semctl");
   exit(1);
}
                                               /* remove shared memory */
if (shmctl(shmid, IPC_RMID, NULL) == -1) {
   perror("shmctl");
   exit(1);
}

exit(0);
}                                              /* end of main */

void P(int *s) {                               /* P(s) routine*/
   struct sembuf sembuffer, *sops;
   sops = &sembuffer;
   sops->sem_num = 0;
   sops->sem_op = -1;
   sops->sem_flg = 0;
   if (semop(*s, sops, 1) < 0) {
      perror("semop");
      exit(1);
   }
   return;
}

void V(int *s) {                               /* V(s) routine */
   struct sembuf sembuffer, *sops;
   sops = &sembuffer;
   sops->sem_num = 0;
   sops->sem_op = 1;
```

```
        sops->sem_flg = 0;
        if (semop(*s, sops, 1) <0) {
          perror("semop");
          exit(1);
        }
        return;
    }
```

```
SAMPLE OUTPUT

process pid = 0, partial sum = 250000
process pid = 26127, partial sum = 250500
The sum of 1 to 1000 is 500500
```

8.7.2 Pthreads Example

In this example, num_thread threads are created, each taking numbers from the list to add to their sums. When all the numbers have been taken, the threads can add their partial results to a shared location sum. For this program, the shared data structure shown in Figure 8.14 is created. The shared location global_index is used by each thread to select the next element of a[]. After index is read, it is incremented in preparation for the next element to be read. The result location is sum, as before, and will also need to be shared and access protected by a lock.

It is important to note that the global index, global_index, should not be accessed outside a critical section. This includes testing whether the index has reached the maximum value. A statement such as

```
while (global_index < array_size) ...
```

requires access to global_index, which could be altered by another thread before the body of the while statement has been executed. In the code, a local variable, local_index, is used to store the currently read value of global_index for both updating the partial summation and detecting whether the maximum value has been reached.

The code uses a mutex lock. A condition variable is not used. A program using the method follows.

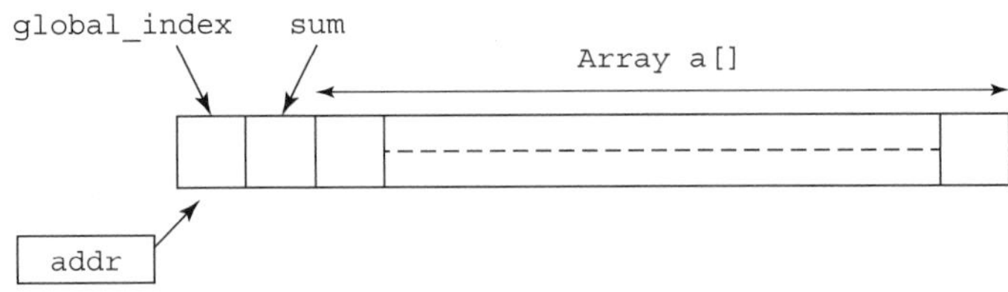

Figure 8.14 Shared memory locations for Section 8.7.2 program example.

```
#include <stdio.h>
#include <pthread.h>
#define array_size 1000
#define num_threads 10
                                    /* shared data */
int a[array_size];                  /* array of numbers to sum */
int global_index = 0;               /* global index */
int sum = 0;                        /* final result, also used by slaves */
pthread_mutex_t mutex1;             /* mutually exclusive lock variable */
void *slave(void *ignored)  {       /* Slave threads */
int local_index, partial_sum = 0;
do {
  pthread_mutex_lock(&mutex1);  /* get next index into the array */
    local_index = global_index;/* read current index & save locally*/
    global_index++;             /* increment global index */
  pthread_mutex_unlock(&mutex1);

  if (local_index < array_size)
      partial_sum += *(a + local_index);

} while (local_index < array_size);

pthread_mutex_lock(&mutex1);     /* add partial sum to global sum */
  sum += partial_sum;
pthread_mutex_unlock(&mutex1);

return ();                          /* Thread exits */
}

main () {
int i;
pthread_t thread[num_threads];              /* threads */
pthread_mutex_init(&mutex1,NULL);           /* initialize mutex */

for (i = 0; i < array_size; i++)            /* initialize a[] */
  a[i] = i+1;

for (i = 0; i < num_threads; i++)           /* create threads */
  if (pthread_create(&thread[i], NULL, slave, NULL) != 0)
    perror("Pthread_create fails");

for (i = 0; i < num_threads; i++)           /* join threads */
  if (pthread_join(thread[i], NULL) != 0)
    perror("Pthread_join fails");

printf("The sum of 1 to %i is %d\n", array_size, sum);
}                                           /* end of main */
```

```
SAMPLE OUTPUT
The sum of 1 to 1000 is 500500
```

Problem 8-9 explores the more efficient method of the slaves taking (up to) 10 consecutive numbers to add as a group so as to reduce the access to the index. Since the threads here do not return values, they could be made detached.

8.7.3 Java Example

The following is a simple Java implementation of the summation problem. This program was written by P. Shah, a University of North Carolina at Charlotte student, to demonstrate the Java monitor method. (We should mention that depending upon the Java implementation, one thread may take all the work.)

```
public class Adder {
   public int[] array;
   private int sum = 0;
   private int index = 0;
   private int number_of_threads = 10;
   private int threads_quit;

   public Adder() {
      threads_quit = 0;
      array = new int[1000];
      initializeArray();
      startThreads();
   }

   public synchronized int getNextIndex() {
      if(index < 1000) return(index++); else return(-1);
   }

   public synchronized void addPartialSum(int partial_sum) {
      sum = sum + partial_sum;
      if(++threads_quit == number_of_threads)
         System.out.println("The sum of the numbers is " + sum);
   }

   private void initializeArray() {
      int i;
      for(i = 0;i < 1000;i++) array[i] = i;
   }

   public void startThreads() {
      int i = 0;
      for(i = 0;i < 10;i++) {
         AdderThread at = new AdderThread(this,i);
         at.start();
      }
}
   public static void main(String args[]) {
      Adder a = new Adder();
```

```
    }

}

class AdderThread extends Thread {
    int partial_sum = 0;
    Adder parent;
    int number;
    public AdderThread(Adder parent, int number) {
        this.parent = parent;
        this.number = number;
    }

    public void run() {
        int index = 0;
        while(index != -1) {
            partial_sum = partial_sum + parent.array[index];
            index = parent.getNextIndex();
        }
        System.out.println("Partial sum from thread " + number + " is "
                + partial_sum);
        parent.addPartialSum(partial_sum);
    }
}
```

8.8 SUMMARY

This chapter discussed the following:

- Process creation
- The concept of a thread and its creation
- Pthreads routines
- How data can be created as shared data
- Methods of controlling access to shared data
- The concept of a condition variable
- Parallel programming language constructs
- OpenMP
- Dependency analysis using Bernstein's conditions
- Factors that affect system performance (synchronization, caches)
- Code examples

FURTHER READING

There are a multitude of invented parallel programming languages. Notable references include Karp and Babb (1988) for early languages based upon FORTRAN, and Wilson and Lu (1996) for languages based upon C++. Skillicorn and Tabia (1995) provide a reprint of important papers. UNIX system calls form the basis of the parallel programming text by Brawer (1989), although we should point out that the heavy cost of creating UNIX processes precludes their use in most realistic parallel programming situations. Pthreads and multithread programming are covered in several books, notably Kleiman, Shah, and Smaalders (1996), Butenhof (1997), Nichols, Buttlar, and Farrell (1996), and Prasad (1997).

OpenMP is described in Chandra et al. (2001). The definitive source for OpenMP is OpenMP Architecture Review Board (2002) from http://www.OpenMP.org.

Using Java for shared memory programming is also an area for further study. A starting point for Java is http://java.sun.com/. Most introductory Java books do not cover threads or synchronization. However, information can be found in Campione, Walrath, and Huml (2001). More specialized books include Lewis and Berg (2000).

BIBLIOGRAPHY

BAL, H. E., J. G. STEINER, AND A. S. TANENBAUM (1989), "Programming Languages for Distributed Computing Systems," *ACM Computing Surveys*, Vol. 21, No. 3, pp. 261–322.

BEN-ARI, M. (1990), *Principles of Concurrent and Distributed Programming*, Prentice Hall, Englewood Cliffs, NJ.

BERNSTEIN, A. J. (1966), "Analysis of Programs for Parallel Processing," *IEEE Trans. Elec. Comput.*, Vol. E-15, pp. 746–757.

BRÄUNL, T. (1993), *Parallel Programming: An Introduction*, Prentice Hall, London.

BRAWER, S. (1989), *Introduction to Parallel Programming*, Academic Press, San Diego, CA.

BUTENHOF, D. R. (1997), *Programming with POSIX® Threads*, Addison-Wesley, Reading, MA.

CAMPIONE, M., K. WALRATH, AND A. HUML (2001), *The Java™ Tutorial 3rd edition: A Short Course on the Basics*, Addison-Wesley, Boston, MA.

CHANDRA, R, L. DAGUM, D. KOHR, D. MAYDAN, J. MCDONALD, AND R. MENON (2001), *Parallel Programming in OpenMP*, Academic Press, San Diego, CA.

CONWAY, M. E. (1963), "A Multiprocessor System Design," *Proc. AFIPS Fall Joint Computer Conf.*, Vol. 4, pp. 139–146.

CULLER, D. E., AND J. P. SINGH (WITH A. GUPTA) (1999), *Parallel Computer Architecture: A Hardware/Software Approach*, Morgan Kaufmann, San Francisco, CA.

DIJKSTRA, E. W. (1968), "Cooperating Sequential Processes," in *Programming Languages*, F. Genuys (ed.), Academic Press, New York, pp. 43–112.

FOSTER, I. (1995), *Designing and Building Parallel Programs*, Addison-Wesley, Reading, MA.

HILL, M. D. (1998), "Multiprocessors Should Support Simple Memory Consistency Models," *Computer*, Vol. 31, No. 8, pp. 29–34.

HOARE, C. A. R. (1974), "Monitors: An Operating System Structuring Concept," *Comm. ACM*, Vol. 17, No. 10, pp. 549–557.

KARP, A., AND R. BABB (1988), "A Comparison of Twelve Parallel Fortran Dialects," *IEEE Software*, Vol. 5, No. 5, pp. 52–67.

KLEIMAN, S., D. SHAH, AND B. SMAALDERS (1996), *Programming with Threads*, Prentice Hall, Upper Saddle River, NJ.

LAMPORT, L. (1979), "How to Make a Multiprocessor Computer That Correctly Executes Multiprocess Programs," *IEEE Trans. Comp.*, Vol. C-28, No. 9, pp. 690–691.

LEWIS, B. AND D. L. BERG (2000), *Multithreaded Programming with Java Technology*, Sun Microsystems Press, Palo Alto, CA.

NICHOLS, B., D. BUTTLAR, AND J. P. FARRELL (1996), *Pthreads Programming*, O'Reilly & Associates, Sebastopol, CA.

OPENMP ARCHITECTURE REVIEW BOARD (2002), *OpenMP C and C++ Application Program Interface Version 2, March 2002*, from http://www.OpenMP.org.

PFISTER, G. F. (1998), *In Search of Clusters: The Ongoing Battle in Lowly Parallel Computing*, Prentice Hall, Upper Saddle River, NJ.

POLYCHRONOPOULOS, C. D. (1988), *Parallel Programming and Compilers*, Kluwer Academic, Norwell, MA.

PRASAD, S. (1997), *Multithreading Programming Techniques*, McGraw-Hill, New York.

SKILLICORN, D. B., AND D. TABIA (1995), *Programming Languages for Parallel Processing*, IEEE CS Press, Los Alamitos, CA.

SUNSOFT (1994), *Pthread and Solaris Threads: A Comparison of Two User Level Threads APIs*, Sun Microsystems, Mountain View, CA.

TERRANO, A. E., S. M. DUNN, AND J. E. PETERS (1989), "Using an Architectural Knowledge Base to Generate Code for Parallel Computers," *Comm. ACM*, Vol. 32, No. 9, pp. 1065–1072.

TOMASEVIC M., AND V. MILUTINOVIC (1993), *The Cache Coherence Problem in Shared Memory Multiprocessors: Hardware Solutions*, IEEE CS Press, Los Alamitos, CA.

WILKINSON, B. (1996), *Computer Architecture Design and Performance*, 2nd edition, Prentice Hall, London.

WILSON, G. V., AND P. LU, eds. (1996), *Parallel Programming Using C++*, MIT Press, Cambridge, MA.

WOLFE, M. (1996), *High Performance Compilers for Parallel Computing*, Addison-Wesley, Redwood City, CA.

PROBLEMS

Many Scientific/Numerical and Real Life programming problems given in other chapters can be implemented using Pthreads and OpenMP as programming assignments. Additional problems are given below, some of which are specific to threads or OpenMP.

Scientific/Numerical

8-1. List the possible orderings of the instructions of the two processes, each having three instructions.

8-2. Write code using Pthreads with a condition variable to implement the example given in Section 8.3.2 for two "action" routines waiting on a "counter" routine to decrement a counter to zero.

8-3. What does the following code do?

```
forall (i = 0; i < n; i++) {
   a[i] = a[i + n];
}
```

8-4. Analyze the code

```
forall (i = 2; i < 6; i++) {
   x = i - 2*i + i*i;
   a[i] = a[x];
}
```

as given in Section 8.3.4 and determine whether any instances of the body can be executed simultaneously.

8-5. Can

```
for (i = 0; i < 4; i++) {
   a[i] = a[i + 2];
}
```

be rewritten as

```
forall (i = 0; i < 4; i++) {
   a[i] = a[i + 2];
}
```

and still obtain the correct results? Explain.

8-6. Explain why each of the following program segments will not work. Rewrite the code in each case so that it will work given $n = 100$ and 11 processors.

(a) For adding a constant 5 to elements of an array a:

```
for (i = 1;i <= n; i++)
   FORK a[i] = a[i] + 5;
```

(b) For computing the sum of the elements of an array a:

```
forall (i = 1;i <= n; i++)
   sum = sum + a[i];
```

8-7. List all possible outputs when the following code is executed:

```
j = 0;
k = 0;
forall (i = 1; i <= 2; i++) {
   j = j + 10;
   k = k + 100;
}
printf("i=%i,j=%i,k=%i\n",i,j,k);
```

assuming that each assignment statement is atomic. (Clue: Number the assignment statements and then find every possible sequence.)

8-8. The following C-like parallel code is supposed to transpose a matrix:

```
forall (i = 0; i < n; i++)
   forall (j = 0; j < n; j++)
     a[i][j] = a[j][i];
```

Explain why the code will not work. Rewrite the code so that it will work.

8-9. As mentioned at the end of Section 8.3.2, basic Pthreads (POSIX.1 standard) do not have a native barrier. Write a barrier routine and test it. Include routines to create and initialize any necessary data structures (shared variables, mutexs, condition variables), and to destroy the data structures.

8-10. The basic Pthreads (POSIX.1 standard) do not have a native read/write lock. A read/write lock is a form of lock which differentiates between read accesses and write accesses, and allows more than one thread to read the data but only one to alter it. When a thread sets a read/write lock, it specifies whether the lock is for a (shared) read access or for (exclusive) write access. The thread will not be allowed to continue if another thread has write access, but it will be allowed to continue otherwise. When multiple threads are waiting on a read/write lock, a precedence has to be established; either read accesses have precedence over write accesses, or vice versa. If read accesses have precedence on write accesses, multiple simultaneous read accesses can occur as soon as possible. If write accesses has precedence, updating the data can occur as soon as possible. Implement a read/write lock in Pthreads.

8-11. The following C-like parallel routine is supposed to compute the sum of the first n numbers:

```
int summation(int n);
{
int sum = 0;
forall (i = 1; i <= n; i++)
   sum = sum + i;
return(sum);
}
```

Why will it not work? Rewrite the code so that it will work given $n = 200$ and 51 processors.

8-12. Determine and explain how the following code for a barrier works (based upon the two-phase barrier given in Chapter 6, Section 6.1.3):

```
void barrier()
{
    lock(arrival);
    count++;
    if (count < n) unlock(arrival)
    else unlock(departure);
    lock(departure);
    count--;
    if (count > 0) unlock(departure)
    else unlock(arrival);
    return;
}
```

Why is it necessary to use two lock variables, `arrival` and `departure`?

8-13. Write a Pthreads or OpenMP program to perform numerical integration, as described in Chapter 4, Section 4.2.2. Compare using different decomposition methods (rectangular and trapezoidal).

8-14. Rewrite the Pthread example code in Section 8.4 so that the slaves will take (up to) 10 consecutive numbers to add as a group to reduce access to the index.

8-15. Condition variables can be used to detect distributed termination. Introduce condition variables into a load-balancing program that has distributed termination, as described in Chapter 7.

8-16. Write a multithreaded program consisting of two threads in which a file is read into a buffer by one thread and written out to another file by another thread.

8-17. Write a Pthreads or OpenMP program to find the roots of the quadratic equation $ax^2 + bx + c = 0$, using the formula

$$x = \frac{-b \pm \sqrt{b^2 - 4ac}}{2a}$$

where intermediate values are computed by different threads. Use a condition variable to recognize when each thread has completed its designated computation.

8-18. If three processes reach their critical sections together, what is the total time the processes spend waiting to enter their critical sections if each critical section takes t_c seconds?

8-19. Rewrite the code given in Problem 8-3 in OpenMP.

8-20. Select one Scientific/Numerical problem given in another chapter and make a comparative study using Pthreads and MPI. Measure the time of execution in each case. Also implement sequentially, and measure the time of execution of this implementation.

8-21. Repeat Problem 8-20, but compare OpenMP and MPI implementations.

8-22. Repeat Problem 8-20, but compare Pthreads and OpenMP.

Real Life

8-23. Write a multithreaded program to simulate two automatic teller machines being accessed by different persons on a single shared account. Enhance the program to allow automatic debits to occur.

8-24. Write a multithreaded program for an airline ticket reservation system to enable different travel agents to access a single source of available tickets (in shared memory).

8-25. Write a multithreaded program for a medical information system accessed by various doctors who may try to retrieve and update a patient's history (add something, etc.), which is held in shared memory.

8-26. Write a multithreaded program for selling tickets to the next concert of the rock group "Purple Mums" in Ericsson Stadium, Charlotte, North Carolina.

8-27. Write a multithreaded program to simulate a computer network in which workstations are connected by a single Ethernet and send messages to each other and to a main server at random intervals. Model each workstation by one thread making random requests for other workstations, and take into account message sizes and collisions.

8-28. Extend Problem 8-27 by providing multiple Ethernet lines (as described in Chapter 1, Section 1.4).

8-29. Write a multithreaded program to simulate a hypercube network and a mesh network, both with multiple parallel communication links between nodes. Determine how the performance changes when the number of parallel links between nodes is increased, and make a comparative study of the performance of the hypercube and mesh using the results of your simulation. Performance metrics include the number of requests that are accepted in each time period. See Wilkinson (1996) for further details and sample results of this simulation.

8-30. Devise a problem that uses locks for protecting critical sections and condition variables and requires less than three pages of code. Implement the problem.

8-31. Write a program to simulate a digital system consisting of AND, OR, and NOT gates connected in various user-defined ways. Each AND and OR gate has two inputs and one output. Each NOT gate has one input and one output. Each gate is to be implemented as a thread that receives Boolean values from other gates. The data for this program will be an array defining the interconnections and the gate functions. For example, Table 8.2 defines the logic circuit shown in Figure 8.15. First establish that your program can simulate the specific logic circuit shown in Figure 8.15, and then modify the program to cope with any arrangement of gates, given that there are a maximum of eight gates.

TABLE 8.2 LOGIC CIRCUIT DESCRIPTION FOR FIGURE 8.15

Gate	Function	Input 1	Input 2	Output
1	AND	Test1	Test2	Gate1
2	NOT	Gate1		Output1
3	OR	Test3	Gate1	Output2

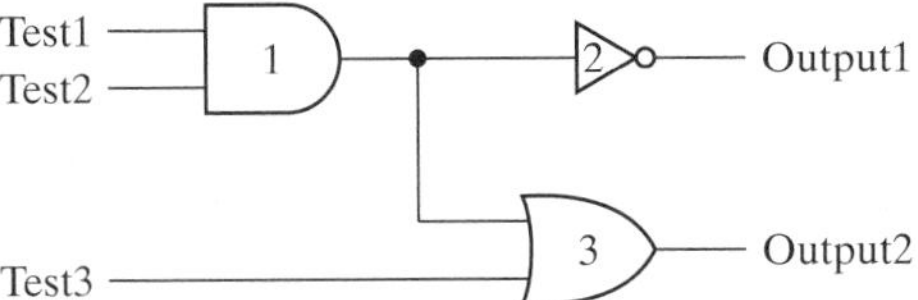

Figure 8.15 Sample logic circuit.

8-32. Write a multithreaded program to implement the following arcade game: A river has logs floating downstream (or to and fro). A frog must cross the river by jumping on logs as they pass by, as illustrated in Figure 8.16. The user controls when the frog jumps, which can only be perpendicular to the riverbanks. You win if the frog makes it to the opposite side of the river, and you lose if the frog lands in the river. Graphical output is necessary, and sound effects are preferable. Concurrent movements of the logs are to be controlled by separate threads. [This problem was suggested and implemented for a short open-ended assignment (Problem 8-30) by Christopher Wilson, a senior at University of North Carolina at Charlotte in 1997. Other arcade games may be amenable to a thread implementation.]

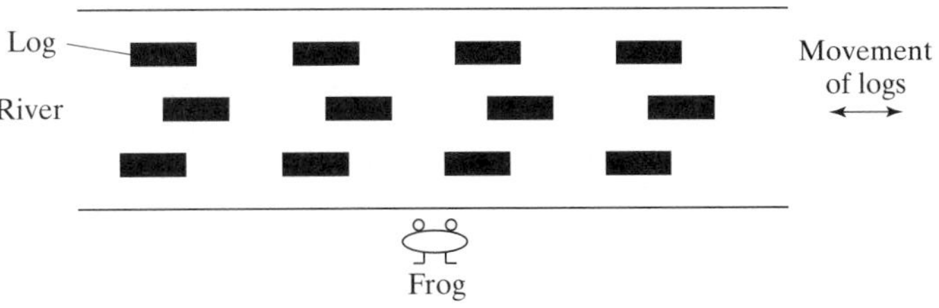

Figure 8.16 River and frog for Problem 8-32.

8-33. In a typical gasoline filling station, there are multiple pumps drawing from a single tank. Slightly complicating the situation, there are usually only two different grades of fuel stored in the tanks: the lowest and highest grades. However, each pump is capable of delivering fuel from the highest-grade tank, fuel from the lowest-grade tank, or a blend of the two for an intermediate grade. Implement a thread-based parallel implementation simulating a large gas station in which up to 20 pumps are all delivering fuel from the two storage tanks, and intermittently a delivery truck adds fuel to the tanks.

8-34. Write a simple Web server using a collection of threads organized in a master-slave configuration. The master thread receives requests. When a request is received, the master thread checks a pool of slave threads to find a free thread. The request is handed to the first free thread, which then services the request, as illustrated in Figure 8.17. [This problem was suggested and implemented for a short open-ended assignment (Problem 8-30) by Kevin Vaughan, a junior at North Carolina State University in 1997.]

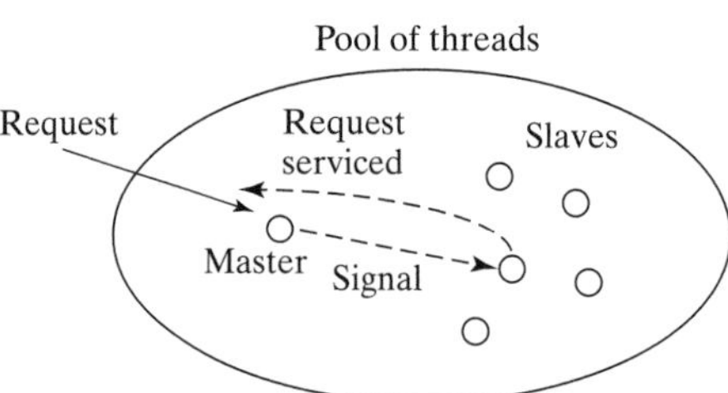

Figure 8.17 Thread pool for Problem 8-34.

8-35. Select one Real Life problem given in another chapter and make a comparative study of using Pthreads and using MPI. Measure the time of execution in each case. Also implement sequentially, and measure the time of execution of this implementation.

8-36. Repeat Problem 8-35, but compare OpenMP and MPI implementations.

8-37. Repeat Problem 8-35, but compare Pthreads and OpenMP.

Chapter 9

Distributed Shared Memory Systems and Programming

This chapter is concerned with using the shared memory programming model on a cluster of computers that has physically distributed and separate memory. From a programming viewpoint, the memory is grouped together and sharable between the processors. This approach is known as *distributed shared memory* (DSM) and can be achieved through software and/or hardware means. We will concentrate upon software means, which can be used with ease on existing clusters at little or no cost except for the effort of installing the software, although the performance of software DSM will generally be inferior to using explicit message-passing on the same cluster. Programming a distributed shared memory system uses the same basic techniques as programming true shared memory systems, as described in Chapter 8, but with additional aspects concerning with the shared memory model is achieved when the memory is physically distributed. Chapter 9 can be studied directly after Chapter 8, or later.

9.1 DISTRIBUTED SHARED MEMORY

In Chapter 8, we described how to program a shared memory multiprocessor system. In this type of multiple processor system, there is a central "shared" memory, and every processor can access it directly. The processors and memory are physically connected together in some manner and form a single high-performance computer system. The shared memory allows data to be directly accessed by each processor as it executes code rather than by sending the data from one computer to another through messages. Shared memory programming is generally more convenient than message-passing programming because it allows data of any size to be accessed by individual processors without having to explicitly send the data to the processor. One can handle complex and large data bases without replication, but access to shared data has to be controlled by the programmer using locks or other means. In both message-passing and shared memory models, processes often need to be synchronized; for example, at places using barriers.

Distributed shared memory (DSM) is the designation for making a group of interconnected computers, each with its own memory, appear as though the physically distributed memory is a single memory with a single address space, as illustrated in Figure 9.1. Once distributed shared memory is achieved, any memory location can be accessed by any of the processors whether or not the memory resides locally, and normal shared memory programming techniques can be used. Of course, one could simply use a shared memory multiprocessor. But traditional bus-connected shared memory multiprocessors have a limited number of processors that can be attached to the bus, so it becomes very difficult to scale them to larger systems. Different, more complex interconnection networks are usually needed. Clusters, in contrast, can very easily be scaled to almost any size. One of the main attractions of DSM on clusters is its economy. Clusters can be established at low cost using commodity interconnects.

In a DSM system implemented on a cluster, messages are still sent between computers to move data between them. However, this message-passing is hidden from the user. The user does not have to specify the messages explicitly in the program. Simply using the appropriate shared memory constructs or routines to access shared data will instigate the necessary message-passing. It will be up to the underlying DSM system to decide what messages to send and whether to replicate data or to actually move it from one computer to another. Various protocols are possible, as will be described.

DSM has some disadvantages. It will definitely provide a lower performance than a true shared memory multiprocessor system, because the interconnects between stand-alone computers will operate much slower than the interconnects within shared memory multiprocessor systems. Of course, the cluster will have a much lower cost for a given number of processors and more scalability. DSM will usually incur a performance penalty when compared to using the cluster with regular message-passing routines, as it would be expected that programmer-inserted message-passing routines would be more efficient than an automated DSM approach. There is some evidence that this is not always true in that DSM systems may be able to take advantage of optimizations or clever protocols that programmers may not recognize for their own programs.

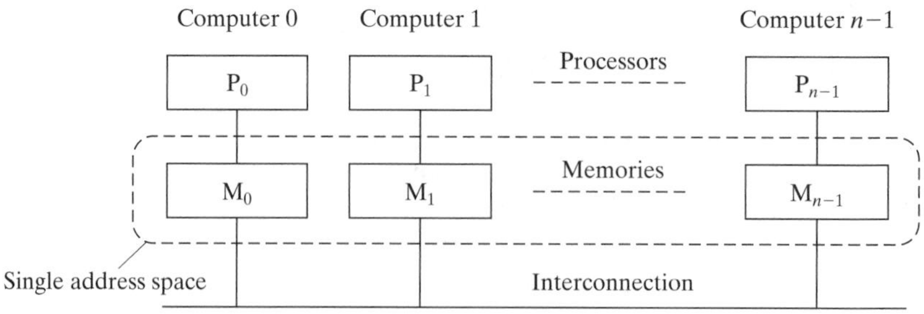

Figure 9.1 Distributed shared memory.

A cluster can be composed of a group of single-processor systems, a group of SMP multiprocessor systems, such as quad Pentium systems, as shown in Figure 9.2, or a combination of single and multiprocessor systems. Some very interesting possibilities arise for programming an SMP cluster. True shared memory programming can be done with each SMP computer by means of either message-passing programming or distributed shared memory programming between the SMP computers. A single DSM environment could be created by fully utilizing the SMP computers.

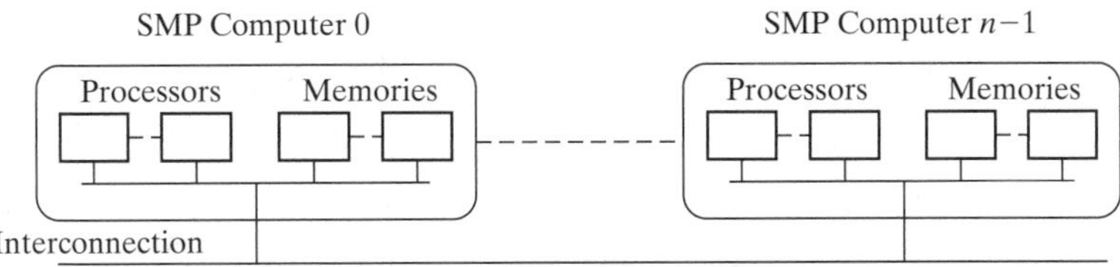

Figure 9.2 SMP cluster.

9.2 IMPLEMENTING DISTRIBUTED SHARED MEMORY

DSM has been studied in the research community since the mid-1980s and can be achieved by software means, hardware means, or combined hardware/software means.

9.2.1 Software DSM Systems

In the software approach, no hardware changes are made to the cluster and everything has to be done by software routines. Usually, a software layer is added between the operating system and the application. The kernel of the operating system may or may not be modified, depending upon the implementation. The software layer can be:

- Page based
- Shared variable based
- Object based

In the page-based approach, the system's existing virtual memory is used to instigate movement of data between computers, which occurs when the page referenced does not reside locally, as illustrated in Figure 9.3. This approach is sometimes called a *virtual shared memory system*. Li (1986) developed perhaps the first page-based DSM system. There have been subsequent page-based systems. TreadMarks, developed at Rice University (Amza et al., 1996), is perhaps the most famous. Another example of a distributed shared memory system that uses the virtual memory mechanism is Locust (Verma and Chiueh, 1998).

Major disadvantages of the page-based approach come from the fact that the unit of data being moved is a complete page, maybe 1024 bytes or more depending upon the underlying virtual memory system, and generally more than the specific data being referenced.

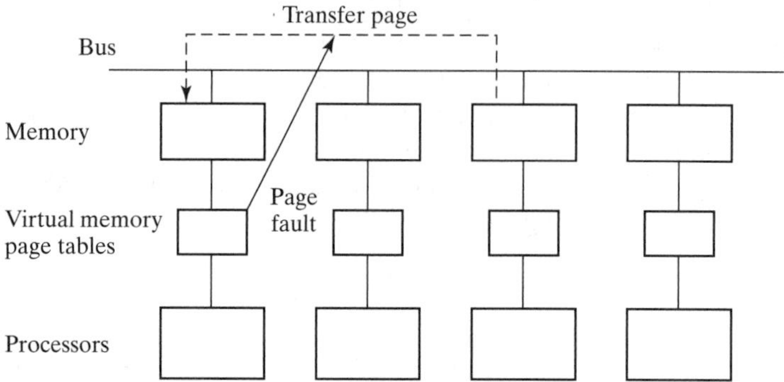

Figure 9.3 Page-based DSM system.

This leads to longer messages than are necessary. Also, false sharing effects appear at the page level and may be even more significant than at the cache level because of the large size of the page. In the context of paged-based systems, false sharing is the situation in which different parts of a page are required by different processors without any actual sharing of information, but the whole page has to be shared by each processor to access the different parts. Finally, page-based systems may not be very portable, since they are generally tied to particular virtual memory hardware and software.

In the shared-variable approach, only variables that are declared as shared are transferred, and this is done on demand. The paging mechanism is not used to cause the transfer. Instead, software routines, called by the programmer directly or indirectly, perform the actions. An example of this approach is Munin (Bennett, Carter, and Zwaenepoel, 1990). Other more recent systems in this category include JIAJIA (Hu, Shi, and Tang, 1999) and Adsmith (Liang, King, and Lai, 1996). The latter is written in C++ but from the perspective of the user is a shared-variable system.We shall describe how the shared-variable approach can be implemented in more detail later. If performance is not a key factor, it can be implemented very easily.

In the object-based approach, the shared data are embodied in objects which include data items and the only procedures (methods) that may be used to access this data. In other aspects, it is the similar to the shared-variable approach and can be regarded as an extension of this approach. It is relatively easy to implement using an object-based language such as C++ or Java and has the advantage over the shared-variable approach of providing an object-oriented discipline.

9.2.2 Hardware DSM Implementation

In the hardware approach, special network interfaces and cache coherence circuits are added to the system to make a memory reference to a remote memory location look like a reference to a local memory location. There are several special-purpose interfaces that support shared memory operations. Examples include Virtual Memory–Mapped Network Interface (Blumrich et al., 1995), Myrinet (Boden et al., 1995), SCI (Hellwagner and Reinefeld, 1999), and the Memory-Integrated Network Interface (Minnich, Burns, and Hady, 1995).

The hardware approach should provide a higher level of performance than the software approach. Software approaches typically add an extra layer of software between the operating system and the user application. Some even use a separate a message-passing layer. Also, software approaches typically use existing commodity interfaces (e.g., Ethernet) and incur significant performance overhead. The purely software approach is more attractive than the hardware approach for teaching purposes, however, because then existing computer systems can be used without modification, and we will concentrate upon the software approach in the following.

9.2.3 Managing Shared Data

There are several ways that a processor could be given access to shared data. The simplest solution is to have a *central server* responsible for all read and write operations on shared data, and to have the processors make requests to this server. All reading and writing of shared data occurs in one place and sequentially; that is, it implements a *single reader/ single writer* policy. This policy is rarely used (except for simple student projects) because it incurs a significant bottleneck in that all requests must go to one place. The problem can be relieved to some extent by having multiple servers, each responsible for a subset of the shared variables. A mapping function is then needed to locate the individual servers.

Normally it is preferable to have multiple copies of data so as to allow simultaneous access to the data by different processors. Then one must address how to maintain these copies using a *coherence* policy. The *multiple reader/single writer* policy allows multiple processors to read shared data but only one to alter the data at any instant, which can be achieved efficiently by replicating the data at sites that require it. Only one site (the *owner*) is allowed to alter the data.

In the multiple reader/single writer policy, when the owner alters the shared data, the other copies are inaccurate. There are two possibilities to handle this situation

- Update policy
- Invalidate policy

In the update policy, all the other copies of the data are immediately altered to reflect the change by a broadcast message. In the invalidate policy, all the other copies of the data are flagged as invalid. If they are subsequently accessed, a response is obtained indicating invalid data, causing the processor to make a request from the owner for the most recent value. The invalidate policy is generally preferred, because messages are only generated when processors try to access updated copies. Any copies of the data that are not accessed subsequently remain invalid. Generally, both policies need to be reliable. Broadcast messages may require individual replies confirming action.

In the multiple reader/multiple writer policy, there can be multiple copies of the data, and different copies can be altered by different processors. This is the most complex scenario and may call for attaching sequence numbers to each write operation to order the write operations. Further details are given by Protic, Tomasevic, and Milutinovic (1996).

9.2.4 Multiple Reader/Single Writer Policy in a Page-Based System

In a page-based system, whenever a shared variable is referenced which does not reside locally, the complete page that holds the variable is transferred. The page is the unit of sharing. A variable stored on a page which is not shared will be moved or invalidated with the page when the whole page is moved because another variable on it is required somewhere else (i.e., false sharing can occur). TreadMarks handles this situation by allowing different parts of the page to be altered by different processes but bringing these changes up-to-date in each copy at synchronization points (i.e., a multiple writer protocol at the page level but not at the shared-variable level). Suppose two processes are writing to different parts of a page. Each process first makes another copy of its page (a *twin*) before altering it. The different copies of the page are only made the same at a synchronization point. This is done by each process creating a record of its page modifications by a word-by-word comparison of the page with its unmodified twin. A "diff" is created which is a run-length encoding of the page modifications. Then each diff is sent to the other process to allow it to update its copy. More details of TreadMarks and this method can be found in (Amza et al., 1996).

9.3 ACHIEVING CONSISTENT MEMORY IN A DSM SYSTEM

The term *memory consistency model* addresses *when* the current value of a shared variable is seen by other processors. There are various models with decreasing constraints to provide potentially higher performance. The most stringent is strict consistency.

Strict Consistency. With strict consistency, when a processor reads a shared variable, it obtains the value produced by the most recent write to the shared variable. Strict consistency is illustrated in Figure 9.4. In this example, x and y are shared variables, and as soon as they are altered, all the other processors are informed of the change. (This could be done by an invalidate message rather than an update message. As mentioned earlier, invalidate is generally preferred over update.)

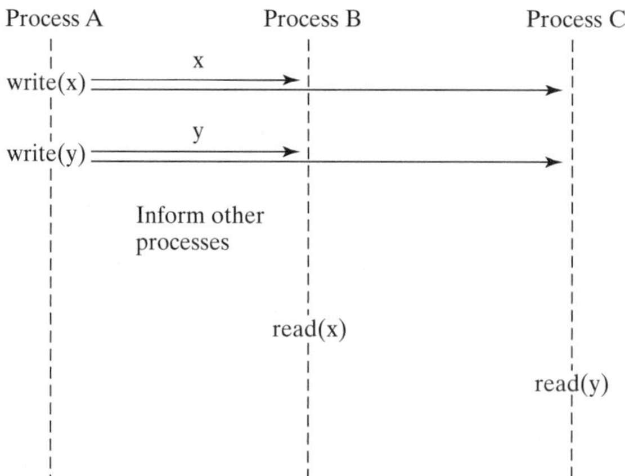

Figure 9.4 Strict consistency.

The major disadvantage of strict consistency is the large number of messages that it generates. And even in this model, there will also be a delay before the invalidate/update is actually seen in the processors because changes cannot be instantaneous. The time of the most recent write will generally be indeterminate, as it will depend upon the time of the execution of the instructions of the individual processors, which are operating independently.

In *relaxed memory consistency*, writes are delayed from being visible to the other processors to reduce the number of messages. There are various relaxed-memory consistency models:

Weak Consistency. Here, synchronization operations are used by the programmer whenever it is necessary to enforce sequential consistency (Chapter 8, Section 8.4.3). The compiler and the processor are allowed in other places to reorder instructions without regard to sequential consistency. This is a quite reasonable model, since any accesses to shared data can be controlled with synchronization operations (locks, etc.).

Release Consistency. This is an extension of weak consistency in which the synchronization operations are specified. The programmer must use the synchronization operators, *acquire* and *release*:

Acquire operation—used before a shared variable or variables are to be read.

Release operation—used after the shared variable or variables have been altered.

Typically, acquire is done with a lock operation, and release by an unlock operation (although not necessarily). Release consistency is illustrated in Figure 9.5. In this example, the shared variables x and y are updated by process 1 and read by process 2.

Lazy Release Consistency. A popular version of release consistency for a DSM system in which the update is only done at the time of acquire rather than at the time of release, as illustrated in Figure 9.6. Lazy release consistency generates fewer messages than release consistency.

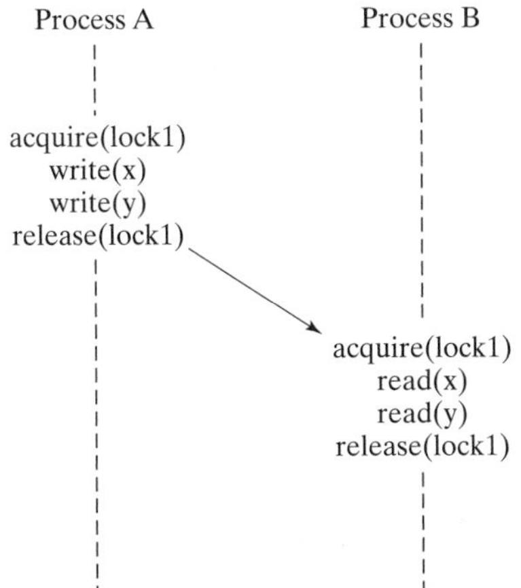
Process A
Process B
acquire(lock1)
write(x)
write(y)
release(lock1)
acquire(lock1)
read(x)
read(y)
release(lock1)

Figure 9.5 Release consistency.

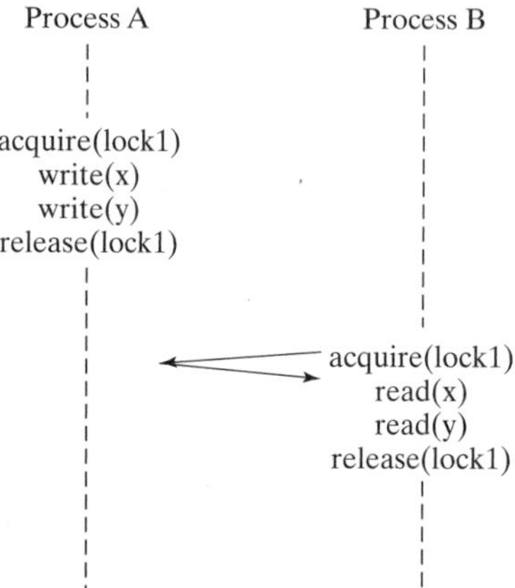
Process A
Process B
acquire(lock1)
write(x)
write(y)
release(lock1)
acquire(lock1)
read(x)
read(y)
release(lock1)

Figure 9.6 Lazy release consistency.

9.4 DISTRIBUTED SHARED MEMORY PROGRAMMING PRIMITIVES

In shared memory programming, there are four fundamental and necessary operations that must be provided, namely:

1. Process/thread creation (and termination)
2. Shared-data creation
3. Mutual-exclusion synchronization (controlled access to shared data)
4. Process/thread and event synchronization

These have to be provided in a DSM system also, typically by user-level library calls.

The set of routines of different DSM systems, such as Adsmith and TreadMarks, are actually very similar to each other. Here we will review common routines found in most DSM systems using generic routine names with the prefix `dsm`. Specific Adsmith routines have the prefix `adsm`. (Note the letters "dsm" in the name A-dsm-ith.) We have used Adsmith for student programming assignments.

9.4.1 Process Creation

A DSM routine such as

```
dsm_spawn(filename, num_processes);
```

would be used to start a new process if dynamic process creation is supported. Processes are then "joined" with, say,

```
dsm_wait();
```

which will cause the process to wait for all its child processes (i.e., the processes it created) to terminate.

9.4.2 Shared Data Creation

A routine or construct is necessary to declare shared data, say:

```
dsm_shared(&x);
```

which provides a pointer to the shared data. DSM systems such as TreadMarks and Adsmith dynamically create memory space for shared data in the manner of a C malloc:

```
dsm_malloc();
```

After use, memory space can be discarded with

```
dsm_free();
```

An elegant way, but not done in TreadMarks or Adsmith, is use a simple shared-data declaration, such as:

```
shared int x;
```

Taking this further, one can apply the object-oriented design throughout and at the interface, whereby shared variables are encapsulated into objects and methods applied to them. However, whatever the declaration, shared data or objects typically have a "home" location, which is the location selected by the creation routine to be nearby the process writing to it. To achieve higher performance, the home location might move (migrate) to be near other processors, depending upon the access patterns.

9.4.3 Shared Data Access

In a DSM system employing a relaxed-consistency model (i.e., most DSM systems), the programmer explicitly needs to prevent competing read/write accesses from different processes with the use of locks or other mechanisms. A typical sequence to increment a shared variable, `sum`, would be

```
dsm_lock(lock1);
dsm_refresh(sum);
   *sum++;
dsm_flush(sum);
dsm_unlock(lock1);
```

where `lock1` is a lock variable associated with `sum`. After locking, `dsm_refresh()` obtains the current value of `sum`. The process increments `sum`, and then `dsm_flush()` updates the home location with a new value for `sum`.

Some accesses to shared data may not be competing. For example, the data is simply read-only (never altered) or the processes are synchronized in such a way that it is not possible for more than one process at a time to access the shared data. In such cases, the accesses do not need to be placed in a critical section. Then the preceding code might become:

```
dsm_refresh(sum);
   *sum ++;
dsm_flush(sum);
```

If the variable is simply read, then a refresh alone would suffice; for example,

```
dsm_refresh(sum);
a = *sum + b;
```

Some systems provide efficient routines for different classes of accesses, differentiated by the use of the shared data. Adsmith, for example, provides for three types of accesses:

- Ordinary Accesses — For regular assignment statements accessing shared variables.
- Synchronization Accesses — Competing accesses used for synchronization purposes.
- Non-Synchronization Accesses — Competing accesses, not used for synchronization.

One early system, Munin (Carter, Bennett, and Zwaenepoel, 1995), took this concept further by differentiating nine types of accesses (later reduced to five). It is left to the programmer to select the appropriate type.

9.4.4 Synchronization Accesses

As with message-passing programming, process synchronization comes in two principal forms, global synchronization and process-process pair synchronization, both of which must be provided. Global synchronization is usually done with a barrier routine, and process-process pair synchronization can be done in the same routine as an option or, better, by separate routines. In message-passing systems, simple synchronous send/receive routines can perform process-process pair synchronization, as described in Chapter 6. Barriers require an identifier to be specified to identify the specific barrier:

```
dsm_barrier(identifier);
```

In systems that use an existing message-passing system, synchronization routines are already available in the message-passing system and could be used. Alternatively, such DSM systems could also provide their own synchronization routines.

9.4.5 Features to Improve Performance

One of the basic goals of research-oriented DSM systems is to devise methods to improve system performance, which usually involves overlapping computations with communications and reducing the number of messages.

Overlapping Computations with Communications. One way to overlap a computation with communication is to start a nonblocking communication before its results are needed, using a "prefetch" routine. The prefetch routine would be inserted as far back in the code as possible, constrained by how far back the data being send is still up-to-date; for example,

```
   .
   .
   .
barrier();
dsm_prefetch(sum);        /* sum known to be up-to-date at this point */
   .
   .
   .
a = *sum + b;
   .
   .
   .
```

The program continues execution after the prefetch while the data is being fetched. At some later point, the data is required. If the data has arrived, it can be used immediately, otherwise the execution stops until the data has arrived.

The prefetch could even be done speculatively, by prefetching the data even if it might not be needed in some circumstances, as in the code:

```
   .
   .
   .
barrier();
dsm_prefetch(sum);        /* sum known to be up-to-date at this point */
   .
   .
   .
if (b == 0) a = *sum + b;
   .
   .
   .
```

Here `sum` would not be needed if `b` is not equal to zero and is simply discarded.

The prefetch mechanism is very similar to the speculative-load mechanism used in some advanced processors that overlaps memory operations with program execution. Memory-load operations take considerable time, and a speculative load is initiated at an earlier point in the program before the data is required. The execution is allowed to continue while waiting for the load to complete. If placed prior to a point in the program where there is a possible change of execution sequence (as in our example for prefetch above), special mechanisms must be in place to handle memory exceptions (error conditions). Similarly, it is possible for an error to occur during the execution of a prefetch in a DSM system that would not occur otherwise. In our sequence above, for example, suppose that at the prefetch point `sum` is invalid if `b` is not equal to zero, but valid if `b` equals zero. If it was prefetched whatever the value of `b`, an exception can occur that would not have occurred without prefetch. The programmer has to establish that prefetch can be used safely.

Reducing the Number of Messages. Routines can be provided to reduce the number of messages by combining common sequences of basic routines ("aggregating" the messages). For example, a critical section previously used four routines:

```
dsm_lock(lock1);
dsm_refresh(sum);
   *sum ++;
dsm_flush(sum);
dsm_unlock(lock1);
```

which could be reduced to two:

```
dsm_acquire(sum);
   *sum ++;
dsm_release(sum);
```

The routine `dsm_acquire(sum)` does what both `dsm_lock(lock1)` and `dsm_refresh(sum)` do together, and similarly `dsm_release(sum)` does what both `dsm_flush(sum)` and `dsm_unlock(lock1)` do together. In both cases, the number of messages can be reduced in the implementation.

Sequences of the same routines, each generating their own messages, can be arranged so that the messages are combined. Efficient routines can also be provided for common operations; for example, routines for shared variables used as accumulators.

9.5 DISTRIBUTED SHARED MEMORY PROGRAMMING

Distributed shared memory programming on a cluster uses the same concepts as shared memory programming on a shared memory multiprocessor system, as described in Chapter 8, but using user level library routines or methods. Take, for example, the heat-distribution problem described in Chapter 6. The solution space is divided into a two-dimensional array of points, and the value of each point is computed by repeatedly taking the average of the four points around it until the values converge on the solution to a sufficient accuracy. A direct interpretation of the code with DSM routines within an SPMD structure, allocating one row to each of $n - 1$ processes, leads to:

```
dsm_sharedarray(*h, n*n);        /* Shared array int h[n][n], size n*n */
dsm_sharedarray(*g, n*n);        /* Shared array int g[n][n], size n*n */
dsm_shared(max_dif);         /*shared variable to test for convergence */
   :
i = processID;                         /* process ID from 1 to n-1 */
do {
   for (j = 1; j < n; j++)
      g[i][j] = 0.25 * (h[i-1][j] + h[i+1][j] + h[i][j-1] + h[i][j+1]);
   dsm_barrier(group);
   for (j = 1; j < n; j++) {        /* find max divergence/update pts */
      dif = h[i][j] - g[i][j];      /* dif in each process */
   if (dif < 0) dif = -dif;
   dsm_acquire(max_dif)
      if (dif < max_dif) max_dif = dif;     /* max_dif a shared variable */
   dsm_release(max_dif);
```

```
        h[i][j] = g[i][j];
        }
        dsm_barrier(group);              /* wait for all processes here*/
    } while (max_dif < tolerance);       /* check convergence */
```

Message-passing occurs that is hidden from the user, and thus there are additional efficiency considerations. Reducing the underlying message-passing is a key aspect. This code calls for two process synchronizations (barriers) and one mutual-exclusion synchronization (acquire/release for a critical section). As pointed out earlier, synchronization points will tend to serialize the execution and significantly increase the execution time, so one should look for ways to reduce the number of synchronization points, especially for executing on clusters. We have described changing the code to be asynchronous, or partially so, in Chapter 6, using chaotic relaxation, and this can be applied to DSM programming also. Finally, one should look at the routines that may be provided to increase performance, such as those described in Section 9.4.5.

9.6 IMPLEMENTING A SIMPLE DSM SYSTEM

It is relatively straightforward to write your own simple DSM system. In this section, we will review how this can be done. The projects at the end of the chapter involving creating your own DSM system are suitable as extended assignments.

9.6.1 User Interface Using Classes and Methods

The first thing to decide upon is the user programming methodology and the user interface. One can following the approach of user level routines, as in TreadMarks and Adsmith and described in Section 9.4. We have experimented with more elegant approaches based upon the object-oriented methodology of C++ and Java. For shared data, wrapper classes might be appropriate. For example in Java, we might write

```
SharedInteger sum = new SharedInteger();
```

which extends the Integer class to provide the methods `lock`, `unlock`, `refresh`, and `flush`, as used in the critical section:

```
sum.lock();
sum.refresh();
   sum++;
sum.flush();
sum.unlock();
```

where the lock and unlock methods implicitly use a lock associated with `sum`. (Of course, one could have separate lock methods, such as `lock1.lock()` and `lock1.unlock()`.)

The approach can be taken even further by having the combined methods `lockandRefresh` and `flushandUnlock`:

```
sum.lockandRefresh();
   sum++;
sum.flushandUnlock();
```

Another very novel approach that we have implemented is to overload the arithmetic operators, so that when one writes

```
x = y + z;
```

where `y` and `z` are shared variables, the appropriate actions automatically take place to refresh `y` and `z`. These are just some of the design alternatives we have designed for our own use.

9.6.2 Basic Shared-Variable Implementation

The simplest DSM implementation is to use a shared-variable approach with user-level DSM library routines, such as those defined earlier, sitting on top of an existing message-passing system, such as MPI. These routines can be embodied into classes and methods as described. The most fundamental user-level DSM routines is the shared-variable read routine and the shared-variable write routine. The write routine could encompass locking and unlocking, or they could be separate routines. The routines could send messages to a central location that is responsible for the shared variables, as shown in Figure 9.7. This corresponds to a single reader/writer protocol. Strictly, locking and unlocking of shared variables are unnecessary, for the central server can only do one thing at a time, and no other

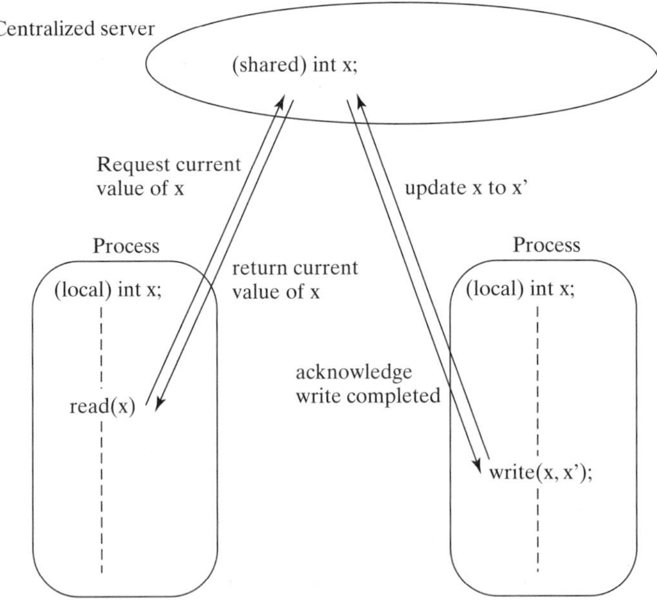

Figure 9.7 Simple DSM system using a centralized server.

process can interfere with its actions. Hence, the code for the server for integer shared variables could be very simple:

```
do {
   recv(&command, &shared_x_name, &data, &source, any_source, any_tag);
   find(&shared_x_name, &x);  /* find shared variable, return ptr to it */
   switch(command)
   case rd:                     /* read routine */
      send(&x, source);         /* no lock needed */
   case wr:                     /* write routine */
      x = data;
      send (&ack, source);      /* seed an acknowledgement update done*/
   .
   .
   .
} while (command != terminator);
```

using our usual pseudocode. The message consists of `&command`, which specifies the requested operation (read, write, or some other operation), `&shared_x_name`, which identifies the shared variable, `data`, which holds the value that will be used to update the shared variable in the case of write, and `&source`, which identifies the process sending the message.

As mentioned, a centralized server will create a bottleneck because it can only respond to one message at a time and generate one message at a time. Such an approach is not used in any reasonably practical system. However, it is a starting point, and it is a relatively simple matter to develop the code to have multiple servers running on different processors, each responsible for specific shared variables, to reduce the bottleneck, as illustrated in Figure 9.8. Then the read and write routines will need to locate the specific

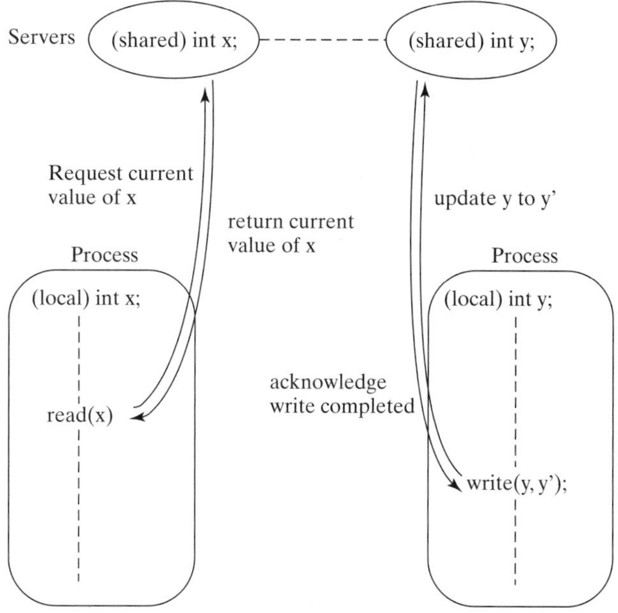

Figure 9.8 Simple DSM system using multiple servers.

server responsible to the shared variable being accessed (through a look-up table or by some other means, such as using a hash function).The approach still uses a single reader/ single writer protocol.

To develop this model further to provide multiple reader capability generally requires replication of the shared data. Let us assume an invalidate policy. Multiple servers are illustrated in Figure 9.9. We retain our model of two routines, read shared variable and write shared variable. The first time the read routine is called, the most recent value of the shared variable is obtained from the server and is kept locally. Having local copies allows multiple processes to read their copies simultaneously. The write routine, as before, updates a shared variable at a server, but now a specific server is responsible for the shared variable. At this time, the other local copies, if existing, are invalidated. The invalidate message is an unexpected message for the receiving process(es) and may require a one-side send or put routine (a send routine that does not need a matching receive, which exists in MPI-2 but needs to be used with extreme care). If the read routine is called again, it will return the value of the local copy if valid, and no message will be sent to the server. If the local copy is invalid, indicating that a more recent value exists, a message will be sent to the server for the most recent value. Asynchronous algorithms may not need the most recent value and can simply use assignment statements to obtain the local copy of x rather than the read routine.

The next step is to eliminate the servers and provide a home location for each shared variable, a process that is responsible for that variable. The read routine requests the most recent value from that process. In fact, no change is necessary to the code; simply map the server and the process designated as the home process for the shared variable to the same

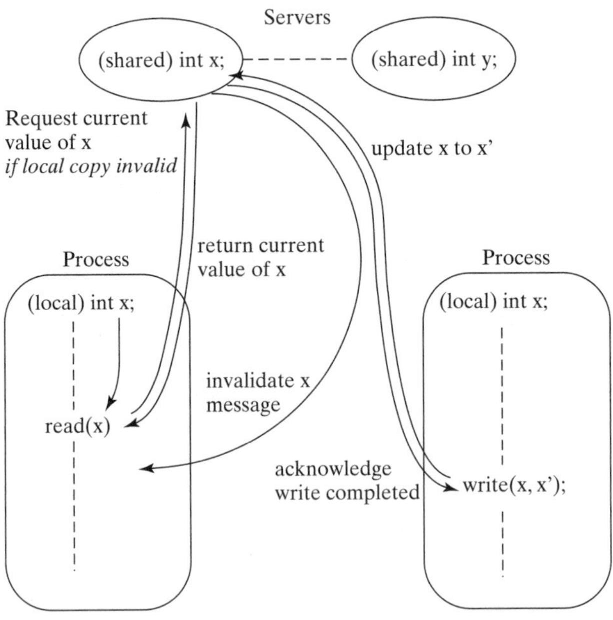

Figure 9.9 Simple DSM system using multiple servers and multiple reader policy.

processor. The advantage of using home locations is that write operations at the home location do not generate any messages.

9.6.3 Overlapping Data Groups

In Chapter 1, we introduced the concept of overlapping connectivity networks in which regions of connectivity are provided and the regions overlap. This leads to a very scalable network that matches many physical applications in science and engineering. Many real-life applications do not need global shared memory but do need local shared memory where the memory access is in overlapping regions. Examples include many simulations of physical systems (e.g., problems in physics, mechanical engineering, weather forecasting). Typically, in such applications, processors performing calculations require communication with logically nearby processors for their results. There are other benefits, including providing a mechanism for detecting logical mistakes in programs.

The concept can be applied to a DSM system by providing regions of data access for the same goals. Let us consider the concept on a cluster of symmetrical multiprocessors (SMPs). A symmetrical multiprocessor is a shared memory multiprocessor in which each processor has the same access time to the shared memory irrespective of the location within the shared memory (i.e., a uniform memory access system). Systems of this kind, with small numbers of processors, are now very cost-effective and are widely employed, especially as Web servers. The concept of overlapping local shared memory takes into account the physical structure of clusters of SMP systems. Software DSM techniques can be used, but with limited access to shared data structures to logically overlapping groups defined by the programmer. A suite of user-level routines can be used. These will interact with the message-passing software on the cluster to give the illusion of shared memory and provide the basic facilities for shared memory programming, namely to create shared data, provide protected access to shared data (locks) and synchronization mechanisms (barriers). However, in contrast to global shared memory systems, the routines have provision for defining overlapping groups of shared data. MPI is very convenient as the underlying message-passing software because it already has the concept communication regions (MPI communicators) that can be used to define data-access regions. The system is illustrated in Figure 9.10.

The overlapping groups are intimately tied to two aspects: existing interconnection structure, and the access patterns of the application. One could define static overlapping groups which are defined by the programmer prior to execution of the program or which

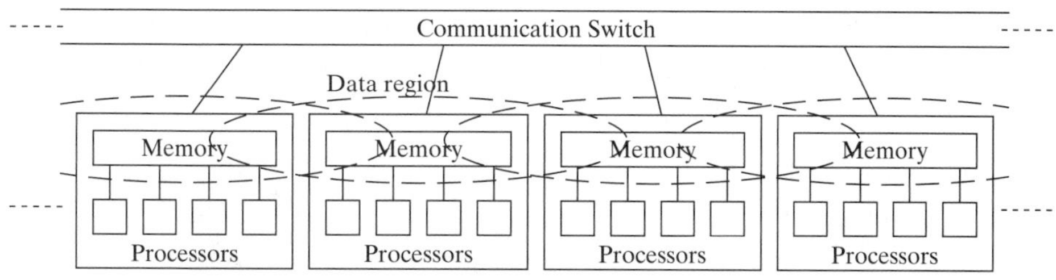

Figure 9.10 Symmetrical multiprocessor system with overlapping data regions.

somehow can be altered or are created by the execution of the program. Static overlapping groups can be declared by parameters in the basic data-access routines. For example,

```
create (data, data_region)
destroy(data, data_region)
read(data, data_region)
write(data, data_region)
```

Finally, shared variables can migrate according to usage, as illustrated in Figure 9.11.

All scalable distributed shared memory systems use some form of hierarchical interconnection structure to interconnect groups of processors. This will inherently create nonuniform access between processors. An example of a scalable interconnection structure is an n-ary tree, which might be applicable to using $\times\, n$ Ethernet switches (100 Mbps or Gigabit Ethernet). A typical commodity Ethernet switch can interconnect 16 computers (a $\times$ 16 switch) and allows a connection to another level of Ethernet switches. Figure 9.12 shows the use of commodity components to form a larger system. In such cases, the overlapping data regions at the edges between separate parts of the tree may incur a significant overhead in communication, whereas the data regions within a part of the tree will be more efficient.

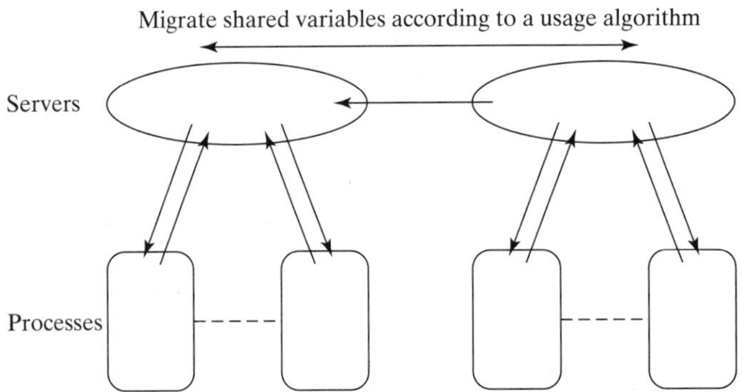

Figure 9.11 Simple DSM system using multiple servers and multiple reader policy.

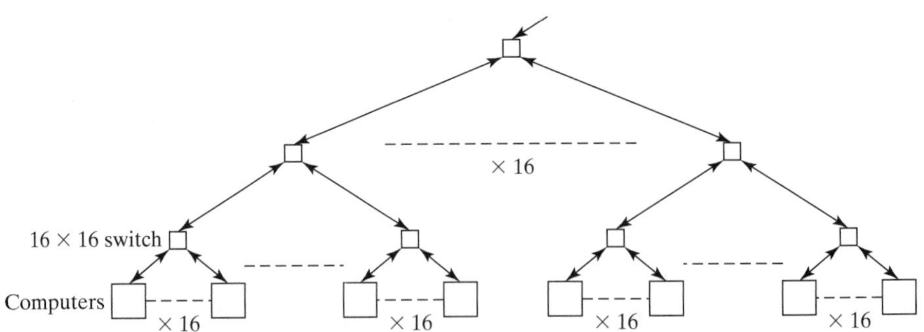

Figure 9.12 Scalable system using commodity switches.

9.7 SUMMARY

This chapter introduced:

- Concept of distributed shared memory (DSM)
- How DSM can be implemented on a cluster
- Various ways of managing the shared data, including reader/writer protocols
- Relaxed-consistency models for DSM systems, notably release and lazy release consistency
- Distributed shared memory programming primitives
- Methods to improve the performance of DSM systems
- Details of simple DSM implementations

FURTHER READING

Articles on distributed shared memory include Judge et al. (1999), Nitzberg and Lo (1991), Protic, Tomasevic, and Milutinovic (1996), and Stumm and Zho (1990). Protic, Tomasevic, and Milutinovic (1998) have produced a collection of important papers on distributed shared memory. It is possible to use shared memory programming tools directly and alone on a cluster if appropriately implemented. For example, a "sizable subset" of OpenMP has been implemented on a network of workstations by Lu, Hu, and Zwaenepoel (1998).

BIBLIOGRAPHY

AMZA, C., A. L. COX, S. DWARKADAS, P. KELEHER, H. LU, R. RAJAMONY, W. YU, AND W. ZWAENEPOEL (1996), "TreadMarks: Shared Memory Computing on Networks of Workstations," *Computer*, Vol. 29, No. 2, pp. 18–28.

BENNETT, J. K., J. B. CARTER, AND W. ZWAENEPOEL (1990), "Munin: Distributed Shared Memory Based on Type-Specific Memory Coherence," *2nd ACM SIGPLAN Symp. Principles & Practice of Parallel Programming*, March 14–16, pp. 168–176.

BLUMRICH, M. A., C. DUBNICKI, E. W. FELTON, K. LI, AND M. R. MESRINA (1995), "Virtual-Memory-Mapped Network Interface," *IEEE Micro*, Vol. 15, No. 1, pp. 21–28.

BODEN, N. J., D. COHEN, R. E. FELDERMAN, A. E. KULAWIK, C. L. SEITZ, J. N. SEIZOVIC, AND W. K. SU (1995), "Myrinet: A Gigabit-per-Second Local Area Network," *IEEE Micro*, Vol. 15, No. 1, pp 29–36.

CARTER, J. B., J. K. BENNETT, AND W. ZWAENEPOEL (1995), "Techniques for Reducing Consistency-Related Communication in Distributed Shared Memory Systems, *ACM Trans. Computer Systems*, Vol. 13, no. 3, pp. 205–243.

HELLWAGNER, H., AND A. REINEFELD (editors) (1999), *SCI: Scalable Coherent Interface*, Springer, Berlin, Germany.

HU, W., W. SHI, AND Z. TANG (1999), "JIAJIA: A Software DSM System Based on a New Cache Coherence Protocol," *Proc. 7th Int. Conf. on High Performance Computing and Networking Europe*, Amsterdam, pp. 463–472. Also available at http://www.ict.ac.cn/chpc/dsm.

LI, K. (1986), "Shared Virtual Memory on Loosely Coupled Multiprocessor," Ph.D. thesis, Dept. of Computer Science, Yale University.

LIANG, W.-Y., C.-T. KING, AND F. LAI (1996), "Adsmith: An Efficient Object-Based DSM Environment on PVM," *Proc. 1996 Int. Symp. on Parallel Architecture, Algorithms and Networks*, Beijing, China, pp. 173–179. Also see http://archiwww.ee.ntu.edu.tw/~wyliang/adsmith.

JUDGE, A., P. NIXON, B. TANGNEY, S. WEBER, AND V. CAHILL (1999), "Distributed Shared Memory," in *High Performance Cluster Computing,* Volume 1, R. Buyya (ed.), Prentice Hall, Upper Saddle River, NJ, Chapter 17, pp. 409–438.

MINNICH, R., D. BURNS, AND F. HADY (1995), "The Memory-Integrated Network Interface," *IEEE Micro*, Vol. 15, No. 1, pp. 11–20.

NITZBERG, B., AND V. LO (1991), "Distributed Shared Memory: A Survey of Issues and Algorithms," *Computer*, Vol. 24, No. 8, pp. 52–60.

PROTIC, J, M. TOMASEVIC, AND V. MILUTINOVIC (1996), Distributed Shared Memory: Concepts and Systems, *IEEE Parallel & Distributed Technology*, Vol. 4, No. 2, pp. 63–79.

PROTIC, J, M. TOMASEVIC, AND V. MILUTINOVIC (1998), *Distributed Shared Memory: Concepts and Systems*, IEEE Computer Society Press, Los Alamitos, CA.

STUMM, M., AND S. ZHO (1990), "Algorithms Implementing Distributed Shared Memory," *Computer*, Vol. 23, No. 5, pp. 54–64.

SUN, X.-H., AND J. ZHU (1995), "Performance Considerations of Shared Virtual Memory Machines," *IEEE Trans. Parallel and Distributed Systems*, Vol. 6, No. 11, pp. 1185–1194.

WILKINSON, B., T. PAI, AND M. MIRAJ (2001), "A Distributed Shared Memory Programming Course," *Int.Workshop on Cluster Computing Education (CLUSTER-EDU_2001)*, IEEE Int. Symp. Cluster Computing and the Grid (CCGrid), Brisbane, Australia, May 16–18.

WOO, S. C., M. OHARA, E. TORRIE, J. P. SINGH, AND A. GUPTA (1995), "The SPLASH-2 Programs: Characterization and Methodological Considerations," *Proc. 22nd Int. Symp. Computer Architecture*, pp. 24–36.

PROBLEMS

In the following, when a DSM program is to be written, use any DSM system that is available to you. The shared memory problems given in Chapter 8 are also suitable for DSM implementation.

Scientific/Numerical

9-1. Write a DSM program to sort a list of n integers using odd-even transposition sort, where n is assumed to be a power of 2. Give a clear explanation of your program.

9-2. Write a DSM program to perform matrix multiplication, dividing each matrix into four submatrices and using four processes. Give a clear explanation of your program.

9-3. Perform a comparative study of using DSM programming and message-passing programming on a problem of your choice.

9-4. Research studies on parallel systems often use benchmark programs. One such suite of programs, SPLASH-2 (Woo, 1995), contains code for applications, such as the Barnes-Hut N-body calculation, L-U factorization of matrices, and simulations. Obtain this suite and evaluate the applications on your DSM parallel/cluster computer system.

9-5. Perform a comparative study of using synchronous iteration and asynchronous iteration to solve the heat-distribution problem described in Chapter 6, Problem 6-14. Write DSM programs for each approach, and determine the improvement in execution speed obtained by using the asynchronous method as described in Section 9.5. Experiment with different numbers of iterations between synchronization points.

Real Life

9-6. The Big-I, the world's largest unknown insurance company, has offices scattered in 35 cities around the world and has over 735,000,000 insurance policies in force, with a total face value of $53.8 trillion. A high-speed inter-office network links Big-I's 35 offices and its central headquarters (located in a secure underground facility somewhere in the Rocky Mountains.) All policy information is kept in a RAID-5 storage system at the headquarters facility.

The agents input information about new policies, changes to existing policies, and customer-relationship changes (marriages/divorces, births, deaths, medical records, court records, etc.) daily. This information may be relevant to a particular customer even though it originated anywhere in the world. For example, Fred Jones, an insured of Big-I in the United States, went on a trip to Paris to celebrate his 50th birthday, became ill, and underwent surgery on the same day his divorce became final in North Carolina. Big-I's agents in both Paris and North Carolina simultaneously want to access/update Fred's records to reflect the new information on both his medical condition and his marital status.

Describe the relevant design aspects of Big-I's central storage system. Describe any changes that will be needed if the central storage system is mirrored at a second underground facility several hundred miles away.

Big-I just got a new CEO who thinks the central storage idea is old-fashioned and wants to use a distributed approach instead. He proposes to have each of the 36 facilities maintain its own local information store, but still be able to enter and access all information on a customer no matter the location at which it is entered/stored: a globally distributed/shared-storage system. Describe a transition plan for distributing the centrally stored information back out to the 35 world offices. Describe how the IT Department of Big-I can simulate the network impact of a distributed shared-storage system versus a centrally stored but (potentially) simultaneously accessed storage system.

9-7. The Adamms family enjoys a very close relationship. Tom and Sue Adamms have been married for 23 years and have eight children, all of whom are active in at least three sports plus church and school. Tom and Sue are both top executives in different divisions of a large insurance firm, Big-I, and their daily calendars typically hold 10–30 appointment/meeting commitments. As the kids have grown and become more involved in activities scheduled by individuals other than Tom and Sue, small disasters have been known to occur! Just last week, Polly (age 9) had scheduled herself for a team soccer match, but that information had not gotten onto either Tom or Sue's calendar. As a result, Polly's team had to forfeit the match when too few players showed up; Polly is still upset a week later.

What are the relevant design aspects of a central calendaring system accessible (and modifiable) by the entire family? What changes need to be made if some individuals are deemed to have priority over others in terms of scheduling? (The children may enter/change items affecting only themselves, but are unable to change items placed on their parent's calendars, for example. Another situation that frequently arises is when Tom needs to be able to enter/change a nonbusiness item on Sue's calendar but is prevented from entering/changing items of a different category: business items.)

DSM Implementation Projects

9-8. Write a DSM system in C++ using MPI for the underlying message-passing and process communication.

9-9. Write a DSM system in Java using MPI for the underlying message-passing and process communication.

9-10. (More advanced) One of the fundamental disadvantages of software DSM system is the lack of control over the underlying message-passing. Provide parameters in a DSM routine to be able to control the message-passing. Write routines that allow communication and computation to be overlapped.

PART II Algorithms and Applications

Chapter 10

Sorting Algorithms

This chapter is concerned with ways to sort numbers. Sorting is usually studied in sequential programming classes, and there are a number of well-known sorting methods. Here we select some sequential sorting algorithms for conversion to a parallel implementation. We also describe sorting algorithms specifically invented for parallel implementation. Finally, some sorting algorithms that have received recent attention for implementation on clusters are considered.

10.1 GENERAL

10.1.1 Sorting

Sorting numbers — that is, rearranging a list of numbers into increasing (or decreasing) order — is a fundamental operation that appears in many applications. If numbers have duplicates in their sequence, sorting is more properly defined as placing the numbers in *nondecreasing* (or nonincreasing) order. Sorting is also applicable to non-numerical values; for example, rearranging strings into alphabetical order. Sorting is often done because it makes searches and other operations easier. Books in a library are sorted into subject/name for ease of searching for specific books.

Two sorting algorithms have already been presented to demonstrate specific parallelizing techniques. Bucket sort demonstrated divide and conquer in Chapter 4, Section 4.2.1, and insertion sort demonstrated a pipeline in Chapter 5, Section 5.2.2. In this chapter, we will look at other sorting algorithms and apply the most suitable parallelizing techniques to them. Many parallel sorting algorithms and parallel implementations of sequential sorting algorithms are synchronous algorithms, in that a group of actions taking place on the numbers must be completed before the next group of actions takes place. Thus, the synchronous iteration techniques described in Chapter 6 are applicable.

10.1.2 Potential Speedup

Quicksort and mergesort are popular sequential sorting algorithms. They are in the family of "comparison-based" sorting algorithms that sort only on the basis of comparing pairs of numbers. The worst-case time complexity of mergesort and the average time complexity of quicksort are both $O(n\log n)$, where there are n numbers. $O(n\log n)$ is, in fact, optimal for any comparison-based sequential sorting algorithm without using any special properties of the numbers. Therefore, the best parallel time complexity we can expect, based upon a sequential sorting algorithm but using p processors, is

$$\text{Optimal parallel time complexity} = \frac{O(n\log n)}{p} = O(\log n) \quad \text{if } p = n$$

An $O(\log n)$ sorting algorithm with n processors was demonstrated by Leighton (1984), based upon an algorithm by Ajtai, Komlós, and Szemerédi (1983), but the constant hidden in the order notation is extremely large. An $O(\log n)$ sorting algorithm is also described by Leighton (1994) for an n-processor hypercube using random operations. Akl (1985) describes 20 different parallel sorting algorithms, several of which achieve the lower bound for a particular interconnection network. But, in general, a realistic $O(\log n)$ algorithm with n processors is a goal that is not easy to achieve with comparison-based sorting algorithms. It may be that the number of processors will be greater than n. Having said that, let us start with traditional comparison-based algorithms.

10.2 COMPARE-AND-EXCHANGE SORTING ALGORITHMS

10.2.1 Compare and Exchange

An operation that can form the basis of several, if not most, classical sequential sorting algorithms is the compare-and-exchange (or compare-and-swap) operation. In a compare-and-exchange operation, two numbers, say A and B, are compared. If $A > B$, A and B are exchanged; that is, the content of the location holding A is moved into the location holding B, and the content of the location holding B is moved into the location holding A; otherwise, the contents of the locations remain unchanged. Compare and exchange is illustrated in the sequential code

```
if (A > B) {
   temp = A;
   A = B;
   B = temp;
}
```

Compare and exchange is well suited to a message-passing system. Suppose the compare and exchange is between the two numbers A and B, where A is held in process P_1 and B is held in process P_2. One simple way of implementing the compare and exchange is for P_1 to send A to P_2, which then compares A and B and sends back B to P_1 if A is larger than B (otherwise it sends back A to P_1). It is not strictly necessary to send A back to P_1, since it already has A, but it does make it easier to have the same number of sends/receives in either case. The method is illustrated in Figure 10.1. The code could be

Process P_1

```
send(&A, P2);
recv(&A, P2);
```

Process P_2

```
recv(&A, P1);
if (A > B) {
   send(&B, P1);
   B = A;
} else
   send(&A, P1);
```

An alternative way is for P_1 to send A to P_2, and P_2 to send B to P_1. Then both processes perform compare operations. P_1 keeps the smaller of A and B, and P_2 keeps the larger of A and B, as illustrated in Figure 10.2. The code for this approach is

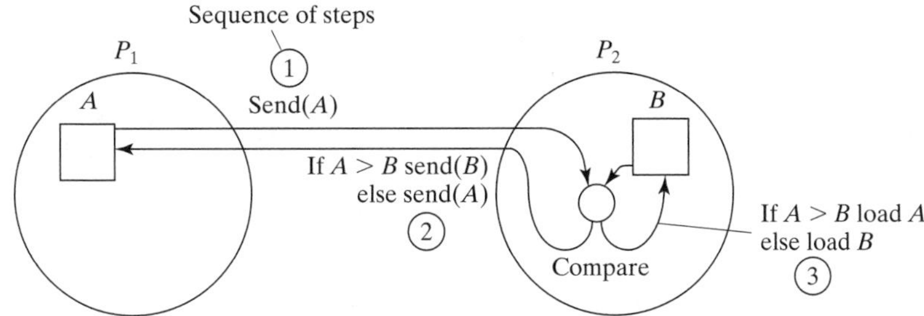

Figure 10.1 Compare and exchange on a message-passing system — Version 1.

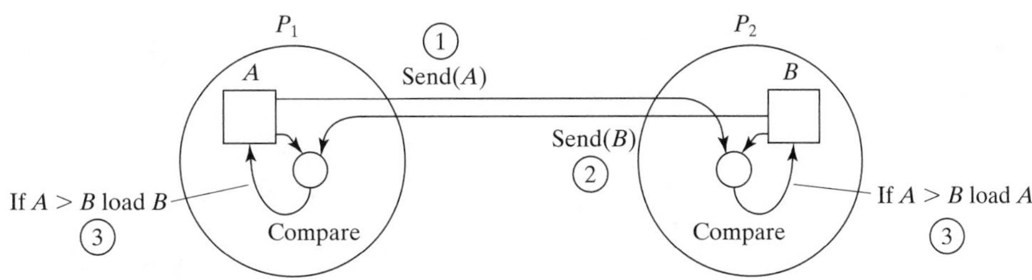

Figure 10.2 Compare and exchange on a message-passing system — Version 2.

Process P_1

```
send(&A, P2);
recv(&B, P2);
if (A > B) A = B;
```

Process P_2

```
recv(&A, P1);
send(&B, P1);
if (A > B) B = A;
```

Process P_1 performs the `send()` first, and process P_2 performs the `recv()` first to avoid deadlock. (In the first version, `send()`s and `recv()`s are naturally in nondeadlock order.) Alternatively, both P_1 and P_2 could perform `send()` first if locally blocking (asynchronous) sends are used and sufficient buffering is guaranteed to exist. Then both processes could initiate their message transfers simultaneously to overlap the message transfer overhead. This is not safe programming in the MPI sense, because deadlock would occur if sufficient buffering were not present.

Note on Precision of Duplicated Computations. The preceding code assumes that the `if` condition, `A > B`, will return the same Boolean answer in both processors; different processors operating at different precisions could conceivably produce different answers if real numbers are being compared. This situation applies wherever computations are duplicated in different processors to reduce message-passing. In our case, message-passing is not reduced, but making the code in each process look similar may enable a single program to be constructed more easily for all processes.

Data Partitioning. Although so far we have assumed that there is one processor for each number, normally there would be many more numbers than processors (or processes). In such cases, a group of numbers would be assigned to each processor. This approach can be applied to all sorting algorithms. Suppose there are p processors and n numbers. A list of n/p numbers would be assigned to each processor. The compare-and-exchange operation can be based upon Figure 10.1 (Version 1) or Figure 10.2 (Version 2). Version 1 is as illustrated in Figure 10.3. Only one processor sends its partition to the other, which then performs the merge operation and returns the lower half of the list back to the first process. Version 2 is illustrated in Figure 10.4. Both processors exchange their groups in this case. One processor will keep n/p smaller numbers, and one processor will keep n/p larger numbers of the total $2n/p$ numbers. The general method is to maintain a sorted list in each processor and merge the stored list with the incoming list, deleting either the top half or the bottom half of the merged list. Again in this method it is assumed that each processor will produce the same results and divide the list exactly the same way. In any event, merging requires $2(n/p) - 1$ steps to merge two lists each of n/p numbers and two message transfers. Merging two sorted lists is a common operation in sorting algorithms.

Compare and exchange can be used to reorder pairs of numbers and can be applied repeatedly to completely sort a list. It appears in quicksort and mergesort. First, though, let us consider a compare-and-exchange algorithm that is less attractive than quicksort or

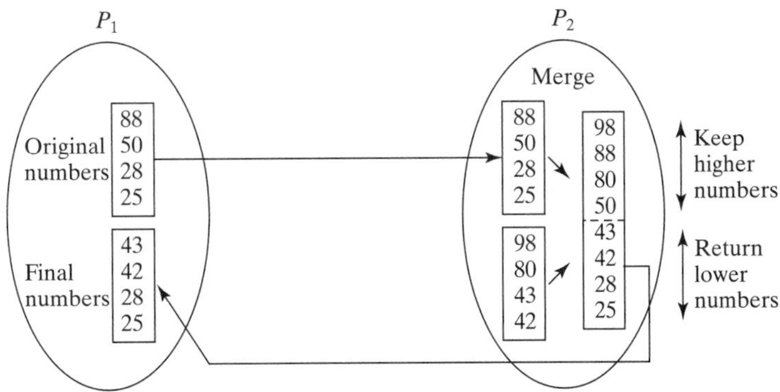

Figure 10.3 Merging two sublists — Version 1.

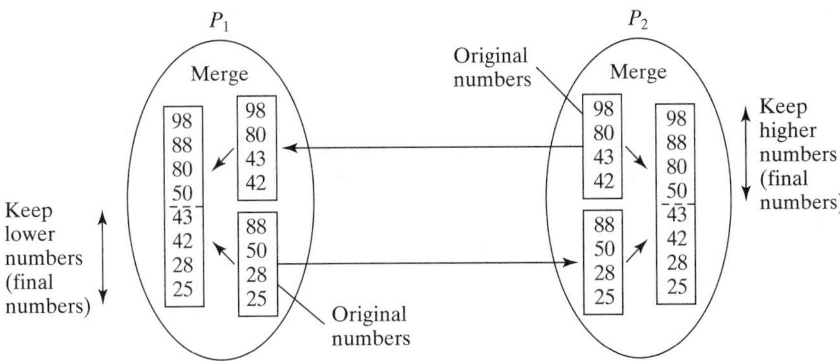

Figure 10.4 Merging two sublists — Version 2.

mergesort for a sequential computer, bubble sort, which is one of the most obvious methods for using compare and exchange.

10.2.2 Bubble Sort and Odd-Even Transposition Sort

In *bubble sort*, the largest number is first moved to the very end of the list by a series of compares and exchanges, starting at the opposite end. We are given the numbers x_0, x_1, x_2, …, x_{n-1}. First, x_0 and x_1 are compared and the larger moved to x_1 (and the smaller to x_0). Then x_1 and x_2 are compared and the larger moved to x_2, and so on until the largest number is x_{n-1}. The actions are repeated, stopping just before the previously positioned largest number, to get the next-largest number adjacent to the largest number. This is repeated for each number. In this way, the larger numbers move ("bubble") toward one end, as illustrated in Figure 10.5 for a sequence of eight numbers.

With n numbers, there are $n - 1$ compare-and-exchange operations in the first phase of positioning the largest number at the end of the list. In the next phase of positioning the

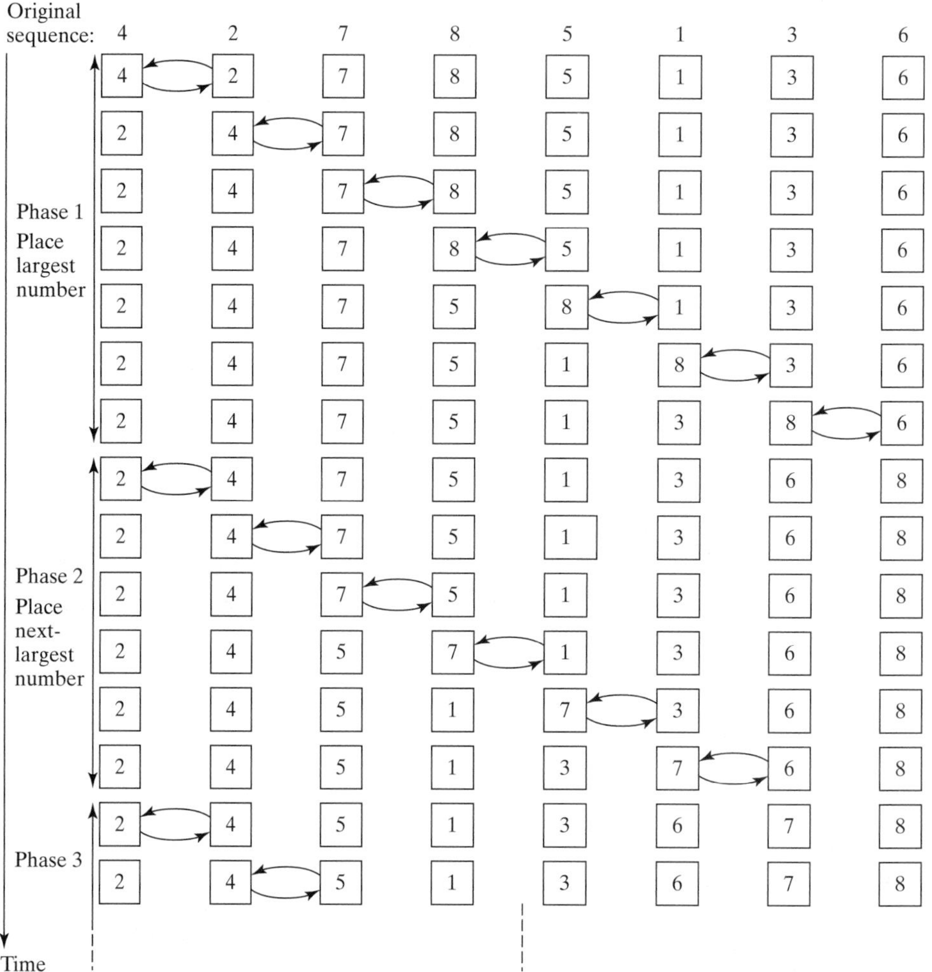

Figure 10.5 Steps in bubble sort.

next largest number, there are $n - 2$ compare-and-exchange operations, and so on. Therefore, the total number of operations is given by

$$\text{Number of compare and exchange operations} = \sum_{i=1}^{n-1} i = \frac{n(n-1)}{2}$$

which indicates a time complexity of $O(n^2)$ given that a single compare-and-exchange operation has a constant complexity, $O(1)$.

Sequential Code. Suppose the numbers are held in the array `a[]`. The sequential code could be

```
for (i = n - 1; i > 0; i--)
  for (j = 0; j < i; j++) {
    k = j + 1;
    if (a[j] > a[k]) {
      temp = a[j];
      a[j] = a[k];
      a[k] = temp;
    }
  }
```

Parallel Code — Odd-Even Transposition Sort. Bubble sort, as written, is a purely sequential algorithm. Each step in the inner loop takes place before the next, and the whole inner loop is completed before the next iteration of the outer loop. However, just because the sequential code uses statements that depend upon previous statements does not mean that it cannot be reformulated as a parallel algorithm. The bubbling action of the next iteration of the inner loop could start before the preceding iteration has finished, so long as it does not overtake the preceding bubbling action. This suggests that a pipeline implementation structure might be beneficial.

Figure 10.6 shows how subsequent exchange actions of bubble sort can operate behind others in a pipeline. We see that iteration 2 can operate behind iteration 1 at the same time if separated by one process. Similarly, iteration 3 can operate behind iteration 2.

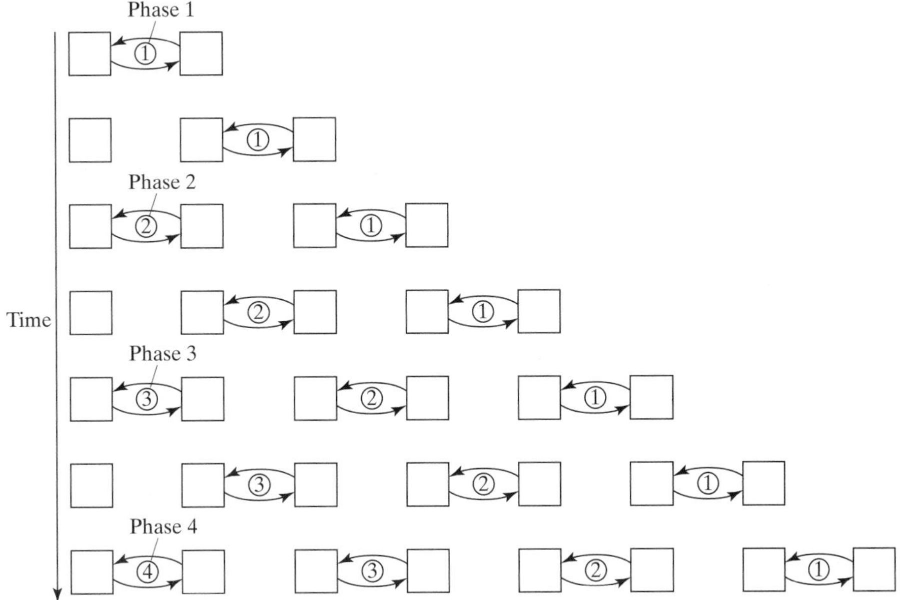

Figure 10.6 Overlapping bubble sort actions in a pipeline.

This idea leads to a variation of bubble sort called *odd-even (transposition) sort*, which operates in two alternating phases, an *even* phase and an *odd* phase. In the even phase, even-numbered processes exchange numbers with their right neighbors. Similarly, in the odd phase, odd-numbered processes exchange numbers with their right neighbors. Odd-even transposition sort normally would not be discussed for sequential programming as it has no particular advantage over normal bubble sort when programmed that way. However, the parallel implementation reduces the time complexity to O(n). Odd-even transposition sort can be implemented on a line network and is optimal for that network (since it requires n steps to reposition a number in the worst case). Odd-even transposition sort applied to a sequence of eight numbers, one number stored in each process, is shown in Figure 10.7.

First let us consider the two distinct alternating phases separately. In the even phase, we have the compare and exchanges: $P_0 \leftrightarrow P_1$, $P_2 \leftrightarrow P_3$, etc. Using the same form of compare and exchange as Version 2 in Section 10.2.1, the code could be

P_i, $i = 0, 2, 4, \ldots, n - 2$ (even) $\qquad$ P_i, $i = 1, 3, 5, \ldots, n - 1$ (odd)

```
recv(&A, Pi+1);             send(&A, Pi-1);        /* even phase */
send(&B, Pi+1);             recv(&B, Pi-1);
if (A < B) B = A;           if (A < B) A = B;      /* exchange */
```

where the number stored in P_i (even) is B, and the number stored in P_i (odd) is A. In the odd phase, we have the compare and exchanges: $P_1 \leftrightarrow P_2$, $P_3 \leftrightarrow P_4$, etc. This could be coded as

P_i, $i = 1, 3, 5, \ldots, n - 3$ (odd) $\qquad$ P_i, $i = 2, 4, 6, \ldots, n - 2$ (even)

```
send(&A, Pi+1);             recv(&A, Pi-1);        /* odd phase */
recv(&B, Pi+1);             send(&B, Pi-1);
if (A > B) A = B;           if (A > B) B = A;      /* exchange */
```

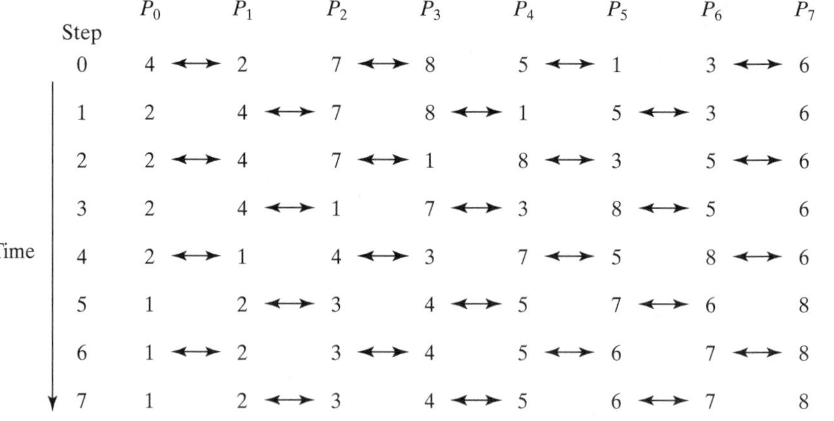

Figure 10.7 Odd-even transposition sort sorting eight numbers.

In both cases, odd-numbered processes execute their `send()` routines first, and even-numbered processes execute their `recv()` routines first. Combining,

P_i, $i = 1, 3, 5, \ldots, n-3$ (odd)

```
send(&A, P_{i-1});
recv(&B, P_{i-1});
if (A < B) A = B;
if (i <= n-3) {
   send(&A, P_{i+1});
   recv(&B, P_{i+1})
   if (A > B) A = B;
}
```

P_i, $i = 0, 2, 4, \ldots, n-2$ (even)

```
recv(&A, P_{i+1});          /* even phase */
send(&B, P_{i+1});
if (A < B) B = A;
if (i >= 2) {               /* odd phase */
   recv(&A, P_{i-1});
   send(&B, P_{i-1});
   if (A > B) B = A;
}
```

These code segments could be combined into an SPMD form in which the identity of the process is used to select the part of the program that a particular processor will execute (Problem 10-5).

10.2.3 Mergesort

Mergesort is a classical sequential sorting algorithm using a divide-and-conquer approach. The unsorted list is first divided in half. Each half is divided in two. This is continued until individual numbers are obtained. Then pairs of numbers are combined (merged) into sorted lists of two numbers each. Pairs of these lists of four numbers are merged into sorted lists of eight numbers. This is continued until the one fully sorted list is obtained. Described in this manner, it is clear that the algorithm will map perfectly into the tree structures of Chapter 4. Figure 10.8 illustrates the algorithm operating on eight numbers. We can see that this construction is the same as the tree structure to divide a problem (Figure 4.3) followed by the tree structure to combine a problem (Figure 4.4). It also follows that the processor allocation in Figures 4.3 and 4.4 can be made.

A significant disadvantage of using a tree construction is that the load is not well balanced among processors. At first one process is active, then two, then four, and so on. At subsequent steps, as the sublists get smaller the processor has less work to do.

Analysis. The sequential time complexity is $O(n \log n)$. There are $2 \log n$ steps in the parallel version, as shown in Figure 10.8, but each step may need to perform more than one basic operation, depending upon the number of numbers being processed. Let us suppose that the sublists are sent to their respective processors and that the merging takes place internally.

Communication. In the division phase, communication only takes place as follows:

Communication at each step	Processor communication
$t_{\text{startup}} + (n/2)t_{\text{data}}$	$P_0 \rightarrow P_4$
$t_{\text{startup}} + (n/4)t_{\text{data}}$	$P_0 \rightarrow P_2$; $P_4 \rightarrow P_6$
$t_{\text{startup}} + (n/8)t_{\text{data}}$	$P_0 \rightarrow P_1$; $P_2 \rightarrow P_3$; $P_4 \rightarrow P_5$; $P_6 \rightarrow P_7$
$\vdots$	

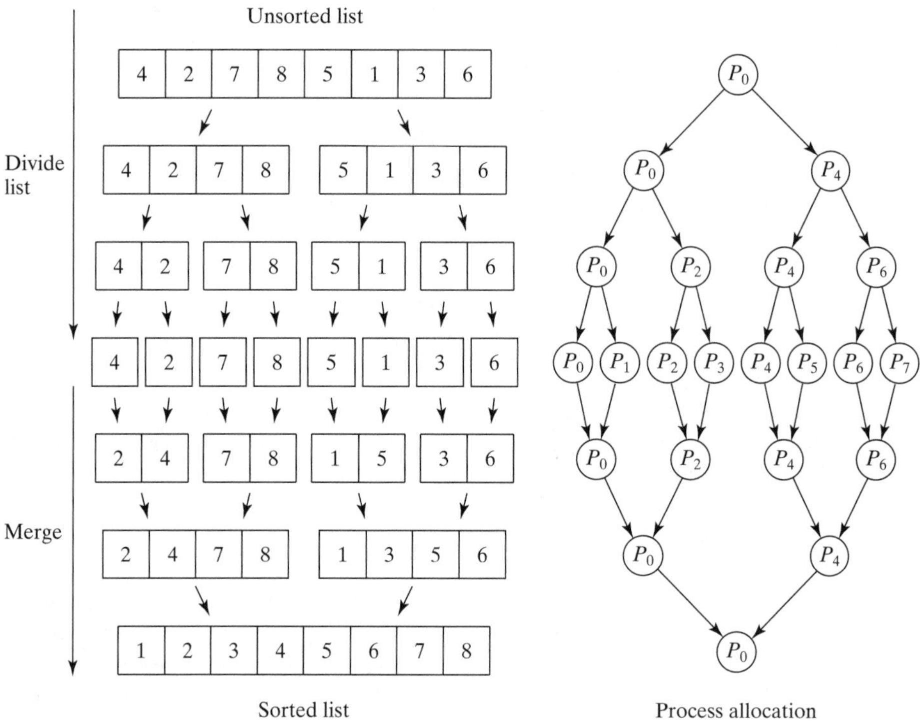

Figure 10.8 Mergesort using tree allocation of processes.

with log p steps, given p processors. In the merge phase, the reverse communications take place:

$$\vdots$$

$t_{\text{startup}} + (n/8)t_{\text{data}}$	$P_0 \leftarrow P_1;\ P_2 \leftarrow P_3;\ P_4 \leftarrow P_5;\ P_6 \leftarrow P_7$
$t_{\text{startup}} + (n/4)t_{\text{data}}$	$P_0 \leftarrow P_2;\ P_4 \leftarrow P_6$
$t_{\text{startup}} + (n/2)t_{\text{data}}$	$P_0 \leftarrow P_4$

again log p steps. This leads to the communication time being

$$t_{\text{comm}} = 2(t_{\text{startup}} + (n/2)t_{\text{data}} + t_{\text{startup}} + (n/4)t_{\text{data}} + t_{\text{startup}} + (n/8)t_{\text{data}} + \ldots\ )$$

or

$$t_{\text{comm}} \approx 2(\log p)t_{\text{startup}} + 2nt_{\text{data}}$$

Computation. Computations only occurs in merging the sublists. Merging can be done by stepping through each list, moving the smallest found into the final list first. In the worst case, it takes $2n - 1$ steps to merge two sorted lists, each of n numbers, into one sorted list in this manner. For eight numbers, the computation consists of

$t_{\text{comp}} = 1$	$P_0;\ P_2;\ P_4;\ P_6$
$t_{\text{comp}} = 3$	$P_0;\ P_4$
$t_{\text{comp}} = 7$	P_0

Hence:

$$t_{\text{comp}} = \sum_{i=1}^{\log p} (2^i - 1)$$

The parallel computational time complexity is O(p) using p processors and one number in each processor. As with all sorting algorithms, normally we would partition the list into groups, one group of numbers for each processor.

10.2.4 Quicksort

Quicksort (Hoare, 1962) is a very popular sequential sorting algorithm that performs well with an average sequential time complexity of O($n\log n$). The question to answer is whether a direct parallel version can achieve the time complexity of O($\log n$) with n processors. We did not manage this with mergesort according to our previous analysis. Now let us examine quicksort as a basis for a parallel sorting algorithm.

To recall from sequential programming, quicksort sorts a list of numbers by first dividing the list into two sublists, as in mergesort. All the numbers in one sublist are arranged to be smaller than all the numbers in the other sublist. This is achieved by first selecting one number, called a *pivot*, against which every other number is compared. If the number is less than the pivot, it is placed in one sublist. Otherwise, it is placed in the other sublist. The pivot could be any number in the list, but often the first number in the list is chosen. The pivot could be placed in one sublist, or it could be separated and placed in its final position. We shall separate the pivot.

The procedure is repeated on the sublists, creating four sublists, essentially putting numbers into regions, as in bucket sort (Chapter 4, Section 4.2.1). The difference is that the regions are determined by the pivots selected at each step. By repeating the procedure sufficiently, we are left with sublists of one number each. With proper ordering of the sublists, a sorted list is obtained.

Sequential Code. Quicksort is usually described by a recursive algorithm. Suppose an array, `list[]`, holds the list of numbers, and `pivot` is the index in the array of the final position of the pivot. We could have code of the form

```
quicksort(list, start, end)
{
  if (start < end) {
    partition(list, start, end, pivot)
    quicksort(list, start, pivot-1);    /* recursively call on sublists*/
    quicksort(list, pivot+1, end);
  }
}
```

`Partition()` moves numbers in the list between `start` and `end` so that those less than the pivot are before the pivot and those equal or greater than the pivot are after the pivot. The pivot is in its final position in the sorted list.

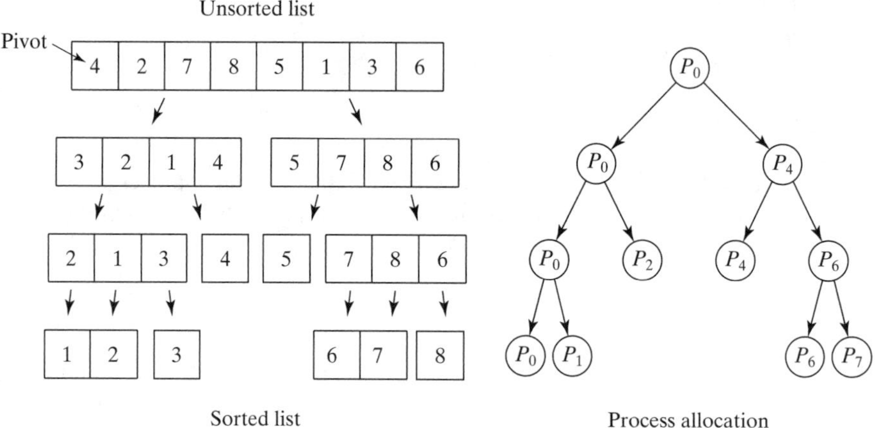

Figure 10.9 Quicksort using tree allocation of processes.

Parallelizing Quicksort. One obvious way to parallelize quicksort is to start with one processor and pass on one of the recursive calls to another processor while keeping the other recursive call to perform. This will create the now familiar tree structure we have seen with mergesort, as illustrated in Figure 10.9. In this example, the pivot is carried with the left list until the final sorting action. Note that the placement of the pivot between two sublists is the final placement of this number, and thus the number need not be considered further in subsequent sorting actions. We could redraw the tree to show the pivot being withheld. Then the sorted list would be obtained by searching the tree in order, as shown in Figure 10.10.

The fundamental problem with all of these tree constructions is that the initial division is done by a single processor, which will seriously limit the speed. Suppose the pivot selection is ideal and each division creates two sublists of equal size.

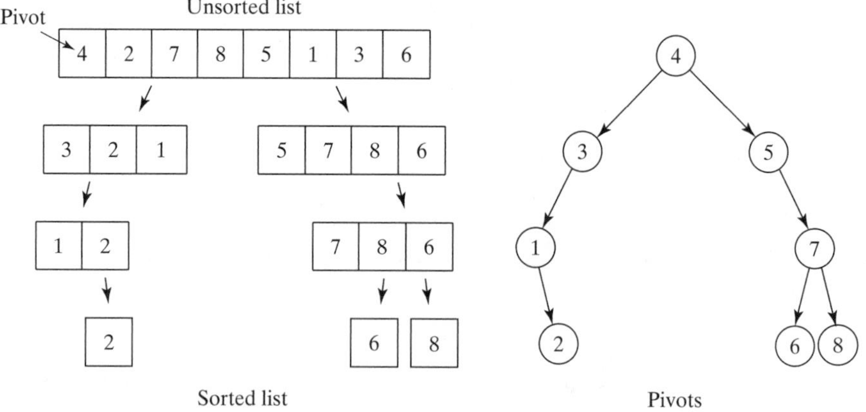

Figure 10.10 Quicksort showing pivot withheld in processes.

Computation. First one processor operates upon n numbers. Then two processors each operate upon $n/2$ numbers. Then four processors each operate upon $n/4$ numbers, and so on:

$$t_{comp} = n + n/2 + n/4 + n/8 + \ldots \approx 2n$$

Communication. Communication also occurs in a fashion similar to mergesort:

$$t_{comm} = (t_{startup} + (n/2)t_{data}) + (t_{startup} + (n/4)t_{data}) + (t_{startup} + (n/8)t_{data}) + \ldots$$
$$\approx (\log p)t_{startup} + nt_{data}$$

The analysis so far is the ideal situation. The major difference between quicksort and mergesort is that the tree in quicksort will not, in general, be perfectly balanced. The tree will be unbalanced if the pivots do not divide the lists into equal sublists. The depth of the tree is no longer fixed at $\log n$. The worst-case situation occurs when each pivot selected happens to be the largest of the sublist. The time complexity then degenerates to $O(n^2)$. If we always choose the first number in a sublist as the pivot, the original ordering of the numbers being sorted is the determining factor in the speed of quicksort. Another number could be used as the pivot. In that case, the selection of the pivot is very important to make quicksort operate fast.

Work-Pool Implementation. The load-balancing techniques described in Chapter 7, notably the work pool, can be applied to divide-and-conquer sorting algorithms such as quicksort. The work pool can hold as tasks the sublists to be divided. First, the work pool holds the initial unsorted list, which is given to the first processor. This processor divides the list into two parts. One part is returned to the work pool to be given to another processor, while the other part is operated upon again. This approach is illustrated in Figure 10.11. It does not eliminate the problem of idle processors, but it deals with the case where some sublists are longer and require more work than others.

Quicksort on the hypercube network as a way to achieve better performance will be be explored in Section 10.3.2.

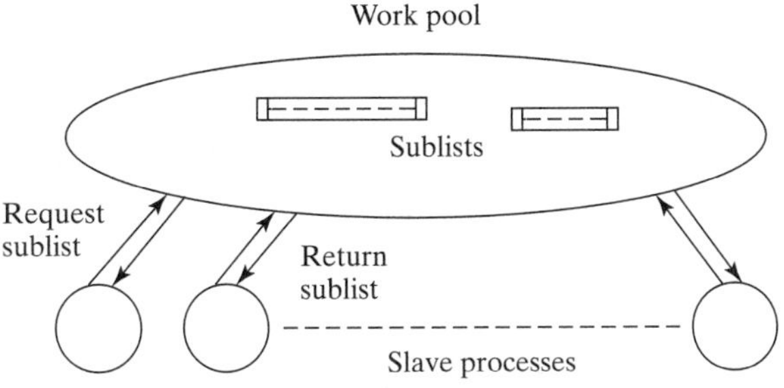

Figure 10.11 Work-pool implementation of quicksort.

10.2.5 Odd-Even Mergesort

The odd-even mergesort algorithm, introduced by Batcher in 1968, is a parallel sorting network based upon his odd-even merge algorithm (Batcher, 1968). The odd-even merge algorithm will merge two *sorted* lists into one sorted list, and this is used recursively to build up larger and larger sorted lists. Given two sorted lists, $a_1, a_2, a_3, \ldots, a_n$ and $b_1, b_2, b_3, \ldots, b_n$ (where n is a power of 2), the following actions are performed:

1. The elements with odd indices of each sequence — that is, $a_1, a_3, a_5, \ldots, a_{n-1}$, and $b_1, b_3, b_5, \ldots, b_{n-1}$ — are merged into one sorted list, $c_1, c_2, c_3, \ldots, c_n$.
2. The elements with even indices of each sequence — that is, $a_2, a_4, a_6, \ldots, a_n$, and $b_2, b_4, b_6, \ldots, b_n$ — are merged into one sorted list, $d_1, d_2, \ldots, d_n$.
3. The final sorted list, $e_1, e_2, \ldots, e_{2n}$, is obtained by the following:

$$e_{2i} = \min\{c_{i+1}, d_i\}$$
$$e_{2i+1} = \max\{c_{i+1}, d_i\}$$

for $1 \le i \le n-1$. Essentially the odd and even index lists are interleaved, and pairs of odd/even elements are interchanged to move the larger toward one end, if necessary. The first number is given by $e_1 = c_1$ (since this will be the smallest of the first elements of each list, a_1 or b_1) and the last number by $e_{2n} = d_n$ (since this will be the largest of the last elements of each list, a_n or b_n).

Batcher (1968) provides a proof of the algorithm. The odd-even merging algorithm is demonstrated in Figure 10.12 for merging two sorted sequences of four numbers into one sorted list of eight numbers. The merging algorithm can also be applied to lists of different lengths, but here we have assumed that the lists are powers of 2.

Each of the original sorted sublists can be created by the same algorithm, as shown in Figure 10.13, and the algorithm can be used recursively, leading to a time complexity of $O(\log^2 n)$ with n processors (Problem 10-15). In this case, pairs of processors perform the compare-and-exchange operations. The whole algorithm can be implemented with hardware units that perform the compare-and-exchange operations, as envisioned by Batcher. It is left as an exercise to draw the final arrangements.

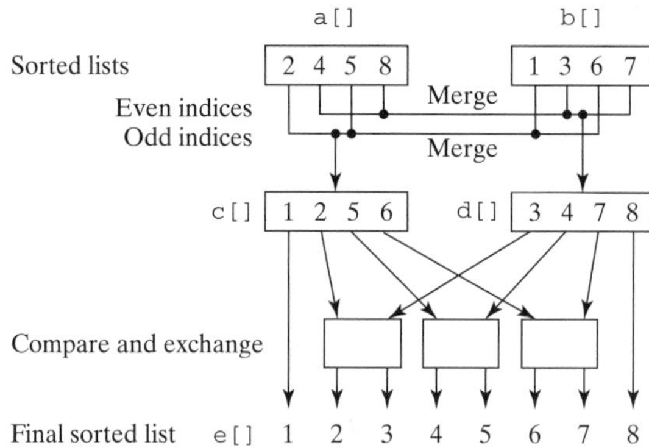

Figure 10.12 Odd-even merging of two sorted lists.

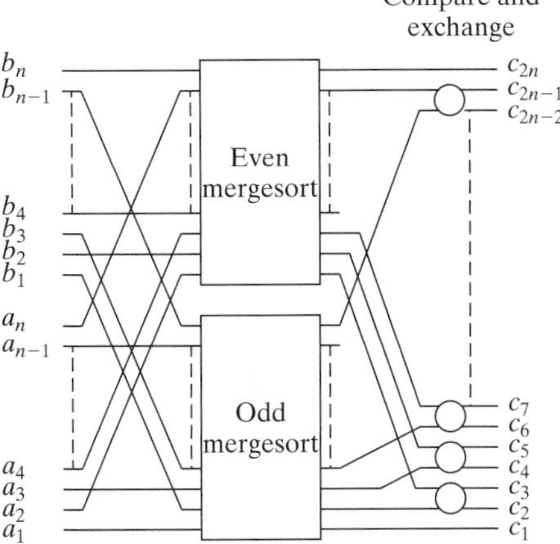

Figure 10.13 Odd-even mergesort.

10.2.6 Bitonic Mergesort

Bitonic mergesort was also introduced by Batcher in 1968 as a parallel sorting algorithm.

Bitonic Sequence. The basis of bitonic mergesort is the *bitonic sequence*, a list having specific properties that will be utilized in the sorting algorithm. A monotonic increasing sequence is a sequence of increasing numbers. A bitonic sequence has two sequences, one increasing and one decreasing. Formally, a bitonic sequence is a sequence of numbers, $a_0, a_1, a_2, a_3, \ldots, a_{n-2}, a_{n-1}$, which monotonically increases in value, reaches a single maximum, and then monotonically decreases in value; for example,

$$a_0 < a_1 < a_2 < a_3, \ldots, a_{i-1} < a_i > a_{i+1}, \ldots, a_{n-2} > a_{n-1}$$

for some value of i ($0 \le i < n$). A sequence is also bitonic if the preceding can be achieved by shifting the numbers cyclically (left or right). Bitonic sequences are illustrated in Figure 10.14. Note that a bitonic sequence can be formed by sorting two lists, one in increasing order and one in decreasing order, and concatenating the sorted lists.

The "special" characteristic of bitonic sequences is that if we perform a compare-and-exchange operation on a_i with $a_{i+n/2}$ for all i ($0 \le i < n/2$), where there are n numbers in the sequence, we get two bitonic sequences, where the numbers in one sequence are

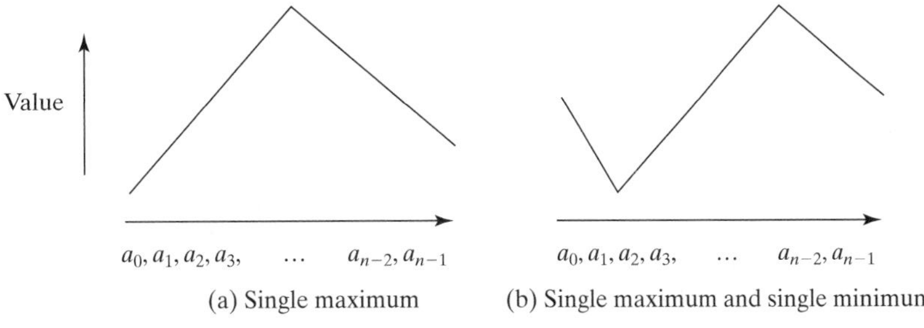

Figure 10.14 Bitonic sequences.

all less than the numbers in the other sequence. For example, starting with the bitonic sequence

$$3, 5, 8, 9, 7, 4, 2, 1$$

and performing a compare and exchange, a_i with $a_{i+n/2}$, we get the sequences shown in Figure 10.15.

The compare-and-exchange operation moves the smaller number of each pair to the left sequence and the larger number of the pair to the right sequence. Note that all the numbers in the left sequence are indeed less than all the numbers in the right sequence, in addition to both sequences being bitonic sequences. It is now clear that given a bitonic sequence, recursively performing compare-and-exchange operations to subsequences will sort the list, as shown in Figure 10.16. Eventually, we obtain bitonic sequences consisting of one number each and a fully sorted list.

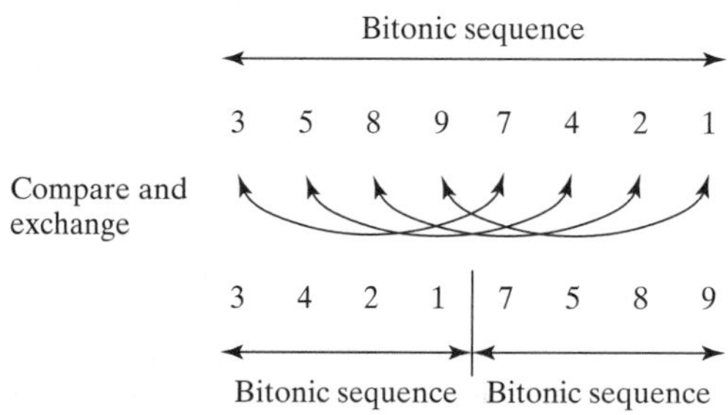

Figure 10.15 Creating two bitonic sequences from one bitonic sequence.

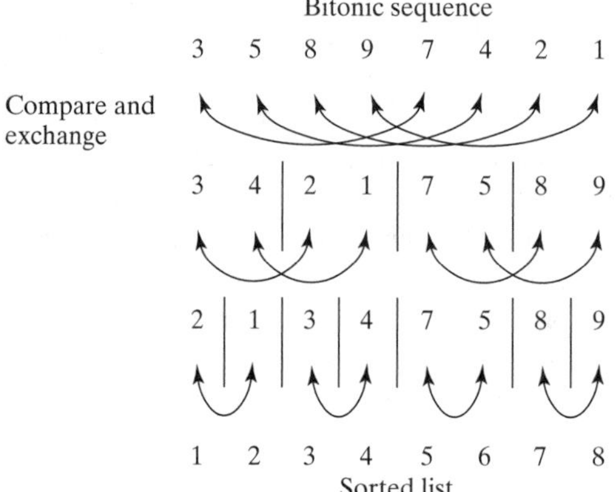

Figure 10.16 Sorting a bitonic sequence.

Sorting. To sort an unordered sequence, sequences are merged into larger bitonic sequences, starting with pairs of adjacent numbers. By a compare-and-exchange operation, pairs of adjacent numbers are formed into increasing sequences and decreasing sequences, pairs of which form a bitonic sequence of twice the size of each of the original sequences. By repeating this process, bitonic sequences of larger and larger lengths are obtained. In the final step, a single bitonic sequence is sorted into a single increasing sequence (the sorted sequence). The algorithm is illustrated in Figure 10.17. Compare-and-exchange operations can create either an increasing sequence or a decreasing sequence, and alternate directions

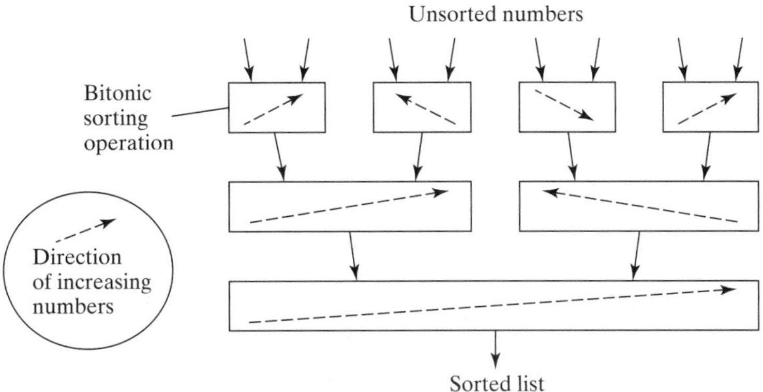

Figure 10.17 Bitonic mergesort.

can form a bitonic sequence with a maximum at the center of the sequence. In Figure 10.17 the first bitonic sequence at the right has a single minimum at the center; the left bitonic sequence has a single maximum at the center. (The algorithm could also work if both sides created bitonic sequences with a maximum at the center.)

First let us expand the algorithm into the basic operations using a numerical example. Figure 10.18 shows bitonic mergesort as applied to sorting eight numbers. The basic compare-and-exchange operation is given by a box, with an arrow indicating which output is the larger number of the operation. The six steps (for eight numbers) are divided into three phases:

Phase 1 (Step 1)	Convert pairs of numbers into increasing/decreasing sequences and hence into 4-bit bitonic sequences.
Phase 2 (Steps 2/3)	Split each 4-bit bitonic sequence into two 2-bit bitonic sequences, higher sequences at the center.
	Sort each 4-bit bitonic sequence into increasing/decreasing sequences and merge into an 8-bit bitonic sequence.
Phase 3 (Steps 4/5/6)	Sort 8-bit bitonic sequence (as in Figure 10.17).

In general, with $n = 2^k$, there are k phases, each of 1, 2, 3, …, k steps. Therefore the total number of steps is given by

$$\text{Steps} = \sum_{i=1}^{k} i = \frac{k(k+1)}{2} = \frac{\log n(\log n + 1)}{2} = \text{O}(\log^2 n)$$

The time complexity of $\text{O}(\log^2 n)$ using n processors (one processor for each number) is attractive. The data can be partitioned, as in all sorting algorithms, to reduce the number of processors with an attendant increase in the number of internal steps. Bitonic mergesort can be mapped onto a mesh and onto a hypercube, as described in Quinn (1994). See also Nassimi and Sahni (1979).

The algorithm is also attractive for implementing in hardware (i.e., as a logic circuit that accepts numbers and sorts them, each compare-and-exchange operation being one

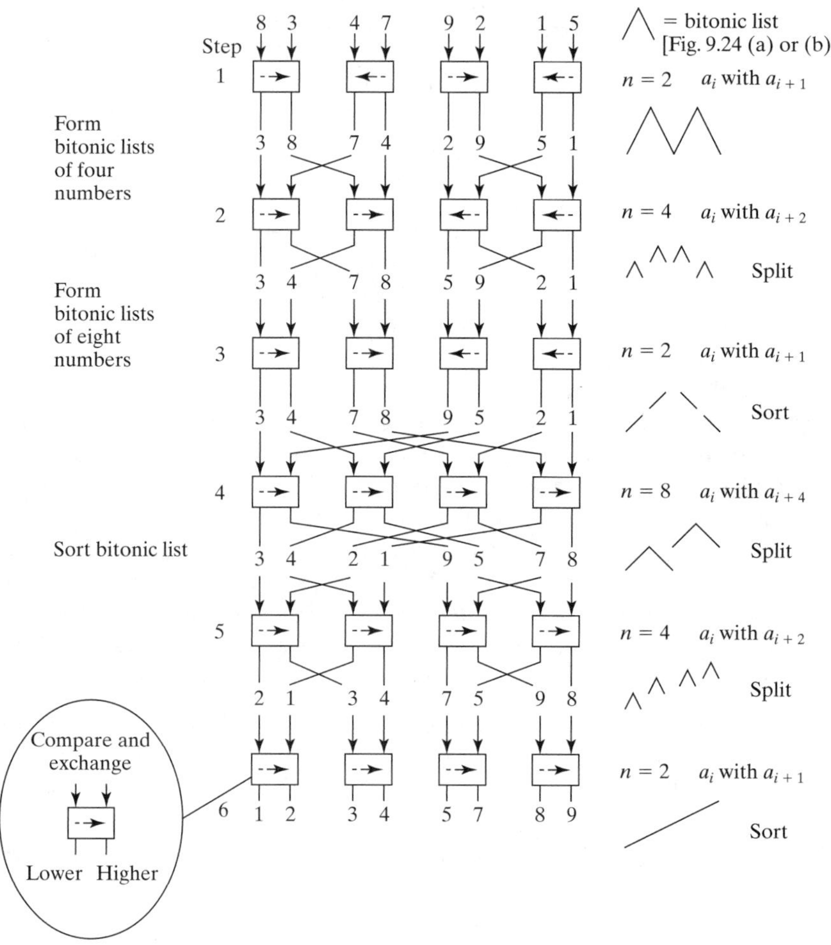

Figure 10.18 Bitonic mergesort on eight numbers.

comparator logic circuit) and is usually described in this context. Each step requires $n/2$ two-input/two-output comparators. The "wiring" in Figure 10.18 can be drawn more directly but is given as shown to clarify the position of numbers that are being compared and their subsequent positions.

10.3 SORTING ON SPECIFIC NETWORKS

Algorithms can take advantage of the underlying interconnection network of the parallel computer. Two network structures have received considerable attention over the years, the mesh and the hypercube, because parallel computers have been built with these networks.

We will describe a couple of representative algorithms. In general, such algorithms are of less interest nowadays because the underlying architecture of the system is often hidden from the user. (However, MPI does provide features for mapping algorithms onto meshes, and one can always use a mesh or hypercube algorithm even if the underlying architecture is not the same.)

10.3.1 Two-Dimensional Sorting

If the numbers are mapped onto a mesh, distinct possibilities exist for sorting them. The layout of a sorted sequence on a mesh could be row by row or *snakelike*. In a snakelike sorted list, the numbers are arranged in nondecreasing order, as shown in Figure 10.19. Numbers can be extracted from the node holding the largest numbers by shifting the numbers toward this node. A one-dimensional sorting algorithm that maps onto a line, such as odd-even transposition sort, could be applied to the numbers leading to an $O(n)$ sorting algorithm on the mesh, but this is not cost-optimal and does not take full advantage of the mesh configuration. The actual lower bound for any sorting algorithm on a $\sqrt{n} \times \sqrt{n}$ mesh is $2(\sqrt{n} - 1)$ steps or $O(\sqrt{n})$, since in the worst case this number of steps is required to reposition a number. Note that the diameter of the network is $2(\sqrt{n} - 1)$.

Scherson, Sen, and Shamir (1986) describe an ingenious sorting algorithm for a mesh architecture called *shearsort*, which requires $\sqrt{n}(\log n + 1)$ steps for n numbers on a $\sqrt{n} \times \sqrt{n}$ mesh. The algorithm is also described in detail in Leighton (1992). First the numbers are mapped onto the mesh. Then a series of phases are performed (1, 2, 3, …). In odd phases (1, 3, 5, …), the following actions are done:

> Each row of numbers is sorted independently, in alternative directions:
>
> > Even rows — The smallest number of each column is placed at the rightmost end and the largest number at the leftmost end.
> >
> > Odd rows — The smallest number of each column is placed at the leftmost end and the largest number at the rightmost end.

In even phases (2, 4, 6, …), the following actions are done:

> Each column of numbers is sorted independently, placing the smallest number of each column at the top and the largest number at the bottom.

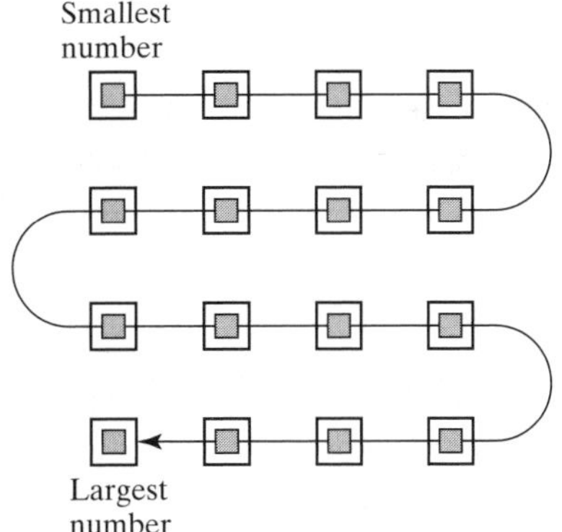

Figure 10.19 Snakelike sorted list.

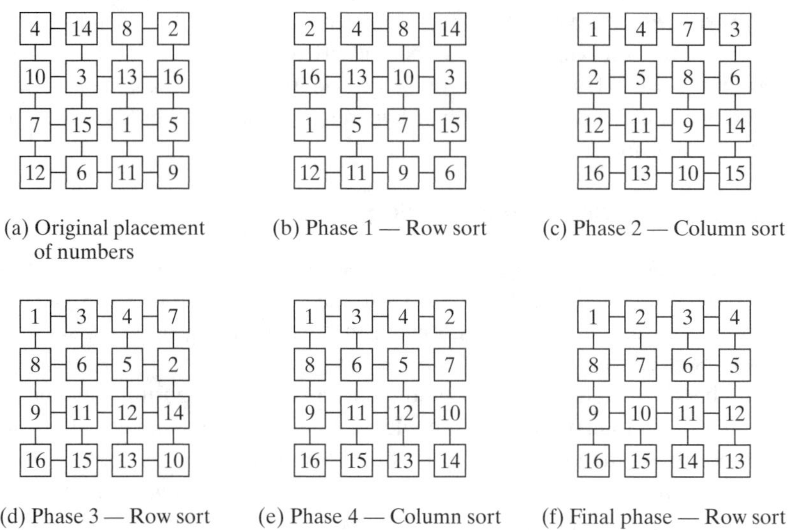

Figure 10.20 Shearsort.

After $\log n + 1$ phases, the numbers are sorted with a snakelike placement in the mesh. (Note the alternating directions of the row-sorting phase, which matches the final snakelike layout.) The algorithm is demonstrated in Figure 10.20 for 16 numbers placed on a 4×4 mesh. The proof is given in Scherson, Sen, and Shamir (1986) and Leighton (1992). Sorting columns and rows can use any sorting algorithm, including odd-even sort. If odd-even sort were used, sorting either columns or rows of $\sqrt{n}$ numbers would require $\sqrt{n}$ compare-and-exchange steps, and the total number of steps would be $\sqrt{n}(\log n + 1)$.

Apart from shearsort, other algorithms have been specifically devised for mapping onto a mesh, as described by Gu and Gu (1994). Existing sorting algorithms can be modified to be mapped onto a mesh. Thompson and Kung (1977) also present sorting algorithms that reach the lower bound of $O(\sqrt{n})$ on a $\sqrt{n} \times \sqrt{n}$ mesh.

Using Transposition. The operations in any mesh algorithm, such as shearsort, which alternate between acting within rows and acting within columns, can be limited to rows by transposing the array of data points between each phase. A transpose operation causes the elements in each column to be in positions in a row. Suppose the elements of array are a_{ij} ($0 \le i < n$, $0 \le j < n$). Elements are moved from below the diagonal in the array to above the diagonal, so that element $a_{ij} = a_{ji}$. The transpose operation is placed between the row operations and column operations, as shown in Figure 10.21. In Figure 10.21(a), operations occur between elements in rows. In Figure 10.21(b), a transpose operation occurs, moving the columns to the rows, and vice versa. In Figure 10.21(c), the operations that were specified on columns now take place on rows.

Figure 10.21 suggests a parallel implementation using a set of processors, where each processor is responsible for sorting one row. For example, consider a $\sqrt{n} \times \sqrt{n}$ array with $\sqrt{n}$ processors, one for each row. There are $\log n + 1$ iterations. In each iteration, each processor can sort its row in $O(\sqrt{n} \log \sqrt{n})$ steps (even one way, odd the other way,

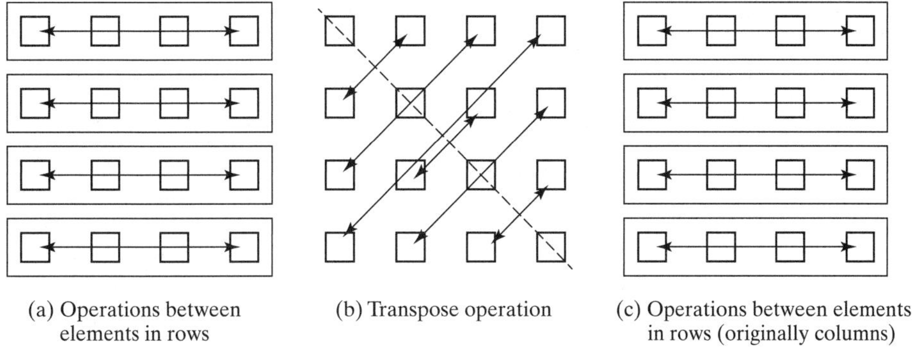

Figure 10.21 Using the transpose operation to maintain operations in rows.

according to the algorithm). The transposition can be achieved with $\sqrt{n}(\sqrt{n} - 1)$ communications or O(n) communications (Problem 10-7). Note that data is exchanged between pairs of processes, each exchange requiring two communications. A single *all-to-all* routine could reduce this if available (see Chapter 4). Then each row is sorted again in $O(\sqrt{n}\log\sqrt{n})$ steps. On a mesh, the overall communication time complexity will be O(n) as it is dominated by the transpose operation. The technique could be used on other structures. For example, each row could be mapped onto one processor of a line structure.

10.3.2 Quicksort on a Hypercube

The hypercube network has structural characteristics that offer scope for implementing efficient divide-and-conquer sorting algorithms, such as quicksort.

Complete List Placed in One Processor. Suppose a list of n numbers is initially placed on one node of a d-dimensional hypercube. The list can be divided into two parts according to the quicksort algorithm by using a pivot determined by the processor, with one part sent to the adjacent node in the highest dimension. Then the two nodes can repeat the process, dividing their lists into two parts using locally selected pivots. One part is sent to a node in the next-highest dimension. This process is continued for d steps in total, so that every node has a part of the list. For a three-dimensional hypercube with the numbers originally in node 000, we have the splits

	Node		Node	
1st step:	000	→	001	(numbers greater than a pivot, say p_1)
2nd step:	000	→	010	(numbers greater than a pivot, say p_2)
	001	→	011	(numbers greater than a pivot, say p_3)
3rd step:	000	→	100	(numbers greater than a pivot, say p_4)
	001	→	101	(numbers greater than a pivot, say p_5)
	010	→	110	(numbers greater than a pivot, say p_6)
	011	→	111	(numbers greater than a pivot, say p_7)

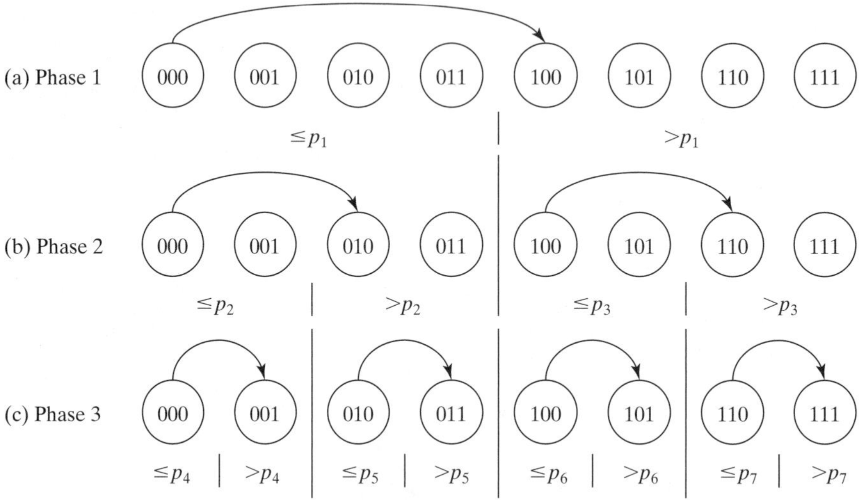

Figure 10.22 Hypercube quicksort algorithm when the numbers are originally in node 000.

The actions are illustrated in Figure 10.22. Finally, the parts can be sorted using a sequential algorithm, all in parallel. If required, the sorted parts can be returned to one processor in a sequence that allows the processor to concatenate the sorted lists to create the final sorted list.

Numbers Initially Distributed Across All Processors. Suppose the unsorted numbers are initially distributed across the nodes in an equitable fashion but not in any special order. A 2^d-node hypercube (d-dimensional hypercube) is composed of two smaller 2^{d-1}-node hypercubes, which are interconnected with links between pairs of nodes in each cube in the dth dimension. These smaller hypercubes can similarly be decomposed into smaller hypercubes (until a single node is reached in each). This feature can be used in a direct extension of the quicksort algorithm to a hypercube as follows. First, consider the hypercube as two subcubes. Processors in the upper subcube have as the most significant bit of their address a 1, and processors in the lower subcube have as the most significant bit of their address a 0. Pairs of processors having addresses 0xxx and 1xxx, where the x's are the same, are "partners." The first steps are

1. One processor (say P_0) selects (or computes) a suitable pivot and broadcasts this to all others in the cube.
2. The processors in the lower subcube send their numbers, which are greater than the pivot, to their partner processor in the upper subcube. The processors in the upper subcube send their numbers, which are equal to or less than the pivot, to their partner processor in the lower cube.
3. Each processor concatenates the list received with what remains of its own list.

Given a d-dimensional hypercube, after these steps the numbers in the lower (d–1)-dimensional subcube will all be equal to or less than the pivot, and all the numbers in the upper (d–1)-dimensional hypercube will be greater than the pivot.

Steps 2 and 3 are now repeated recursively on the two (d–1)-dimensional subcubes. One process in each subcube computes a pivot for its subcube and broadcasts it throughout its subcube. These actions terminate after log d recursive phases. Suppose the hypercube has three dimensions. Now the numbers in the processor 000 will be smaller than the numbers in processor 001, which will be smaller than the numbers in processor 010, and so on, as illustrated in Figure 10.23. The communication patterns are also illustrated in the hypercube in Figure 10.24 for a three-dimensional hypercube.

To complete the sorting, the numbers in each processor need to be sorted sequentially. Finally, the numbers have to be retrieved from the processors by visiting them in numeric order. Since there is not always a direct link between adjacent processors in numeric order, it may be more convenient to use the construction shown in Figure 10.25, which leaves the sorted numbers in a sequence of processors having increasing Gray code order. It is left as an exercise to investigate larger hypercubes (Problem 10-13).

Pivot Selection. As with all formulations of quicksort, the selection of the pivot is important, and more so for multiprocessor implementations. A poor pivot selection could result in most of the numbers being allocated to a small part of the hypercube, leaving the rest idle. This is most deleterious in the first split. In the sequential quicksort algorithm, often the pivot is simply chosen to be the first number in the list, which could be obtained in a single step or with O(1) time complexity. One approach to improve the pivot selection is to take a sample of a numbers from the list, compute the mean value, and select the median as the pivot. If we were to select the median as the pivot, the numbers sampled

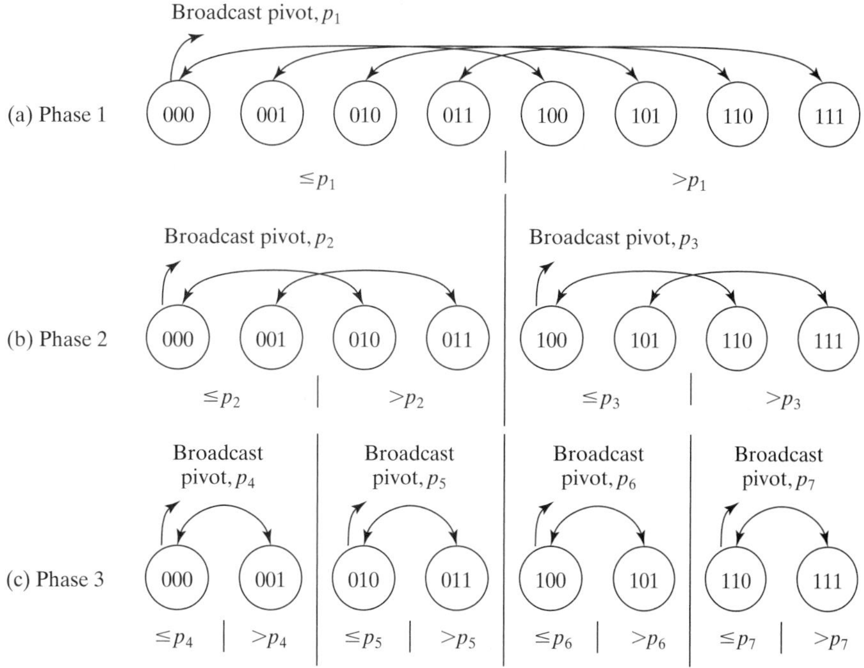

Figure 10.23 Hypercube quicksort algorithm when numbers are distributed among nodes.

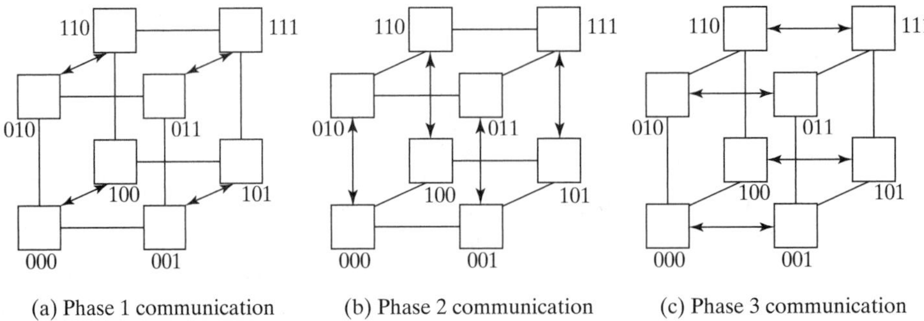

Figure 10.24 Hypercube quicksort communication.

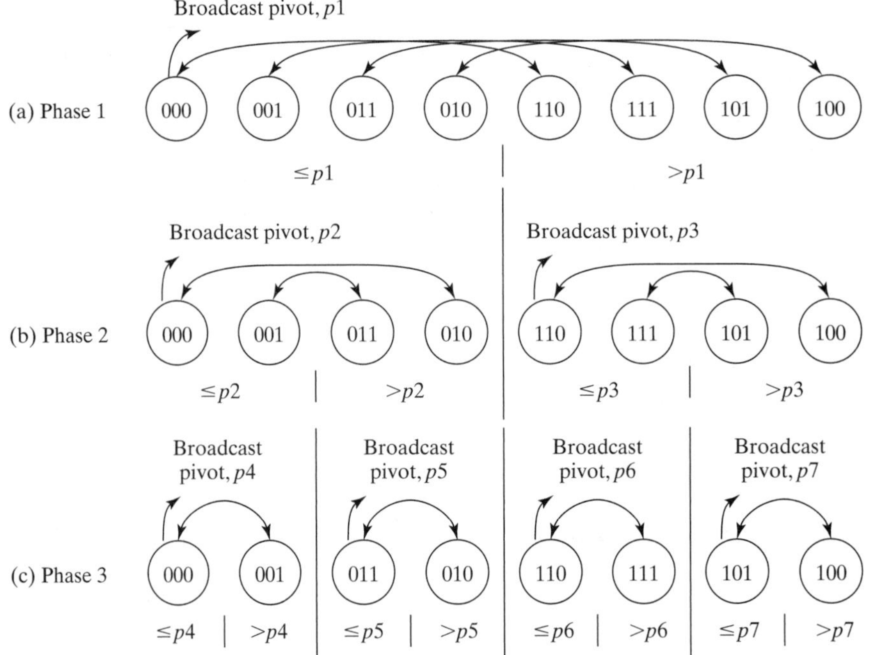

Figure 10.25 Quicksort hypercube algorithm with Gray code ordering.

would need to be sorted at least halfway through to find the median. We might choose a simple bubble sort, which can be terminated when the median is reached.

Hyperquicksort. Another version of the hypercube quicksort algorithm always sorts the numbers at each stage to maintain sorted numbers in each processor. Not only does this simplify selecting the pivots, it eliminates the final sorting operation. This formulation of quicksort on a hypercube is called *hyperquicksort* (Wagar, 1987) and maintains sorted numbers at each stage.

10.4 OTHER SORTING ALGORITHMS

We began this chapter by giving the lower bound for the time complexity of a sequential sorting algorithm based upon comparisons as $O(n\log n)$ (actually $\Omega(n\log n)$, but we have been using big-O notation throughout). Consequently, the time complexity of a parallel sorting algorithm based upon comparisons is $O((\log n)/p)$ with p processors or $O(\log n)$ with n processors. In fact, there are sorting algorithms that can achieve better than $O(n\log n)$ sequential time complexity and thus are very attractive candidates for parallelization, but they often assume special properties of the numbers being sorted. But first, let us look at one sorting algorithm, rank sort, that does not achieve a sequential time of $O(n\log n)$, but can be parallelized easily to achieve a parallel time of $O(n)$ with n processors and $O(\log n)$ with n^2 processors, and leads us onto linear sequential time algorithms which can be parallelized to achieve $O(\log n)$ parallel time and are attractive algorithms for clusters.

10.4.1 Rank Sort

In rank sort (also known as *enumeration sort*), the number of numbers that are smaller than each selected number is counted. This count provides the position of the selected number in the list; that is, its "rank" in the list. Suppose there are n numbers stored in an array, `a[0]` … `a[n-1]`. First `a[0]` is read and compared with each of the other numbers, `a[1]` … `a[n-1]`, recording the number of numbers less than `a[0]`. Suppose this number is x. This is the index of the location in the final sorted list. The number `a[0]` is copied into the final sorted list, `b[0]` … `b[n-1]`, at location `b[x]`. Then the next number, `a[1]`, is read and compared with each of the other numbers, `a[0]`, `a[2]`, …, `a[n-1]`, and so on. Comparing one number against $n - 1$ other numbers requires at least $n - 1$ steps if performed sequentially. Doing this with all n numbers requires $n(n - 1)$ steps, an overall sequential sorting time complexity of $O(n^2)$ (not exactly a good sequential sorting algorithm!).

The actual sequential code might look like

```
for (i = 0; i < n; i++) {        /* for each number */
   x = 0;
   for (j = 0; j < n; j++)       /* count number of numbers less than it */
      if (a[i] > a[j]) x++;
   b[x] = a[i];                  /* copy number into correct place */
}
```

with two `for` loops each iterating for n steps. The code given will actually fail if duplicates exist in the sequence of numbers, because duplicates will be placed in the same location in the sorted list, but the code can be easily modified to handle duplicates as follows:

```
for (i = 0; i < n; i++) {        /* for each number */
   x = 0;
   for (j = 0; j < n; j++)       /* count number of numbers less than it */
      if (a[i] > a[j] || (a[i] == a[j] && j < i)) x++;
   b[x] = a[i];                  /* copy number into correct place */
}
```

This code places duplicates in the same order as in the original sequence. Sorting algorithms that place duplicates in the same order as they were in the original sequence are called *stable sorting algorithms*. In the following, for simplicity, we will omit the modification of the code to handle duplicates. We should also point out that rank sort can be coded in a fashion that achieves O(n) sequential time complexity if the numbers are only integers. The code requires an additional array for each possible value of the numbers. We shall look at this implementation under the name of *counting sort* in Section 10.4.2.

Using n Processors. Suppose we have n processors. One processor would be allocated to one of the numbers and could find the final index of one number in O(n) steps. With all the processors operating in parallel, the parallel time complexity would also be O(n). In `forall` notation, the code would look like

```
forall (i = 0; i < n; i++) {          /* for each number in parallel*/
   x = 0;
   for (j = 0; j < n; j++)            /* count number of nos less than it */
      if (a[i] > a[j]) x++;
   b[x] = a[i];                       /* copy number into correct place */
}
```

The linear parallel time complexity, O(n), is good, but we can do even better if we have more processors.

Using n^2 Processors. Comparing one selected number with each of the other numbers in the list can be performed using multiple processors. For example, the structure shown in Figure 10.26 could be used. Here, $n - 1$ processors are used to find the rank of one number, and with n numbers, $(n - 1)n$ processors or (almost) n^2 processors are needed. A single counter is needed for each number. Incrementing the counter is done sequentially in Figure 10.26 and requires a maximum of n steps (including one step to initialize the counter). Therefore, the total number of steps would be given by $1 + n$ (the 1 for the processors in parallel). A tree structure could be used to reduce the number of steps involved in incrementing the counter, as shown in Figure 10.27. This leads to an O($\log n$) algorithm with n^2 processors for sorting numbers. The actual processor efficiency of this method is

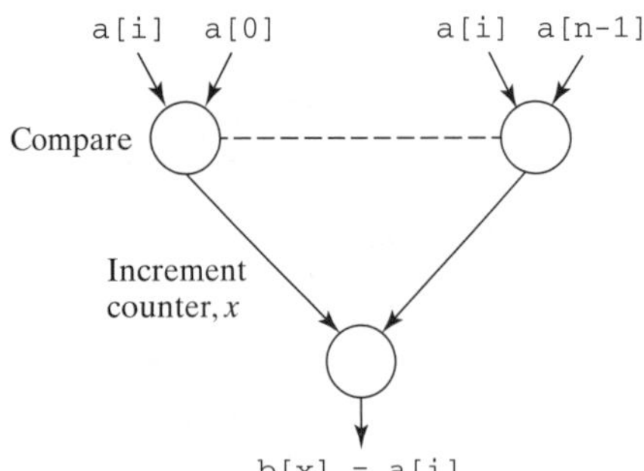

Figure 10.26 Finding the rank in parallel.

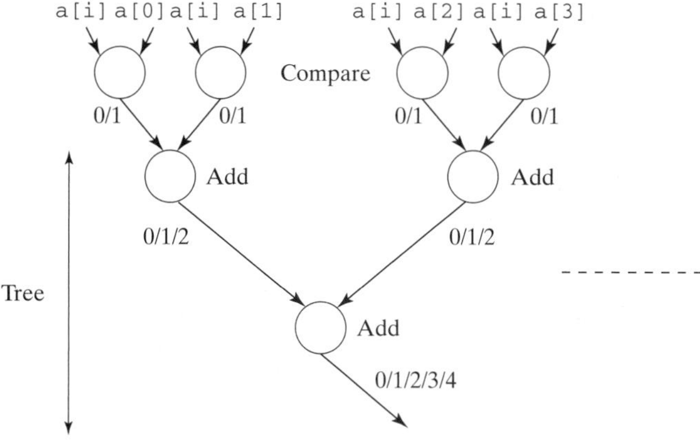

Figure 10.27 Parallelizing the rank computation.

relatively low (again left as an exercise to determine). In theoretical models of parallel computations, only one step is needed to perform the increment operations and combine their results. In these models, it is possible to reduce the time complexity of rank sort to O(1). O(1) is, of course, the lower bound for any problem. However, we do not explore theoretical models here.

Rank sort, then, can sort in O(n) with n processors or in O(log$n$) using n^2 processors. In practical applications, using n^2 processors will be prohibitive. The algorithm requires shared access to the list of numbers, making the algorithm most suitable to a shared memory system. The algorithm could be implemented with message-passing, in which a master process responds to requests for numbers from slaves, as shown in Figure 10.28.

Of course, we could reduce the number of processors by partitioning the numbers into groups, say m numbers in each group. Then only n/m processors would be needed to rank each group of numbers (without parallelizing the comparison operation). The number of operations that each processor performs would increase by a factor of m. Such data partitioning applies to many sorting algorithms and is common because the number of numbers, n, is usually much larger than the number of processors available.

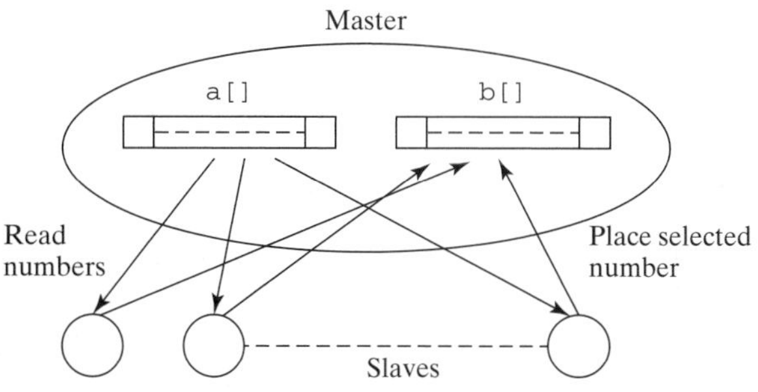

Figure 10.28 Rank sort using a master and slaves.

10.4.2 Counting Sort

If the numbers to be sorted are integers, there is a way of coding the rank sort algorithm described in Section 10.1.3 to reduce the sequential time complexity from $O(n^2)$ to $O(n)$. Coren, Leiserson, and Rivest (1990) refer to the method as *counting sort*. Counting sort is naturally a stable sorting algorithm (i.e., it will place identical numbers in the same order as in the original sequence). As in the rank sort code in Section 10.4.1, the original unsorted numbers are stored in an array `a[]`, and the final sorted sequence is stored in array `b[]`. The algorithm uses an additional array, say `c[]`, having one element for each possible value of the numbers. Suppose the range of integers is from 1 to m. The array has element `c[1]` through `c[m]` inclusive. Now let us work through the algorithm in stages.

First, `c[]` will be used to hold the histogram of the sequence, that is, the number of each number. This can be computed in $O(m)$ time with code such as:

```
for (i = 1; i <= m; i++)
   c[i] = 0;
for (i = 1; i <= m; i++)
   c[a[i]]++;
```

In the next stage of the algorithm, the number of numbers less than each number is found by preforming a prefix sum operation on array `c[]`. In the prefix sum calculation, given a list of numbers, $x_0, \ldots, x_{n-1}$, all the partial summations (i.e., x_0; $x_0 + x_1$; $x_0 + x_1 + x_2$; $x_0 + x_1 + x_2 + x_3$; …) are computed, as first mentioned in Chapter 6, Section 6.2.1. Now, though, the prefix sum is computed using the histogram originally held in `c[]` in $O(m)$ time, as described below:

```
for (i = 2; i <= m; i++)
   c[i] = c[i] + c[i-1];
```

In the final stage of the algorithm, the numbers are placed in the sorted order in $O(n)$ time, as described below:

```
for (i = 1; i <= n; i++) {
   b[c[a[i]]] = a[i];
   c[a[i]]--;                    // done to ensure stable sorting
}
```

The complete code has $O(n + m)$ sequential time complexity. If m is linearly related to n, as it is in some applications (see below for an example), the code has $O(n)$ sequential time complexity. Figure 10.29 shows counting sort operating upon a sequence of eight numbers. Highlighted here is the movement of the first number in the sequence. The other numbers are moved in the same fashion.

Parallelizing counting sort can use the parallel version of the prefix sum calculation which requires $O(\log n)$ time with $n - 1$ processors (see Chapter 6, Section 6.2.2). The final sorting stage can be achieved in $O(n/p)$ time with p processors or $O(1)$ with n processors by simply having the body of the loop done by different processors.

Counting sort is a very efficient algorithm when there are few different numbers and they are all integers. In the next section, we shall use counting sort in the radix sort algorithm.

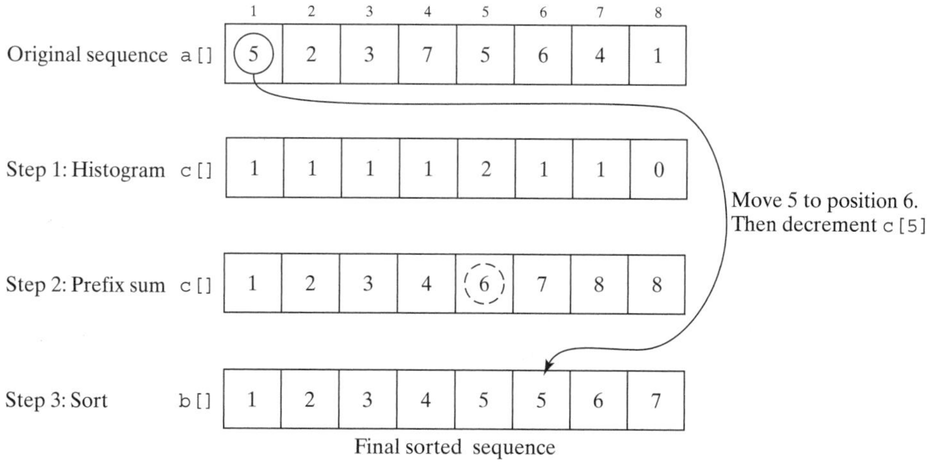

Figure 10.29 Counting sort.

10.4.3 Radix Sort

Radix sort assumes that the numbers to be sorted are represented in a positional digit representation, such as binary and decimal numbers. The digits represent values, and the position of each digit indicates its relative weighting (i.e., what to multiple the value by, the base 10 in decimal, the base 2 in binary). The positions are ordered from the least significant digit through to the most significant digit. Radix sort starts at the least significant digit (rather than the more intuitive method of the most significant digit) and sorts the numbers according to their least significant digits. The sequence is then sorted according to the next least significant digit, and so on until the most significant digit, after which the sequence is sorted. For this to work, it is necessary to maintain the order of numbers with the same digit, that is, one must use a stable sorting algorithm.

Radix sort can sort on individual digits of the number or on groups of digits. Figure 10.30 shows radix sort sorting on individual decimal digits. A example of sorting on individual bits of binary numbers is shown in Figure 10.31. In this case, it requires

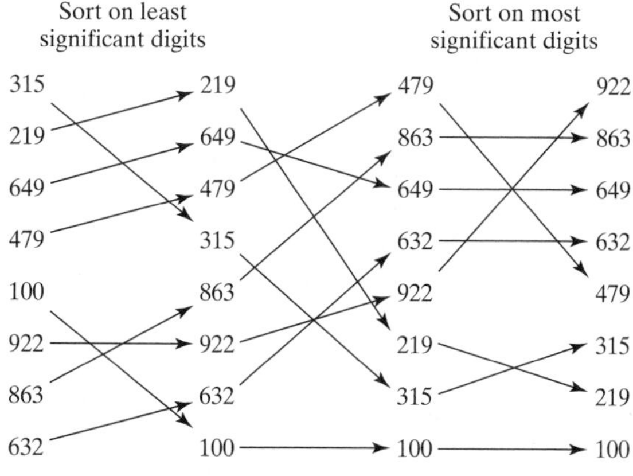

Figure 10.30 Radix sort using decimal digits.

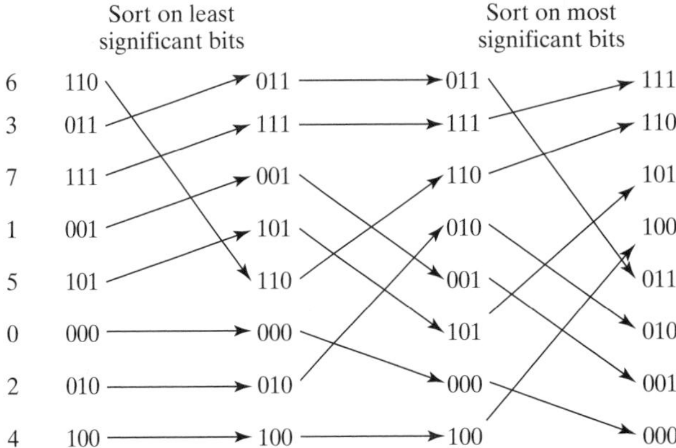

Figure 10.31 Radix sort using binary digits.

b phases if there are b bits in each number. Note that the order of numbers with the same bit value (0 or 1 in this example) is maintained. Radix sort would normally be applied to groups of binary digits at each stage rather than only considering one bit at each stage. In general, b-bit numbers can be sorted in radix sort by sorting on groups of r digits at a time and there are $\lceil b/r \rceil$ phases in that case. The time complexity of radix sort will depend upon the algorithm for sorting at each pass; the algorithm must be a stable sort. Given the small range of numbers, counting sort is suitable, but it is not the only choice because it does not sort in place (i.e., it requires additional storage for numbers as they are sorted).

Suppose that counting sort is used in radix sort. As mentioned in Section 10.4.2, counting sort has an $O(n + m)$ sequential time complexity operating on n integers each within the range of 1 to m. Given r-bit numbers, the range is potentially 1 to $2^r - 1$. There are $\lceil b/r \rceil$ phases where there are b bits on the complete numbers. Hence the sequential time complexity is $O(b/r(n + 2^r))$. If b and r are constants,[1] the sequential time complexity is $O(n)$; that is, again linear time complexity.

Radix sort can be parallelized by using a parallel sorting algorithm in each phase of sorting on bits or groups of bits. We have already mentioned parallelized counting sort using prefix sum calculation, which leads to $O(\log n)$ time with $n - 1$ processors and constant b and r. Radix sort with counting sort is used by Bader and JáJá (1999) in their study of programming clusters of SMPs.

Consider the example of sorting on binary digits, as in Figure 10.31 (i.e., with $r = 1$). A clever way to parallelize this radix sort is to use the prefix-sum calculation for positioning each number at each stage. When the prefix-sum calculation is applied to a column of bits, it gives the number of 1's up to each digit position because the digits can only be 0 or 1 and the prefix calculation will simply add the number of 1's. A second prefix calculation can also give the number of 0's up to each digit position by performing the prefix calculation on the digits inverted (sometimes called a *diminished prefix-sum* calculation). In the case where the digit of the number considered is a 0, the diminished prefix-sum calculation provides the new position for the number. In the case where the digit is a 1, the result of normal prefix-sum calculation plus the largest diminished prefix calculation gives the final

[1] There is a relationship between n and b. Given no duplicates, $n \leq 2^b$, i.e., $b \geq \log_2 n$. However, computers normally operate with a fixed number of bits to represent numbers no matter how many numbers there are.

position for the number. For example, if the number under consideration has a 1 and there were four numbers with a 0 plus two previous numbers with a 1, diminished prefix calculation gives 4 and normal prefix-sum calculation gives 3, resulting in the seventh position for the number (counting from position 1). Clearly this algorithm again leads to O(log$n$) time with $n - 1$ processors, but it does require b phases as $r = 1$.

10.4.4 Sample Sort

Sample sort is an old idea (Frazer and McKellar, 1970), as are many basic sorting ideas. It has been discussed in the context of quicksort and bucket sort. In the context of quicksort, sample sort takes a sample of s numbers from the sequence of n numbers. The median of this sample is used as the first pivot to divide the sequence into two parts, as required as the first step by the quicksort algorithm, rather than the usual first number in the list. For speed, all the pivots for subsequent steps can be found at the same time. For example, the upper and lower quartile points can be used as pivots for the first two subsequent sublists. This method addresses the problem of badly selected pivots in quicksort unevenly dividing the lists.

Sample sort has also been applied to bucket sort, as described in Chapter 4, Section 4.2. The fundamental problem in bucket sort is the same as in quicksort: unevenly divided lists. In bucket sort, if the numbers are not equally distributed, more numbers will fall into some buckets than others. In the worst case, all the numbers fall into one bucket, reducing the potential linear sequential time complexity to that of the comparison sorting algorithm used to sort n numbers (i.e., O($n$log$n$)). The basic problem is that the range of numbers for each bucket is fixed and chosen by dividing the complete range of numbers into equal regions.

The objective of sample sort is to divide the ranges so that each bucket will have approximately the same number of numbers. It does this by using a sampling scheme which picks out numbers from the sequence of n numbers as splitters that define the range of numbers for each bucket. If there are m buckets, $m - 1$ splitters are needed. These can be found by the following method. The numbers to be sorted are first divided into n/m groups. Each group is sorted, and a sample of s equally spaced numbers is chosen from each group. This creates ms samples in total, which are then sorted, and $m - 1$ equally spaced numbers are selected as splitters. The method for selecting the splitters is shown in Figure 10.32. After the range for each bucket is set by the splitters, the algorithm continues in the same fashion as in bucket sort (the buckets are sorted and the results concatenated).

The method can be parallelized in much the same way as bucket sort, by assigning one group of n/m numbers and one bucket to each processor ($p = m$). The mp numbers can be sent to one processor for sorting, although there are other possibilities. The larger the value for s, the greater the number of numbers used in the final splitter. If $s = m - 1$, less than $2n/m$ numbers will be in any one bucket. There are variations in the sample sort described, in which very high oversampling is done to take advantage of regular collective operations and achieve superior performance on clusters (see Helman, Bader, and JáJá, 1998).

10.4.5 Implementing Sorting Algorithms on Clusters

Efficient implementation on clusters calls for the use of broadcast and other collective operations, such as gather, scatter, and reduce, provided in message-passing software such as

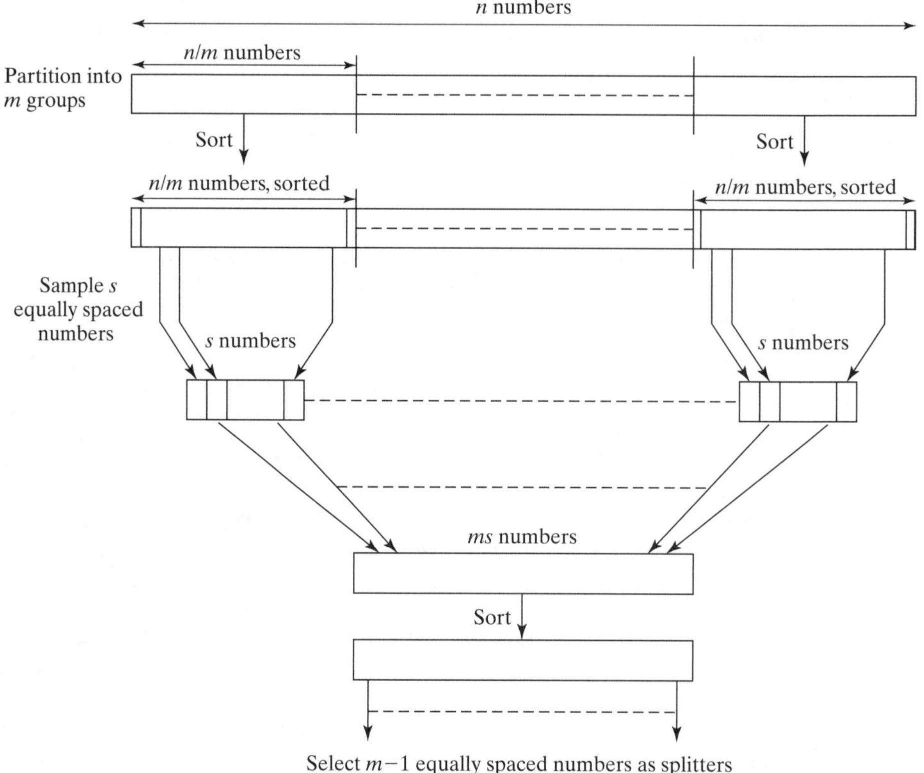

Figure 10.32 Selecting spliters in sample sort version of bucket sort.

MPI, rather than non-uniform communication patterns that require point-to-point communication, because collective operations are expected to be implemented efficiently. The distributed memory of a cluster does not favor algorithms requiring access to widely separated numbers. Algorithms that require only local operations are better, although in the worst case, all sorting algorithms finally have to move numbers from one end of the sequence to the other.

Processors always have cache memory, and it is better to have an algorithm that operates upon a block of numbers that can be placed in the cache. In consequence, one will need to know the size and organization of the cache, and this has to become part of the algorithm as parameters. Finally, with the advent of clusters of SMP processors (SMP clusters), algorithms need to take into account that the groups of processors in each SMP system may operate in a shared memory mode where the shared memory is only within each SMP system, whereas each system may communicate with other SMP systems in the cluster in a message-passing mode. Taking this into account again requires parameters such as number of processors within each SMP system and size of the memory in each SMP system. More information on algorithms on SMP systems can be found in Bader and JáJá (1999).

10.5 SUMMARY

This chapter described several ways that sorting can be done with multiprocessors. We began by stating that the lower bound of comparison-based sorting algorithms implemented sequentially is $O(n \log n)$ and for parallel implementation is $O(\log n)$ with n processors. We then considered compare-and exchange operations and sorting algorithms:

- Bubble sort
- Odd-even transposition sort
- Mergesort
- Quicksort, including on a hypercube
- Odd-even mergesort
- Bitonic mergesort

We then briefly looked at representative sorting algorithms that take advantage of specific interconnection networks:

- Shearsort (on a mesh)
- Quicksort on a hypercube

Finally, we explored sorting algorithms that do not use compare-and-exchange operations:

- Rank sort
- Counting sort, for integers only

and algorithms that obtain superior parallel performance when parallelized:

- Radix sort
- Sample sort

FURTHER READING

There are very many sorting algorithms and variations not covered in this chapter. We have selected those which are most common, representative of the technique, or have the potential for parallelization. Richards (1986) provides a list of 373 papers on parallel sorting up to the early 1980s. Akl (1985) has also written a book devoted entirely to parallel sorting algorithms. Subsequent papers proposing sorting algorithms include Blackston and Ranade (1993) and Bolorforoush et al. (1992). Survey papers have been published on parallel sorting, notably Bitton et al. (1984) and Lakshmivarahan, Dhall, and Miller (1984), the latter concentrating totally upon sorting networks.

In this second edition, we have reordered the material and added two well-known sorting algorithms, radix sort and sample sort, because of the attention recently given them as the basis for sorting on clusters and, in particular, SMP clusters, although the full details of cluster implementation are omitted because of their complexity. Further details can be found in Helman, Bader, and JáJá (1998). Sample sort is described by Shi and Schaeffer (1992).

BIBLIOGRAPHY

AJTAI, M., J. KOMLÓS, AND E. SZEMERÉDI (1983), "An O($n \log n$) Sorting Network," *Proc. 15th Annual ACM Symp. Theory of Computing*, Boston, MA, pp. 1–9.

AKL, S. (1985), *Parallel Sorting Algorithms*, Academic Press, New York.

BADER, D. A., AND J. JÁJÁ (1999), "SIMPLE: A Methodology for Programming High Performance Algorithms on Clusters of Symmetric Multiprocessors (SMPs), *J. Par. Dist Computing*, Vol. 58, pp. 92–108.

BATCHER, K. E. (1968), "Sorting Networks and Their Applications," *Proc. AFIPS Spring Joint Computer Conference*, Vol. 32, AFIPS Press, Reston, VA, pp. 307–314.

BITTON, D., D. J. DEWITT, D. K. HSIAO, AND J. MENON (1984), "A Taxonomy of Parallel Sorting," *Computing Surveys*, Vol. 16, No. 3 (September), pp. 287–318.

BLACKSTON, D. T., AND A. RANADE (1993), "SnakeSort: A Family of Simple Optimal Randomized Sorting Algorithms," *Proc. 1993 Int. Conf. Par. Proc.*, Vol. 3, pp. 201–204.

BOLORFOROUSH, M., N. S. COLEMAN, D. J. QUAMMEN, AND P. Y. WANG (1992), "A Parallel Randomized Sorting Algorithm," *Proc. 1992 Int. Conf. Par. Proc.*, Vol. 3, pp. 293–296.

CORMEN, T. H., C. E. LEISERSON, AND R. L. RIVEST (1990), *Introduction to Algorithms*, MIT Press, Cambridge, MA.

FRAZER, W. D., AND A. C. MCKELLAR (1970), "Samplesort: A sampling approach to minimal storage tree sorting," *J. ACM*, Vol. 17, No. 3 (July), pp. 496–567.

FOX, G., M. JOHNSON, G. LYZENGA, S. OTTO, J. SALMON, AND D. WALKER (1988), *Solving Problems on Concurrent Processors,* Volume 1, Prentice Hall, Englewood Cliffs, NJ.

GU, Q. P., AND J. GU (1994), "Algorithms and Average Time Bounds of Sorting on a Mesh-Connected Computer," *IEEE Trans. Par. Distrib. Syst.*, Vol. 5, No. 3, pp. 308–314.

HELMAN, D. R., D. A. BADER, AND J. JÁJÁ (1998), "A Randomized Parallel Sorting Algorithm with an Experimental Study, *Journal of Parallel and Distributed Computing*, Vol. 52, No. 1, pp. 1–23

HIRSCHBERG, D. S. (1978), "Fast Parallel Sorting Algorithms," *Comm. ACM*, Vol. 21, No. 8, pp. 538–544.

HOARE, C. A. R. (1962), "Quicksort," *Computer Journal*, Vol. 5, No. 1, pp. 10–15.

JÁJÁ, J. (1992), *An Introduction to Parallel Algorithms*, Addison-Wesley, Reading, MA.

LAKSHMIVARAHAN, S., S. K. DHALL, AND L. L. MILLER (1984), "Parallel Sorting Algorithms," *Advances in Computers*, Vol. 23, pp. 295–354.

LEIGHTON, F. T. (1984), "Tight Bounds on the Complexity of Parallel Sorting," *Proc. 16th Annual ACM Symposium on Theory of Computing*, ACM, New York, pp. 71–80.

LEIGHTON, F. T. (1992), *Introduction to Parallel Algorithms and Architectures: Arrays, Trees, Hypercubes*, Morgan Kaufmann, San Mateo, CA.

NASSIMI, D., AND S. SAHNI (1979), "Bitonic Sort on a Mesh-Connected Parallel Computer," *IEEE Trans. Comp.*, Vol. C-28, No. 2, pp. 2–7.

QUINN, M. J. (1994), *Parallel Computing Theory and Practice*, McGraw-Hill, NY.

RICHARDS, D. (1986), "Parallel Sorting — A Bibliography," *SIGACT News* (Summer), pp. 28–48.

SCHERSON, I. D., S. SEN, AND A. SHAMIR (1986), "Shear-Sort: A True Two-Dimensional Sorting Technique for VLSI networks," *Proc. 1986 Int. Conf. Par. Proc.*, pp. 903–908.

SHI, H, AND J. SCHAEFFER (1992), "Parallel Sorting by Regular Sampling," *Journal of Parallel and Distributed Computing*, Vol. 14, pp. 361–372.

THOMPSON, C. D., AND H. T. KUNG (1977), "Sorting on a Mesh-Connected Parallel Computer," *Comm. ACM*, Vol. 20 (April), pp. 263–271.

WAGAR, B. (1987), "Hyperquicksort: A Fast Sorting Algorithm for Hypercubes," *Proc. 2nd Conf. Hypercube Multiprocessors*, pp. 292–299.

WAINWRIGHT, R. L. (1985), "A Class of Sorting Algorithms Based on Quicksort," *Comm. ACM*, Vol. 28, No. 4, pp. 396–402. Also see "Technical Correspondence," *Comm. ACM*, Vol. 29, No. 4, pp. 331–335.

PROBLEMS

Scientific/Numerical

10-1. Rewrite the compare-and-exchange code given in Section 10.2.1 to eliminate the message-passing when exchanges are not needed.

10-2. Implement both methods of compare-and-exchange operations described in Section 10.2.1 (i.e., Version 1 and Version 2), operating upon blocks of four numbers. Measure the performance of the methods. Devise an experiment to show that it is possible to obtain erroneous results on a heterogeneous system with computers having different arithmetic precisions (if available).

10-3. Determine the processor efficiency of the O(log n) algorithm based upon the rank sort described in Section 10.1.3 for sorting numbers.

10-4. Fox et al. (1988) present a method of compare and exchange in which individual numbers are exchanged between the processors, say P_0 and P_1. Suppose each processor has four numbers in its group. Processor P_0 sends the largest number in its group to processor P_1, while processor P_1 sends the smallest number of its group to processor P_0. Each processor inserts the received number into its group, so that both still have n/p numbers. The actions are repeated with the new largest and smallest numbers. The algorithm is most conveniently implemented using a queue with a pointer to the top or bottom, as illustrated in Figure 10.33.

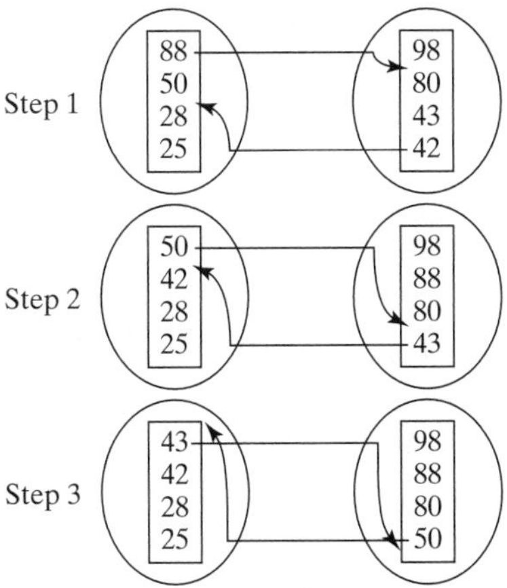

Figure 10.33 Compare-and-exchange algorithm for Problem 10-4.

The algorithm can terminate when the insertions would be at the top and bottom of the groups, as shown. The maximum number of communication steps would be when all the numbers in the left list were initially larger than all of the numbers in the other group (a maximum of x steps with x numbers in each group). Write a parallel program to implement Fox's method and evaluate it compared to the methods described in the text.

10-5. The following is an attempt to code the odd-even transposition sort of Section 10.2.2 as one SPMD program.

Process P_i

```
evenprocess = (i % 2 == 0);
evenphase = 1;
for (step = 0; step < n; step++, evenphase = !evenphase){
  if ((evenphase && evenprocess) || (!evenphase) && !evenprocess)) {
    send(&a, Pi+1);
    recv(&x, Pi+1);
    if (x < a) a = x;              /* keep smaller number */
  } else {
    send(&a, Pi-1);
    recv(&x, Pi-1);
    if (x > a) a = x;              /* keep larger number */
  }
}
```

Determine whether this code is correct, and if not, correct any mistakes.

10-6. The odd-even transposition sort of Section 10.2.2 was described on the assumption of an even number of numbers and processors. What changes to the code would be necessary to allow an odd number of numbers and processors?

10-7. Show that there are $\sqrt{n}(\sqrt{n} - 1)$ communications for a transpose operation on a $\sqrt{n} \times \sqrt{n}$ array, as stated in Section 10.3.1.

10-8. Write a parallel program to implement shearsort.

10-9. Write a parallel program to find the kth smallest number of a set of numbers. Use a parallel version of quicksort, but apply it only to the set of numbers containing the kth smallest number. See Cormen, Leiserson, and Rivest (1990) for further discussion on the problem.

10-10. There have been many suggestions of ways to improve the performance of sequential quicksort (see, for example, Wainwright, 1985 and the references therein). The following are two suggestions that have appeared in the literature:

1. Rather than selecting the first number as the pivot, use the median of a group of three numbers picked randomly ("median-of-three" technique).
2. The initial set of numbers is divided into two parts using the first number as the pivot. While the numbers are being compared with the pivot, the sum of the numbers in each of two parts is computed. From these sums, the mean of each part is computed. The mean of each part is used as the pivot for this part in the next partitioning stage. The process of computing two means is done in subsequent stages for the next pivots. This algorithm is called the meansort algorithm.

Determine empirically the prospects for parallelizing these methods.

10-11. Draw the exchanges of numbers for a four-dimensional hypercube, using the parallel hypercube described in Section 10.2.6, that leaves the results in embedded ring order. Determine a general algorithm to handle a hypercube of any size.

10-12. Draw the compare-and-exchange circuit configuration for the odd-even mergesort algorithm described in Section 10.2.7 to sort 16 numbers. Sort the following sequence by hand using the odd-even mergesort algorithm:

12 2 11 4 9 1 10 15 5 7 14 3 8 13 6 16

10-13. Repeat Problem 10-12 for bitonic mergesort.

10-14. Compare Batcher's odd-even mergesort algorithm (Section 10.2.5) and his bitonic mergesort algorithm (Section 10.2.6), and assess their relative advantages for parallel implementation on a message-passing multicomputer.

10-15. Prove that the time complexity of odd-even mergesort is $O(\log^2 n)$ with n processors.

10-16. Identify those sorting algorithms in Chapter 10 that operate in place (i.e., do not use additional storage for the numbers as they are sorted. In place algorithms will reduce the storage requirements, and this factor may be important when sorting a large number of numbers.

10-17. Would radix sort work if the sorting operated from the most significant digit to the least significant digit? Discuss.

10-18. Implement two sorting algorithms in MPI and compare their performance.

10-19. Read the paper by Helman, Bader, and JáJá (1998) and implement their sorting algorithm in MPI.

Real Life

10-20. Fred has a deck of 52 playing cards that have been thoroughly shuffled. He has asked you to determine several things related to reordering them:

1. What modification to bitonic mergesort will be needed to sort the cards, given that there are four suits (spades, hearts, clubs, and hearts)?
2. How many friends will Fred have to invite over (and feed) to carry out a modified bitonic mergesort in parallel, and how many steps will each friend have to carry out?

10-21. One way to find matching entries in two files is first to sort the contents of the files and then to step through the files comparing entries. Analyze this method compared to simply comparing each entry of one file with each entry of the second file without sorting. Write a parallel program to find matching entries of two files by first sorting the files.

10-22. Sorting algorithms can create any permutation of an input sequence by simply numbering the input elements in the required order and sorting on these numbers. Write a parallel program that randomizes the contents of a document file for security purposes by first numbering the words in the file using a random-number generator and then sorting on the numbers. (Refer to Chapter 3 for details of random numbers.) Is this a good method of encoding a file for security purposes? Write a parallel program that restores the document file to its original state.

Chapter 11

Numerical Algorithms

In this chapter, we study a selection of important numerical problems:

- Matrix multiplication
- The solution of a general system of linear equations by direct means
- The solution of sparse systems of linear equations and partial differential equations by iteration

Some of the techniques for these problems were introduced in earlier chapters to describe specific parallel programming techniques. Now we will develop the techniques in much more detail and introduce other programming techniques.

11.1 MATRICES — A REVIEW

The underlying basis for many scientific problems is the matrix. Let us review the mathematical concept of a matrix. A *matrix* is a two-dimensional array of numbers (or variables representing numbers). An $n \times m$ matrix has n rows and m columns of elements. An $n \times m$ matrix **A** is shown in Figure 11.1. This structure will be familiar from sequential programming as a two-dimensional array, and an array would typically be used to store a matrix.

11.1.1 Matrix Addition

Matrix addition simply involves adding corresponding elements of each matrix to form the result matrix. Given the elements of **A** as $a_{i,j}$ and the elements of **B** as $b_{i,j}$, each element of

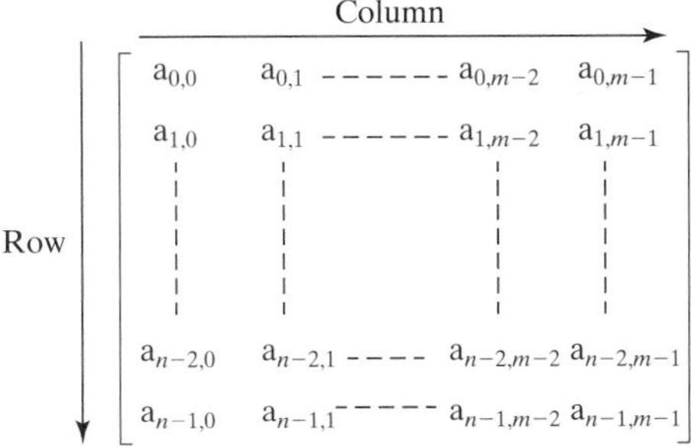

Figure 11.1 An $n \times m$ matrix.

C is computed as

$$c_{i,j} = a_{i,j} + b_{i,j}$$
$$(0 \le i < n, 0 \le j < m)$$

11.1.2 Matrix Multiplication

Multiplication of two matrices, **A** and **B**, produces the matrix **C**, whose elements, $c_{i,j}$ $(0 \le i < n, 0 \le j < m)$, can be computed as follows:

$$c_{i,j} = \sum_{k=0}^{l-1} a_{i,k} b_{k,j}$$

where **A** is an $n \times l$ matrix and **B** is an $l \times m$ matrix. Each element of the ith row of **A** is multiplied by an element of the jth column of **B**, and the products summed together to obtain the value of the element in the ith row and jth column of **C**, as illustrated in Figure 11.2. The number of columns in **A** must be the same as the number of rows in **B**, but otherwise the matrices can be of different sizes. Matrices can also be multiplied by constants (all elements multiplied by the same constant).

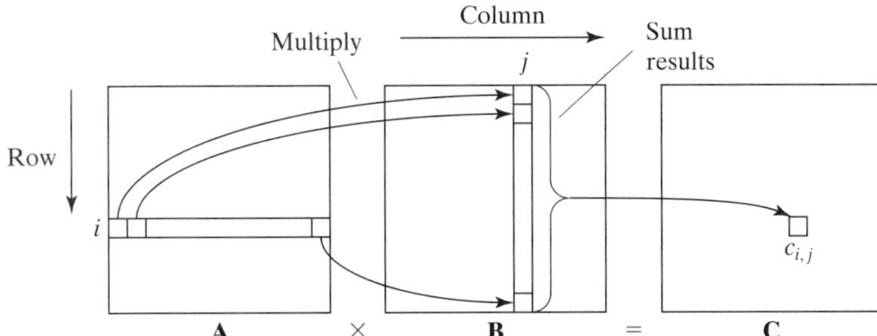

Figure 11.2 Matrix multiplication, **C** = **A** × **B**.

11.1.3 Matrix-Vector Multiplication

A *vector* is a matrix with one column; that is, an $n \times 1$ matrix. Matrix-vector multiplication follows directly from the definition of matrix-matrix multiplication by making **B** an $n \times 1$ matrix. The result will be an $n \times 1$ matrix (vector), as shown in Figure 11.3. Alternatively,

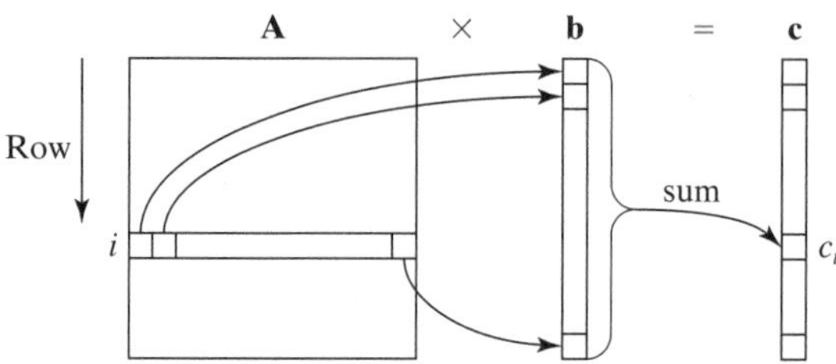

Figure 11.3 Matrix-vector multiplication $\mathbf{c} = \mathbf{A} \times \mathbf{b}$.

A could be a vector with one row (i.e., a $1 \times n$ matrix) and **B** an $n \times m$ matrix. Vector-matrix multiplication follows directly, resulting in a $1 \times m$ matrix (vector).

11.1.4 Relationship of Matrices to Linear Equations

Matrices appear frequently in mathematical formulations of many everyday problems encountered in engineering, business, and the sciences. The system of linear equations described in Chapter 6, Section 6.3.1, can be written in matrix form:

$$\mathbf{Ax} = \mathbf{b}$$

The matrix **A** holds the a constants, **x** is a vector of the unknowns, and **b** is a vector of the b constants. Matrix multiplication can be used to transform systems of linear systems (Kreyszig, 1962). Matrices and matrix operations can appear in other situations. For example, matrices can be used to find the shortest path between vertices in a graph.

11.2 IMPLEMENTING MATRIX MULTIPLICATION

11.2.1 Algorithm

Sequential Code. For convenience, let us assume throughout that the matrices are square ($n \times n$ matrices). From the definition of matrix multiplication given above, the sequential code to compute $\mathbf{A} \times \mathbf{B}$ could simply be

```
for (i = 0; i < n; i++)
  for (j = 0; j < n; j++) {
    c[i][j] = 0;
    for (k = 0; k < n; k++)
      c[i][j] = c[i][j] + a[i][k] * b[k][j];
  }
```

This algorithm requires n^3 multiplications and n^3 additions, leading to a sequential time complexity of $O(n^3)$. (For computational efficiency, a temporary variable, say `sum`, could be substituted for `c[i][j]`, so that an address calculation is not specified within each iteration of the inner `for` loop.)

Parallel Code. Parallel matrix multiplication is usually based upon the direct sequential matrix multiplication algorithm. Even a superficial look at the sequential code reveals that the computation in each iteration of the two outer loops is not dependent upon any other iteration, and each instance of the inner loop could be executed in parallel. Hence, with $p = n$ processors (and $n \times n$ matrices), we can expect a parallel time complexity of $O(n^2)$, and this is easily obtainable. It is also quite easy to obtain a time complexity of $O(n)$ with $p = n^2$ processors, where one element of **A** and one of **B** are assigned to each processor. These implementations are cost-optimal [since $O(n^3) = n \times O(n^2) = n^2 \times O(n)$]. As we will show, it is even possible to obtain $O(\log n)$ with $p = n^3$ processors by parallelizing the inner loop, though this is not cost-optimal [since $O(n^3) \neq n^3 \times O(\log n)$]. $O(\log n)$ is actually the lower bound for parallel matrix multiplication according to Moldovan (1993). The time complexities quoted here are for the computation. Unfortunately, any additional communication overhead can be very significant.

Partitioning into Submatrices. Usually, we want to use far fewer than n processors with $n \times n$ matrices because of the size of n. Then each processor operates upon a group of data points (data partitioning). Partitioning can be done very easily with matrix multiplication. Each matrix can be divided into blocks of elements called *submatrices*. These submatrices can be manipulated as if they were single matrix elements (Fox et al., 1988). Suppose the matrix is divided into s^2 submatrices (s across and s down). Each submatrix has $n/s \times n/s$ elements, say $m \times m$ elements ($m = n/s$). Using the notation $A_{p,q}$ as the submatrix in submatrix row p and submatrix column q, we simply replace the inner accumulation in the previous code with a matrix multiplication; that is,

```
for (p = 0; p < s; p++)
  for (q = 0; q < s; q++) {
    Cp,q = 0;                          /* clear elements of submatrix */
    for (r = 0; r < m; r++)            /* submatrix multiplication and */
      Cp,q = Cp,q + Ap,r * Br,q;       /* add to accumulating submatrix */
  }
```

The line

```
Cp,q = Cp,q + Ap,r * Br,q;
```

means multiply submatrix $A_{p,r}$ and $B_{r,q}$ using matrix multiplication, and add to submatrix $C_{p,q}$ using matrix addition. The inner loop is, in fact, composed of additional loops. The arrangement is known as *block matrix multiplication* and is central to all parallel implementations when using fewer than n processors. Block matrix multiplication is illustrated in Figure 11.4. Note that submatrix addition simply involves adding corresponding elements of two submatrices to form the result submatrix. Block matrix multiplication of two 4×4 matrices each divided into four 2×2 submatrices is shown in Figure 11.5. This construction actually suggests a recursive solution, but there are several different ways to implement the basic matrix multiplication algorithm, and we shall look at them now.

11.2.2 Direct Implementation

One way to implement the matrix multiplication algorithm is to allocate one processor to compute each element of **C**. Then n^2 processors would be needed. One row of elements of

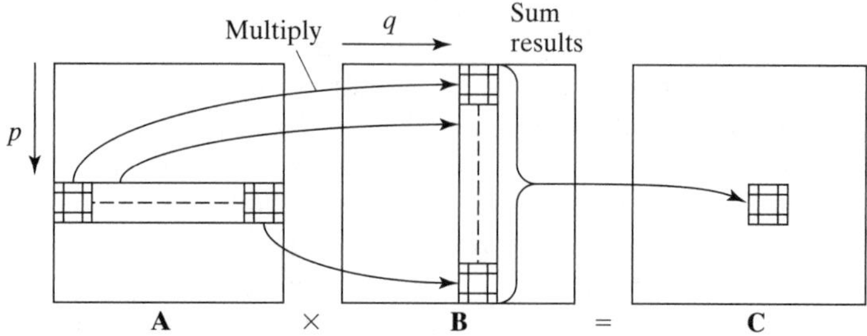

Figure 11.4 Block matrix multiplication.

$$\left[\begin{array}{cc|cc} a_{0,0} & a_{0,1} & a_{0,2} & a_{0,3} \\ a_{1,0} & a_{1,1} & a_{1,2} & a_{1,3} \\ \hline a_{2,0} & a_{2,1} & a_{2,2} & a_{2,3} \\ a_{3,0} & a_{3,1} & a_{3,2} & a_{3,3} \end{array}\right] \times \left[\begin{array}{cc|cc} b_{0,0} & b_{0,1} & b_{0,2} & b_{0,3} \\ b_{1,0} & b_{1,1} & b_{1,2} & b_{1,3} \\ \hline b_{2,0} & b_{2,1} & b_{2,2} & b_{2,3} \\ b_{3,0} & b_{3,1} & b_{3,2} & b_{3,3} \end{array}\right]$$

(a) Matrices

$$\overset{A_{0,0}}{\begin{bmatrix} a_{0,0} & a_{0,1} \\ a_{1,0} & a_{1,1} \end{bmatrix}} \times \overset{B_{0,0}}{\begin{bmatrix} b_{0,0} & b_{0,1} \\ b_{1,0} & b_{1,1} \end{bmatrix}} + \overset{A_{0,1}}{\begin{bmatrix} a_{0,2} & a_{0,3} \\ a_{1,2} & a_{1,3} \end{bmatrix}} \times \overset{B_{1,0}}{\begin{bmatrix} b_{2,0} & b_{2,1} \\ b_{3,0} & b_{3,1} \end{bmatrix}}$$

$$= \begin{bmatrix} a_{0,0}b_{0,0} + a_{0,1}b_{1,0} & a_{0,0}b_{0,1} + a_{0,1}b_{1,1} \\ a_{1,0}b_{0,0} + a_{1,1}b_{1,0} & a_{1,0}b_{0,1} + a_{1,1}b_{1,1} \end{bmatrix} + \begin{bmatrix} a_{0,2}b_{2,0} + a_{0,3}b_{3,0} & a_{0,2}b_{2,1} + a_{0,3}b_{3,1} \\ a_{1,2}b_{2,0} + a_{1,3}b_{3,0} & a_{1,2}b_{2,1} + a_{1,3}b_{3,1} \end{bmatrix}$$

$$= \begin{bmatrix} a_{0,0}b_{0,0} + a_{0,1}b_{1,0} + a_{0,2}b_{2,0} + a_{0,3}b_{3,0} & a_{0,0}b_{0,1} + a_{0,1}b_{1,1} + a_{0,2}b_{2,1} + a_{0,3}b_{3,1} \\ a_{1,0}b_{0,0} + a_{1,1}b_{1,0} + a_{1,2}b_{2,0} + a_{1,3}b_{3,0} & a_{1,0}b_{0,1} + a_{1,1}b_{1,1} + a_{1,2}b_{2,1} + a_{1,3}b_{3,1} \end{bmatrix}$$

$$= C_{0,0}$$

(b) Multiplying $A_{0,0} \times B_{0,0}$ to obtain $C_{0,0}$

Figure 11.5 Submatrix multiplication.

A and one column of elements of **B** are needed for each processor, as shown in Figure 11.6. Using a master-slave approach, these elements could be sent from the master processor to the selected slave processors. Note that some of the same elements must be sent to more than one processor. Using submatrices, one processor would compute one $m \times m$ submatrix of C.

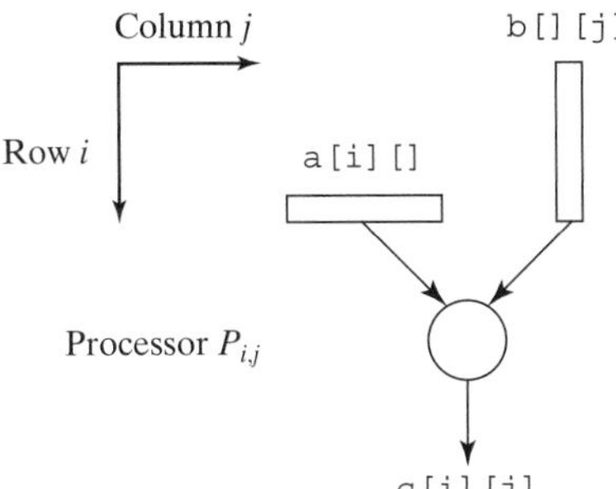

Figure 11.6 Direct implementation of matrix multiplication.

Analysis

Communication. Let us assume that $n \times n$ matrices are used but not submatrices. (Submatrices will be considered next.) With separate messages to each of the n^2 slave processors, each processor will receive one row of elements and one column of elements; that is, $2n$ elements. In addition, each slave will return one of the elements of **C** to the master processor, giving a communication time of

$$t_{\text{comm}} = n^2(t_{\text{startup}} + 2nt_{\text{data}}) + n^2(t_{\text{startup}} + t_{\text{data}}) = n^2(2t_{\text{startup}} + (2n + 1)t_{\text{data}})$$

The use of a master processor to collect results serializes this collection.

We can see that selective transmission of **A** and **B** elements involves excessive communication overhead and dominates the communication time. A single broadcast of the two complete matrices to each slave would usually, in fact, result in a reduced communication overhead depending upon the broadcast algorithm. A broadcast along a single bus would yield

$$t_{\text{comm}} = (t_{\text{startup}} + n^2t_{\text{data}}) + n^2(t_{\text{startup}} + t_{\text{data}})$$

The dominant time now is in returning the results, as t_{startup} is usually significantly larger than t_{data}. A gather routine should reduce the time in returning results if an efficient algorithm is used, such as one using a tree structure, as described in Chapter 2, Section 2.3.4.

Computation. The computation occurs only in the slaves. Each slave performs in parallel n multiplications and n additions; that is,

$$t_{\text{comp}} = 2n$$

The performance can be improved by using a tree construction so that n numbers can be added in $\log n$ steps using n processors. Figure 11.7 shows computing $c_{0,0}$ with 4×4 matrices. Thus, we can obtain a computational time complexity of $O(\log n)$ using n^3 processors instead of a computational time complexity of $O(n)$ using n^2 processors.

Submatrices. In every method, we can substitute submatrices for matrix elements to reduce the number of processors. Let us select $m \times m$ submatrices and $s = n/m$, that is, s rows and columns of $m \times m$ submatrices. Then there are s^2 submatrices in each matrix and s^2 processors.

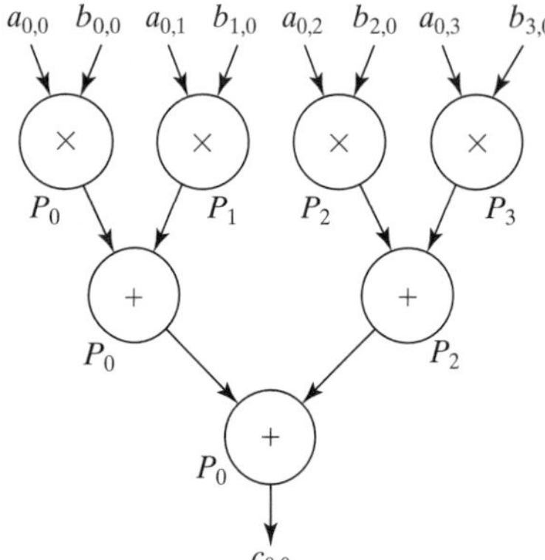

Figure 11.7 Accumulation using a tree construction.

Communication. Each of the s^2 slave processors must separately receive one row and one column of submatrices, consisting of m^2 elements each. In addition, each slave processor must separately return a C submatrix to the master processor (m^2 elements), giving a communication time of

$$t_{\text{comm}} = s^2\{2(t_{\text{startup}} + nmt_{\text{data}}) + (t_{\text{startup}} + m^2t_{\text{data}})\} = (n/m)^2\{3t_{\text{startup}} + (m^2 + 2\text{nm})t_{\text{data}}\}$$

Again, the complete matrices could be broadcast to every processor. As the size of the matrices, m, is increased (and in consequence the number of processors is decreased), the data transmission time of each message increases but the actual number of messages decreases. It is left as an exercise to determine whether this function has a minimum value, given m as a variable (Problem 11-1).

Computation. The total number of arithmetic operations remains essentially unchanged. Each slave performs in parallel s submatrix multiplications and s submatrix additions. One sequential submatrix multiplication requires m^3 multiplications and m^3 additions. A submatrix addition requires m^2 additions. Hence

$$t_{\text{comp}} = s(2m^3 + m^2) = \text{O}(sm^3) = \text{O}(nm^2)$$

Throughout, we assume that the result location is initially cleared and then values are added, so that the number of additions is the same as the number of values to be added to the accumulating sum.

11.2.3 Recursive Implementation

The block matrix multiplication algorithm suggests a recursive divide-and-conquer solution, as described by Horowitz and Zorat (1983) and Hake (1993). The method has significant potential for parallel implementations, especially shared memory implementations.

First, consider two $n \times n$ matrices, **A** and **B**, where n is a power of 2. (Problem 11-2 explores how to handle matrices when n is not a power of 2.) Each matrix is divided into four square submatrices, as was shown in Figure 11.5. Suppose the submatrices of **A** are labeled A_{pp}, A_{pq}, A_{qp}, and A_{qq}, and the submatrices of **B** are labeled B_{pp}, B_{pq}, B_{qp}, and B_{qq}

(p and q identifying the row and column positions). The final answer requires eight pairs of submatrices to be multiplied, $A_{pp} \times B_{pp}$, $A_{pq} \times B_{qp}$, $A_{pp} \times B_{pq}$, $A_{pq} \times B_{qp}$, $A_{qp} \times B_{pp}$, $A_{qq} \times B_{qp}$, $A_{qp} \times B_{pq}$, $A_{qq} \times B_{qq}$, and pairs of results to be added, as shown in Figure 11.8. The same algorithm could do each submatrix multiplication by decomposing each submatrix into four sub-submatrices, and so on. Hence, the algorithm can be written in recursive form:

```
mat_mult(A, B, s)
{
if (s == 1)                    /* if submatrix has one element */
   C = A * B;                  /* multiply elements */
else {                         /* else continue to make recursive calls */
   s = s/2;                    /* the number of elements in each row/column*/
   P0 = mat_mult(A_pp, B_pp, s);
   P1 = mat_mult(A_pq, B_qp, s);
   P2 = mat_mult(A_pp, B_pq, s);
   P3 = mat_mult(A_pq, B_qq, s);
   P4 = mat_mult(A_qp, B_pp, s);
   P5 = mat_mult(A_qq, B_qp, s);
   P6 = mat_mult(A_qp, B_pq, s);
   P7 = mat_mult(A_qq, B_qq, s);
   C_pp = P0 + P1;                /* add submatrix products */
   C_pq = P2 + P3;                /* to form submatrices of final matrix */
   C_qp = P4 + P5;
   C_qq = P6 + P7;
}
return (C);                       /* return final matrix */
}
```

Each of the eight recursive calls can be performed simultaneously and by separate processors. More processors can be assigned after further recursive calls. Generally, the number of processors needs to be a power of 8 if each processor is to be given one task of the tasks created by the recursive calls. The level of recursion can be limited by stopping, not when s (the number of elements on each row and column of each submatrix) is 1, but at some higher number dictated by the number of processors available. With eight processors, it may be better to stop the recursion at the first level (i.e., make $s = n/2$) (Hake, 1993) because any further division of the problems still requires the tasks to be mapped onto these processors.

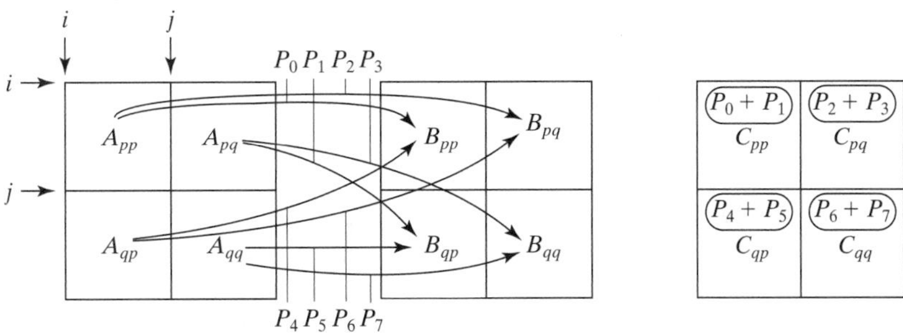

Figure 11.8 Submatrix multiplication and summation.

A very advantageous aspect of the method is that at each recursive call, the size of the data being passed is reduced and localized. This is ideal for the best performance of a multiprocessor system with cache memory. The method is especially suitable for shared memory systems, because specific message-passing is not part of the algorithm. In contrast, the matrix multiplication algorithms in the next sections have message-passing characteristics as part of the algorithms and are more applicable in message-passing systems.

11.2.4 Mesh Implementation

The most natural message-passing architecture for matrix operations is a two-dimensional mesh, where each node in the mesh computes one element (or submatrix) of the result array. The mesh connections will enable messages to pass between adjacent nodes in the mesh simultaneously. Even if the underlying architecture is not a mesh, a mesh can be modeled by appropriate numbering of the processors, although message contention and greater delays may exist. For example, using workstations on a single Ethernet line will certainly cause message contention with mesh algorithms, which would not occur when using an actual mesh computer with separate links between nodes. This performance aspect means that large blocks of elements (submatrices) will need to be processed in each node to reduce the internode communication.

There are several possible ways that matrix multiplication can be developed for a mesh organization. We will describe two methods, namely Cannon's algorithm and the systolic approach. Another matrix multiplication algorithm was devised by Fox; details can be found in Fox et al. (1988).

Cannon's Algorithm. Cannon's algorithm (Cannon, 1969) uses a mesh of processors with wraparound connections (a torus) to shift the **A** elements (or submatrices) left and the **B** elements (or submatrices) up, as illustrated in Figure 11.9. All the shifts are with wraparound. For clarity, we will refer to elements of the arrays **A** and **B**, though submatrices would normally be used. The algorithm can be described by the following steps:

1. Initially processor $P_{i,j}$ has elements $a_{i,j}$ and $b_{i,j}$ $(0 \le i < n,\ 0 \le j < n)$.
2. Elements are moved from their initial position to an "aligned" position. The complete ith row of **A** is shifted i places left, and the complete jth column of **B** is shifted j places upward. This has the effect of placing the element $a_{i,j+i}$ and the element $b_{i+j,j}$ in processor $P_{i,j}$, as illustrated in Figure 11.10. These elements are a pair of those required in the accumulation of $c_{i,j}$.

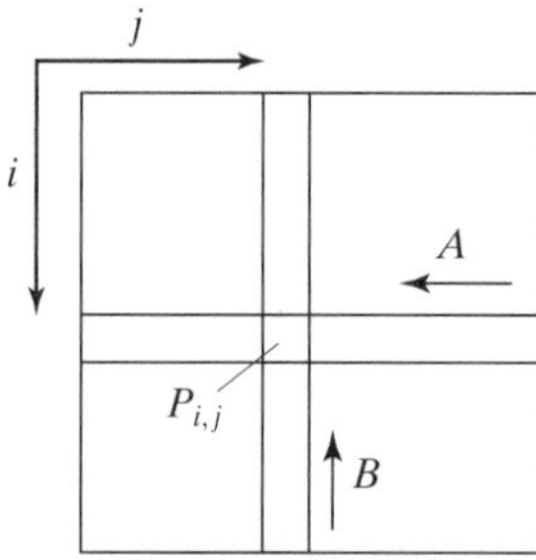

Figure 11.9 Movement of A and B elements.

3. Each processor, $P_{i,j}$, multiplies its elements.
4. The ith row of **A** is shifted one place left, and the jth column of **B** is shifted one place upward. This has the effect of bringing together the adjacent elements of **A** and **B**, which will also be required in the accumulation, as illustrated in Figure 11.11.
5. Each processor, $P_{i,j}$, multiplies the elements brought to it and adds the result to the accumulating sum.
6. Step 4 and 5 are repeated until the final result is obtained ($n - 1$ shifts with n rows and n columns of elements).

Additional storage for partial results is unnecessary with this algorithm.

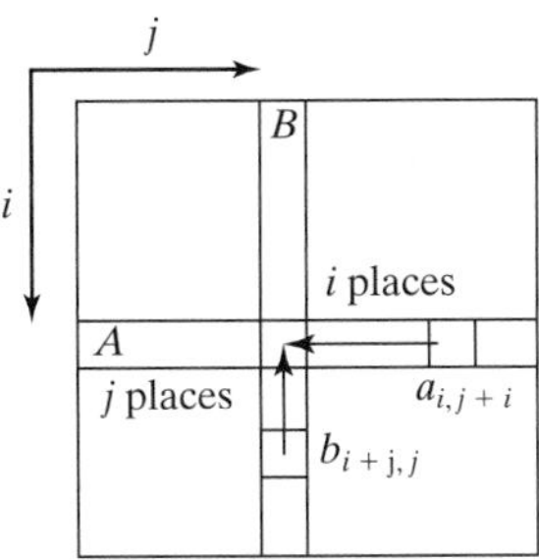

Figure 11.10 Step 2 — Alignment of elements of A and B.

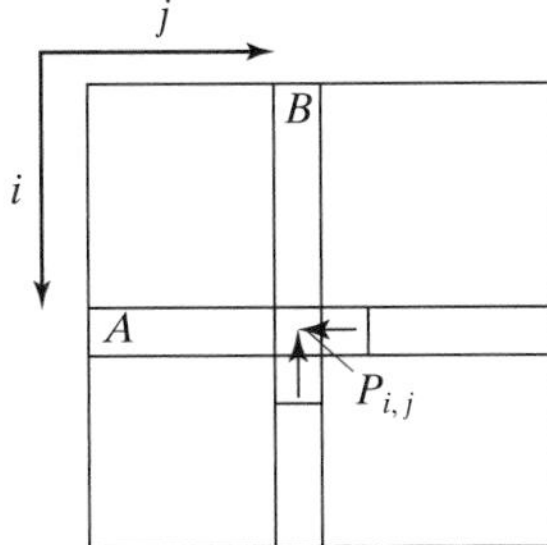

Figure 11.11 Step 4 — One-place shift of elements of A and B.

Analysis

Communication. Returning to submatrices, given s^2 submatrices, each of size $m \times m$, the initial alignment requires a maximum of $s - 1$ shift (communication) operations for **A** and **B** each. After that, there will be $s - 1$ shift operations for **A** and **B** each. Each shift operation involves $m \times m$ elements. Hence

$$t_{comm} = 4(s - 1)(t_{startup} + m^2 t_{data})$$

or a communication time complexity of $O(sm^2)$ or $O(mn)$.

Computation. Each submatrix multiplication requires m^3 multiplications and m^3 additions. Therefore, with $s - 1$ shifts,

$$t_{comp} = 2sm^3 = 2m^2 n$$

or a computational time complexity of $O(m^2 n)$.

Two-dimensional Pipeline — Systolic Array. The word *systolic* has been borrowed from the medical field—just as the heart pumps blood, information is pumped through a systolic array in various directions, and at regular intervals. In the two-dimensional systolic array considered here, information is pumped from left to right and from top to bottom. The information meets at internal nodes where the processing occurs. The same information passes onward (left to right, or downward).

Figure 11.12 shows a systolic array used to multiply two 4 × 4 matrices, **A** and **B**. The elements of **A** enter from the left, and the elements of **B** enter from the top. The final product terms of **C** will be held in the processors, as shown. A suitable numbering of processors uses *x* and *y* coordinates starting at (0, 0) in the top-left corner. Each processor, $P_{i,j}$, repeatedly performs the same algorithm (after c is initialized to zero):

```
recv(&a, Pi,j-1);          /* receive from left */
recv(&b, Pi-1,j);          /* receive from right */
c = c + a * b;             /* accumulate value for ci,j */
send(&a, Pi,j+1);          /* send to right */
send(&b, Pi+1,j);          /* send downwards */
```

which accumulates the required summations.

Let us consider what happens at $P_{0,0}$. First, $a_{0,0}$ and $b_{0,0}$ enter $P_{0,0}$, to produce $c_{0,0} = a_{0,0}b_{0,0}$. Both $a_{0,0}$ and $b_{0,0}$ are passed onward, $a_{0,0}$ right to $P_{0,1}$, and $b_{0,0}$ down

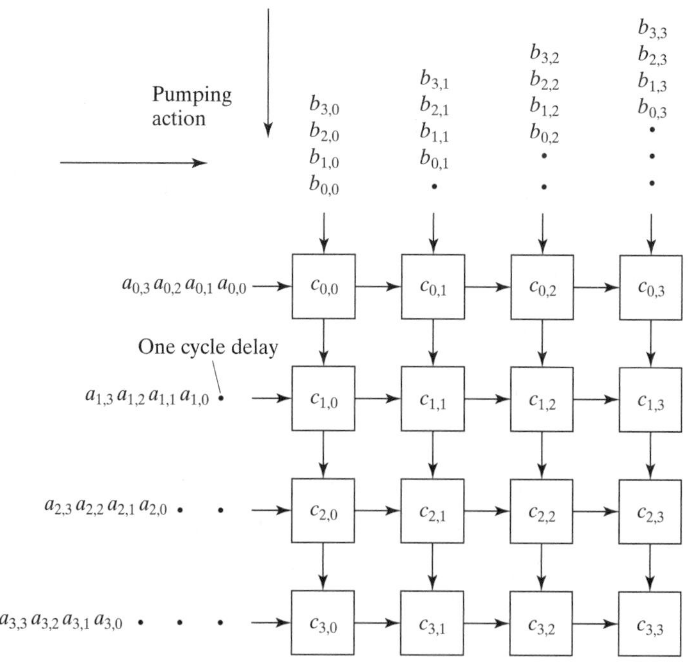

Figure 11.12 Matrix multiplication using a systolic array.

to $P_{1,0}$. Next, $P_{0,0}$, receives $a_{0,1}$ from the left and $b_{1,0}$ from above. After these numbers are multiplied, the product is added to $c_{0,0}$, and $a_{0,1}$ and $b_{1,0}$ are passed onward. Continuing with each of the other numbers that enter from left and top, finally after four "cycles," we get the required result:

$$c_{0,0} = a_{0,0}b_{0,0} + a_{0,1}b_{1,0} + a_{0,2}b_{2,0} + a_{0,3}b_{3,0}$$

$P_{0,1}$ operates in a similar manner but receives numbers from $P_{0,0}$ to the left one cycle later. Hence, the numbers from the top are also delayed by one cycle. $P_{0,1}$ starts with multiplying $a_{0,0}$ and $b_{0,1}$ and after four cycles obtains the value for $c_{0,1}$; i.e.,

$$c_{0,1} = a_{0,0}b_{0,1} + a_{0,1}b_{1,1} + a_{0,2}b_{2,1} + a_{0,3}b_{3,1}$$

A similar computation occurs with each of the other processors. Although there is no common clock signal, the computation operates in a synchronous fashion, timed by the `send()`s and `recv()`s. It is necessary to produce the elements of **A** and **B** at the inputs, as shown in Figure 11.12. The staggered layout of the elements is simply to indicate the timing. The method is also applicable to submatrix decomposition. Then the submatrices are used in place of the matrix elements.

Analysis. The analysis is quite similar to that for Cannon's algorithm and is left as an exercise (Problem 11-3).

Matrix-Vector Multiplication. Clearly, the methods for matrix multiplication can be applied to matrix-vector multiplication by simply using one column of the matrix **B**. A systolic array for matrix-vector multiplication is shown in Figure 11.13.

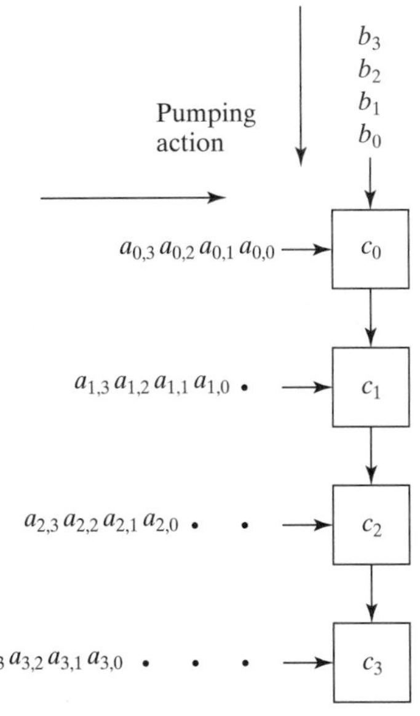

Figure 11.13 Matrix-vector multiplication using a systolic array.

11.2.5 Other Matrix Multiplication Methods

The $O(n^3)$ time complexity of sequential matrix multiplication can be improved very slightly by a clever method originated by Strassen (1969). This method is given in Problem 11-4 and is also described in textbooks on algorithms, such as Aho, Hopcroft, and Ullman (1974) and Cormen, Leiserson, and Rivest (1990). It results in a time complexity of $O(n^{2.81})$. Subsequently, researchers have come up with slight improvements on this time complexity ($O(n^{2.376})$). However, the added complexities of these methods do not generally warrant using them unless n is really large. Hake (1993) presents the results of using the basic divide-and-conquer matrix multiplication algorithm and Strassen's algorithm on a Cray-Y-MP; they show a slightly improved execution speed using Strassen's method. Matrix multiplication can also employ a three-dimensional array.

11.3 SOLVING A SYSTEM OF LINEAR EQUATIONS

11.3.1 Linear Equations

Suppose we have a system of linear equations:

$$
\begin{array}{lcll}
a_{n-1,0}x_0 + a_{n-1,1}x_1 + a_{n-1,2}x_2 & \cdots & + a_{n-1,n-1}x_{n-1} & = b_{n-1} \\
 & \vdots & & \\
a_{2,0}x_0 + a_{2,1}x_1 + a_{2,2}x_2 & \cdots & + a_{2,n-1}x_{n-1} & = b_2 \\
a_{1,0}x_0 + a_{1,1}x_1 + a_{1,2}x_2 & \cdots & + a_{1,n-1}x_{n-1} & = b_1 \\
a_{0,0}x_0 + a_{0,1}x_1 + a_{0,2}x_2 & \cdots & + a_{0,n-1}x_{n-1} & = b_0
\end{array}
$$

which, in matrix form, is

$$\mathbf{Ax} = \mathbf{b}$$

The objective of solving this system of equations is to find values for the unknowns, x_0, x_1, …, x_{n-1}, given values for $a_{0,0}$, $a_{0,1}$, …, $a_{n-1,n-1}$, and b_0, …, b_n (i.e., the matrix A and vector b). In some applications, some of the values in matrix A may be zero. Matrices are regarded as *dense matrices* if most of the elements in the matrix are nonzero, and as sparse matrices if a significant number of the elements is zero. The reason the two are differentiated is that less computationally intensive and perhaps more space-efficient methods are available for sparse matrices. Perhaps a more accurate definition of *dense* and *sparse* is whether the simpler computational methods that take advantage of the zero entries can be applied to the matrix.

Throughout this section, we will assume that the matrix **A** is dense. The equations will then be solved *directly* by mathematical manipulation. In Section 11.4, we will explore *iterative* methods for problems in which the matrix **A** is sparse. We have already seen methods of solving a system of linear equations in previous chapters, in connection with specific parallel programming techniques. A general system of linear equations was solved by iteration in Chapter 6, Section 6.2.1, a method that is particularly suitable for a sparse matrix **A**. An upper triangular system of linear equations was also solved by back substitution using a pipeline in Chapter 5, Section 5.2.4. In fact, solving an upper triangular system of linear equations is the final step in solving a general system of linear equations using the direct technique called Gaussian elimination, which will be described next, together with the possibilities of parallelizing Gaussian elimination.

11.3.2 Gaussian Elimination

The objective of Gaussian elimination is to convert the general system of linear equations, as given in Section 11.3.1, into a triangular system of equations. The method uses the characteristic of linear equations that any row can be replaced by that row added to another row multiplied by a constant. The procedure starts at the first row and works toward the bottom row. At the ith row, each row j below the ith row is replaced by row j + (row i) $(-a_{j,i}/a_{i,i})$. The constant used for row j is $-a_{j,i}/a_{i,i}$. This has the effect of making all the elements in the ith column below the ith row zero because

$$a_{j,i} = a_{j,i} + a_{i,i}\left(\frac{-a_{j,i}}{a_{i,i}}\right) = 0$$

Figure 11.14 shows the situation when row i is being considered. Row i is called the *pivot row*. At this stage, all the columns to the left of column i below the diagonal will have already been set to zero by previous actions. All the columns to the right of column i below the diagonal will be set to zero by subsequent actions. Once the procedure has continued to the last row, the resultant system will be an upper triangular system.

Unfortunately, the procedure does not exhibit good stability on digital computers. In particular, if $a_{i,i}$ is zero or close to zero, we will not be able to compute the quantity $-a_{j,i}/a_{i,i}$. The procedure must be modified into so-called *partial pivoting* by swapping the ith row with the row below it that has the largest absolute element in the ith column of any

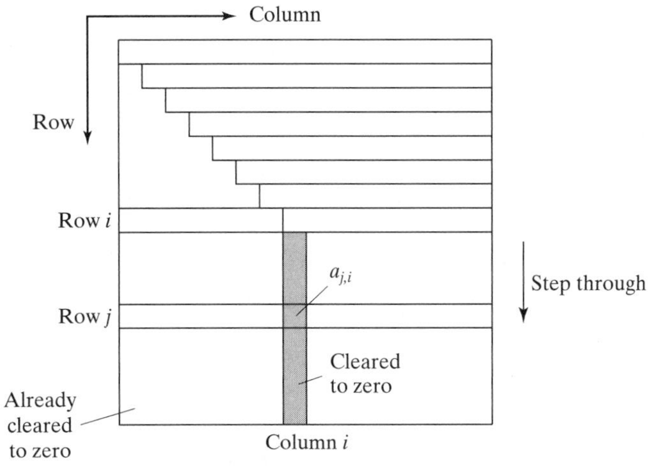

Figure 11.14 Gaussian elimination.

of the rows below the *i*th row if there is one. (Reordering equations will not affect the system.) Then the Gaussian elimination procedure takes place on the *i*th row. The numerical stability has to be checked at each step through the procedure and cannot be done prior to the start of the Gaussian elimination. In the following, we will not consider partial pivoting, which will incur additional computations.

Sequential Code. The following is an outline of the sequential code to implement Gaussian elimination without partial pivoting:

```
for (i = 0; i < n-1; i++)          /* for each row, except last */
   for (j = i+1; j < n; j++) {     /* step through subsequent rows */
      m = a[j][i]/a[i][i];         /* Compute multiplier */
      for (k = i; k < n; k++)      /* modify last n-i-1 elements of row j */
         a[j][k] = a[j][k] - a[i][k] * m;
      b[j] = b[j] - b[i] * m;      /* modify right side */
   }
```

The time complexity is $O(n^3)$.

11.3.3 Parallel Implementation

Looking at the sequential code, clearly there is scope for parallelization. The inner loop modifying row j involves independent operations on the elements of row j. One way to partition the problem is to arrange for each processor to hold and operate on one row of elements. This requires n processors for n equations. Before a processor can operate on its row, it must receive the elements from row i, which can be achieved through a broadcast operation. First, processor P_0 (holding row 0) broadcasts elements of its row to each of the other $n - 1$ processors. Then these processors compute their multipliers and modify their rows. The procedure is repeated with each of P_1, P_2 … P_{n-2} broadcasting elements of their rows. The elements of row i broadcast by P_i are `a[i][i+1]`, `a[i][i+2]`, …, `a[i][n-1]`, and `b[i]`, a total of $n - i + 1$ elements, for $0 \leq i < n - 1$, as shown in Figure 11.15. Processors P_{i+1} to P_{n-1} inclusive receive the broadcast message (at total $n - i - 1$ processors) and operate upon $n - i + 1$ elements of their rows.

Analysis

Communication. Suppose the broadcast messages could be done in one step. There are $n - 1$ broadcast messages that must be performed sequentially because the rows are altered after each broadcast. The *i*th broadcast message contains $n - i + 1$ elements. Hence, the total message communication is given by

$$t_{\text{comm}} = \sum_{i=0}^{n-2} (t_{\text{startup}} + (n - i + 1)t_{\text{data}}) = \left((n-1)t_{\text{startup}} + \left(\frac{(n+2)(n+1)}{2} - 3\right)t_{\text{data}}\right)$$

or a time complexity of $O(n^2)$. For large n, the data time t_{data} could dominate the overall communication time in the early stages. In practice, each broadcast message requires more than one step, depending upon the underlying system architecture.

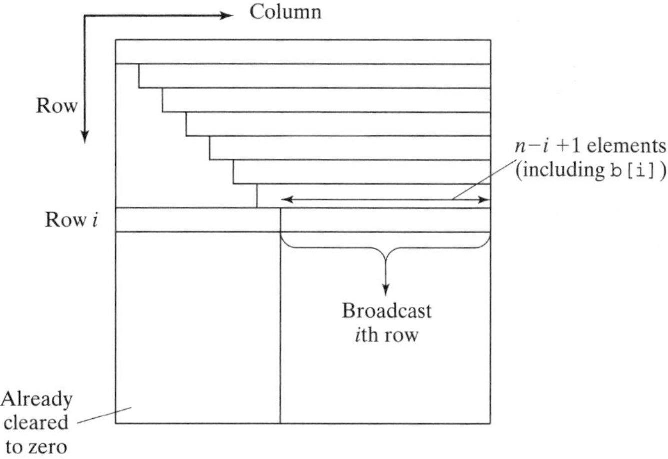

Figure 11.15 Broadcast in parallel implementation of Gaussian elimination.

Computation. After a row has been broadcast, each processor P_j beyond the broadcast processor P_i will receive the message, compute its multiplier, and operate upon $n-j+2$ elements of its row. Ignoring the computation of the multiplier, there are $n-j+2$ multiplications and $n-j+2$ subtractions. Hence, the computation consists of

$$t_{\text{comp}} = 2\sum_{j=1}^{n-1}(n-j+2) = \frac{(n+3)(n+2)}{2} - 3 = \text{O}(n^2)$$

Note that the efficiency will be relatively low because none of the processors before the processor holding row i participate in the computation again. At first, $n-1$ processors will have computation, then $n-2$ processors, then $n-3$ processors, and so on. At each step less work need be done. It is left as an exercise to derive the efficiency (Problem 11-15).

Pipeline Configuration. The processors could be formed into a pipeline configuration, as shown in Figure 11.16.

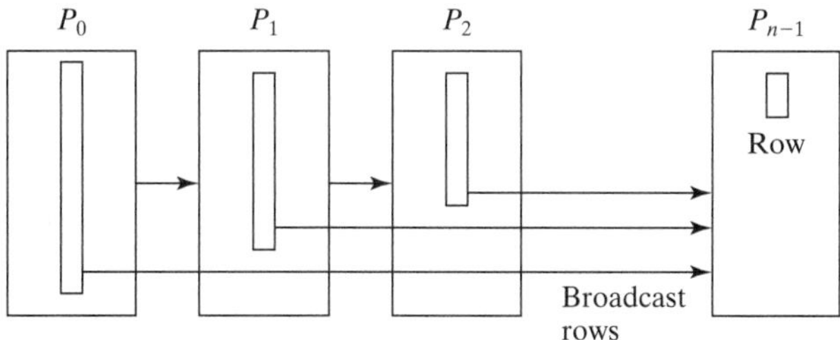

Figure 11.16 Pipeline implementation of Gaussian elimination.

Partitioning. To reduce the number of processors to less than n, we can partition the matrix into groups of rows for each processor, such as the so-called *strip partitioning* shown in Figure 11.17. With p processors, each processor holds n/p rows. Unfortunately,

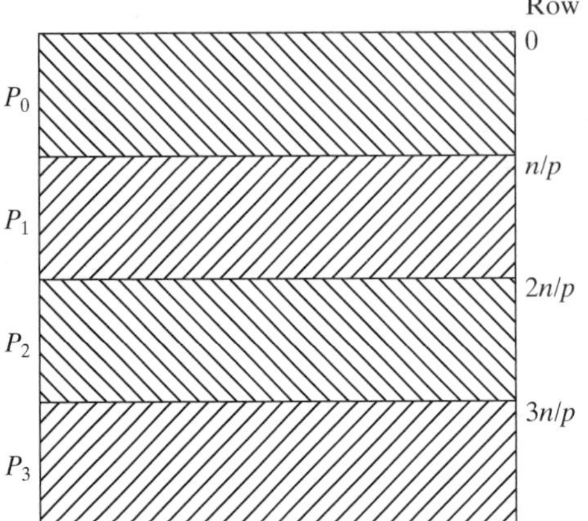

Figure 11.17 Strip partitioning.

again processors do not participate in the computation after their last row is processed. An alternative, which actually equalizes the processor workload, is the *cyclic-striped partitioning*, as shown in Figure 11.18. Now each processor will have some activity for a greater period. For example, P_0 is assigned rows 0, n/p, $2n/p$, $3n/p$ and is active until row $3n/p$ is passed. P_1 is assigned rows 1, $n/p + 1$, $2n/p + 1$, $3n/p + 1$ and is active until row $3n/p + 1$ is passed. A final way the matrix could be partitioned is in a checkerboard fashion, as we partitioned processors for matrix multiplication.

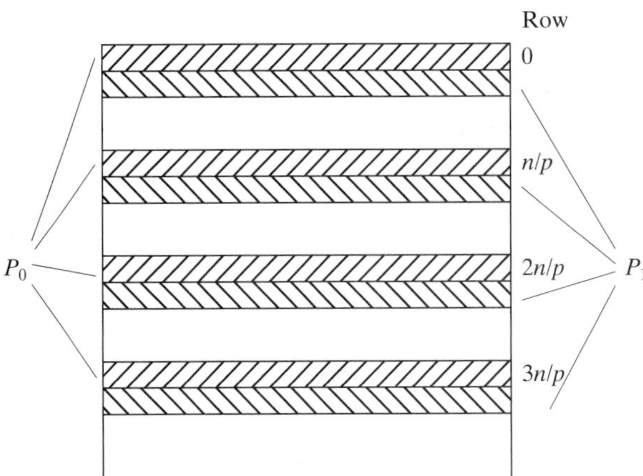

Figure 11.18 Cyclic partitioning to equalize workload.

11.4 ITERATIVE METHODS

In this section, we explore methods of solving both a system of linear equations and partial differential equations by iteration. We show the relationship between solving partial differential equations by a discrete method and solving a system of linear equations.

11.4.1 Jacobi Iteration

The basic *Jacobi iteration method* has already been introduced, in Chapter 6, Section 6.3.1, in the context of local synchronization. Given a general system of n linear equations:

$$\mathbf{Ax} = \mathbf{b}$$

Jacobi iterations are described by the following iteration formula:

$$x_i^k = \frac{1}{a_{i,i}}\left[b_i - \sum_{j \neq i} a_{i,j} x_j^{k-1}\right]$$

where the superscript indicates the iteration; that is, x_i^k is kth iteration of x_i and x_j^{k-1} is the (k-1)th iteration of x_j ($0 \le i < n$, $0 \le j < n$). The iteration formula is simply the ith equation rearranged to have the ith unknown on the left side.

Thus, we have given two methods for solving the system of linear equations: a direct method (Gaussian elimination) and an iterative method. The time complexity of the direct method is significant at $O(n^2)$ with n processors. The time complexity of the iteration method will depend upon the number of iterations and the required accuracy.

The iterative method has a particular application in solving a system of sparse linear equations; that is, a system of linear equations in which the equations do not have many terms. Such equations appear in solving partial differential equations. A good example of a fundamental partial differential equation is Laplace's equation:

$$\frac{\partial^2 f}{\partial x^2} + \frac{\partial^2 f}{\partial y^2} = 0$$

The objective is to solve for f over the two-dimensional space having coordinates x and y. The following methods can also be applied to Poisson's equation, another fundamental equation, which is similar to Laplace's equation except that the right-hand side is a function. Problem 11-8 explores the changes that are necessary.

For a computer solution, *finite difference* methods are appropriate. Here the two-dimensional solution space is "discretized" into a large number of solution points, as shown in Figure 11.19. If the distance between the points in the x and y directions, Δ, is made small

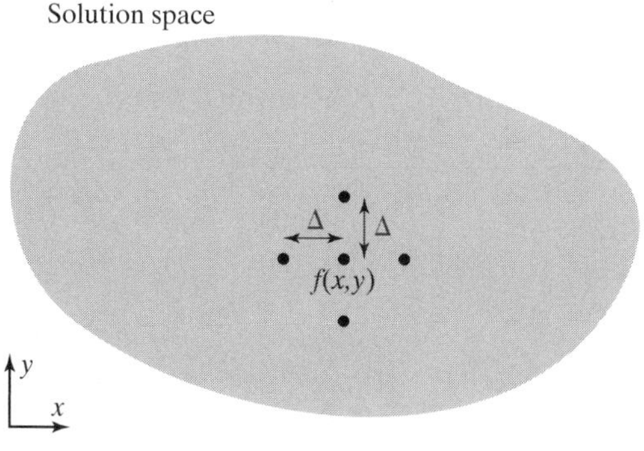

Figure 11.19 Finite difference method.

enough, the central difference approximation of the second derivative can be used:

$$\frac{\partial^2 f}{\partial x^2} \approx \frac{1}{\Delta^2}[f(x+\Delta, y) - 2f(x, y) + f(x-\Delta, y)]$$

$$\frac{\partial^2 f}{\partial y^2} \approx \frac{1}{\Delta^2}[f(x, y+\Delta) - 2f(x, y) + f(x, y-\Delta)]$$

[See Bertsekas and Tsitsiklis (1989) for proof.] Substituting into Laplace's equation, we get

$$\frac{1}{\Delta^2}[f(x+\Delta, y) + f(x-\Delta, y) + f(x, y+\Delta) + f(x, y-\Delta) - 4f(x, y)] = 0$$

Rearranging, we get

$$f(x, y) = \frac{[f(x-\Delta, y) + f(x, y-\Delta) + f(x+\Delta, y) + f(x, y+\Delta)]}{4}$$

that is, the result used in Chapter 6, Section 6.3.2.

The formula can be rewritten as an iterative formula:

$$f^k(x, y) = \frac{[f^{k-1}(x-\Delta, y) + f^{k-1}(x, y-\Delta) + f^{k-1}(x+\Delta, y) + f^{k-1}(x, y+\Delta)]}{4}$$

where $f^k(x, y)$ is the value obtained from kth iteration, and $f^{k-1}(x, y)$ is the value obtained from the $(k-1)$th iteration. By repeated application of the formula, we can converge on the solution, as we saw in Chapter 6.

As in Chapter 6, we will assume that the solution space is square and the solution points are arranged in rows. Let m be the number of points on each row, so that there are m rows and the array has $m \times m$ points. For computational convenience, the boundaries are made of points, but the points have known values. The boundary points are used in computing points adjacent to the boundaries and are included in the $m \times m$ array. Suppose the points are numbered from 1 in so-called *natural order*, which is row by row in the mesh. The first row has the points $x_1, x_2, x_3, \ldots, x_m$. The next row has the points $x_{m+1}, x_{m+2}, x_{m+3}, \ldots, x_{2m}$ and so on, as shown in Figure 11.20 for 100 points with 10 points on each row (including boundaries whose values are known).

Relationship with a General System of Linear Equations. The ith point is computed from the ith equation. This equation has the points x_i, x_{i-1}, x_{i-m}, x_{i+1}, and x_{i+m} using natural ordering:

$$x_i = \frac{x_{i-m} + x_{i-1} + x_{i+1} + x_{i+m}}{4}$$

or

$$x_{i-m} + x_{i-1} - 4x_i + x_{i+1} + x_{i+m} = 0$$

which is a linear equation with five unknowns (except those with boundary points). In general form, the ith equation becomes:

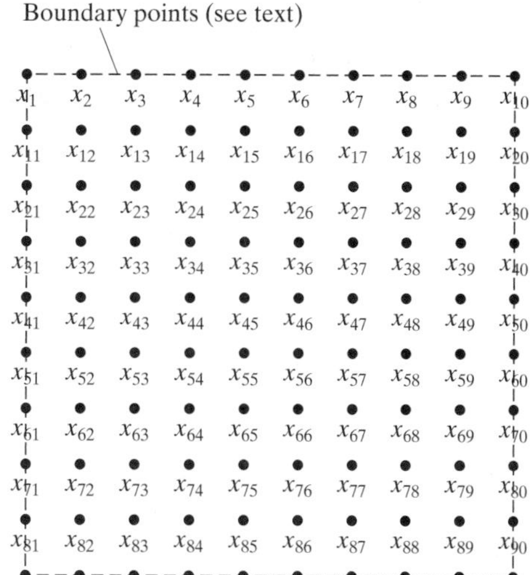

Figure 11.20 Mesh of points numbered in natural order.

$$a_{i,i-m}\,x_{i-m} + a_{i,i-1}\,x_{i-1} + a_{i,i}\,x_i + a_{i,i+1}\,x_{i+1} + a_{i,i+m}\,x_{i+m} = 0$$

where $a_{i,i} = -4$, and $a_{i,i-m} = a_{i,i-1} = a_{i,i+1} = a_{i,i+m} = 1$.

The matrix-vector form of equations is shown in Figure 11.21. The vector **x** includes known boundary variables (and four unused corner points). Similarly, the matrix **A** includes the boundary values (and unused entries). For example, in Figure 11.20, the variables x_1, x_2, x_3, x_4, x_5, x_6, x_7, x_8, x_9, x_{10}, x_{11}, x_{20}, x_{21}, x_{30}, x_{31}, x_{40}, x_{41}, x_{50}, x_{51}, x_{60}, x_{61}, x_{70}, x_{71}, x_{80}, x_{81}, x_{90}, x_{91}, x_{92}, x_{93}, x_{94}, x_{95}, x_{96}, x_{97}, x_{98}, x_{99}, and x_{100} in **x** are set to 1, and the corresponding $a_{i,i}$ entries in **A** are boundary constants. The general characteristics of **A** can be seen. The diagonal element is –4, and this is surrounded by a 1 on each side, and further entries of 1 are n elements away from the diagonal on each side. Only equations with unknowns on the diagonal are used in the solution, and the boundary values in these equations can be moved to the right side as constants.

For an array with many points, the matrix is very large and sparse. In such cases, iterative methods are attractive because they use less memory and can more quickly reach an acceptable solution.

Convergence Speed. Unfortunately, Jacobi iterations may converge slowly, depending upon the matrix (and in some instances will not converge!). According to Leighton (1992), for certain classes of matrices, such as diagonally dominant matrices (matrices in which the diagonal element on each row exceeds the sum of the absolute values of the other elements on the row), Jacobi relaxation will converge "to a good solution" in log n steps. In these cases, the parallel time complexity is potentially O(log n) with n processors, which is better than using Gaussian elimination. Of course, this all depends upon the convergence rate. Let us now look at potentially faster convergence methods.

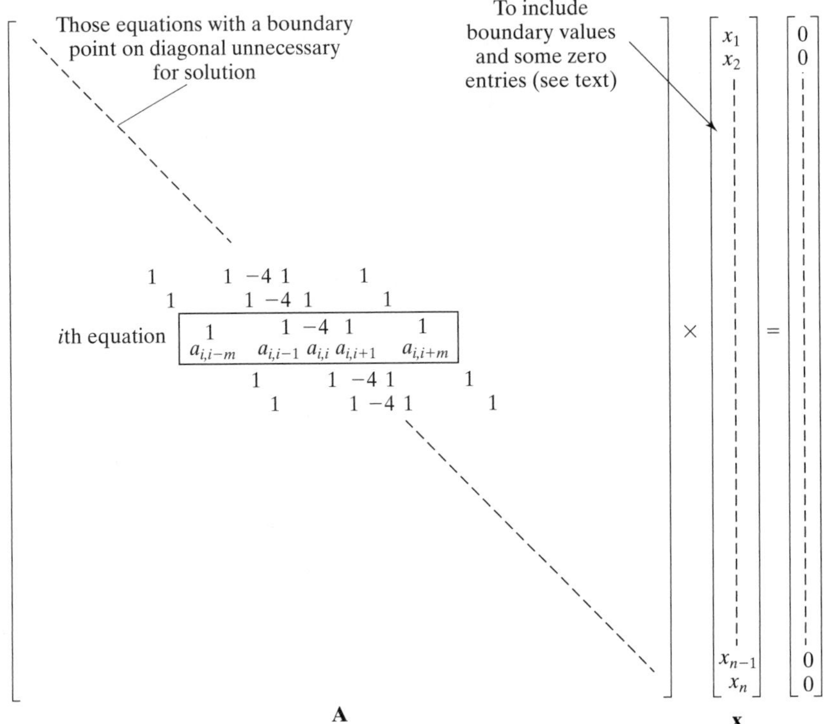

Figure 11.21 Sparse matrix for Laplace's equation.

11.4.2 Faster Convergence Methods

Gauss-Seidel Relaxation. One way to attempt a faster convergence is to use some of the newly computed values to compute other values in the iteration. Suppose we compute the values sequentially in natural order, x_1, x_2, x_3, and so on. When x_i is being computed, $x_1, x_2, \ldots, x_{i-1}$ will have already been computed, and these values could be used in the iteration formula for x_i, together with the previous values of $x_{i+1}, x_{i+2}, \ldots, x_n$, which have not yet been recomputed. This method is known as the *Gauss-Seidel relaxation* method. It usually (but not necessarily) has a higher convergence rate than the basic Jacobi method and is particularly convenient for sequential programming since each point can be computed in a specific sequential order.

Gauss-Seidel iteration employs the following iteration formula:

$$x_i^k = \frac{1}{a_{i,i}}\left[b_i - \sum_{j=1}^{i-1} a_{i,j}x_j^k - \sum_{j=i+1}^{n} a_{i,j}x_j^{k-1}\right]$$

where the superscript indicates the iteration; that is, the kth iteration uses values from the kth iteration and values from the (k–1)th iteration. For Laplace's equation with natural ordering of unknowns, the formula reduces to

$$x_i^k = (-1/a_{i,i})[a_{i,i-n}\,x_{i-n}^k + a_{i,i-1}x_{i-1}^k + a_{i,i+1}x_{i+1}^{k-1} + a_{i,i+n}\,x_{i+1}^{k-1}]$$

(Note that $a_{i,i} = -4$.) At the kth iteration, two of the four values (of the points before the ith element) are taken from the kth iteration, and two values (of the points after the ith element) are taken from the $(k-1)$th iteration. Using the original finite difference notation, we have

$$f^k(x, y) = \frac{[f^k(x-\Delta, y) + f^k(x, y-\Delta) + f^{k-1}(x+\Delta, y) + f^{k-1}(x, y+\Delta)]}{4}$$

Of course, to be able to use this formula, we must have computed certain values from the kth iteration before computing other values, which suggests that each computation must be performed in a prescribed order. In the Gauss-Seidel method, the update is in natural order. Hence, the computation will sweep across the mesh of points, as illustrated in Figure 11.22. This is not a very convenient characteristic for parallelizing the method (except perhaps for a linear pipeline solution). However, the ordering can be changed to make the method more amenable to parallelization.

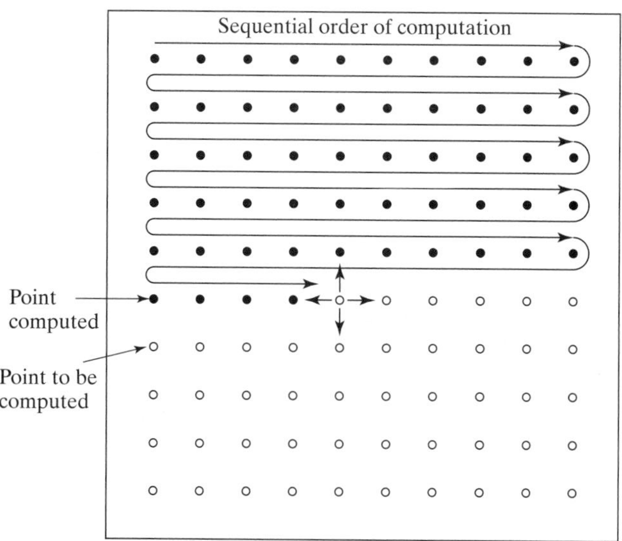

Figure 11.22 Gauss-Seidel relaxation with natural order, computed sequentially.

Red-Black Ordering. In red-black ordering, the mesh of points is divided into "red" points and "black" points, which are interleaved, as shown in Figure 11.23. The black points are computed using four neighboring red points. The red points are computed using four neighboring black points. The computation is organized in two phases that are repeated until the values converge. First, the black points are computed. Next, the red points are computed. All the black points can be computed simultaneously, and all the red points can be computed simultaneously. The black points can be identified by the subscript (i, j) when $i + j$ is even (say), and the red points when $i + j$ is odd. Clearly, this method is amenable to parallelization.

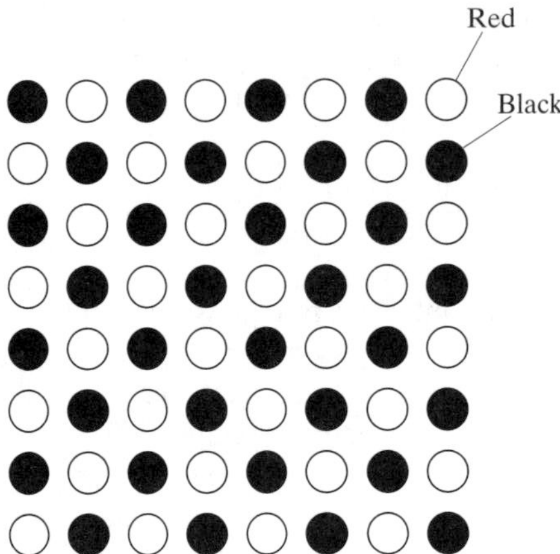

Figure 11.23 Red-black ordering.

Parallel Code. Using a forall construct to describe parallelism, the code could be of the form

```
forall (i = 1; i < m; i++)
  forall (j = 1; j < m; j++)
    if ((i + j) % 2 != 0)                    /* compute red points */
      f[i][j] = 0.25*(f[i-1][j] + f[i][j-1] + f[i+1][j] + f[i][j+1]);
forall (i = 1; i < m; i++)
  forall (j = 1; j < m; j++)
    if ((i + j) % 2 == 0)                    /* compute black points */
      f[i][j] = 0.25*(f[i-1][j] + f[i][j-1] + f[i+1][j] + f[i][j+1]);
```

where the array has $(m - 1) \times (m - 1)$ interior data points. It would be more computationally efficient to avoiding using the mod operator, perhaps by using two separate arrays, one for black points and one for red points. This modification is left as an exercise (Problem 11-11).

Processor Assignment. If we were to assign one processor to each point, each of the processors would be idle half of the time. A more efficient allocation would be to assign one processor to a pair of adjacent points, one red and one black. Now $(m - 1)^2/2$ processors would be needed for $(m - 1)^2$ points.

Large Partitions. Normally, we would want to use fewer processors than number of points in the mesh. The red-black ordering described here can be extended to *a red-black checkerboard,* as described by Fox et al. (1988), in which the mesh is divided into red regions and black regions, each holding not one point but a group of adjacent points. Then the red regions can be computed simultaneously, and the black regions can be computed simultaneously. The points within red and black regions are computed sequentially by individual processors.

Higher-Order Difference Methods. So far, we have used four neighboring points in the computation. In an attempt to increase the speed of convergence and accuracy, more distant points could be used in the computation. The following update formula:

$$f^k(x, y) =$$

$$\frac{1}{60}\Big[16f^{k-1}(x-\Delta, y) + 16f^{k-1}(x, y-\Delta) + 16f^{k-1}(x+\Delta, y) + 16f^{k-1}(x, y+\Delta)$$

$$-f^{k-1}(x-2\Delta, y) - f^{k-1}(x, y-2\Delta) - f^{k-1}(x+2\Delta, y) - f^{k-1}(x, y+2\Delta)\Big]$$

uses eight nearby points to update a point, as shown in Figure 11.24, the so-called *nine-point (star) stencil* (rather than the five-point "star" stencil previously). Here, we are counting the central point in the stencil size; this point can be used in iteration formulas (see, for example, Problem 11-10.)

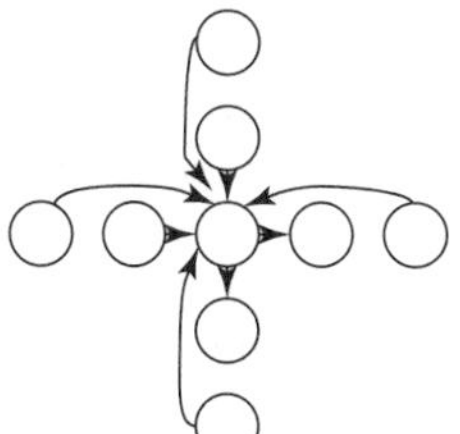

Figure 11.24 Nine-point stencil.

There are several alternative stencils. For example, the nine-point stencil is like the five-point star stencil except that it also uses the nearest diagonals; the 13-point star stencil uses the points of the nine-point star and also the nearest diagonals. There is a trade-off between more computation per step and fewer steps to converge. The most obvious way to map processors onto the mesh of points is either to use a column of points for each processor or to divide the mesh into a checkerboard, with each processor having one square group of points. Terrano, Dunn, and Peters (1989) showed that the optimum way is, in fact, to arrange each processor to have a polygon whose edges are defined by the points in the stencil that are the farthest from the center. For example, a simple five-point star stencil creates a diamond-shaped polygon. Mapping several points onto one processor still leads to a diamond shape for each processor.

Overrelaxation. Improved convergence can be obtained by adding the factor $(1 - \omega)x_i$ to either the Jacobi or the Gauss-Seidel formula to obtain so-called *Jacobi overrelaxation* or *Gauss-Seidel successive overrelaxation*, respectively. The factor ω is the *overrelaxation parameter.* The Jacobi overrelaxation formula (for the general system of linear equations) is

$$x_i^k = \frac{\omega}{a_{ii}}\left[b_i - \sum_{j \neq i} a_{ij}x_i^{k-1}\right] + (1-\omega)x_i^{k-1}$$

where $0 < \omega < 1$. The Gauss-Seidel successive overrelaxation (for the general system of linear equations) is

$$x_i^k = \frac{\omega}{a_{ii}}\left[b_i - \sum_{j=1}^{i-1} a_{ij}x_i^k - \sum_{j=i+1}^{N} a_{ij}x_i^{k-1}\right] + (1-\omega)x_i^{k-1}$$

where $0 < \omega \leq 2$. If $\omega = 1$, we obtain the Gauss-Seidel method.

Multigrid Method. So far, we have used a fixed number of points. In the *multigrid method*, the iterative process operates on a grid of points as previously, but the number of points is altered at stages during the computation. First, a coarse grid of points is used (i.e., the solution space is divided into relatively few points). With these points, the iteration process will start to converge quickly. At some stage, the number of points is increased to include the points of the coarse grid and extra points between the points of the coarse grid. The initial values of the extra points can be found by interpolation. The computation continues with this finer grid. The grid can be made finer and finer as the computation proceeds, or the computation can alternate between fine and coarse grids. The coarser grids take distant effects into account more quickly and provide a good starting point for the next finer grid.

For convenience, the grid sizes will usually be powers of 2. Suppose the finest grid has $2^r \times 2^r$ points. The next coarse grid will have $2^{r-1} \times 2^{r-1}$ points, and the next coarser grid $2^{r-2} \times 2^{r-2}$ points. Figure 11.25 shows one coarse grid point allocated to each processor. Leighton (1992) suggests that a suitable number of different levels of grids is $\log r$, that is, the grid sizes are $2^k \times 2^k$ for $1 < k \leq \log r$.

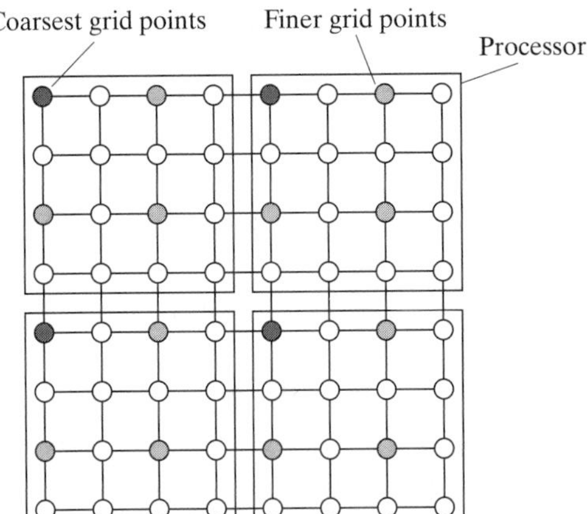

Figure 11.25 Multigrid processor allocation.

In some problems, it may be better to have different grid sizes (point separations) at different places within the solution space. The grid size could be adapted to suit the local computation (so-called *adaptive grid* methods). More details of such methods can be found in various research papers; for example, De Keyser and Roose (1997).

11.5 SUMMARY

This chapter discussed in detail numerical topics introduced in earlier chapters:

- Different parallel implementations of matrix multiplication (direct, recursive, mesh)
- Solving a system of linear equations using Gaussian elimination and its parallel implementation
- Solving partial differential equations using Jacobi iteration
- Relationships with systems of linear equations
- Faster convergence methods (Gauss-Seidel relaxation, red-black ordering, higher-order difference methods, overrelaxation, multigrid method)

FURTHER READING

The primary authoritative reference on parallel numerical methods is Bertsekas and Tsitsiklis (1989). Other senior undergraduate/graduate-level texts devoted to parallel numerical algorithms include Freeman and Phillips (1992), Modi (1988), and Smith (1993). Grama et al. (2003) offer significant treatment on parallel methods using dense and sparse matrices. Chaudhuri (1992) features a chapter on matrix computations, including a treatment of Boolean matrices. Other topics for further study include the conjugate gradient method and the finite element method. An excellent source of additional information on parallel methods is Van de Velde (1994). A text on iterative solution of linear systems is Young (1971). Texts dedicated to multigrid methods include Hackbrush (1985).

BIBLIOGRAPHY

AHO, A. V., J. E. HOPCROFT, AND J. D. ULLMAN (1974), *The Design and Analysis of Computer Algorithms*, Addison-Wesley, Reading, MA.

AVILA, J. (1994), "A Breadth-First Approach to Parallel Processing for Undergraduates," *Conf. Par. Computing for Undergraduates*, Colgate University, June 22–24.

BERTSEKAS, D. P., AND J. N. TSITSIKLIS (1989), *Parallel and Distributed Computation Numerical Methods*. Prentice Hall, Englewood Cliffs, NJ.

CANNON, L. E. (1969), *A Cellular Computer to Implement the Kalman Filter Algorithm*, Ph.D. thesis, Montana State University, Bozman, MT.

CHAUDHURI, P. (1992), *Fundamentals of Parallel Algorithms*, Prentice Hall, Englewood Cliffs, NJ.

CORMEN, T. H., C. E. LEISERSON, AND R. L. RIVEST (1990), *Introduction to Algorithms*, MIT Press, Cambridge, MA.

DE KEYSER, J., AND D. ROOSE (1997), "A Software Tool for Load Balanced Adaptive Multiple Grids on Distributed Memory Computers," *Proc. 6th Distrib. Memory Comput. Conf.*, IEEE CS Press, Los Alamitos, CA, pp. 122–128.

FOX, G., M. JOHNSON, G. LYZENGA, S. OTTO, J. SALMON, AND D. WALKER (1988), *Solving Problems on Concurrent Processors,* Volume 1, Prentice Hall, Englewood Cliffs, NJ.

FREEMAN, T. L., AND C. PHILLIPS (1992), *Parallel Numerical Algorithms*, Prentice Hall, London.

GRAMA, A., A. GUPTA, G. KARYPIS, AND V. KUMAR (2003), *Introduction to Parallel Computing,* 2nd edition, Benjamin/Cummings, Redwood City, CA.

HACKBRUSH, W. (1985), *Multigrid Methods with Applications*, Springer-Verlag, New York.

HAKE, J.-F. (1993), "Parallel Algorithms for Matrix Operations and Their Performance on Multiprocessor Systems," in *Advances in Parallel Algorithms*, L. Kronsjö and D. Shumsheruddin, eds., Halsted Press, New York.

HOROWITZ, E., AND A. ZORAT (1983), "Divide-and-Conquer for Parallel Processing," *IEEE Trans. Comput.*, Vol. C-32, No. 6, pp. 582–585.

KREYSZIG, E. (1962), *Advanced Mathematics*, Wiley, New York.

LEIGHTON, F. T. (1992), *Introduction to Parallel Algorithms and Architectures: Arrays, Trees, Hypercubes*, Morgan Kaufmann, San Mateo, CA.

MODI, J. J. (1988), *Parallel Algorithms and Matrix Computations*, Oxford University Press, Oxford, England.

MOLDOVAN, D. I. (1993), *Parallel Processing from Applications to Systems*, Morgan Kaufmann, San Mateo, CA.

MURTHY, C. S. R., K. N. B. MURTHY, AND S. ALURU (2000), *New Parallel Algorithms for Direct Solution of Linear Equations*, Wiley, New York.

SMITH, J. R. (1993), *The Design and Analysis of Parallel Algorithms.* Oxford University Press, Oxford, England.

STRASSEN, V. (1969), "Gaussian Elimination Is Not Optimal," *Numerische Mathematik*, Vol. 13, pp. 353–356.

TERRANO, A. E., S. M. DUNN, AND J. E. PETERS (1989), "Using an Architectural Knowledge Base to Generate Code for Parallel Computers," *Comm. ACM*, Vol. 32, No. 9, pp. 1065–1072.

VAN DE VELDE, E. F. (1994), *Concurrent Scientific Computing*, Springer-Verlag, New York.

WILSON, G. V. (1995), *Practical Parallel Programming*, MIT Press, Cambridge, MA.

YOUNG, D. M. (1971), *Iterative Solution of Large Linear Systems*, Academic Press, Boston, MA.

PROBLEMS

Scientific/Numerical

11-1. Determine whether the communication time derived in Section 11.2.2 has a minimum value when the size of the submatrices is variable.

11-2. Modify the recursive matrix multiplication algorithm to cope with $n \times n$ matrices, where n is not a power of 2.

11-3. Analyze the systolic array for matrix multiplication as described in Section 11.2.4, deriving equations for the computation and for the communication.

11-4. Strassen's method for matrix multiplication, $\mathbf{C} = \mathbf{A} \times \mathbf{B}$, where

$$\mathbf{A} = \begin{bmatrix} a_{11} & a_{12} \\ a_{21} & a_{22} \end{bmatrix}$$

$$\mathbf{B} = \begin{bmatrix} b_{11} & b_{12} \\ b_{21} & b_{22} \end{bmatrix}$$

$$\mathbf{C} = \begin{bmatrix} c_{11} & c_{12} \\ c_{21} & c_{22} \end{bmatrix}$$

is given as follows:

$$\begin{aligned}
Q_1 &= (a_{11} + a_{22})(b_{11} + b_{22}) \\
Q_2 &= (a_{21} + a_{22})b_{11} \\
Q_3 &= a_{11}(b_{12} - b_{22}) \\
Q_4 &= a_{22}(-b_{11} + b_{21}) \\
Q_5 &= (a_{11} + a_{12})b_{22} \\
Q_6 &= (-a_{11} + a_{21})(b_{11} + b_{12}) \\
Q_7 &= (a_{12} - a_{22})(b_{21} + b_{22}) \\
c_{11} &= Q_1 + Q_4 - Q_5 + Q_7 \\
c_{21} &= Q_2 + Q_4 \\
c_{12} &= Q_3 + Q_5 \\
c_{22} &= Q_1 + Q_3 - Q_2 + Q_6
\end{aligned}$$

Derive a recursive parallel program for this method.

11-5. One application of matrix-vector multiplication is *convolution*, which finds application in digital signal processing and image processing (see Chapter 12). Given a sequence of constants, $w_1, w_2, \ldots, w_n$, and a data input sequence, $x_1, x_2, \ldots, x_{N+n-1}$, the convolution operation produces an output sequence, $y_1, y_2, \ldots, y_N$, as given by

$$y_i = \sum_{j=1}^{n} x_{i-j+n} \times w_j$$

where $1 \le i \le N$. This computation can be described in matrix-vector multiplication form:

$$\begin{bmatrix} y_1 \\ y_2 \\ y_3 \\ y_4 \end{bmatrix} = \begin{bmatrix} x_5 & x_4 & x_3 & x_2 & x_1 \\ x_6 & x_5 & x_4 & x_3 & x_2 \\ x_7 & x_6 & x_5 & x_4 & x_3 \\ x_8 & x_7 & x_6 & x_5 & x_4 \end{bmatrix} \begin{bmatrix} w_1 \\ w_2 \\ w_3 \\ w_4 \\ w_5 \end{bmatrix}$$

(for $N = 4$, $n = 5$). Develop a parallel program structure for convolution.

11-6. Determine the partial differential equation that each of the following finite difference equations solve:

$$x_i = \frac{x_{i-1} + x_{i+1}}{2}$$

$$x_i = \frac{x_{i-1} - 2x_i + x_{i+1}}{2}$$

11-7. Develop the finite difference equation to solve the partial differential equation

$$\frac{\partial^2 f}{\partial x^2} + \frac{\partial^2 f}{\partial y^2} + \frac{\partial^2 f}{\partial z^2} = 0$$

by substituting the central difference approximation given in Section 11.4. Write a parallel program to solve this equation with fixed boundary values and solution dimensions being entered.

11-8. Write down the five-point and nine-point Jacobi convergence formulas for Poisson's equation:

$$\frac{\partial^2 f}{\partial x^2} + \frac{\partial^2 f}{\partial y^2} = g(x, y)$$

11-9. Draw the complete contents of the array **A** and vector **x** in Figure 11.21 for a 3×3 mesh of points.

11-10. Write parallel programs to implement both of the following Jacobi iteration formulas and determine which converges fastest:

$$f^k(x, y) = \frac{[f^{k-1}(x-\Delta, y) + f^{k-1}(x, y-\Delta) + f^{k-1}(x+\Delta, y) + f^{k-1}(x, y+\Delta)]}{4} \quad \text{or}$$

$$f^k(x, y) = \frac{[4f^{k-1}(x, y) + f^{k-1}(x-\Delta, y) + f^{k-1}(x, y-\Delta) + f^{k-1}(x+\Delta, y) + f^{k-1}(x, y+\Delta)]}{8}$$

11-11. Rewrite the red-black ordering pseudocode in Section 11.4.2 to avoid using the mod operator.

11-12. Develop a linear pipeline solution for the Gauss-Seidel method described in Section 10.5.1 and write a parallel program to implement it.

11-13. Make a comparative study of Jacobi iterative methods using 5-, 9-, and 13-point stencils. Establish the trade-offs between computational effort and number of iterations.

11-14. Write parallel programs to solve Laplace's equation using each of the following three ways:

1. Standard Jacobi iteration
2. Red-black iteration
3. Multigrid Jacobi iteration

Use a 256×256 mesh of points initialized along the four edges to 10.0, 5.0, 10.0, and 5.0. Stop iterations when the differences between iteration values are all less than 0.01. Use 16 processes. For the standard and red-black iteration methods, partition the problem into 16 columns of 16×256 points each, one column for each of the 16 processes. For the multigrid iteration, start with a grid size of 16×16 and increase the grid size by a factor of 2 every 10 iterations until the maximum grid size is reached. Continue iterations until the solution is obtained. Experiment with other coarse-to-fine strategies.

11-15. Derive the system efficiency when implementing Gaussian elimination with the strip partition and the cyclic partition, as described in Section 11.3.2.

Real Life

11-16. Write a parallel program to solve the room temperature distribution problem described in Problem 6-15 (Chapter 6) but by the direct means of Gaussian elimination and back substitution rather than by iteration. Only the Gaussian elimination need be computed in parallel; the back substitution may be done on one processor. First, determine the elements of the array **A** of the system of linear equations, **Ax** = 0. Since this array will always have nonzero elements along the diagonal, partial pivoting should be unnecessary. Next, decompose the problem so that 10 consecutive rows are handled by one process.

11-17. Write a parallel program for the room temperature distribution problem described in Problem 6-15, but allow for finer grid sizes nearer the fireplace. Provide for user control over the grid sizes. Experiment with adaptive grids.

11-18. Figure 11.26 shows a printed circuit board with various electronic components mounted that generate heat and are at the temperatures indicated. Write a parallel program that computes the temperature distribution. Choose your own components, board dimensions, and component placement for this problem. The idea for this problem came from Avila (1994).

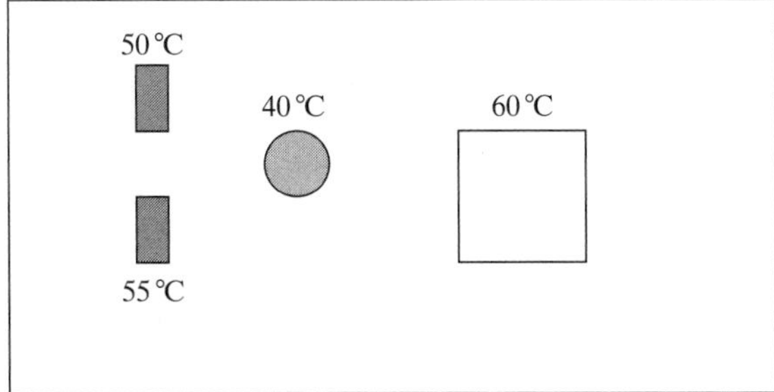

Ambient temperature at edges of board = 20°C

Figure 11.26 Printed circuit board for Problem 11-18.

Chapter 12

Image Processing

This is a "speciality" chapter providing information that can be used for parallel programming projects. Included are topics in image processing that have the potential for significant parallelism. We begin with so-called *low-level preprocessing operations* that are done at a very early stage of image enhancement. Sometimes straight lines (and curves) need to be identified, and we will describe an algorithm for doing this, called the *Hough transform*. Finally, we will describe transforming the stored image into the frequency domain using the discrete Fourier transform. A computationally fast way of performing the transformation is the *fast Fourier transform* (FFT). The material on the Fourier transform is applicable to a wide range of applications in addition to image processing.

12.1 LOW-LEVEL IMAGE PROCESSING

Low-level image processing operates directly on a stored image to improve or enhance it and to help human and computer recognition of the image. Such image processing is used in many applications, including medical diagnosis, police fingerprints, viewing components for manufacturing defects, and the film industry, to name a few. Images are first captured by cameras or other sensors and stored digitally. The stored image consists of a two-dimensional array of *pixels* (picture elements). Many low-level image-processing operations assume monochrome images and refer to pixels as having *gray-level* values or *intensities*. The gray level has a range from a minimum value to a maximum value (the *grayscale*). Typically, the grayscale is normalized to start at zero for black and 255 for white, which requires an 8-bit pixel. Color images typically use three values, one for each of the primary colors (red, green, and blue), or use the pixel value to point to a look-up table, as mentioned in Chapter 3, Section 3.2.1.

We will assume that the stored image uses a coordinate system whereby the origin is at the top-left corner, as shown in Figure 12.1. The pixels of the image are stored in a two-dimensional array, a *pixmap*, say `p[i][j]`, and individual pixel intensities can be found by referencing the array. While there is essentially a one-to-one correspondence between the image and the stored information, large image files may employ either a compressed format or a color look-up table stored with the image to reduce the storage requirements. Before any image-processing operation can be performed, the file must be uncompressed and the information laid out in a two-dimensional array.

Many of the different operations that can be performed on the stored information begin with *low-level processing*. Low-level processing uses the individual pixel values to modify the image in some way. Often such operations are embarrassingly parallel. For example, an image typically has "noise," unwanted variations produced by the sensors or environment, which alter the actual pixel values. Ideally, this noise should be removed, leaving only the required image. The operations for doing this are termed *noise cleaning* or *noise reduction*. Since the exact pixel values of the image are not known (otherwise why use sensors to detect them?), an experimental approach is necessary. Another example is the detection of edges in an image as an aid to recognition. An edge is a significant change in intensity. In *edge detection*, the changes in intensity in the image are enhanced or highlighted. Other low-level operations include labeling pixels as belonging to a specific object, and object *matching*, in which an object is compared in some fashion with a known object. A simple form of matching is *template matching*, whereby the image is compared with a stored template.

Sometimes the pixels associated with straight lines and curves need to be identified. An efficient method of doing this is by using the *Hough transform*. The Hough transform uses the pixels' coordinates to identify the equations of the most likely lines. Therefore we will characterize the Hough transform as low-level image processing (though not "preprocessing"). The Hough transform is very suitable for parallel implementation.

It may be advantageous in some applications to transform the image from the original *spatial domain* into the *frequency domain*; for example, for filtering the digital image. Such transformations also operate upon the pixel values to produce a new set of values relating to the frequency content of the digitized image. We shall look at such transformations at the end of this chapter.

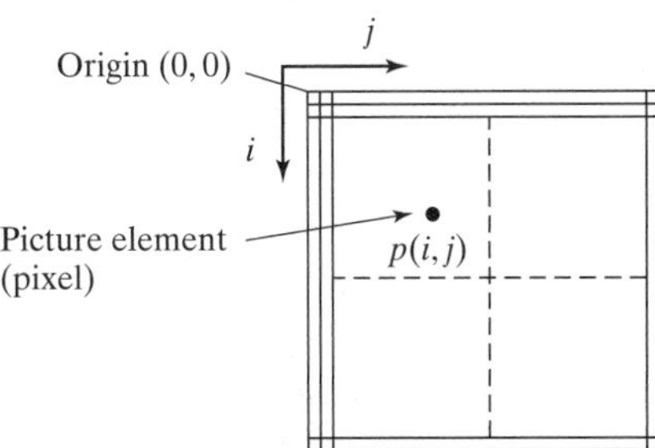

Figure 12.1 Pixmap.

Computational Requirements. Before beginning with the various low-level operations, let us first look at why parallel processing may be necessary. Suppose a pixmap has 1024×1024 pixels. With such a pixmap and 8-bit pixels, the storage requirement is

2^{20} bytes (1 Mbytes), not an unreasonable size for today's technology. A more critical factor is the speed of computation. Suppose that each pixel must be operated upon just once. Then 2^{20} operations are needed in the time of one frame. Today's computers are fast, but this would take 10 ms, even at 10^{-8}second/operation (10ns/operation). In real-time applications, the speed of computation must be at the frame rate (typically 60–85 frames/second). All the pixels in the image must be processed in the time of one frame; that is, in 12–16 ms. Typically, many high-complexity operations must be performed, not just one operation. The demands upon sequential computers are so overwhelming that special-purpose image-processing hardware has often been developed. Such special-purpose hardware continues to be developed using signal-processing chips. However, these systems do not have the flexibility that a true parallel computer can provide. Also, special-purpose hardware may be difficult to adapt to a new image-processing algorithm.

12.2 POINT PROCESSING

Image-processing operations can be divided into those that produce an output based upon the value of a single pixel (*point processing*), those that produce an output based upon a group of neighboring pixels (*local operations*), and those that produce an output based upon all the pixels of the image (*global operations*). Point operators do not need the values of the other pixels in the image, so parallelizing point processing is simple and totally embarrassingly parallel. Local operations are also highly parallelizable. Examples of *point processing* include *thresholding*, *contrast stretching*, and *gray-level reduction.*

Thresholding. In single-level thresholding, pixels with values above a predetermined threshold value are kept and others below the threshold are reduced to 0; that is, given a pixel, x_i, the operation on each pixel is

$$\text{if } (x_i < \text{threshold})\ x_i = 0;\ \text{else } x_i = 1;$$

Contrast Stretching. In contrast stretching, the range of gray-level values is extended to make the details more visible. Given the pixel of value x_i within a range x_l and x_h, the contrast is stretched to the range x_H to x_L by multiplying x_i by

$$x_i = (x_i - x_l)\left(\frac{x_H - x_L}{x_h - x_l}\right) + x_L$$

In medical images, for example, dense structures such as bone commonly absorb far more of the incident energy ("illumination" by X-ray, ultrasound, or other technology) than soft structures such as muscle or organs. Contrast stretching is frequently used to scale the soft tissue portion of the grayscale (perhaps only 5%–20% of the range). When this is done, the least dense soft-tissue grayscale value is at one extreme of the displayable pixel intensity, and the most dense soft-tissue grayscale value is at the other end. Contrast stretching is also applied to the dense structures such as bone to enable the viewing of small variations in density associated with hairline fractures.

Gray-Level Reduction. In gray-level reduction, the number of bits used to represent the gray level is reduced, perhaps to reduce the storage requirements. A simple method would be to truncate the less significant bits. This method would only work well and maintain sufficient information if the full range of gray levels is well represented in the image.

12.3 HISTOGRAM

The variations of gray levels can be found by creating a *histogram* of the image. A histogram could be used before thresholding to determine a suitable threshold level. Producing a histogram is a global operation because all the pixel values are needed in the operation. However, histograms are, in fact, extremely useful. A histogram of an image consists of a function showing the number of pixels in the image at each gray level. A histogram might look like the one shown in Figure 12.2.

The sequential code to produce a histogram might simply be

```
for(i = 0; i < height_max; x++)
  for(j = 0; j < width_max; y++)
    hist[p[i][j]] = hist[p[i][j]] + 1;
```

where the pixels are contained in the array `p[][]` and `hist[k]` will hold the number of pixels having the *k*th gray level.

The sequential code is similar to that described in Chapter 8 for adding numbers to an accumulating sum, and similar parallel solutions can be used for computing histograms. The inner loop could be unfolded and mapped onto individual processors. For shared memory solutions, the statement `hist[p[i][j]] = hist[p[i][j]] + 1` would need to be placed in a critical section. Generally, we would have individual processors perform local accumulations before adding to a global accumulation, to reduce delays in accessing global locations. For message passing, partial accumulations could be done by separate processors and a master process used in place of the critical section to do the final accumulation.

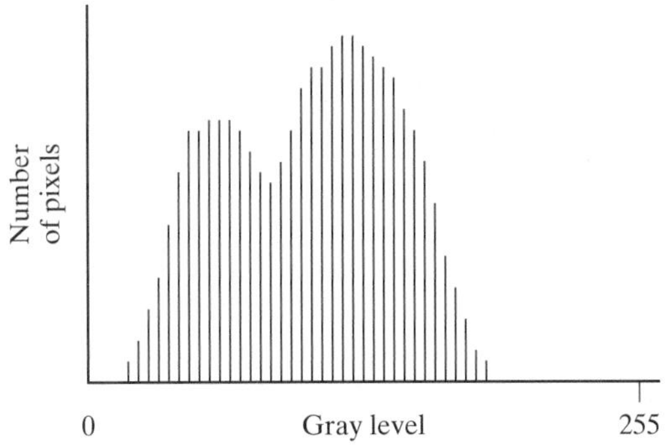

Figure 12.2 Image histogram.

12.4 SMOOTHING, SHARPENING, AND NOISE REDUCTION

Now let us look at the next level of preprocessing operations — namely, *smoothing*, *sharpening*, and *noise reduction*. These operations require the values of neighboring pixels and hence are local operations. The stored image may contain random noise or results of other undesirable effects. *Smoothing* suppresses large fluctuations in intensity over the image area and can be achieved by reducing the high-frequency content. *Sharpening* accentuates the transitions, enhancing the detail, and can be achieved in two ways. One approach is to reduce the low-frequency content. The other is to accentuate changes through differentiation. *Noise reduction* suppresses a noise signal present in the image. The noise signal itself could be of various forms and may be a random signal completely uncorrelated with the image signal. Smoothing will reduce noise but also blur the image. One way to reduce a completely random noise signal is by capturing the images more than once and taking the average of each pixel value. It can be shown easily that as the number of images used is increased, the averaged image becomes closer to the noise-free image (assuming that the noise is uncorrelated) (Gonzalez and Woods, 1992). This method requires each image to be in exactly the same position.

12.4.1 Mean

A simple smoothing technique is to take the *mean* or *average* of a group of pixels as the new value of the central pixel. (The word *mean* is more suggestive — halfway between extremes.) This requires a local operation with access to a group of pixels around the pixel to be updated. A common group size is 3×3, as shown in Figure 12.3. Given a 3×3 group, the computation is

$$x_4' = \frac{x_0 + x_1 + x_2 + x_3 + x_4 + x_5 + x_6 + x_7 + x_8}{9}$$

where x_4' is the new value for x_4.

Sequential Code. The mean operation needs to be performed on all the pixels, using the original values of the pixels, and suggests nine steps to compute the average for each pixel, or $9n$ for n pixels [a sequential time complexity of $O(n)$].

Parallel Code. Suppose first that one processor is assigned for each pixel (not likely given the number of pixels, except for some very specialized image-processing hardware). A direct parallel implementation would require each processor to perform nine steps with all the processors operating simultaneously. Since the accesses to the pixel data are solely read accesses (except for the final update, which is to unique pixels), no conflicts occur for shared memory implementations.

x_0	x_1	x_2
x_3	x_4	x_5
x_6	x_7	x_8

Figure 12.3 Pixel values for a 3×3 group.

The parallel version can take advantage of the ability of each processor to compute a partial sum for its neighboring processors as well as itself. Let the values of the pixels be x_0, x_1, x_2, x_3, x_4, x_5, x_6, x_7, and x_8, as given in Figure 12.3. The number of steps can be reduced by separating the computation into four data transfer steps, as shown in Figure 12.4.

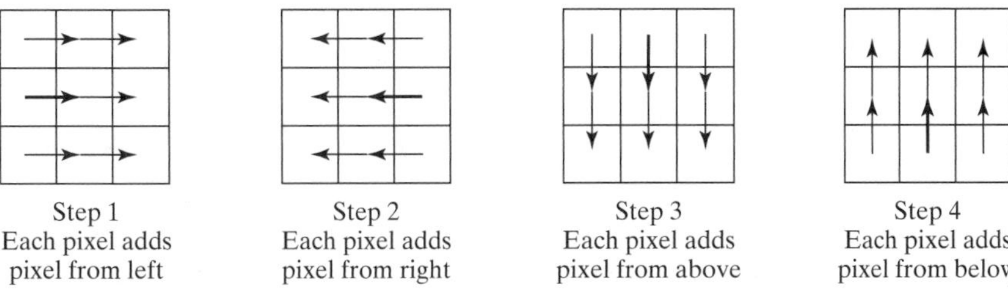

Figure 12.4 Four-step data transfer for the computation of mean.

Each processor performs the following four steps in lock-step fashion:

Step 1 Each processor receives the value of the pixel from its left and adds that value to the value of its pixel to form an accumulating sum. The center processor (x_4) forms the accumulating sum, $x_3 + x_4$.

Step 2 Each processor receives the value of the pixel from its right and adds that value to its accumulating sum. The center processor forms the accumulating sum, $x_3 + x_4 + x_5$.

Step 3 Each processor receives the *accumulated value at step 2* from above it and adds that value to its accumulating sum. It must also retain the original accumulated value for the next step. The center processor forms the accumulating sum, $x_0 + x_1 + x_2 + x_3 + x_4 + x_5$, and retains $x_3 + x_4 + x_5$ separately.

Step 4 Each process receives the *accumulated value at step 2* from below it and adds that value to its accumulating sum. The center processor forms the accumulating sum, $x_0 + x_1 + x_2 + x_3 + x_4 + x_5 + x_6 + x_7 + x_8$.

Figure 12.5 shows the results after each of these steps. Finally, each process divides its accumulating sum by 9 to obtain their means, a total of four communication/adds steps and one divide step for n pixels. Clearly, the algorithm can be used with each processor handling a group of pixels, but with increased communication and arithmetic steps within each processor (Problem 12-1).

Note that this computation naturally suggests the single-instruction multiple-data model, SIMD, since each process will perform the same operation at the same time. For general-purpose multiprocessor systems, a single-program multiple-data model, SPMD, is applicable.

12.4.2 Median

The mean method just described tends to blur edges and other sharp details. For noise reduction, an alternative is to replace the pixel value by the *median* of the neighborhood

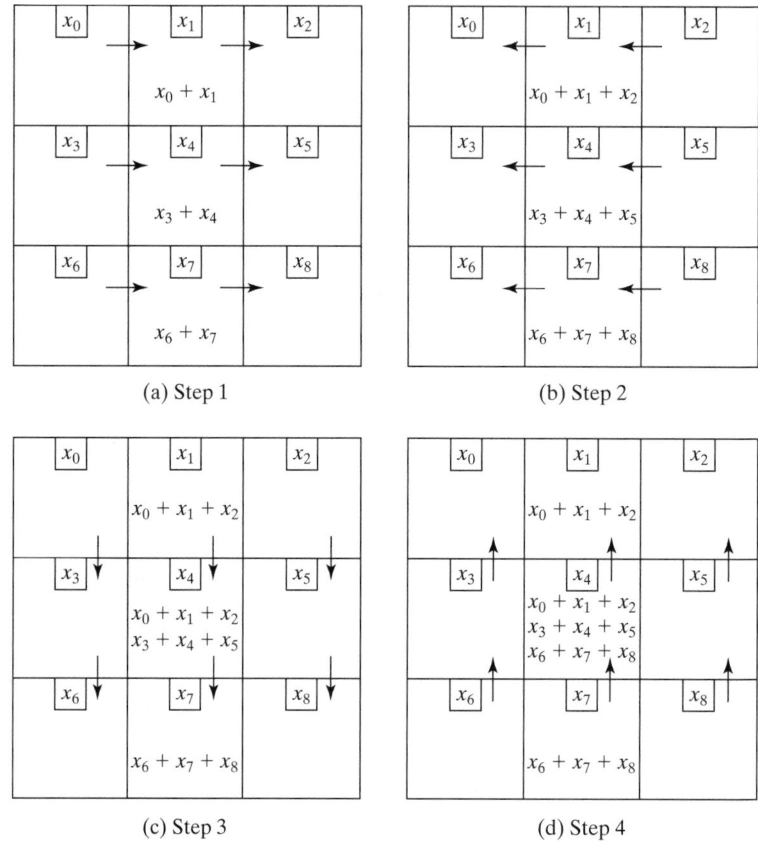

Figure 12.5 Parallel mean data accumulation.

pixels, which is more effective at maintaining the edge sharpness when the image is a strong "spike-like" image (Gonzalez and Woods, 1992). The median can be found by ordering the pixel values from smallest to largest and choosing the center pixel value (assuming an odd number of pixels). With a 3×3 group, suppose the values in ascending order are y_0, y_1, y_2, y_3, y_4, y_5, y_6, y_7, and y_8. The median is y_4. This operation suggests that all the values in the group must first be sorted, and then the fifth element taken to replace the original value of the pixel. Using a sequential sorting algorithm such as bubble sort, in which the lesser values are found first in order, sorting could, in fact, be terminated after the fifth-lowest value is obtained. In this case, the number of steps for finding each median is given by $8 + 7 + 6 + 5 + 4 = 30$ steps, or $30n$ for n pixels.

Parallel Code. One of the mesh sorting algorithms, such as shearsort (Chapter 10, Section 10.2.3), could be used. Shearsort separates sorting into two repeating phases, sorting contents of rows and sorting contents of columns, but alternative rows are sorted in opposite directions. Alternatively, and especially for ease of parallel operation and greater speed, an approximate sorting algorithm could be used in which rows and columns are sorted once but the rows are all sorted in the same direction. In each stage, bubble sort can be used effectively and would require three steps. First, a compare-and-exchange operation is performed on each of the rows, requiring three steps. For the ith row, we have

$$\begin{aligned} x_{i,j-1} &\leftrightarrow x_{i,j} \\ x_{i,j} &\leftrightarrow x_{i,j+1} \\ x_{i,j-1} &\leftrightarrow x_{i,j} \end{aligned}$$

where $x_{i,j}$ is the value held in the element at row i and column j, and $\leftrightarrow$ means "compare and exchange if the left gray level is greater than the right gray level" (the normal bubble sort action to bubble the largest to the right side). Then the columns are sorted using three compare-and-exchange operations. For the jth column, we have

$$\begin{aligned} x_{i-1,j} &\leftrightarrow x_{i,j} \\ x_{i,j} &\leftrightarrow x_{i+1,j} \\ x_{i-1,j} &\leftrightarrow x_{i,j} \end{aligned}$$

The whole process is shown in Figure 12.6. The value in $x_{i,j}$ is taken to be the fifth-largest pixel value. This algorithm does not always select the fifth-largest value. For example, if the fifth-largest value is x_2 (in Figure 12.1) and it is also the largest in its row, it will remain in its original position and not be selected by this algorithm. However, the algorithm is a reasonable approximate algorithm and only requires six steps for the whole image if there is one processor for each pixel. Again, clearly the algorithm can be used with each processor handling a group of pixels. Problem 11-2 explores the accuracy of the algorithm.

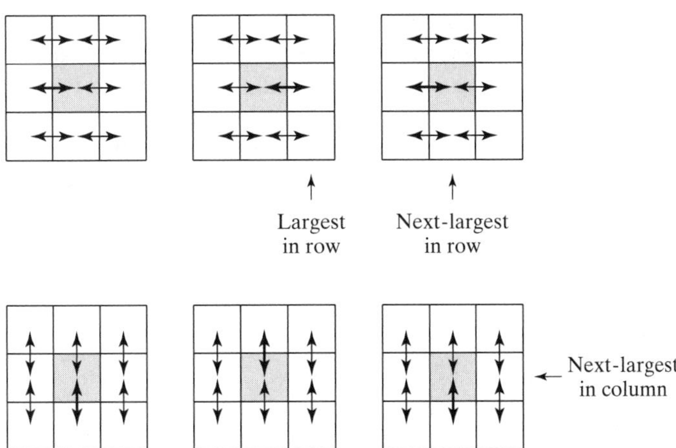

Figure 12.6 Approximate median algorithm requiring six steps.

12.4.3 Weighted Masks

The simple mean method of Section 12.4.1 could be described by a weighted 3×3 mask that describes the amount of each pixel value used in the averaging. For convenience of notation, suppose the weights are w_0, w_1, w_2, w_3, w_4, w_5, w_6, w_7, and w_8, and the pixel values are x_0, x_1, x_2, x_3, x_4, x_5, x_6, x_7, and x_8. The new center pixel value, x_4', is given by

$$x_4' = \frac{w_0x_0 + w_1x_1 + w_2x_2 + w_3x_3 + w_4x_4 + w_5x_5 + w_6x_6 + w_7x_7 + w_8x_8}{k}$$

The scale factor, $1/k$, is set to maintain the correct grayscale balance in the image after the operation. Often, k is given by $w_0 + w_1 + w_2 + w_3 + w_4 + w_5 + w_6 + w_7$. The summation of products, w_ix_i, from two functions, w and x, is the (discrete) *cross-correlation* of f with w (written as $f \otimes w$) (Haralick and Shapiro, 1992).

The operation with a 3×3 mask is depicted in Figure 12.7. The 3×3 mask is applied to all the pixels of the image. Those pixels at the border of the image will not have a full set of neighboring pixels. The simplest solution is to extend the image one pixel along each side and assign a fixed value to these pixels, say to be the same as the nearest pixel, or even just zero. (Note: every local image-processing algorithm has to be concerned with boundary conditions.)

Mask

w_0	w_1	w_2
w_3	w_4	w_5
w_6	w_7	w_8

$\otimes$

Pixels

x_0	x_1	x_2
x_3	x_4	x_5
x_6	x_7	x_8

=

Result

	x_4'	

Figure 12.7 Using a 3×3 weighted mask.

Although 3×3 is a common mask size for all image-processing operations, other sizes are possible; for example, 5×5, 9×9, and 11×11. Usually, an odd number is chosen so that there is a central pixel. For the mean operation of Section 12.4.1, all the weights are 1, as in the mask shown in Figure 12.8, and the scale factor is 1/9. However, the weights need not be 1, nor all the same. For example, the mask shown in Figure 12.9 could be used for noise reduction, and many other masks are possible. By making the weights negative, a sharpening effect can be achieved. A sharpening mask is shown in Figure 12.10. The computation done with this mask is

$$x_4' = \frac{8x_4 - x_0 - x_1 - x_2 - x_3 - x_5 - x_6 - x_7 - x_8}{9}$$

$k = 9$

1	1	1
1	1	1
1	1	1

Figure 12.8 Mask to compute mean.

$k = 16$

1	1	1
1	8	1
1	1	1

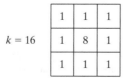

Figure 12.9 A noise-reduction mask.

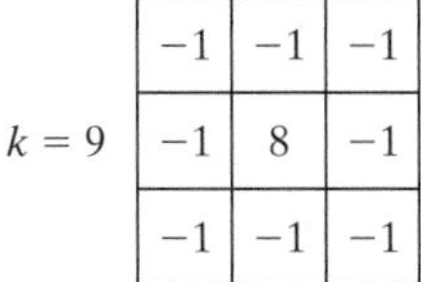

$k = 9$

−1	−1	−1
−1	8	−1
−1	−1	−1

Figure 12.10 High-pass sharpening filter mask.

If certain conditions are met regarding the weights, the computation can be separated into a row operation followed by a column operation. See Haralick and Shapiro (1992) for more details of this technique and many other masks for various purposes.

12.5 EDGE DETECTION

For computer recognition, identifying objects from other objects in the image often involves highlighting the edges of the object (*edge detection*), where an edge is a significant change in the gray-level intensity.

12.5.1 Gradient and Magnitude

Let us first consider a one-dimension gray-level function, $f(x)$ (say along a row). If the function, $f(x)$, were differentiated, the first derivative, $\partial f/\partial x$, measures the gradient of the transition and would be a positive-going or negative-going spike at a transition. The direction of the transition (either increasing or decreasing) can be identified by the polarity of the first derivative, as shown in Figure 12.11. Also shown here is the second derivative, $\partial^2 f/\partial x^2$, which crosses zero at the site of the transition and might be useful to identify the exact position of the transition.

An image is a two-dimensional discretized gray-level function, $f(x,y)$. The change in gray level has a *gradient magnitude* (or simply *gradient*) and a *gradient direction* described

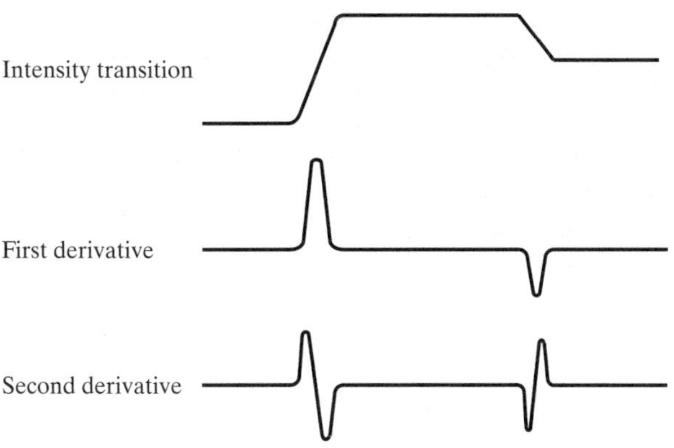

Figure 12.11 Edge detection using differentiation.

by an angle, here with respect to the y-axis, as shown in Figure 12.12. For a two-dimensional function, $f(x,y)$, the gradient (magnitude) of $f(x,y)$, ∇f, is given by

$$\nabla f = \sqrt{\left(\frac{\partial f}{\partial x}\right)^2 + \left(\frac{\partial f}{\partial y}\right)^2}$$

and the gradient direction is given as an angle by

$$\phi(x, y) = \tan^{-1}\left(\frac{\frac{\partial f}{\partial y}}{\frac{\partial f}{\partial x}}\right)$$

where ϕ is the angle with respect to the y-axis (see Figure 12.12). The gradient can be approximated to

$$\nabla f \approx \left|\frac{\partial f}{\partial y}\right| + \left|\frac{\partial f}{\partial x}\right|$$

for reduced computational effort.

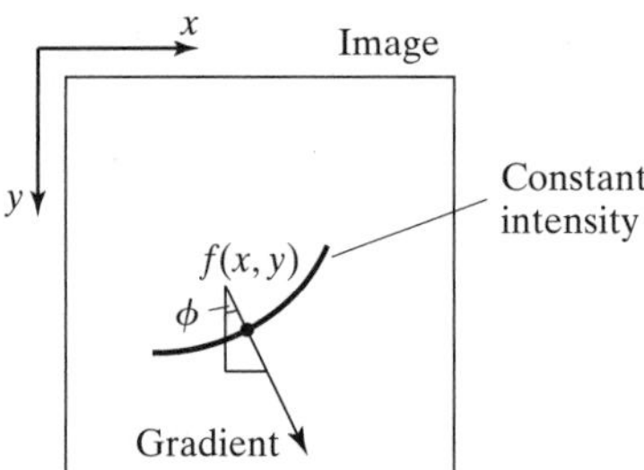

Figure 12.12 Gray-level gradient and direction.

12.5.2 Edge-Detection Masks

For discrete functions, the derivatives are approximated by differences. The derivatives can be implemented digitally in several ways using weighed masks. The term $\partial f/\partial x$ is the difference in the x-direction, and $\partial f/\partial y$ is the difference in the y-direction. Hence, we could take the difference between neighboring pixel gray levels in a row and the difference between neighboring pixels in a column. Suppose we have a set of 3×3 pixel values, as shown in Figure 12.3. We might consider computing the approximate gradient using pixel values x_5 and x_3 (to get $\partial f/\partial x$) and x_7 and x_1 (to get $\partial f/\partial y$),

$$\frac{\partial f}{\partial x} \approx x_5 - x_3$$

$$\frac{\partial f}{\partial y} \approx x_7 - x_1$$

so that

$$\nabla f \approx |x_7 - x_1| + |x_5 - x_3|$$

Two masks are needed, one to obtain $x_7 - x_1$ and one to obtain $x_5 - x_3$. The absolute values of the results of each mask are added together. Negative weights would be used to obtain subtraction. (Scale factors for obtaining derivatives are not shown throughout; they would be chosen to obtain the appropriate contrast.)

Prewitt Operator. Better results can be obtained by using more pixel values. For example, the approximate gradient could be obtained from

$$\frac{\partial f}{\partial y} \approx (x_6 - x_0) + (x_7 - x_1) + (x_8 - x_2)$$

$$\frac{\partial f}{\partial x} \approx (x_2 - x_0) + (x_5 - x_3) + (x_8 - x_6)$$

Then

$$\nabla f \approx |x_6 - x_0 + x_7 - x_1 + x_8 - x_2| + |x_2 - x_0 + x_5 - x_3 + x_8 - x_6|$$

which requires using the two 3×3 masks shown in Figure 12.13, known as the *Prewitt operator*. Again, the absolute values of the results of each mask are added together.

Sobel Operator. A very popular edge-detection operator is the Sobel operator, using two 3×3 masks, as shown in Figure 12.14. Here the derivatives are approximated to

$$\frac{\partial f}{\partial y} \approx (x_6 + 2x_7 + x_8) - (x_0 + 2x_1 + x_2)$$

$$\frac{\partial f}{\partial x} \approx (x_2 + 2x_5 + x_8) - (x_0 + 2x_3 + x_6)$$

Operators implementing first derivatives will tend to enhance noise. However, the Sobel operator also has a smoothing action. Two-mask operators such as Sobel provide both $\partial f/\partial x$ and $\partial f/\partial y$ and allow the gradient (∇f) and the gradient direction (ϕ) to be readily calculated. Figure 12.15 shows an image and the effect of the Sobel operator.

−1	−1	−1
0	0	0
1	1	1

−1	0	1
−1	0	1
−1	0	1

Figure 12.13 Prewitt operator.

−1	−2	−1
0	0	0
1	2	1

−1	0	1
−2	0	2
−1	0	1

Figure 12.14 Sobel operator.

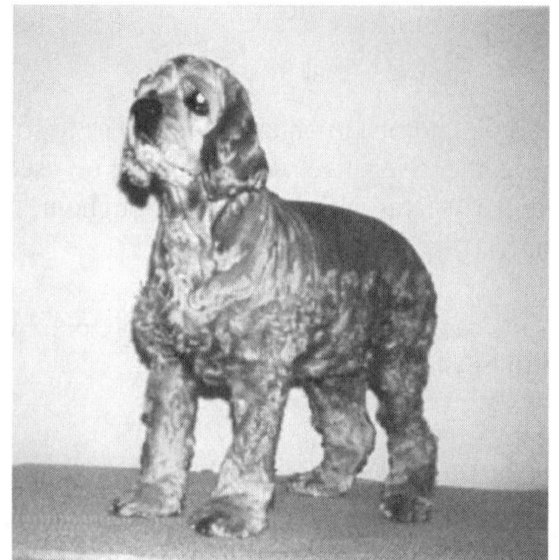

(a) Original image (Annabel)

(b) Effect of Sobel operator

Figure 12.15 Edge detection with Sobel operator.

Parallel Code with Two Masks. Since the results of the two masks are independent of each other, it is clear that both could be performed simultaneously given sufficient resources. A parallel implementation can use the four steps shown in Figure 12.5 for each mask, except that now weights are associated with the additions.

Laplace Operator. Rather than using first-order derivatives, a second-order derivative could be considered for edge detection, since an edge results in a recognizable output (a positive and negative going pulse; see Figure 12.11). The Laplace second-order derivative is defined as

$$\nabla^2 f = \frac{\partial^2 f}{\partial x^2} + \frac{\partial^2 f}{\partial y^2}$$

which can be implemented approximately in more than one way using differences. It could be approximated to

$$\nabla^2 f = 4x_4 - (x_1 + x_3 + x_5 + x_7)$$

which can be obtained with the single mask shown in Figure 12.16. The central pixel, x_4, is updated accordingly using four adjacent pixels, as illustrated in Figure 12.17 ($x_4' = 4x_4 - x_1 - x_3 - x_5 - x_7$). Note that the computation will yield zero for a constant

0	−1	0
−1	4	−1
0	−1	0

Figure 12.16 Laplace operator.

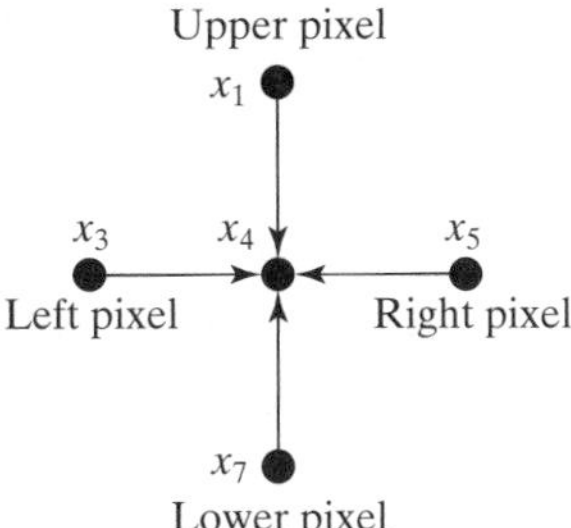

Figure 12.17 Pixels used in Laplace operator.

gray level across the mask. A threshold is usually applied after the Laplace operator (or any other edge-detection operator) to get either black or white pixels. Figure 12.18 shows the effect of the Laplace operator on the original image in Figure 12.11 (without noise). Unfortunately, the Laplace operator is generally too sensitive to noise for edge- detection. The results of the Laplace operator for edge detection can be improved by applying a threshold operator after the Laplace operator (Problem 12-7). In fact, thresholding can often improve all edge-detection methods and has been applied to the images here.

Figure 12.18 Effect of Laplace operator.

12.6 THE HOUGH TRANSFORM

The purpose of the Hough transform (Hough, 1962) is to find the parameters of equations of lines that most likely fit the sets of pixels in an image. The Hough transform can form a basis for template matching and for converting an object into a set of vectors for recognition or other purposes. Edge detection will, in theory, delineate objects, but edge detection as so far described is likely to leave some gaps in the edges, and the Hough transform could be used to fill in the gaps. The Hough transform operates upon all the pixels in the image and is a global operation rather than a local operation like the ones treated in the preceding section.

A line is described by the equation

$$y = ax + b$$

where the parameters, a and b, each uniquely describe a particular line, a the slope and b the intercept on the y-axis. This equation is of the conventional *slope-intercept* form. A single pixel has an infinite number of lines that could pass through it. If a and b are discretized, a finite set of lines will exist. One could search for all the lines of all the points and maybe find the most likely lines in the image, those with the most pixels mapped onto them, but computationally this would be prohibitively expensive [an $O(n^3)$ algorithm].

However, suppose the equation of the line is rearranged as

$$b = -xa + y$$

Figure 12.19 shows the line plotted in the original (x, y) plane and also plotted using the parameters (a, b) as coordinates in the so-called *parameter space*. (For clarity, we have returned briefly to the conventional x-y coordinate orientation rather than with the origin at the upper-left corner.) In the parameter space, a line is indicated as a single point. It follows that *every* point that lies on a specific line in the x-y space (i.e., with specific values for a and b) will map into same point in the parameter space. Therefore, we can find the number of points on each possible line in the x-y space by simply counting when a mapping maps onto a point in the a-b space.

Now let us see how this might be implemented. Many lines can pass through a single point in the original x-y space, and each will map onto a different point in the a-b space, only limited by the precision of a and b. In fact, a single point (x_1, y_1) can be mapped onto the points of a line

$$b = -x_1 a + y_1$$

in the a-b space. In the mapping process, discrete values will be used to a coarse prescribed precision and the computation is rounded to the nearest-possible a-b coordinates. For example, a and b could each be divided into 100 values. An accumulator or counter is associated with each (a, b) value. The mapping process is done for every point in the x-y space. A record is kept of the a-b points that have been obtained by incrementing the corresponding accumulator. Thus, each accumulator will have the number of pixels that map into a single point in the parameter space, and we can determine the number of pixels that are on each possible line in the x-y space. Finally, to find the most likely lines in the x-y space, the points in the parameter space with locally maximum numbers of pixels are chosen as lines.

Unfortunately, this method will fail for vertical lines (i.e., with the slope, a, infinite, and with the y intercept, b, infinite) and with lines that approach this extreme. To avoid the

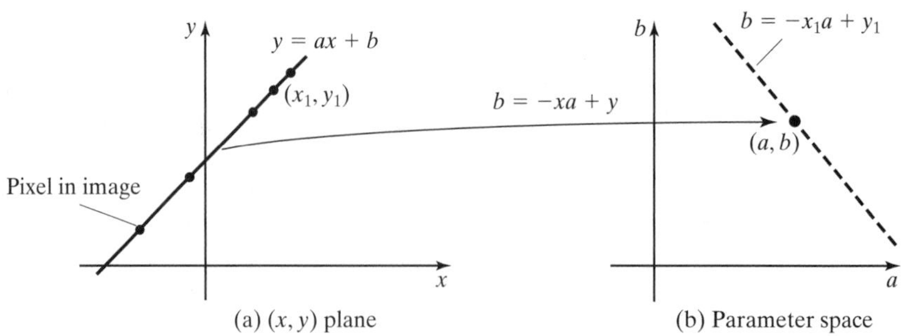

Figure 12.19 Mapping a line into (a, b) space.

problem, as suggested by Duda and Hart (1972), the line equation is rearranged to polar coordinates (the *normal representation*):

$$r = x \cos \theta + y \sin \theta$$

where r is the perpendicular distance to the origin in the original (x, y) coordinate system, and θ is the angle between r and the x-axis, as shown in Figure 12.20. The θ value will be in degrees and very conveniently will also be the *gradient angle* of the line (with respect to the x-axis). Each line will map to a single point in the (r, θ) space. A vertical line will simply map into a point where $\theta = 0°$ if a positive intercept with the x-axis, or $\theta = 180°$ if a negative intercept with the x-axis. A horizontal line has $\theta = 90°$. Each point in the x-y space will map into a curve in the (r, θ) space; that is, (x_1, y_1) maps into $r = x_1 \cos \theta + y_1 \sin \theta$.

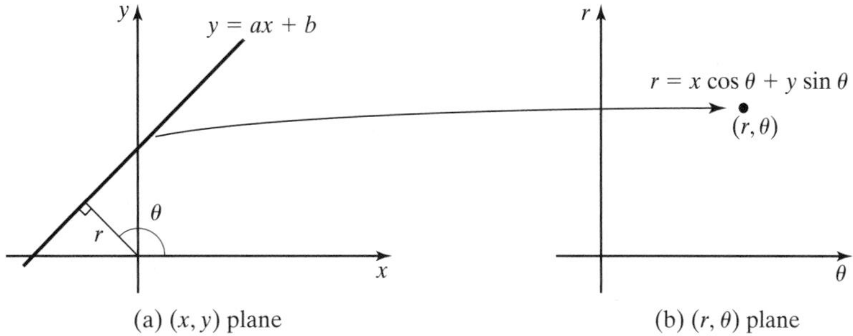

Figure 12.20 Mapping a line into (r, θ) space.

We should point out that it is not necessary to use the normal representation. For example, Krishnaswamy and Banerjee (1997) use the conventional slope-intercept form of equation in their work, but avoid the possibility of infinite values by dividing the slopes into four regions, 0 to $\pi/4$, $\pi/4$ to $\pi/2$, $\pi/2$ to $3\pi/4$, and $3\pi/4$ to π. Lines with the slopes of lines to 0 to $\pi/4$ are treated normally, while in the other regions the coordinates are altered. See Krishnaswamy and Banerjee (1997) for more details.

Implementation. Figure 12.21 shows the normal representation using the image coordinate system with the origin at the top-left corner. Note here that x and y can only be positive. The parameter r is constrained to be positive also. The range of values for θ is 0° to 360°, although in this image coordinate system, θ cannot be between 180° and 270°. The range of values of r will depend upon the original range of x and y.

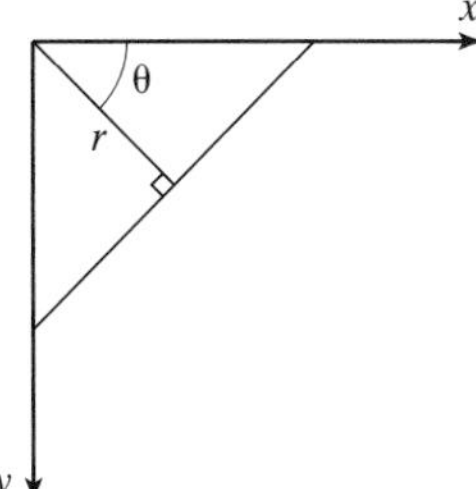

Figure 12.21 Normal representation using image coordinate system.

The parameter space is divided into small rectangular regions. One accumulator is provided for each region. The number of regions will depend upon the desired discretized precision. Suppose r is divided into increments of 5, and θ is divided into 10° increments. Then each region is $10° \times 5$ and has one accumulator associated with it, say acc[r][θ], as shown in Figure 12.22. Accumulators of the regions that a pixel maps into are incremented. This process must be done for all the pixels in the image. The computational effort will depend upon the number of regions. If all values of θ were tried (i.e., incrementing θ through all its values), the computational effort would be given by the number of discrete values of θ, say k intervals. With n pixels the complexity is $O(kn)$. Although essentially a linear complexity for fixed k, it may still be worth reducing the complexity.

The computational effort can be reduced significantly by limiting the range of lines for individual pixels using some criteria. A single value of θ could be selected based upon the gradient of the line. The gradient angle can be found using a gradient operator such as the Sobel operator (Section 12.5.2). Once we have this value, a single accumulator can be found to increment. Now only one computational step is required for each pixel, and the complexity for n pixels is $O(n)$.

Usually, we wish to know the end points of the lines, and this can be found by recording the pixels that actually map onto the line. This list can be examined to find the furthest pixels on the line.

Sequential Code. The sequential code could be of the form

```
for (x = 0; x < xmax; x++)                  /* for each pixel */
  for (y = 0; y < ymax; y++) {
    sobel(x, y, dx, dy);                    /* find x and y gradients */
    magnitude = grad_mag(dx, dy);           /* find magnitude if needed */
    if (magnitude > threshold) {
      theta = grad_dir(dx, dy);             /* atan2() fn */
      theta = theta_quantize(theta);
      r = x * cos(theta) + y * sin(theta);
      r = r_quantize(r);
      acc[r][theta]++;                      /* increment accumulator */
      append(r, theta, x, y);               /* append point to line */
    }
  }
```

Finally, when all the pixels have been considered, the values held in each accumulator will give the number of pixels that can map onto the corresponding line. The most likely lines are those with the most pixels, and accumulators with the local maxima are chosen. An algorithm for choosing the local maxima must be devised.

Parallel Code. Clearly, the preceding sequential code has significant potential for parallelization. Since the computation for each accumulator is independent of the other accumulations, it could be performed simultaneously, although each requires read access to the whole image. A shared memory implementation does not need critical sections because the accesses are all read accesses, but delays and contention may occur due to simultaneous requests to locations.

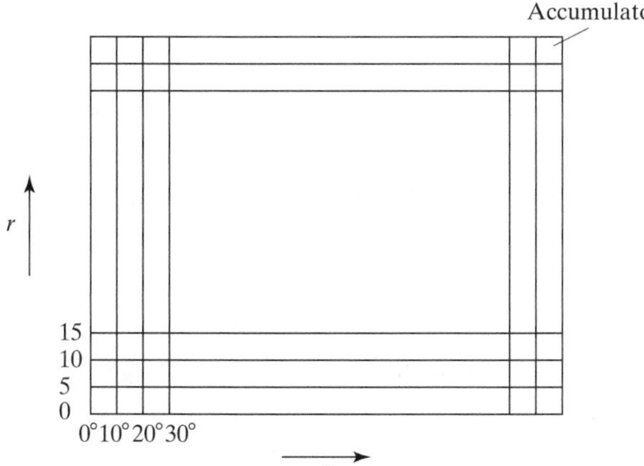

Figure 12.22 Accumulators, acc[r][θ], for the Hough transform.

12.7 TRANSFORMATION INTO THE FREQUENCY DOMAIN

A periodic (time) function, $x(t)$, can be decomposed into a series of sinusoidal waveforms of various frequencies and amplitudes. This decomposition was developed by Fourier in the early 1800s and is called the *Fourier series*. The *Fourier transform* produces a continuous function of frequencies, $X(f)$, of the original function, $x(t)$. There are many applications for the Fourier transform in science and engineering, including digital signal processing and image processing. Image processing is of particular interest here, although what is said applies to all Fourier transform application areas. In the area of image processing, the Fourier transform (and especially the fast Fourier transform, a fast algorithm for implementing the Fourier transform) is used in image enhancement, restoration, and compression.

The image is a two-dimensional discretized function, $f(x, y)$, but first let us consider the one-dimensional continuous case. The two-dimensional case is solved by application of the one-dimensional case in both dimensions, as will be shown. For completeness, let us first review the results of the Fourier series and Fourier transform concepts from first principles. All the derivations of the equations, including the mathematical rigor, can be found in Elliott and Rao (1982) and many other texts on Fourier series and transforms.

12.7.1 Fourier Series

The Fourier series is a summation of sine and cosine terms and can be written as

$$x(t) = \frac{a_0}{2} + \sum_{j=1}^{\infty}\left(a_j \cos\left(\frac{2\pi jt}{T}\right) + b_j \sin\left(\frac{2\pi jt}{T}\right)\right)$$

T is the period ($1/T = f$, where f is a frequency). The Fourier coefficients, a_j and b_j, can be found from specific direct integrals. By some mathematical manipulation, we can get the more convenient description of the series:

$$x(t) = \sum_{j=-\infty}^{\infty} X_j e^{2\pi ij\frac{t}{T}}$$

where X_j is the jth Fourier coefficient in a complex form and $i = \sqrt{-1}$. The complex Fourier coefficients can also be computed from specific integrals.

12.7.2 Fourier Transform

Continuous Functions. With a little mathematical work, the preceding summation can be developed into an integral:

$$x(t) = \int_{-\infty}^{\infty} X(f)e^{2\pi if}df$$

where $X(f)$ is a continuous function of frequency. The function $X(f)$ can be obtained from

$$X(f) = \int_{-\infty}^{\infty} x(t)e^{-2\pi ift}dt$$

$X(f)$ is the *spectrum* of $x(t)$, or more simply the *Fourier transform* of $x(t)$. Instead of discrete frequencies, as in the Fourier series, we now have a continuous frequency domain even to frequencies with an infinite period (and negative frequencies!). See Elliott and Rao (1982) for more details.

The original function, $x(t)$, can obtained from $X(f)$ using the first integral given, which is the *inverse Fourier transform* and is similar in form to the Fourier transform. Hence, any algorithm implementing the Fourier transform is also applicable for the inverse Fourier transform.

Discrete Functions. For all digital computer implementations of Fourier transforms, the input function $x(t)$ must be sampled and stored as a set of discrete values, say x_0, $x_1, x_2 \ldots x_{N-1}$ for N samples. The previous Fourier transform can be developed for functions having a set of N discrete values by replacing the integral with a summation, leading to the *discrete Fourier transform* (DFT), given by

$$X_k = \frac{1}{N}\sum_{j=0}^{N-1} x_j e^{-2\pi i\left(\frac{jk}{N}\right)}$$

and the *inverse discrete Fourier transform*, given by

$$x_k = \sum_{j=0}^{N-1} X_j e^{2\pi i\left(\frac{jk}{N}\right)}$$

for $0 \le k \le N - 1$. The N (real) input values, $x_0, x_1, x_2, \ldots, x_{N-1}$, produce N (complex) transform values, $X_0, X_1, X_2, \ldots, X_{N-1}$.

Scale Factor. N is a scale factor. Since in most applications a function will be transformed, processed, and returned to its original form, the scale factor could be performed during the transform or during the inverse transform (or $\sqrt{N}$ used in each transform). Sometimes the discrete Fourier transform is given without the scale factor being explicitly shown; that is,

$$X_k = \sum_{j=0}^{N-1} x_j e^{-2\pi i\left(\frac{jk}{N}\right)}$$

We will omit the scale factor except in Section 12.7.5 on the fast Fourier transform.

Positive and Negative Coefficients. As pointed out by Cochran et al. (1967), in addition to variations in the use of scale factors, some workers use positive coefficients in the transform and negative coefficients in the inverse transform, rather than the negative coefficients in the transform and positive coefficients in the inverse transform used here. (Note: $e^{i\theta} = \cos\theta + i\sin\theta$ and $e^{-i\theta} = \cos\theta - i\sin\theta$.)

Time Complexity. The summation can be computed easily, especially if the values for the exponential terms are stored in a look-up table, but it still requires N^2 multiplications and additions for N points as this equation is written; that is, sequential complexity of $O(N^2)$. This sequential complexity has been generally regarded as prohibitively expensive, especially for large N, but fortunately an algorithm has been developed, known as the *fast Fourier transform*, that reduces the complexity to $O(N \log N)$. This algorithm will be described in Section 12.7.5, but first let us look at the image-processing application of the discrete Fourier transform.

12.7.3 Fourier Transforms in Image Processing

In image processing, the input will be a set of pixels forming a two-dimensional function that is already discrete. In this section, we will use the coordinates j and k (rather than x and y used earlier). The pixel at coordinate (j, k) is $x(j, k)$.

A two-dimensional Fourier transform is

$$X_{lm} = \sum_{j=0}^{N-1} \sum_{k=0}^{M-1} x_{jk} e^{-2\pi i\left(\frac{jl}{N} + \frac{km}{M}\right)}$$

where j and k are row and column coordinates, $0 \le j \le N-1$ and $0 \le k \le M-1$. For convenience, let us assume that the image is a square array, where $N = M$. The equation can be rearranged into

$$X_{lm} = \sum_{j=0}^{N-1} \left[\sum_{k=0}^{N-1} x_{jk} e^{-2\pi i\left(\frac{km}{N}\right)} \right] e^{-2\pi i\left(\frac{jl}{N}\right)}$$

The inner summation is a one-dimensional DFT operating on N points of a row to produce a transformed row. The outer summation is a one-dimensional DFT operating on N points of a column. We might write

$$X_{lm} = \sum_{j=0}^{N-1} X_{jm} e^{-2\pi i\left(\frac{jl}{N}\right)}$$

Hence, the two-dimensional DFT can be divided into two sequential phases, one operating on rows of elements and one operating on columns of (transformed) elements, as shown in Figure 12.23, and only a one-dimensional DFT algorithm need be implemented. Clearly, the process could start with columns and then use rows. The choice may depend upon how the original data is stored for efficient parallel implementation (Fox et al., 1988). Since row transforms are independent of each other, and column transforms are independent of each other, a significant opportunity for parallelism exists.

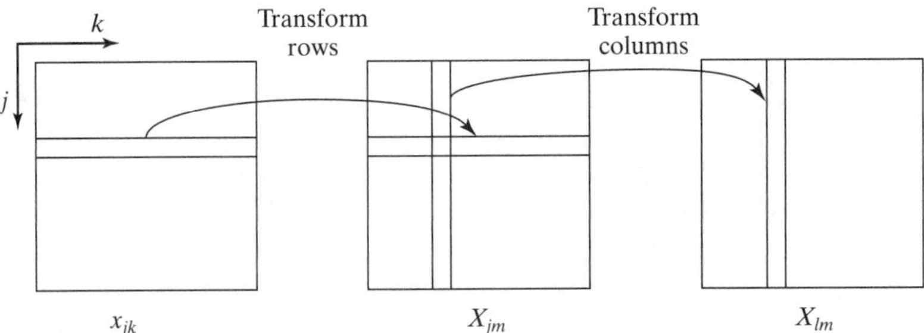

Figure 12.23 Two-dimensional DFT.

Figure 12.23 suggests an implementation of the two-dimensional DFT: a one-dimensional DFT, followed by a transpose operation, followed by the same DFT operation. (Transpose was first introduced in Chapter 4, Section 4.2.1, and can be implemented with all-to-all routines.)

Applications. A very wide range of image processing and analysis can be done in the frequency domain. One application for the DFT is in frequency filtering, which is applicable to both smoothing and edge detection (low-pass and high-pass filters). Frequency filtering was achieved earlier with weighted masks, which can be described by the *convolution* operation:

$$h(j, k) = g(j, k) * f(j, k)$$

(the same operation as the cross-correlation operation for symmetrical masks; Haralick and Shapiro, 1992), where $g(j, k)$ describes the weighted mask (filter), and $f(j, k)$ describes the image. It can be shown that the Fourier transform of a product of functions is given by the convolution of the transforms of the individual functions (the so-called frequency convolution theorem; Brigham, 1988). Hence, the convolution of two functions can be obtained by taking the Fourier transforms of each function, multiplying the transforms

$$H(j, k) = G(j, k) \times F(j, k)$$

(element by element multiplication), where $F(j, k)$ is the Fourier transform of $f(j, k)$, and $G(j, k)$ is the Fourier transform of $g(j, k)$, and then taking the inverse transform to return the result into the original spatial domain. This way of filtering requires much more computational effort than using a simple weight mask in the spatial domain, but other more complex operations could be performed. Convolution can also take place between two complete images to produce a new image in the manner illustrated in Figure 12.24. Note that the two transforms are independent of each other and can be performed in parallel.

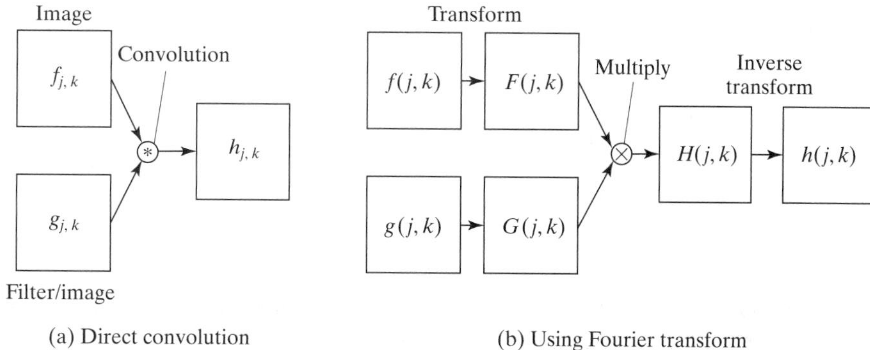

Figure 12.24 Convolution using Fourier transforms.

12.7.4 Parallelizing the Discrete Fourier Transform Algorithm

There is a clever, faster algorithm for the Fourier transform, which we will consider in the next section, but first let us consider the basic DFT algorithm and how to parallelize it. Starting from

$$X_k = \sum_{j=0}^{N-1} x_j e^{-2\pi i\left(\frac{jk}{N}\right)}$$

and using the notation $w = \mathrm{e}^{-2\pi i/N}$,

$$X_k = \sum_{j=0}^{N-1} x_j w^{jk}$$

The w terms are called the *twiddle factors*. Each input value has to be multiplied by a twiddle factor. The inverse transform can be obtained by replacing w with w^{-1}.

Sequential Code. The sequential code to generate all N points of the DFT could have the form

```
for (k = 0; k < N; k++) {                  /* for every point */
   X[k] = 0;
   for (j = 0; j < N; j++)                 /* compute summation */
      X[k] = X[k] + w^(j * k) * x[j];
}
```

where `X[k]` is the kth transformed point, `x[k]` is the kth input for `N` points, and $w = e^{-2\pi i/N}$. The summation step requires complex number arithmetic. Since each summation step uses the raised power of `w` of the preceding step multiplied by w^k (i.e., $w^{(j-1)*k} * w^k = w^{j*k}$), the code could be rewritten as

```
for (k = 0; k < N; k++) {
   X[k] = 0;
   a = 1;
   for (j = 0; j < N; j++) {
      X[k] = X[k] + a * x[j];
      a = a * wk;
   }
}
```

where `a` is a temporary variable.

Parallel Code. There are several ways this code could be parallelized. Here we will briefly mention the obvious master-slave approach, the less obvious pipeline approach, and finally the matrix-vector product method.

Elementary Master-Slave Implementation. For a simple *master-slave approach*, one slave process of N slave processes could be assigned to produce one of the transformed values; that is, the kth slave process produces `X[k]`. The required values for `a` could be precomputed for each process by the master process, as shown in Figure 12.25, though we might just let each slave compute its values simultaneously. The approach requires each slave to have a copy of all the input points, and thus the memory requirement has increased N-fold. (The elements could be requested from the master when needed, but this would significantly increase the message passing.) The parallel time complexity with N (slave) processes is $O(N)$, which is cost-optimal for an $O(N^2)$ sequential algorithm implemented directly. Unfortunately, the number of data points is likely to be much larger than the number of available processes. In that case, more than one summation would need to be done by each slave process.

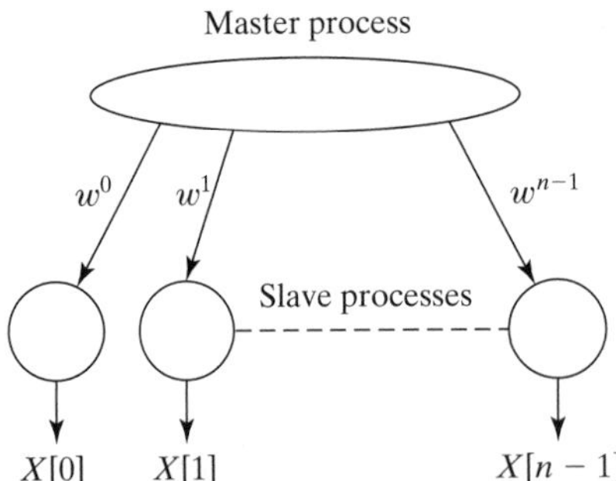

Figure 12.25 Master-slave approach for implementing the DFT directly.

Pipeline Implementation. The algorithm could be implemented using a *pipeline* structure since each iteration of the inner loop uses a value from the preceding iteration. Unfolding the inner loop for `X[k]`, we have

```
X[k] = 0;
a = 1;
X[k] = X[k] + a * x[0];
a = a * wᵏ;
X[k] = X[k] + a * x[1];
a = a * wᵏ;
X[k] = X[k] + a * x[2];
a = a * wᵏ;
X[k] = X[k] + a * x[3];
a = a * wᵏ;
    ⋮
```

Each pair of statements

```
X[k] = X[k] + a * x[0];
a = a * wᵏ;
```

could be performed by a separate pipeline stage, as illustrated in Figure 12.26. The pipeline and its timing are shown in Figure 12.27.

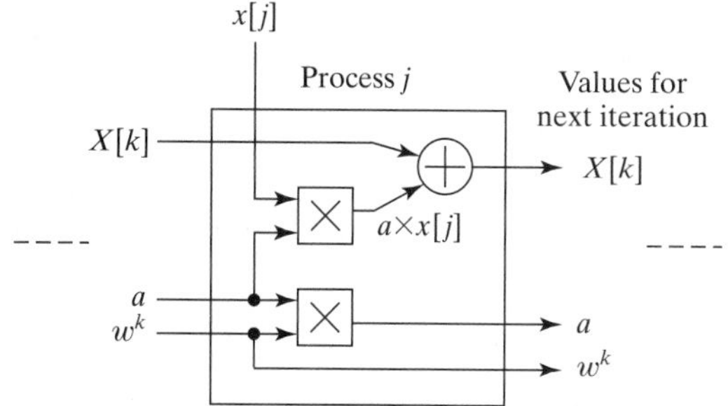

Figure 12.26 One stage of a pipeline implementation of DFT algorithm.

Apart from our method, there are several other ways to pipeline the computation, as described by Thompson (1983).

DFT as a Matrix-Vector Product. The kth element of the discrete Fourier transform is given by

$$X_k = x_0w^0 + x_1w^1 + x_2w^2 + x_3w^3 + \ldots x_{N-1}w^{N-1}$$

and the whole transform can be described by a matrix-vector product:

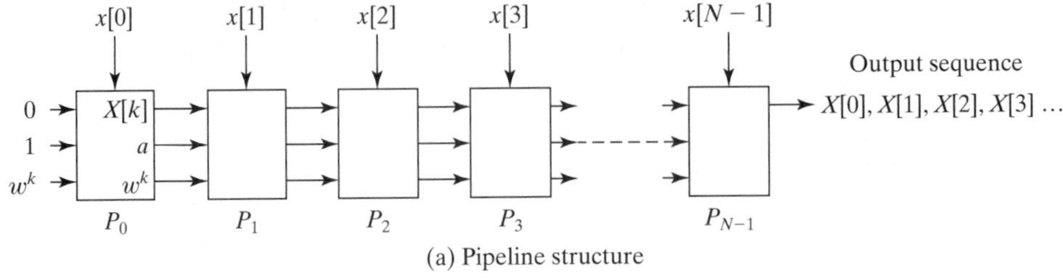

(a) Pipeline structure

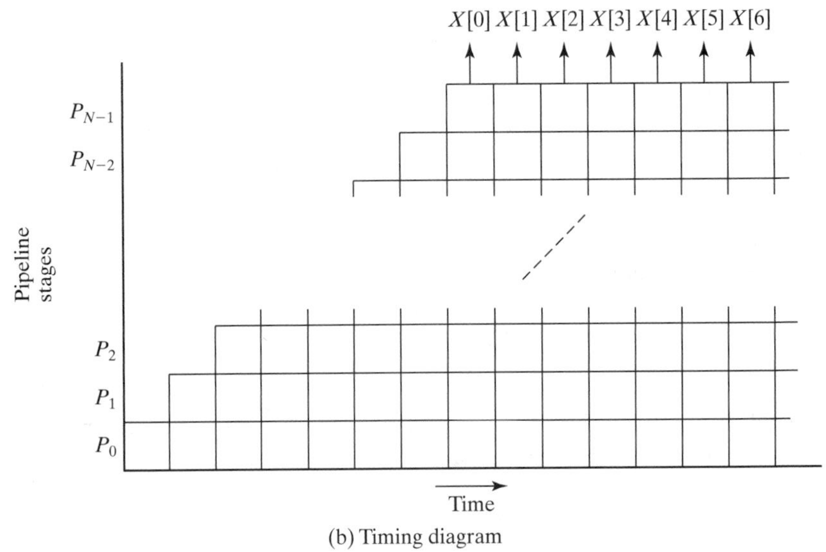

(b) Timing diagram

Figure 12.27 Discrete Fourier transform with a pipeline.

$$\begin{bmatrix} X_0 \\ X_1 \\ X_2 \\ X_3 \\ \vdots \\ X_k \\ \vdots \\ X_{N-1} \end{bmatrix} = \frac{1}{N} \begin{bmatrix} 1 & 1 & 1 & 1 & \cdots & 1 \\ 1 & w & w^2 & w^3 & \cdots & w^{N-1} \\ 1 & w^2 & w^4 & w^6 & \cdots & w^{2(N-1)} \\ 1 & w^3 & w^6 & w^9 & \cdots & w^{3(N-1)} \\ \vdots & \vdots & \vdots & \vdots & \cdots & \vdots \\ 1 & w^k & w^{2k} & w^{3k} & \cdots & w^{(N-1)k} \\ \vdots & \vdots & \vdots & \vdots & \cdots & \vdots \\ 1 & w^{N-1} & w^{2(N-1)} & w^{3(N-1)} & \cdots & w^{(N-1)(N-1)} \end{bmatrix} \begin{bmatrix} x_0 \\ x_1 \\ x_2 \\ x_3 \\ \vdots \\ x_k \\ \vdots \\ x_{N-1} \end{bmatrix}$$

(Note that $w^0 = 1$.) Hence, the parallel methods of producing a matrix-vector product, as described in Chapter 11, can be used for the discrete Fourier transform. Some of the w terms can be reduced, as explored in Problem 12-15.

12.7.5 Fast Fourier Transform

The FFT is a fast method of obtaining a discrete Fourier transform and has a time complexity of $O(N \log N)$ instead of $O(N^2)$. It is usually credited to Cooley and Tukey (1965), though subsequence correspondence in the literature showed that in fact the underlying ideas are much older and can be traced back to the early 1900s (Cooley, Lewis, and Welch, 1967; Gonzalez and Woods, 1992). In the following, it is assumed that N is a power of 2.

Let us start with the discrete Fourier transform equation with the scale factor to demonstrate that the scale factor does not affect the derivation of the algorithm:

$$X_k = \frac{1}{N}\sum_{j=0}^{N-1} x_j w^{jk}$$

where $w = e^{-2\pi i/N}$. There are many formulations of the fast Fourier transform. For example, Swarztrauber (1987) describes eight formulations. Generally, the summation is successively divided into parts by a divide-and-conquer approach. We will describe the version that starts by dividing the summation into the following two parts:

$$X_k = \frac{1}{N}\left[\sum_{j=0}^{(N/2)-1} x_{2j} w^{2jk} + \sum_{j=0}^{(N/2)-1} x_{2j+1} w^{(2j+1)k}\right]$$

where the first summation processes the x's with even indices, and the second summation processes the x's with odd indices. Rearranging, we get

$$X_k = \frac{1}{2}\left[\frac{1}{(N/2)}\sum_{j=0}^{(N/2)-1} x_{2j} w^{2jk} + w^k \frac{1}{(N/2)}\sum_{j=0}^{(N/2)-1} x_{2j+1} w^{2jk}\right]$$

or

$$X_k = \frac{1}{2}\left[\frac{1}{(N/2)}\sum_{j=0}^{(N/2)-1} x_{2j} e^{-2\pi i\left(\frac{jk}{N/2}\right)} + w^k \frac{1}{(N/2)}\sum_{j=0}^{(N/2)-1} x_{2j+1} e^{-2\pi i\left(\frac{jk}{N/2}\right)}\right]$$

Each summation can now be recognized as an $N/2$ discrete Fourier transform operating on the $N/2$ even points and the $N/2$ odd points, respectively. Therefore

$$X_k = \frac{1}{2}\left[X_{\text{even}} + w^k X_{\text{odd}}\right]$$

for $k = 0, 1, \ldots N-1$, where X_{even} is the $N/2$-point DFT of the numbers with even indices, $x_0, x_2, x_4, \ldots$, and X_{odd} is the $N/2$-point DFT of the numbers with odd indices, $x_1, x_3, x_5, \ldots$.

Now, suppose k is limited to $0, 1, \ldots N/2-1$, the first $N/2$ values of the total N values. The complete sequence can be divided into two parts:

$$X_k = \frac{1}{2}\left[X_{\text{even}} + w^k X_{\text{odd}}\right]$$

and

$$X_{k+N/2} = \frac{1}{2}\left[X_{\text{even}} + w^{k+N/2}X_{\text{odd}}\right] = \frac{1}{2}\left[X_{\text{even}} - w^{k}X_{\text{odd}}\right]$$

since $w^{k+N/2} = -w^k$, where $0 \le k < N/2$. Hence, we could compute X_k and $X_{k+N/2}$ using two $N/2$-point transforms, as illustrated in Figure 12.28.

Each of the $N/2$-point DFTs can be decomposed into two $N/4$-point DFTs, and the decomposition could be continued until single points are to be transformed. A 1-point DFT is simply the value of the point. The computation has to be done for each transformed point and is often depicted in the form shown in Figure 12.29 for a 4-point transform. The twiddle factors are not shown here, but it should be noted that different values occur at different stages depending upon the number of numbers being used in X_{even} and X_{odd} and the specific X transform output index. Finding the twiddle factors is eased by recognizing that as the number of numbers reduces by factors of 2, the powers of w increase correspondingly ($w = e^{2\pi i/(N/2)}$, $e^{2\pi i/(N/4)} = w^2$, $e^{2\pi i/(N/8)} = w^4$, etc.). The 1/2 scale factors are also omitted for clarity and would not exist if a scale factor were not present in the original DFT equation.

The decomposition of a 16-point DFT is outlined in Figure 12.30. Note that the elements are initially selected in *bit-reversal order.* That is, the binary pattern for the indices is the reverse of normal numerical order; that is, 0 and 8 are combined (0000 and 1000 instead of 0000 and 0001, and so on). The flow of results for the 16-point FFT is shown in Figure 12.31.

Sequential Code. The sequential time complexity is essentially O(N log N), since there are log N steps and each step requires a computation proportional to N, where there are N numbers. The algorithm can be implemented recursively or iteratively.

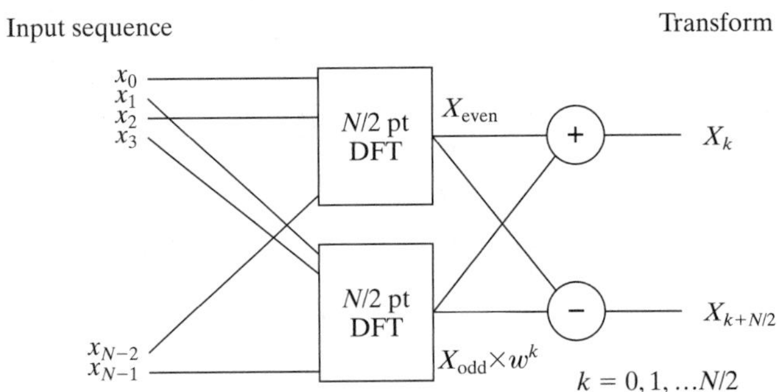

Figure 12.28 Decomposition of N-point DFT into two $N/2$-point DFTs.

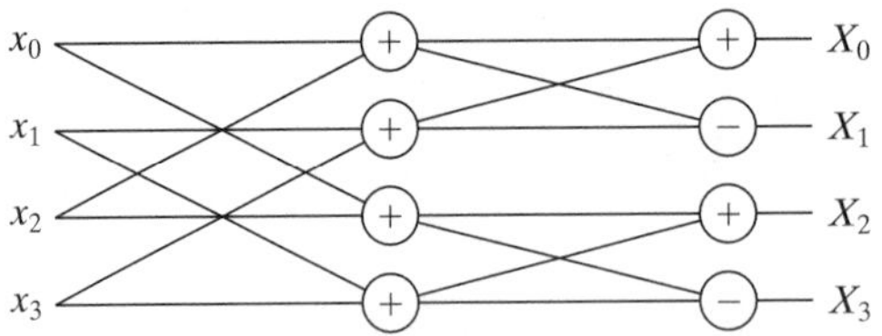

Figure 12.29 Four-point discrete Fourier transform.

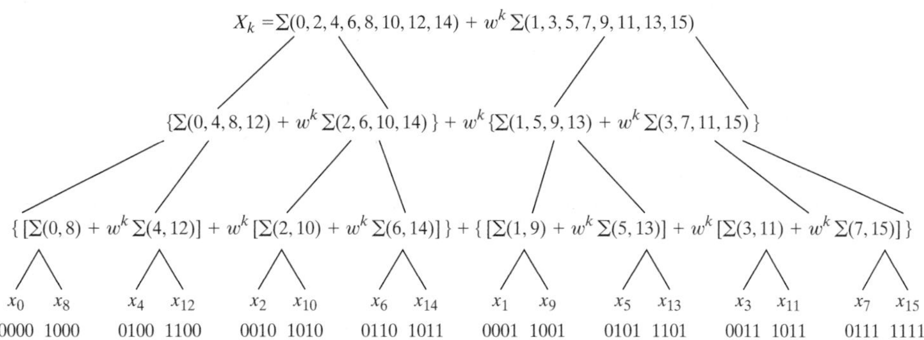

$X_k = \Sigma(0, 2, 4, 6, 8, 10, 12, 14) + w^k\,\Sigma(1, 3, 5, 7, 9, 11, 13, 15)$
$\{\Sigma(0, 4, 8, 12) + w^k\,\Sigma(2, 6, 10, 14)\} + w^k\,\{\Sigma(1, 5, 9, 13) + w^k\,\Sigma(3, 7, 11, 15)\}$
$\{[\Sigma(0, 8) + w^k\,\Sigma(4, 12)] + w^k\,[\Sigma(2, 10) + w^k\,\Sigma(6, 14)]\} + \{[\Sigma(1, 9) + w^k\,\Sigma(5, 13)] + w^k\,[\Sigma(3, 11) + w^k\,\Sigma(7, 15)]\}$
x_0 x_8 x_4 x_{12} x_2 x_{10} x_6 x_{14} x_1 x_9 x_5 x_{13} x_3 x_{11} x_7 x_{15}
0000 1000 0100 1100 0010 1010 0110 1011 0001 1001 0101 1101 0011 1011 0111 1111

Figure 12.30 Sixteen-point DFT decomposition.

Parallelizing the FFT Algorithm. Since the FFT has a sequential time complexity of O(N log N), the ideal cost-optimal parallel time complexity would be O(log N) with N processors. Here we will describe two ways it can be done, one called the *binary exchange algorithm* by Gupta and Kumar (1993), and one using a transpose operation. between row and columns operations.

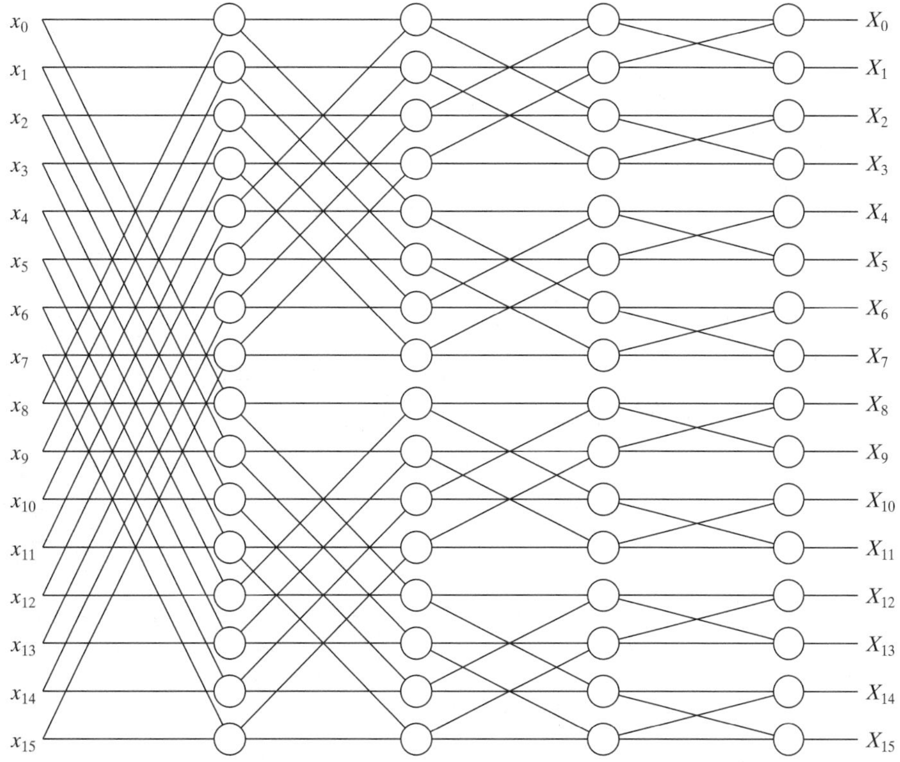

Figure 12.31 Sixteen-point FFT computational flow.

Binary Exchange Algorithm. Referring to Figure 12.31, suppose one processor were allocated to each data point ($x[j]$ for the jth process) that is one row in Figure 12.31. Each process would finally produce one transformed point. The connection pattern of Figure 12.31 comprises so-called *butterfly* connections, which would map onto a hypercube perfectly if each processor is allocated to one row, since results are passed to processes having an address that differs by only one bit at each stage. For example, processor 0 will communicate with processor 8 in the first communication step, then processor 4 in the next communication step, processor 2 in the next communication step, and finally with processor 0 in last communication step.

Indeed, even if the number of processors is less than the number of data points, and each processor is allocated a group of data points, the interprocessor communication pattern has the same characteristics. Suppose there are p processors and N data points. Each processor has N/p rows. If N and p are both powers of 2, the numbering of processors downward takes on the most significant $\log p$ digits of the data point indices. The remaining bits identify the data point within the group. This is illustrated in Figure 12.32 for $N/p = 4$.

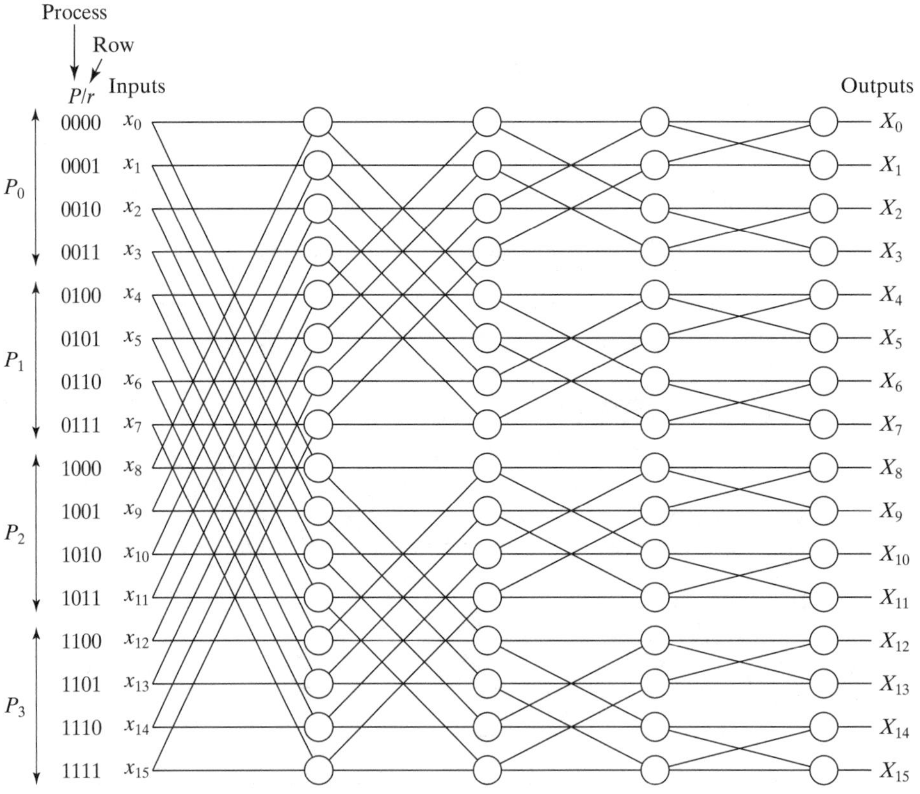

Figure 12.32 Mapping processors onto 16-point FFT computation.

Analysis

Computation. Given p processors and N data points, at each step each processor will compute N/p points, and each point requires one multiplication and addition. With $\log N$ steps, the parallel time complexity is given by

$$t_{\text{comp}} = O(N \log N).$$

Communication. If $p = N$, communication occurs at each step and there is one data exchange between pairs of processors at each of the $\log N$ steps. Suppose a hypercube or another interconnection network that allows simultaneous exchanges is used. In that case, the communication time complexity is given by

$$t_{\text{comm}} = O(\log N)$$

If $p < N$, communication between processors only occurs during the first $\log p$ steps. In the first step, all p processors make exchanges. In the next set, only half of the processors make data exchanges, in the next, a quarter of the processors, and so on. If an interconnection network that will allow simultaneous exchanges is used, the communication time complexity is simply given by

$$t_{\text{comm}} = O(\log p)$$

Of course, these complexities will be become much worse if the interconnection network forces the communication to be serialized.

Transpose Algorithm. Suppose $N = p$ (for now) and again each processor starts with one data point. For the sake of illustration, suppose there are 16 data points. If the processors are organized as a two-dimensional array, say in row major order, communications would first take place between processors in each column, and then communication would take place in processors in each row. Suppose a processor is allocated to each column, as illustrated in Figure 12.33. During the first two steps, all communication would be within a processor, as shown. During the last two steps, the communication would be between processors. In the *transpose algorithm*, between the first two steps and the last two steps, the array elements are transposed, that is, the elements down each column are moved across a row, as shown in Figure 12.34. After the transpose, the last two steps proceed but now

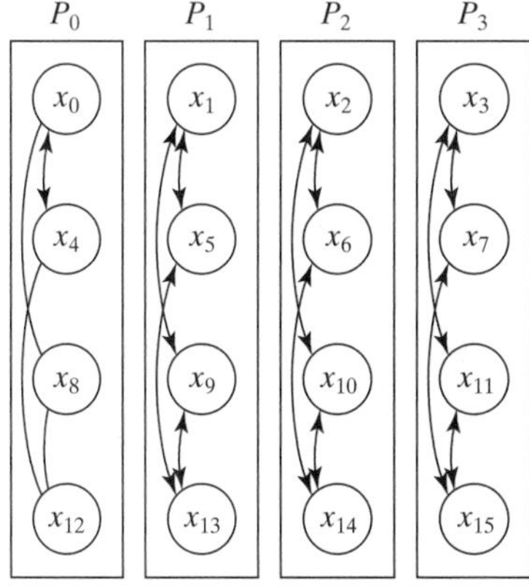

Figure 12.33 FFT using transpose algorithm — first two steps.

involve communication only within the processors, as shown in Figure 12.35. The only communication between processors is to transpose the array.

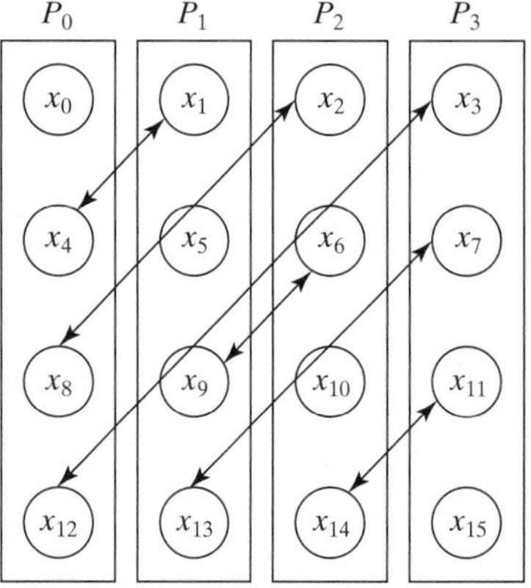

Figure 12.34 Transposing array for transpose algorithm.

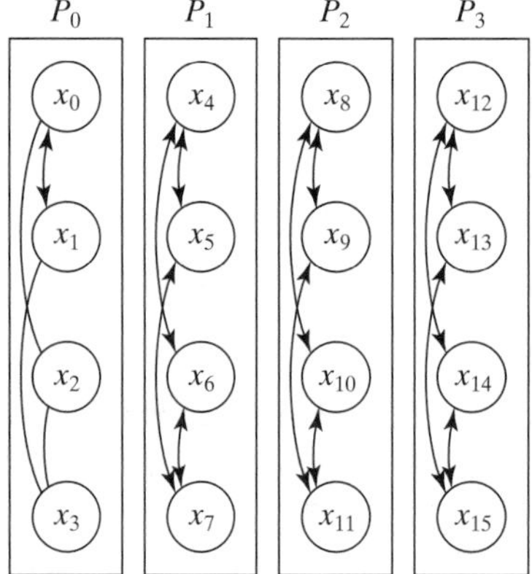

Figure 12.35 FFT using transpose algorithm — last two steps.

12.8 SUMMARY

This chapter covered the following aspects of image processing in the context of parallel programming:

- Basic low-level preprocessing operations (thresholding, contrast stretching, histograms, smoothing, sharpening, noise reduction)
- Edge detection using masks (notably the Sobel and Laplace operators)
- Hough transform
- Discrete Fourier transform and fast Fourier transform

FURTHER READING

Several texts are devoted to image processing, including Gonzalez and Woods (1992), Haralick and Shapiro (1992), Jain (1989), Sonka, Hlavac, and Boyle (1993), Castleman (1996), and Bässmann and Besslich (1995). A research text on multiprocessor implementations is Uhr et al. (1986).

Low-level preprocessing is described in papers such as Davis (1975), Sahoo, Soltani, and Wong (1988), and Weszka (1978). Hardware implementations can be found in Ercan and Fung (1996). Median algorithms can be found in Cole and Yap (1985) and Sen (1990). There are other image-processing operations not considered here. For example, shrinking algorithms reduce the area of an object down to possibly 1 pixel, which enables objects to be easily counted. Rao, Prasada, and Sarma (1976) describe a parallel shrinking algorithm using binary weighted masks. Arcelli and Levialdi (1972) consider shrinking in three dimensions.

Hough transforms have been implemented in various ways. Shared memory implementations are discussed in Choudhary and Ponnusamy (1991). Interesting applications include Carlson, Evans, and Wilson (1994).

The source for the FFT is Cooley and Tukey (1965). Many other papers have appeared subsequently on various aspects of FTTs, including Gupta and Kumar (1993), Illingworth and Kittler (1988), Norton and Silberger (1987), Swarztrauber (1987), and Thompson (1983). Textbooks on the FFT include Elliott and Rao (1982) and Brigham (1988).

BIBLIOGRAPHY

ARCELLI, C., AND S. LEVIALDI (1972), "Parallel Shrinking in Three Dimensions," *Comput. Graphics Image Process.*, Vol. 1, pp. 21–30.

BÄSSMANN, H., AND P. W. BESSLICH (1995), *Ad Oculos Digital Image Processing*, International Thomson Publishing, London, England.

BORN, G. (1995), *The File Formats Handbook*, International Thomson Computer Press, London, England.

BRIGHAM, E. O. (1988), *The Fast Fourier Transform and Its Application*, Prentice Hall, Englewood Cliffs, NJ.

CARLSON, B. D., E. D. EVANS, AND S. L.WILSON (1994), "Search Radar Detection and Track with Hough Transform Part I: System Concept, Part II Detection Statistics, Part III Detection Performance with Binary Integration," *IEEE Trans. Aerospace and Electronic Syst.*, Vol. 30, No. 1, pp. 102–125.

CASTLEMAN, K. R. (1996), *Digital Image Processing*, Prentice Hall, Upper Saddle River, NJ.

CHOUDHARY, A. N., AND R. PONNUSAMY (1991), "Implementation and Evaluation of Hough Transform Algorithms on a Shared Memory Multiprocessor," *J. Par. Distribut. Comput.*, Vol. 12, No. 2, pp. 178–188.

COCHRAN, W. T., J. W. COLLEY, D. L. FAVIN, H. D. HELMS, R. A. KAENEL, W. W. LANG, G. C. MALING, D. E. NELSON, C. M. RADER, AND P. D. WELCH (1967), "What Is the Fast Fourier Transform," *IEEE Trans. Audio Electroacoustics,* Vol. AU-15, No. 2, pp. 45–55.

COLE, R., AND C. M. YAP (1985), "A Parallel Median Algorithm," *Inform. Process. Letters*, Vol. 20, pp. 137–139.

COOLEY, J. W., P. A. W. LEWIS, AND P. D. WELCH (1967), "Historical Notes on the Fast Fourier Transform," *IEEE Trans. Audio Electroacoustics*, Vol. AU-15, No. 2, pp. 76–79.

COOLEY, J. W., AND J. W. TUKEY (1965), "An Algorithm for the Machine Calculation of Complex Fourier Series," *Math. Comput.*, Vol. 19, pp. 297–301.

DAVIS, L. (1975), "A Survey of Edge Detection Techniques," *Computer Graphics and Image Processing*, Vol. 4, pp. 248–270.

DUDA, R., AND P. HART (1972), "Use of Hough Transformations to Detect Lines and Curves in Pictures," *Comm. ACM*, Vol. 15, No. 1, pp. 11–15.

ELLIOTT, D. F., AND K. R. RAO (1982), *Fast Transforms, Algorithms, Analyses, Applications*, Academic Press, New York.

ERCAN, M. F., AND Y. F. FUNG (1996), "Low-Level Processing on a Linear Array Pyramid Architecture," *Computer Architecture Technical Committee Newsletter,* June, 9–15, pp. 9–11.

FOX, G., M. JOHNSON, G. LYZENGA, S. OTTO, J. SALMON, AND D. WALKER (1988), *Solving Problems on Concurrent Processors,* Volume 1, Prentice Hall, Englewood Cliffs, NJ.

GONZALEZ, R. C., AND R. E. WOODS (1992), *Digital Image Processing,* Addison-Wesley, Reading, MA.

GUPTA, A., AND V. KUMAR (1993), "The Scalability of FFT on Parallel Computers," *IEEE Trans. Par. Distrib. Syst.,* Vol. 4, No. 8, pp. 922–932.

HARALICK, R. M., AND L. G. SHAPIRO (1992), *Computer and Robot Vision*, Volume 1, Addison-Wesley, Reading, MA.

HOUGH, P. V. C. (1962), *A Method and Means for Recognizing Complex Patterns,* U.S. Patent 3,069,654.

HUERTAS, A., W. COLE, AND R. NEVATIA (1990), "Detecting Runways in Complex Airport Scenes," *Comput. Vision, Graphics, Image Proc.*, Vol. 51, No. 2, pp. 107–145.

ILLINGWORTH, J., AND J. KITTLER (1988), "Survey of the Hough Transform," *Computer Vision, Graphics, and Image Processing*, Vol. 44, No. 1, pp. 87–116.

JAIN, A. K. (1989), *Fundamentals of Digital Image Processing*, Prentice Hall, Englewood Cliffs, NJ.

KRISHNASWAMY, D., AND P. BANERJEE (1997), "Exploiting Task and Data Parallelism in Parallel Hough and Radon Transforms," *Proc. 1997 Int. Conf. Par. Proc.*, pp. 441–444.

MANDEVILLE, J. R. (1985), "A Novel Method for Analysis of Printed Circuit Images," *IBM J. Res. Dev.*, Vol. 29, Jan., pp 73–86.

NORTON, A., AND A. J. SILBERGER (1987), "Parallelization and Performance Analysis of the Cooley-Tukey FFT Algorithm for Shared Memory Architectures," *IEEE Trans. Comput.*, Vol. C-36, No. 5, pp. 581–591.

RAMIREZ, R. W. (1985), *The FFT: Fundamentals and Concepts*, Prentice Hall, Englewood Cliffs, NJ.

RAO, C. V. K., B. PRASADA, AND K. R. SARMA (1976), "A Parallel Shrinking Algorithm for Binary Patterns," *Comput. Graphics Image Process.*, Vol. 5, pp. 265–270.

SAHOO, P. K., S. SOLTANI, and A. K. C. WONG (1988), "A Survey of Thresholding Techniques," *Computer Vision, Graphics and Image Processing*, Vol. 41, pp. 233–260.

SEN, S. (1990), "Finding an Approximate Median with High Probability in Constant Parallel Time," *Inform. Process. Letters*, Vol. 34, pp. 77–80.

SONKA, M., V. HLAVAC, AND R. BOYLE (1993), *Image Processing, Analysis and Machine Vision*, Chapman and Hall, London, England.

SWARZTRAUBER, P. N. (1987), "Multiprocessor FFTs," *Parallel Computing*, Vol. 5, pp. 197–210.

THOMPSON, C. D. (1983), "Fourier Transforms in VLSI," *IEEE Trans. Comput.*, Vol. C-32, No. 11, pp. 1047–1057.

UHR, L., Editor (1987), *Parallel Computer Vision*, Academic Press, Boston, MA.

UHR, L., K. PRESTON JR., S. LEVIALDI, AND M. J. B. DUFF (1986), *Evaluation of Multicomputers for Image Processing,* Academic Press, Boston, MA.

WESZKA, J. S. (1978), "A Survey of Threshold Selection Techniques," *Computer Graphics and Image Processing*, Vol. 7, pp. 259–265.

PROBLEMS

Scientific/Numerical

12-1. Determine the parallel time complexity for computing the mean according to the algorithm described in Section 12.4.1 for p processors and n image pixels.

12-2. Determine the circumstances in which the median algorithm described in Section 12.4.2 will find the median and the circumstances in which it will not find the median. What is the worst-case position inaccuracy in finding the median?

12-3. Figure 12.36 shows an image that has changes in intensity. A 3×3 mask is moved over an image. Work through the results of Sobel operator masks moving across this image to find the gradient magnitude and gradient angle at various places. Assume that the gray area has a value of 0, the white area has a value of 255, and at least 50 percent of the pixel area must be highlighted to be recognized.

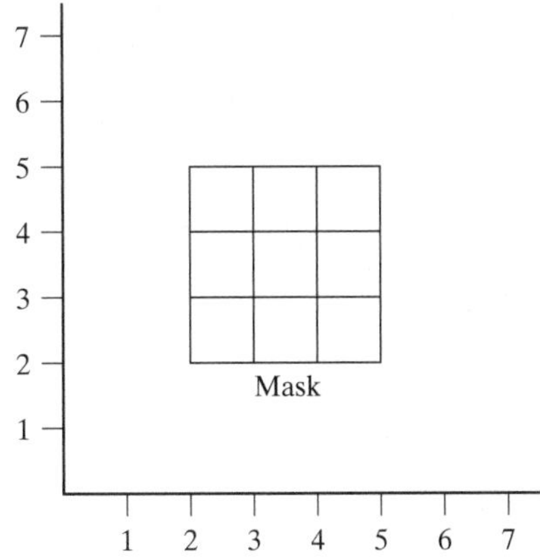

Figure 12.36 Image for Problem 12-3.

12-4. All of the masks in this chapter are 3×3 masks, but other sizes are possible, such as 5×5, 7×7, 9×9, 11×11, and 13×13 masks. Write a program to implement weighted mask filtering to cope with any $m \times m$ mask in which the size of the mask (m odd) and its contents are entered as input. Apply this program to an image and experiment with different masks.

12-5. Write a parallel program to perform edge detection of an image file stored in a standard uncompressed format such as the PPM (portable pix map) or PGM (portable gray map) file format. For viewing, it may be necessary to convert the image into a format such as gif format; such conversions can be done with system utilities. (See also system "man" pages and Born, 1995.)

12-6. Read in a PPM file in P6 format (full color), and write a parallel program to reduce the image to grayscale by taking the average of the red, green, and blue values for each pixel:

$$\text{pixel value} = \frac{\text{red value} + \text{green value} + \text{blue value}}{3}$$

12-7. Write a program to implement the Laplace operator. Experiment with subsequent thresholding to obtain edge detection. In addition to using the left-right-up-down neighboring points, experiment with points that are neighbors to these points.

12-8. Suppose edge detection has already been done on an image creating a binary image (1 at an edge and 0 elsewhere). Develop an algorithm and write a parallel program that fills the object, as delineated by the enclosed edges, with 1's. One way of doing this is to start with a single seed placed within the object and fill adjacent pixels recursively until the edges are reached.

12-9. Write a parallel program for the Hough transform using the normal representation for lines, and evaluate the program on sample images.

12-10. In the Hough transform, as an alternative to simply incrementing the accumulators, the gradient operator also provides the gradient magnitude, ∇f, allowing the gradient to be added to the accumulator instead. Investigate this method empirically and compare to simply incrementing the accumulators.

12-11. Read the paper by Krishnaswamy and Banerjee (1997) describing using the slope-intercept form of equation for lines in images for the Hough transform, and make a detailed comparison of that method compared to using the normal representation of Duda and Hart (1972).

12-12. Determine the computation time of the pipelined discrete Fourier transform implementation described in Section 12.7.4.

12-13. Show that the result of a one-point discrete Fourier transform is simply the value of the point.

12-14. Since the fast Fourier transform is a divide-and-conquer algorithm, it can be considered as a tree. Develop the connections in the form of a tree.

12-15. Prove that the matrix-vector formulation for discrete Fourier transform described in Section 12.7.4, for $N = 4$, is

$$\begin{bmatrix} X_0 \\ X_1 \\ X_2 \\ X_3 \end{bmatrix} = \frac{1}{4}\begin{bmatrix} 1 & 1 & 1 & 1 \\ 1 & w & w^2 & w^3 \\ 1 & w^2 & 1 & w^2 \\ 1 & w^3 & w^2 & w \end{bmatrix}\begin{bmatrix} x_0 \\ x_1 \\ x_2 \\ x_3 \end{bmatrix}$$

Write parallel programs for $N = 4$ using the matrix-vector formulation and the FFT formulation, and measure the execution speeds.

Real Life

12-16. You have been commissioned by a major film studio to develop a really fast "morphing" package that will change one image into another image. You come up with the idea of having two images, the original image and the final image, and changing each pixel on the original image to become closer and closer to the pixels of the final image in a lock-step SIMD fashion. This method is certainly embarrassingly parallel, although it may not create a very smoothly changing shape. Experiment with the method and demonstrate it to the studio using pictures of actors (or your friends).

12-17. NASA has given you the task of writing a really fast image-recognition program, fast enough that a Venusian CAT (Commercial Access Transport) is able to capture touchdown sites from topographic images made by the VERMIN satellite (VEnusian Radar Imaging and Networking satellite) while passing over the mapped area at a speed of 1000 km/hour. The VERMIN image maps are of a 5 km × 5 km area and have 0.5 m resolution both horizontally and in altitude. Appropriate landing sites are areas in which there is a 1.5 m maximum altitude variation within a 25 m circle. (Fairly large and relatively flat areas are needed for the CAT to land gracefully.) Create sample image maps of imperfect terrain; NASA will send you detailed VERMIN maps once your firm has demonstrated the capabilities of its CATs. For background information, read the paper on detecting runways by Huertas, Cole, and Nevatia (1990).

12-18. A manufacturer of printed circuit cards is having significant problems with broken printed circuit tracks on its boards and has commissioned you, as an independent programmer, to find a way to inspect images of the boards automatically as they leave the manufacturing line and recognize broken tracks. You know that all the tracks are straight in one direction or can turn 90 degrees to that direction. Develop a strategy for recognizing the break in the tracks and write a parallel program using realistic test images. For interest, read Mandeville (1985).

12-19. Tom's favorite activity is putting together 1,000-piece puzzles (odd, but uniquely shaped cardboard pieces that are die-cut from a single complete scene). Using shape and coloration as cues, Tom picks up two pieces and tries to fit them together, possibly rotating one or the other. Sometimes Tom misjudges, and the two pieces don't fit together properly; he then has to put the two pieces back on the board and try again. When they do fit together, Tom places them on the board, where they are then considered to be a single piece. Tom then repeats the process. Since developing an interest in computer science in general, and parallel programming in particular, Tom has rigged up a video camera over a small table on which he has spread all pieces of the current puzzle on which he is working. This camera is linked to one of his N computers (yes, he has N home computers, ranging from a now ancient 2 GHz P4 to a 64-CPU P9 with its 256-bit data path and a 12 GHz clock) producing a compact 30,000 × 30,000 pixel image. Tom's goal is to have the N computers working in parallel to produce a list of directions for assembling this puzzle in the fewest steps.

(Easy) List all of the aspects of computer science that need to be brought together in order for Tom to solve this parallel computing problem; explain the role each plays.

(Harder) Outline an approach Tom could use to solve this puzzle problem on his N computers. Identify the steps he needs to take, but do not actually carry out the programming that would produce the puzzle-assembly directions.

(Still harder) Outline what would need to be done if the shapes of the pieces were not unique.

(Difficult) Implement such a puzzle-solver on whatever parallel system you have available.

Chapter 13

Searching and Optimization

This chapter is concerned with searching and optimization methods. First, we consider *branch-and-bound methods*. Parallel implementations can draw upon several techniques introduced in earlier chapters. Then we examine in detail a quite different approach: using *genetic algorithms*. We discuss both the underlying techniques of genetic algorithms and various parallelization approaches. Finally, we look at the *hill climbing* technique as applied to a banking optimization problem. As with Chapter 12, this chapter provides information that can be used for parallel programming projects.

13.1 APPLICATIONS AND TECHNIQUES

Combinatorial search and optimization techniques are characterized by looking for a solution to a problem from among many potential solutions. For many search and optimization problems, exhaustive search is not feasible. Instead, some form of directed search is undertaken. In addition, rather than only the best (optimal) solution, a good nonoptimal solution is often sought.

Classical computer science problems tackled by combinatorial search and optimization techniques include the traveling salesperson problem, the 0/1 knapsack problem, the n-queens problem, and the 15- and 8-puzzles. In the traveling salesperson problem, the goal is to find the shortest route that starts at one city and visits each of a list other cities exactly once before returning to the first city. In the 0/1 knapsack problem, objects are assigned profit values and the goal is to pack a knapsack with selected objects to maximize the profit. The notation "0/1" is used to indicate that the object is either selected in its entirety (1) or is not selected (0). The goal of the n-queens problem is to place n queens on an $n \times n$ chessboard in an arrangement whereby none of the queens can attack any other. In the 8-puzzle, eight numbered tiles, 1 to 8, are placed on a 3×3 board having one empty space. The goal is to move one tile at a time, but only into an empty space, so that the tiles are finally in row major order (i.e., 1, 2, 3 in order on the top row, 4, 5, and 6 in order on the second row, and 7 and 8 in order on the bottom row). The 15-puzzle is similar except with 15 tiles on a 4×4 board. All these problems are characterized by a huge number of permutations, and a search through all of them would be very time-consuming. In cases such as the knapsack problem and the traveling salesperson problem, a (worst-case) polynomial time algorithm is not known and the decision problems are classified as NP-complete.

There are also many serious applications in commerce, banking, and industry. For example, search and optimization techniques have been used for financial forecasting, airline fleet and crew assignment, and VLSI chip layout. The problem of VLSI layout is similar in concept to the knapsack problem. The goal is to lay out components on a VLSI chip in an arrangement that minimizes chip area, given the shape of each component. Constraints include the chip being a rectangle. Placing the components in different positions will result in different unused spaces. There will be additional constraints in real designs, such as chip aspect ratio (length/width ratio) and wiring between components. Combinatorial search and optimization techniques also find application for processor register assignments made by compilers and multiprocessor scheduling.

There are several search and optimization techniques that can be used on the problems described above, including

- Branch-and-bound search
- Dynamic programming
- Hill climbing
- Simulated annealing
- Genetic algorithms

In this chapter, we will outline the branch-and-bound technique, one of the fundamental sequential search and optimization techniques, and then consider genetic algorithms in some detail. Later, we will consider an example of hill climbing. We will not investigate the other methods for parallelization. Parallel dynamic programming can be found in Quinn (1994), and parallel simulated annealing can be found in Witte, Chamberlain, and Franklin (1991). A comparison of genetic algorithms, simulated annealing, and hill climbing can be found in Michalewicz (1996).

13.2 BRANCH-AND-BOUND SEARCH

13.2.1 Sequential Branch and Bound

The actions of branch-and-bound search can be described by a *state space tree*. The root of this tree represents the starting point. From the root to the next level represents individual choices made toward the solution of the problem; for example, in selecting one object in the knapsack problem or one component and its place for VLSI layout. Once this choice is made, another choice is selected and the search process moves down to the next level of the tree.

In essence, the problem is being divided into subproblems, which themselves are then divided in a divide-and-conquer manner. The nodes become subproblems to be solved.

A generic state space tree is illustrated in Figure 13.1 that would be applicable to many problems. There are n choices that can be made initially, C_0 to C_{n-1}. For the knapsack problem, each choice would be the object first selected. For the traveling salesperson problem, each choice would be the next city to select in the route. For the n-queens problem, it would be the position of the first queen. The construction of the tree as described is problem dependent and is called a *dynamic tree* (Horowitz and Sahni, 1978). The state space tree can also be formulated as a binary tree by making a TRUE/FALSE decision at each node. For example, in the knapsack problem, the choices at each node are either to select or not select a particular object. This form of tree is called a *static tree*.

The state space tree could be explored by a *depth-first* method — starting at, say, the left side, downward from one node to the next-lower node, then continuing as far as possible from left to right. The search tree could also be explored using a *breadth-first* method by expanding each level from left to right before moving to the next-lower level. Normally, an exhaustive search of all the nodes would be prohibitively expensive, so strategies are used to reduce the search. The common strategy called *best-first* directs the search down the paths most likely to lead to the best solution. The search does not proceed at all down paths that cannot lead to a better solution than already found. By avoiding unpromising search paths, the state space tree is *pruned*.

Pruning is a key part of the search method to reduce the search space, but it requires one to decide whether a better solution might exist further down the state space tree. For this, a *bounding function* or *cut-off function* must be devised. As each node is reached, the bounding function is evaluated that provides a lower bound (for minimization problems) or an upper bound (for maximization problems) for any further search. In the case of the knapsack problem, the bounding function would yield the maximum possible profit; for the VLSI layout, it would yield the minimum possible chip area. The result of the bounding function would be compared to the best solution so far obtained.

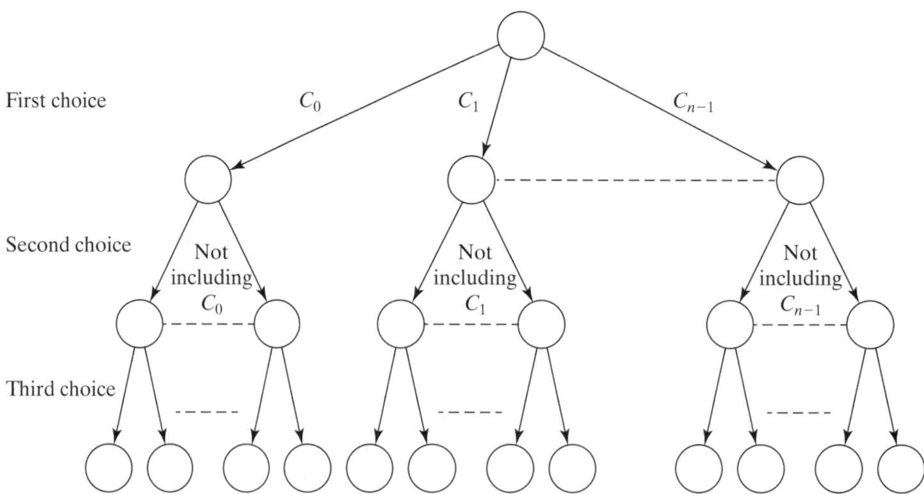

Figure 13.1 State space tree.

When a node is reached but not all its children have been explored, the node is a called a *live node*. A live node in which the children are currently being explored is called an *E-node* (being expanded). When all the children have been explored, the node becomes a *dead node*. In branch and bound, all the children of an E-node become live nodes. A list of live nodes is maintained in a queue as the search proceeds, and the queue is used in the search algorithm. Sometimes the queue is called an *open list*. (If necessary, dead nodes are placed on a *closed list*; for example, to check for duplicates.) For a best-first strategy, the queue would be a *priority queue*, in which more promising live nodes are placed at the front of the queue and are considered first.

In *backtracking* (which is usually regarded as distinct from branch and bound), when a search should not proceed downward any further, the search moves back to a higher level to continue the search at that level; that is, it "backtracks." An appropriate data structure to implement this mechanism is a (last-in-first-out) stack for holding nodes that have been visited.

13.2.2 Parallel Branch and Bound

State space trees would appear to be very amenable to parallelization. For example, separate processors could search different parts of the state space tree independently. The most natural approach would be to allocate a portion of the state space tree from a node downward to one processor. This processor could then perform a search in its area of the search tree. A depth-first search partitioned into multiple independent depth-first searches is usually called *parallel depth-first search*, although strictly the parallelism creates a breadth-first wavefront throughout the tree as each processor moves from one live node to the next downward. It might also be feasible to introduce parallelism in the evaluation of the bounding function and in the selection of the next E-node.

Unfortunately, several issues make the parallelization more complex and less efficient than one would first imagine. Branch-and-bound search requires the current lower (or upper) bound as created by the bounding function to be known by all the processors in order for them to prune their portions of the tree optimally at any instant. The level at which to prune changes during the search as better solutions are found.

In addition, the size of the state space tree in any partition is not known in advance. Load balancing becomes a significant issue, and the load-balancing techniques described in Chapter 7 are applicable. The (open list) queue is a shared data structure that is similar to the vertex queue in the shortest-path problem described in Section 7.4. Indeed the shortest-path problem could be regarded as a search and optimization problem, since the objective is to search for the best path through the graph. Usually solutions to the shortest-path problem are grouped with other graph algorithms, such as finding connected components. A fundamental difference between graph searching and the state space search techniques described in this chapter is that in graph searching, the graph is known before the search begins, whereas the structure of the state space tree is not known before the search begins.

Concurrent Queue Access. For a shared memory implementation, the queue must be protected from simultaneous access, and the shared data techniques using locks in Chapter 8 are applicable. However, the resultant serialization will significantly limit the potential speedup. As pointed out by Rao and Kumar (1988), the maximum speedup that can be achieved is given by

$$S(n) \le \frac{t_{\text{queue}} + t_{\text{comp}}}{t_{\text{queue}}}$$

where t_{queue} is the mean time to access the queue, and t_{comp} is the mean subproblem (node) computation time. This result comes essentially from Amhahl's law (Chapter 1, Section 1.2.2).

Rather than place a lock around the complete queue, one could place a lock around each entry in the queue. When one processor accesses the first item on the queue, it is locked. The next processor must access the next item in the queue after being blocked from the first. As we have mentioned, a best-first strategy uses a priority queue. A priority queue could be implemented by maintaining a sorted list after each insertion or deletion. However, this approach would have an $O(n \log n)$ time complexity. Priority queues can also be implemented using a *heap* data structure, which has more efficient insertion and deletion. A heap is a complete binary tree that has the characteristic that each node holds a value at least as large as the values held by its children. In the context of a priority queue, the parent has higher priority than its children (or at least as high if more than one node could have the same priority). Hence, the root holds the highest-priority item. An algorithm to insert a new item starts by inserting the item at the bottom of the heap (the first free leaf node on the lowest level, left to right). The item is then moved up the tree in a series of compares and exchanges until a position can be found that maintains the heap characteristic. Deletion of the highest-priority node (the root) involves replacing the root with the last item of the heap and then moving it downward until the heap characteristic exists again. These insertion and deletion algorithms only have $\log n$ steps but require access to more than one node. Rao and Kumar (1988) describe an approach in which concurrent access is achieved by locking only a portion of the heap, called a *window* (three nodes for insertion and one node for deletion). Additional status information must be stored in each node to control multiple access to the heap. The reader is referred to Rao and Kumar (1988) for more details.

To avoid the problems of a centralized queue, one could distribute the queue among processors and have them broadcast better nodes to each other at intervals. Such strategies would be used in message-passing systems. Janakiram, Agrawal, and Mehrotra (1988) have investigated (in the context of backtracking) processors selecting children nodes at random rather than in a fixed order to reduce the interprocessor communication.

Speedup Anomalies. When a sequential search is done by the depth-first method, the processor starts at the root and traverses the leftmost path first and then the next path downward, and so on, until it finds the solution. When p processors are operating independently on separate downward paths, it may be that one processor very quickly finds a feasible solution. In that case, it is possible for the parallel speedup to be greater than p (superlinear speedup). This is known as an *acceleration anomaly.* Conversely, a feasible solution may be in a position in the tree where it cannot be reached in $1/p$ of the time that it would be reached with a single processor. Then the speedup becomes less than p. This is known as a *deceleration anomaly* if the speedup is still more than 1. It is possible for the speedup to be less than 1. In that case, the anomaly is called a *detrimental anomaly.* Lai and Sahni (1984) and Li and Wah (1986) have studied in detail how these anomalies might occur. See also Wah, Li, and Yu (1985).

13.3 GENETIC ALGORITHMS

13.3.1 Evolution and Genetic Algorithms

Genetic algorithms have their theoretical roots in biology and are an attempt to mimic the process of natural evolution in a population of individuals. While the exact mechanisms behind natural evolution are not very well known, some aspects have been studied in significant depth. One of the principal research areas in biology for some time now has been the study of chromosomes: the information carriers containing the characteristics of a living being. Although there is some uncertainty surrounding the way in which chromosomes dictate the properties of living organisms, there is little doubt that they in fact do uniquely determine them.

Evolution is a process that works at the chromosome level, through the reproductive process, rather than on the living individuals themselves. When individuals in a population reproduce, portions of the genetic information of each parent (portions of the parents' chromosomes) are combined to generate the chromosomes of their offspring. In this way, the offspring carry genetic-makeup information that is a blend of their parents' information, and exhibit a corresponding blend of the parental characteristics. Combining chromosomes from the parents to produce offspring is the predominant mechanism by which chromosome patterns change. This inheritance of some portion of the characteristics from each parent is termed *crossover.*

In addition, an occasional random change may occur in the chromosome pattern of a particular individual: an effect termed *mutation*. Mutations may lead to individuals whose chromosome patterns are significantly different from either parent. A mutation may enhance survivability or impair it, compared to the individual's parents. The most significant aspect of mutation is that it causes an abrupt change in the individual's viability that is not directly related to that of the parents. Since there appear to be many more ways to degrade an individual's survivability than to improve it, massively occurring mutations tend to degrade the viability of the population over time. Rarely occurring mutations will occasionally produce a favorable change, yet will not overwhelm the population with unfavorable changes.

As with all changes to an organism's chromosomes, there will be a change in the way the organism interacts with its environment. On occasion these changes improve the viability of the adapted organism relative to its ancestors, leading to an increased likelihood of its surviving and passing on some of its chromosome information to its offspring. Naturally, there will be occasions as well in which the changes reduce the organism's viability and thereby decrease its chances of passing that information to its offspring. Mutation is generally believed to play a significant, although infrequent, role in natural evolution as compared to crossover.

When the mutation rate is relatively low, the unfit individuals tend to die out before passing their traits on to their offspring. Conversely, the more fit individuals generally succeed in passing their traits to future generations. However, when the mutation rate is relatively large, large numbers of individuals whose characteristics are randomly different from the characteristics of the preceding generation are introduced. This leads to degeneration of the population in nature, and to instability, or nonconvergence, in the computer implementation of genetic algorithms.

Over time, changes in chromosomes produce variants that may differ significantly from the members of the original organism strain. In general, changes that enhance the viability of the strain in some way tend to predominate over time. For example, in species of birds in which the female provides the primary care for the eggs in a nest, the feather coloration of the females is generally subdued in comparison to that of the males. In this manner, the females blend into their surroundings rather than call attention to themselves as the males do. The lifespan of individuals who blend into their surroundings while sitting motionless on a nest for long periods tends to be greater than the lifespan of those who call a predator's attention to themselves. As such, females tend to pass their subdued-coloration chromosomes to more offspring. Eventually, the population becomes weighted toward those characteristics that tend to be associated with increased lifespan.

The theory proposed by Charles Darwin in 1859 in his classic work on evolution, the theory of natural selection, is more commonly known as "survival of the fittest." Just as in the preceding bird example, in any population of a species the "stronger" or "more fit" individuals are more likely to survive and subsequently to pass on to their offspring those traits that led to their survival. It is certainly possible for an extremely fit individual to fail to survive long enough to reproduce! An example would be the individual who just happens to be in "the wrong place at the wrong time" and is prematurely turned into a food source for another species. As the pundits have noted, the race does not always go to the fastest, or the fight to the strongest, but on average it sure pays to bet on those outcomes.

The repeated application of the principles of crossover and mutation, each time followed by the production of a "next generation" based on the relative fitness of the reproducing members, is termed a genetic algorithm. Just as in nature, this approach toward optimization of a "population of solutions" tends over time to produce good solutions. The next sections describe in detail how genetic algorithms may be implemented.

Genetic algorithms are computational approaches to problem solving that are modeled after the biological process of evolution. The algorithm first creates an initial population of solutions (*individuals*). These solutions are then evaluated, using an application-specific criterion of *fitness*, to characterize them from "most fit" to "least fit." A subset of the population is selected, using criteria that tend to favor the more fit individuals. This subset is then used to produce a new generation of offspring. Finally, a small number of individuals in this next generation are subjected to random *mutations*.

The processes of selection, crossover, and mutation are then repeated, producing a number of generations. The underlying presumption is that, as in nature, individuals in a population will tend to evolve and improve in fitness so long as the more fit individuals in a given generation are used to produce the next generation. While genetic algorithms are not guaranteed to find the optimum solution, they are generally excellent at quickly finding solutions that are pretty good.

13.3.2 Sequential Genetic Algorithms

The following is a pseudocode outline of the components of a sequential genetic algorithm:

```
generation_num = 0;
initialize Population(generation_num);
evaluate Population(generation_num);
set termination_condition to False;
while (not termination_condition) {
    generation_num++;
    select Parents(generation_num) from Population(generation_num - 1);
    apply crossover to Parents(generation_num) to get
         Offspring(generation_num);
    apply mutation to Offspring(generation_num) to get
         Population(generation_num);
    evaluate Population(generation_num) and update termination_condition;
}
```

Several issues have been somewhat glossed over to this point in the discussion. Among them are

- How one represents an individual or potential solution in terms of "chromosomes"
- How one produces the initial population of potential solutions
- How one evaluates each potential solution to determine its fitness
- How one determines the condition(s) under which the repetition terminates
- How one selects individuals to become "parents" of the next generation, and the actual production of next-generation individuals

Once these have been explored, the issues involving parallelizing the sequential approach will be considered.

13.3.3 Initial Population

To demonstrate the first steps in the genetic algorithm method, let us consider the simple problem of determining the maximum of the function

$$f(x, y, z) = -x^2 + 1{,}000{,}000x - y^2 - 40{,}000y - z^2$$

over an integer domain of −1,000,000 to +1,000,000 for each variable. (The variables, x, y, and z are restricted to integer values for additional simplicity.)

It so happens that there is a direct solution to this problem that facilitates verification of the results obtained by other techniques. In practice, of course, since they do not guarantee the optimum solution, one would only apply search and optimization techniques to problems for which a simple closed-form solution did not exist. Using simple algebra, f can be factored into a form in which the maximum may be seen by inspection

$$f(x, y, z) = 2504 \times 10^8 - (x - 500{,}000)^2 - (y + 20{,}000)^2 - z^2$$

In this form, it is apparent that the maximum of $f(x, y, z)$, 250,400,000,000, occurs when x is 500,000, y is −20,000, and z is 0, since those coordinate values make the squared terms zero and any other coordinate values reduce f by subtracting something from the 2504×10^8 term. But let us suppose that such a direct solution is unavailable. (As indicated, we use this function as our test case so that the computer solution can be readily checked against the actual solution; any function could be used.)

Due to the computational size of the problem, the "immediately obvious" exhaustive search approach of simply calculating the function value corresponding to every possible coordinate is impractical. There are $(2{,}000{,}001)^3$ coordinates to be evaluated, and even if the function value corresponding to each could be computed in 100 ns (highly optimistic for any reasonable evaluation function), it would take more than 200,000,000 hours on a single processor. Even if we were able to speed up the process by a factor of 10,000 through parallel implementation of this algorithm, we still would have to wait more than two years for a solution.

Data Representation. The first step in determining the initial population of potential solutions is to choose a suitable data representation for an individual. In early genetic algorithm work, the potential solutions were simply strings of 1's and 0's. More recent work has extended the representations to include floating point, Gray code, and integer strings (Michalewicz, 1996). For simplicity, we will use binary strings.

The ith potential solution will consist of a three-tuple (x_i, y_i, z_i), in which each component of the three-tuple has one of the 2,000,001 possible integers in the interval $-1{,}000{,}000 \leq \text{component\_value} \leq +1{,}000{,}000$. Since

$$2^{20} < 2{,}000{,}001 \leq 2^{21}$$

21 bits are needed to represent each of the three components. A single potential solution (i.e., a chromosome, or individual) will simply be the 63 bits consisting of the concatenation of the (x_i, y_i, z_i) representations.

Suppose $x = +262{,}408_{10}$, $y = +16{,}544_{10}$, and $z = -1{,}032_{10}$. Using the "sign plus magnitude" representation, the binary representation for each of the numbers is

$$x = 001000000000100001000$$
$$y = 000000100000010100000$$
$$z = 100000000010000001000$$

where the leftmost bit of each number is the sign (0 denoting positive values, 1 denoting negative values) and the remaining bits represent the magnitude. Note that this choice of representations ensures that the magnitudes must fall between $-1{,}048{,}575$ and $+1{,}048{,}575$, or $\pm 2^{20}$. Concatenating into a binary string, we get the representation of a potential solution

001000000000100001000000000100000010100000100000000010000001000

Now that we have determined the length of a potential solution, 63 bits, we may easily introduce an initial population of them using a pseudorandom generator.

Evaluation. Next, we use the values of x, y, and z in our function to assess the fitness of this individual:

$$f(x, y, z) = -x^2 + 1{,}000{,}000x - y^2 - 40{,}000y - z^2$$

$$f(262408, 16544, -1{,}032) = -(262{,}408)^2 + 1{,}000{,}000 \times 262{,}408 - (16{,}544)^2 - 40{,}000 \times 16{,}544 - (-1{,}032)^2$$

$$= -68{,}857{,}958{,}464 + 262{,}408{,}000{,}000 - 273{,}703{,}936 - 661{,}760{,}000 - 1{,}065{,}024$$

$$= 192{,}613{,}512{,}576$$

This evaluation process would be repeated for every individual in the population, calculating the function value, or fitness, corresponding to each. These individuals are then ranked according to how well they did at maximizing the function. That is, individuals whose fitness, as evaluated by this function, is greater than 192,613,512,576 would be ranked more fit than this individual, while those evaluating to a lower value would be ranked as less fit.

Constraints. Naturally, since our variable domain is restricted to ±1,000,000, any individual whose x, y, or z values fall outside that interval is considered to be of such low fitness that there is no reason even to compute its function value in anticipation of its possibly becoming a parent. That is, its equivalent in nature would be that of a stillborn individual. There are other ways to handle restricted domains on individuals. The defect that caused the individual to fall outside the ±1,000,000 interval could be "surgically repaired" (changing one or more bits to correct the defect). Alternatively, the generated individual can be mapped into the restricted domain prior to fitness evaluation with some simple scaling of each coordinate:

$$\text{Scaled coordinate} = -1{,}000{,}000 + \frac{\text{coordinate}}{2^{21}} \times (2{,}000{,}000)$$

Solution constraints on individuals as applied to genetic algorithms are discussed further in Michalewicz (1996).

Number of Individuals. Finally there is the issue of how many individuals should be placed in the initial population. In general, a small number of individuals decreases the likelihood of obtaining a good solution in a reasonable number of generations, while a large number increases the computation required for each generation. It is not uncommon for an initial population to be made up of 20 to 1000 pseudorandom potential solutions. For this example, that would mean the production of 20 to 1000 pseudorandomly generated binary strings, each of which is 63 bits long.

13.3.4 Selection Process

Again, modeling after nature, it should be possible for any individual to be selected to become a parent of an offspring in the next generation. However, as in nature, a more fit individual is presumed to have a somewhat greater chance of being selected than one that is less fit. This bias toward the more fit individuals is termed *selective pressure*.

At first glance it might appear that a high degree of selective pressure (e.g., choosing only the most fit portion of the population to produce offspring for the next generation) would be highly desirable. However, for problems in which there may be local optima, this may result in the process converging rapidly to a local optimum and totally missing the global optimum. The opposite situation, too little selective pressure, results in very slow convergence or even nonconvergence; neither situation is desirable.

Based on its having demonstrated relatively satisfactory performance in many applications, one of the leading candidates for use in applying selective pressure is *tournament selection.*

Tournament Selection. In this approach each individual is equally likely to be chosen at random from the general population and entered into a tournament. A set of k such individuals is chosen for each tournament, and the fitness of each is evaluated. The most fit individual from this set of k individuals is deemed to be the overall tournament winner and will become a parent to the next generation of individuals. In all, n such tournaments are conducted to determine the n individuals that will be used to produce the next generation, which keeps the population size the same as the preceding population size.

Clearly, when k is 1 there is no selective pressure at all; each member of the population is equally likely to be used to produce the next generation. When k is large, the amount of selective pressure is likewise large, since only the individual determined to be the most fit out of k randomly chosen individuals will be selected to become a parent. More typically, a value of 2 is used for k, reminiscent of a medieval joust (or tournament) by two knights.

13.3.5 Offspring Production

Once the more fit individuals have been selected from the present generation through a series of tournaments, their chromosomes must be combined to determine the composition of the individuals who will make up the population of the next generation. The process of combining portions of the chromosomes from each parent to produce the chromosomes of the children is crossover. While there are several common crossover forms, our discussion will be limited to single-point crossover.

Single-Point Crossover. In single-point crossover, a randomly located cut is made at the pth bit in the m-bit chromosome patterns of each parent, A and B. This cut divides each parent's pattern into two parts. Child number 1 has its pattern made from the first p bits of parent A's pattern, followed by the last $m - p$ bits of parent B's pattern. Child number 2 has its pattern made from the first p bits of parent B, followed by the last $m - p$ bits of parent A's pattern. As the term implies, portions of the parents' chromosome patterns *cross over* in the process of forming the children. This is illustrated in Figure 13.2. For example, consider two individuals that have been selected to be parents. Each has 63-bit chromosome patterns

$$A = 001100101000000100001\ 010010100000010101010\ 000111111100000011000$$

and

$$B = 000001000000101000001\ 101000001010101010101\ 000110001010101010000.$$

If the cut is made after the fifteenth bit, the two portions of the parents' chromosomes are

Parent A (first 15 bits): 001100101000000

Parent A (last 48 bits): 100001010010100000010101010000111111100000011000

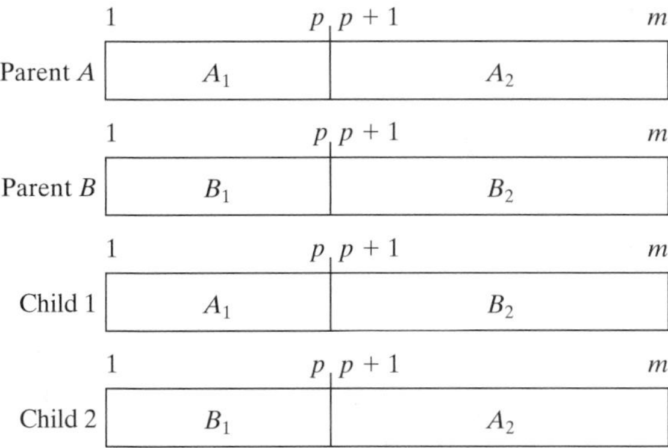

Figure 13.2 Single-point crossover.

Parent *B* (first 15 bits): 000001000000101

Parent *B* (last 48 bits): 000001101000001010101010101000110001010101010000

Applying crossover, a pair of children are created:

Child 1: 001100101000000 000001101000001010101010101000110001010101010000

and

Child 2: 000001000000101 100001010010100000010101010000111111100000011000

The children's *genes*, the individual bits of their chromosomes, are a blend of the genes of their parents. Due to the selection process having a bias toward choosing the more fit individuals from the current generation, the children are characterized by a blend of more fit parents' characteristics. As in nature, crossover slowly tends to force the population toward stronger (i.e., more fit) individuals. Since this is a gradual, relatively predictable change, crossover is usually encouraged in genetic algorithms and typically occurs at each generation.

While we have discussed only single-point crossover in this example, it should be noted that researchers have investigated other alternatives. Some of these include multipoint crossover, in which several cuts are made and smaller portions of the chromosomes are intermingled, and uniform crossover, in which each bit, or gene, is randomly selected from either parent. The use of gene sharing from a pool of parents in which each gene of an offspring is selected from a parent randomly chosen from the pool has also been investigated.

Mutation. Unlike crossover, mutation occurs at the isolated gene level within a chromosome. This can be thought of as similar to the effects that disease, radiation, or the ingestion of various controlled substances might have on a living organism. Mutation tends to bring about major unpredictable changes in the fitness of an individual.

In the initial example of maximizing a function, a single-bit change in the leftmost position of the 21-bit pattern of x, y, or z, would induce a sign change in that component of a coordinate, but the magnitude would remain the same. A single-bit change in the second position from the left (the position weighted by 2^{19}) would cause a change in magnitude of

524,288 for x, y, or z. However, a single-bit change in the rightmost position would cause a change in magnitude of only 1.

Since the effect of a single-bit mutation on an individual's x, y, or z component may range all the way from minimal (± 1) to extreme (±1,000,000), depending upon which bit is changed, it is clear that mutation can be an extremely powerful factor in influencing an individual's fitness. When the probability of mutation is high, the chances of a relatively fit individual changing characteristics (and thereby being dramatically degraded in fitness) are likewise high. In the extreme, high rates of mutation may result in the nonconvergence of the genetic algorithm.

Since the changes in an individuals's fitness due to mutation may be very dramatic and much less predictable than the effects of crossover, the chances of mutations occurring are generally kept small in a genetic algorithm. This allows mutated individuals to be introduced into the population, but at a rate slow enough to prevent them from continually shifting the population away from convergence on an optimum solution. Through selection and crossover, the effects of mutations are gradually incorporated into the population as a whole. When it is beneficial (i.e., the mutation improves the fitness of an individual), the mutated individual's likelihood of being selected to help produce the next generation of individuals is increased. This automatically results in the propagation of beneficial mutations and the dying out of the nonbeneficial mutations.

13.3.6 Variations

The preceding sections by no means exhaust the variations that have been explored in producing members of the next generation. Instead of producing the next generation solely from crossover and mutation on the current generation, one might

- Carry over a few of the most fit individuals from this generation to be a part of the next generation
- Randomly create a few new individuals in each generation rather than only generating randomized individuals at the initiation of the algorithm
- Allow the population size to vary from one generation to the next

13.3.7 Termination Conditions

Several strategies have been employed in terminating genetic algorithms, ranging from a simple count of the number of generations to attempts to determine how close the solution is to convergence. In the simplest case, the production of successive generations is carried out s times. While this is an easy enough termination condition to implement, it suffers from two obvious deficiencies. In one extreme the population may have converged already to a solution in far fewer than s generations, while in the other it may still have a long way to go before converging satisfactorily.

Since the optimal solution is unknown a priori, one cannot simply measure the difference between the current best solution and the optimum to decide whether to terminate. On the other hand, one can borrow a technique from the field of numerical analysis in which the results of successive iterations are examined, and a decision to terminate is then based on the degree of improvement between successive generations. Just as various numerical algorithms may exhibit oscillation around a solution rather than further convergence, so may genetic algorithms. Since such oscillation has been experimentally confirmed both in the situation where the difference in probability of selection of individuals is nearly the same (minimal selective pressure) and in the high-mutation-rate situation, some care must be taken in relying solely on this form of termination.

Yet another termination condition may be based on the degree of similarity of the individuals within the population. Since their similarity increases as the population of individual-solution candidates converges toward an optimal solution, measuring the diversity in the population serves to measure convergence as well. It is not uncommon for a genetic algorithm to incorporate multiple termination conditions.

13.3.8 Parallel Genetic Algorithms

Conceptually, the problem of adapting genetic algorithms to multiple processors is straightforward. Two approaches immediately come to mind:

1. Let each processor operate independently on an isolated subpopulation of the individuals, periodically sharing its best individuals with the other processors through *migration*, or
2. Let each processor do a portion of each step of the algorithm — selection, crossover, and mutation — on the common population.

Isolated Subpopulations. In the first approach each processor independently generates its own initial subpopulation of individuals. Each processor then carries out k generations of individuals:

- Handling the evaluation of fitness
- Selecting the individuals from its subpopulation to be used to produce its next generation
- Performing the crossover and mutation computations on its subpopulations.

After k such generations ($k \geq 1$), the processors share their best individuals with the other processors.

Migration Operator. When migration is incorporated, changes in a population come not only from inheriting portions of one's parents' genes, albeit with occasional random mutations, but also from the introduction of new species into the population. In nature, this movement between subpopulations is often a survival response, although humankind has (sometimes unwittingly) accelerated the process by providing a transportation mechanism. A few examples of transported species include the rabbits introduced into Australia and the zebra mussels introduced into the St. Lawrence River system and the Great Lakes region of North America. In genetic algorithms, the migration operator is responsible for several tasks needed to implement the exchange of individuals between subpopulations. Such tasks include

- Selecting the emigrants
- Sending the emigrants
- Receiving the immigrants
- Integrating the immigrants

Sending and receiving selected individuals can be done relatively easily in a message-passing parallel environment. It is the selecting and integrating of the individuals that provides interesting results. Selecting the best individuals to migrate from each subpopulation, and integrating the received individuals into the population in place of the worst individuals, will cause a faster convergence. Therefore, it would seem likely that by passing copies of a number of the more fit individuals from one subpopulation to another subpopulation, replacing the worst individuals would achieve convergence even faster. However, selecting and integrating in such a manner eventually places too much selective pressure on the population and might hinder the results produced. Once again, selective pressure should not be so great that the results progress toward a local optimum instead of the global optimum.

Introducing migration also introduces a communication overhead. As with other parallel computations using message passing, when the communication time begins to dominate the total computation time, the performance of the parallel algorithm suffers. Therefore, both the frequency and the volume of information communicated between slave processes should be considered.

Migration Models. The most popular approaches for modeling migration are

- The island model
- The stepping-stone model

In the *island model*, individuals are allowed to be sent to any other subpopulation, as illustrated in Figure 13.3. There are no restrictions on where an individual may migrate. In the *stepping-stone model*, migration is limited by allowing emigrants to move only to neighboring subpopulations. This concept is illustrated in Figure 13.4. The stepping-stone model reduces communication overhead by limiting the number of destinations to which emigrants may travel, and thereby limiting the number of messages. The island model allows more freedom, and in some ways represents a better model of nature. However, there is significantly more communication overhead and delay when implementing such a model.

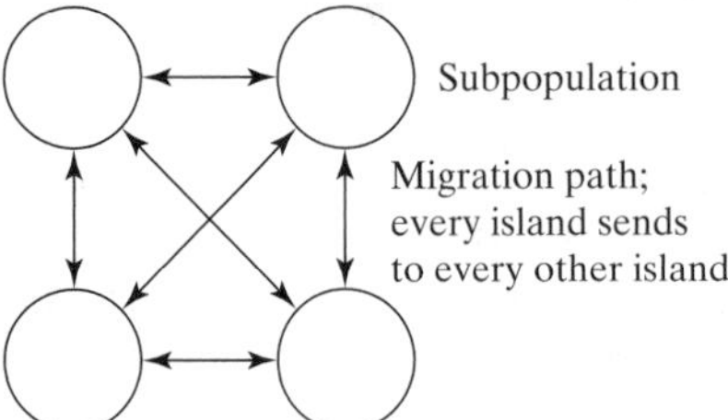

Figure 13.3 Island model.

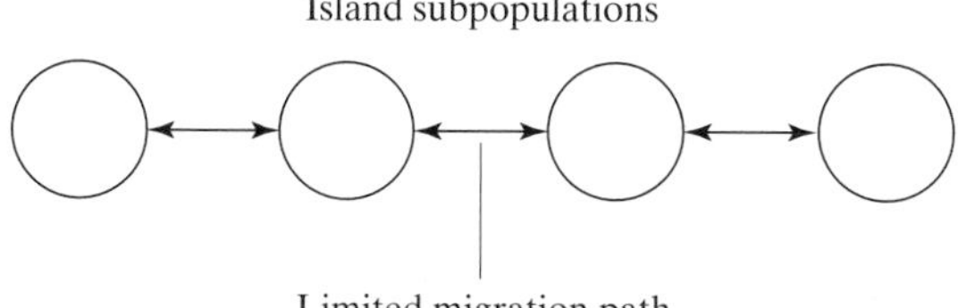

Figure 13.4 Stepping-stone model.

Parallel Implementation. The following pseudocode describes the implementation of the slave process:

```
set generation_num to 0;
initialize Population(generation_num);
evaluate fitness of Population(generation_num);
while (not termination_condition) {
   generation_num++;
   select Parents(generation_num) from
      Population(generation_num - 1);
   apply crossover to Parents(generation_num) to produce
      Offspring(generation_num);
   apply mutation to Offspring(generation_num) to get
      Population(generation_num);
   apply migration to Population(generation_num);
   evaluate Population(generation_num);
}
```

Each slave program executes the preceding pseudocode to produce results that are returned to the master program. The master program then performs some analysis before producing the final results.

The island and stepping-stone models both have advantages and drawbacks. The obvious advantage is that, except for the communication of best individuals, which occurs only once in every k generations, both are embarrassingly parallel in nature. That is, by using p processors, each operating independently on (population_size/p) subpopulations of individuals, one could potentially speed up the computation of the k generations by a factor of p.

Such isolated parallelism has even been used to attempt to explain the (apparently) missing links in the fossil record. Cohoon et al. (1987) proposed an implementation based on the theory of "punctuated equilibria," which provided a foundation for the theory that new species are likely to form quickly in subpopulations following a change in the environment. These changes might occur, for example, as a result of migration introducing new genetic material into the population. Cohoon et al. observed that when a substantial number of individuals migrated between isolated subpopulations, new solutions were found shortly after the migration occurred, just as the fossil records seem to indicate that major developments occurred in nature over relatively short periods.

Since the overall parallelism is interrupted every k generations so that information about the most fit individuals may be communicated, somewhat less than a p-fold speedup is possible under this approach. Whether information about the most fit individuals is communicated to all the other processors or only to ones deemed adjacent will affect the actual speedup. The interprocessor communication architecture also may be a factor.

Under the stepping-stone model, even the interprocessor communication that occurs after the kth generation is reduced by restricting communication to a processor's nearest neighbors, rather than permitting each processor to communicate with every other processor.

As computationally advantageous as the embarrassingly parallel approach may be, it suffers from a flaw: the relatively isolated nature of the population subsets. The isolation of the subsets increases the possibility that each will converge to its own local optimum rather than to a global optimum and perhaps completely miss the global solution. In addition, the reduced number of individuals making up each population subset increases the number of generations needed to achieve convergence.

As an aside, the isolation/local-optima phenomenon in genetic algorithms is believed to have occurred in nature as well! Geologists studying plate tectonics (the large sections of the earth's crust that move around, over, and into each other) have produced computer projections of past plate movements. One of the plates that has long been isolated from contact with others makes up the bulk of the Australian continent. Biologists have long noted the number of species unique to that region, including wingless birds and large hopping mammals. Evolution, occurring in parallel in isolated regions, does not necessarily result in similar solutions in each of the regions! Rather, differing local optima may well be the result.

Of course, the obvious mechanism to reduce the effective isolation, increased interprocessor communication, introduces its own disadvantage. An increase in the sequentially occurring (communication) portion of the algorithm and a decrease in the effective speedup over the case using multiple, but isolated, processors is the result.

Parallelizing a Common Population. As an alternative to this isolated subpopulation parallelism, one could simply implement the genetic operators in parallel on the global population. For example, if there were a way to provide information on the individuals to every processor, then the processors could perform selection, crossover, and mutation in parallel.

Clearly, if we utilize tournament selection, the processors may operate on independent pairs of individuals. Similarly, each processor could work independently on a subset of the selected individuals to perform the crossover and mutation operations and evaluate the resulting fitnesses. Unfortunately, while this effectively parallelizes the genetic operations, it may well do little to speed up the overall computation! Much depends upon the time needed to compute the various operations (selection, crossover, and mutation), compared to the time to distribute the population information to all the processors plus the time to communicate the results of the selection process. In many cases genetic operators require little intensive computation, and the resulting overall process speedup is effectively communication limited.

Shared Memory Systems. If the individuals were stored in shared memory, each processor has access to the population and may read/modify individuals in the process of carrying out the genetic algorithm. By assigning individuals to specific processors, it may be possible to minimize the memory-access contention that would otherwise require synchronization, thereby avoiding most of the serializing effects. Aside from synchronization between generations, which would introduce some serialization, each processor is free to carry out its computations on its local subpopulation in parallel with the others. Since communication between processors occurs at essentially the speed of accessing memory, one would expect the solution time of a genetic algorithm on such a system to be reduced compared to that of a distributed processor system.

Distributed Processor Systems. If all the workstations in a distributed processor system lie on the same subnet, then their interprocessor communications will be competing for the network resources. The simple task of communicating each processor's most fit individuals to the others will involve contention for network bandwidth and result in serializing a portion of the genetic algorithm. Minimizing the serial portions through the use of isolated subpopulations has historically been the approach of choice to maximize the parallelism.

On the other hand, it may not be necessary to minimize the subpopulation intercommunication if it is feasible to segregate the processors into a number of subnets. Doing this makes each subnet capable of carrying on communication among its processors independent of the other subnets. Effectively, this parallelizes (at the subnet level) at least a portion of the interprocessor communication in addition to parallelizing (at the individual processor level) the computation required by the genetic algorithm's operators.

Yet another mechanism for achieving at least partial parallelism in communication is to interconnect the processors in a two- or three-dimensional ring, or torus. This limits the communication to what occurs between processors deemed adjacent by virtue of their interconnections and corresponds to the stepping-stone model of isolated subpopulations. By limiting the interprocessor communication to the migration of individuals between adjacent subpopulations, while permitting each processor to work independently on its subpopulation in parallel with the others, much of the serializing effect of communication is eliminated. Marin, Trelles-Salazar, and Sandoval (1994) showed that near-linear speedup could be attained with a half dozen processors and claimed that it can scale up to larger workstation networks as well.

13.4 SUCCESSIVE REFINEMENT

There are many alternative searching algorithms that could have been employed to find a good solution to our optimization problem. One of the most intuitive applies successive refinement to the search grid. Initially, a grid spacing is chosen that permits a brute-force examination of the search volume in very little time. In the context of the problem just looked at, the grid size might have started with an examination of every ten-thousandth point. Since the volume spanned −1,000,000 to +1,000,000 on each edge, a search increment of 10,000 would mean that we only evaluate about $200 \times 200 \times 200$ points, or perform a little under 10^7 function evaluations. If the best K points are retained, and a cube centered on each is evaluated using a finer grid spacing, say an increment of size 100, it will require about $K \times 10^6$ additional function evaluations.

Again, retaining the K best points in each of the K subvolumes and exhaustively searching a grid of size 100^3 around each will result in about $K^2 \times 10^6$ additional function evaluations. If the 10 best points are retained each time, this approach will have terminated after about 10^8 function evaluations. While this approach has a significantly smaller number of evaluations than would be required for a fully exhaustive examination of every point in the volume, 10^8 versus some 10^{19}, it is still somewhat computationally intensive and does not guarantee that the point that optimizes the function will be located. However, the total number of function evaluations needed for a genetic algorithm solution typically is several orders of magnitude fewer. (See Problem 13-1.)

This approach parallelizes readily. The original volume may be divided into K subvolumes, and each of K processors searches its assigned subvolume in an embarrassingly parallel fashion. When this portion of the algorithm is completed, each sends its candidates for the K best points back to the master. The master determines which K of the K^2 points represent the K best and redistributes them to the slaves. Each slave then works on its own subvolume in parallel with its peers.

Schraudolph and Belew (1992) apply this successive-refinement concept to genetic algorithms. Their approach was to use relatively low precision, say 5 bits, for each coordinate. When it appeared that the most significant bit of the coordinates had stabilized, they stripped it out and saved it, shifted the remaining bits one position to the left, and added a new least significant bit. This corresponds to dividing the original interval in half in each coordinate. They then restarted the genetic algorithm optimization using the reduced search space.

13.5 HILL CLIMBING

Another common approach to searching and optimization is based on the same algorithm a human might use to locate a local maximum; for example, to find the top of a hill when hiking, blindfolded or in a heavy fog or snowstorm, in the woods. Past experience might suggest that one way to reach the top is always to move in a direction that is uphill, or at least never to head downhill. Following that approach will guarantee that you never move to a lower point than you are presently standing on and, depending upon the terrain, may actually permit you to reach the highest point in the woods.

However, it is more likely that you will instead reach the top of a small rise (a local maximum). Since all the terrain immediately surrounding you is lower (and your rule does not allow you to move lower), you will never cross the little valley and climb up the mountain on the other side. An algorithm that produces the correct result only under ideal conditions does not have much appeal. What can be done to modify it?

Instead of thinking about the problem as a single hiker located at a single point, following the local terrain to the local peak, suppose we generalize it to n hikers starting at n random points. If each hiker follows the hiking algorithm of never moving downward from his or her starting location, each will move to a local maximum. Intuitively, the more hikers we have and the better dispersed their starting points, the greater the likelihood of at least one of them reaching the top of the highest hill in the woods. Granted, this approach does not guarantee that any hiker will reach the highest point. However, by increasing the number of hikers and ensuring that their starting points are randomized, one can make the likelihood of missing the peak arbitrarily small.

In essence this is the heart of the Monte Carlo search technique. As mentioned in Chapter 3 (Section 3.2.3), the name is derived from a primary feature of Monte Carlo: its casinos. Conceptually we "roll the dice," generating a random starting location for a hiker. Since the difference between a lucky roll (starting a hiker on the side of the highest peak) and an unlucky roll (starting the hiker on the side of a small hill and thereby precluding reaching the highest peak) is pure luck when the starting position is randomly chosen, the name seems appropriate!

The solution can be implemented either in a static assignment approach or by a dynamic work-pool approach. In the first case, we simply divide up the area to be searched among the different processors and let each generate the random starting points and follow the hiker's movements to a local maximum. Each processor then reports back its findings, and the master determines which has found the highest point. The second case recognizes that some hikers will have longer traversals than others before reaching their local peak, or that some may climb faster than others (corresponding to faster processors). Either way, some processors may finish before others. The natural solution to the problem of keeping the processors busy is to divide the area to be searched into smaller segments and parcel out a new segment to be searched as a processor finishes the segment it had been working on and reports its findings.

13.5.1 Banking Application

A frequently occurring question for the financial management in any large firm dealing with the public is, "Where should our customers send their payments?" When most commerce was relatively local, the answer was apparent: "Directly to the firm!" However, with the national (and increasingly international) nature of commerce, it is just as apparent that the former answer was naive.

There is a mailing delay that occurs between the date a customer sends the firm a payment and the date the firm receives it. In addition, there is a processing delay between when the firm receives it and when it deposits the payment with its bank. Finally, there is yet another delay while the bank processes the collection of funds through the national and/or international banking system and credits the payment to the firm's bank account. Under optimum conditions (a local customer whose check is drawn on the same bank with which the firm has its account), the firm receives the payment the day after the customer mails it, deposits it before the bank processing cut-off time that day, and receives credit to its account as of midnight that evening. Less ideal conditions nationally might involve a three- to five-day mailing delay, missing that day's cut-off for processing at the bank, and a one- to three-day federal funds-clearing delay before receiving credit for the payment. The delay between the customer's initial mailing of a payment and the firm's subsequent collection of funds, multiplied by the amount of the payment, is termed a *float*. The weighted average collection delay, or *float-days*, is only increased when national boundaries are crossed between customer and firm.

While the four to nine+ additional float-days may not appear significant to an individual customer (and may even be welcome!), when a large number of payments involving perhaps tens of millions of dollars per day is involved, the firm takes a different viewpoint. For an interest rate of 8 percent/year, each day that can be shaved off the average float-days on $10,000,000 of outstanding daily payments amounts to $800,000 per year either of additional income to the firm or, alternatively, of $10,000,000 the firm does not have to borrow to finance its operations.

Recognizing the problem, several national and international banks have provided distributed collection facilities known as lockboxes. For a fee, the bank will set up a number of lockboxes around the United States as well as in the various other countries in which the firm does business. The bank staffs each lockbox facility, retrieves the firm's mail from the post office several times a day, opens it, and deposits the payments to the firm's account. The firm then directs its customers to mail their payments to the lockbox that will provide the fastest collection of the customers' funds. Thus, this optimization problem is simply one of determining the appropriate number and placement of lockboxes to minimize the average float.

In the general case there are n cities that are potential lockbox sites; for example, there are well over a hundred in the United States alone and hundreds more internationally. The problem of determining the optimum number and location of the lockboxes is conceptually simple:

```
set Float_days to 1000;
for (i = 1; i <= MaxLockboxes; i++)
  for (all possible placements of i lockboxes) {
    compute CurrentFloat_days;
    if (Float_days > CurrentFloat_days) {
      Float_days = CurrentFloat_days;
      Save i and lockbox placement pattern;
    }
  }
```

The primary computational problem is that, while there are only n places to position the first lockbox, there are $n(n-1)/2$ ways to position two of them, and in general there are $n!/((k!)(n-k)!))$ ways to place k such lockboxes. Considering only 200 cities as potential lockbox candidate sites and only six lockboxes to be placed in those cities, there are roughly 8×10^{10} lockbox location evaluations to be done to compute the average float. In addition, the computation involved with each such lockbox arrangement is nontrivial.

Since mail delays vary between two points depending on the day of the week the item is mailed, the bank typically gathers mailing data on an ongoing basis to use in this computation. The result is a three-dimensional array of mailing data that has the size $n \times n \times 7$. The array subscripts identify the region from which the receivable was mailed, the region to which it was mailed, and the day of the week the item was mailed. The value in an array element represents the average number of days of mail delay that elapsed from the time the item was mailed until it was delivered.

To evaluate the optimal number and location of lockboxes for a firm, one must know the pattern of receivables (payments being sent to the firm). The bank takes a statistically significant subset of the firm's receivables and categorizes them by originating location, day of the week the item was postmarked, and payment amount.

In the simplest case, the evaluation of the average float for a particular configuration of lockbox locations consists of first assigning each originating region to a single lockbox. The choice of mailing destination is based on the sampled receivables data, and to avoid confusion, each customer in a region will be instructed to send payments to the same lockbox location. For each originating region, the destination lockbox with the lowest average mail delay for this firm's actual receivables pattern (in which each payment is weighted by its amount and date mailed) will be selected to receive its items. The algorithm used to compute the average float-days for a particular *k*-lockbox siting pattern is

```
TotalFloat = 0;
for all_receivables {
   accumulate amount_date-mailed weighted mail delay to each lockbox;
   accumulate each_region's_total_payments;
   accumulate number_of_items_mailed_from_region;
   accumulate TotalReceivables;
}
for each_region {
   determine destination_lockbox;
   determine AverageMailDelay;
}
for (i = 1; i <= n; i++)
   TotalFloat = TotalFloat + Total_amount_i * AverageMailDelay_i;
CurrentFloat_days = TotalFloat/TotalReceivables;
```

If the evaluation of the float-days associated with a particular siting pattern of lockboxes could be done in 100 microseconds (rather optimistic), one is looking at nearly 2000 years to evaluate all possible combinations of siting six lockboxes among 200 potential locations. Clearly, even a parallelization improvement by as much as a factor of 1000 is not sufficient to make the algorithm just described practical.

13.5.2 Hill Climbing in a Banking Application

If we approach the problem from a different perspective, we may have a better chance of finding a good solution in a reasonable amount of computational time. Instead of trying to evaluate exhaustively every possible placement of *k* lockboxes in *n* potential locations, let us think of this as representing a *k*-dimensional terrain and apply hill climbing.

Just as the hikers moved on an *x*-*y* plane in whatever direction promised the greatest local improvement in altitude, this problem may be set up as one of determining the incremental change in lockbox locations that produces the greatest reduction in float-days. By changing the locations incrementally, we will eventually reach a solution that represents a local minimum in float-days.

Just as was the case with the hikers, we will randomly generate *m* initial starting points. In this case they correspond to siting *m* configurations of *k*-lockboxes. For each initial *k*-lockbox siting pattern, we will determine which change in one lockbox location will provide the greatest reduction in float-days, and repeatedly adopt that change.

```
for (i = 1; i <= m; i++) {
   Generate random siting pattern, p_m, of k lockboxes
      from n possibilities;
   Compute fd = FloatDays(p_m);      /* float for starting pattern */
   for (j = 1; j <= k; j++) {        /* vary each of the K lockboxes */
      x = 1;                         /* set a continuation flag */
      while (x != 0) {               /* loop while improvement is possible */
```

```
            x = 0;                    /* clear flag */
            for(s=1;s<=(n-k);s++){    /*try all possible lockbox j placements*/
               Evaluate fd_Temp as the FloatDays of placements of lockbox j;
               if (fd_Temp < fd) {    /* see whether float improved*/
                  x = 1;              /* keep looping if improvement was made*/
                  fd = fd_Temp;       /* save float_days for this placement */
                  Save placement_s;   /* save placement that was responsible */
               }
            }
         }
      }
   }
```

Since m is a constant, analogous to the number of hikers looking independently for the peak, this involves $O(n)$ entries into the `while` loop. The number of loops within the `while` will be at worst exponential rather than factorial, and in practice far better than that, and most local optima are reached within a few tens of loops.

13.5.3 Parallelization

As indicated earlier, the parallelization is now direct. We may either distribute different "seeds" to each of p processes and have each generate m/p random placements of k lock-boxes, or employ the work-pool approach discussed earlier. In the latter case, each process would request additional starting placements to work on when it finishes its initial set.

13.6 SUMMARY

This chapter introduced the following concepts:

- Branch-and-bound technique
- Parallel genetic algorithms
- Successive refinement
- Hill climbing

This chapter introduced the following important genetic algorithm terms:

- Crossover
- Mutation

FURTHER READING

In the branch-and-bound section of this chapter, we did not explore specific problems, but rather simply outlined the basic techniques. The knapsack problem is very commonly used to describe search and optimization techniques and can be found in many texts. There is even a text devoted entirely to this problem (Martello and Toth, 1990). Similarly, the traveling salesperson problem is treated exclusively in Lawler et al. (1985).

An early survey of the branch-and-bound method is found in Lawler and Wood (1966). Treatment of parallel branch-and-bound methods can be found in Lai and Sprague (1985), Kumar and Kanal (1984), and Wah, Li, and Yu (1985). Wah and Ma (1982) and Mohan (1983) have investigated parallel best-first strategies. Various parallel graph and tree-searching algorithms can be found in Quinn and Deo (1984).

A particularly good introduction to genetic algorithms can be found in Michalewicz (1996). Other texts include Bäck (1995), Fogel (1995), Goldberg (1989), and Mitchel (1996). Further information on parallel genetic algorithms can be found in Chipperfield and Fleming (1996). Applications to management appear in Biethahn and Nissan (1995), and to engineering appear in Dasgupta and Michalewicz (1997). In addition, several journals address genetic algorithms and parallel search and optimization, including *IEEE Transactions on Evolutionary Computation.*

BIBLIOGRAPHY

BÄCK, T. (1995), *Evolutionary Algorithms in Theory and Practice,* Oxford University Press, New York.

BÄCK, T., D. B. FOGEL, AND Z. MICHALEWICZ, editors (1997), *Handbook of Evolutionary Computation,* Oxford University Press, New York.

BIETHAHN, J., AND V. NISSAN, editors (1995), *Evolutionary Algorithms in Management Applications,* Springer-Verlag, Berlin, Germany.

CHIPPERFIELD, A., AND P. FLEMING (1996), "Parallel Genetic Algorithms," in *Parallel and Distributed Computing Handbook,* A. Y. H. Zomaya, editor, McGraw-Hill, NY.

COHOON, J., S. HEDGE, W. MARTIN, AND D. RICHARDS (1987), "Punctuated Equilibria: A Parallel Genetic Algorithm," in *Proc. Second Int. Conf. on Genetic Algorithms,* J. J. Grefenstette editor, Lawrence Erlbaum Associates, Hillsdale, NJ.

DASGUPTA, D., AND Z. MICHALEWICZ, editors (1997), *Evolutionary Algorithms for Engineering Applications,* Springer-Verlag, Berlin, Germany.

FOGEL, D. B. (1995), *Evolutionary Computation: Toward a New Philosophy of Machine Intelligence,* IEEE Press, Piscataway, NJ.

GOLDBERG, D. E. (1989), *Genetic Algorithms in Search, Optimization, and Machine Learning,* Addison-Wesley, Reading, MA.

HOROWITZ, E., AND S. SAHNI (1978), *Fundamentals of Computer Algorithms,* Computer Science Press, Potomac, MD.

JANAKIRAM, V. K., D. P. AGRAWAL, AND R. MEHROTRA (1988), "A Randomized Parallel Backtracking Algorithm," *IEEE Trans. Comput.*, Vol. 37, No. 12, pp. 1665–1676.

KUMAR, V., AND L. KANAL (1984) "Parallel Branch-and-Bound Formulations for AND/OR tree Search," *IEEE Trans. Pattern Analysis and Machine Intelligence,* Vol. PAMI-6, No. 6 (November), pp. 768–778.

LAI, T.-H., AND S. SAHNI (1984), "Anomalies in Parallel Branch-and-Bound Algorithms," *Comm. ACM,* Vol. 27, No. 6, pp. 594–602.

LAI, T.-H., AND A. SPRAGUE (1985), "Performance of Parallel Branch-and-Bound Algorithms," *IEEE Trans. Comput.*, Vol. C-34, No. 10, pp. 962–964. Also see extended paper in *Proc. 1985 Int. Conf. Par. Proc.*, pp. 194–201.

LAWLER, E. L., J. K. LENSTRA, A. H. G. R. KAN, AND D. B. SHMOYS, editors (1985), *The Traveling Salesman Problem: A Guided Tour of Combinatorial Optimization*, Wiley, New York.

LAWLER, E. L., AND D. E. WOOD (1966), "Branch-and-Bound Methods: A Survey," *Operations Research*, Vol. 14, pp. 699–719.

LI, G.-J., AND B. W. WAH (1986), "Coping with Anomalies in Parallel Branch-and-Bound Algorithms," *IEEE Trans. Comput.*, Vol. C-35, No. 6, pp. 568–573.

MARIN, F., O. TRELLES-SALAZAR, AND F. SANDOVAL (1994), "Genetic Algorithms on Lan-Message Passing Architectures Using PVM: Application to the Routing Problem," in *Parallel Problem Solving from Nature–PPSN III, Lecture Notes in Computer Science*, Y. Davidor, H. P. Schwefel, and R. Manner, editors, Vol. 866, Springer-Verlag, Berlin, Germany.

MARTELLO, S., AND P. TOTH (1990), *Knapsack Problems: Algorithms and Computer Implementation*, Wiley, Chichester, England.

MICHALEWICZ, Z. (1996), *Genetic Algorithms + Data Structures = Evolution Programs,* 3rd edition, Springer-Verlag, Berlin, Germany.

MITCHEL, M. (1996), *An Introduction to Genetic Algorithms,* MIT Press, Cambridge, MA.

MOHAN, J. (1983), "Experiences with Two Parallel Programs Solving the Traveling Salesman Problem," *Proc. 1983 Int. Conf. Parallel Processing*, pp. 191–193.

QUINN, M. J. (1994), *Parallel Computing, Theory and Practice*, 2nd edition, McGraw-Hill, New York.

QUINN, M. J., AND N. DEO (1984), "Parallel Graph Algorithms," *Computing Surveys*, Vol. 16, No. 3 (Sept.), pp. 319–348.

RAO, V. N., AND V KUMAR (1988), "Concurrent Access of Priority Queues," *IEEE Trans. Comput.*, Vol. 37, No. 12, pp. 1657–1665.

SCHRAUDOLPH, N., AND R. BELEW (1992), "Dynamic Parameter Encoding for Genetic Algorithms," *Machine Learning*, Vol. 9, No. 1, pp. 9–21.

SCHWEFEL, H.-P. (1995), *Evolution and Optimum-Seeking,* Wiley, Chichester, England.

WAH, B. W., G.-J. LI, AND C. F. YU (1985), "Multiprocessing of Combinational Search Problems," *Computer*, Vol. 18, No. 6, pp. 93–108.

WAH, B. W., AND Y. W. MA (1982), "MANIP — A Parallel Computer System for Implementing Branch-and-Bound Algorithms," *Proc. 8th Ann. Int. Symp. Comput. Architecture*, pp. 239–262.

WITTE, E. E., R. D. CHAMBERLAIN, AND M. A. FRANKLIN (1991), "Parallel Simulated Annealing Using Speculative Computing," *IEEE Trans. Parallel and Distributed Systems*, Vol. 2, No. 4, pp. 483–494.

PROBLEMS

Scientific/Numerical

13-1. Write a parallel program to solve the 8-queens problem; that is, find all the positions of eight queens on an 8×8 chessboard such that no two queens can attack each other (not on the same column or diagonal). Since each queen must be placed on a different row of the chessboard, each solution can be represented by the column position of each queen; that is, an 8-tuple $(x_1, x_2, \ldots, x_i, \ldots, x_8)$, where x_i is the column position of queen i. The constraint of x_i is

$1 \le x_i \le 8$. Also note that two queens at positions (a, b) and (c, d) cannot be on the same diagonal if $a - b = c - d$ or $a + b = c + d$.

13-2. Write a parallel program using a genetic algorithm approach to find the maximum of the function $f(x, y, z) = -x^2 + 1{,}000{,}000x - y^2 - 40{,}000y - z^2$ (as used in Section 13.3.3). Modify the program so that the user may input any three-dimensional function. Instrument the code to determine the number of evaluations your program makes of $f(x, y, z)$.

13-3. Write a parallel program to find the maximum of the preceding function, using the successive-refinement algorithm discussed in Section 13.2.8.

Real Life

13-4. Shortpath Realty has a collection of PCs connected together in its main office. Shortpath needs a parallel program so that its real estate agents can plan a schedule of showing houses to minimize the traveling time required. Develop suitable test data and the program.

13-5. Mike was doing just fine traveling around Europe until he discovered a *Bäckerei* with dozens of delicious-looking pastries and breads. He needs to fill a small bag with edibles for a train ride he is about to take, but he has several constraints:

1. He wants variety; no more than two of any item,
2. He wants the maximum number of calories, which is not necessarily related to the item volume, and
3. He cannot exceed the volume limit of the bag.

Develop a parallel program to select quickly the items for his trip from the set of 5-tuples describing the *Bäckerei* items for sale (length, width, thickness, item type, calorie value). In addition to the program, develop a set of 20 test-data items and use them to check your program.

13-6. Given a set of rectangles in which the area of the ith one is given by A_i, write a parallel program to position the rectangles in a large rectangle, subject to the conditions that

1. The individual rectangles must not overlap,
2. All n smaller rectangles must be included in the large one, and
3. The area of the larger one is to be a minimum.

(Note: This is a simplified version of the problem of laying out an integrated circuit. The more complex layout problem has more conditions related to relationships between the smaller rectangles.)

13-7. Nat-Ex, a nationwide parcel delivery company, is reassessing the placement of its hubs that collect and distribute parcels. Ideally, the hubs should be situated at strategic places across the country to minimize costs and delivery times. You have been commissioned to make a study of possible alternative sites for the hubs and decide to write a parallel program based upon genetic algorithms. You assume that the number of parcels being received is directly proportional to the population, and for a first approximation only the major cities are considered. Write the program, developing suitable input data and constraints. One constraint is the number of hubs.

13-8. A problem rather similar to Problem 13-7 is the siting of airline hubs. Write a parallel program to help an airline find the hub locations that will maximize its profits. Again, input data and constraints must be developed.

13-9. A recently discovered planetoid, Geometrica, has a most unusual surface. By all available observations the surface can be modeled by the formula

$$h = 35{,}000\ \sin(3\theta)\sin(2\rho) + 9700\ \cos(10\theta)\cos(20\rho) - 800\ \sin(25\theta + 0.03\pi) + 550\ \cos(\rho + 0.2\pi)$$

where h is the height above or below sea level, θ is the angle in the equatorial plane (defines longitude on Earth), and ρ is the angle in the polar plane (defines latitude on Earth).

1. Write a sequential program to use hill climbing to find the (θ, ρ) position of the highest point above sea level on Geometrica's surface.
2. Develop an embarrassingly parallel solution to 1.
3. Develop a work-pool parallel solution to Part 1 under the assumption that workstations of dramatically varying capabilities are being used to solve the problem.
4. Compare the simulated times required for a solution under the preceding three approaches.

13-10. A commonly occurring problem, known as "bin packing," consists of trying to put k objects of varying characteristics into a smaller number of categories, or "bins." While this is commonly encountered in sending a set of presents to a favorite relative on a holiday (you have to find the lowest-cost box that will hold all the items), or in industry (a set of machines having different capacities and speeds must be assigned to produce different products optimally), you have been approached to solve a different problem. It has come to the attention of an enterprising (and wealthy) individual that the game of blackjack fits this model also: Each player is trying to obtain anywhere from two to ten or more playing cards whose face values add to 21 or less, while staying at or above the sum of the face values of the dealer's cards. The face values of all previously played cards are known, as are the number of cards of each face value in the deck. You have been hired to outline a serial algorithm for computing the likelihood that the next card you are dealt will "bust" your hand (result in the sum of face values totaling more than 21) and then to outline a parallel algorithm.

13-11. An enterprising entrepreneur has concluded that the ideal opportunity for him to combine his love of dogs with a vast fortune is to corner the market for a new breed of dog: the Softie. Characteristics of the Softie are as follows:

A.	Length of coat:	8 in. or longer
B.	Coat characteristics:	Extremely soft (or softer)
		Brown areas on a white background
		White paws
		Black tail
C.	Tail characteristics:	Short (4 in.–6 in.)
		Points straight up
D.	Weight:	Extremely large: 90 kg or heavier
E.	Foot characteristics:	Pawprint area in excess of 9 sq in.
		Fully webbed between toes
F.	Disposition:	Extremely mild tempered

Each of these characteristics has a range when viewed across all dogs:

A. Can be represented by eight bits in which 00000000 corresponds to a hairless dog, 11111111 corresponds to a hairlength of 10.2 in., and 11001000 corresponds to 8 in.

B. Can be represented by six softness bits (in which 000000 corresponds to the ultimate in softness), 000111 is extremely soft, and 111111 is the ultimate in stiffness; three background brightness bits, in which 000 is bright and 111 is dark; three background color bits, in which white is 000 and brown is 001 and all other colors are covered by the remaining six combinations; three foreground brightness bits (000 is bright); three foreground color bits (000 is white, 001 is brown, 010 is red, 011 is yellow, 111 is black, and the remaining bit patterns are other colors); one bit for paw color, in which 0 corresponds to white and 1 is "anything else"; one bit for tail color, in which 0 corresponds to "anything else" and 1 corresponds to black.

C. Can be represented by 10 bits, in which eight are related to tail length (00000000 corresponds to a tailless variety, and 11111111 corresponds to a tail-length of 25.5 in. or longer) and two denote tail appearance: 00 corresponds to pointing straight up, 01 corresponds to pointing horizontally, 10 corresponds to pointing straight down, and 11 corresponds to the highly undesirable curly-tailed appearance.

D. Can be represented by 10 bits, in which the first seven correspond to a weight in kg and the second three correspond to a weight in increments of $^1/_8$ kg. Thus, a weight characteristic of 0000101011 would be a weight of $5^3/_8$ kg.

E. Can be represented by 10 bits, seven bits of which correspond to pawprint area and three to the fraction webbed. In this example, 0000000 corresponds to a pawprint area of 0.5 sq in., 1111111 corresponds to a pawprint area of 13.2 sq in., and 0100011 corresponds to a pawprint area of 4.0 sq in. In the final three bits, 000 corresponds to 1/8 webbed, and 111 corresponds to fully webbed.

F. Can be represented by six bits, in which 000000 corresponds to the ultimate in mild-tempered disposition, 000100 is extremely mild tempered, and 111111 is "meaner than a junkyard dog" — the ultimate in non-mild-temperedness!

Thus, in total, one needs 64 bits to represent an individual dog in this population. One such dog might be

11001000 001011 000000 111001 01 1000000011 001101100 0100011 011 000100

whose characteristics are

11001000	8 in. coat
001011	Slightly more stiff than desirable
000000	Background color is bright white
111001	Foreground color is dark brown
01	White paws and black tail
1000000011	12.8 in. long, curly-tailed
001101100	13.5 kg weight
0100011	4 sq in. pawprint area
011	50 percent webbed
000100	Extremely mild mannered

In short, this dog has some desirable characteristics (its coat is pretty good, its paw size is fine, and its temperament is fine) and some that are undesirable (coat is a little stiffer than the standard, the tail is curly, the dog is extremely small compared to the standard, and it won't be as good a water dog as desired due to its less than fully webbed toes).

The entrepreneur is anxious to hedge his bets on this project and has hired both you and a competitor to develop Softies. Your competitor has a single large kennel complex in which he plans to house 500 dogs; you have opted for five independent kennel locations each housing 100 dogs. Both of you plan to visit animal shelters and take the first 500 nonspayed/neutered dogs you find (i.e., you will start off the initial population with "random" characteristics).

Both your competitor and you plan to keep the population sizes constant in your kennels while breeding successive generations of dogs. You both plan to have each kennel location retain its two parents in the current generation that best match the standard for the Softie breed. In addition, since a pair of parents may have multiple offspring in a given litter (corresponding to making multiple "cuts" and crossovers), both of you plan to give away (to your friends) the offspring that least conform to the standards for Softies, as needed, to keep your local populations constant.

The major difference between the two approaches you and your competitor are using is that he has a single large population while you have five independent kennel "subcontractors" each working with an isolated subpopulation. He will simply produce n generations of offspring; your subcontractors each will produce five generations of offspring in isolation, and only then send their two most fit dogs to their neighbors (A sends one to B and one to E, B sends one to A and one to C, etc.), as in the island model.

1. Write a single-processor genetic algorithm solution modeled after your competitor's approach. Run it with several random initial populations and compute the average number of generations it takes before 10 percent of the population (50 dogs) meets the standards for Softies.
2. Write a multiprocessor genetic algorithm solution modeled after your approach. As in Part 1, run this with several random initial populations and compute the average number of generations it takes before a total of 50 dogs from your kennels meet the standards for Softies.

Hint: You will need to construct an evaluation function that incorporates all of these characteristics, such that a dog meeting the characteristics of the Softie standard will exhibit a greater fitness than one that does not.

13-12. The 1535 Senators and Representatives of the newly established country of Nella are all under consideration to receive soft-money campaign-financing contributions, expressed in local currency called the kerf, from a major firm that is encountering some regulatory challenges to the continued sale of its products. It is known that the Senators and Representatives all have their own criteria for assessing such contributions. For example, one might feel that all contributions from this firm should be returned (definitely a minority viewpoint)! Another might feel that all contributions should be gratefully accepted in light of the superb work he is doing. A few others might have varying thresholds above which they would reject contributions, fearing that accepting might unfairly prejudice their vote on matters concerning this firm.

While the potential benefit to the firm is a matter of considerable debate, the firm believes that some Senators and Representatives are more influential than others and therefore considers it important to show them as much support through the contribution process as possible. Unfortunately, the firm does not have enough money left after fighting the regulatory agencies to be able to fully support all the congressional representatives to the upper limit they might accept. Thus, the firm must be somewhat more selective in allocating its budget for contributions.

The firm's political consultants and attorneys have established an evaluation function that they believe describes each Congress member's Support-Interest-as-a-function-of-campaign-Kerfs, SI(Ci, Ki). This function takes into consideration not only the individual's contribution acceptance threshold, but also weights the expected "friendliness to the firm" as a result of the contributions by the influence the Congress member has overall in the legislative process. What the firm has lacked up to this point is a mechanism to relate the SI(Ci,Ki) function to a particular allocation of kerfs among the individuals. As a renowned expert in the application of genetic algorithms, you have been hired to find the optimum allocation of kerfs to the individual Congress members subject to the firm's budget limit.

After a bit of thought you devise a serial genetic algorithm. Each individual in the genetic algorithm sense is a set of 1500 kerf-amounts, which sum to the total firm budget for this phase. You randomly generate (subject to the budget limits) the kerf-amounts going to each of the 1535 Congress members to produce one genetic algorithm individual, and repeat that to generate 1000 campaign contribution allocations: 1000 genetic algorithm individuals. Fortunately, you quickly recognize that you need a factor of 10 speedup in computation to be able to find an optimum allocation of kerfs among the Congress members in time for your presentation to the firm later today.

Outline a parallel genetic algorithm approach using the networked workstations sitting idle on the desks of ex-employees of the firm who have been downsized as a result of the unfavorable regulatory activities.

13-13. After several recent consolidations in the international banking sector, one of the largest banks, BankWorld, has a problem. It handles some 35 billion credit card transactions per day and has found that while its central computer is still able to record the transactions and process the monthly statements, it has no unused cpu cycles with which to analyze customer spending patterns. It has come to the attention of the board of directors of BankWorld that you have skills in the use of networks of workstations to solve problems like the one the bank is facing.

Specifically, BankWorld has in excess of 8000 Terabytes (8 million gigabytes) of online storage containing last year's credit card purchase history. This data is the raw point-of-purchase information but is totally unsorted. Each item contains the business ID number, customer account number, date, and amount. BankWorld's internal marketing department proposes to mine this historical data and organize it in ways that will enable BankWorld to earn additional revenue.

As your overall task, BankWorld wants you to design a parallel computing approach to analyzing this data. You are to produce a mailing list of all customers who charged a cumulative total of at least $500 at any combination of home product centers within the past year. BankWorld's marketing department believes that it can sell copies of the mailing list (of all good home product center customers) back to each of these stores, which will in turn use the lists to send advertising circulars to the customers. Without stopping to analyze the privacy issues involved, you immediately jump into the task of summing purchases, by customer, from a list of businesses identified as being home product centers.

Sketch an algorithm for applying the several thousand idle workstations (made available through the staff reductions occasioned by the latest merger) to this task. Specifically, identify what a typical networked workstation will be doing, how workstation actions will be coordinated, and how the results will be merged to produce the desired mailing list. Keep in mind that each workstation has a very limited amount of local memory: 512 Mbyte of RAM and 48 Gbyte of disk. Any approach that requires more storage than that on any single workstation is doomed to failure!

13-14. Convert the genetic algorithm example of searching within a volume for the point that maximizes an evaluation function into a hill-climbing problem, implement the solution, and compare it to the time required for an equivalent-accuracy genetic algorithm solution:

1. As a sequential approach, and
2. As a parallel approach.

13-15. Convert the hill-climbing solution to the banking application into a genetic algorithm problem, implement the solution, and compare it to the time required for an equivalent-accuracy hill-climbing solution:

1. As a sequential approach, and
2. As a parallel approach.

Appendix A

Basic MPI Routines

The following is a collection of MPI routines that is sufficient for most programs in the text. A very large number of routines are provided in MPI. The routines described here are divided into preliminaries (those for establishing the environment and related matters), basic point-to-point message-passing, and collective message-passing. The complete set of routines and additional details can be found in Gropp, Lusk, and Skjellum (1999), Gropp, Lusk, and Thakur (1999), and Gropp et al. (1998).

PRELIMINARIES

```
int MPI_Init(int *argc, char **argv[])
```

ACTIONS: Initializes MPI environment.

PARAMETERS:

`*argc`	argument from `main()`
`**argv[]`	argument from `main()`

```
int MPI_Finalize(void)
```

ACTIONS: Terminates MPI execution environment.

PARAMETERS: None.

```
int MPI_Comm_rank(MPI_Comm comm, int *rank)
```

ACTIONS: Determines rank of process in communicator.

PARAMETERS:

`comm`	communicator
`*rank`	rank (returned)

```
int MPI_Comm_size(MPI_Comm comm, int *size)
```

ACTIONS: Determines size of group associated with communicator.

PARAMETERS:

`comm`	communicator
`*size`	size of group (returned)

```
double MPI_Wtime(void)
```

ACTIONS: Returns elapsed time from some point in past, in seconds.

PARAMETERS: None.

POINT-TO-POINT MESSAGE-PASSING

MPI defines various datatypes for `MPI_Datatype`, mostly with corresponding C datatypes, including

`MPI_CHAR`	`signed char`
`MPI_INT`	`signed int`
`MPI_FLOAT`	`float`

```
int MPI_Send(void *buf, int count, MPI_Datatype datatype, int dest, int tag,
MPI_Comm comm)
```

ACTIONS: Sends message (blocking).

PARAMETERS:

`*buf`	send buffer
`count`	number of entries in buffer
`datatype`	data type of entries
`dest`	destination process rank
`tag`	message tag
`comm`	communicator

```
int MPI_Recv(void *buf, int count, MPI_Datatype datatype, int source,
int tag, MPI_Comm comm, MPI_Status *status)
```

ACTIONS: Receives message (blocking).

PARAMETERS:

`*buf`	receive buffer (loaded)
`count`	max number of entries in buffer
`datatype`	data type of entries
`source`	source process rank
`tag`	message tag
`comm`	communicator
`*status`	status (returned)

In receive routines, `MPI_ANY_TAG` in `tag` and `MPI_ANY_SOURCE` in `source` matches with anything. The return status is a structure with at least three members:

`status -> MPI_SOURCE`	rank of source of message
`status -> MPI_TAG`	tag of source message
`Status -> MPI_ERROR`	potential errors

```
int MPI_Isend(void *buf, int count, MPI_Datatype datatype, int dest, int tag,
MPI_Comm comm, MPI_Request *request)
```

ACTIONS: Starts a nonblocking send.

PARAMETERS:

`*buf`	send buffer
`count`	number of buffer elements
`datatype`	data type of elements
`dest`	destination rank
`tag`	message tag
`comm`	communicator
`*request`	request handle (returned)

Related:

`MPI_Ibsend()`	Starts a nonblocking buffered send
`MPI_Irsend()`	Starts a nonblocking ready send
`MPI_Issend()`	Starts a nonblocking synchronous send

```
int MPI_Irecv(void *buf, int count, MPI_Datatype datatype, int source,
int tag, MPI_Comm comm, MPI_Request *request)
```

ACTIONS: Begins a nonblocking receive.

PARAMETERS:

`*buf`	receive buffer address (loaded)

`count`	number of buffer elements
`datatype`	data type of elements
`source`	source rank
`tag`	message tag
`comm`	communicator
`*request`	request handle (returned)

```
int MPI_Wait(MPI_Request *request, MPI_Status *status)
```

ACTIONS: Waits for an MPI send or receive to complete and then returns.

PARAMETERS:

`*request`	request handle
`*status`	status (same as return status of `MPI_recv()` if waiting for this.

Related:

`MPI_Waitall()`	Wait for all processes to complete (additional parameters)
`MPI_Waitany()`	Wait for any process to complete (additional parameters)
`MPI_Waitsome()`	Wait for some processes to complete (additional parameters)

```
int MPI_Test(MPI_Request *request, int *flag, MPI_Status *status)
```

ACTIONS: Tests for completion of a nonblocking operation.

PARAMETERS:

`*request`	request handle
`*flag`	true if operation completed (returned)
`*status`	status (returned)

```
int MPI_Probe(int source, int tag, MPI_Comm comm, MPI_Status *status)
```

ACTIONS: Blocking test for a message (without receiving message).

PARAMETERS:

`source`	source process rank
`tag`	message tag
`comm`	communicator
`*status`	status (returned)

```
int MPI_Iprobe(int source, int tag, MPI_Comm comm, int *flag, MPI_Comm
*status)
```

ACTIONS: Nonblocking test for a message (without receiving message).

PARAMETERS:

`source`	source process rank
`tag`	message tag

comm	communicator
*flag	true if there is a message (returned)
*status	status (returned)

GROUP ROUTINES

```
int MPI_Barrier(MPI_Comm comm)
```

ACTIONS: Blocks process until all processes have called it.

PARAMETERS:

comm	communicator

```
int MPI_Bcast(void *buf, int count, MPI_Datatype datatype, int root, MPI_Comm
comm)
```

ACTIONS: Broadcasts message from root process to all processes in `comm` and itself.

PARAMETERS:

*buf	message buffer (loaded)
count	number of entries in buffer
datatype	data type of buffer
root	rank of root

```
int MPI_Alltoall(void *sendbuf, int sendcount, MPI_Datatype sendtype, void
*recvbuf, int recvcount, MPI_Datatype recvtype, MPI_Comm comm)
```

ACTIONS: Sends data from all processes to all processes.

PARAMETERS:

*sendbuf	send buffer
sendcount	number of send buffer elements
sendtype	data type of send elements
*recvbuf	receive buffer (loaded)
recvcount	number of elements each receives
recvtype	data type of receive elements
comm	communicator

Related:

MPI_Alltoallv()	Sends data to all processes, with displacement

```
int MPI_Gather(void *sendbuf, int sendcount, MPI_Datatype sendtype, void
*recvbuf, int recvcount, MPI_Datatype recvtype, int root, MPI_Comm comm)
```

ACTIONS: Gathers values for group of processes.

PARAMETERS:

`*sendbuf`	send buffer
`sendcount`	number of send buffer elements
`sendtype`	data type of send elements
`*recvbuf`	receive buffer (loaded)
`recvcount`	number of elements each receives
`recvtype`	data type of receive elements
`root`	rank of receiving process
`comm`	communicator

Related:

`MPI_Allgather()`	Gather values and distribute to all
`MPI_Gatherv()`	Gather values into specified locations
`MPI_Allgatherv()`	Gather values into specified locations and distribute to all

`MPI_Gatherv()` and `MPI_Allgatherv()` require additional parameter: `*displs` – array of displacements, after `recvcount`.

```
int MPI_Scatter(void *sendbuf, int sendcount, MPI_Datatype sendtype,
void *recvbuf, int recvcount, MPI_Datatype recvtype, int root, MPI_Comm comm)
```

ACTIONS: Scatters a buffer from root in parts to group of processes.

PARAMETERS:

`*sendbuf`	send buffer
`sendcount`	number of elements send, each process
`sendtype`	data type of elements
`*recvbuf`	receive buffer (loaded)
`recvcount`	number of recv buffer elements
`recvtype`	type of recv elements
`root`	root process rank
`comm`	communicator

Related:

`MPI_Scatterv()`	Scatters a buffer in specified parts to group of processes.
`MPI_Reduce_scatter()`	Combines values and scatter results.

```
int MPI_Reduce(void *sendbuf, void *recvbuf, int count, MPI_Datatype
datatype, MPI_Op op, int root, MPI_Comm comm)
```

ACTIONS: Combines values on all processes to single value.

PARAMETERS:

`*sendbuf`	send buffer address
`*recvbuf`	receive buffer address

`count`	number of send buffer elements
`datatype`	data type of send elements
`op`	reduce operation. Several operations, including
	`MPI_MAX` Maximum
	`MPI_MIN` Minimum
	`MPI_SUM` Sum
	`MPI_PROD` Product
`root`	root process rank for result
`comm`	communicator

Related:

`MPI_Allreduce()`	Combine values to single value and return to all.

BIBLIOGRAPHY

GROPP, W., S. HUSS-LEDERMAN, A. LUMSDAINE, E. LUSK, B. NITZBERG, W. SAPHIR, AND M. SNIR (1998), *MPI—The Complete Reference*, Volume 2, *The MPI-2 Extensions*, MIT Press, Cambridge, MA.

GROPP, W., E. LUSK, AND A. SKJELLUM (1999), *Using MPI Portable Parallel Programming with the Message-Passing Interface*, 2nd edition, MIT Press, Cambridge, MA.

GROPP, W., E. LUSK, AND R. THAKUR (1999), *Using MPI-2 Advanced Features of the Message-Passing Interface*, MIT Press, Cambridge, MA.

SNIR, M., S. W. OTTO, S. HUSS-LEDERMAN, D. W. WALKER, AND J. DONGARRA (1998), *MPI—The Complete Reference*, Volume 1, *The MPI Core*, MIT Press, Cambridge, MA.

Appendix B

Basic PThread Routines

The following is a collection of Pthread routines that is sufficient for most programs in the text. Additional details can be found in Butenhof (1997), Kleiman, Shah, and Smaalders (1996), Nichols, Buttlar, and Farrell (1996), and Prasad (1997).

THREAD MANAGEMENT

The header file `<pthread.h>` contains the type definitions (`pthread_t` etc.) and function prototypes.

```
int pthread_create(pthread_t *thread, const pthread_attr_t *attr, void
*(*routine)(void *), void *arg)
```

ACTIONS: Creates thread.

PARAMETERS:

`thread`	thread identifier (returned)
`attr`	thread attribute (NULL for default attributes)
`routine`	new thread routine

```
void pthread_exit(void *value)
```

ACTIONS: Terminates the calling thread.

PARAMETERS:

`value`	returned to threads that have already issued `pthread_join()`

```
int pthread_join(pthread_t thread, void **value)
```

ACTIONS: Causes thread to wait for specified thread to terminate.

PARAMETERS:

`thread`	thread identifier (returned)
`value`	new thread routine

```
int pthread_detach(pthread_t thread)
```

ACTIONS: Detaches a thread.

PARAMETERS:

`thread`	thread to detach

```
int pthread_attr_init(pthread_attr_t *attr)
```

ACTIONS: Initializes a thread attribute object to default values.

PARAMETERS:

`attr`	thread attribute object

```
int pthread_attrsetdetachedstate(pthread_attr_t *attr, int state)
```

ACTIONS: Specifies whether a thread created with `attr` will be detached.

PARAMETERS:

`attr`	thread attribute
`state`	not detached – `PTHREAD_CREATE_JOINABLE` detached – `PTHREAD_CREATE_DETACHED`

```
int pthread_attr_destroy(pthread_attr_t *attr)
```

ACTIONS: Destroys a thread attribute object.

PARAMETERS:

`attr`	thread attribute object

```
pthread_t pthread_self(void)
```

ACTIONS: Returns the ID of the calling thread.

PARAMETERS: None

```
int pthread_equal(pthread_t thread1, pthread_t thread2)
```

ACTIONS: Compares two thread IDs, `thread1` and `thread2`, and returns zero if they are equal, otherwise returns nonzero.

PARAMETERS:

`thread1`	thread
`thread2`	thread

```
int pthread_once(pthread_once_t *once_ctr, void (*once_rtn) void)
```

ACTIONS: Executes specified routine if it has not been called before. Ensures that the routine is only called once. Useful for initialization. For example, mutex locks should only be initialized once.

PARAMETERS:

`once_ctr`	variable used to determine whether once_routine called before (a global variable that should be initialized to `PTHREAD_ONCE_INIT` (e.g., `static pthread_once_t once_ctr = PTHREAD_ONCE_INIT;`)
`once_rtn`	routine to be executed once

THREAD SYNCHRONIZATION

Mutual Exclusion Locks (Mutex Locks)

```
int pthread_mutex_init(pthread_mutex_t *mutex,
const pthread_mutexattr_t *attr)
```

ACTIONS: Initializes mutex with specified attributes.

PARAMETERS:

`mutex`	mutex
`attr`	attributes — NULL default

```
int pthread_ mutex_destroy(pthread_mutex_t *mutex)
```

ACTIONS: Destroys a mutex.

PARAMETERS:

`mutex`	mutex

```
int pthread_mutex_lock(pthread_mutex_t *mutex)
```

ACTIONS: Locks an unlocked mutex (and becomes owner of mutex). If already locked, blocks until thread that holds mutex releases it.

PARAMETERS:

`mutex`	mutex

```
int pthread_mutex_unlock(pthread_mutex_t *mutex)
```

ACTIONS: Unlocks a mutex. If any thread waiting for mutex, one is awakened. If more than one thread waiting, thread chosen dependent upon thread priority and scheduling.

PARAMETERS:

`mutex`	mutex

```
int phread_mutex_trylock(pthread_mutex_t *mutex)
```

ACTIONS: Locks an unlocked mutex (and becomes owner of mutex). If already locked, returns immediately with EBUSY.

PARAMETERS: `mutex` mutex

Condition variables

```
int pthread_cond_init(pthread_con_t *cond, const pthread_condattr_t *attr)
```

ACTIONS: Creates a condition variable with specified attributes.

PARAMETERS: `cond` condition variable

`attr` attributes, NULL — default

```
int pthread_cond_destroy(pthread_cond_t *cond)
```

ACTIONS: Destroys a condition variable.

PARAMETERS: `cond` condition variable

```
int pthread_cond_wait(pthread_cond_t *cond, pthread_mutex_t *mutex)
```

ACTIONS: Waits for a condition, awakened by a signal or broadcast. The mutex is unlocked before the wait and relocked after the wait. (The mutex should be locked by the thread prior to the call.)

PARAMETERS: `cond` condition variable

`mutex` mutex

```
int pthread_cond_timedwait(pthread_cond_t *cond, pthread_mutex_t *mutex,
const struct timespec *abstime)
```

ACTIONS: Waits for a condition with a time-out. Similar to `pthread_cond_wait()`, except routine returns with locked mutex if the system time equal to or greater than a specified time occurs.

PARAMETERS: `cond` condition variable

`mutex` mutex

`abstime` time before returning if condition not occurring.

To set time to 5 seconds:

```
abstime.tv.sec = time(NULL) + 5;
abstime.tv.nsec = 0;
```

```
int pthread_cond_signal(pthread_cond_t *cond)
```

ACTIONS: Unblocks one thread currently waiting on condition variable. If more than one thread waiting, thread chosen dependent upon thread priority and scheduling. If no threads are waiting, the signal is not remembered for subsequent threads.

PARAMETERS: `cond` condition variable

```
pthread_cond_broadcast(pthread_cond_t *cond)
```

ACTIONS: Similar to `pthread_cond_signal()`, except all threads waiting on condition are awakened.

PARAMETERS: `cond` condition variable

Though the actions of "wake-up" routines may call for only one thread to be awakened, it may be possible on some multiprocessor systems for more than one thread to awaken, and hence this should be taken into account in the coding.

BIBLIOGRAPHY

BUTENHOF, D. R. (1997), *Programming with POSIX® Threads*, Addison-Wesley, Reading, MA.

KLEIMAN, S., D. SHAH, AND B. SMAALDERS (1996), *Programming with Threads*, Prentice Hall, Upper Saddle River, NJ.

NICHOLS, B., D. BUTTLAR, AND J. P. FARRELL (1996), *Pthreads Programming*, O'Reilly & Associates, Sebastopol, CA.

PRASAD, S. (1997), *Multithreading Programming Techniques*, McGraw-Hill, New York.

Appendix C

OpenMP Directives, Library Functions, and Environment Variables

The following is the collection of C/C++ directives, library functions, and environment variables that together make up OpenMP. Additional details can be found in Chandra et al., (2001) and the document *OpenMP C and C++ Application Program Interface Version 2 March 2002* (OpenMP Architecture Review Board, 2002). There are some discrepancies between these two references, partly because OpenMP has been slightly modified from version 1 and version 2. The document *OpenMP C and C++ Application Program Interface Version 2 March 2002* is used as the definitive document for this appendix.

GENERAL

OpenMP compiler directives begin with `#pragma` and are followed by `omp`, a name, optional clauses, and terminated with a new line. Some clauses can occur in different directives and are defined separately. Some directives apply to a structured block (statement or statements). A construct consists of a compiler directive followed by the structured block.

Notation

`[clause] ...`	One or more optional clauses from those listed subsequently. Clauses can be in any order. They can be separated by commas in OpenMP version 2. Items within a list in clauses are comma-separated.
`structured_block`	A single or compound statement (with single entry and exit points).

PARALLEL REGIONS

```
#pragma omp parallel [clause] ...
     structured_block
```

ACTIONS: Creates multiple threads, each one executing the specified `structured_block`.

CLAUSES:

```
if (scalar_expression)
private(variable_list)
firstprivate(variable_list)
default(shared or none)
shared(variable_list)
copyin(variable_list)
reduction(operator : variable_list)
num_threads(integer_expression)
```

WORK-SHARING

Threads are not created by work-sharing constructs. The existing threads are used. Generally, the `parallel` construct would precede work-sharing constructs. There is no explicit barrier at the end of these constructs.

```
#pragma omp for [clause] ...
     for_loop
```

ACTIONS: Causes the iterations of the `for` loop, `for_loop`, to be divided among the exiting threads in the team. The `for` loop must be of canonical form:

```
for (initial_expression; boolean_expression;
   increment_expression)
```

where each expression must be of a simple form, as described in *OpenMP C and C++ Application Program Interface Version 2 March 2002* (OpenMP Architecture Review Board, 2002). A form loop such as:

```
for (i = 0; i < 10; i++)
```

would be acceptable. Here, `i` must not be modified within the loop

CLAUSES:

```
private(variable_list)
firstprivate(variable_list)
lastprivate(variable_list)
reduction(operator : variable_list)
ordered
schedule(kind, chunk_size)
nowait
```

The `for` directive can be combined with the `parallel` directive on one line, that is. `parallel for` and `parallel sections` directives. All the clauses in `parallel` and `for` can be used in `parallel for` except `nowait`.

```
#pragma omp sections [clause] ...
{
          #pragma omp section
              structured_block
          #pragma omp section
              structured_block
                  :
}
```

ACTIONS: The `section` constructs are shared among the existing threads in the team. Each `section` construct is executed once.

CLAUSES: Occur only in `sections` construct, and can be:

```
private(variable_list)
firstprivate(variable_list)
lastprivate(variable_list)
reduction(operator : variable_list)
nowait
```

The `sections` directive can be combined with the `parallel` directive on one line, that is, `parallel for` and `parallel sections` directives. All the clauses in `parallel` and `sections` can be used in `parallel sections` except `nowait`.

```
#pragma omp single [clause] ...
     structured_block
```

ACTIONS: The structured block is executed by one thread of the team only.

CLAUSES:

```
private(variable_list)
firstprivate(variable_list)
copyprivate(variable_list)
nowait
```

DIRECTIVES/CONSTRUCTS

In general, a team of threads needs to be established before using directives that involve more than one thread by using the `parallel` directive, unless otherwise specified.

```
#pragma omp atomic
     expression_statement
```

ACTIONS: The statement, `expression_statement`, is executed by the thread in a manner such that the memory location updated by this statement is done atomically, that is, without interference from other threads. The statement must be in one of the following simple forms:

```
x binary_op= expression
x++
++x
x--
--x
```

CLAUSES: There are no clauses.

```
#pragma omp barrier
```

ACTIONS: Threads wait until all threads have reached the barrier, and then all threads execute the statements after the barrier together.

CLAUSES: There are no clauses.

```
#pragma omp critical name
     structured_block
```

ACTIONS: The structured block is executed by one thread at a time. Threads wait until no other thread is executing the structured block, and then one threads is selected to proceed. The selection process is not defined in OpenMP.

CLAUSES: The optional clause `name` identifies the critical section. If omitted, the critical section maps to the one unnamed critical section.

```
#pragma omp flush (variable_list)
```

ACTIONS: Creates a synchronization point in which all current read and write operations on the variables listed are allowed to complete and values written back to memory. All the variables in the list are brought up-to-date in the thread calling the flush directive. This is usually needed if shared variables are altered by other threads because of the use of registers to hold shared variables locally. Note that this directive does not automatically operate on all threads having access to the variables. Each thread must call the directive separately according to Chandra et al. (2001), although this point is not clear from OpenMP Architecture Review Board (2002). If the variable list is omitted, all accessible variables are brought up-to-date in the thread. This occurs automatically in various other constructs, as noted in Chapter 8.

CLAUSES: There are no clauses.

```
#pragma omp master
      structured_block
```

ACTIONS: The structured block is executed by the master thread only. There is no barrier at the beginning or end of the construct.

CLAUSES: There are no clauses.

```
#pragma omp ordered
      structured_block
```

ACTIONS: This directive can only be used within a `for` or `parallel for` construct. Then the structured block is executed in the order that would occur if the loop were executed sequentially. Normally, there would be other parts of the body of the loop outside the `ordered` construct which is still executed in parallel.

CLAUSES: There are no clauses.

```
#pragma omp threadprivate(variable_list)
```

ACTIONS: The variables in the list are made private to a thread. They are initialized once at some unspecified point beforehand. The `threadprivate` directive would be called prior to any parallel construct, and the `threadprivate` variables so defined would persist from one parallel region to the next (assuming a fixed number of threads), that is, their values can be used in subsequent parallel regions.

CLAUSES: There are no clauses.

CLAUSES

`copyin(variable_list)`

Each variable in the list is assigned the value of the corresponding variable in the master thread. The variables in the list must be `threadprivate` variables. This clause can appears in the `parallel` construct (and in consequence, `parallel for` and `parallel sections`).

`copyprivate(variable_list)`

Added to OpenMP version 2 and used only in the `single` construct. The value of each variable in the list at the end of execution of the structured block in each member of the team is set to that is of the thread executing the single structured block. This provides an alternative mechanism to using a shared variable to broadcast values to members of the team. May be useful when using a shared variable would be difficult.

`default(shared or none)`

The clause `default(shared)` specifies all variables as shared except for those otherwise declared as `threadprivate` (or `const`). The clause `default(none)` will generate an error message if any variable is not explicitly declared as shared or private (or its variations, firstprivate or lastprivate) or listed in a reduce clause. Without a default clause, the effect is the same as if a `default(shared)` were specified. The default clause can appear in the `parallel` construct (and, in consequence, the `parallel for` and `parallel sections`).

`firstprivate(variable_list)`

The variables in `variable_list` are created as private variables to each thread in the same manner is if declared in private clause, except that the variables are initialized to values from the values of the corresponding variables in the master thread prior to execution of the construct. This clause can appear in all directives.

`if (scalar_expression)`

If the expression evaluates to zero, the multiple structured blocks are executed sequentially, otherwise they are executed in parallel. This feature allows a parallel or sequential execution to be decided at runtime. This clause can appears in the `parallel` construct (and in consequence, `parallel for` and `parallel sections`).

`nowait`

Used only in `for`, `parallel for`, and `sections` constructs. Causes threads not to wait for other threads at the end of the construct and allows them to proceed to the next statement when finished.

`num_threads(integer_expression)`

Added to OpenMP version 2 and appears only in the `parallel` construct. If this clause is present, it takes precedence over other ways of specifying the number of threads (i.e., the `omp_set_num_threads()` library function and the environment variable `OMP_NUM_THREADS`), and requests the number of threads given by `integer_expression`.

`ordered`

Used only in `for` and `parallel for` constructs and necessary when the loop contains an ordered directive (only one or none allowed). Requiring an `ordered` clause in addition to an `ordered` directive is for the interests of compiler efficiency. See `ordered` directive under synchronization directives for the actions of an `ordered` directive.

`private(variable_list)`

The variables in `variable_list` are created as private variables to each thread. Each thread has a personal copy of these variables. This clause can appear in all directives.

`reduction(operator : variable_list)`

The operator can be any of the operators, +, -, *, &, |, ^, &&, or ||. A private copy of each variable in the list is created for each thread, initialized according to the operator (0 for +, -, |, ^, and ||, 1 for * and &&, and all 1's for &). At the end of the execution of the construct, each variable in the master thread holds its initial value combined with the final value of the private copies using the specified operator. This clause can appear in every clause except `single`.

`schedule(kind, chunk_size)`

This clause is only used in `for` and `parallel for` constructs, and defines how the iterations of the loop are divided among the threads. The parameter `kind` can be:

`static` The iterations are divided into blocks of size `chunk_size` which are statically assigned to threads in a round-robin fashion. If `chunk_size` omitted, the iterations are divided into approximately equal-sized blocks with one block assigned to each thread.

`dynamic` The iterations are divided into blocks of size `chunk_size` which are assigned to threads as they become free. If `chunk_size` omitted, it is assumed to be of size equal to 1.

`guided` When `chunk_size` is specified as greater than 1, iterations are assigned to threads in block of exponentially decreasing size until a block size of `chunk_size` is reached. If `chunk_size` equals 1, the size of each block is given approximately by (number of unassigned iterations)/(number of threads). If `chunk_size` is not specified, it is assumed to be 1.

`run_time` the environment variable `OMP_SCHEDULE` determines the scheduling. (`chunk_size` is not used in `run_time`.)

For example, if `OMP_SCHEDULE` is set to "guided, 8", with

```
setenv OMP_SCHEDULE "guided, 8"
```

`kind` = `guided` and `chunk_size` = 8.

`shared(variable_list)`

The variables in `variable_list` are shared among the threads. Each thread has access these variables. This clause can appears in the `parallel` construct (and, in consequence, `parallel for` and `parallel sections`).

LIBRARY FUNCTIONS

To use the following, include:

```
#include <omp.h>
```

which also has two types, `omp_lock_t` and `omp_nest_lock`, for locks.

Execution environment functions

```
int omp_get_dynamic(void)
```

ACTIONS: Returns a nonzero value if dynamic adjustment is enabled, otherwise it returns zero.

PARAMETERS: None.

```
int omp_get_nested(void)
```

ACTIONS: Returns a nonzero value if nested parallelism is enabled, otherwise it returns zero.

PARAMETERS: None.

```
int omp_get_num_threads(void)
```

ACTIONS: Returns the number of threads currently in a team when called from a parallel region.

PARAMETERS: None.

```
int omp_get_max_threads(void)
```

ACTIONS: Returns the maximum number of threads that could be used in a team if a parallel region is encountered without a `num_threads` clause.

PARAMETERS: None.

```
int omp_get_num_procs(void)
```

ACTIONS: Returns the number of processors available to the program.

PARAMETERS: None.

```
int omp_in_parallel(void)
```

ACTIONS: Returns a nonzero value if called from within a parallel region, otherwise returns zero.

PARAMETERS: None.

```
void omp_set_dynamic(int dynamic_threads)
```

ACTIONS: If `dynamic_threads` is set to a nonzero value, the number of threads may be altered during the execution of the program to achieve best system utilization (dynamic adjustment). If `dynamic_threads` is set to zero, this feature is disabled. The actual number of threads is fixed for the duration of a parallel region.

PARAMETERS: `dynamic_threads` disable/enable feature (zero/non-zero).

```
void omp_set_nested(int nested)
```

ACTIONS: If `nested` is set to a nonzero value, nested parallelism is enabled. If `nested` is set to zero, this feature is disabled and nested parallel regions are serialized and executed by the current thread.

PARAMETERS: `nested` disable/enable feature (zero/non-zero)

```
void omp_set_num_threads(int num_threads)
```

ACTIONS: Sets the default number of threads to use in subsequent parallel regions (unless `num_threads` clause present).

PARAMETERS: `num_threads` Number of threads

```
int omp_thread_num(void)
```

ACTIONS: Returns the thread number of the thread. Threads are numbered from 0 to `omp_get_num_threads()` - 1, with the master thread being thread 0.

PARAMETERS: None.

Lock functions:

These functions manipulate lock variables. They are grouped in pairs, one for simple locks of the type `omp_lock_t` and one for nestable locks of type `omp_nest_lock`. They all have the same parameter, the lock variable.

```
void omp_init_lock(omp_lock_t *lock)
void omp_init_nest_lock(omp_nest_lock_t *lock)
```

ACTIONS: Allocate and initialize lock (for a simple lock, to unlocked, for a nestable lock, to zero).

```
void omp_destroy_lock(omp_lock_t *lock)
void omp_destroy_nest_lock(omp_nest_lock_t *lock)
```

ACTIONS: Uninitialize lock (deallocate and free lock).

```
void omp_set_lock(omp_lock_t *lock)
void omp_set_nest_lock(omp_nest_lock_t *lock)
```

ACTIONS: The thread is blocked until the specified lock is available. Then the lock is locked and the thread continues. For a nested lock, the thread is blocked until the specified lock is available or it is already owned by the thread and the nesting count is incremented.

```
int omp_test_lock(omp_lock_t *lock)
int omp_test_nest_lock(omp_nest_lock_t *lock)
```

ACTIONS: The lock is set, if possible. For a simple lock, returns a nonzero value if the lock can be set, otherwise it returns zero. For a nestable lock, the function returns the new nesting count if the lock can be set, otherwise it returns zero.

```
void omp_unset_lock(omp_lock_t *lock)
void omp_unset_nest_lock(omp_nest_lock_t *lock)
```

ACTIONS: The thread is released from ownership of the lock. For a nestable lock, the nesting count is also decremented.

Timing

The following were added to OpenMP version 2 and are similar to MPI timing routines.

```
double omp_get_wtick(void)
```

ACTIONS: Returns the number of seconds between successive clock ticks

PARAMETERS: None.

```
double omp_get_wtime(void)
```

ACTIONS: Returns the elapsed wall clock time in seconds from some time in the past.

PARAMETERS: None.

ENVIRONMENT VARIABLES

The environment variables are set before execution, typically with the `setenv` statement.
`OMP_DYNAMIC` - Enables/disables dynamic adjustment (TRUE/FALSE)
`OMP_NESTED` - Enables/disables nested parallelism (TRUE/FALSE)
`OMP_NUM_THREADS` - Sets the number of threads to use (specified as an integer)
`OMP_SCHEDULE` - Sets the runtime schedule type and chunk size (specified in a string)

BIBLIOGRAPHY

CHANDRA, R, L. DAGUM, D. KOHR, D. MAYDAN, J. MCDONALD, AND R. MENON (2001), *Parallel Programming in OpenMP*, Academic Press, San Diego, CA.

OPENMP ARCHITECTURE REVIEW BOARD (2002), *OpenMP C and C++ Application Program Interface Version 2 March 2002*, from http://www.OpenMP.org.

Index

G

H

I

J

N

O

P

Q

R

S

T

U

V

W